Y0-BTB-670

THE ROLE OF GOVERNMENT IN EAST ASIAN ECONOMIC DEVELOPMENT

The Role of Government in East Asian Economic Development

Comparative Institutional Analysis

Edited by

MASAHIKO AOKI
HYUNG-KI KIM
and
MASAHIRO OKUNO-FUJIWARA

CLARENDON PRESS · OXFORD
1997

Oxford University Press, Great Clarendon Street, Oxford OX2 6DP
Oxford New York
Athens Auckland Bangkok Bogota Bombay
Buenos Aires Calcutta Cape Town Dar es Salaam
Delhi Florence Hong Kong Istanbul Karachi
Kuala Lumpur Madras Madrid Melbourne
Mexico City Nairobi Paris Singapore
Taipei Tokyo Toronto

and associated companies in
Berlin Ibadan

Oxford is a trade mark of Oxford University Press

Published in the United States by
Oxford University Press Inc., New York

British Library Cataloguing in Publication Data
Data available

Library of Congress Cataloging in Publication Data
The role of government in East Asian economic development: comparative institutional analysis/edited by Masahiko Aoki, Hyung-Ki Kim, and Masahiro Okuno-Fujiwara.
p. cm.
Includes bibliographical references.
1. East Asia—Economic policy—Case studies. I. Aoki, Masahiko, 1938– . II. Kim, Hyung-Ki, 1936– III. Okuno-Fujiwara, Masahiro.
HC460.5.R65 1997 338.95—dc20 96–29000
ISBN 0–19–829213–9

1 3 5 7 9 10 8 6 4 2

Typeset by Best-set Typesetter Ltd., Hong Kong
Printed in Great Britain by Biddles Ltd., Guildford & King's Lynn

Dedicated to the Fond Memory of the Late Hyung-Ki Kim

PREFACE

This book is the result of a project cosponsored by the Economic Development Institute (EDI) at the World Bank and by the Center for Economic Policy Research at Stanford University. The project was conceived in the autumn of 1993 with the objective of advancing an understanding of the role of the government in East Asian development. Initially we specifically set the following three aims:

1. In contrast to the traditional view that regards government and the market as alternative resource allocation mechanisms, to treat government as an integral element of the economic system, functioning sometimes as a substitute and other times as a complement of other institutional elements (e.g., private order organizations, markets, and various intermediaries).
2. To explore generic characteristics of East Asian economies in comparison to economies in other regions, while recognizing the diversity of institutional settings across East Asian economies.
3. To try to understand the role of government in East Asian economic development through interactions among economic theory, development economics, political science, and economic history.

However, we fully realize that an attempt to advance a coherent alternative paradigm of East Asian economic development incorporating all three of these aims was perhaps not fully possible yet. These aims were set only as a guide for exploring a new perspective of East Asian development with the collective efforts and expertise of scholars from different disciplines and countries.

Some of the eventual contributors to the project and other participants met on December 18 and 19, 1993, in Hakone, Japan, to design the project, select chapter topics, and identify possible writers. On September 16 and 17, 1994, the writers of the chapters met, together with outside commentators, at the Stanford Japan Center in Kyoto to discuss first drafts. Drafts were rewritten, in some cases with complete changes in subject and an overhaul of contents. On February 10 and 11, 1995, we gathered once more at Stanford University to invite critical comments from outside experts for finalizing drafts. Chapter 1 was drafted after the conference with the objective of relating the contents of the chapters to each other and synthesizing common themes whenever possible, while respecting the diversity of views and approaches adopted by the authors. We hope that the contributions prepared, discussed, and enriched over the course of almost two years and finally assembled in this volume will present useful material for the advancement of East Asian economic studies in particular, and of development economics in general.

We, and all the authors, greatly benefited from the expertise, insight, and constructive comments made by other participants who kindly attended the initial planning session and/or the two workshops: Pranab Bardhan, University of California, Berkeley; Ha-Joon Chang, University of Cambridge; Zhiyuan Cui, Massachusetts Institute of Technology; Dennis De Tray, World Bank; Albert Fishlow, University of California, Berkeley; K. C. Fung, University of California, Santa Cruz; Yujiro Hayami, Aoyama-Gakuin University; Ken-ichi Imai, Stanford Japan Center; Yoshihiko Kono, Overseas Economic Cooperation Fund; Paul Krugman, Stanford University; Jisoon Lee, Seoul National University; Ronald McKinnon, Stanford University; Saha Dhevan Meyanathan, World Bank; Akira Morita, Chiba University; Michio Muramatsu, Kyoto University; Ken-ichi Ohno, University of Tsukuba; Kosuke Ohyama, University of Tsukuba; Dani Rodrik, Columbia University; Gérard Roland, Université Libre de Bruxelles; Paul Sheard, Osaka University; Vinod Thomas, World Bank; Ikuo Kume, Kobe University; Wing Thye Woo, University of California, Davis; Pan Yotopoulos, Stanford University (all the affiliations are at the time of participation). Luke Gower (Bank of Japan), Ian Michael Woolford (Osaka University), and James Minifie (Stanford University) took notes of the lively and intense discussions at the initial planning sessions and the subsequent workshops, making them available to the project participants for contemplating and improving their manuscripts during interim periods. Martha Walsh of the University of Washington carefully copy-edited the chapters while maximally respecting the individual styles of the writers from a number of countries.

Most of the funding for this project was provided by the Policy and Human Resources Development Trust Fund established at the World Bank. Additional funding was provided by the Program on the Economy of Japan at the Center for Economic Policy Research at Stanford University. We benefited from project administration by the staff at our three institutions, especially by Deborah Carvalho, Deborah Johnston, and Christy R. Drexel at Stanford University, Hiromi Tojima at the University of Tokyo, and Latifah Alsegaf at EDI. Andrew Schuller has rendered great sympathy and interest in the project from its inception and engineered early publication of its output from Oxford University Press, for which we thank him.

It was with great sorrow and regret that we received the news of the death of Hyung-Ki Kim, one of the co-organizers of this project, on the eve of its completion. We worked well together from the beginning of the project to his final days. He contributed substantially to the academic aspect of the project, co-authoring a chapter based on his valuable experience as an industrial policy administrator in the Korean government as well as providing constructive comments to every author during the course of the project.

Throughout the project, all the participants from different countries were able to build a strong sense of collegiality, facilitating productive and candid academic exchange, for which all of us owe very much to Mr. Kim's warm personality and kind consideration of the project. In spite of the great loss inflicted on us by his sudden death, however, his dedicated and able assistant, Latifah Alsegaf, assumed the administrative responsibility for the fulfillment of the project. We are much comforted by her attentive service.

We, the authors, wish to dedicate the present volume to our fond memory of Hyung-Ki Kim's great humanity and contributions to development economics.

Masahiko Aoki
Masahiro Okuno-Fujiwara

October 15, 1995

CONTENTS

CONTRIBUTORS

MASAHIKO AOKI, Tomoye and Henri Takahashi Professor, Department of Economics, Stanford University, USA

YOON JE CHO, Senior Counsellor to the Deputy Prime Minister and Minister of Finance and Economy (at the time of project implementation), currently Senior Fellow, Korean Institute of Public Finance, Korea

EDMUND TERENCE GOMEZ, Lecturer, Faculty of Economics and Administration, University of Malaya, Malaysia

THOMAS HELLMANN, Assistant Professor, Graduate School of Business, Stanford University, USA

JOMO K. S., Professor, Faculty of Economics and Administration, University of Malaya, Malaysia

HYUNG-KI KIM, deceased, September 20, 1995; formerly Division Chief, Studies and Training Design Division, Economic Development Institute, World Bank

LAWRENCE J. LAU, Kwoh-Ting Li Professor of Economic Development, Department of Economics, Stanford University, USA

JUN MA, Public Policy Specialist, Economic Development Institute, World Bank

KIMINORI MATSUYAMA, Professor, Department of Economics, Northwestern University, USA

KEVIN MURDOCK, Assistant Professor, Graduate School of Business, Stanford University, USA

MASAHIRO OKUNO-FUJIWARA, Professor, Faculty of Economics, University of Tokyo, Japan

TETSUJI OKAZAKI, Associate Professor, Faculty of Economics, University of Tokyo, Japan

YINGYI QIAN, Assistant Professor, Department of Economics, Stanford University, USA

JOSEPH STIGLITZ, Chairman, Council of Economic Advisors to the President; and Joan Kenney Professor, Department of Economics, Stanford University, USA

JURO TERANISHI, Professor, Institute of Economic Research, Hitotsubashi University, Japan

BARRY R. WEINGAST, Senior Fellow, Hoover Institution; and Professor, Department of Political Science, Stanford University, USA

MEREDITH WOO-CUMINGS, Associate Professor, Department of Political Science, Northwestern University, USA

INTRODUCTION

The role of government in East Asian economic development has been one of the most contentious issues in economics. Until recently there has not been consensus among economists on whether government intervention in the market process played any positive role in the phenomenal economic growth in that region over past decades. Some have forcibly argued that East Asian economic development can primarily be explained by the macroeconomic stability that provided proper incentives for investment and saving as well as high human capital accumulation, while the intervention of government in specific industries was at best irrelevant, or, worse, had a harmful or distortive effect on the allocation of resources. In the sense that this view approves only of those government actions that facilitate the development and efficiency of markets, it was referred to as the market-friendly view by the World Bank's *World Development Report 1991*.

The other pole of the argument may be found in the so-called developmental-state view. According to this view, market failure associated with coordinating resource mobilization, allocating investment, and promoting technological catch-up at the developmental stage is so pervasive that state intervention is necessary to remedy it. Adherents of this view argue that strong states in the East Asian economies succeeded in fulfilling these objectives by deliberately "getting the prices wrong" (Amsden 1989) in order to boost industries that would not otherwise have thrived (see Johnson 1982 for Japan, Amsden 1989 for Korea, Wade 1990 for Taiwan). This view has been relatively more popular among political scientists and in public forums, but has never become the mainstream view in economics.

The publication in 1993 of a World Bank study, *The East Asian Miracle: Economic Growth and Public Policy*, may be regarded as a watershed in the debate. The World Bank had been officially committed to the market-oriented, noninterventionist development approach in its loan conditionality and policy dialogues. Therefore, the following admission of the study came as news: "each of the HPAEs [high-performing Asian economies] maintained macroeconomic stability *and* accomplished three functions of growth: accumulation, efficient allocation, and rapid technological catch-up. They did this with *combinations of policies*, *ranging from market-oriented to state-led,* that varied both across economies and over time" (World Bank 1993:10; emphasis added). As Rodrik (1994:14) put it, "Thanks to the bank's study, it will no longer be fashionable to argue that the East Asian economies did so well because their governments intervened so little, or that they would have grown even faster had their governments intervened less. This is an extremely valuable service, because the debate on East Asia can now move on to a higher plateau of common understanding."

The project culminating in the present book was initially planned around the time of the publication of *The East Asian Miracle.* Some of the authors in this project had participated in the earlier World Bank project by preparing background papers, discussing ongoing research and draft reports, presenting papers at seminars, etc. All of us strongly felt the simple division of thought on East Asian economic development between the market-friendly and developmental-state views was unproductive and unfortunate. For that reason, we regarded the attempt of the Bank's study to explore a middle ground by reconciling the market-friendly approach with a cautious, nuanced version of the state interventionist view as a useful step. But at the same time, we felt there still were many things left undone. Some of us thought that the analysis of the Bank's study did not go deep enough or that its emphasis was misplaced. Others thought, more ambitiously, that the Bank's attempt to reconcile the two views was eclectic and that a synthesis would require a more integrative or alternative approach. However, at the inception of the present project there was not a clear, coherent consensus among participants about what the role of government in East Asian economic development was and how it should be analyzed.

Thus, it was not the purpose of the present project to try to prematurely construct a new paradigm of the East Asian miracle. However, the project was designed from the outset in such a way that some advancement could be made beyond *The East Asian Miracle.* The authors of the chapters included in this project do not speak with one voice about the fundamentals underlying the success of the East Asian economies, and the papers reflect the range of opinions represented by their views in spite of the systematic design of the project. But, diverse as they are in nuance and content, we are hopeful that subtle unifying themes and common methodological interests run throughout the book.

To repeat, the market-friendly view maintains that the state should confine its economic activity only to fostering market coordination, while the developmental-state view asserts that the state can be an important substitute (in fact the only substitute) for market coordination which often fails at the developmental stage of the economy. Although they seem to represent two polar views on the role of government, they have conceptually two things in common. First, they take the market and state control as only two mechanisms to solve resource allocation problems. Second, they regard Walrasian market equilibrium—the idealized outcome of "complete" market coordination—as the universalistic norm. They are different only in that the market-friendly view regards the norm to be undisturbed by state action, while the developmental-state view regards state activism as indispensable to achieving the norm. We emphasize a third view.

Market failure can be more pervasive than the market-friendly view tends to suggest, but this does not unconditionally justify the immediate substitution of state-led coordination for market coordination. Coordination failures in the economy can be more general than market failures—that is, the failure of price signals to achieve efficient allocation. In resolving coordination problems, various private institutions other than markets evolve, including the organization of firms, trade associations, financial intermediaries, labor and farmers' organizations, business customs, etc. The primary role of government in East Asia is not so much in directly intervening in resource allocation as in fostering the development of those institutions and interacting with them.

However, government is not a neutral, omnipotent agent that can correct market or organizational failures. Government itself is constrained in its capacity to process information. Also, government itself is an agent (or, more correctly, a collection of agents) with particular interests and incentives molded through private-sector interactions under particular developmental and historical conditions. In short, government is not a neutral arbiter exogenously attached to the economic system to correct the failure of private coordination, but is an endogenous (integral) element of the system with the same informational and incentive constraints as other economic agents in the system. Therefore, the effectiveness of government in promoting the efficiency of private coordination cannot be taken for granted.

Thus, some contributions in this volume try to identify the conditions, if any, under which government may play an active role in coordination. Other contributions try to identify conditions under which government can enhance the development of private-sector institutions through which private coordination, within and across organizations, operates to resolve market failures. Still other contributions try to trace the motivational cause of government action and explain the outcome of its interactions with the private sector. The same government action may succeed in facilitating economic development under certain developmental, historical, and internal, as well as external, conditions, but may fail under other conditions.

From such a perspective, we all recognize that *comparative institutional analysis* can be a useful approach. In contrast to the conventional approach based on a market–government dichotomy, we assert the importance of taking the role of institutions (including, but not limited to, markets) seriously and analyzing the workings of those institutions with the same rigor as markets. Because the ways in which a cluster of institutions evolves and the role government plays in that evolution are not uniform even among East Asian economies, however, comparative and historical studies must constitute an integral element of analysis of the role of government.

Let us briefly introduce each chapter.

The first chapter, by Masahiko Aoki, Kevin Murdock, and Masahiro Okuno-Fujiwara amplifies the view expressed in this introduction, both discussing unifying themes that run throughout the volume and delineating the diversity and differences of thought that appear as well.

Immediately following the introductory chapter, Part I assembles four chapters related to issues of "Market Failures and Government Activism." Chapter 2 by Lawrence Lau, entitled "The Role of Government in Economic Development: Some Observations from the Experience of China, Hong Kong, and Taiwan," presents a comprehensive list of policy instruments the government used in mobilizing resource inputs, allocating them more efficiently (moving to the production frontier), and shifting the production frontier outward. Issues involved in the use of each instrument are illustrated with rich facts from the greater Chinese economic zone.

Chapter 3 by Tetsuji Okazaki, entitled "The Government-Firm Relationship in Postwar Japanese Economic Recovery: Coordinating the Coordination Failure in Industrial Rationalization," describes, on the basis of newly available historical documents, the workings of a government-sponsored deliberation council for resolving particular investment coordination problems facing Japan in the postwar economic recovery period. Based on historical analysis, it identifies historical and institutional conditions under which the deliberation council may function as a device for resolving well-defined coordination problems.

Chapter 4 by Hyung-Ki Kim and Jun Ma, entitled "The Role of Government in Acquiring Technological Capability: The Case of the Petrochemical Industry in East Asia," is a comparative case study of the petrochemical industry in Japan, Korea, and Taiwan in which scale economies, needs for coordination among upstream and downstream activities, and large investment requirements may call for substantive government intervention at the developmental stage. Governments in these economies were involved in selection of the upstream entry, but at the same time encouraged unbundled (unpackaged) imports of foreign technology and participation of domestic engineers in project design from the outset to nurture indigenous engineering capability. They contrast this approach to those adopted by China, Brazil, and India, where governments also intervened heavily but generated very different outcomes, and derive some lessons to restrain unproductive rent-seeking behavior under the condition of government control.

Chapter 5 by Kiminori Matsuyama, entitled "Economic Development as Coordination Problems," fundamentally questions the value of state activism as a solution to coordination failure. It contends that coordination failure arises because no one can know the exact nature of the problem he or she is trying to solve. Because of this lack of knowledge, the logic of coordination failures does not justify centralized policy activism. Centralized coordination would pose the greatest danger of interfering with private experiments to discover an even better way of coordination.

Part II introduces "The Market-Enhancing View." It departs from the conventional analysis based on a dichotomy between markets and government and instead addresses the role of government in facilitating private-sector coordination. This view recognizes that a significant fraction of economic activity is coordinated not by markets or within a government bureaucracy but rather by decentralized, private-sector organizations such as firms and intermediaries. The role of government in promoting these private-sector institutions to complement their activities is the focus of this part. Chapter 6 by Thomas Hellmann, Kevin Murdock, and Joseph Stiglitz, entitled "Financial Restraint: Toward a New Paradigm," introduces the new concept of financial restraint: a set of financial policies that create rent opportunities in the banking and production sectors. They argue that these rents may curtail a bank's moral hazard behavior and enhance incentives for monitoring and for savings mobilization. Consequently, more efficient credit allocation and financial deepening is induced under financial restraint than under either *laissez-faire* policies or financial repression.

Chapter 7 by Yoon Je Cho, entitled "Government Intervention, Rent Distribution, and Economic Development in Korea," examines the workings of financial restraint in a historical perspective. It divides the postwar developmental process of Korea into three phases: the 1950s when large rents were created by overvalued foreign exchange rates and import restrictions; the 1960s, characterized by financial restraint *par excellence*; and the 1970s when the government promoted heavy and chemical industries utilizing financial repression (in the sense of highly repressed rates). For each phase, Cho examines the mechanism in which rents were created and distributed, measures the relative size of rents, and assesses their impact on growth, industrial structure, moral hazard behavior of banks and firms, and risk bearing by various parties.

Chapter 8 by Masahiko Aoki, entitled "Unintended Fit: Organizational Evolution and Government Design of Institutions in Japan," focuses on nanoscopic, intra-organizational coordination. It posits that the spontaneous order of cross-task coordination based on information sharing within the firm has been one important source of total factor productivity growth in postwar Japan. The institutional apparatus that the government had originally designed for the centralized control of wartime production did not work as intended, but it evolved as a supporting framework for decentralized private coordination after its democratic transformation during postwar reform.

Chapter 9 by Yingyi Qian and Barry R. Weingast, entitled "Institutions, State Activism, and Economic Development: A Comparison of State-Owned and Township-Village Enterprises in China," poses the question of why the latter enterprises perform more efficiently than the former. The latter type are controlled by the lowest level of governments (township or village governments), while the former are controlled by higher levels of government (central or provincial governments). The institutional environment affects the incentives of each type of government control. In particular, Qian and Weingast emphasize that the local governments (township-village enterprises) cannot bail out ailing firms with inexpensive loans or protect them with trade barriers. This in turn affects the incentives of the managers and workers because punishment for failure is credible. Thus, China's special form of decentralization, "market-preserving federalism, Chinese style," accounts for the positive incentives at the lowest level of government.

The last four chapters comprising Part III deal with "The Political Economy of Development and Government-Private Interactions." Traditionally the macroscopic discussion of coordination has centered on investment, relegating saving to a secondary position. In contrast, Chapter 10 by Juro Teranishi, entitled "Sectoral Resource Transfer, Conflict, and Macrostability in Economic Development: A Comparative Analysis," spotlights the saving side and argues that the difference in the pattern of financing industrialization may have serious impact on the development performance of the economy. It specifically focuses on the policy-based, as well as market-based, mobilization of agricultural savings in East Asia, Latin America, and Sub-Saharan Africa. Across these three regions, the degree of resource shift, from the rural sector through direct and indirect taxation, does not vary much. But there is a significant difference between East Asia and the other two regions in the ways the adverse effects of the resource transfer were politically compensated. In Latin America and Sub-Saharan Africa, divisible benefits (rents) were supplied by the government to win the support of particular interest groups (large landlords or tribes). In contrast, in East Asia the adverse effects were mitigated by investment in infrastructure which enhanced the productivity of small landholding farmers. It examines the effects of this difference on macrostability, the transformation of the rural sector, market-induced savings, etc.

Why did such differences occur? Chapter 11 by Meredith Woo-Cumings, entitled "The Political Economy of Growth in East Asia: A Perspective on the State, Market, and Ideology," discusses the impact of differences in initial conditions and international environments on the developmental strategy between Latin America and East Asia (Korea and Taiwan). She elucidates the unique imprint of Japanese colonial legacies on the bureaucratic nature of the state in Korea and Taiwan and its relations with business and agrarian interests—a subject long neglected by economists in spite of its importance. She also discusses how the specific geopolitical positions of these two economies affected their developmental strategies as well as their capabilities to extract "rent" from the United States in the Cold War.

As mentioned before, the highly bureaucratic nature and growth-oriented strategy of the Northeast Asian states have been made possible by the relative homogeneity of their populations. What if such a condition did not exist? Chapter 12 by Jomo K. S. and Edmund Terence Gomez, entitled "Rents and Development in Multiethnic Malaysia," discusses the trade-offs involved between two types of rents in the context of resource-rich, ethnically diverse Malaysia: one primarily generated for postcolonial industrial development and the other generated for redistributive goals, mainly along interethnic lines. They describe how the two types of rents have interacted with each other, alternated in influence, and affected the efficiency of the development process in successive phases. While admitting that redistributive policy has enhanced human capital accumulation among Malays or Bumiputeras and reduced political tension, they note that redistributive rents have induced various unproductive rentier behaviors.

Chapter 13 by Masahiro Okuno-Fujiwara, entitled "Toward a Comparative Institutional Analysis of the Government-Business Relationship," lays out an abstract model of broad government activities, which encompass the legislative, administrative, and litigative branches of the government, and analyzes the interactions among the intragovernment organizations as well as between the government and private business. The analysis captures the government-business relationship in the bargaining-theoretic framework by focusing on the actions of the administrative branch, and identifies three alternative regimes of the relationship: rule based, relation based, and authoritarian. An important dimension of distinction is the relative importance of *ex ante* policy rules versus *ex post* negotiation to revise them, as well as the degree of separation of power within the three branches of government and/or within the administrative branch, which determines the bargaining power of the government. The chapter assesses the merits and demerits of those regimes in terms of various criteria and applies the results to evaluate the development performance of the relation-based Japanese system contrasted with the rule-based United States system.

As suggested by the brief introduction of each chapter above, the topics dealt with and approaches adopted by each author are diverse and wide ranging. We try, however, in Chapter 1 to relate the contents of the chapters to each other and contrast them, whenever applicable, with the approach taken by *The East Asian Miracle.* We hope this will help place our possible contributions to development economics in perspective.

Masahiko Aoki
Hyung-Ki Kim
Masahiro Okuno-Fujiwara

REFERENCES

AMSDEN, A. H. (1989), *Asia's Next Giant: South Korea and Late Industrialization*, Oxford University Press, Oxford.

JOHNSON, C. (1982), *MITI and the Japanese Miracle*, Stanford University Press, Stanford.

Rodrik, D. (1994), "King Kong Meets Godzilla: The World Bank and The East Asian Miracle," in Miracle or Design, *Overseas Development Council Policy Essay No. 11*, Washington, 15–56.

Wade, R. (1990), *Governing the Market: Economic Theory and the Role of the Government in East Asian Industrialization*, Princeton University Press, Princeton.

World Bank (1991), *World Development Report 1991*, World Bank, Washington.

——(1993), *The East Asian Miracle: Economic Growth and Public Policy*, Oxford University Press, Oxford.

1

Beyond *The East Asian Miracle*: Introducing the Market-Enhancing View

MASAHIKO AOKI, KEVIN MURDOCK,
AND MASAHIRO OKUNO-FUJIWARA

In the Introduction, we made a critical comment on the market-friendly view and the developmental-state view. Both views regard government and the market as alternative mechanisms for resource allocation. The market-friendly view expects that most economic coordination can be achieved through the market mechanism and that when markets alone are insufficient, other private-sector organizations, such as intrafirm coordination, will suffice. The role of government in this view is limited to providing a legal infrastructure for market transactions and providing goods subject to extreme market failure (for example, when markets are missing for public goods such as a clean environment). In contrast, the developmental-state view regards market failures as more pervasive for developing economies (for example, due to the lack of liquid capital markets) and thus looks to government intervention as a substitute mechanism for the resolution of these more prevalent market failures. Both views look to markets as the initial basis for organization and recognize that markets alone are imperfect. Where they differ significantly is in the mechanism by which market imperfections are resolved. The market-friendly view expects that most market imperfections can be resolved by private-sector institutions, whereas the developmental-state view looks to government intervention as the solution. In this sense, these two views consider the role of government and that of the market (or, more broadly, market-based institutions) as substitutes, with competing roles for the resolution of market failures.

We suggest a third view: the market-enhancing view. Instead of viewing government and the market as the only alternatives, and as mutually exclusive substitutes, we examine the role of government policy to facilitate or complement private-sector coordination. We start from the premise that private-sector institutions have important comparative advantages *vis-à-vis* the government, in particular in their ability to provide appropriate incentives and to process locally available information. We also recognize that private-sector institutions do not solve all important market imperfections and that this is particularly true for economies in a low state of development. The capabilities of the private sector are more limited in developing economies. The market-enhancing view thus stresses the mechanisms whereby government policy is directed at improving the ability of the private sector to solve coordination problems and overcome other market imperfections.

In analyzing the capability of government to facilitate private-sector coordination, the behavior of government should be treated as constrained by its limited information-processing capacity and the incentives of government can be seen to be influenced by the political economy of its institutions and interactions with the private sector. This implies that government should be regarded as an endogenous player interacting with the economic system as a coherent cluster of institutions rather than a neutral, omnipotent agent exogenously attached to the economic system with the mission of resolving its coordination failures.

The purpose of this introductory chapter is to amplify the view summarized above by referring to relevant parts of the contributions included in this volume. We start this task by summarizing basic elements of *The East Asian Miracle* (World Bank 1993; hereafter referred to as *EAM*) in Section 1.1. In Section 1.2, we discuss the potential role of government in resolving coordination failures and in particular highlight the difference between coordinating movements that bring economic activity toward the production possibilities frontier and those that attempt to coordinate activities aimed at expanding the frontier. The market-enhancing view is discussed in Section 1.3, with specific examples of how government policy can complement decentralized coordination. Contingent rents are an important policy mechanism that government can use to promote private-sector coordination. Section 1.4 contrasts the use of contingent rents with the more traditional policy of direct subsidies.

Section 1.5 presents a framework (Figure 1.1) for analyzing the different roles of the private sector and government in coordinating economic activity. Each of the three views discussed in this chapter—the market-friendly view, the market-enhancing view, and the developmental-state view—can be analyzed within this framework by examining the mechanisms whereby market failures are resolved. The market-friendly view emphasizes the role of private-sector institutions, the developmental-state view emphasizes government intervention, whereas the market-enhancing view emphasizes the role of government policy in promoting private-sector coordination.

Section 1.6 addresses the political-economy structures of East Asian economies to better understand the political basis of the policies pursued by government. Section 1.7 examines the motivations of government and the bureaucracy embedded in it, discussing analysis aimed at endogenizing the incentives of government. Section 1.8 concludes with a comment on our common methodology, comparative institutional analysis.

1.1 ELEMENTS OF *THE EAST ASIAN MIRACLE*

As mentioned in the Introduction, *EAM* also tries to explore a third way between the market-friendly view and the developmental-state view. We are sympathetic with the basic orientation and agree with some of the analytical conclusions presented in *EAM*. At the same time, however, we feel that other parts of the analytical conclusions are eclectic, incomplete, or misleading. We are hopeful that clarifying differences between our approach and that of *EAM* may be helpful in placing our view in perspective.

Getting the Fundamentals Right

EAM regards the policy choice of government in the high-performing Asian economies (HPAEs) as "a combination of fundamental and interventionist policies" (p. 15). Fundamental policies are those that encourage macroeconomic stability, high investment in human capital, stable and secure financial systems, limited price distortions, and openness to foreign technology and agricultural development. *EAM* emphasizes, along the line of the market-friendly view, that "getting the fundamentals right" should be the first order of business by any government and judges that governments in HPAEs have indeed done that. However, it also contends that "these fundamental policies do not tell the entire story. In most of these economies [HPAEs], in one form or another, the government intervened—systematically and through multiple channels—to foster development, and in some cases the development of specific industries" (p. 5). *EAM* considers that specific interventions by the government may be rationalized as a response to various coordination failures that can result in market failures, especially during early stages of development.

The Importance of Government-Private Sector Intermediaries

While the developmental-state models emphasize solely the role of state machinery, such as the Ministry of International Trade and Industry (MITI) in Japan, the Economic Planning Agency in Korea, and development banks in many HPAEs, *EAM* recognizes that various intermediaries between government and the private sector, such as "deliberation councils" (a kind of forum between government officials and representatives of the private sector), played important roles in resolving possible market coordination failures by facilitating information exchange, in realizing an efficient allocation of credit under the condition of information asymmetry, and in other ways. *EAM* claims that "developmental-state models overlook the central role of government-private sector cooperation" (p. 13).

The Principle of Shared Growth

EAM recognizes that relatively equal income distribution has accompanied high growth in the HPAEs. It argues that leaders of the HPAEs, while tending to be either authoritarian or paternalistic, followed the "principle of shared growth" to establish their legitimacy and win the support of society at large, promising that as the economy expanded all groups would benefit. It argues that, under the shared growth approach, education was brought to all groups and through this accumulation of human capital, which also contributed to a high-quality civil service, the economy enjoyed a rising stock of skilled workers and entrepreneurship capabilities.

Export-Push Strategy

In order to get the fundamentals right and to be able to pursue the shared growth objective without hampering the efficient management of the economy, competent and relatively honest bureaucrats have to be recruited and insulated from political pressures. Otherwise, unproductive rent-seeking activities of special interest groups seeking to capture possible economic gains created by selective government interventions would proliferate. *EAM* argues that the adoption of the export-push strategy, supported by export credits, etc., prevented resource-wasteful rent-seeking activities. Essentially, the subsidies made available by these government interventions were allocated by a contest mechanism, with demonstrated export success determining the winners. Since export markets are competitive, these subsidies were allocated to efficient firms and thus promoted efficiency. *EAM* claims that "*Export-push strategies* have been by far the most successful combination of fundamentals and policy interventions and hold the most promise for other developing economies" (p. 24). It asserts that among other state interventions widely practiced in East Asia, "promotion of specific industries generally did not work . . . Mild financial repression combined with directed credits has worked in certain situations but carries high risks" (p. 24).

These elements of *EAM* are certainly a step forward from simple neo-classical models or developmental-state models that focused on market mechanism or state activism as the only alternatives, and can serve as a starting point for further studies. Below, we present discussions and critical comments on these elements as a way of introducing the issues discussed in this volume.

1.2 "COORDINATION FAILURES" AND THE GOVERNMENT

EAM *on Missing Markets*

The basic logic of *EAM* for substantiating the positive role of government intervention is a familiar one: it identifies various problems of coordination failure that arise in competitive markets, especially during the early stages of development, and then interprets some of the interventionist policies as responses to such failures. Familiar though the concept of coordination failure may be, the discussions of coordination problems in *EAM* are extensive and highly sophisticated.[1]

Traditionally, economists have found a rationale for government intervention in various forms of incomplete information due to missing markets. A classical example is that current prices do not convey adequate information about the future prospects of investment when the development of capital markets is not mature, or when multiple investment projects of large scale are highly complementary. Other examples may be found in cases where spill-over effects related to learning are diffuse (e.g., external effects of education, the nonappropriability of technological knowledge, and the regional clustering of specialized skills). Direct intervention in the market mechanism, or creation of quasi-markets, through taxes and subsidies has traditionally been considered a standard means to cope with these problems.

Is the Coordination of Expectations Always Good?

When a coordination problem involves many parties, spontaneous, multilateral negotiations may be too costly to resolve the problem. If what is necessary is the coordination of expectations among existing private agents who are to be engaged in complementary projects, this may be most efficiently performed in a group activity such as a deliberation council. Ultimately, mutually profitable investment plans may emerge and become apparent to all private parties concerned. Public credits could then be provided to facilitate the implementation of the emergent investment plans. Chapter 3 by Okazaki describes how a deliberation council succeeded, operating in the special circumstances of the postwar recovery period of Japan where a necessary coordination problem among existing industries was fairly clearly identified and formulated. However, we caution that government-mediated information exchanges and expectation coordination may not necessarily be helpful for avoiding coordination failures in other circumstances. Rather, it may succeed only in implementation of inferior solutions.

Suppose, for example, that technological and market opportunities are uncertain and that information about those opportunities will evolve only over time. Investment decisions must be adjusted on the basis of emergent information, but the capacity to process such information is limited for everybody. Suppose that the profit opportunities of those projects are either positively or negatively correlated (i.e., they are affected by common random events that evolve over time). Under such a situation, the values of information exchange and expectation assimilation crucially depend on whether these projects are technologically complementary or substitutes. If they are complementary, information and expectation assimilation will lead to a collective choice of a mutually consistent investment configuration. Coordination of expectations among independent agents improves the outcome, even if the expectation turns out to be inaccurate *ex post*, by minimizing costs of coordination failure. However, if projects are substitutes and they compete for scarce resources, decentralized investment decisions based on differentiated expectations will yield a better social outcome. In this case, if the expectation was inaccurate *ex post*, assimilated expectations would only ensure that all agents uniformly chose an inappropriate level of investment.

During early stages of development, investment projects may more likely be characterized as complementary, such as in the classic example in which the profitability of a steel plant is contingent on the availability of a sufficient power supply and vice versa. The case dealt with by Okazaki in Chapter 3 was precisely characterized by a high degree of complementarity among steel, marine transportation, coal, and shipbuilding, because of the special circumstance of recovery of the war-damaged economy. However, as the economy develops to a more technologically advanced stage so that technological and market opportunities become more uncertain, there emerge various projects that are mutually substitutable and compete for resources. As an example, in the emergent multimedia industry, the standard of communications has not yet been firmly established and alternative means of communication, such as the telephone network, cable network, satellite transmission, wireless transmission, etc., compete for a dominant position. In such a case, *de facto* standardization may be defined and redefined among competing business alliances drawn from different industries and organized around particular alternatives. Theoretically, such decentralized private coordination is expected eventually to yield a better outcome in comparison to the scheme where the standard is uniquely and collectively defined by a deliberation council.

A similar example can be drawn from the development of the high-density television (HDTV) industry. The Japanese Ministry of Post and Communications mediated the agreement among Japanese firms to an analog standard and made significant investments in promoting that standard. In the United States, multiple firms competed to define the United States standard using alternative approaches and ultimately a more advanced, digital standard was developed. The policy adopted by the United States government was much closer to what we describe as the market-enhancing view in this chapter. The United States government held a contest to determine the standard, selecting from among proposals generated by private-sector consortiums. The winner expected to generate large rents associated with licensing fees for the use of the standard.

A more subtle example could be found in the "staggered entry" approach discussed by Kim and Ma in Chapter 4. Under this scheme MITI allowed one or a few firms at a time to enter specific markets of the petrochemical industry to control "excess competition." They interpret such a government strategy to have been effective for assuring large-scale investment as well as motivating incumbent firms to develop technological competency by the threat of potential competition from new entrants. Their analysis is carefully documented and their interpretation is highly nuanced. However, an often-made alternative claim has been that such a government approach was not adopted as a well-thought-out *ex ante* strategy, but as an *ex post* compromise between MITI, incumbent firms, and those who sought new entry. The involvement of MITI in the development of the industry was also costly, in the sense that it created general optimism among individual firms and inhibited autonomous risk assessment of future market opportunities by new entrants. This led to the excess-capacity expansion dramatically manifested after the oil shock in the early 1970s.

The Economics of Coordination Failure Does Not Justify Government Intervention

Chapter 5 by Kiminori Matsuyama goes beyond the orthodox modeling of economics and poses an even more fundamental question for the role of government in coordination. In the traditional market-failure literature, as well as more modern asymmetric information models, the stock of knowledge in the economy is regarded as fixed, although there is a barrier to its transmission because of missing markets or for incentive reasons. The Fundamental Welfare Theorem, on which the traditional market-failure argument ultimately relies, assumes that the technological potential of each firm is exogenously determined by engineering science (and thus represented by a production function). If so, climbing up the hill of the profit contour with the guidance of price signals (with the help of government when some markets are missing) will eventually lead to the efficiency frontier of production.

However, currently known production possibilities actually represent only a portion of infinitely many possibilities. These productive possibilities have been discovered through numerous experiments of economic agents who aspire to be rational, but who are limited in their ability to acquire, transmit, and interpret information. So, there is the possibility that nobody notices the presence of coordination failures. The economy may have climbed up a hill thanks to market competition (and sometimes with the help of government intervention), but there is no guarantee that the economy has climbed the highest hill and, further, nobody knows precisely where the highest hill is located. With such a lack of knowledge on comparative economic systems, it is better that many coordination experiments (including organizational experiments) are allowed so that the chance of discovering a higher hill will never be lost. If a monolithic coordination mechanism is imposed by a single entity (the government), the probability of discovering a more efficient mechanism is greatly diminished. Thus Matsuyama argues that economics of coordination failure does not justify any greater role of government in coordination.

1.3 THE MARKET-ENHANCING VIEW

As pointed out already, it has conventionally been thought that government control and the market mechanism are alternative mechanisms for solving resource-allocation problems. When the market fails to implement an efficient solution, government interventions may be called for as the substitute. In this regard, there does not seem to be a fundamental difference between neoclassical orthodoxy (the market-friendly view) and the developmental-state view. The difference may be reduced to a matter of degree in perceived market failures and in the perceived ability of the government to intervene successfully. Neoclassical orthodoxy holds that government intervention should be limited to, and is warranted only in a very narrow scope, i.e., when markets fail to exist (e.g., pollution) or diffusive externalities are present (e.g., investment in education). The developmental-state view considers market failures to be more pervasive, possibly extending to the sphere of major investment decisions in strategic industries due to the underdevelopment of capital markets (see Chapter 4 by Kim and Ma). It is hard to draw an unambiguous line between them.

The issue raised by Matsuyama in Chapter 5 may be interpreted that "coordination failures" and "market failures" should not be casually identified, because the former may be much more fundamental and broad. For example, the case of pollution can be perceived by anybody as an obvious failure of the market to exist. But coordination failures may arise because of the lack of knowledge of possible market and technological opportunities so that they cannot be easily recognized. They may be gradually resolved through decentralized private experiments including those by nongovernmental organizations. Here may arise an alternative view of government. One possible role of government may be to complement and foster private-order coordination rather than to substitute for it. By broadly interpreting the meaning of markets to cover private-order coordination, we may characterize this as the market-enhancing view. From this perspective, it is not the government's responsibility to solve the coordination problem. Rather, *the government's role is to facilitate the development of private-sector institutions that can overcome these failures*. We consider two examples, starting with a somewhat more traditional case in which knowledge is given but asymmetrically distributed among private agents. We then proceed to a case in which information may be created and new combinations of activities may be generated by cooperation within private-order organizations. Our interest lies in the potential role of government in these cases.

Information Asymmetry and the Banks

In considering coordination problems, *EAM* goes beyond the traditional argument of missing markets by entertaining the notion of information asymmetry. For example, in credit markets, those who bid higher interest rates are not necessarily the ones who actually yield the highest return to the bank, because their willingness to pay a high interest rate may signal a high risk of default. Therefore, credit cannot be allocated efficiently through a Walrasian auction market. In this situation, a coordination problem arises because information is asymmetrically distributed—borrowers know their own risk characteristics, but creditors do not, yet a competitive market cannot provide incentives for truthful revelation of information by borrowers. Financial intermediaries may evolve in response to this problem. Banks monitor the credit standings of borrowers, and loan to firms that maintain good reputations with the bank. This argument was first developed by Stiglitz and Weiss (1981) and is further elaborated in Chapter 6 of the present volume by Hellmann, Murdock, and Stiglitz.

Their theory suggests that market failures may sometimes be resolved by the creation of a private institution (in their case, private banks), which can act as an information-processing mechanism partially to overcome these information asymmetries. Banks, of course, have creditors of their own—depositors. To insure that banks invest depositors' funds wisely and invest in the information-gathering and monitoring of their borrowers, banks must have long-run incentives. Hellmann, Murdock, and Stiglitz argue that these incentives may be provided by a set of government interventions that they characterize as "financial restraint," comprising deposit regulation, entry restriction, and stable macro policy. The set of policies results in a real interest rate that is positive, but lower than the competitive rate.

Financial restraint should not be confused with financial repression. In financial repression, which has been much discussed, high inflation created by government induces the transfer of wealth from the household sector to the government, which becomes in turn the object of rent-seeking activities among various interest groups who seek to influence the government. In contrast, the policy objective of financial restraint is to create "rent opportunities" in the private sector and, in particular, for financial intermediaries (banks). These rent opportunities are created because deposit-rate control induces a wedge between lending rates and deposit rates. Banks capture these rents by increasing their deposit base and by monitoring their loan portfolios.

Financial restraint increases the "franchise value" of banks. In each period that a bank maintains a high-performing loan portfolio, it captures the rent opportunity created by lower deposit rates. Were the bank to increase the riskiness of its portfolio, it would risk the loss of this future stream of rents. Thus, financial restraint creates incentives that reward diligent monitoring and penalize risky loans (moral hazard behavior).

Rent opportunities create additional long-run incentives for banks. In particular, rents may compensate for the cost banks incur in accumulating reputational capital by rescuing firms that are viable in the long run, but temporarily financially distressed. Such rescue operations may be particularly valuable when the assets of firms are highly specific, such as human assets geared toward organizational coordination based on information sharing as typically observed in Japan. From this perspective, "mild" government intervention combined with a stable macro policy is complementary to a matrix of organizational coordination and bank-firm relationships that may involve an active role of banks in the corporate governance structure (see Chapter 8 in this volume by Aoki).

Financial restraint may have its own costs, as well as benefits, such as the distortion of portfolio selection by households and the eventual decline of a bank's monitoring incentives and capability due to its market power. In Korea and Japan, the very high value of real estate may, in part, have been accounted for by the deposit-rate regulation combined with the repression of the bond market. Chapter 7 by Cho describes how financial restraint worked in Korea in historical perspective.[2]

One contentious issue could be whether financial restraint is required to generate the bank rents necessary to support "relational banking" activities (e.g., the bank's continual monitoring of borrowers, rescue operations when called for, etc.). By using a repeated game model, Dinc (1995) recently showed that the bank rents that can sustain relational banking may be generated endogenously. In his model, rents are extracted from the entrepreneur (the borrowing firm) rather than from savers. If bank rents are too high, relational banking cannot be supported, because there is no incentive for the entrepreneur to maintain relational banking. If bank rents are too low, however, relational banking does not arise, because banks are not motivated to monitor and rescue when necessary. Thus, rents must be within a certain range for relational banking to be supported. In Dinc's model, the repression of bond markets (preventing bond financing) enlarges the range of parameter values for which relational banking can be viable. In that sense, government intervention in the bond markets may be complementary to the emergence of the relational banking institution.

Indeed, the Japanese government adopted such a policy in the beginning of the high-growth period in which banks played a significant role in corporate financing and monitoring. A further result of this model is the path-dependent nature of institutional evolution: once reputational capital is sunk by banks, even if the high-rent opportunity is removed by the deregulation or internationalization of financial markets, relational banking may survive. Policy-induced rents to create the institutional basis for relational banking may thus be necessary only at an early stage of development.

Fit between Spontaneous Private Organization and Government-Designed Institutions

Although the traditional "market failures" literature looked to government intervention as the only alternative to market coordination, the private firm is also an organization that evolved in response to market-coordination failure—it internalizes decisions that cannot be simply mediated by market prices (Coase 1937). If, however, the firm's coordination method is simply dictated by engineering imperatives, development economics need not deal with it explicitly. However, as Leibenstein (1966) forcefully argued three decades ago, this may not be the case. Leibenstein observed wide productivity differences across developing economies—"X-inefficiency"—that can be attributable to neither technological differences nor market failure, but to various internal factors associated with the organization of the firm.

Although traditional economics treated organizational coordination within the firm as a black box, organization within the firm actually occupies a substantial component of coordination taking place in the economy. The mode of organizational coordination in a particular firm is molded through interactions between, and the amalgamation of, entrepreneurial insights and direction, managerial and engineering design, workers' experiences, etc. As a result, the form of organizational coordination that takes place within each firm may differ from one firm to another, across industries, and between economies, depending on the historical path.

However, over time certain particular organizational modes gain a competitive advantage in markets and become dominant in each particular economy. Which mode becomes dominant may depend on various factors, such as "fitness" with the engineering and market requirements of dominant industries; available skills of managers, engineers, and workers; the way in which financial institutions perform monitoring and provide financing *vis-à-vis* firms; and so on. In turn, the supply of skill types may be conditioned by the educational system, and the structure of financial institutions may be affected by government regulation. This observation suggests that there is a complementarity relationship between the private coordination taking place within an organization (and across organizations) and the way the institutional environment is shaped. In this perspective, the government does not substitute for private coordination, but may play a complementary role in shaping an institutional environment conducive to a particular type of organizational coordination.

This argument is amplified and illustrated in Chapter 8 by Aoki. He argues that a unique convention of organizational coordination evolved in Japan in the last 50 years or so and that it holds a key for understanding the cross-industrial pattern of Japan's total factor productivity growth. That convention relies heavily on information sharing at the grass-roots level of the organization and may be contrasted with the dominant mode of organizational coordination in the West which is based on information differentiation and task specialization. Aoki's chapter tries to clarify the logic of how such an organizational mode is complemented by the matrix of surrounding institutions. However, an irony of history is that those institutions were originally designed by the government for another purpose: the centralized control of resource mobilization and allocation. Before they became supporting institutions for the new organizational convention, they had to undergo a fundamental change in the postwar reform, which resulted in a particular type of political decentralization (see also Chapter 13 by Okuno-Fujiwara).

Framing Decentralized Experiments: Fiscal Federalism, Chinese Style

Another story in which the efficiency of the firm's coordination is crucially conditioned by the frame of government is provided in Chapter 9 by Qian and Weingast. They take as a starting point the following observation: in China, small township and village enterprises (TVEs—a form of rural entrepreneurship) are gaining market share and realizing significant productivity increases, while large state-owned enterprises (SOEs) are stagnant. The latter are centrally controlled by the national government or by a provincial government. These governments stand ready to rescue SOEs financially distressed for political reasons and therefore these governments have no credible commitment to discipline the incompetency and moral hazard behavior of management or a low level of effort by workers. On the other hand, township and village governments, which act as *de facto* holding companies of TVEs under their jurisdiction, do not have the ability to create money and therefore are subject to a hard budget constraint. Qian and Weingast argue that this consequence of fiscal federalism creates incentives for higher entrepreneurial effort by the TVEs and earnest effort by workers.

Their analysis, based on recent developments in China, may suggest broader lessons for the role of an activist government concerned with economic development and/or the transition from a socialist economy. Reform or transition need not be directed by a centralized, national government. In a large economy, decentralization serves as a better mechanism for creating appropriate incentives for productive private experiments that foster economic prosperity. At the same time, the complete withdrawal of government from coordination activities (and thus a total reliance on market coordination) may not be feasible if private-sector institutions are not sufficiently developed to fill the void left by government withdrawal. This idea is discussed further in Section 1.5 of this chapter.

1.4 RENTS AND SUBSIDIES

A Taxonomy of Rents

One of the most prominently discussed issues in development economics has been that government intervention creates artificial returns that may be captured through unproductive "rent-seeking" activities by various private interest groups. This ultimately distorts the market mechanism, making it difficult, if not impossible, to get the fundamentals right, and inhibits the development process. Some argue that an important underpinning of East Asian success is that unproductive rent-seeking behavior is less conspicuous than in other areas. In contrast, the model of Hellmann, Murdock, and Stiglitz suggests that "rent opportunities" created by government may have provided incentives for banks to monitor private firms and promoted financial deepening. How can such rents be differentiated from rents inducing unproductive rent-seeking behavior? To discuss this and other related issues, we identify a number of competing concepts of "rent."

The classical and neoclassical concept of "(economic) rent" is defined as returns to an economic factor whose supply is naturally fixed. It is determined as the residual after all variable inputs have been purchased at market-determined prices. "Quasi-rent" is a transitory rent that accrues to a resource whose supply is temporarily fixed. Organizational innovation and technological innovation whose supply will eventually become diffused in the economy may be thought of as examples. To capture the quasi-rents available from these activities, private agents will engage in entrepreneurial and innovative activities.

There are "(policy-induced) rents" that can be created by government intervention in market processes and that are defined as returns above the competitive rate. For example, government can create an artificial scarcity of goods, for example, by means of import quotas. Alternatively, government may provide subsidies to certain key industries and/or preferential tax treatment for those who qualify according to a criterion decided politically. In such a case, the distribution of the rationed goods and/or the granting of subsidies may become instruments of political favoritism, allocated on the basis of political, tribal, and family ties, etc. Activity designed to capture policy-induced rents may divert scarce resources away from productive use.

The costs incurred from this induced misallocation of resources may well exceed the possible benefits, if any, from limiting the supply of goods. An influential policy prescription forged by such thinking has been that it is essential for developing economies to restrain rent-seeking behavior by removing state intervention in the competitive market process as much as possible. The so-called structural adjustment policy that the World Bank imposed on debtor nations as a condition for its loans made such a view the orthodoxy.

Suppose that government policies create rent *opportunities* in the private sector, opportunities to gain returns in excess of those generated by a competitive process, instead of by a direct transfer of wealth. Recall the model of Hellmann, Murdock, and Stiglitz. The policy of financial restraint does not automatically transfer wealth to financial intermediaries as in the case of a direct subsidy, but creates an opportunity for extra profits, which may be realized by a bank's own efforts to expand its deposit base and to monitor private firms. A similar example may be found in the patent system. When the market fails to provide sufficient quasi-rents for investments in research, the government may create (by the design of the patent system) opportunities for quasi-rents for inventors. The patent system is distinguished from the standard subsidy scheme in that quasi-rents are provided only on the condition of commercialization of inventive activity rather than on inventive activity itself.

Another example is the use of export subsidies. When policy-induced rents are distributed on a discretionary basis, such as with import quotas, private agents may allocate their efforts away from productive activities to attempt to capture policy-induced rents. However, if policy-induced rents are provided on the condition of fulfillment of an objective criterion, they may induce private agents to supply more goods that are undersupplied in the competitive process. Using the phrase "performance-indexed reward," *EAM* suggests an idea similar to "contingent rents." *EAM* notes that a wide range of government assistance in the form of subsidies, access to rationed credits and foreign exchanges, tax exemptions, etc., was provided to businesses in East Asia on the basis of export "contests." *EAM* considers such contests to be effective in limiting unproductive rent-seeking behavior because of the transparency of the rule. Rewarding the agent with better performance will preserve competition among the recipients. However, this argument entails an export-push bias, which we discuss below.

The Coordinating Role of Contingent Rents

The discussion in the previous subsection suggests a new concept of "contingent rents," i.e., the realization of rents contingent on performance or outcome, e.g., the mobilization of savings, commercialization of inventions, or increase of exports. Measurement of performance or outcome may be based on a fairly objective criterion or a more or less discretionary one. In this subsection, we discuss two issues: First, we inquire whether the failure of cooperation arising from a "prisoner's dilemma" situation can be rectified by the use of contingent rent, and, further, can possibly be better than that achieved by a nonconditional subsidy. Second, we inquire under what conditions the efficient management of contingent rent can be made credible when it is based on the judgment of whether cooperation has been achieved.

Many economic activities involve the joint decisions of multiple independent agents. When the investment or effort choice of each agent affects the other, the coordination of input decisions is necessary to achieve economic efficiency. Consider, for example, the case where both parties must make some kind of fixed investment that benefits both parties. If each side invests without considering the benefits that accrue to the other, the investment choice will be lower than that which maximizes the joint return from investment. If the two sides could commit to cooperate, then they could both choose efficient levels of investment. Conversely, if one party believed the other intended to cooperate unconditionally, it could maximize its *private* return with a lower level of investment. Thus, many coordination problems have the same strategic structure as the prisoner's dilemma.

By cooperation, the two parties are able to generate high pay-offs for both. If they do not cooperate, the level of pay-offs will be lower for both parties. But, because there are short-term advantages for each party from unilaterally defecting from cooperation, if the two parties interact only once, both will defect. Conversely, if the two parties expect to meet repeatedly, such a defection may trigger the other party to retaliate by withdrawing cooperation in the future. It is well known that, if this game of "cooperate or defect" is repeated infinitely over time, cooperation can emerge if both parties are sufficiently farsighted. Therefore, relational transactions among the fixed members can be a mechanism to resolve the type of coordination problem addressed here (see Chapter 13 of this volume by Okuno-Fujiwara). However, there are circumstances when both parties are sufficiently myopic (nearsighted) that cooperation will not be self-enforcing. Lau argues in Chapter 2 of this volume that "one important role of the government is to enforce contracts and commitments that are not 'self-enforcing.'" Let us pursue this idea and ask under what conditions the government itself is motivated to play such a role, instead of assuming that the government, which creates law, will unconditionally choose to impose laws that facilitate efficient private transactions, rather than to exploit this power in a predatory manner.

A model recently developed by Murdock (1996) is suggestive for this class of problems. The model analyzes how to overcome a hold-up problem (a one-sided prisoner's dilemma problem as described below) between the firm and its workers (*à la* Grout 1984), but the basic idea is applicable in any strategic interaction of a prisoner's dilemma nature. The firm makes a (partially) sunk investment in its capital stock. After the firm invests, the workers may extract extra income from the firm because the firm cannot costlessly redeploy its capital. This induces the firm to choose a low investment level, because the firm internalizes the cost of hold-up into its investment decision. If the workers could credibly commit to not hold up the firm, then the firm could invest efficiently and both parties would earn higher incomes. In this framework, the firm's choices are to invest "high" (i.e., choose the efficient level of investment) or "low" (invest expecting to be held up), whereas the workers' options are to "cooperate" (refrain from holding up the firm) or "defect" (hold up the firm).

The government, which is modeled as a "strategic" agent maximizing fiscal revenue, can choose one of four policies: it can offer a "contingent rent" to the firm conditional on cooperation (the market-enhancing approach), it can provide a per-unit subsidy for specific capital (the neoclassical solution), it can remain neutral (doing nothing), or it can hold up the firm as well (the predatory approach). The difference between the four policies may be visualized as follows. Suppose that a pay-off matrix of the conventional prisoner's dilemma type is given, with rows representing the firm's "high or low" strategy choice and columns representing workers' "cooperate or defect" strategy choice. The cooperative equilibrium is where the firm invests high and the workers cooperate. The adversarial equilibrium is where the firm invests low and the workers defect. Even though the income for both the firm and the workers is higher under cooperation, this equilibrium may not be stable—because the workers always have a one-period incentive to defect (the value that the workers can extract from the firm by holding it up after it has invested high). Cooperation can only be sustained when the future value of cooperation (the capitalized value of the difference in income between the cooperative and adversarial equilibria) exceeds the one-period incentive to defect. Contingent rents increase the incremental value of cooperation, by providing a reward only when cooperation is achieved, whereas a per-unit subsidy has almost no effect on the *incremental* value of cooperation (because the subsidy increases investment in both the cooperative *and* the adversarial equilibria).

The contingent-rent policy, where the firm is offered a bonus subsidy payment for achieving cooperation and high investment, when feasible, will increase income for all three parties—the firm, the workers, and the government. This is feasible because the policy induces the firm to choose a more efficient investment level and the returns from cooperation are shared among all three parties. The neoclassical policy, to subsidize the cost of capital, would increase investment to a more efficient level, if it were implemented. The government may choose not to do so, however, because the general subsidy cost to the government exceeds its incremental revenue.[3]

The final policy option for government is to act as a predator, extracting income from the firm by holding it up as well. This action induces the firm to choose an even lower level of investment than in the adversarial case (when it is being held up only by the workers), further reducing the surplus of investment. Government, however, increases the share of the surplus it captures—its income consists of that it extracts directly from the firm plus whatever it collects through its tax apparatus. In contrast, government revenue for each of the other three policies depends solely on what it collects via taxes. Consequently, whether government chooses to act as a predator or to promote the private sector depends critically on the quality of its tax apparatus. A revenue-maximizing government with a poor tax apparatus will always choose to act as a predator. Thus, the quality of the bureaucracy is an important institutional prerequisite for enabling the government's incentives to be directed at enforcing private contracts and promoting the private sector.

Contingent Rents Versus Straight Subsidy

It is worth emphasizing that the comparative advantage of contingent rents *vis-à-vis* the standard tax-subsidy policy is that contingent rents facilitate private-sector resolution of coordination problems. If the performance criterion to be pursued by government is merely the quantity of exports, the government may as well adopt a uniform export-subsidy scheme such as access to low-rate export financing. However, when the problem involves one of coordination, the government must provide inducement for building the reputation of private partners. In this instance, mere simulation of the market mechanism (the introduction of unconditional and universal subsidies applied to particular goods) will not mitigate inducement for defection from cooperation. As pointed out, the private sector can overcome cooperation problems when the gains from cooperation are sufficiently large. Thus, unconditional subsidies do not promote private-sector coordination because they do not alter the relative returns to cooperation in comparison to the adversarial equilibrium.

Anecdotal evidence that supports such an interpretation is abundant in East Asia. The Japan Development Bank provided low-rate credits not only to export industries, but also to enterprises whose market bases were primarily domestic. However, it seldom provided credits to enterprises whose reputations were marred by adversarial industrial relations. Because the Ministry of Finance awarded licenses in Japan for new bank branches, and because bank branches were highly profitable due to the practice of financial restraint, the Ministry of Finance could threaten the reduction of rent opportunities for banks that shirked their duties for monitoring and prudence. For example, in the main bank system of Japan, banks were expected to rescue firms suffering from temporary financial distress. Banks that shirked this responsibility would have difficulty acquiring bank licenses in the future. In this way, the bureaucrats of the Ministry of Finance also benefited from increased tax revenues, as well as lucrative post-retirement job opportunities in the profitable banking sector (Aoki and Patrick 1994).

Finally, we may add a critical comment on the alleged informational efficiency of the standard tax-subsidy scheme in general. This scheme seems to require less information than the administration of contingent rents. However, the real world is full of informational imperfection, and incentive problems must be coped with properly in order for this policy measure to work as designed. Unfortunately, the same problem perceived in a classical writing of Hayek (1945) on the command economy may also hinder the efficient management of tax/subsidy measures. For example, production subsidies need to be awarded in proportion to the amount of outputs. They may merely accelerate the volume of production without providing incentives for, e.g., the renewal of production facilities. Subsidies for investment in research and development may not create incentives for generating really innovative products. The patent system, which requires much more detailed and specialized information processing for its administration, may perform better in this respect. Also, competition in the real world is multidimensional. In the Arrow–Debreu static general-equilibrium world, all goods are assumed to be homogenous, each good being assured of a thick market without intertemporal effect. This implicit assumption implies there is a unique price for each good established by perfect competition independent of producers' reputation, etc. In reality, service after sale, quality reputation, and other factors are also important elements of competition. Must subsidies then be based on multidimensional criteria? As the incomplete contract theory suggests, subsidies contingent on many facets of competition may not be possible to specify. For these reasons, the alleged informational efficiency of standard tax subsidies *vis-à-vis* contingent rents based on a simple criterion may not be self-evident.

1.5 THE LOCUS OF COORDINATION ACTIVITY

The preceding sections describe a broad set of microeconomic policies potentially available to the government of a developing economy. It is the purpose of this section to clarify how these policies relate to each other and to elucidate the circumstances under which they may be applied.

Earlier, we characterized the distinction between the market-friendly view and the developmental-state view as one where market and government were substitutes. Here we can be more precise by what we mean by substitutes: the market-friendly view emphasizes that coordination problems should be resolved by market-based institutions whereas the developmental-state view emphasizes that many important coordination problems should be resolved by government. The two views consider markets and government as rival institutions for determining the locus of coordination in the economy.

This need not be the case. The market-enhancing view emphasizes the role of government action in promoting private-sector coordination. Thus, government and the private sector are not rivals, competing for control over economic activity. It is interesting to note that in the countries of East Asia, despite their activist governments, the size of the public sector is quite small relative to Western standards. The role of the government was not to substitute for, but to facilitate private-sector coordination.

The Matrix of Coordination Activity

Figure 1.1 describes a spectrum of the locus of coordination activity, with rows indicating spheres where coordination takes place, and columns indicating mechanisms of coordination. At the upper left corner lie Walrasian markets in which coordination can be achieved merely through the mediation of price signals. A prerequisite for these markets to function well is that the property rights to all goods are well defined and enforced, for which the state is ultimately responsible (a point emphasized by early North; see North and Thomas 1973). Also, the monitoring and enforcement by the government to regulate the emergence of monopoly is necessary for Walrasian markets to achieve efficiency. These are the fundamental, complementary roles of the government to frame the basis of market coordination. In addition, in the case of public goods or goods with diffusive externalities, markets are incomplete and government intervention to facilitate provision of these goods, or to create quasi-markets, may actually facilitate private-sector coordination in other areas (consider, for example, government provision of road and highway infrastructure or Pigouvian taxes on pollutants).

At the other extreme in the lower right corner is a command economy, where all coordination takes place under the quantity direction of a centralized government. An example of this in East Asia could be the Chinese economy before it started the transition to a market economy in the late 1970s. Somewhat close to this regime is the Japanese wartime economy when the government directed the flow of resources to war production. The government bureaucrats at that time tried to emulate the Soviet planning system, but this effort failed because of the lack of price incentives on the side of the private sector (Okazaki 1993; see also Chapter 8 by Aoki in this volume). Discretionary import control may fall into this category, although the quantity control may be limited to particular markets. It is well known that such a mechanism can lead to unproductive rent-seeking behavior, which will be discussed in the next section. Over all, at the bottom right

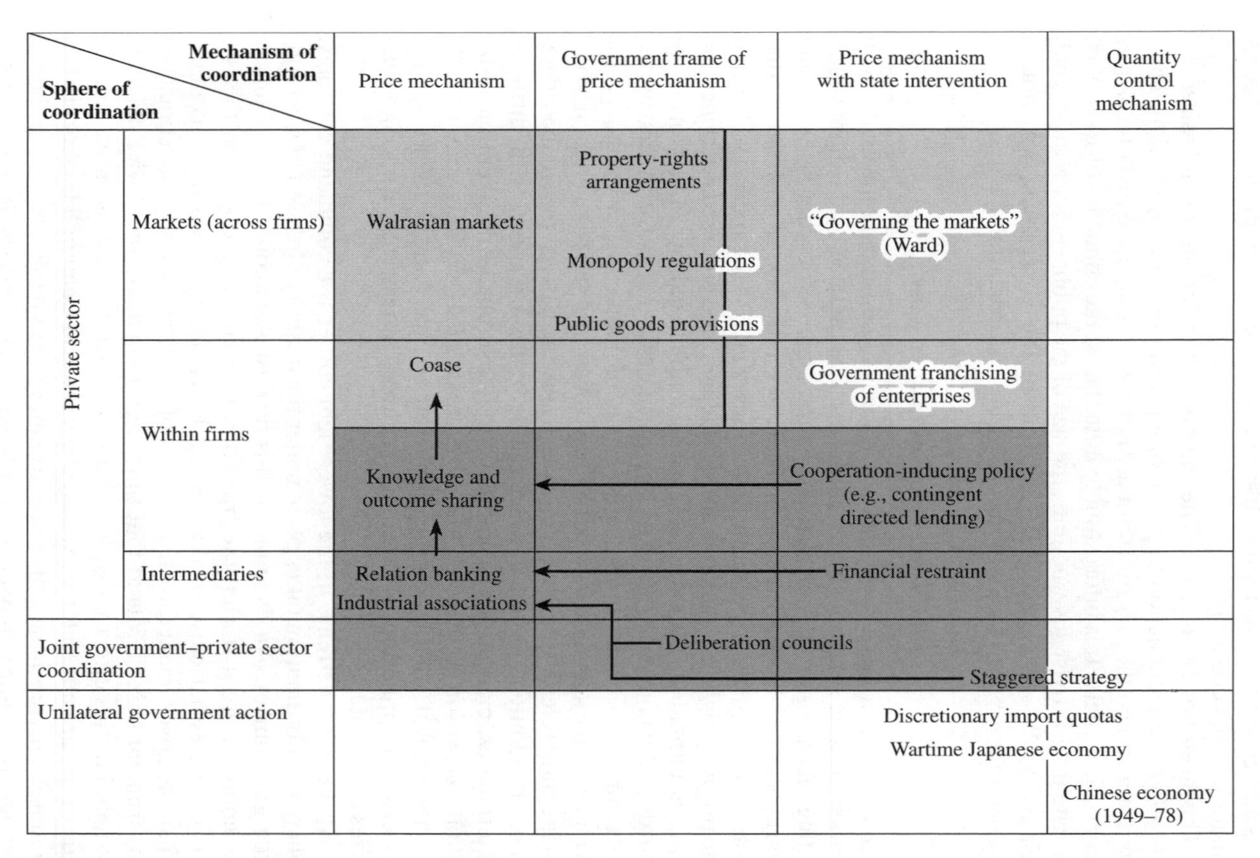

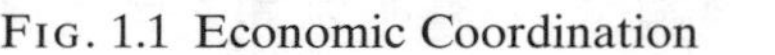
FIG. 1.1 Economic Coordination

corner, government tends to be predatory, extracting resources from the private (or household) sector to finance its own activity.

Although the Walrasian market economy and the command economy were two major objects of study within the framework of the old "comparative economic system" *à la* Bergson, these are obviously not the only two methods of achieving coordination. As Coase (1937) discussed, the firm is a private-sector institution (a contractual arrangement) that arises to coordinate activities that may not be achieved through market transactions. Similarly, when the coordination problem involves a diffuse set of agents involved in an activity characterized by increasing returns to scale and asymmetric information, another set of private-sector institutions will arise to act as intermediaries, as is the case in the financial sector with banks.

It is upon the upper left region (light-shaded) that proponents of the market-friendly view focus. The primary means of resolving coordination problems emphasized in this view are markets and firms, with a government frame of competition and provision of public goods. The proponents of this view tend to underplay the significance of intermediaries (say, banks), *vis-à-vis* markets (say, securities markets). Implicit in this emphasis is that this set of coordination activities is sufficient to solve most important coordination problems. A further embedded assumption of this view is that future private-sector innovations will ultimately solve additional problems through a process of experimentation. They regard market-based coordination, with private-sector organizations (particularly firms) serving to resolve coordination problems that the economy faces.

In contrast, the developmental-state view has a more pessimistic perspective on the ability of the market mechanism to solve coordination problems, expecting these failures to be pervasive. This view emphasizes the need for government systematically to "get the prices wrong" (Amsden 1989) or to "govern the market" (Wade 1990) in order to facilitate the development process. In contrast to the Walrasian model of the world in which the number of players is fixed, they even consider that, unless the government creates viable players (firms), the development process may not even take off. Presumably they consider the government to have better information and judgment than the private sector and to be capable of guiding markets "unilaterally" and wisely. The upper right area (shaded with diagonal lines) in Figure 1.1 indicates that, according to the developmental-state view, markets are heavily intervened in and governed by the state.

Although the market-friendly view and the developmental-state view capture certain aspects of the East Asian economic development process, we consider the perceptions and concerns of both to be too biased toward the sphere of market coordination. They differ only in arguing that market failures are taken care of by the minimum action of government framing the market mechanism (the market-friendly view) or that market failures are so pervasive that comprehensive corrective actions in markets by government are called for (the developmental-state view).

In contrast, the market-enhancing view points out that one cannot understand essential ingredients of East Asian development without attending to the intermediate region of Figure 1.1 highlighted with shadow. The importance of this region is made clear first by recognizing the ability of the private sector to coordinate a large fraction of economic activity (whether across markets, within firms, using intermediaries, or jointly with government), while at the same time recognizing the potential for government to facilitate the development of private-sector institutions. This idea is best captured by looking at the entries in the "price mechanism with state intervention" column of the figure under the "markets" row and then following the arrows. Various policy instruments, as discussed in the previous sections, such as contingent rents, financial restraint, deliberation councils, and staggered-entry strategies, induce coordination and cooperation in the private-sector institutions. In this view, government policy is not aimed directly at introducing a substitute mechanism for resolving market failures, but rather at increasing the capabilities of private-sector institutions to do so. It should now be clear how the government acts to complement private institutions, rather than as a substitute for the market mechanism.

The Role of Government as a Function of Stage of Development

In our view, policy should have a bias to using private-sector institutions to resolve coordination problems whenever feasible. The private sector has built-in self-regulating features, such as competition, entry, and exit, that the government does not have. Furthermore, private-sector agents are much better able to respond to local information than can a centralized institution. This preference for the private sector should narrow the scope of policy discussion to only those coordination problems that remain unresolved by the private sector and create a boundary for government activism.

This boundary, however, may depend on the level of development of the economy. When the economy is in a low state of development, the availability of intermediaries is limited, the capabilities of firms are modest, and even the efficiency of markets is hampered by poor integration and underdevelopment of property-rights arrangements in the economy. Under these circumstances, the ability of the private sector to solve challenging coordination problems is suspect, and there may be significant scope for government policy to facilitate development. As the economy matures, however, the ability of the private sector improves and the scope for policy becomes more limited. As Dinc's path-dependent theory suggests, even if government intervention may facilitate the emergence of a private-sector intermediary (in his case, relational banking), once it is established, it may survive even after government regulations are removed or the economy is open to more competitive external environments. Another example we suggested was that, when the source of coordination failure is easily recognizable, joint government-private coordination may be effective. This condition is most likely to hold when the economy is in a low state of development. It is important to recognize, however, that when technologies are advanced and exploration into new technological opportunities becomes highly uncertain, standard setting, with the heavy involvement of government, even if performed jointly with the private sector, may result in higher costs when a mistake is made. The previous discussion of standard setting in the high-definition television industry in both Japan and the United States emphasized this point.

An Application to Transition Economies

Analysis of policy based on this matrix of economic coordination may also be helpful for considering the role of government as an economy makes the transition from a command economy to a market-based economy. The countries of the former Soviet Union and of Eastern Europe attempted to make a rapid transition to a market economy, effectively attempting to move the locus of coordination activity from the lower right extreme of the matrix to the upper left extreme of Figure 1.1. Unfortunately, after years of state control, the capabilities of private-sector institutions were limited. For example, mushrooming banks in Russia had no experience in evaluating loans on a competitive basis and the governance institutions of firms were poorly developed, with the consequence that insiders gained control of most firms' assets, reducing incentives for efficient restructuring.

In contrast, the transition taking place in China has proceeded much more slowly, with a gradual decrease in the direct role of the government in coordinating economic activity and a concomitant rise in the role of more decentralized institutions. Chapter 9 by Qian and Weingast in this volume discusses this transition, in particular because township-village enterprises are a government-owned form of decentralized coordination. It may be understood as a gradual move from the bottom right corner to the central region of the market-enhancing policy arena. As Aoki discusses in Chapter 8 in this volume, it is somewhat analogous to the path the Japanese economy traveled from the command economy during the war to the post-war market economy.

Three Caveats

We would like to record three caveats. First, the schematic representation in Figure 1.1 is obviously simplified, as it is constructed for organizing a conceptual framework. The boundary between different spheres and mechanisms of coordination may not be readily apparent, and the method by which each of these forms of coordination is actually achieved will depend in large part on important institutional features of the economy.

Second, when we state that less government intervention is desirable as the economy develops, we do not mean that every economy will eventually converge to the upper left Walrasian extreme. Even within highly developed economies, coordination failure will be pervasive, as Matsuyama argues in Chapter 5 in this volume. These coordination failures may become even more difficult to resolve as technological and market opportunities become more uncertain and complex. Hence, diverse private experiments involving various types of private organizations will play a larger role. The organizational forms by which an economy will arrange such private experiments will be partially path dependent (historically conditioned), but government may play a certain role in determining the direction in which the economy will evolve within such constraints.

Third, even if private-sector institutions geared toward market coordination are underdeveloped, it does not automatically guarantee the effectiveness of state activism or even call for unconditional state intervention. The government must be capable of performing the required coordination tasks and it must also be motivated to do so in the public interest. The capability and incentives of government are shaped by the political-economy structure in which they are embedded.

In the rest of this chapter we turn to the issues related to the structure of political economy and path dependence.

1.6 THE POLITICAL ECONOMY OF EAST ASIAN DEVELOPMENT

The Absence of a Dominant Economic Class as an Initial Condition

As already noted, *EAM* maintains that economic contests, as well as non-contest-based policies, require the insulation of a professional, well-disciplined bureaucracy from the push and pull of politics. However, we can find professional civil services that are even more merit based in many former British colonies such as India. The communist elites in China have been highly insulated from external pressures, but their performance pales in comparison with that of their East Asian counterparts in realizing shared economic growth without corruption or predatory behavior. Meanwhile, we observe that Japanese civil servants have been placed under increasing criticism both from abroad and at home for their inactiveness, excessively conservative regulations stifling private experiments, etc. Is that mainly because the bureaucrats themselves have turned into a powerful interest group? Or is there another reason? The "insulation of elite civil servants" does not seem to be an unambiguously positive characteristic of a bureaucracy.

In our opinion, the issue is related to *EAM*'s "shared-growth" interpretation of the development process in East Asia. *EAM* posits that continued equal distribution of the fruits of growth is the legitimizing objective of a neutral bureaucracy and its great achievement. In challenge to this view, Rodrik (1994) argues that the relative equality of income, schooling, and wealth (landholding) was an important initial condition, rather than a consequence, of economic development in East Asia. Sachs (1985) concludes from a comparison of Latin America and East Asia that equal income distribution can become an important determinant of the quality of macroeconomic management, as the government may be less susceptible to rent-seeking behavior of certain specific interest groups. We want to amplify their arguments from a slightly different angle.

Neoclassical economics is concerned with market processes in which anonymous resource holders exchange their services for final goods. The firm is no more than a mechanical intermediary to transform those services into final goods. The corresponding neoclassical model of government is also a black box through which pluralistic interests of resource holders are aggregated and by which market failures can be accordingly corrected. However, for understanding the development process of the economy, it is often useful to use the "classical" concepts of resource holders distinguished by the type of resource they control, such as capitalists, landlords, workers, and peasants, rather than the neoclassical notion of anonymous resource holders, and analyze how they are capable of influencing the political process to acquire political rents to their advantage.

From such a perspective, Northeast Asian economies seem to have a unique initial condition of economic development: the absence of a dominant economic class. This is a very important thesis, developed in this volume by Meredith Woo-Cumings in Chapter 11 for the case of Korea and Taiwan, but the characteristic also applies to postwar Japan as well as partially to Hong Kong.

Before the postwar development process took off in those economies, there were no individual capitalists who had amassed enormous assets and controlled the supply of financial and industrial capital. In Japan, the controlling power of *zaibatsu* capitalists had already been restrained by the military-bureaucrat alliance during wartime (Okazaki 1993) and was finally annihilated in the postwar period. In Korea and Taiwan, as Woo-Cumings lucidly describes, the Japanese imperialist government systematically suppressed the rise of individual capitalists. Therefore, foreign aid (and foreign direct investment by overseas Chinese in the case of Hong Kong) aside, demands for the initial financing of industrial development was only met by the mobilization of savings from numerous households.

Neither did large landlords exist who ruthlessly exploited or drove peasants from the farmland. In Japan, Korea, and Taiwan, sweeping land reforms were implemented after World War II to hold the (potential) tide of peasant revolts in check and, consequently, small-scale landholding by cultivating farmers became dominant. Finally, there was no organized labor to raise minimum wages through collective action. In Japan, workers sometimes took control of factories immediately after the war when incumbent management lost the authority and ability to manage. In 1947 unionized workers even attempted to stage a general strike under the communist leadership to defend jobs that were threatened. However, industrial actions were politically suppressed on the eve of the Korean War with the backing of the political might of the Occupation Army. After that, workers were domesticated within the scope of their own enterprises. In Korea and Taiwan, the organization of workers, at an industrial or enterprise level, was not tolerated.

The absence of a politically powerful, dominant economic class was indeed an important historical condition that profoundly constrained postwar economic development in Northeast Asia. And, it was indeed this condition that made political leaders and a nonelective, permanent bureaucracy in Northeast Asia appear to be autonomous, and not the reverse. It is true that political leaders and bureaucrats were most responsive to the interests of business leaders. Political scientists used to describe the situation in Japan in the 1950s as an "iron triangle" of bureaucrats, business, and political elites. However, bureaucrats and business elites were not from exclusive origins. They ascended to the positions at the apex of a relatively homogeneous society on the basis of educational screening and the merit of demonstrated administrative and/or managerial ability, not uncommonly with family roots in the rural hinterland. The ruling political party was dominated by ex-bureaucrats, and after the collapse of the political ambition of the empire, there was no independent voice from political elites. Bureaucrats thus were able to treat the government of their country as if it were the management of a household—*oikonomos*. In Korea and Taiwan, political leaders ascended from a military background but, for them as well, the building up of the countries' industrial power was regarded as the first order of business given their geopolitical positions in the Cold War.

Furthermore, political leaders and bureaucrats in these economies had no incentive to distribute political rents in favor of any particular economic class, because if that class were to become sufficiently powerful in the future, the favored class might thereby be able to threaten these leaders' autonomy someday in the future. Thus the "shared growth" phenomenon in Northeast Asia seems to be a profoundly path-dependent phenomenon that evolved from the unique historical conditions prevailing immediately after the Pacific War. It was not something intrinsic to a Confucian tradition of the East Asian bureaucracy.

Because of its apparent autonomy, the permanent bureaucracy in the East Asian state is sometimes characterized as "strong." Paradoxically, however, it may be also regarded as "weak." Both strength and weakness arise from the same source—the absence of a dominant economic class, which amounted to the relative equality of power among various interest groups. The bureaucracy, which has legitimized its control by the equal payment of growth dividends to all economic classes, may become inhibited, by inertia, from making any radical move that would disproportionately hurt any specific economic interest. We discuss below the growing evidence of such weakness in the contemporary Japanese bureaucracy.

Integral Development of the Rural Economy and the Market-Enhancing Role of Rural Entrepreneurship

One of the important consequences of the absence of a politically powerful class in East Asia, particularly that of large landlords and organized labor, was the evolution of a more integral linkage between the rural sector and the urban sector, instead of the drastic destruction of peasant farming and the resulting massive immigration of the rural population to the urban center. Chapter 10 by Juro Teranishi describes the macrobackground of this process. He finds little difference between Latin America and Sub-Saharan Africa on one hand and East Asia on the other in that industrial development was largely financed by the transfer of resources from the rural sector in the form of direct and indirect taxes. However, in Latin America and Africa, (urban-based) governments compensated particular groups of the rural sector, landlords in the case of Latin America and politically influential tribes in the case of Africa, by the supply of divisible goods (such as subsidies for machinery, fertilizer, etc.). In contrast, East Asian governments delivered rural expenditures more in the form of indivisible infrastructure (such as irrigation and transportation). The rural areas of East Asia could be better characterized as many small, independent farms. Thus, the government could best deliver value to these interests by providing public goods, such as infrastructure. The consequence was a steady and universal increase in the productivity of small-scale farming.

A microeconomic outcome of the steady, universal improvement of rural productivity was the continual thrust of the "rural-based entrepreneur," a concept introduced by Hayami (1993). Instead of merely utilizing cheap labor in traditional farming, these rural entrepreneurs link the new productive potential of the rural sector to the advanced industrial sector and urban markets by creating new economic activities in the rural sector, while relying on traditional community ties as a means of mitigating contract-enforcement costs which can otherwise be costly when the institutions of market and property rights have not been fully developed. Such rural-based entrepreneurship seems to be a generic feature found throughout East Asia, and may take various forms ranging from rural subcontractors in Japan, commercial middlemen in Indonesia (Hayami and Kawagoe 1993), food-processing entrepreneurs in Taiwan, to local administrators who organize the thriving TVEs in rural China today (Chapter 9 by Qian and Weingast).

The role of the rural entrepreneur is the subject of another World Bank study directed by Professor Yujiro Hayami (1993). We only stress here that the steady integral development of the rural economy is one of the most important elements of East Asian development. Because income growth was not concentrated in the urban sector, migration from rural to urban areas was more gradual. Consequently, there was not a rapid rise in urban poverty, so political pressure never developed for significant government consumption aimed at mitigating urban poverty. This facilitated more stable macroeconomic policies, because the economy did not face a massive reallocation of resources in concentrated time periods. Further, because rural incomes rose in parallel with urban incomes, domestic markets expanded rapidly. We turn now to the implications of this feature.

Is the Story of Export-Push Strategy Really Telling?

An important implication of the gradual transition and the universal growth of rural incomes was the sustained growth of domestic markets for industrial products. *EAM*'s emphasis on the "export-push" strategy is somewhat misleading in this light. For example, in Japan the leading export industries of various phases of economic development (textile and garment industries in the prewar period and the 1950s; shipbuilding and electric appliances in the 1960s; cars, manufacturing machinery, semiconductors, and electronics products in the 1970s and 1980s) were those industries whose products had been first widely marketed and tested in domestic markets. They were not necessarily nurtured by government industrial policy (except for shipbuilding) because of their intrinsic export capability. A tentative econometric study by Aoki and Nakamura using corporate data from the Nikkei Electronic Economic Data System between 1965 and 1973 did not reject the hypothesis that the car and electric machinery industries were not the beneficiaries of low interest rates. It was, rather, the power industry, a public monopoly, and the declining textile and shipbuilding industries that paid relatively lower "effective" interest costs (after taking into account the effects of compensated balances) during that period.

Through learning by doing made possible by marketing products to the growing domestic markets, manufacturers in the car and electric machinery industries were able to improve productivity and subsequently become competitive in international markets. Ironically, the role of government in this process was not an export-promoting policy for those industries, but the protection of domestic markets through implicit and explicit regulations on new entry. In slighting the important implications for industrial learning made possible through the integral development of the rural sector, on the one hand, and overemphasizing "a result of the export policies of the HPAEs . . . [on] high rates of productivity-based catching up and TFP [total factor productivity] growth" (p. 316), on the other, *EAM* may be deriving a somewhat misleading lesson for other developing economies. *EAM*'s "export fetishism" has been thoroughly, and rightly in our opinion, criticized by Rodrik (1994:33–42).

Rents as an Affirmative Action Instrument

It is often claimed that the East Asian type of government intervention is effective, because populations there are rather homogenous in ethnic and economic backgrounds. This chapter has suggested that the absence of a dominant economic class and the associated tendency toward assimilation in educational and income opportunities was an important initial condition preceding development in the Northeast Asian economies. But the presence of such a condition may not be necessary for "successful" government intervention in the developmental process, measured in terms of the per-capita growth rate.

Chapter 12 by Jomo K. S. and Gomez describes how the government of Malaysia intervened in the market, primarily by means of the incorporation of public enterprises and favorable government treatment of Bumiputera or Malay enterprises, with the objective of promoting economic opportunities for economically disadvantaged Malays *vis-à-vis* the economically dominant ethnic Chinese. As a consequence of this process, combined with the impressive economic growth of the nation as a whole, the position of the Malay majority has dramatically improved. For example, according to statistics Jomo and Gomez cite, the proportion of Bumiputeras in professions increased from 4.9 per cent in 1970 to 31.9 per cent in 1992, and their proportion in ownership of share capital rose from 1.6 per cent in 1970 to 18.2 per cent in 1992. The improved performance for the Bumiputera ethnic group did not come without costs, however. The country was troubled by capital flight and increasing public debt, especially from the mid-1970s to the mid-1980s, and ethnic Chinese engaged in unproductive rent-seeking to develop connections with influential Bumiputera policymakers. Nevertheless, only a small proportion of such rents has been wasted through dissipation, while Malaysia's relatively abundant resource rents realized an impressive 6.9 per cent average growth in gross domestic product between 1971 and 1990, rising to over 8 per cent between 1988 and the present. Since the end of the 1980s, the government has liberalized and modified its affirmative action program by various means, including privatizing public enterprises, but Jomo and Gomez claim this process has not been less redistributive to the politically influential. These two authors open up an important research agenda on trade-offs between government interventions for the purpose of development and those for the purpose of redistribution.

1.7 A NEW RESEARCH AGENDA: ENDOGENIZING THE GOVERNMENT

Incentives of the Government

In the neoclassical approach, government is conceptualized as a neutral arbiter potentially capable of intervening in the market process to correct various market failures. Obviously such an assumption is not useful for understanding the actual development process of any economy. Needless to say, the government may have its own incentives. More realistically, each government branch may have a different objective formed through interaction with various private interests and the political-economic process may reflect intricate interplays of conflicting interests, public and private. The theory of unproductive rent-seeking behavior was an attempt to capture one type of this process prevalent in many developing economies. Making explicit the incentives of the government and analyzing its consequence for government–private sector interaction is certainly a very important new research agenda for East Asian economies. This volume contains a few works that take steps in that direction.

As already noted, Chapter 9 by Qian and Weingast enquires why there is such a large performance differential between two types of government-owned enterprise, SOEs and TVEs, and finds an answer in the differences in the incentives of the governments of different levels that control the two types of enterprise. Township and village governments have proper incentives to discipline TVEs. They have no incentives either to protect TVEs by trade barriers or to bail out failing TVEs. Qian and Weingast argue that the institutional environment of governments, "fiscal federalism, Chinese style," effectively removes such incentives from township and village governments.

The model by Murdock (1995) referred to above in connection with contingent rents also assumes that government has its own incentives: to maximize its revenues. For fulfilling that purpose, government may have the option of exploiting its power in a predatory manner. His analysis shows that, only when government has an information-processing capability and a high-quality tax-collection apparatus, will it refrain from acting as a predator on the private sector. A recent attempt by the Chinese government to move from a rather ambiguous profit-contracting system entailing much-publicized bribery to a formal corporate tax system may reflect the long-term interest of the central government to facilitate further growth and thereby secure a solid fiscal foundation for the government. The fate of such a move would crucially hinge upon the capability of the government to create a quality tax apparatus.

Institutional Inertia of Bureau-Pluralism

A conventional notion is that unproductive rent-seeking behavior is not prevalent in East Asia because of the relative neutrality of bureaucracy. *EAM* seems to subscribe to this view. We have stressed that in Northeast Asia there is no dominant economic class. However, that does not imply that there is no room for rents to play a role in distribution nor that distribution is entirely determined through competitive government-administered "contests." *EAM* claims that the relatively small income differential between rural and urban incomes in East Asia is the result of a flexible labor market. However, this characterization is not correct at least for the cases of Japan and Korea. It is largely a result of heavy market interventions by the government, such as the price-support policy of a major agricultural crop, rice. Income protection is not limited to the rural sector, but also extended to other low-productivity sectors such as wholesale and retail in the forms of strict entry regulation (by potentially more efficient newcomers), credit subsidies, opportunities for tax evasion, as well as government-administered risk-sharing schemes such as employment adjustment and equipment-scrapping subsidies to declining industries.

Chapter 8 by Aoki characterizes such redistributional mechanisms in Japan as "bureau-pluralism" in the sense that pluralistic interests are protected by the mediation of government bureaucracy. Quasi-rents acquired through organizational and technological innovation by the advanced, high-productivity sectors, such as the machinery industry, are redistributed evenly to backward, low-productivity sectors, such as agriculture, wholesale and retail, declining industries, through the distortion of the price mechanism dramatically manifested in huge foreign–domestic price differentials and through tax-subsidy schemes. Government protection in Japan is not primarily directed toward export industries, but rather toward the unproductive segment of the economy.

Such redistribution mechanisms certainly contributed to the expansion of domestic markets for consumption goods and, through producers' learning by doing made possible by the expanding domestic markets, contributed to a larger opportunity for the advanced high-productivity sector to gain quasi-rents from international markets. However, such a process cannot continue indefinitely as the relative presence of the economy becomes large in the world market. Ever-growing export efforts by the advanced industries, combined with the protected markets of the low-productivity sector, has led to an increasing balance-of-payments surplus, eventually resulting in the rapid appreciation of domestic currency far exceeding purchasing power parity. As a result, the continuing protection of low-productivity sectors will mitigate the ability of the export industry to compete effectively in the international market and induce it to shift its mature production operations abroad. From the perspective of Asia as a whole, increasing transplants by Japanese industry are a manifestation of the workings of the principle of classical comparative advantage. Yet, for Japan it is a dilemma in that the maintenance of relative income distribution through bureau-pluralism undermines the very viability of the process. However, the Japanese bureaucracy seems to be too "weak" to undertake an initiative to correct it.

In the theory of bureau-pluralism, it is assumed that each administrative bureau absorbs the interests of constituent private groups and represents them in intrabureaucratic processes such as budgetary allocation and national economic planning. One of most important incentives for each bureau to act as the quasi-agent of jurisdictional private interests is that bureaucrats may get postretirement jobs in the private sector, the practice known as *amakudari* (Aoki 1988). A subtle difference between this practice and the revolving-door practice in other economies is that these post-retirement jobs cannot be arranged privately, but by the ministry itself. Thus, potential private-government collusion may be institutionalized, if not in the form of private bribery.

Comparative Regimes of Government-Private Interactions

Interactions between the private sector and the government (especially its administrative organ) are more explicitly analyzed in a comparative perspective in Chapter 13 by Okuno-Fujiwara. The mode of these interactions varies across economies, depending on institutional structures historically formed, and this difference may have important implications for economic development. Okuno-Fujiwara uses the bargaining game theoretic framework to highlight implications of the relative importance of *ex ante* rules versus *ex post* renegotiation in determining the outcome of business-government interactions. Whether emergent outcomes, jointly determined by the actions of concerned parties and stochastic events, can be flexibly negotiable may depend on the possibility of side payments (transfer of incomes among bargaining partners). Even though such possibility may have the opportunity to make both parties better off, if side payments are blocked, *ex ante* rules may prevail.

Okuno-Fujiwara identifies United States institutions as having a rule-based system in which *ex ante* rules play a relatively more important role in determining the outcome, while Japanese institutions have the relation-based system in which a limited *ex post* flexibility is made possible by repeated interactions among a closed group of players. This difference is traced to a difference in the way power is allocated within the government, to the "preference" of the government (its administrative organ), and to the institutional structure in which the government-business relationship is embedded. If the judicial branch of the government is relatively autonomous, the discretionary modification of an *ex post* outcome by negotiation between a private agent and a government agency may be effectively challenged in court by a third party who would be hurt by such a move. As a result, the administrative organ may prefer to follow *ex ante* rules. On the other hand, if membership at the negotiation table with the government is fixed over time, even if outright side payment is not feasible, an average outcome over time may exhibit a certain degree of flexibility by concessions and reciprocation over time.

Using this analytical framework, Okuno-Fujiwara proceeds to identify three different political regimes relevant not only for a comparison of the United States and Japan, but also for the analysis of authoritarian governments. He also argues that the government-business relationship in postwar Japan may have contributed to the success of industrialization in the 1950s and 1960s, but its efficacy may be declining. These observations suggest that the performance characteristics of a particular type of state activism and their implications for economic development may be dependent on external environments as well as historical conditions to a significant degree, a point we made in Section 1.5 above.

1.8 WHY COMPARATIVE INSTITUTIONAL ANALYSIS?

Although *EAM* made a major contribution for understanding the experiences of economic development in East Asia in particular and deriving general lessons from these experiences, there remained many points to be explored further and developed afresh and, in certain respects, to be debated or challenged. During the course of this project, we have come to realize more and more that East Asian economies are diverse and a unifying theorizing of their development is not easy, at least not at this moment. Therefore, the objective of this project has been not to try to present a coherent and systematic alternative or a new grand paradigm of the East Asian miracle. The following chapters are therefore diverse in their foci, methods, and policy implications. However, we feel there is a common ground bonding us: the methodology of *comparative institutional analysis.* This approach literally involves three elements: comparison, institutions, and analysis (see Aoki 1996).

In contrast to the *EAM* approach which basically posits the dichotomy of the market versus the government and views the possible role of government as substituting for the market when the latter fails to coordinate economic activities, we have argued that coordination failure is more pervasive because of the incompleteness of markets, information asymmetry, bounded rationality, and limited knowledge. Therefore, various institutions, besides government and the market, emerge in an economy as a response. In this perspective, we have also argued, government may not be an omnipotent, neutral substitute for the market. Depending on its environment and capability, it may perform a complementary role to help other institutional elements of the economy to emerge and function. In other environments, it may be motivated to behave in a predatory manner and suppress the evolution of private experiments and institutions that may contribute to the vigorous development of the economy. Recent advances in institutional analysis indicate that each economy may be viewed as a system of interdependent institutions. However, because of the bounded rationality and limited knowledge of economic agents, there may not be a single most efficient economic system, like an idealized Walrasian equilibrium, to which each economy tends to (or should) converge. Rather, there may be multiple economic systems that have evolved from different historical conditions.

An important point is that these multiple systems may not be easily Pareto-rankable on a single dimension of productive efficiency. Criteria for comparing multiple systems may include, besides productive efficiency, various distributive characteristics (relative equality, incentive compatibility, the provision of a safety net). Also, each system may differ in selecting firms over time. Some systems may be more susceptible to Type I errors—potentially viable firms are weeded out prematurely—while other systems may be more susceptible to Type II errors—inefficient firms are rescued and not sufficiently disciplined. Each system may also be different in how new experiments are performed: some systems may be flexible in switching to a new method of coordination, may excel in incremental improvement, or may be hostile to any new private experiment. A system may perform better in some dimensions than in others.

Thus, once one drops the time-honored axiom of the perfect rationality of economic agents, one cannot make the Walrasian equilibrium an analytical benchmark and diagnose real economies by a deductive method. We need to engage in earnest comparative study. We hope that the following chapters dealing with various aspects of diverse Asian economies and their implicit or explicit comparisons with each other, as well as with other types of system, will amply show that there cannot easily be a simple standard model with which the performance of each system can be diagnosed.

However, saying that comparison is important does not imply that assembling a catalogue of different systems of institutions suffices or that analytical technique is irrelevant. On the contrary. If information imperfection and bounded rationality are the major reasons for the emergence of multiple systems, it becomes important for understanding the workings of economic systems to specify explicitly how information is distributed among different types of agents in each system, and to analyze how available information is utilized consistent with the incentives of each agent and how certain patterns of information flows come to evolve and become self-enforcing. For the analysis of such context-specific models based on comparative and historical information, economic tools of game theory and contract theory (information economics), which have made remarkable progress in recent years, will be quite useful. Also, if the formation of the economic system is path dependent, as we have discussed for Northeast Asia, historical analysis that analyzes the evolutionary path of the system should become an integral element of comparative study. Indeed, dialogue between theoretical analysis and historical analysis is an important component of the present volume (Aoki 1996).

While the comparison of various systems has its own specific value for the understanding of each of them, it may also have generic value. Comparative studies may function as a sort of substitute for laboratory experiments which are impossible for the social sciences. It was not rare in our discussion in and out of conferences for somebody to make a general hypothetical statement about some aspect of the role of government explicitly or implicitly based on the experience of a single economy, but invited refutation on the basis of the experience of another economy. Trying to derive a generic proposition that may be valid for a set of economies and identifying conditions that make the proposition true is analogous to collecting experimental samples and seeking a common property among them by controlling irrelevant factors. In this way, we may be safeguarded from making premature claims that may be *ex post* rationalizable only for certain economies. In this regard, we hope that the Asian perspectives developed in the following chapters are helpful in disclosing certain limits of the neoclassical approach which evolved primarily in Anglo-American academia.

NOTES

[1] See pp. 90–93 of *EAM* for the general argument, p. 188 on coordination problems related to aligning interests of various private actors to the principle of shared growth, pp. 197–98 on coordination problems that hinder human capital formation, pp. 211–12 on coordination problems that hinder saving, p. 276 on coordination failures in financial markets, and pp. 293–95 on coordination failures in international markets.

[2] A book on the Japanese main-bank system, based on another World Bank project, also contains several chapters relevant to this issue. See Aoki and Patrick (1994).

[3] The intuition for this result is understandable when one considers that the government must subsidize the entire capital stock of the firm to induce a marginal increase in investment. This subsidy cost dwarfs the incremental government revenue due to more efficient investment. In comparison, contingent rents can be

modest because they are designed to alter the strategic incentives of the parties, rather than to compensate the firm for the strategic cost of being held up by the workers.

REFERENCES

AMSDEN, A. H. (1989), *Asia's Next Giant: South Korea and Late Industrialization*, Oxford University Press, Oxford.

AOKI, M. (1988), *Information, Incentives and Bargaining in the Japanese Economy*, Cambridge University Press, Cambridge.

——(1996), "Toward a Comparative Institutional Analysis: Motivations and Some Tentative General Insights," presidential address delivered at the annual meeting of the Japan Association of Economics and Econometrics (1995), *Japanese Economic Review*, 47:1–19.

——and PATRICK, H., eds. (1994), *The Japanese Main Bank System: Its Relevance for Developing and Transforming Economies*, Oxford University Press, Oxford.

COASE, R. (1937), "The Nature of the Firm," *Economica*, N.S. 4:386–405.

DINC, S. (1996), "Bank Competition, Relational Banking, and Integration of Financial Systems," Ph.D. dissertation submitted to Stanford University.

GROUT, P. (1984), "Investment and Wages in the Absence of Legally Binding Contracts: A Nash Bargaining Approach," *Econometrica*, 52:449–60.

HAYAMI, Y. (1993), "In Search of Rural Entrepreneurship in Asia: Concept and Approach," paper presented at a World Bank project on rural entrepreneurship, Hakone, Japan.

——and KAWAGOE, T. (1993), *The Agrarian Origins of Commerce and Industry*, St. Martin's Press, New York.

HAYEK, F. (1945), "The Use of Knowledge in Society," *American Economic Review*, 35:519–30.

LEIBENSTEIN, H. (1966), "Allocative Efficiency vs. 'X-efficiency,'" *American Economic Review*, 56:392–415.

MURDOCK, K. (1996), "The Determinants of Cooperative and Predatory Government Policy Regimes," a chapter in a Ph.D. dissertation submitted to Stanford University.

NORTH, D. and THOMAS, R. P. (1973), *The Rise of the Western World*, Cambridge University Press, Cambridge.

OKAZAKI, T. (1993), "The Japanese Firm under the Wartime Planned Economy," *Journal of the Japanese and International Economies*, 7:175–203.

RODRIK, D. (1994), "King Kong Meets Godzilla: The World Bank and The East Asian Miracle," in Miracle or Design, *Overseas Development Council Policy Essay No. 11*, Washington, 15–56.

SACHS, J. (1985), "External Debt and Macroeconomic Performance in Latin America and East Asia," *Brookings Papers on Economic Activity*, (II), 523–73.

STIGLITZ, J. and WEISS, A. (1981), "Credit Rationing in Markets with Imperfect Information," *American Economic Review*, 71:393–410.

WADE, R. (1990), *Governing the Market: Economic Theory and the Role of the Government in East Asian Industrialization*, Princeton University Press, Princeton.

World Bank (1993), *The East Asian Miracle: Economic Growth and Public Policy*, Oxford University Press, Oxford.

PART I

MARKET FAILURES AND GOVERNMENT ACTIVISM

2

The Role of Government in Economic Development: Some Observations from the Experience of China, Hong Kong, and Taiwan

LAWRENCE J. LAU

2.1 INTRODUCTION

The role of the government in the highly successful development of the East Asian economies, including Japan, is an extremely broad subject with many different aspects. It is also a subject of considerable controversy. While all the governments, including the usually considered *laissez-faire* government of Hong Kong, have played important roles, there is in fact great diversity in their policies, actions, and outcomes.[1]

One can approach this subject in many ways. For example, one can take a "functional" approach and examine all of the functions that a government can or should fulfill in a developing economy, including the design and maintenance of the economic environment, the regulation of the economy, the enforcement of laws and contracts, and the provision of public goods such as infrastructure and education.[2] Another approach is the positive approach which poses the questions: What have these governments actually done (or not done)? How have their policies worked? Under what circumstances? In this study, I mostly rely on the positive approach. Of course, it is taken as a given that at least one of the objectives of government is to promote the development of the economy.

More specifically, I focus on the policies adopted and implemented by the governments of China, Hong Kong, and Taiwan in the process of their economic development. I choose these three economies because of the strong economic linkages among them—they are already among the largest trading partners and foreign direct investors of one another—because of their shared cultural and historical heritage and ethnic affinity, and because of the demonstration effects of each economy on the others. I organize the discussion along the lines of how these governments have affected the growth of these economies.

Broadly speaking, three sources of growth of an economy can be identified: (1) increases in tangible inputs such as capital, labor, and human capital;[3] (2) increases in efficiency, both technical and allocative; and (3) increases in intangible inputs such as R&D capital, or adoption of new managerial methods or organizational forms for production.[4] The distinction between increases in efficiency and increases in intangible inputs is not particularly clear-cut, especially if the intangible input in question can only be measured indirectly, e.g., by the "residual" method. However, it is useful to maintain the hypothetical distinction between movements to the production possibility frontier, which is related to the efficient allocation and utilization of available resources, and movements of the production possibility frontier, which is presumably due to intangible inputs (and luck). I examine the government policies adopted for augmenting each source of economic growth as well as their successes or failures. Along the way, I also identify the types of instruments used by the various governments in the implementation of their policies and evaluate their relative effectiveness. However, I am pragmatic in asking only whether a given policy has done some good, or is better in comparison with an alternative one, rather than whether it is optimal, recognizing that in the real world there are so many constraints that we are in practice dealing with only the *n*th best policy.

In real terms, the gross domestic products (GDPs) of Hong Kong and Taiwan over the postwar period and China since it began its process of economic reform in 1979 grew at an average annual rate of approximately 9 per cent. To put this performance in perspective, we may note that during the two decades of the most rapid economic growth in the history of the United States (approximately 1870–90), real GDP grew at a rate of approximately 5 per cent per annum.[5] Of all other countries, only Japan (1955–76) and South Korea ever experienced a comparable rate of real economic growth over as long a period.[6]

A question mentioned earlier—under what circumstances?—turns out to be important. No policy, or sets of policies, no matter how brilliant, can work for all countries and at all times. Initial conditions as well as external circumstances influence the suitability and effectiveness of government policies and hence affect their choice. For example, if capital per unit of labor, or capital intensity, is low, then a policy that promotes saving and investment clearly makes sense. However, if capital intensity is already very high, then a policy that promotes R&D activities, or, in fact, invests in R&D activities, may be more necessary. The total amount of investable funds and the quality and quantity of human resources in the economy are also relevant considerations in determining the appropriate role of the government, especially if the capital requirements of minimum-efficient-scale plants are large relative to the total capital (physical as well as human) available. In the latter case, the government will have to make, whether consciously or by default, some choices that will have serious long-term consequences for the economy. Problems of this type are likely to be much more acute in the beginning phase of economic development when capital markets are small and underdeveloped. However, over time, there is also a tendency for the size of the minimum-efficient-scale plants to grow because of technological progress.

The potential size of the domestic market also makes a big difference. The size of the domestic market, relative to the minimum-efficient-scale plant, determines the nature of and the potential social benefits, if any, from any government intervention and/or coordination.[7] In general, the larger the effective size of the economy, the less nonmarket coordination will be required. However, the size of the domestic economy should not be viewed as an unmitigated blessing. For a large economy, there is the question of controllability. The organization of the flow of information and authority within the economy, which is in turn a function of the technology, becomes critical. There is an appropriate degree of decentralization and devolution corresponding to the structure of information flows. Finally, the potential size of the domestic market also determines directly the amount of "rents" that can be created and/or distributed by the government through its policies.[8]

The initial size distribution of the enterprises also has a significant and lasting effect on the appropriate role of the government. For example, if the economy consists of a large number of small enterprises, as in Hong Kong and Taiwan, the government will have to take a more active role in the promotion of R&D—simply enacting an R&D investment tax credit will have very little effect because none of the small enterprises has the capital or is able to accept the long gestation period and risk inherent in R&D projects. However, for an economy dominated by a small number of large, well-capitalized enterprises, such as South Korea, an R&D tax credit may well be very effective.[9]

Other initial conditions that may matter include whether there is still surplus labor, the level of per capita income, the savings ratio, agriculture's share of GDP, whether the government budget is in surplus or deficit, the government's capacity to raise revenue, the private sector's share of GDP and capital stock, the extent of marketization, the public's tolerance for inflation, and the degree of tax compliance.

2.2 AUGMENTING THE INPUTS

How do the governments of the three economies attempt to augment their inputs of production, such as capital, labor, and human capital? I discuss each of the inputs in turn.

Capital

In order for the fixed capital stock to increase, there must be fixed investment. Fixed investment is financed from saving, both domestic and foreign. However, except for Hong Kong, foreign saving is not quantitatively important, so that domestic saving is the principal source of investment funds in these economies.[10]

Increasing Savings

Saving behavior can depend very much on past historical experiences as well as cultural factors. All three economies achieved very high saving rates, of between 35 and 40 per cent, after a certain threshold of per capita real GDP was reached. Before 1979, this high saving rate was partially achieved in China through a restriction of consumption opportunities. However, more recent data show that Chinese household consumption is voluntarily restrained, perhaps in anticipation of future expenditures on big-value items such as consumer durables and housing, or for ceremonial needs such as birthday celebrations, weddings, and funerals. Consumer durables as well as residential housing are relatively expensive in all of these economies. Moreover, savings accounts in China, as well as those in Taiwan, are virtually free of bank default risk because of explicit and implicit deposit insurance.[11] In addition, the rate of interest has almost always been positive in real terms in Taiwan, providing additional incentive to save. If there was any financial repression in Taiwan, it was probably quite mild. In China, the longer-term savings deposits are indexed to domestic inflation, thus guaranteeing a nonnegative real rate of return.

Saving (and investment) is further encouraged by the macroeconomic stability maintained by the different governments in their respective economies (except for China, but it tries). This has been achieved, in both Hong Kong and Taiwan, by almost always, at least until recent years, adopting a conservative fiscal policy and running a budget surplus. Monetary policy in Taiwan is targeted on a positive real rate of interest. China has a negative real rate of interest on bank loans (but not on savings deposits), which has since the beginning of 1995 become slightly less negative. The saving graces for China are the indexation of longer-term savings deposits and the lack of competition for bank savings as there is a dearth of alternative financial instruments available to households.

Real wages in all three economies are somewhat repressed—the labor unions have been, until recently, kept weak. It should be remarked that wage repression has the same "beneficial" consequences as "mild" financial repression. In particular, it augments business, as opposed to household, savings.[12]

Inflation can sometimes be used as a means of forced saving as well as subsidizing borrowers, mostly enterprises, in these economies. As a method of forced saving, it has not been important in all three economies. However, in China, it may be viewed as a method of subsidizing the net borrowers, which are by and large the state-owned enterprises. The subsidy takes the form of a negative real rate of interest.[13]

Savings can be further augmented through the encouragement of foreign investment, both direct and portfolio. Foreign investment is facilitated by a stable exchange rate (achieved by both Hong Kong and Taiwan), by the freedom of capital movements (always true in Hong Kong but gradually attained in Taiwan), and through special concessions such as tax holidays, capital and profit repatriation rights, and special rights to import equipment and material inputs. Because of its complete freedom of capital movements, Hong Kong has always functioned as a safe haven for capital from Southeast Asian countries, especially for the overseas Chinese residents there.

Increasing Investments

Aggregate saving is not necessarily equal to aggregate investment—there can be both inflows and outflows. In addition, investment is not necessarily translated into capital stock: only fixed investment is, change in stocks is not. Fixed investment, of both domestic and foreign origin, is promoted by special tax incentives, such as tax holidays, in Taiwan and in China, although China has traditionally had a large excess demand for fixed investment. In addition, special privileges are available in the Special Economic Zones, such as Shenzhen, in China. Hong Kong provides industrial estates for the establishment of factories and offers complete freedom to export and import. Technical assistance is provided by the government in Taiwan to enterprises undertaking pioneering or new investment projects. A relatively pliant labor force and "wage repression" in these economies have also helped.

Fixed investment is also promoted by macroeconomic stability. When inflation rises, the ratio of fixed investment to total investment declines, indicating a rise in the change in stocks, that is, an increase in hoarding activities at the expense of fixed capital formation. Inflation and expectation of inflation also discourage long-term investments. The stable exchange rates maintained by Hong Kong and Taiwan also favor investment because they reduce one major risk for foreign as well as domestic producers for the export market. The export orientation of Hong Kong and Taiwan also facilitates foreign direct investment because it assures that the foreign exchange will be available when repatriation time arrives.

However, loans, with the exception of short-term loans for export financing, were until recently not generally available from government banks in Taiwan to private enterprises—so that in fact the commercial banking system is not used very much to promote fixed investment. This is left for development banks such as the China Development Corporation and the Chiao Tung Bank (formerly the Bank of Communications). Similarly, during the initial stage of the economic development of Hong Kong, commercial banks were unimportant as a source of loans for fixed investment although they were active in providing working capital loans.

Since 1984, commercial banks in China, almost all government-owned, have become the principal source of finance for the fixed investment projects of state-owned enterprises, replacing direct budgetary allocations. Unfortunately, many of the fixed investment projects undertaken by the state-owned enterprises did not turn out well, resulting in massive nonperforming loans on the books of the commercial banks in China. The Chinese banks provided virtually no financing to non-state-owned enterprises.

Labor

The rates of growth of the labor force in China, Hong Kong, and Taiwan have been quite rapid, but both Hong Kong and Taiwan have experienced labor shortages and rising wages since the 1980s. The use of foreign contract labor has become quite common in Hong Kong and Taiwan. All three economies have had substantial and successful family-planning programs.[14] According to long-term projections of the Chinese economy, in the year 2020, the proportion of the Chinese labor force employed in the agricultural sector will still be 33 per cent, even though the agricultural sector will only account for 7 per cent of the GDP then.[15] Thus, labor *per se* will continue to be in "surplus" in China for a long time to come. The challenge for China is to create employment for the new entrants to its rapidly growing labor force—approximately 16 million new jobs are needed every year. For China, the emphasis must be on augmenting the quality, rather than the quantity, of its labor force.

The female labor force participation rates in all three economies are already quite high, especially among the below-40 cohorts. Further significant increases are not very likely and the growth of the labor forces in these countries will mostly follow the growth of the working-age population.

Human Capital

Universal compulsory primary education, financed by the government, was achieved in Taiwan sometime in the early 1960s. It was subsequently extended to 9 years and then to 12 years. The constitution of Taiwan actually mandates the spending of 15 per cent of the annual government budget on education. Universal secondary education was also mostly achieved in Hong Kong, but with a greater reliance on the private sector. Private education has always been an important component of Hong Kong's educational system. Taiwan has a stronger tertiary educational system than Hong Kong—its enrollment rates have been much higher. But Hong Kong is in the process of catching up, with the government establishing several new universities recently.

In China there is a potential deficiency in the supply of human capital. As an unintended consequence of the new economic prosperity in China, which is mostly concentrated in the coastal regions, the poorer rural areas of China are short on funds for education and unable to attract teachers. The demand for labor in the rural areas further erodes the incentive for many rural parents to send their children to school. Illiteracy is still a serious and increasingly important problem in the poorer rural areas of China. Tertiary educational opportunities are still relatively scarce in China. In both Hong Kong and Taiwan, the public educational system is supplemented by private institutions. It may well be that China will have to allow a similar development, given the emphasis on the quality and not the quantity of labor.

2.3 ALLOCATING RESOURCES EFFICIENTLY

An allocation of resources is said to be efficient if no additional output can be produced without increasing at least one input, and no input can be decreased without decreasing at least one output. Under constant or decreasing returns to scale and competitive markets, and profit and utility maximization, efficiency is assured by the well-known Welfare Theorem. However, the Welfare Theorem breaks down if there are increasing returns to scale, other nonconvexities, informational asymmetry, or other externalities, and/or significant market power on either the supply side or the demand side of the economy. In that case, neither the market nor a bargaining solution by economic agents acting in their own self-interest will necessarily assure the efficiency of the economy. The role of the government is to help achieve an efficient allocation of resources (and thereby increase aggregate output). It should therefore adopt policies and actions that will lead to an efficient outcome—for example, one that corresponds to a solution to the full-information cooperative game, with the government possibly lending credibility to the commitments through its power of enforcement of contracts or more generally as a potential dispenser of economic favors. By thus adding value, the government is also able to create rents and in the process distribute any such rents to support the efficient outcome. For example, the returns to the land input, assuming that it is fixed in supply, are all rent. The government can modify the distribution of rents through property and capital gain taxation so that land is allocated to its socially highest and best use (subject to incentive compatibility constraints). Similarly, royalties on natural resources are also a form of rent.

There is a distinction between a permanent (one-time) allocation of rent and a repeated allocation of rent. Under repeated allocation, some care has to be taken to assure that there will actually be competition in the market. Precisely because the government has the power of creating and allocating rents, it runs the risk of being coopted by rent seekers and/or by current rent recipients.

I examine the role of the government in achieving economy-wide efficiency by separating it into two parts: achieving technical efficiency within each industry and enterprise and achieving allocative efficiency across industries and enterprises. But first, I discuss several factors that have significant influence on the incentives and abilities of the economic agents to achieve efficiency.

The Structure of Ownership

In both Hong Kong and Taiwan, the predominant mode of ownership of enterprises is private, in fact, family owned. Almost all of the successful large enterprises in both Hong Kong and Taiwan, even the publicly listed ones, with the possible exception of the public utilities in Taiwan, are family controlled.[16] The only major exceptions that come to mind are the Hong Kong and Shanghai Banking Corporation in Hong Kong, and the China Steel Corporation, as well as the government-owned banks and financial institutions in Taiwan. In China, it is the nonstate sector (consisting of collective—including the township and village—enterprises, foreign-owned enterprises, joint-venture enterprises, and private, including individual, enterprises) that has been the most dynamic and successful over the past 15 years. Even though there has been no significant privatization in China, the nonstate sector now accounts for well over half of Chinese GDP, compared to less than 10 per cent in 1979.[17] Hong Kong has always operated as a private-enterprise economy: its public utilities—electricity, gas, and transportation—have always been privately owned and operated but publicly regulated.

With Taiwan, the reliance on the private sector was by no means inevitable—the share of the public sector in terms of the value of industrial assets in the early 1950s was almost 90 per cent![18] However, early in the economic development drive of Taiwan (the late 1950s), there was considerable internal debate within its government of the relative merits of public versus private ownership, and it was decided at the highest level of the government that the new investments (initially mostly in export-oriented industries) would be undertaken by private rather than state-owned enterprises, except in naturally monopolistic industries such as public utilities.[19] It is a remarkable testimony of the success of this policy that the more rapid growth of the private sector in Taiwan has resulted in the public sector's share of industrial assets declining to below 15 per cent in the 1980s, again without any significant privatization of public enterprises. Even in China, the managers of many township and village enterprises, whose legal ownership status is still not clearly defined, often manage the enterprises and dispose of assets as if they are the actual owners of these enterprises. In practice, these enterprises are like partnerships, with the original residents of the township or village being the beneficial owners/partners. It is significant to note that workers from outside the township or village are typically put on finite-term contracts and have no tenure, pension, or other rights, as distinct from workers from the same township or village itself.[20]

The choice of private over public ownership for enterprises other than public utilities turned out to have enormous economic significance. First, the effectively family-owned nature of these private enterprises implies that they are owner managed.[21] There is thus no "agency problem"—the interests of the owner and the manager are identical.[22] The owner-managers of these enterprises, who are interested in maximizing their own profits in the *long run* (or equivalently, present value), have an incentive to be efficient in both their production and investment decisions. They know that they have to put their own equity capital at risk, because no one, including the government, is going to make good any losses that they may incur. They thus have the incentives to maximize profit, minimize loss, and most importantly pay careful attention to the consequences of their actions, especially with respect to their investments, unlike the managers of state-owned enterprises.[23] Their investment plans are sensitive to the real rate of interest whereas those of state-owned enterprises run by managers with few ownership interests typically are not.

Empirically, the transition of Chinese agriculture from a collective system to an essentially private individual household system (with land leases) resulted in large gains in efficiency of the order of between 30 and 40 per cent from 1979 to 1985, holding inputs constant. Efficiency gains of such a magnitude are very, very significant. This early success of the Chinese agricultural reform laid the foundations of its subsequent success in the other (mostly nonstate) sectors, including the township and village enterprises.

The Market Environment

Hong Kong has always been a private-enterprise, free-market economy, even though the government does intervene from time to time and most notably has maintained a fixed exchange rate *vis-à-vis* the US dollar since 1984.[24] The government of Taiwan has been more activist or interventionist, but by and large it has been content to let the market work where it can. China is probably the least marketized of the three, but even there, very few commodities are currently still under price control or rationing, and the prices of most tradable goods in China, including energy and grains, are now at or near world-market levels.

In order to make the market work, however, one needs more than private enterprise and a determination by the government not to intervene. The government must also assure that there is the transportation and communication infrastructure to make the one market a reality; that is why infrastructural development is such an important role for the government. The government must also assure that there is sufficient meaningful competition. It can influence the degree of competition in a market by regulating entry, licensing capacity, restricting foreign equity, controlling imports of goods as well as imports of technology, and promoting the creation of indigenous technological capabilities. The government also needs to provide services for standardization, inspection, and certification. One simple example of standardization is traffic signals—it does not matter whether one goes on green and stops on red, or vice versa—but someone has to decide one way or the other and to enforce it. Actually, during the Cultural Revolution in China, for a brief period, it was decreed that one should go on red (the revolutionary color) and stop on green. It also worked. In any case, setting standards and conventions is a highly important and socially productive activity of the government. (Setting the gauge of railroad tracks and the voltage of the household electricity supply are other examples.)

In Hong Kong, a free port, the market works the best of the three economies, although as I have already mentioned there is the fixed exchange rate and the banking cartel has been able to set the ceiling on the rate of interest on savings deposits at a low level. The market in Taiwan is becoming more and more open. However, there are still monopolistic or oligopolistic elements in the distribution systems as well as in construction (basically the nontradable sectors). China is still far from being a competitive market, both because of infrastructural bottlenecks and because of significant monopolistic elements in the economy. Wholesale trade is still monopolized. There are still foreign trade export and import and service monopolies established and maintained by the government. For example, despite the split-up of the former Civil Aviation Administration of China and the proliferation of new airline companies,[25] the airline industry in China is still dominated by regional monopolies. Overall, though, there has been impressive progress—exchange rates have been unified as are many other prices. Trades are becoming more and more anonymous (the same price regardless of the parties). And regulations are becoming more transparent.

In the three economies, commercial banks are not relied upon as a primary source of equity capital—they specialize in providing working capital—except in China where since 1984 they have had to provide state-owned enterprises with loans to finance fixed investment in lieu of direct allocations from the government budget. The financial market in Hong Kong is one of the most competitive in the world. If there is any financial repression in Hong Kong, it is done by the Foreign Exchange Banks Association, headed by the Hong Kong and Shanghai Bank. This association functions as a deposit-rate-setting cartel. In Taiwan, financial repression is practically absent, but not credit rationing. However, all the commercial banks in Taiwan were government owned until the late 1980s, when a large number of new private commercial banks were allowed to be established. Bank loans are generally used for working capital rather than long-term investment purposes. For large enterprises, the development banks, including Chiao Tung Bank (formerly Bank of Communications) and the China Development Corporation, may be tapped. Small and medium-sized enterprises are financed by equity investment and loans from the informal credit market. China is the only economy with bank lending rates significantly below the market. Even there, because of the existence of indexation for longer-term savings deposits, the degree of financial repression is not as severe as it might otherwise be. Instead, most of the "rents" result from credit rationing, with the state-owned enterprises most favored. Financial repression and credit rationing may be viewed as a reallocation of rents between lenders and borrowers, savers and investors. In China the rents appear to have gone mostly to the loss-making state-owned enterprises.[26]

Finally, it is worth noting that the export orientation and more general participation in the world market through international trade provide the competitive pressure for the exporting enterprises in China, Hong Kong, and Taiwan to be efficient. The predominant export orientation of Hong Kong, Taiwan, and the coastal provinces of southern China, coupled with the commodity nature of their products, means that most of the enterprises have to compete internationally with the enterprises of other countries, in third-country markets, over which neither they nor their governments have much control. The discipline imposed by the fiercely competitive world market keeps the enterprises lean, mean, and honest. With the increasing openness of the domestic markets, the enterprises will be subject to even more intense competitive pressure to be efficient and rent-seeking activities will be reduced. Perhaps the critical difference between the policies of import substitution and export promotion lies in the fact that under import substitution, there is little or no competitive pressure on the enterprises, whereas under export promotion, enterprises in one country have to compete with enterprises all over the world. While it is true that inefficient export enterprises can still be directly subsidized, an explicit, direct subsidy is much more noticeable and more difficult to sustain in the long run than an import tariff or restriction. There is also much less rent to be sought and appropriated on the open world market.

Coordination Externalities

Often, there may be efficient economic outcomes that are not supportable through the market or through bargaining, cooperatively or noncooperatively, among economic agents acting in their own self-interests alone. This is especially important when there is the possibility of multiple economic equilibria. Multiple economic equilibria can arise from "nonconvexities," complementarity, information asymmetry, or the lack of credible commitments. One useful role of the government is to create conditions that are conducive to the achievement of the efficient economic outcome that otherwise is not achievable and to guarantee its implementation through its powers of enforcement. This may be broadly referred to as "coordination."

At its most elementary level, coordination means using or sharing the same information among the economic agents, so that the adverse effects of information asymmetry can be overcome. Put in these terms, it always pays to coordinate—it cannot do any harm. However, coordination is necessary only in so far as the information to be used or shared does not consist solely of information available in the market; for example, the market may provide information about the price and quantity of a good, but not necessarily information about the (individual) supply and demand functions. Coordination makes it possible for the different economic agents to use and share such information and thereby reduce uncertainty.[27] Coordination is much more important for investment decisions than for current production decisions: this is especially so if investment is not readily reversible.

However, nonmarket coordination does not necessarily need to involve the government. For example, private signaling, which can be done without the intercession of the government, can be an effective form of coordination, or at least attempted coordination. Economic agents may also find it advantageous to reveal their response functions to one another, thus saving learning and testing time. Collusion among economic agents can also be viewed as a form of privately but not necessarily socially beneficial coordination. Coordination, whether private or public, can lead to either private or social benefit, or both. Nor is government coordination necessarily preferable to private coordination, but it is more credible because it can assure the credibility of commitments made not only by itself but also by other economic agents through its powers of enforcement. It also tends to remove the gaming aspects that make private information appear fuzzy and unreliable and thereby inhibit the achievement of an efficient economic outcome.

For example, banks can avoid overinvestment in certain industries, or overlending to certain enterprises, through an exchange of information. Such an exchange of information does not necessarily have to be organized by the government. It can be done through credit bureaus and rating agencies, and through the practice of loan syndication. But the government can help by imposing exposure limits for individual banks. It can also compel truthful reporting and use its audit and investigative powers to ensure compliance.

For another example, there may be benefits generated by *simultaneous* expansion of all industries, so that one industry's additional supply will be taken up as another industry's additional demand and altogether the additional earnings of the workers will increase the aggregate final demand. In other words, the incomes generated by the new economic activities created can in turn provide the demands, directly and indirectly, for the goods produced. Of course, the domestic market must be large enough. For example, it is not possible for manufacturers in Hong Kong to get rich by relying on sales to one another and their own workers only; the domestic market is simply too small. This is not true of China. Such a "bootstrap" strategy that does not work for much smaller economies may actually work in China. However, in order for these so-called coordination externalities to be realized, all industries must share the common knowledge or belief that a simultaneous expansion will be forthcoming. This is a coordination problem—for example, the announcement or formulation of an economic plan may provide the signal. Announced economic growth and money supply targets can also serve as coordinating signals, to the extent that they are credible.

More concretely, consider how the Chinese economy emerged from its recession of 1989–91. Publicity about Deng Xiao-Ping's visit to southern China in early 1992, as well as statements attributed to him, provided precisely the signal for the convergence of public expectations of a resumption of economic expansion, stimulating the subsequent boom that continues today.[28] This experience shows how it is possible for concerted actions prompted by a common expectation to move the economy into fast forward again, provided that the economy is large enough. This is a good example of the importance of coordination when there are multiple equilibria—one low-growth and one high-growth. In the absence of Deng's southern visit, the recovery in China from the recession caused by the Tiananmen incident would not have occurred so soon—it might not have occurred at all. As it was, it also made the Chinese economic reform totally irreversible.[29]

An example of failure of coordination is the almost complete absence of interenterprise trade credit among nonstate enterprises in China. The famous interenterprise, or "triangular," debts in China are almost exclusively debts among state-owned enterprises. The nonstate enterprises typically neither extend trade credit to nor receive trade credit from other enterprises in China. Most transactions among these enterprises are done on a "cash-on-delivery" basis. The insistence on cash on delivery is a defensive measure on the part of these nonstate enterprises, reflecting serious information asymmetry, and cannot be consistent with efficiency. Total trades, and transactions, would rise if short-term trade credit were made available. It would appear that if a credible credit bureau or rating agency, like a Dun and Bradstreet, backed by either the government or one or more government banks (so as to compel truthful revelation), can be organized to provide credit information in China, it would greatly increase the volume of transactions and hence the overall efficiency of the economy.

Another role for the government is to reduce transaction costs. When the number of economic agents is large, there can be tremendous economies in adopting a government-imposed solution to a bargaining game situation.

Achieving Technical Efficiency

What are some measures that can be undertaken by the government that will move the economy closer to its production possibility frontier?

There is no question that reducing red tape increases efficiency. "Red tape" is a relic of the days when the government had to provide employment to a large number of people and carve up or make work for them. Both China and Taiwan have made special provisions to expedite foreign investment applications. But if it is possible to streamline the procedure for foreign investors, it should be possible to reduce red tape for all, including domestic, enterprises. Also relevant is whether the style of government is discretion based or rule based. A discretion-based system is open to "rent-seeking" and corruption. Hong Kong has already put in place a rule-based system. Taiwan is moving in that direction. However, even in the early phase of Taiwan's economic development, rent-seeking was not particularly prevalent, partly because the central government was dominated by people from the mainland, whereas the private sector, where most of the potential rent-seekers would be, was dominated by people whose families had been resident in Taiwan for a long time. Even China, where traditionally government regulation is stated "permissively" as opposed to "prohibitively," that is, one can only do what one is explicitly "permitted" to do, is under some pressure to increase the transparency of its decision processes. It may be noted that in the transition from a discretion-based system to a rule-based system, kinship and long-term friendship rooted in shared cultural norms can provide the bases for the implicit contracts necessary to support economic transactions in the absence of explicit rules and regulations or established customs. This is one of the reasons why the initial foreign investors in China have been almost exclusively members of overseas Chinese communities.

What one can say is that with increasing democratization, turnover in the government has become a real possibility in Taiwan. Under these circumstances, when longevity of the government or the bureaucracy can no longer be assumed, it is better for enterprises to have a rule-based system rather than a discretion-based system. This is especially the case if the real power does not reside in the permanent bureaucracy as in Japan and the United Kingdom. A rule-based system is also preferable to a discretion-based system if there are many players in the economic system.

Creating New Institutions and Drafting New Laws

The government can make new laws and create new institutions that facilitate and support economic development. These can be laws with regard to property rights, which can provide for greatly variegated forms of ownership. For example, in most jurisdictions under the influence of English common law, the mineral rights in the ground are not the property of the owner of the land but belong to the state. Land in Hong Kong (the island itself) is mostly covered by leases, for 999 years, when it is initially sold by the government. By contrast, the land in the New Territories of Hong Kong used to be covered by leases that would expire in 1997. The property sector, which is so important for the Hong Kong economy, owed its start to two developments in the 1950s. First, the government of Hong Kong abolished rent control on *new* residential buildings. Second, it perfected the laws governing the condominium ownership of separate units in a building, thus making it possible for individuals to own their own individual units. Real estate ownership in Hong Kong had previously been confined only to those who could purchase an entire building, which severely limited the demand. These two developments ushered in a great expansion in residential building. The same condominiumization concept was later also adopted in Taiwan.[30] China also adopted a transferable land lease system with durations of 15 years and up.

Another piece of legislation that may seem draconian made writing bad checks a criminal offense prosecutable by the government rather than a civil matter between the check issuer and recipient. This legislation helped enormously in popularizing the use and acceptance of checks. One cannot possibly imagine how one could operate with currency alone in today's Hong Kong and Taiwan.

Social Safety Net, Income Distribution, and Social Welfare Programs

It is a responsibility of the government to provide a social safety net, defined broadly. A social safety net reduces risks to workers and the population in general. It is more efficient for the government to assume this responsibility both because of economies of scale and because it has lower transaction costs. An alternative system run by the enterprises individually, say, will face serious complications as workers change jobs, are between jobs, or simply become disabled and unemployable. The government should also pay attention to the distribution of income to make sure that the gap between the rich and poor does not become so excessive that it may breed social and political instability, and to the equality of access to opportunities to make sure that sufficient social mobility, and hence hope, exists in society.

Traditionally, social welfare programs are provided only for very low-income households in Hong Kong and Taiwan. However, with increasing democratization, the governments of both Hong Kong and Taiwan are faced with increasing demands for social welfare programs. While some social welfare programs can enhance productivity and efficiency, others detract from it. Thus, social welfare programs must be carefully designed. One important aspect of these programs is that in order for them to work, they must be compulsory for everyone. Thus, the government needs to be involved so that its coercive power can be invoked. Left on a voluntary basis, many such programs cannot survive financially because of the possibilities of the free-rider (moral hazard) and adverse selection problems.

For example, if contribution to and participation in a retirement program is voluntary, then there will be people who may reason that even if they do not participate during their working years, society will ultimately still have to provide for them in their old age—it cannot possibly let them starve—so that they are better off not joining the program now but they will still be able to benefit later. This means that those who do participate will wind up paying more than they would receive actuarially in order to keep the program solvent. This removes the incentive for anyone to join the program, unless he or she is certain that everyone will participate. This is why the government has to make it compulsory.[31]

Infrastructural Investment

The social overhead capital such as electric utilities, transportation and communication facilities, and industrial parks all require a huge amount of investment, which cannot be afforded by individual private enterprises, especially in the early stage of economic development. Moreover, many of these industries are natural monopolies because of the existence of significant economies of scale (relative to the size of the domestic market) and thus in any case need to be publicly regulated even if they are privately owned.[32] Infrastructural projects are usually undertaken by the government rather than by private investors because of factors such as nonappropriability, lack of sufficient capital, long gestation period, or inability to bear the risk given the capital position. In other words, the social benefits of the infrastructural investment (but not necessarily the privately appropriable benefits) exceed the social costs. Thus, infrastructure should be an area of primary, and some would argue exclusive, focus of government investment.

Examples of successful infrastructural projects include the Hsinchu Science-Based Industrial Park in Taiwan, which is modeled after the Stanford Industrial Park. The park now produces several billion US dollars worth of output a year. China is trying to do the same thing in an area located adjacent to the Chinese Academy of Sciences in Zhongguancun, a suburb of Beijing.

Sometimes infrastructural investment projects also act as signals for coordinated expansion in an industry, a cluster of industries, or a geographical area as well as a tangible demonstration of a government commitment. When potential investors see that an infrastructural project is being developed, they know that the benefits of a related private investment will be enhanced and the costs lowered. In addition, they also know that other investors also know. This will set off a stampede to undertake complementary new investment projects, helping to realize the economies of agglomeration and simultaneous expansion.

The existence of complementarities is a major reason for coordination. The use of turnkey infrastructural projects, under which a consortium of investors is asked to deliver a finished, operating facility, can be viewed as a way of solving a complex coordination problem in a developing economy. The establishment of special geographical areas—such as the export-processing zone in Kaohsiung[33] and the Science-Based Industrial Park in Hsinchu, Taiwan; the Special Economic Zones of China (Shenzhen, Zhuhai, Shantou, Xiamen and Hainan);[34] and the Suzhou project run by Singapore—represents an attempt by the respective governments to implement, in one place, a complete package of complementary policies in an administratively efficient manner as well as to signal publicly a credible commitment to do so. All of these aforementioned projects have been very successful, with the exception of the Suzhou project for which it is still too early to tell.

Consumer and Environmental Protection

The area of consumer and environmental protection is one where the government must take a leading role. The problem with consumer and environmental protection is that every individual has only a very small stake and except for the most dedicated does not have sufficient incentive to become actively involved. By contrast, the enterprises that victimize consumers and pollute the environment or have the potential of doing so have every incentive to resist any control or sanction. However, recently, both movements have been coming to the fore in Hong Kong and Taiwan and the politicians there are beginning to take notice. Unfortunately, China still lags far behind in both consumer and environmental protection. Note, however, that in standard national income and product accounts, consumer and environmental protection are all costs and not benefits. Thus, greater expenditures on consumer and environmental protection will be reflected in lower measured real GDP and economic efficiency. New measures of real GDP or GNP are required in order to reflect the benefits of a cleaner, healthier, and safer environment.

Efficient Allocation across Industries

A necessary condition for overall efficiency of the economy is an efficient allocation of resources, including fixed investment and capital, across industries. The selection, or targeting, of industries for favored treatment in order to promote investment in them by the government is often referred to as an industrial policy.

There are many reasons why an industrial policy may be justified, for example, the differences between social and private risk and time preferences,[35] the need to accelerate learning and change (because of externalities), and the existence of complementarities. Moreover, industrial expertise is much more industry specific than country specific. A successful entrepreneur would much prefer to move to a different country to continue in the same industry than to engage in a new industry in the same country. The government may therefore have an important role in the promotion of new industries.

In China, prior to 1984, the entire industrial sector was state owned. All the investments were planned by the State Planning Commission. More recently, with the growth of the nonstate sector and the devolution of economic decision-making power, greater attention has been paid to industrial policy. Industrial policy in Hong Kong is rather limited, if it exists at all, although in recent years the government has greatly expanded tertiary educational institutions as well as its support for research and development. In Taiwan, credit rationing is definitely used to support industries that the government wants to start—these are referred to as pioneering industries. From time to time, lists of pioneering industries are published and bureaucrats scour the island for potential investors. In addition to credit rationing, industrial policy in Taiwan is often carried out through the support of industrial R&D at national research laboratories such as the Industrial Technology Research Institute. Of course, protection, in the form of tariffs, quotas, and import permits, is also used to favor certain industries. For example, until recently, China Steel Corporation had long been allowed to approve all import permits for steel! One notable failure of industrial policy in Taiwan is an attempt to promote Taiwanese large trading firms along the lines of the Japanese firms of Marubeni, Mitsubishi, and Mitsui. Despite the many incentives provided, it has not been successful. Direct investment by the government, or by government development banks, in favored industries in the form of a state-owned or -controlled enterprise, is also done. For example, China Steel Corporation, established in the mid-1970s, was majority owned by the government of Taiwan.

The export industries and enterprises have been favored in the early phase of Taiwan's industrialization and China's economic reform. In Taiwan, this is done through preferential interest rates for the finance of production for exports. There are also other miscellaneous advantages such as the rebating of import duties on inputs used in production for exports and reduction of port fees, etc. Chinese export enterprises also receive preferential treatment such as the rebating of import duties on inputs and until January 1995 they were allowed to retain part of the foreign exchange they earned. In Hong Kong, there has been no explicit government support for exports, but export orders are often accompanied by letters of credit from foreign banks which can be used as "security" to finance production for exports at the Hong Kong banks. The export orientation of the three economies, one can say, is also a form of industrial policy.

Efficient Allocation across Enterprises

First, the government has to take into account the existence of increasing returns to scale which render the usual market allocation inefficient. For example, if the size of the market will support it, it is better to have one enterprise build one minimum-efficient-scale plant than to have two build two sub-minimum-efficient-scale plants. This is where the government can and should intervene to prevent potentially inefficient and possibly ruinous competition. However, if the government then creates a monopoly, it must also take steps to ensure that the enterprise selected does not overuse its monopoly power to the detriment of the consumers of the output produced. (For example, the world price can be used as a benchmark and the government can approve imports if the price charged by the enterprise exceeds the world price by a significant amount.)

In order to implement its industrial policy, the government must also be able to identify and enlist promising entrepreneurs/enterprises to undertake selected industrial projects in the early stage of its industrial development. The story of how Y. C. Wang of Formosa Plastics was chosen, which may be apocryphal, is well known. After approaching a member of a prominent wealthy family about investing in a plastics project and being turned down, the government turned to the individual with the largest bank account balance in the Bank of Taiwan, who happened to be a Mr. Wang. Today, the Formosa Plastics Group is the largest private industrial group in Taiwan. In practice, the government has the ability to create as well as allocate rents, through taxation and subsidies, franchising, preferential loans, and land grants, especially in the early stage of economic development, when markets are small and underdeveloped (and hence noncompetitive).

The selection of Formosa Plastics was a one-time choice. A one-time choice often has to be based on expectations, because there are, in fact, no performance data until the enterprise has been selected, although one can sometimes rely on the track record of related activities in the past. It is also possible to reward an enterprise *ex post*, such as awarding a government contract to the most profitable enterprise in an industry. However, sometimes it is necessary to select enterprises continually, based on performance, which must be appropriately defined. The government may in fact run a tournament among the participating enterprises and reward the winners with "rents" in accordance with the results.[36] Examples of rewards or "performance-based rents" may include export quotas, preferential loans, and monopoly franchises. Such rents share a common characteristic, that is, the value of the "rents" depends positively on the efficiency of the enterprises being awarded the "rents."

The allocation of textile import quotas imposed by the United States and the European Union is a good example of performance-based rents. In Hong Kong, the quotas are given to the exporters in the year in which the quota system is imposed. They then become the property of the initial quota-holders and can be bought, sold, and "leased." In effect, this is a one-time selection of enterprises and transfers all the rents from the potential manufacturers to the quota-holders. Many such quota-holders in Hong Kong are known to have closed their factories immediately and live on the "rentals" generated by their quotas. By contrast, in Taiwan, the quota-holders are allowed to retain only 80 per cent of their initial quotas, with the remaining 20 per cent being returned to the government, which then puts it into a pool to be awarded through open competition on the basis of the highest unit value achieved on *bona fide* new export orders. This competitive bidding system provides the incentive for manufacturers to innovate and to try to increase the added value of their products (and as a side benefit reduces the tendency for exporters to understate their export revenue in order to circumvent capital export control and tax laws). It also has the advantage of being transparent and independent of bureaucratic discretion, which in turn reduces "rents" as well as rent seeking. The 80 per cent annual quota retention also provides the incentive for investment in new manufacturing machinery.[37] In February 1994, a similar bidding system was introduced for the allocation of the quotas on some export commodities in China, replacing an administrative examination and approval system used heretofore. All enterprises—foreign, joint venture, and domestic—are permitted to participate in the quota bidding in China.

Other examples of "performance-based rents" include investment tax credits, accelerated depreciation, and tax holidays for *new* enterprises. Essentially, all of these benefits and special privileges are of no value to the new enterprises and of no cost to the government unless the new enterprises turn out to be successful and have large and otherwise taxable profits.

In Hong Kong, the natural monopolies such as broadcasting, communication, electric power, mass transportation, etc. are awarded franchises for fixed durations based on a competitive bidding process. There is presumably not too much economic rent created. In Taiwan, the natural monopolies are state enterprises. There are also informally sanctioned oligopolies, for example, the cement industry. In China, wholesale trade is completely monopolized.

However, not all rents are "performance based." There is another type of rent, which may be referred to as "transition-facilitating rent," that is used to compensate vested interests so as to obtain their support for reforms that enhance the overall efficiency of the economy. For example, a two-track price system for manufactured goods was introduced in China in 1984. It essentially allowed a parallel free market for the above-plan-quota outputs of state-owned enterprises while the within-plan-quota outputs continued to be sold at the lower official prices to authorized purchasers. The introduction of these parallel free markets, coupled with the expansion of producer autonomy, greatly stimulated supply and alleviated shortages of food products and other consumer goods in China. By 1986, only a handful of consumer goods, compared to hundreds in the late 1970s and early 1980s, still needed to be rationed. In the past several years, the prices of such basic goods and services as grains, energy, and transportation were also adjusted upward continually to reflect true scarcity costs. Today, the prices of more than 97 per cent of consumer goods and 80 per cent of producer goods are determined in the free market.

Similarly, dual markets have been permitted to exist for foreign exchange in China since the mid-1980s. Prior to 1994, there was an official exchange rate, available only for certain limited approved transactions, as well as an officially sanctioned swap rate that was determined in markets around the country among exporters and importers qualified to trade in those markets. The supply of foreign exchange in the swap markets was provided by the exporters through the foreign-exchange earnings they were allowed to retain. The swap rate was, not surprisingly, significantly higher than the official rate. At the same time, foreign visitors to China were required to use foreign exchange certificates (FECs), which were available at the official exchange rate, rather than the *renminbi*, the domestic currency. The dual exchange rate system functioned until January 1, 1994, when the two exchange rates—the official rate and the swap rate—were merged into a single rate, with its level determined in a market consisting of exporters and importers, and the FECs were finally withdrawn from circulation. The best way to characterize the current exchange-rate system is that it is "trade accounts convertible" but not "capital accounts convertible." The exchange rate itself is not determined by a free float, but rather by a "dirty" float, which is, however, not uncommon among both developed and developing economies.

The two-track price system, with one price market determined and the other one fixed, is a major factor in the relatively smooth transition of the Chinese economy from a centrally planned one to a mostly market one. Under this system, efficiency is immediately achieved because, on the margin, everything is bought and sold at the free-market price. Thus, the value of an additional unit of any good is the same to all potential users. However, users who used to be allocated a good at the low fixed official price are no worse off than before, because they are given the same old quantity allocation at the same old low price. In fact, they are better off because they can now sell the same good at the higher price in the free market and pocket the difference, if they wish. Thus, the rights of the pre-existing vested interests are fully protected—"grandfathered"—under the two-track price system, at least during the transitional period. Not only does this neutralize any potential opposition, but it actually creates a constituency for the free market, which is now perceived as a source of effortless instant profit. Of course, the two-track price system can also be viewed as a system of market prices under which some purchasers are given a subsidy equal to the difference between the market price and the initial fixed price per unit of the good times the quantity of the *initial* allocation. It is "rent," pure and simple, to the recipients of the "subsidy" because no social value is created. The two-track price system also potentially breeds corruption because whoever is granted a subsidy reaps an effortless instant profit and therefore has an incentive to try to influence the grantor. But it does not in itself cause a distortion in the allocation of resources.

It is, however, important to note that the quantity of the good under "subsidy" is frozen at the initial level and in many instances the "transition-facilitating rents" are phased out after a predetermined number of years, exploiting the difference between the rates of time preference of the central government on the one hand and the state-owned enterprises and their managers on the other. With rapid economic growth, the free market accounts for an increasingly greater proportion of the total sales of the good over time, until the proportion of fixed-price transactions becomes so small that it is no longer material and the two-track price system in effect becomes a single market-price system. This has indeed been the experience of China for both the market for goods and the market for foreign exchange.

Efficient Allocation through Government Coordination

One important role of the government is to enforce contracts and commitments that are not "self-enforcing." Let us consider the case of two investment projects—an upstream project and a downstream project in, say, the petrochemical industry, so that one would be the exclusive supplier and the other would be the exclusive customer. Neither investment project would proceed if the other one did not (if only one went forward, it would have either no market or no supplier and hence would not be viable). This is a version of the classic "prisoner's dilemma" two-person game with its well-known inefficient noncooperative solution. One possibility is for a single enterprise to invest in both projects, thus internalizing the efficiency gains. If there were no capital, or risk-bearing constraints, this might be a good solution, with the government auctioning off the rights or otherwise selecting an enterprise to invest in the bundled project. However, if no enterprise can be found that has the capacity to invest in the bundled project, then only a cooperative solution between two enterprises is possible. However, since the cooperative game has the structure of a bilateral monopoly, the distribution of the gain from trade (or allocation of rent) between the two parties is not determinate and must be agreed upon by both parties. The problem arises with the enforcement of such an agreement. If the two parties are not of approximately equal financial strength, predatory behavior may arise on the part of the stronger party in the future after the investment projects are completed. The government would have a role to play, not so much as an arbitrator for the distribution of rent, but as a credible neutral guarantor of the rent distribution scheme agreed upon by both parties. What the government could do, for example, is to permit the downstream enterprise to import the intermediate input if the upstream enterprise overcharged and to impose an excise tax on the output of the downstream enterprise if it underpaid. It is clear that in the noncooperative two-enterprise case, without some kind of government intervention, the projects would not go forward.[38]

On the whole, the governments of Hong Kong and Taiwan tend to be less interventionist than, say, those of Japan and South Korea. While this difference may be due partly to ideology (more so for Hong Kong), it may also be due to the fact that Hong Kong and Taiwan are much smaller economies and their own domestic markets may be too small to create or support a great deal of rents. The fact that there are many relatively small (nonstate) enterprises in Hong Kong and Taiwan (and now China) also suggests fairly intense competition and therefore a low level of potential rents that can be distributed by the government. Overall, rents tend not to be so important in Hong Kong and Taiwan. Whatever rents exist are to be found in the nontradable sectors, often associated with land and real estate ownership.

The key to successful government coordination lies in the credibility of its commitments, including the commitments to enforce explicit and implicit agreements among independent contracting parties. The government must therefore use its credibility wisely and in particular should avoid engaging in predatory behavior that undermines its future credibility.

2.4 SHIFTING THE PRODUCTION POSSIBILITY FRONTIER

To the extent that technical progress is embodied,[39] any policy that increases the quantity of gross domestic fixed investment shifts the production possibility frontier upward. Other measures that shift the production possibility frontier include R&D investments and reorganizations.

R&D and Technology

In the 1970s, Taiwan, which had heretofore largely eschewed an industrial policy, set up a number of national research institutes and dramatically increased its funding of large-scale industrial R&D projects. One of the research institutes, the Industrial Technology Research Institute, has been responsible for initiating or reviving several major industries, including bicycles, sporting goods, computers and computer peripherals, and semiconductors. Hong Kong is relatively late to this game although it recently set up a new Hong Kong University of Science and Technology which has an R&D arm that works closely with industry. China has strong scientific and technological capabilities in the Chinese Academy of Sciences and in its national defense establishment. However, it needs to become more market oriented and cost conscious in order to play an important role in economic development.

Industrial policy is not infrequently linked to R&D and science and technology policies. The personal computer industry in Taiwan provides a successful example of government-financed R&D and industrial policy. In the early 1980s, the personal computer industries in Hong Kong and Taiwan consisted mostly of "pirates" who simply copied foreign designs (frequently through reverse engineering) without licenses or payment of royalties. All that activity was stopped as a result of legal actions on the part of the United States and other computer manufacturers. Then the Industrial Technology Research Institute of Taiwan came along and developed its own BIOS chip for the personal computer, which enabled the personal computer industry in Taiwan to continue (under foreign licensing). In Hong Kong, where such R&D effort was lacking, the personal computer industry never recovered. The Industrial Technology Research Institute also went on to develop a version of the notebook computer for a consortium of small computer manufacturers in Taiwan. The very successful semiconductor industry in Taiwan was also incubated in the Industrial Technology Research Institute.

It has long been recognized that the basic issue in the financing of R&D is appropriability. To the extent that the gains from R&D cannot be captured by the enterprise engaging in the R&D itself, the social returns will be greater than private returns, and there will be circumstances under which the government should finance, organize, and support these activities. The situation is further complicated if an industry consists of only small and medium-sized enterprises. In this case, even if in principle the gains are appropriable, in practice, no one single enterprise will have sufficient resources to finance an investment with a large capital requirement, long gestation period, and uncertain outcome and the ability to bear the risks to enable it to capture the appropriable gains eventually. This sets up a *prima facie* justification for government intervention in R&D and for the support of pioneering industries.[40] Government investment in R&D, whether directly through government laboratories, or indirectly by financially supporting R&D projects at universities and in private industry, can also be viewed as an attempt to create comparative advantage. However, one also needs to take into account that the case for government-sponsored R&D is strongest when the direction for the search is more or less known. When the direction is not clear, there is a risk that government sponsorship may send the wrong signal, that is, may prematurely and unduly lead to a concentration of both private and public resources in a limited direction only, with the result that the cost of a mistake, when it occurs, may be large. In general, when the direction for the search is not clear, diversification is probably warranted regardless of whether the R&D effort is publicly or privately sponsored.[41]

Technology Transfer

Foreign direct investment can also bring in new technology, and in principle can shift the production possibility frontier. The use of imported new equipment should also have the same effect. However, Kim and Lau (1992a, 1992b, 1994b, 1994c, 1995) find that there is virtually no technical progress, that is, no shift in the production possibility frontier in the East Asian newly industrialized economies in the postwar period, and that all of their economic growth can be attributed to growth in inputs—physical capital, labor, and human capital, with physical capital the most important. This finding is most surprising and is at variance with one of the conclusions of the World Bank (1993). It is, however, supported by the earlier results of Tsao (1982, 1985, 1986) for Singapore even though the results of Young (1992) for Hong Kong and Singapore are mixed (see also the discussion in Krugman 1994). There are many possible explanations of why there has been no measured technical progress in the East Asian newly industrialized economies, in contrast to the experience of the industrialized economies of France, Germany, Japan, the United Kingdom, and the United States, two of which are the most convincing. First, the East Asian newly industrialized economies had not done much R&D until relatively recently, so one should not expect to be able to measure too much of an effect, given the long gestation period of R&D investments. Second, while foreign direct investment and the use of imported new capital equipment and technology increase gross output, they do not necessarily increase added value above a normal return to the capital, and thus there are no "excess" returns to be measured. Another way of putting this is that the transferer of the technology and the (foreign) manufacturer of the new capital equipment have been able to appropriate substantially all of the gains from the use of the new technology.

Strategic R&D

Sometimes R&D can be used strategically. It is the standard practice in the technology transfer world to cross-license. In order to cross-license, an enterprise must have an invention, a patent, something to cross-license to another enterprise. This means that it is important to have done some R&D

before one comes to the table. In addition, an indigenous R&D effort often has the effect of coaxing a reluctant technology transferer to transfer the technology. This is especially the case with regard to the technology of so-called "critical components." There have been many instances in which an enterprise in a developed country has initially refused to transfer a technology, but upon learning that an indigenous investment was about to be launched based on the results of an indigenous R&D effort, readily agrees to either establish a joint venture or license. Frequently the purely indigenous venture would then fail. But from a social point of view, the R&D effort has actually paid off even if the directly related venture itself has failed.

Finally, as long as a country does R&D itself and is in the business of cross-licensing, it will have the incentive to enforce intellectual property rights. This is exactly what has happened in Taiwan. In time, this will happen in China also.

Reorganization

Reorganization and the introduction of new modes of production are also measures that can shift the production possibility frontier. For Hong Kong and Taiwan, whatever changes there have been are more evolutionary. They include the gradual transformation of the family enterprise to an enterprise with professional managers, the adoption of new inventory management and quality-control methods, and the use of computer equipment in not only finance and accounting but also design and manufacturing. For China, the changes have been more radical. A major component of the Chinese economic reform that began in 1979 consists of the devolution of economic decision-making power and the creation of new modes of economic organization for production. The intent of such decentralization was to raise the efficiency and productivity of the production units by increasing their autonomy and providing the proper incentives. The foundation of this decentralization effort is the "contract responsibility system." In rural areas, the contract responsibility system was implemented at the farm household level. It gave the individual farm household the autonomy to farm the land allocated to it on a long-term lease as it saw fit, in return for a commitment to pay its *pro rata* share of agricultural taxes and meet its *pro rata* share of delivery quotas. For all practical purposes, the new system amounted to a return of individual private farming, except that the farm households did not (and most still do not) have legal title to the land, only a lease.

The contract responsibility system, coupled with the agricultural price and market reforms, was immediately and immensely successful, generating huge increases in productivity in agriculture of the order of 30–40 per cent within a few years. In turn, the high productivity in agriculture assured the supply of food and financial resources that enabled the reallocation of the labor force from agriculture to industry. In addition, private and collective township and village enterprises (TVEs), as well as foreign and joint-venture enterprises, that engaged in industrial and service activities were permitted to be established. These TVEs turned out to be the fastest-growing sector of the Chinese economy during the years of reform. As of 1993, the gross value of industrial production of the TVEs constituted almost 45 per cent of the gross value of the entire Chinese industrial production.

In the urban areas, the planning authority that was at one time concentrated in the State Planning Commission in Beijing was devolved to the provincial and local government levels in 1984. It would probably have been better, from an economic point of view, if the authority had been devolved to the enterprise levels, but that was not to be. An attempt was made to extend the contract responsibility system to the state-owned manufacturing enterprises. However, the contract responsibility system failed to elicit the same improvement in efficiency and productivity there as in the rural areas, except in small service establishments, although it did increase the outputs of certain goods. The inefficiency of the state-owned enterprises and the resulting losses remain major problems in the Chinese economy. As part of the urban economic reform, small private and collective (nongovernment) enterprises were also allowed, especially in the service sector. Some of the successful ones went on to become relatively large private or collective enterprises.

It is important to note that it is mostly the new enterprises established since 1979 and/or the new economic activities initiated since then that are responsible for the phenomenal economic success of China during the past 15 years. Most of these new organizations face hard budget constraints and hence have a strong incentive to be efficient. For example, the TVEs, even though they are organized and run by the administration of the former communes, in practice operate very much like a private partnership under managing partners. They typically receive no subsidies from the central or provincial governments but thus enjoy a high degree of autonomy. Their advantage over their urban counterparts lies in the natural social safety net in rural areas—every rural resident has the right to a lease on agricultural land and to farm it—which in turn implies that the wage rates paid by the TVEs can be flexible downward and that little or no new social infrastructure is necessary.

As a result of the much faster growth of the more efficient nonstate, including collective, township and village, private, joint-venture, and foreign-owned sectors, the state-owned sector has been contracting relative to the other sectors. In fact, even without any significant privatization, the state-owned sector now accounts for well under half of Chinese GDP, compared to more than 90 per cent in 1979.

2.5 CONCLUDING REMARKS

The role of government in the economic development of China, Hong Kong, and Taiwan has been diverse and multifaceted. However, one has to conclude that the role of the government has been important in the three economies, albeit in each in a different way. Yet the commonalities are also striking—many similar policies and measures have been adopted in the different economies, albeit at different times, reflecting the differences in their relative stages of economic development (e.g., the unification of the dual exchange rates, the use of special economic zones, the textile quota allocation system). The similarities stem from the demonstration effects of each economy on the others and from mutual learning and emulation, reinforced by the strong economic linkages among China, Hong Kong, and Taiwan, as well as the cultural and ethnic affinity among their respective citizens.

There are, of course, also major differences across the three economies. On the one hand, the relative lack of support for tertiary education and for R&D by the government in Hong Kong has resulted in the superiority that Taiwan has in high-technology industries. On the other hand, the freedom of capital movements, the low tax rate, and the adherence to the rule of law, coupled with a relatively relaxed regulatory regime, have contributed to Hong Kong's success as a leading financial center in East Asia. The free-trade policy of Hong Kong has also resulted in a much more even development in Hong Kong, whereas the economies of both China and Taiwan are characterized by dualism—the existence, side by side, of an efficient, externally oriented sector and an inefficient, domestic nontradable and service sector.

The differences among the three economies will probably never disappear. In a sense, they will specialize in accordance with their respective comparative advantages, even though, as noted, these comparative advantages arose partly in response to government policies and actions. But precisely because these comparative advantages are creatable, the economies that are currently ahead in their respective dimensions must continue to innovate. Taiwan today is producing and exporting what Japan was producing and exporting a decade ago. China today is producing what Taiwan was producing a decade ago. Shanghai will be looking to replace or at least supplant Hong Kong's role as a financial center serving the Chinese economy within the next couple of decades. It is this continuous competitive pressure that makes it necessary for governments to plan ahead and pursue forward-looking policies.

More generally, what distinguishes China and Taiwan on the one hand and Hong Kong on the other is the role of ideology and the East Asian tradition of a high degree of personalization of government. Both ideology—communism in China, the Three People's Principles in Taiwan—and the high degree of personalization of government in these East Asian societies mandate activism, at least superficially, for the heads of the governments, at all levels, especially in response to a perceived need. Benign neglect is not a politically feasible option. It may be reasonably expected that the role of government will increase in Hong Kong after 1997, not so much because of its reversion to Chinese sovereignty, but because of the larger role its citizens, mostly of Chinese ethnic origin, will play in its own governance.

NOTES

[1] Even in Hong Kong, with its strong tradition of *laissez-faire*, the government has kept the exchange rate fixed relative to the US dollar since the early 1980s, undertaken prudential supervision of the banking sector and the securities markets, and provided infrastructure such as public schools and hospitals, housing for low-income households, industrial estates as potential factory sites, and roads, subways, and airports.

[2] See, for example, the remarks by Hyung-Ki Kim at the World Bank Workshop on the Role of Government in the Evolution of System Change, December 18–19, 1994, Tokyo, Japan.

[3] For all three economies the land input is virtually fixed over time.

[4] Examples include the adoption of the just-in-time inventory method or quality-assurance circles.

[5] See Abramovitz and David (1973:431, Table 2).

[6] See International Monetary Fund, *International Financial Statistics Yearbook* (Washington: International Monetary Fund), various issues.

[7] For example, if the potential domestic market is not large enough, then the protection granted to an infant industry may have to become permanent, unless it becomes export oriented and internationally competitive.

[8] For example, the values of import or monopoly franchises (such as cement or steel manufacturing) are directly related to the size of the domestic market.

[9] It should be remarked that the size distribution of enterprises can be substantially influenced by government ideologies and policies as well as by new technologies and can undergo significant changes over time.

[10] However, foreign resources can be pivotal in making possible the initial "big push." For example, in the 1950s, loans from the former Soviet Union to China were crucial in financing China's very successful First Five-Year Plan (1953–57). Similarly, US aid to Taiwan was very important from the early 1950s to 1965.

[11] For example, postal savings in Taiwan are guaranteed by the government. In fact, no depositors have ever lost any money from the failure of formal financial institutions in Taiwan. Nor, for that matter, have depositors in China.

[12] The basic idea is that the marginal propensity to save out of profits by firms is higher than the marginal propensity to save out of incomes by households. A

redistribution from the households to the firms therefore increases the aggregate saving rate of the economy.

[13] The real rate of interest in Hong Kong has been negative for quite some years. However, this is not due to government control of the financial and money markets. Rather, a banking cartel in Hong Kong sets the nominal rate of interest on deposits.

[14] Family-planning programs were less successful in the rural areas in China in recent years.

[15] See Lau (1995).

[16] Even the largest non-Chinese-owned enterprises in Hong Kong, Jardine Matheson and Swire, are controlled by the Keswick and the Swire families, respectively.

[17] Perhaps it is not as important whether an enterprise is public or private, as whether it has a soft or a hard budget constraint, to use a terminology introduced by Janos Kornai (1980). Enterprises that have hard budget constraints take into account seriously the negative consequences of their actions on their profit; enterprises with soft budget constraints do not care about their losses or potential losses because they expect to be bailed out by the government at the end.

[18] See Lau and Song (1992).

[19] Apparently this debate also occurred in South Korea in the early 1960s and was also concluded in favor of private enterprise.

[20] However, the rights, if any, of residents emigrating from the township and village remain to be determined.

[21] At a later stage, when the family enterprises have expanded so much that they require nonfamily members as executives, there may be an "agency problem" to the extent that the objectives of the owners and the nonowner managers do not coincide. Unavoidable economic inefficiency may result from such incompatibility—resources must then be devoted to assure that the agents (the nonowner managers) behave in a way so as to advance the objectives of the principal (the owners).

[22] Agency problems may arise if the managers are not themselves substantial owners. In a large private, but publicly owned corporation, the interests of the owners and the professional managers may diverge. Consequently, the managers may not be responsive to the needs of the owners (shareholders) and instead may pursue their own interests. Such conflicts of interest frequently lead to inefficiency. In many ways, large private corporations with many small shareholders in which the managers do not have a significant stake have an incentive structure not unlike that of state-owned enterprises. The losses are borne by the shareholders and any glory goes to the managers. There is thus a natural tendency, on the part of the managers, to overinvest and to take inordinate risks not to mention elaborate perks and privileges at the expense of the shareholders.

[23] However, there are potential limits to the expansion of a family-owned enterprise with a highly centralized process of decision making. At some point, the efficiency gain resulting from the alignment of the interests of the owner and the manager may be offset by the diseconomies of scale associated with overcentralized decision making and by the inability to recruit the best talents. Thus, at some scale, an enterprise with diffused ownership and professional (nonowner) management may become more efficient than a similar enterprise under family ownership and management.

[24] The exchange rate of the Hong Kong dollar has been maintained at a fixed parity to the US dollar of HK$7.8 per US$ since 1984. Moreover, the rate itself appeared to have been simply pulled out of a hat just to head off a free fall of the Hong Kong dollar during a crisis of confidence in Hong Kong.

[25] The number of airlines in China currently exceeds 30.

[26] Part of the rent is also skimmed by bank officers with the authority to approve loans.

[27] For example, standardization, setting of a fixed exchange rate, and setting the schedule for rotating power outages under conditions of chronic excess demand for electricity are all different forms of nonmarket coordination.

[28] In fact, Deng's southern visit coordinated not only China but also Hong Kong and Taiwan, which stepped up their direct investments in China in response. I owe this point to K. C. Fung.

[29] The declared commitment by the United States to win the race to send a man to the moon in the aftermath of the successful launch of the Sputnik satellite by the Soviet Union in 1957 also served as a coordinating signal to the military-industrial-scientific complex.

[30] It may be noted that even in the United States, condominiumization is a relatively recent concept that did not gain currency until the 1970s. Previously, most nonrental multiple-residential-unit buildings were owned jointly by the individual unit-owners as a "cooperative," under which legal structure the buying, selling, and financing of the units were extremely complex and difficult.

[31] One partial remedy is to institute a "means test" to impose some nonpecuniary costs to the free-riders.

[32] If these infrastructural activities were to be priced at marginal cost, the enterprise would operate at a loss—this is a well-known proposition in public finance.

[33] Established in the late 1960s, the Kaohsiung Export-Processing Zone is the first export-processing zone of its kind in the world.

[34] Twenty-six per cent of foreign direct investment in China is located in the special economic zones.

[35] The society as a whole should be close to being risk neutral whereas individuals and firms are risk averse to various degrees. The social rate of discount is also likely to be lower than the private rate of discount.

[36] In the 1960s, the US Department of Defense actually ran a tournament between two aircraft manufacturers based on their prototypes to determine which one would receive the actual order for many more of the same model.

[37] If the quotas turn over every year, it will be too uncertain for any manufacturer to want to invest in manufacturing equipment with a long life.

[38] Note that in this example there is no information asymmetry or imperfection. What we have is an *ex post* reopening of the negotiations after the capital costs are sunk. In this case, the party with the greater financial resources would have the upper hand as it could outlast the other party in a stalemate. As long as this possibility is known it would doom the agreement in the absence of the government assuming a guarantor's role to both sides.

[39] Kim and Lau (1992a, 1994a) find that technical progress, to the extent that it exists, is mostly embodied in new capital goods.

[40] It is interesting to compare South Korea and Taiwan in this regard. In South

Korea, most of the industrial R&D is carried out in the large conglomerates such as Samsung, Hyundai, Daewoo, and Lucky-Goldstar (recently renamed the LG Group).

[41] This was pointed out to me by Masahiko Aoki.

REFERENCES

ABRAMOVITZ, M. and DAVID, P. A. (1973), "Reinterpreting Economic Growth: Parables and Realities," *American Economic Review*, 63:428–39.

KIM, J.-I. and LAU, L. J. (1992a), "The Importance of Embodied Technical Progress: Some Empirical Evidence from the Group-of-Five Countries," working paper, Department of Economics, Stanford University.

——(1992b), "The Sources of Economic Growth of the Newly Industrialized Countries on the Pacific Rim," paper presented at the Conference on the Economic Development of the Republic of China and the Pacific Rim in the 1990s and Beyond, Taipei, May 25–28.

——(1994a), "The Sources of East Asian Economic Growth Revisited," working paper, Department of Economics, Stanford University.

——(1994b), "The Sources of Economic Growth in the East Asian Newly Industrialized Countries," *Journal of the Japanese and International Economies*, 8:235–71.

——(1994c), "The Sources of Economic Growth of the Newly Industrialized Countries on the Pacific Rim," in L. R. Klein and C.-T. Yu, eds., *The Economic Development of ROC and the Pacific Rim in the 1990s and Beyond*, World Scientific Publishing Co., Singapore, 65–103.

——(1996), "The Sources of Asian-Pacific Economic Growth," *The Canadian Journal of Economics,* 29:S448–S454.

KORNAI, J. (1980), *Economics of Shortage*, North-Holland, Amsterdam.

KRUGMAN, P. (1994), "The Myth of Asia's Miracle," *Foreign Affairs*, 73:62–78.

LAU, L. J. (1995), "Global Impacts of Chinese Economic Growth," paper presented at the Aspen Strategy Group Conference on "The Growth of Chinese Power and Implications for U.S. Policy," Aspen, Colorado, August.

——and SONG, D.-H. (1992), "Growth versus Privatization—An Alternative Strategy to Reduce the Public Enterprise Sector: The Experiences of Taiwan and South Korea," working paper, Department of Economics, Stanford University.

TSAO, Y. (1982), "Growth and Productivity in Singapore: A Supply Side Analysis," Ph.D. diss., Harvard University.

——(1985), "Growth without Productivity: Singapore Manufacturing in the 1970s," *Journal of Development Studies*, 18:25–38.

——(1986), "Sources of Growth Accounting for the Singapore Economy," in C.-Y. Lim and P. J. Lloyd, eds., *Singapore: Resources and Growth*, Oxford University Press, New York, 17–44.

World Bank (1993), *The East Asian Miracle: Economic Growth and Public Policy*, Oxford University Press, Oxford.

YOUNG, A. (1992), "A Tale of Two Cities: Factor Accumulation and Technical Change in Hong Kong and Singapore," in O. J. Blanchard and S. Fischer, eds., *National Bureau of Economic Research Macroeconomics Annual*, The MIT Press, Cambridge, Mass., 13–54.

3

The Government-Firm Relationship in Postwar Japanese Economic Recovery: Resolving the Coordination Failure by Coordination in Industrial Rationalization

TETSUJI OKAZAKI

As East Asian economies have achieved remarkable growth, the experience of Japan has again attracted wide attention as an example of the "East Asian Miracle." At the same time, the Japanese economy has also been seen as a model for transforming socialist economies. Since the early 1980s, research on Japan's industrial policy by both political scientists and economists has focused on the government-firm relationship. (Johnson 1982, Tsuruta 1982, Komiya *et al.* 1984, Ito *et al.* 1988, and a more recent work (World Bank 1993) have aroused new interest in this relationship.)

The most recent research has taken into account the possibility of government failure as well as market failure (Matsuyama ch. 5 in this volume, Okuno-Fujiwara and Hori 1994). It is not easy for the government to identify market failure precisely, and government intervention itself may bring about rent-seeking activities in the private sector. One important implication of this new research is that the performance of industrial policy substantially depends on institutional and fundamental conditions. In order to clarify why a policy succeeded or failed, and to know the transferability of Japanese industrial policy to other countries, we must have a detailed understanding of these fundamental and institutional conditions.

In this chapter I examine these conditions, taking the case of industrial rationalization policy in Japan in the early 1950s. This was the central policy of the Ministry of International Trade and Industry (MITI) in the 1950s. The Japanese economy, which had been a controlled economy during and after World War II, had just been transformed into a market economy (Okazaki and Okuno-Fujiwara 1993). As I discuss below, the newly formed Japanese market economy was faced with serious coordination failure because of complementarity among industries, economies of scale, and incomplete information (Murphy, Shleifer, and Vishny 1989, Matsuyama 1991).

MITI intended to coordinate the coordination failure by an industrial rationalization policy.

To examine this issue, we can use the large volume of first-hand materials from the Economic Stabilization Board (Keizai Antei Honbu) and the Council for Industrial Rationalization (Sangyō Gōrika Shingikai) under MITI. With these inside materials, we can shed light into the black box where industrial policy was drawn up and implemented. We can thus clarify subtle aspects of the government-firm relationship in postwar Japan. The availability of abundant inside information is an important advantage in taking a historical case-study approach.

The material discussed in this chapter is organized as follows. Section 3.1 identifies the coordination failure faced by the Japanese economy. In Section 3.2, I examine the role of the Council for Industrial Rationalization in solving the coordination failure problem. Section 3.3 examines the role of the government and other institutions in implementing the industrial rationalization policy and Section 3.4 presents my conclusions.

3.1 COORDINATION FAILURE IN THE JAPANESE ECONOMY IN THE EARLY 1950S

Let us first examine several macro and sectoral characteristics of the Japanese economy during the first half of the 1950s. Before 1955, when the so-called rapid growth started, the investment rate (private investment/GNP) began an upward trend in 1950 (Figure 3.1). In the latter half of the 1940s, most of the growth in Japan's GNP had been absorbed by consumption, and the investment rate remained low (Okazaki and Yoshikawa 1993:69–70). The first half of the 1950s can be regarded as the starting point of the postwar accumulation of capital.

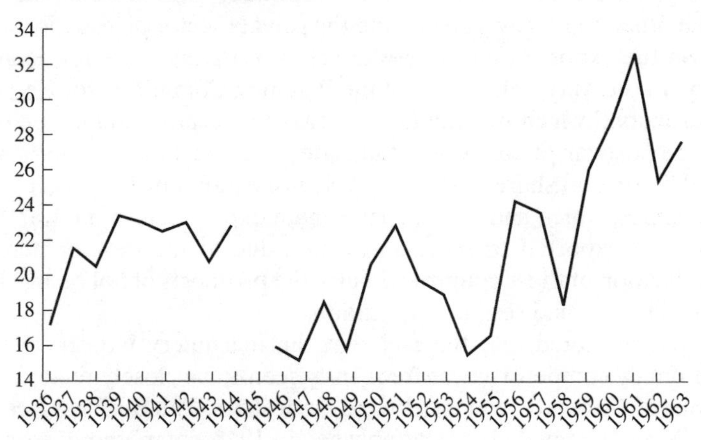

FIG. 3.1 Private Investment/GNP in Japan, 1936–1963

Investment in the 1950s, which includes the first half of the rapid economic growth period, was characterized by a correlation between industries. Yoshikawa (1992:78–79) accounts for rapid growth in 1966–85 by the growth of domestic demand, and he points out the high correlation of investment between industries. When the same calculations are made with data from the 1950s, the high correlation becomes even more evident (Table 3.1). This means that investment resumed simultaneously in each industry during the first half of the 1950s. At the same time, the relative weight of heavy industries in production began to increase. It is notable that this take-off toward rapid growth during the first half of the 1950s was just after the transition from a controlled economy to a market economy. The Japanese economy seemed to have carried out the transition smoothly.

However, if we consider the historical process in more detail, we can see that the transition to a market economy and taking off to sustainable growth were by no means easy tasks even for Japan. In April 1949 the regime of foreign exchange shifted from multiple exchange rates, which had given substantial *de facto* subsidies to Japanese industries, to a single exchange rate ($1 = ¥360). According to a survey by the Economic Stabilization Board (ESB), the exchange rates for the main products at the beginning of 1949 were as shown in Table 3.2. While textile products were appreciated under ¥360, many machinery products were depreciated. Thus, the ESB and the Ministry of Commerce and Industry (a predecessor of MITI) expected that machinery—including sewing machines, watches, bicycles, radios, cameras, and ships—could not be exported if the exchange rate was fixed at $1 = ¥360. This would have resulted in fulfilling only 70–80 per cent of the export plan. In addition, in accordance with the Dodge plan of the Allied Occupation, subsidies for the metal industry were also to be cut off, which would result in an increase in the price of the raw materials for machinery. This would make exports of machinery still more difficult.[1]

On the other hand, government and the private sector placed high expectations on the export of machinery to act as a driving force for economic recovery. In the May 1949 report of the Planning Committee for Economic Reconstruction,[2] which was the first general deliberative council on industries in the postwar period, it was calculated that machinery exports would hold a 21.5 per cent share of the total value of exports by the target year of 1953.[3] Textiles, which had been Japan's main export before the war, could no longer be exported to India and China due to the development and industrialization of those countries.[4] Thus, the prospects of not being able to export machinery had serious implications.

It should be noted that the fact that the machinery industry was not internationally competitive was frequently seen to be closely related to the conditions of "forward" and "backward" industries. The Business Research Society (Kigyo kenkyukai) was established in 1948, composed of corporate managers, administrators, and researchers, to "study the problems involved in maintaining and developing important industries under domestic and

TABLE 3.1 Correlation of Investment by Industry, 1953–1962 and 1963–1973

(a) 1953–1962

	Electricity	Steel	Shipping	Textiles	Chemicals	Ceramics	Machinery	Metals	Mining	Transport.	Gas	Fisheries	Ave.
Electricity	1.000												0.559
Steel	0.569	1.000											0.499
Shipping	0.235	0.740	1.000										0.370
Textiles	0.723	0.306	0.175	1.000									0.578
Chemicals	0.732	0.718	0.596	0.788	1.000								0.704
Ceramics	0.545	0.323	0.112	0.852	0.728	1.000							0.490
Machinery	0.733	0.892	0.673	0.675	0.906	0.650	1.000						0.651
Metal	0.562	0.656	0.435	0.756	0.919	0.743	0.822	1.000					0.633
Mining	0.590	0.389	0.270	0.364	0.527	0.001	0.381	0.468	1.000				0.364
Transportation	0.793	0.504	0.371	0.955	0.866	0.777	0.816	0.783	0.418	1.000			0.647
Gas	0.260	0.382	0.337	0.033	0.334	0.160	0.313	0.175	0.078	0.186	1.000		0.202
Fisheries	0.409	0.007	0.126	0.730	0.631	0.503	0.305	0.648	0.513	0.651	–0.032	1.000	0.408

(b) 1963–1973

	Electricity	Steel	Shipping	Textiles	Chemicals	Ceramics	Machinery	Metals	Mining	Transport.	Gas	Fisheries	Ave.
Electricity	1.000												–0.079
Steel	0.206	1.000											0.349
Shipping	0.054	–0.027	1.000										0.044
Textiles	–0.255	0.427	–0.405	1.000									0.164
Chemicals	0.085	0.453	0.188	0.410	1.000								0.224
Ceramics	–0.381	0.422	–0.593	0.513	0.301	1.000							0.148
Machinery	–0.296	0.699	–0.202	0.505	0.493	0.650	1.000						0.276
Metals	–0.217	0.672	0.067	0.494	0.656	0.303	0.711	1.000					0.252
Mining	–0.257	–0.033	0.838	–0.290	–0.102	0.468	–0.108	0.126	1				0.096
Transportation	–0.051	0.215	0.139	0.304	0.330	0.132	–0.050	0.060	–0.095	1.000			0.100
Gas	0.004	0.662	0.095	0.304	0.041	0.182	0.664	0.275	0.201	0.003	1.000		0.284
Fisheries	0.238	0.139	0.332	–0.208	–0.396	–0.367	–0.028	–0.370	0.304	0.113	0.691	1.000	0.041

Source: Japan Development Bank.

TABLE 3.2 Exchange Rates by Commodities, 1949

Textiles	
Cotton yarn	250
Cotton cloth (raw)	250
Cotton cloth (pre-dyed)	300
Cotton cloth (bleached)	300
Cotton cloth (printed)	300
Knitted cotton	300
Rayon staple	420
Rayon cloth A	250
Rayon cloth B	420
Rayon muffler	350
Staple fiber	350
Machinery	
Freight car	372
Passenger car	381
Catcher boat	520
Steel ship	530
Wooden ship	300
Automobile parts	542
Spinning machine and parts	320
Weaving machine	240

Source: Survey by the Economic Stabilization Board.

international conditions."[5] In 1949 the Society was entrusted with research on "rationalization" (*gōrika*), "economic independence" (*jiritsuka*), and "industrial finance" (*sangyō kin'yū*) by ESB, the Ministry of Finance (MOF), and MITI, and it set up three committees to examine these topics.[6]

At the first committee meeting on "economic independence," the machinery manufacturers brought up the problem of the price and quality of steel.[7] The director of the Automobile Industry Association said that steel made up 16 per cent of automobile costs and that the steel industry should recognize that the price of steel was the biggest problem for the automobile industry. The association also requested improvement in the quality of steel, because the automobile industry currently could not use the steel as delivered; it could only be used after being treated by the automobile enterprises. Hitachi Manufacturing Co. claimed that, when the exchange rate was fixed at $1 = ¥360, electrical machinery could be exported only by using steel at prices reduced by subsidies. Hitachi wished for drastic rationalization of the steel industry to make the export of machinery possible. At the fourth committee meeting, Ishikawajima Heavy Industries Co. claimed that reducing the costs of shipbuilding enterprises by half would only result in a 20 per cent decrease in the total cost of ships, and that therefore a sufficient reduction in the cost of ships would not be possible without rationalization of each related industry and the Japanese economy as a whole.[8]

In sum, the machinery manufacturers perceived a reduction in the price of their main input, steel, as the key to the international competitiveness of their products. On the other hand, at the same committee meeting, Nippon Steel Co. pointed out that in order to reduce the cost of steel, it would be necessary to save on shipping costs by using Japanese ships and to reduce the price of coal.[9]

The request to use Japanese ships was urgent for the iron and steel industry. On a different occasion, the chairman of Nippon Kokan Co. claimed that in 1949, the shipping costs for raw materials were $2.6 million, 33 per cent of material costs, while this cost would have been $1.5 million if Japanese ships could have been used. The company was thus eager to have the Japanese merchant fleet reconstructed.[10] Yet from the shipping enterprises' point of view, there was a need for a decrease in the price of ships, which in turn meant a need for the rationalization of the shipbuilding and related industries.[11] As Kosai (1990:297) and Nakagawa (1992:116–29) have pointed out, the coal, steel, shipbuilding (machinery), shipping, and other industries were connected through input-output relations, and this interdependent relationship brought about high costs.

Another aspect of interdependence can be seen in that the production or investment level of one industry affected another industry's production level through market size, which in turn affected cost through economies of scale. This problem was also taken up as an issue by enterprises at that time. The Japan Federation of Industries (JFI; Nihon Sangyō Kyōgikai), which was one of the largest organizations of major industrial enterprises, took up the problem of the international competitiveness of Japanese industries, focusing on machinery and steel. In June 1949, JFI, hearing that the government was planning to reduce steel subsidies, held a conference with steel producers and the enterprises that purchased steel and surveyed the effects of a price increase on steel in the steel-purchasing industries.[12]

The associations of the steel-purchasing industries responded that total cessation of subsidies would lead to a 20–70 per cent increase in the cost or price of their products. A majority of the steel-purchasing industries also said that the effects of a price increase on steel could not be absorbed through their own rationalization. The reason they offered was that further cost reduction was difficult in the face of decreasing rates of operation due to a decline in domestic demand and poor performance of exports. It is notable that the Federation of the Machinery Industry requested a policy for promoting investment in order to increase demand for machinery.[13] The machinery manufacturers supposed that investment toward rationalization in the various industries would reduce not only costs in those industries, but also the cost of machinery, through expanding the domestic market for machinery and the economies of scale.[14]

Another point raised by the JFI survey concerned economies of scale. In its response, the automobile industry claimed that the shortage of electricity was preventing an increase in the rate of operation, making a decrease in costs difficult. At the time, there were regulations on the supply of electricity, and this acted as a bottleneck preventing automotive firms from taking advantage of economies of scale.

Putting all of these together, the problems faced by Japanese industries and enterprises in 1948–50 can be illustrated by Figure 3.2. The costs of various industries were pushed up both by the small market size and by high input prices; as a result, the export of machinery, which had gained a wide consensus as being the key to the recovery and future growth of the Japanese economy, stagnated. Because the interdependent relationships were complex and wide ranging, the self-motivated independent actions of each industry and enterprise alone would likely not result in the resolution of this vicious cycle. This can be regarded as a typical case of coordination failure due to complementarity and scale economy. This type of coordination failure can be solved, if trade is free and without transportation costs. But most of the goods in question at that time, namely coal, iron ore, and steel,

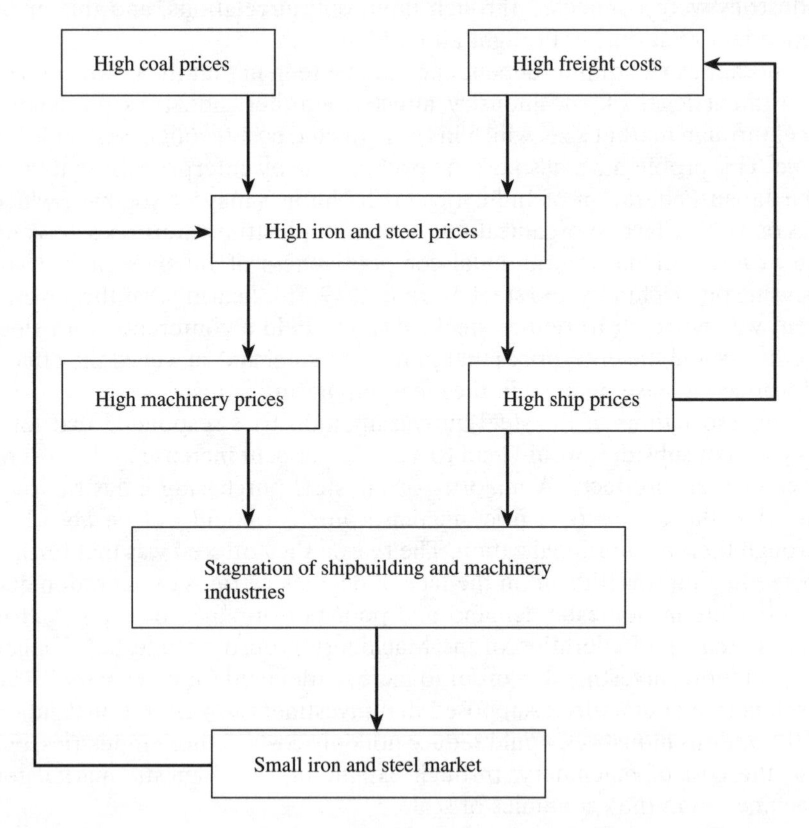

FIG. 3.2 Interrelationship of the Problems of Japan's Industries in the Early 1950s

were bulky cargo, and high shipping costs were an important link in the vicious cycle. Furthermore, importing coal was politically difficult because of pressure from the coal-mining enterprises and trade unions.[15] The policy of industrial rationalization was started under these conditions.

3.2 THE COUNCIL FOR INDUSTRIAL RATIONALIZATION AND THE DRAFTING OF THE RATIONALIZATION PLANS

The industrial rationalization policy started with a September 1949 cabinet decision.[16] In accordance with this decision, the Council for Industrial Rationalization (CIR) was established in December as an advisory organization for the Minister of International Trade and Industry. CIR at the time consisted of a Coordination Branch, a General Branch, and 29 other sectoral branches. The latter were composed of representatives from the industrial associations and leading enterprises of each industry (Table 3.3). In many cases the representatives from the enterprises were their presidents. This composition reflected MITI's intention to formulate its industrial rationalization policy on the basis of a wide range of knowledge from both the public and private sectors.[17] In May 1950, expert committees were appointed for each branch. Most of the expert committee members came from industrial associations and leading enterprises (Table 3.4), and many of the members from the enterprises were ordinary directors and department chiefs. The General Branch had many expert committee members from financial institutions, particularly in its funds section, described below. The council gathered widely from the private sector those persons with managerial and technical information.

It is important to note MITI's aim for the operation of CIR. It intended the council to take up the following three issues.[18]

1. Find the aspects to be rationalized in each enterprise and industry, and set a target input coefficient and cost for each industry.
2. Investigate the problem areas in eliminating the barriers to rationalization and forming the conditions necessary for rationalization.
3. Investigate the rational arrangement of industries from an industrial-structure perspective, especially the rational interdependence of the basic industries important for industrial rationalization.

The first issue was to be investigated in the sectoral branches, while the second and third issues would be taken up by the respective relevant sectoral branches and then coordinated at the Coordination Branch. The fact that the third issue was taken up and coordinated at the Coordination Branch was intended to reflect the fact that the problems faced in each industry were interrelated, as discussed in Section 3.1. One important purpose of CIR can be said to have been finding a path for resolving the vicious

TABLE 3.3 Membership of the Council for Industrial Rationalization

Branch	Total	General Association	Industrial Association	Financial Institution	Industrial Firm	Others
Total	100	3	32	2	53	10
Coordination	10	2	0	2	5	1
General	10	1	0	0	1	8
Cotton	3	0	3	0	0	0
Silk	3	0	3	0	0	0
Synthetic fibers	3	0	1	0	2	0
Flax and wool	3	0	1	0	2	0
Clothes	3	0	3	0	0	0
Fabrics	3	0	3	0	0	0
Paper	3	0	2	0	1	0
Rubber	1	0	0	0	1	0
Ceramics	3	0	0	0	3	0
Leather	1	0	1	0	0	0
Daily necessities	4	0	2	0	2	0
Industrial machinery	4	0	1	0	3	0
Electric machinery	2	0	1	0	1	0
Communicating machinery	2	0	0	0	2	0
Precision machinery	5	0	3	0	2	0
Vehicles	2	0	2	0	0	0
Forge and foundry	2	0	0	0	2	0
Organic chemicals	2	0	1	0	1	0
Inorganic chemicals	2	0	0	0	2	0
Oils and fats	2	0	1	0	1	0
Chemical fertilizers	3	0	2	0	0	1
Iron and steel	4	0	0	0	4	0
Processed steel	2	0	0	0	2	0
Coal	4	0	1	0	3	0
Gas and coke	3	0	0	0	3	0
Mining	2	0	1	0	1	0
Metals	3	0	0	0	3	0
Petroleum	2	0	0	0	2	0
Electricity	4	0	0	0	4	0

TABLE 3.4 Expert Staff of the Council for Industrial Rationalization

Branch	General Association	Industrial Association	Financial Institution	Industrial Firm	Others
Total	11	122	15	596	13
Coordination	0	1	3	2	0
General	11	5	12	19	11
Cotton	0	0	0	21	0
Silk	0	3	0	17	0
Synthetic fibers	0	3	0	17	0
Flax and wool	0	9	0	12	0
Clothes	0	18	0	0	1
Fabrics	0	0	0	20	0
Paper	0	10	0	24	0
Rubber	0	1	0	21	0
Ceramics	0	1	0	26	0
Leather	0	4	0	17	0
Daily necessities	0	11	0	18	0
Industrial machinery	0	4	0	33	0
Electric machinery	0	1	0	30	0
Communicating machinery	0	2	0	25	0
Precision machinery	0	5	0	21	0
Vehicles	0	11	0	13	0
Forge and foundry	0	4	0	15	0
Organic chemicals	0	5	0	21	0
Inorganic chemicals	0	4	0	26	0
Oils and fats	0	2	0	18	0
Chemical fertilizers	0	0	0	24	0
Iron and steel	0	4	0	21	0
Processed steel	0	1	0	19	0
Coal	0	6	0	19	0
Gas and coke	0	1	0	18	0
Mining	0	1	0	20	0
Metal	0	2	0	23	0
Petroleum	0	3	0	14	0
Electricity	0	0	0	22	0

cycle among industries, by looking into the rationalization strategies of each industry and by coordination at the Coordination Branch.

The sectoral branches of CIR met frequently in early 1950, as shown in Table 3.5. As is well known, in 1950 there was emphasis on the discussion of steel and coal. Therefore, I shall consider these industries in detail. The Iron and Steel Branch was set up in January 1950 and comprised four sections (general, management, accounting, and trade). According to the intermediate report of the Iron and Steel Branch given to the expert committee of the Coordination Branch on February 17,[19] the Iron and Steel Branch settled on its steering policy on February 4, and decided to examine the measures necessary to make steel exports possible after subsidies were eliminated. At the branch meeting, it was clarified that the price gap for steel in relation to Europe and the United States was increasing. It was also pointed out that processing costs accounted for only 20 per cent of total steel costs and that

TABLE 3.5 Frequency of Meetings in Each Branch Council of the Council for Industrial Rationalization (December 1949–April 1950)

Branch	
Total	162
Coordination	5
General	8
Cotton	0
Silk	0
Synthetic fibers	0
Flax and wool	2
Clothes	0
Fabrics	0
Paper	10
Rubber	2
Ceramics	9
Leather	8
Daily necessities	62
Industrial machinery	4
Electric machinery	9
Communicating machinery	8
Precision machinery	1
Vehicles	3
Forge and foundry	3
Organic chemicals	4
Inorganic chemicals	1
Oils and fats	0
Chemical fertilizers	1
Iron and steel	8
Processed steel	10
Coal	2
Gas and coke	2
Mining	0
Metal	0
Petroleum	0
Electricity	0

reducing this was not enough to make Japanese steel internationally competitive. The high price of raw materials, especially coal, was stressed as a cause of the high steel cost, with the cost of coal accounting for 50 per cent of the total steel cost. The price of domestic coal provided to factories was $14–15 compared to $7 in the United States.

Having received this report, the expert committee of the Coordination Branch debated the steel and coal issue in depth.[20] First, in supplementing the report, a member of the expert committee from Nippon Steel Co. said there was a limit to the amount of rationalization in each iron and steel enterprise, and that the future was not promising in light of the current price of coal. In addition, a representative of MITI expressed the view that "if the current situation was maintained, all other industries would go under and only the coal industry would remain . . . the issue of coal prices was a central problem to industrial rationalization [and] as long as the vicious cycle between the coal enterprises and related industries could not be broken, the problem would not be resolved." It was determined that once the Iron and Steel Branch and the Coal Branch could agree on quantified targets respectively, the Coordination Branch would take the issue up for discussion. Thus, the rationalization plans for steel and coal of the two interrelated industries would be looked into and coordinated, as had been intended by MITI from the beginning.

The initial conclusions of the Iron and Steel Branch were summarized in the intermediate report given in April 1950.[21] This report confirmed the statements made by the member of the expert committee from Nippon Steel Co. mentioned above. It was stated that "the conclusion has been reached that the high price of coal, which is the main input for the iron and steel industry, prevents that industry from being internationally competitive, regardless of severe rationalization within the industry." The Iron and Steel Branch gave quantified reasoning for this conclusion (Table 3.6). At the current coal price, the elimination of subsidies would result in domestic steel prices largely exceeding steel prices in Europe and the United States. Data indicated that reducing all possible production costs for a given year would still not lower steel prices enough to be able to export. Furthermore, it was stated that if imported and domestic coal prices fell to international levels, steel exports would be possible without subsidies, and that this fact indicated that much of the reason for steel being internationally uncompetitive was the high coal price. As a conclusion, the Iron and Steel Branch stressed that "if the high coal price continues and subsidies are eliminated,

TABLE 3.6 Estimates of Iron and Steel Prices by the Council for Industrial Rationalization, 1950 (yen/ton)

	Export Price	Cost Excluding Subsidy		C + Export Charge
		Before Rationalization	After Rationalization	
	(A)	(B)	(C)	
Pig iron		19,022	16,550	
Bar	23,400	35,580	27,820	30,880
Plate	30,600	39,170	30,610	33,490
Sheet	43,200	44,460	37,200	42,960
Pipe	50,400	61,065	48,400	51,610

Source: Interim report of the Iron and Steel Branch of the Council for Industrial Rationalization.

not only will steel not be exported, but machinery and other industries that use steel as an input will also not be able to export. This will decrease domestic demand, which will force the iron and steel industry to reduce operations and increase production costs." This is precisely the vicious cycle that was discussed in the Section 3.1.

The intermediate report of the Iron and Steel Branch was explained at the expert committee of the Coordination Branch in April 1950 and a report issued on the 25th.[22] The first interesting point of this report was that the industrial rationalization plans of the coal industry were taken into consideration. The high price of coal was found to be a result of decreased efficiency due to poor mining facilities, restrictions on labor hours, degenerating natural conditions, and changes in the composition of the labor force. The report claimed that in order to resolve the high coal price, there was an immediate need to mechanize the facilities of coal mines and to remove conditions leading to low efficiency. The report sought at least ¥23.1 billion in investment in fiscal year 1950.

Second, the report quantitatively examined the influence of the high steel price on the international competitiveness of the shipbuilding industry. Even at the existing steel price lowered by subsidies, with the steel for shipbuilding priced at ¥18,500 per ton, the cost of a large ship built in Japan exceeded that of one built in Great Britain. If subsidies were eliminated, the cost of steel for shipbuilding would become ¥36,500 per ton and the price of a Japanese ship would further increase by 13 per cent. Based on this, the report stated that measures for rationalization for shipbuilding should be looked into. Thus, CIR not only coordinated the industrial rationalization plans of the iron and steel and coal industries, but it also intended to coordinate the shipbuilding industry along with them.

On April 28, the Coordination Branch debated the industrial rationalization plans for the shipbuilding, iron and steel, and coal industries.[23] Regarding shipbuilding, one member stated that "the price of ships is high. To build ships is meaningless, if the ships cannot stand the competition. I want a ship that is competitive." MITI's vice-minister stated that "under current conditions, we will not be able to export ships. We will immediately meet with the Ministry of Transport and discuss this issue." Some members claimed that the main cause for the high cost of ships was high prices for steel and coal. After debating the issue, MITI's administrative vice-minister stated that "we would like to make the Coal Branch issue its intermediate report soon." As mentioned above, the rationalization plans of the steel industry had been examined quantitatively, so quantified plans for the rationalization of the coal industry, which were to be coordinated with that of the steel industry, were sought as soon as possible.

The intermediate conclusion of the Coordination Branch was issued on June 17, 1950.[24] This report calculated the target coal price that would have been necessary in order for steel prices to be internationally competitive.

By calculating whether coal prices could be lowered to that level, the rationalization plans for the steel and coal industries were coordinated. The price of steel bars for export in FY 1953 was projected at $60 (¥21,600). In order to achieve this target price, the price of pig iron had to be $33 (¥11,880), and the price of coal had to be ¥2,800 for coking coal, or ¥2,300 for gas-producing and other coal. On the other hand, by FY 1953, the coal price was expected to decrease by 18 per cent. This expectation was consistent with the data in a report dated June 20, issued by the Coal Branch.[25] However, despite the decrease in the cost of coal, the price of coking coal would be as high as ¥3,700. Thus, even if the rationalization plans for the iron and steel and coal industries were carried out simultaneously, steel would not be internationally competitive.

After such a pessimistic report had been issued, the Coordination Branch revised its rationalization plans. In the report by the expert committee of the Coordination Branch,[26] the coal price necessary for steel to be exported was recalculated. If the steel industry concentrated production in efficient works and used oil, the target price of coal could be relaxed as follows: coking coal, ¥3,000; gas-producing coal, ¥2,900; and other coal, ¥2,500 (Table 3.7). In the coal-mining industry, by concentrating production in high-efficiency mines and by postponing repayment of liability from the Reconstruction Finance Bank, the price of coking coal could be reduced to ¥3,200–3,300. This reduction, coupled with a deflationary trend due to falling coal prices and a mixing of cheap imported coal, would make possible the export of steel.

The report drawn up by the Steel Branch on June 22, 1950,[27] provided data that supported the above claim. It stated that with coking coal priced at ¥3,000, gas-producing coal at ¥2,900, and other coal at ¥2,500, the price of a steel bar would be $60 (¥21,600). This conclusion was reconfirmed at the June 24 Coordination Branch meeting and was authorized by a decision of the cabinet on August 18.[28]

TABLE 3.7 Rationalization Plan for the Coal and Steel Industries by the Council for Industrial Rationalization, 1950 (yen)

	1950	1953
Steel		
International price	21,600	21,600
Total cost	25,230	24,300
Index of processing cost	100	76
Required coal price		
Coal for blast furnace		3,000
Coal for open hearth		2,900
Coal for other purposes		2,500

Source: Council for Industrial Rationalization.

In this way, with rationalization of not only the steel industry but also the coal industry, prospects improved for the steel industry to become internationally competitive. This rationalization was authorized by the cabinet. An additional point to note is that this conclusion seems to have created the prospect of the shipbuilding industry becoming internationally competitive as well. In May 1950 the Research Committee on Steel for Shipbuilding formed by the Bureau of Shipping within the Ministry of Transport (MOT), ESB's Bureau of Construction and Transportation, and 12 major shipbuilding enterprises drew up a report.[29] It specified that in order for Japanese ships to be competitive with European ships, the shipbuilding industry would need to be rationalized and, at the same time, the price of steel for shipbuilding would have to fall to below ¥27,000.

The Research Committee claimed that this condition could be met if the price of steel plates was ¥24,090 and the standard shipbuilding fee could be reduced to ¥2,900. The price of steel plates was not shown in the Coordination Branch conclusions on the industrial rationalization of the steel and coal industries, but this can be estimated from the June 20 report of the expert committee of the Coordination Branch, by calculating the relative price of steel plates and steel bars. The price of steel bars was ¥21,600, thus steel plates would have been ¥24,622. Therefore, we can say that, along with the rationalization of the steel and coal industries, rationalization of the shipbuilding industry would create the prospect of the industry becoming internationally competitive.

The above-mentioned report of June 24 by the Coordination Branch planned investment in facilities in the amount of ¥42 billion for the iron and steel industry and ¥40 billion for the coal industry for their rationalization. The planned investment is shown in Table 3.8. In light of the above facts, we can see that CIR, through the efforts of government and private members, was able to develop an investment plan that took into account the rationalization of related industries. This investment effect would allow the steel and shipbuilding industries to become internationally competitive. In other words, CIR assimilated and coordinated information from the various enterprises and industries and found a path through which the selected industries—the industries that were to act as the engines for economic recovery—could escape from the vicious cycle. The council also formulated the path for investment plans.

It should be noted that this whole process implies that causes of the coordination failure included not only complementarity and economies of scale (discussed in Section 3.1), but also incomplete information. It was not easy to know that simultaneous investment in related industries could really break the vicious cycle. In order to see that, the coordinated experiment carried out at CIR was necessary. However, it was not an incentive to private enterprises. In other words, there was a failure in coordinating the experiment, and the government played the role of resolving this problem.[30]

TABLE 3.8 Three-Year Investment Plan by the Council for Industrialization Rationalization, 1950 (million yen)

Commodity	
Iron and steel	
Total	42,031
Blast furnace	6,259
Steelmaking	4,098
Rolling	26,465
Power	2,055
Transportation	1,592
Housing etc.	1,561
Coal	
Total	40,000
Machine	10,173
Others	29,827

Source: Iron and Steel Branch, "Targets and Measures for Reducing the Cost of Iron and Steel;" Coal Branch, "On Rationalization of the Coal Industry."

3.3 IMPLEMENTATION OF THE INDUSTRIAL RATIONALIZATION PLANS

The examination and creation of the rationalization plans by CIR affected each enterprise's investment plans. Furthermore, the government played a substantial role in implementing the investment plans. Let us look at this issue with respect to the steel industry.[31] The effect of the rationalization plan for the steel and coal industries can be seen by checking the company histories of several leading enterprises. For example, at Yawata Steel Co., established by the break-up of Nippon Steel Co., plans for the modernization of facilities had been developed. After becoming aware of the government's rationalization plan, the firm announced a three-year plan for the modernization of facilities.[32] Nippon Kokan Co., aware that subsidies for steel would be stopped, set up in September 1949 a Rationalization Promotion Committee for the process of making pig iron. Then, in accordance with CIR's conclusion, a new three-year plan was set up for modernizing facilities, starting in 1951.[33] Kawasaki Steel Co., which had had a plan to introduce an integrated production process from pig iron to steel since the establishment of the enterprise in 1950, applied for loans from the Counterpart Funds (*Mikaeri Shikin*)[34] to construct the Chiba works with blast furnaces after the conclusion of CIR.[35]

MITI found that the total of these investment plans over three years came to ¥121.1 billion.[36] Even taking into account the inflation caused by the Korean War, the investment was far larger than CIR had anticipated.

We cannot deny that the progressive stance of private enterprises toward investment for rationalization and the boom from the Korean War had an effect on this figure. But, as the company histories show, we should not overlook the fact that the conclusions reached by CIR and the decision of the cabinet were the impetus for major enterprises simultaneously to draw up and announce three-year rationalization plans.

In implementing each enterprise's rationalization investment plans, there was an important constraint, namely, fundraising. Concerning the ¥121.1 billion plan, MITI's Bureau of Iron and Steel stated "there is room for consideration as there may be problems in overlapping facilities, procurement of raw materials, and the ability to raise funds. There is also the problem of too much of the investment funds relying on public funds."[37] In resolving the problem of fundraising, the literature emphasizes the role of company management (Yonekura 1991:296). Needless to say, the abilities of management were important in raising funds. However, it is also important to note that the framework within which the enterprises operated was formed by the relationship with the government, public agencies, and private financial institutions led by the main banks. Let us examine the Chiba Steel Works project of Kawasaki Steel Co., which was the focus of the First Rationalization Plan for the Iron and Steel Industry.

As pointed out in the above-mentioned Bureau of Iron and Steel document, the First Rationalization Plan for the Iron and Steel Industry relied heavily on public funds. In April 1951, the Japan Development Bank (JDB) was established. In order to screen projects for JDB loans, MITI again requested that enterprises submit their rationalization plans. Thus Kawasaki Steel Co. reissued plans for the Chiba Steel Works. MITI evaluated this plan as follows.[38] Due to the lack of steel scrap, an increase in the operation of blast furnaces was necessary. But it was open to question whether the closed furnaces should be renovated or totally new facilities constructed. While constructing two 500-ton blast furnaces would require ¥10 billion, operating the closed furnaces would require only ¥2 billion.

But MITI supposed there would be good reasons to construct new blast furnaces. First, it was apparent that due to lack of steel scrap, the rational future model for iron and steel production would be continuous process. It is desirable for a large open-hearth steelmaker to use integrated production. Second, the fundamental modernization of the blast furnace process would be best served by the construction of a new blast furnace works. On this point, the Bureau of Iron and Steel of MITI stated that:

> currently the iron and steel enterprises with blast furnaces are working hard to improve the raw material processing facilities and the transportation facilities. But under a preexisting factory layout, there are limits to improvements. In order to truly modernize facilities, plans should be drawn up for a new location because the modernization of the blast furnaces starts with the rationalized layout of the factory

and facilities. Thus, if funds will allow, we would like to build model plants, and by this measure the modernization of the steel industry would leave its mark.

This meant that MITI appreciated Kawasaki Steel's plan for the Chiba Works and thought that if funds allowed, the plan should be promoted. MITI's attitude had a substantial effect on the fundraising for the project. In evaluating the Chiba project, JDB worked carefully, recruiting the former head of the technology department of Nippon Steel Co. as a technical advisor. JDB also took information from MITI into account, including its above-mentioned evaluation of the Chiba project and its outlook for the future demand and supply of steel. In February 1952, MITI approved Kawasaki Steel's Chiba Works project and at the same time recommended it to JDB for loans.[39] In response, JDB decided to provide loans to the Chiba project.

The JDB loan was approved by the policy board of the Bank of Japan (BOJ). Two points from this process should be stressed. First, at the meeting of the policy board, MITI supported JDB loans for the Chiba project. Thus, MITI consistently provided financial institutions with positive information on the Chiba project. Second, the JDB loan was made possible in the end as a result of the approval by BOJ.

With confirmation of the JDB loans, Dai-ichi Bank, the main bank of Kawasaki Steel Co., decided on its financial support to the Chiba Works project in February 1953, providing a ¥250-million loan and recommending the project to other banks.[40] As a result, that June, a loan consortium was organized by the private banks, with Dai-ichi Bank as a manager. Thus Dai-ichi Bank played the typical role of a main bank as a delegated monitor.[41] The following points should be noted. First, the Chiba project had already been screened by MITI, JDB, and BOJ. Furthermore, there was a wide consensus that the Japanese iron and steel industry (integrated production) would be made internationally competitive by the rationalization plan (discussed in Section 3.2). It can be said that the main bank's monitoring function was supported by these complementary screening mechanisms.

Second, the functions of the main bank were complemented in a direct manner. When the loan consortium was organized, the loan mediation division of BOJ supported Dai-ichi Bank by loan mediation. Loan mediation by BOJ started in 1947 and until the beginning of 1950 almost all cooperative loans went through BOJ mediation (Okazaki 1994).[42] Although loan mediation was contracted by the policy of the Allied Occupation in May 1950, for the Chiba Works project, BOJ initiated this measure. This meant that the ability of Dai-ichi Bank to organize a loan consortium was complemented by BOJ. This point is important because it is crucial counterevidence to the accepted view that BOJ consistently opposed and disrupted the Chiba project (Calder 1993). On the contrary, BOJ played a positive role in implementation of the Chiba project.

Thus, we have seen the role of such public agents as MITI, JDB, and BOJ in fundraising for investment in the case of the iron and steel industry. In addition, we can show that MITI and CIR generally coordinated industrial enterprises with financial institutions. On March 29, 1950, the expert committee of the Coordination Branch of CIR looked into the demand for capital funds. The Industrial Funds Section of the Bureau of Firms within MITI reported to the committee the amount of capital funds demand by industry and the prospects for fundraising. The total capital funds demanded amounted to ¥148.5 billion.

At the meeting of the expert committee of the Coordination Branch on April 10, 1950, the Industrial Funds Section explained the revised prospect for demand and supply of funds by industry (Table 3.9).[43] The data were based on questionnaires sent to some 1,200 enterprises under MITI's jurisdiction.[44] MITI screened and curtailed the plans for the enterprises, from ¥150 billion to ¥116.8 billion, taking the effective demand for the products into account.[45] The explanation by the Industrial Funds Section on the investment projects was rather detailed and included MITI's evaluation of the projects.

As to the fundraising plan in Table 3.9, the Industrial Funds Section stated that "the ¥3.5 billion to be raised from private banks and the ¥1.11 billion of the funds to be raised from the Counterpart Fund are open to question."[46] At the expert committee meeting that day, the chief of the First Section of Firms in MITI's Bureau of Firms expressed the view that "raising more than ¥9 billion would be difficult." In the end, they offered the following opinion to the Coordination Branch: "Without the ¥9 billion investment for industrial rationalization in FY 1950, not only the growth of

TABLE 3.9 Plan for Funds Allocation by MITI, 1950 (million yen)

	Demand Total	Fundraising Plan				
		Total	Capital	Debenture	Private Loan	Public Loan
Iron and steel	9,852	8,475	1,508	1,257	3,200	2,510
Coal	11,336	9,756	1,922	1,144	2,342	4,348
Electricity	34,920	33,155	1,563	4,195	5,106	22,291
Mining	13,523	12,053	741	2,540	7,922	850
Chemicals	20,181	18,264	1,210	1,648	12,751	2,655
Machinery	4,195	4,087	101	747	3,039	200
Textiles	10,341	9,943	263	1,373	7,107	1,200
Miscellaneous goods	7,728	6,187	273	481	5,226	207
Gas and coke	4,721	4,621	500	520	3,601	0

Source: Industrial Funds Section of MITI, "Table of Demand for Industrial Funds in 1950," in *Ishikawa Ichiro monjo* (Documents of Ishikawa Ichiro) held at the library, Faculty of Economics, University of Tokyo.

exports but also maintaining the base of Japan's industrial independence will become impossible."[47]

The Coordination Branch approved the expert committee's opinion in a meeting on April 28. The details were to be worked out in the Fund Section of the General Branch.[48] The Fund Section was established in April 1950 and was composed of representatives of major industries and enterprises along with representatives of BOJ, the Industrial Bank of Japan, and major private banks (Table 3.10).[49] The Fund Section was to look into seven issues, including "the methods and limits of fundraising, mainly for industrial rationalization." At this point, detailed explanations of the investment projects and MITI's evaluation of them were provided to the members participating from the major financial institutions, thus filling the information gap that existed among financial institutions, industries, and MITI. Removal of this gap would decrease the loan risk for financial institutions.

Along with fundraising, there was another constraint to resolve concerning investment for rationalization, namely, the size of the market. It is true that, as discussed in Section 3.2, the investment for rationalization in related industries led to the machinery and steel industries becoming internationally competitive, and consequently led to solving the problem of market size. But, in the process of rationalization, there remained a problem. At first, MITI considered providing subsidies during the three-year rationalization plan and made a budgetary request. But this request was not approved by the cabinet. Consequently, the price of steel increased sharply,[50] and the problem of high steel price remained (Japan Association of Iron and Steel Industry 1958:104). The chairman of the Hitachi Manufacturing Co. expressed his opinion that "because Japanese diesel generators were beaten

TABLE 3.10 Membership of the Funds Section of the General Branch

Nobuo Noda	Seikei University
Teizo Horikoshi	Federation of Industrial Associations
Sohei Nakayama	Industrial Bank of Japan
Hiroshi Hara	Bank of Japan
Mansaku Takeda	Nihon Kangyo Bank
Toshio Nakamura	Chiyoda (Mitsubishi Bank)
Hideo Kajiura	Industrial Bank of Japan
Yusuke Saito	Association of Chemical Industry
Toru Kondo	Mitsui Mining Co.
Teiichi Yamaguchi	Yawata Steel Co.
Kazuo Iwata	Tokyo Shibaura Electric Co.
Torao Nakaya	Federation of Industrial Associations
Goro Koyama	Teikoku (Mitsui) Bank

Source: "Record of the First Meeting of the Funds Section of the General Branch," in *Ishikawa Ichiro monjo*, K47-1 (Documents of Ishikawa Ichiro), held at the library, Faculty of Economics, University of Tokyo.

by the United States, United Kingdom, and West Germany last year [1950], the bidding prices of Japanese electric machinery have been higher than those of other countries, which has been caused by the high steel price. If we are not able to solve this problem, we will not be able to export heavy electric machinery."[51]

In order to cope with this situation, the head of the Section of Machinery Policy in MITI's Bureau of Machinery stated in the Association of Iron and Steel Industry's bulletin that "the rationalization of the machinery industry is necessary for the development of raw materials, fuel, and for all other industries. And in order to achieve rationalization, the cooperation of related industries, especially the raw materials industries, is necessary. If the steel and machinery industries must cooperate as one, economic independence cannot be accomplished."[52] In response to this, the iron and steel industry stated that "we feel that we greatly benefit from Japan's machinery being exported and from the machinery industry expanding. The iron and steel industry should consult with the machinery industry, and do its best to cooperate, from a long-run view."[53]

With coordination by MITI's Bureau of Iron and Steel and Bureau of Machinery and MOT's Bureau of Shipping, the steel and machinery industries met and agreed upon a 10–20 per cent decrease in the price of steel (Japan Association of Iron and Steel 1959:105–6). Additionally, with regard to the shipbuilding industry, the government decided to issue a tentative measure to reduce the cost of shipbuilding in August 1953.[54] The government reduced the interest on JDB loans and Counterpart Fund loans for the iron and steel industry, which were *de facto* subsidies, and these in turn resulted in a decrease in the price of the steel used for shipbuilding.[55] Thus, we can say that there was government coordination among enterprises and industries, not only in drawing up the rationalization plans, but in their implementation as well.

3.4 CONCLUDING REMARKS

In the first half of the 1950s, the Japanese economy resumed capital accumulation and reestablished the heavy-industry base. This process was not an easy one. When the Japanese economy was in transition to a market economy following the Dodge plan, heavy industries were faced with the problems of high cost and small scale. This in turn impeded investment for rationalization, and the Japanese economy became mired in a vicious cycle that could not be escaped by the self-motivated conduct of the private enterprises alone. Complementarity among industries, economies of scale, and incomplete information caused this coordination failure. To resolve the coordination failure, coordination by the government played an important role. The Council for Industrial Rationalization was a body wherein cooperation between government and private enterprises could create a path to escape the vicious cycle. The path was formulated and developed into the plans for simultaneous investment in related industries. This process can be interpreted as a coordinated experiment by the government and private enterprises, which was one of the essential aspects of the government-firm relationship in postwar Japan. The discovery of the path resulted in private enterprises progressively making rationalization plans. In the implementation process, the government coordinated fundraising and market creation.

In concluding, let me discuss the conditions for the effectiveness of industrial policy in this case. It should be noted that the coordination problem was relatively clear. There was broad consensus on the desirable future industrial structure, and there was also common understanding of the impediments to it. First, this was because of the fundamental conditions of the Japanese economy at that time. On the one hand, the competitiveness of the textile industry, which was unskilled-labour-intensive was challenged by developing countries, and there were abundant skilled workers who had accumulated experience in the machinery industry during the war. Second, institutions for information exchange had developed in the private sector. During the war, sectoral associations and their federation were established and these were succeeded by their postwar counterparts. Information exchange through these institutions contributed to a common understanding of the problems the individual industries faced and the interrelationships among them.

Moreover, the government had favorable institutional conditions. First, many experts from various leading enterprises and industry associations took part in the Council for Industrial Rationalization. This made it possible for the government to gather and check information from the private sector. Second, there were many technical officials in MITI as a legacy of the war economy and therefore MITI itself had the ability to evaluate the technology and technological capacity of the enterprises. Third, in policy implementation, the government made use of the ability of the financial institutions. The function of JDB is well known. In addition, through loan mediation by BOJ and the Funds Section of the Council for Industrial Rationalization, private financial institutions were induced to collaborate with the industrial policy.[56] These fundamental and institutional conditions were thought to prevent any government failure in drawing up and implementing the industrial policy and to guarantee its effectiveness.

NOTES

I would like to thank Masahiko Aoki, Ha-Joon Chang, Masahiro Okuno-Fujiwara, Hyung-Ki Kim, Ikuo Kume, Kiminori Matsuyama, Chiaki Moriguchi, Paul Sheard, Tetsushi Sonobe, Juro Teranishi, Ryuhei Wakasugi, and other participants of the

World Bank Conferences in Kyoto (1994) and Stanford (1995), and the TCER Hakone Conference (1994, 1995).

[1] Japan Federation of Industries, "Tan'itsu kawase reto no settei to yushutsu sangyō" (Setting the single exchange rate and export industries), *Nissankyo geppō* (JFI monthly), May 1949, p. 3.

[2] See Okazaki (1993a).

[3] Keizai Fukkō Keikaku Iinkai (Planning Committee for Economic Reconstruction), "Keizai Fukkō Keikaku Iinkai hōkoku-sho" (Report of the Planning Committee for Economic Reconstruction), in Arisawa (1990).

[4] Keizai Fukkō Keikaku Iinkai, "Keizai fukkō keikaku daiichiji shian" (First draft of the plan for economic reconstruction), May 1948, in Arisawa (1990:73).

[5] "Kigyō Kenkyūkai kaisoku" (Prospectus of the Business Research Society), in *Keizai antei honbu shiryō* (Documents of the ESB), which is available at the library of the Faculty of Economics, University of Tokyo. *Zenkoku kakushu dantai meikan* (Directory of Associations), 1993 ed. (Tokyo: Shiba Inc., 1992), vol. 1, p. 338.

[6] Kigyō Kenkyū Kai (Business Research Society), "Gōrika Iinkai dai-ikkai kaigi yō roku" (Summary proceedings of the first meeting of the Committee on Rationalization), in *Keizai antei honbu shiryō* (see note 5 above).

[7] Kigyō Kenkyū Kai, "Sangyō jiritsusei no kenkyū" (Research on independence of industries), ibid.

[8] Kigyō Kenkyū Kai, "Jiritsuka Iinkai (shō-iinkai) dai-yonkai kaigo yōroku" (Summary proceedings of the fourth meeting of the subcommittee of the Committee on Independence), ibid.

[9] Kigyō Kenkyū Kai, "Sangyō jiritsusei no kenkyū" (see note 7 above).

[10] Kawada Shigeru, "Tekkō gyō to kaiun" (The iron and steel industry and shipping), *Nissankyo geppō*, Nov. 1949 (see note 1 above).

[11] Tanaka Tokujiro (chairman of Tokyo Marine Co.), "Nihon keizai no jiritsuka to genka kaiun no shomondai" (Independence of the Japanese economy and present problems in shipping), ibid.

[12] JFI, "Dai-gojūgokai teirei rijikai yōroku" (Summary proceedings of the 55th meeting of the ordinary board of directors), in *Ishikawa Ichiro monjo* (Documents of Ishikawa Ichiro), which is available at the library of the Faculty of Economics, University of Tokyo.

[13] JFI, "Tekkō kakaku hikiage ni yoru jūyō bumon ni oyobosu eikyō chōsa hōkoku gaiyō" (Summary report of the research on the influence of a rise in steel price on the demanding industries), Aug. 2, 1949, ibid.

[14] At a symposium held by JFI at the beginning of 1950, the chairman of Shibaura Kyodo Kogyo Co. stated that "the main reason the machinery industry is facing problems in improving efficiency, compared to other industries, is that there are very few orders." *Nissankyo geppō*, Mar. 1950 (see note 1 above).

[15] It is well known that restructuring of the coal-mining industry eventually caused the 1960 Miike Labor Dispute, one of the most serious labor disputes in postwar Japan.

[16] "Sangyō gōrika ni kansuru ken" (On industrial rationalization), MITI (1991:509).

[17] Bureau of Firms, MITI, "Sangyō Gōrika Shingikai setchi yōkō" (Outline of the establishment of the Council for Industrial Rationalization), Nov. 20, 1949, *Ishikawa Ichiro monjo*, K47-1 (see note 12 above).

[18] "Sangyō gōrika ni kansuru ken" (On industrial rationalization), in *Ishikawa Ichiro monjo*, K47-2.

[19] "Sangyō Gōrika Shingikai sōgō bukai dai-ni kai senmon bukai gijiroku" (Proceedings of the second meeting of the expert committee of the Coordination Branch), ibid.

[20] Ibid.

[21] Iron and Steel Branch of CIR, "Tekkō gyō no gōrika ni tsuite" (On rationalization of the iron and steel industry), in *Ishikawa Ichiro monjo*, V-9.

[22] "Tekkō gyō oyobi sekitan kōgyō no gōrika ni tsuite no mondaiten" (Problems concerning the industrial rationalization of the steel and coal industries), ibid.

[23] "Sangyō Gōrika Shingikai sōgō bukai dai-ni kai gijiroku" (Proceedings of the second meeting of the Coordination Branch), in *Ishikawa Ichiro monjo*, K47-2.

[24] "Tekkō gyō oyobi sekitan kōgyō no gōrika ni tsuite" (On the rationalization of the steel and coal industries), MITI (1992:523).

[25] "Sekitan kōgyō no gōrika keikaku ni tsuite" (On the rationalization plans of the coal industry).

[26] "Tekkō gyō oyobi sekitan kōgyō no gōrika ni tsuite" (On the rationalization of the steel and coal industries), June 20, 1950, *Ishikawa Ichiro monjo*, K47-2.

[27] "Tekkō seisanhi teika no mokuteki to hōtō ni tsuite" (On the goals and measures for reducing the cost of steel), ibid.

[28] "Tekkō gyō oyobi sekitan kōgyō gōrika shisaku yōkō" (Summary of plans for rationalization of the steel and coal industries).

[29] Bureau of Shipping, MOT, "Zōsen yo kozai kakaku ni tsuite" (On the prices of steel for shipbuilding), in *Ishikawa Ichiro monjo*, K47-2.

[30] On this point, I am indebted to Professor Tetsushi Sonobe (Tokyo Municipal University) for his comments. Discussion with Professor Masahiro Okuno-Fujiwara was also quite helpful.

[31] For a more detailed analysis, see Okazaki (1995a).

[32] Japan Steel Co., *Hōnō totomo ni: Yawata Seitetsu Kabushi Kaisha shashi* (History of Yawata Steel Co.) (Tokyo: Japan Steel Co., 1981), p. 16.

[33] Nippon Kokan Co., *Nippon Kokan Kabushiki Kaisha yonjū-nen shi* (40-year history of Nippon Kokan Co.) (Tokyo: Nippon Kokan Co., 1952), p. 421.

[34] The Counterpart Funds were reserved from the sale of commodities provided as assistance by the United States. They were used for public purposes by the Japanese government under the supervision of the General Headquarters of the Supreme Command for the Allied Powers.

[35] Kawasaki Steel Co., *Kawasaki Seitetsu Kabushiki Gaisha nijūgo-nen shi* (25-year history of Kawasaki Steel Co.) (Kobe: Kawasaki Steel Co., 1976), p. 73.

[36] Iron and Steel Bureau, MITI, "Tekkō gyō no genjō to gōrika keikaku" (The present situation and the rationalization plans of the iron and steel industry) (1951), p. 56.

[37] Ibid., p. 57.

[38] Ibid., pp. 61–62.

[39] *Kawasaki Seitetsu Kabushiki Gaisha nijūgo-nen shi* (see note 35 above).

[40] Ibid., pp. 558–59.

[41] On the function of main banks, see Aoki et al. (1995).

[42] On loan mediation by BOJ, see Okazaki (1994).

[43] "Sangyō gōrika shingikai sōgō bukai dai-yon kai senmon bukai gijiroku" (Proceedings of the fourth meeting of the expert committee of the Coordination Branch, CIR), April 10, 1950, in *Ishikawa Ichiro monjo*, K47-1.

[44] "Shōwa nijūgo-nendo shōyō sangyō setsubi shikin ni tsuite" (Demand for industrial capital funds in FY 1950), April 8, 1950; Industrial Funds Section, Bureau of Firms, MITI, "Showa nijūgo-nendo shōyō sangyō setsubi shikin sōkatsu-hyō" (Summarized tables of the demand for industrial capital funds in FY 1950), April 5, 1950; "Nijgo-nendo sangyō setsubi shikin gyōshubetsu setsumei" (Explanation of industrial capital funds in FY 1950 by industry), March 30, 1950, ibid.

[45] "Shōwa nijōgo-nendo Tsūshō Sangyō Shō shōkan jigyō shōyō shikin ni tsuite" (On demand for funds by industries under MITI's jurisdiction), April 28, 1950, ibid.

[46] "Shōwa nijūgo-nendo shōyō sangyō shikin ni tsuite" (On demand for industrial funds in FY 1950), April 8, 1950, ibid.

[47] "Sangyō gōrika shingikai sōgō bukai dai-yon kai senmon bukai gijiroku," ibid.

[48] "Sangyō gōrika shingikai sōgō bukai dai-ni kai gijiroku" (Proceedings of the second meeting of the Coordination Branch of CIR), April 28, 1950, in *Ishikawa Ichiro monjo*, K47-2.

[49] "Gōrika shingikai ippan bukai shikin bunkakai dai-ichi kai kaigo keika" (Proceedings of the first meeting of the Fund Section of the General Branch of CIR), April 12, 1950, in *Ishikawa Ichiro monjo*, K47-1.

[50] Kojima Keizo (chief of the Heavy Industry Section, Third Division, Ministry of Prices), "Sentetsu hojokin haishi to sono eikyō" (Abolition of the subsidies for pig iron and its influence), in *Nissankyo geppō*, November 1950 (see note 1 above).

[51] Kurata Chikara, "Jukikairui no yushutsu shinkō taisaku" (Measures for promoting exports of heavy machinery), in *Nissankyo geppō*, June 1951 (see note 1 above).

[52] Hidaka Jun'nosuke, "Kikai kōgyō no genjō to mondai" (Present siituation and problems of the machinery industry), in *Tekkōkai* (Society of Iron and Steel), February 1952, p. 33.

[53] Kuwahara Suetaka (chief of research division, Yawata Steel Co.), "Tekkō kakaku no mondaiten" (Problems of iron and steel prices), in *Tekkōkai*, July 1951, p. 18.

[54] "Zōsen kosuto hikisage ni kansuru zantei sochi."

[55] *Tekkōkai*, March 1954.

[56] The Industrial Funds Branch was established in CIR in 1957, which extended the council's function to coordinate the industrial and financial sectors. See Okazaki (1995b and 1995c).

REFERENCES

Aoki, M., Patrick, H., and Sheard, P. (1995), "The Japanese Main Bank System: An Introductory Overview," in M. Aoki and H. Patrick, eds., *The Japanese Main Bank System and Its Relevance for Developing and Transforming Economies*, Oxford University Press, Oxford.

ARISAWA, H., ed. (1990), *Shiryo Sengo Nihon no Keizai Seisaku Koso* (Materials on the economic policy plans in postwar Japan), vol. 2, University of Tokyo Press, Tokyo.

CALDER, K. (1993), *Strategic Capitalism: Private Business and Public Purpose in Japanese Industrial Finance*, Princeton University Press, Princeton.

ITO, M., KIYONO, K., OKUNO-FUJIWARA, M., and SUZUMURA, K. (1988), *Sangyō seisaku no keizai bunseki* (Economic analysis of industrial policy), University of Tokyo Press, Tokyo.

Japan Association of Iron and Steel (1959), *Sengo tekkō shi* (History of the postwar iron and steel industry), Nihon Tekkō Renmei, Tokyo.

JOHNSON, C. (1982), *MITI and the Japanese Miracle*, Stanford University Press, Stanford.

KOMIYA, R., OKUNO-FUJIWARA, M., and SUZUMURA, K., eds. (1984), *Nihon no sangyō seisaku* (Japanese industrial policy), University of Tokyo Press, Tokyo.

KOSAI, Y. (1990), "Kōdō seichō e no shuppatsu" (Take-off to high growth), in Takafusa Nakamura, ed., *"Keikakuka" to "minshuka"* (Planning and democratization), Iwanami Shoten, Tokyo.

MATSUYAMA, K. (1991), "Increasing Returns, Industrialization, and Indeterminacy of Equilibria," *Quarterly Journal of Economics*, 106:617–50.

——(1995), "Economic Development as Coordination Problem," unpublished manuscript, Northwestern University.

Ministry of International Trade and Industry (MITI), ed. (1992), *Tsūshō sangyō seisaku shi* (History of industrial policies), vol. 2. Tsūshō Sangyō Chōsakai, Tokyo.

MURPHY, K., SHLEIFER, A., and VISHNY, R. (1989), "Industrialization and the Big Push," *Journal of Political Economy*, 97:1003–26.

NAKAGAWA, K. (1992), *Sengo Nihon no kaiun to zōsen* (Shipping and the shipbuilding industries in postwar Japan), Nihon Keizai Hyōronsha, Tokyo.

OKAZAKI, T. (1993a), "Nihon no seifu-kigyō kan kankei" (The government-firm relationship in postwar Japan), *Soshiki kagaku*, 26(4).

——(1993b), "Kigyō shisutemu" (Corporate system), in T. Okazaki and M. Okuno-Fujiwara, eds., *Gendai Nihon keizai shisutemu no genryū* (Origins of the contemporary Japanese economic system), Nihon Keizai Shinbunsha, Tokyo.

——(1995a), "Sengo Nihon ni okeru sangyō no kokusai kyōsō-ryoku to sono seidōteki kiso: tekkō gōrika keikaku to hikaku yui kogo no henka" (International competitiveness of postwar Japanese industries and its institutional foundations: rationalization plans of the iron and steel industry and the change of comparative advantage structure), Discussion Paper Series, Faculty of Economics, University of Tokyo, 95-J-2.

——(1995b), "Evolution of the Financial System in Postwar Japan," *Business History*, 37(2).

——(1995c), "Fund Allocation Policy in Postwar Japan," EUI Colloquium Papers 608/95.

——(1996), "Sengo keizai fukkō ki no kinyū shisutemu to Nihon Ginkō yūshi assen" (Financial system in the postwar reconstruction period and the role of BOJ loan mediation), *Keizasaku Ronshu*, 60–4.

——and OKUNO-FUJIWARA, M. (1993), "Gendai Nihon no keizai shisutemu to sono rekishiteki genryū," in T. Okazaki and M. Okuno-Fujiwara, eds., *Gendai Nihon keizai shisutemu no genryū* (Origins of the contemporary Japanese economic system), Nihon Keizai Shinbunsha, Tokyo.

—— and YOSHIKAWA, H. (1993), "Sengo infureshon to Dodge rain" (Postwar hyperinflation and the Dodge plan), in Y. Kosai and J. Teranishi, eds., *Sengo Nihon no keizai kaikaku* (Economic reform in postwar Japan), University of Tokyo Press, Tokyo.

OKUNO-FUJIWARA, M. and HORI, Y. (1994), "Sangyō seisaku no kinō to rironteki hyō ka" (Role of industrial policy and its theoretical evaluation), *MITI Research Review*, 4.

TSURUTA, T. (1982), *Sengo Nihon no sangyō seisaku* (Industrial policies in postwar Japan), Nihon Keizai Shinbunsha, Tokyo.

World Bank (1993), *The East Asian Miracle: Economic Growth and Public Policy*, Oxford University Press, Oxford.

YONEKURA, S. (1991), "Tekkō" (Iron and steel industry), in S. Yonekawa, ed., *Sengo Nihon keieishi* (Business history in postwar Japan), Toyo Keizai Shinposha, Tokyo.

YOSHIKAWA, H. (1992), *Nihon keizai to makuro keizaigaku* (Japanese economy and macroeconomies), Toyo Keizai Shinposha, Tokyo.

4

The Role of Government in Acquiring Technological Capability: The Case of the Petrochemical Industry in East Asia

HYUNG-KI KIM AND JUN MA

As Gerschenkron (1962) observed, in spite of many handicaps, the relatively backward countries have the one great asset of the technological knowledge accumulated by advanced countries. However, developing countries cannot take advantage of this asset unless they develop the technological competence to search for appropriate technologies and to select, absorb, adapt, and improve imported technologies. Such a capacity has externalities, that is, its social benefits far exceed the private benefits. Hence, the role of government in facilitating the process of acquiring technological competence is crucial (Westphal 1981, Rosenberg and Frishtak 1985). It is particularly critical when the technology is highly sophisticated, entails substantive set-up costs and scale economies, as well as strong backward and forward linkages, as in the case of sectors such as iron and steel and petroleum and its derivatives.

Further, absorption of sophisticated technology takes time; during this gestation lag, an enterprise requires protection from imports, in accordance with the well-known infant-industry argument. Further, when there are strong interlinkages among different sectors and/or enterprises, there exists the problem of coordinated development; the social benefits of such coordinated development are much greater than the private benefits can potentially be. Here again, there is a role for the state to act as a catalyst for coordinating the investment behavior of related sectors or enterprises (O'Driscoll 1977, Drazen 1990). In addition to these arguments, government intervention also finds support in the case of "strategic interdependence in international markets" (Brander and Spence 1985).

While there are theoretical grounds for the state to intervene in the development of technology-intensive industries, strong counterarguments also exist, indicating possible government failures. Two of these counterarguments are most notable. The first argument, or the "rent-seeking" argument, contends that government intervention creates economic rents for parties that receive the privileges (e.g., a monopolist position, government-directed credits, subsidies, etc.), and induce rent-seeking activities that are socially wasteful. According to Vergara and Babelon (1990), capacity-licensing policy in India has increased the existing protection of established producers, who have organized to lobby against granting licenses to new entrants; consequently, grants of new licenses have often lagged behind demand, and existing producers have tended to operate in a sellers' market with little incentive to innovate or improve productivity.

The second argument against government intervention, the "government coordination failure" argument, claims that coordination failure by the market (due to, for example, various forms of externalities) does not justify policy activism. In his chapter in this volume (Chapter 5), Matsuyama argues that efficient government coordination requires information about a large number of activities performed by a large number of people, and about a large number of possible equilibrium outcomes. Such information is not likely to be available. In Matsuyama's words, "There is no way for the society [government] to search in a systematic way for the global optimum, or other local optima that are more efficient." Therefore, government coordination failure is inevitable due to the informational problem.

Most arguments for and against active government intervention are purely theoretical, and very few empirical works have proved any of them. Results from the few existing econometric works are largely inconclusive (as cited in Rodrik 1993) and at best show that the infant industry theory "is not disproved" (Westphal 1981). Krueger and Tuncer (1982) compare sectoral total factor productivity (TFP) growth rates in a cross-section of Turkish industries and report no systematic tendency for more protected industries to have higher TFP growth than less protected industries. Conclusions derived from institutional studies that look at industrial policy in general are often vulnerable to criticism because many policies succeed in one sector but fail in another in the same country. To obtain more convincing results, an alternative approach seems necessary.

This chapter uses case studies to assess the role of government in the acquisition of technological capability in the petrochemical industries in three East Asian economies, where technology capabilities are broadly defined as including those for operating production facilities (production capability), for expanding capacity and establishing new production facilities (investment capability), and for developing technologies (innovation capability).[1] On the basis of detailed discussions on the policy formation and implementation process, this chapter highlights the efforts made by the East Asian governments to overcome government failures due to rent-seeking activities or informational problems. In particular, we identify certain institutional mechanisms that allowed the East Asian governments to do so. We find that government failures are not absolute. Rent seeking can be controlled when government intervention is based on well-specified and effectively enforced rules. Government coordination failures can be minimized when the number of players involved is small, the homogeneity of products is high, and channels that permit information exchange between the government and the private sector function effectively. Most of these conditions existed in the East Asian cases we investigate.

The three economies chosen for this study are: Japan, the Republic of Korea (hereafter Korea), and Taiwan. All have enjoyed rapid growth in petrochemical production, and some have experienced rapid export expansion over the past decades. None of the three governments adopted a *laissez-faire* approach in developing its petrochemical industry. In contrast to what has been suggested by neoclassical economics, they imposed strict control over market entry and technology imports during the early stages of the industries' development, though not for the same reasons. They have also experienced the process of going from strict government controls to a liberalization of these controls. This chapter also contrasts the experiences of these three high-performing economies to those of India and Brazil, where governments also intervened heavily in the petrochemical industry but witnessed very different outcomes.

We had several reasons for choosing the petrochemical industry as an illustration. First, this industry is often one of the major targets for promotional policy. Second, the petrochemical industry generally calls for massive transfers of technology and capital from advanced economies for its operation. During the first phase (1955–60) of promoting the petrochemical industry in Japan, royalty payments for the licensing of technologies amounted to US$35 million, as compared to US$23 million spent for imports of equipment (Petrochemical Industrial Association of Japan 1990:37), illustrating the importance of technology licensing. Governments often use control over technology imports as an important policy tool in controlling market entry, as well as in acquiring the requisite technological know-how for enhancing local capability in plant design, engineering, and operation. Third, the industry is strongly characterized by large initial capital investments, rapidly changing technology, and a high degree of integration with other petroleum- or chemical-related businesses,[2] thereby necessitating the reliance on foreign investment or supplier credits. While the private sector is financially constrained, as was the case for the East Asian economies in their early stages, government can play a role in ensuring the industry's long-term efficiency and competitiveness through controls over market entry, direct provisions of financing schemes, and other support measures. Fourth, the industry is highly dependent on both petroleum producers and downstream producers. Between and among these producers, it is important to have a mechanism that coordinates and synchronizes the investment and innovation activities among the upstream, midstream, and downstream sectors. These reasons prompt governments to take a more interventionist policy stance in the petrochemical industry than in many other sectors, although the extent varies widely among them.

This chapter is organized as follows. Section 4.1 briefly reviews the development performance of the petrochemical industries in the three East Asian economies. Section 4.2 describes the methods of government control, particularly those concerning market entry, technology transfers, and technology absorption, in the three economies. Section 4.3 discusses the mechanisms through which government policies impacted the development of the East Asian petrochemical industries and minimized the possibility of government failures. These include creating incentives for innovation using contingent entry, ensuring economies of scale and avoiding excessive competition, securing favorable terms and conditions for domestic firms in technology transfers, promoting "unpackaging" of imported technologies, and promoting research and development (R&D) activities. The last section presents conclusions.

4.1 A BRIEF HISTORY OF THE EAST ASIAN PETROCHEMICAL INDUSTRY

The petrochemical industry in East Asia is of recent origin. Taking Japan, Korea, and Taiwan as a whole, their share of world ethylene production was only 2.4 per cent in 1960, and Japan was the only producer in East Asia at that time. Between 1960 and 1992, this share increased eightfold to 20.0 per cent, indicating the extraordinary swiftness of the industry's development in these economies relative to other parts of the world.[3]

In Japan, the leader among the three economies, even as late as 1960, the petrochemical industry's share of total output of the chemical industry was a mere 6.5 per cent in value (MITI 1962). Japan succeeded in developing its petrochemical industry at an astonishing pace in the 1950s and 1960s, under strong government intervention. In 1966, Japan's petrochemical industry surpassed the chemical fertilizer sector in terms of output value, becoming the leading sector of the chemical industry. Between 1960 and 1970, Japan's share of world ethylene production rose from 2.4 per cent to 17.3 per cent, making Japan the second-largest ethylene producer in the world, next to the United States.[4] Since the early 1970s, Japan has emerged as one of the world's major exporters of petrochemical technologies.

Since the late 1970s, the petrochemical industries in Korea and Taiwan have developed at a rapid pace and reduced the predominance of Japan considerably. In 1983 Japan accounted for 76 per cent of Asian ethylene capacity. It also held 89 per cent of styrene capacity, 69 per cent of polyolefins, and 62 per cent of polyvinyl chloride (PVC). Ten years later, it accounted for only 46 per cent of Asian ethylene, 53 per cent of styrene, 40 per cent of polyolefins, and 37 per cent of PVC capacity (Tattum 1993). While ethylene production in Japan still grew in quantity, its share in world ethylene production declined from 17 per cent to 13 per cent between 1970 and 1992. The increase in the share of East Asia ethylene production since 1980 came largely from Korea, Taiwan, and China.

Korea's petrochemical industry was initiated in the early 1970s as part of government efforts to launch an industrial modernization program and as a result of the enactment of the Petrochemical Development Act. Building from scratch in the early 1970s, Korea achieved a production capacity of 600,000 tons per year for ethylene and 347,000 tons per year for propylene in 1988. In less than 20 years since the first petrochemical plant was built with foreign technology and capital, Korea has acquired the ability to design, construct, and operate such petrochemical complexes. In the 1980s, the annual growth rate of almost all major petrochemical products exceeded 10 per cent. Since the late 1980s ethylene capacity has increased dramatically. By May 1994, Korea had a total ethylene capacity of 3.57 million tons per year, slightly surpassing the combined capacity of East and West Germany in 1990 (Petrochemical Industrial Association of Korea 1994).

Taiwan's petrochemical industry, relative to other sectors in its economy, also grew rapidly. If the chemical materials sector as well as chemical products and plastic products are included, the share of the entire chemical industry in the manufacturing sector and the gross domestic product (GDP) rose from 5.5 per cent and 1.1 per cent in 1960, to 10.8 per cent and 3.2 per cent in 1970, and to 15.2 per cent and 5.4 per cent in 1989, respectively. From 1970 to 1990, the annual average growth rates of synthetic fiber materials, plastic, and synthetic fibers were 28.6 per cent, 18.8 per cent, and 25.3 per cent respectively (Chu 1994). Ethylene production increased at an annual average rate of 21 per cent between 1970 and 1985, but stagnated between 1986 and 1992 due to domestic disputes over the environmental impact of naphtha-cracking projects. Recently Taiwan completed its fifth naphtha-cracking plant and approved six cracking plants to be built by Formosa Plastics Group, Taiwan's biggest private conglomerate. According to the Formosa Plastics Group's plan, Taiwan will double its ethylene capacity between 1994 and 1998 (Petrochemical Industrial Association of Taiwan 1994). In terms of domestic R&D capacity, however, Taiwan lagged behind Japan and Korea and still relies heavily on imported technologies for new petrochemical projects.

4.2 POLICIES TO PROMOTE TECHNOLOGY ACQUISITION

The petrochemical industry has the reputation of being extremely capital intensive and of employing very sophisticated technology. In the early stages of development, the petrochemical industries in the East Asian economies had two features: technologies were the most important production input, and most technologies were not available domestically. These features meant that governments could effectively implement their industrial policies by controlling technology imports; both the licensing of foreign technology and the use of foreign exchange were under government control. The following subsections look at three aspects of such controls: who took part in formulating the development plan and who made the decisions as to the deployment of policy instruments, how firms were selected to enter the industry and to import technologies, and how foreign technologies and their suppliers were selected and what criteria were used in arriving at such decisions.

Policy Formation

All three East Asian governments have or formerly had agencies at the national level to formulate the development plans of the petrochemical industries. In the late 1940s, Japan's Council on Reconstruction of the Textile Industry—composed of government officials, manufacturers' representatives, and academics—worked out the development plan; the Ministry of Commerce and Industry (later the Ministry of International Trade and Industry, [MITI]) announced a policy listing the types of products to be encouraged (vinylon and nylon). In the late 1950s, MITI decided to promote another important synthetic fiber, polyester (Ozawa 1980). It was also MITI that worked out a policy to develop petrochemical products as raw materials for the two pillars of the organic synthetic chemical industries, synthetic fiber and synthetic resin. The ministry singled out a particular product for domestic production in the 1950s—low-density, high-pressure process polyethylene, which is a raw material for plastics used in such items as containers, furniture, and electric insulation. In June 1955, MITI adopted a petrochemical guideline for the development of this industry, which laid the groundwork for implementing the Petrochemical Industry Phase I Plan. This plan started in autumn 1955 and ended in 1960 with the completion of the Nihon Gosei ethylene plant (see Petrochemical Industrial Association of Japan 1990:6).

MITI's plan had four stated objectives: to provide a stable supply of intermediate raw materials to the growing synthetic fiber and plastic industries, to save foreign exchange by substituting domestic production, to reduce the price of petrochemical products, and to meet the expectations of improved quality. To these ends, MITI evolved promotional and regulatory policy regimes covering investment coordination, support to enterprises, and creation of a favorable business environment. Importation of foreign technologies was the major part of the development plan (Peck 1976). At the end of 1964, the Petrochemical Cooperative Discussion Group was established to provide guidance to MITI and the industry; it comprised government officials, industrialists, and third-party individuals. The committee established criteria for minimum economic scale for ethylene and secondary products such as polyethylene.

The government of Korea started planning an integrated petrochemical complex in the early 1960s. Its initial coordinator was the government's Economic Planning Board, an agency responsible for the introduction of foreign private capital as well as the management of foreign public loans. The coordinating responsibility was later transferred to the Ministry of Commerce and Industry. Arthur D. Little, Inc., was engaged to study the proposal for the petrochemical industry in 1966. It identified the products that had sufficient demand within Korea; estimated their costs of manufacture at different rates of output; and recommended that minimal plant sizes for their production (32,000 tons in ethylene, for example) be located at an integrated complex adjacent to a petroleum refinery, so as to minimize the cost of transporting intermediates and to provide a common source of inputs, such as utilities and maintenance (Enos and Park 1987). On the basis of this report, the government included major projects (petrochemical refineries and ethylene crackers) in the nation's second Five-Year Plan starting from 1966. But it made significant modifications to the initial capacity during actual implementation in light of the subeconomical scale.

In Taiwan, before the mid-1950s, there was little government planning in the petrochemical industry. Small-scale private firms used natural gas as the raw material to produce PVC, vinyl chloride monomer, and chemical fertilizers. In the late 1950s, the Ministry of Economic Affairs (MEA) planned the first naphtha-cracking plant to produce ethylene. The plan delineated the plant's location, financing scheme, technologies, and which companies were to receive the outputs. Similar planning procedures were applied to the next four naphtha crackers. The Industrial Development Bureau of the ministry has been responsible for approving investment applications in the downstream sectors (Wade 1990). The decisions of the Industrial Development Bureau have been based on the recommendations of the Investment Review Committee which is composed of officials from MEA, industrialists, and experts from academia.

Selecting Domestic Players

All three East Asian governments have controlled the market structure of the petrochemical industry by limiting the number of firms allowed to enter. However, each has adopted a different approach in selecting entrants. In Japan, MITI adopted the "staggered entry" approach, as it did for the synthetic fiber industry. Under this approach, it used the technology-import screening mechanism and allocation of foreign exchange as devices to let companies enter the industry at intervals.[5] The criteria that MITI used to select the entrants were laid out in its four-pronged directions for the promotion of the petrochemical industry (MITI 1990:490–92). These directions were made on the basis of the responses from the Petrochemical Industry Technical Consultative Group, formed under the auspices of MITI in November 1954 and consisting of 18 experts from industry, academia, and research communities, and in light of the demand for petrochemical products forecast by the Light Industry Bureau of MITI.

These directions were to:

1. realize as the objective a system of supplying the main petrochemical products as forecast at the level of international prices;
2. promote those firms that had formulated plans for petrochemical plants with:
   a. sufficient technological and managerial background to implement the plans efficiently,
   b. profitability in using international prices as sales prices even when accelerated depreciation is applied,
   c. superior technological content in plans,
   d. sound financial plans, and
   e. the possibility of realizing the plans without necessarily increasing oil-refining capacity greatly;
3. if the sum of the projected outputs by plans meeting the above criteria exceeds the estimated demand by a big margin, give priority to those plans judged to be advantageous to the country—in such terms as estimated supply prices, size of the output, potential for future growth, dependence on foreign exchange, and affiliation with foreign capital—provided that the individual products do not greatly exceed estimated demand; and
4. to the extent possible, avoid drastic effects on existing industries that face competition from the petrochemical industry and its products.

On the basis of these directions, the policymakers for the petrochemical industry decided to deploy the following policy instruments:

1. provision of loans, as needed, from the Japan Development Bank for facilities;
2. provision of special depreciation measures to enable accelerated depreciation of the facilities;
3. approval of the requisite foreign technology;
4. designation of which petrochemical industry firms would be eligible for tax exemptions under the articles of the Corporate Law; and
5. provision of duty exemptions for and allocation of foreign exchange for the importation of equipment and facilities.

In an effort to avoid excessive investment in production facilities and to deal with the proliferation of small firms with no international competitiveness, the Petrochemical Cooperative Discussion Group was established in December 1964. The fact that the group's decisions were to be honored by both MITI and the industry represents an institutional innovation in interests mediation for setting "promotion standards" in Japan. Such novel cooperation (through a discussion group) was clearly a departure from the more traditional route of regulation by MITI through legislation of industry-specific business law.

Some of the early decisions made by the group, which in turn were implemented by MITI, were quite significant. For instance, the group's guideline for the establishment or expansion of ethylene production facilities was largely responsible for the selection of new plans for ethylene plants.[6] After making the first decisions on the appropriate scales of petrochemical plants in January 1967, the group was again asked by MITI in June 1968 to consider its new proposal to put the minimum capacity of ethylene plants at 300,000 tons per year (about 17 per cent of the 1968 industrial capacity) and to require sound provision for the production of derivatives (secondary products), as well as firm sales plans. At the same time, the proposal called for the supply of naphtha, the raw material for ethylene, to be piped from oil refineries, that is, from combinards. The group accepted the proposal and after deliberations transformed it into a new guideline in light of the vast gaps that existed between individual plant capacities in Japan which were only about 100,000 tons per year and those in the West, which were 450,000–500,000 tons per year at Mobil, Union Carbide, Du Pont, and ICI plants.

The new guideline prompted some local companies to make upward adjustments in their planned capacities to the level of 300,000 tons per year from 100,000 tons per year, for which they obtained MITI's approval. MITI's new approach then was to approve those investment plans in petrochemical products, ethylene in particular, that were to have joint investment by two or more companies and such approval would be granted to companies on a rotating basis. That is, as the plans for investment firmed up, MITI granted approval on a staggered basis, just as it did for the synthetic fiber industry. The entry pattern of ethylene producers under the staggered approach is shown in Table 4.1. With increases in both domestic and foreign demand, a rush to invest in ethylene followed. Between 1969 and 1972, nine ethylene-cracking plants went into operation, with the first 300,000-ton ethylene plant of Maruzen Petrochemical in March 1969 and the ninth 300,000-ton plant of Sanyo Ethylene Co. in April 1972. By the time the massive expansion of ethylene capacity was completed in early 1972, the industry was already facing depressed demand, largely attributable to the Nixon shock, which, among other factors, led to an appreciation of the yen, to the detriment of export growth. In fact, the Cooperative Discussion Group had already decided in October 1971 on an investment moratorium.

The case of polyethylene also illustrates how MITI applied the staggered entry approach in accordance with decisions reached by the Petrochemical

TABLE 4.1 Entry of Ethylene Production and Distribution of Industrial Capacity, Selected Years, 1958–1974[a] (% of total industrial capacity)

Company	Before 1958	1958	1960	1962	1964	1966	1968	1970	1972	1974
Producer No. 1	62.5	25.3	26.1	19.1	10.9	18.4	12.8	11.9	9.3	
Producer No. 2	37.5	15.2	17.9	13.2	11.9	14.3	9.8	14.1	11.0	
Producer No. 3	n.a.	31.7	16.3	23.9	13.7	13.5	8.5	9.3	9.3	
Producer No. 4	n.a.	27.8	26.7	19.6	11.2	12.3	16.2	18.1	14.2	
Producer No. 5	n.a.	n.a.	13.0	14.3	11.4	13.8	8.7	5.4	10.5	
Producer No. 6	n.a.	n.a.	n.a.	9.9	5.7	2.8	1.8	1.1	6.2	
Producer No. 7	n.a.	n.a.	n.a.	n.a.	6.0	9.7	16.3	10.2	9.2	
Producer No. 8	n.a.	n.a.	n.a.	n.a.	8.2	8.0	6.8	12.2	9.6	
Producer No. 9	n.a.	n.a.	n.a.	n.a.	10.0	6.7	12.7	8.0	6.2	
Producer No. 10	n.a.	n.a.	n.a.	n.a.	n.a.	n.a.	n.a.	6.4	4.0	3.1
Producer No. 11	n.a	n.a.	n.a.	n.a.	n.a.	n.a.	n.a.	n.a.	5.8	6.2
Producer No. 12	n.a.	n.a.	n.a.	n.a.	n.a.	n.a.	n.a.	n.a.	n.a.	6.2

n.a.: Not applicable.
[a] Those companies that built, for the first time, 300,000-ton capacity ethylene plants during phases I or II of the Petrochemical Industrial Promotion.
Source: Quoted in MITI (1990), vol. 10, p. 357.

Cooperative Discussion Group. The group established a criterion for minimum economic scale for each company that would produce derivatives (secondary products), such as polyethylene. The scale for production of low-density polyethylene was set at 30,000 tons annually, about 5 per cent of the 1968 capacity and 3.4 per cent of 1970 capacity (Peck 1976). From 1958 to 1970 the number of polyethylene producers increased from one to ten. New entrants appeared at regular intervals and paralleled the growth in demand. The first entrant allowed to "monopolize" the industry was the Sumitomo Group, which in 1955 established Sumitomo Chemical Company with technology purchased from Imperial Chemical Industries of Britain. In 1957 the Mitsubishi Group was chosen to follow with technology acquired from BASF of the former West Germany. Three years later it was the Mitsui Group's turn; with technology obtained from Du Pont of the United States, it set up Mitsui Polychemical. Still later, other groups and other companies from the same industrial group were gradually allowed to enter the industry—all with the help of foreign technology (Ozawa 1980). The last three entrants had a capacity of about 30,000 tons annually, the minimum economic scale determined by MITI. Existing firms expanded, but the share of capacity held by the four firms that entered before 1962 declined to 63 per cent by 1970 (Peck 1976).

Japan effectively implemented its staggered approach through its technology-licensing policy both in the synthetic fiber and petrochemical industries in part because Japanese producers were dependent on the acquisition of foreign licenses, and because the foreign patent holders happened to prefer to license either one or a limited number of Japanese firms on an exclusive basis. If foreign licensors had insisted on offering only multifirm licensing agreements with a large number of Japanese firms,

MITI would have had no power to limit the number of entrants. The exclusive licensing arrangement for the first entrants meant that the second group had to wait for the availability of new alternative sources of technologies; as a result, MITI actually had little freedom with respect to the timing of the second group's entry (Ozawa 1980).[7]

Japan gradually liberalized its control over technology imports after the late 1960s, with the government withdrawing most of its previous reservations with respect to the provisions of the OECD Code of Liberalization of Current Non-Trade Transactions in 1968 and 1969. While the fifth liberalization measure—which allowed automatic approval for even 100 per cent equity participation by foreigners—was announced in 1975, the liberalization of technology imports for the petrochemical industry, regulated under the Foreign Capital Law, actually took place earlier: ethylene technology from January 1972, and its derivatives beginning in 1973. These moves constituted part of Japan's response to the growing surplus in its balance of payments.

In terms of means of technology imports, during the 1950s and 1960s, Japan favored purchasing technology licenses and importing equipment, rather than foreign direct investment (FDI). It believed that restricting FDI was necessary for maintaining the independence of the industrial sector. Japan's Foreign Capital Control Law, promulgated in 1951, states that the government will approve a foreign investment in Japan and return the interest and principle of the investment only if the foreign capital is considered beneficial to obtaining economic independence, sound economic development, and improvement of international balance of payments (Wada 1976).

In Korea, the government decided that the industry should produce petrochemicals based on a one-item, one-firm principle. The government stated that selected firms should employ the most recent state-of-the-art technology used in the industrialized countries, by means of joint ventures with foreign firms. In the early 1960s, the government decided that the first petrochemical complex be started with public enterprises. In 1960, Chungju Fertilizer Company (subsequently, the Korea General Chemical Corporation), which operated two fertilizer plants, was chosen to be the first entrant, responsible for the utility center and the polyethylene, vinyl chloride monomer, acrylnitrole, and caprolactam plants. Chungju Fertilizer Company was chosen because it employed the nation's largest group of chemical engineers, whose expertise was necessary in evaluating the technical and economic terms of any foreign offer (Enos 1984). At the same time, the government decided that Korea Oil Corporation, 75 per cent of the equity of which was held by the state-owned Korea Development Bank, was to build the naphtha-cracking center (which produces ethylene), leaving five plants for participation by private firms (Kim 1994). The reason Korea Oil Corporation was chosen to build the first ethylene plant was to enable the government to ensure internationally competitive prices of ethylene for the downstream plants by effectively passing the costs on to gasoline and diesel oil.

In line with the government's plan to induce foreign direct investment into the petrochemical sector as much as possible to benefit from the inflow of capital and technology, the Petrochemical Industry Promotion Committee (made up of the vice-ministers of related ministries, the president of the Korea Oil Corporation, and an expert from academia) formulated the following guidelines:

1. Seek funds separately from foreign local sources, and then integrate them after negotiations are concluded.
2. Pursue a 50–50 equity distribution and in operations between foreign and local partners, ensuring consensual decision making.
3. Transform some portion of technology royalties into equity investment, and transform the basis for technology royalties into royalties based on the running of plants (instead of offering a lump sum).
4. Supply any foreign exchange requirements over and above the investment for facilities and plants via commercial loans or by the investors themselves or by the arrangements of concerned investment.
5. Allow any single investor to invest in more than two plants.
6. Permit investment by consortia of two or more foreign firms.
7. Require foreign investors to follow the policies of the Korean government and abide by the following directions:
   a. plans for the promotion of the industry are to be formulated by the Korean government,
   b. the Korean government is to select the investors,
   c. related support facilities for the petrochemical complex must be concentrated, and
   d. the petrochemical plants must be located in an industrial estate as a complex.
8. The appropriate ratio between assets and liabilities of the investors will be maintained at 30 to 70.

In the late 1980s, the Korean government abandoned this one-item, one-firm principle when it liberalized the investment-licensing policy in the petrochemical sector. Almost all major conglomerates rushed into the lucrative petrochemical sector, resulting in a sixfold increase in capacity from 1988 to 1994 (Petrochemical Industrial Association of Korea 1994).

Taiwan relied primarily on the government-owned China Petrochemical Corporation (CPC) during the early stage of the petrochemical industry's development. In the early 1960s, when the industry was almost nonexistent, private capital was weak and unable and unwilling to undertake the upstream projects, mainly naphtha crackers. The government planned the projects and created CPC which built and operated the naphtha crackers.

Between 1973 and 1994, CPC built all five naphtha crackers, and the government, upon negotiating with the private sector, decided which private firms would set up facilities to process its flow of output.

During the planning stage of each naphtha cracker, the Industrial Development Bureau of MEA called discussion meetings with potential private-sector investors in the mid- or downstream sectors. The planned figures for petrochemical materials to be produced by the cracking plant and the number/size of downstream production needed to absorb these raw materials were announced. The discussions between the Industrial Development Bureau and the downstream investors normally led to an agreement on which firms were to receive the raw materials (e.g., ethylene) from CPC's new cracking plant and to construct the mid- or downstream plants (e.g., those producing polyethylene). If more mid- or downstream investors than necessary insisted on entering, the Industrial Development Bureau would (1) persuade some of them to drop out on the basis of financial and technology capacity; or (2) encourage several investors to invest jointly in one project.[8]

For example, in 1969, when the plan for the fourth naphtha cracker was formulated, the government requested that the private sector submit applications for investing in midstream and downstream projects. Twenty-two companies submitted 32 investment plans. After extensive discussions between the Industrial Development Bureau and investors, 19 projects were approved (Lee 1980). In 1990 the Formosa Plastics Group, a private conglomerate, was given approval to build the sixth naphtha-cracking plant, but the project was later delayed until 1993. Construction of the project started in 1994 and is expected to finish in 1998. Until today, CPC has enjoyed monopoly status in the upstream sector (naphtha crackers). By getting private capital involved in the mid- and downstream sectors, the government also granted these companies a near-monopoly franchise (Chu 1994).

Selecting Foreign Technologies and Suppliers

In addition to control over market entry, the three East Asian governments also had important roles in selecting foreign technology suppliers. In Japan, MITI's influence over terms and conditions has often been realized through its direct participation in royalty negotiations in technology transfers. The mid-1960s, when royalty rates were lowest, represented the period of the most intensive MITI intervention. Its approval requirement served to reduce competition among Japanese firms, especially since MITI sometimes informally designated a particular Japanese firm to negotiate with a specific foreign company. In addition, MITI would delay its approval or make it conditional upon revisions that would lower rates. The success of such interventions was reflected in the strong criticism from technology suppliers

(Peck 1976). MITI's intervention in technology imports had several features.

First, MITI restricted foreign direct investment during the 1950s and 1960s. It favored other means of technology imports, such as purchasing technology licenses and importing equipment, rather than FDI. Second, MITI favored "unpackaged" technology transfers rather than "packaged" ones. Instead of importing entire plants, Japan's technology imports concentrated on individual items in the form of patent rights, detailed drawings, operating instructions, manuals, and interchange of personnel between the Japanese buyers and foreign sellers. In the 1950s and the first half of the 1960s, MITI favored the use of class B technology agreements—agreements of less than one year or that allow royalty payments only in yen. The total number of class B technology imports between 1950 and 1964 was 3,388, while the number of class A technology agreements—agreements with the terms of contract or terms of payment equal to or more than one year—was 3,068.[9] Although most of the class A technologies were also unpackaged, the degree to which the class B contracts unpackaged the technologies was obviously higher. By breaking down the elements of a technology as much as was practical, the Japanese engineers had participated, and often took initiatives, in all stages of detailed design, basic design, construction, and operation.

Third, MITI also objected to technology agreements that limited exports. This may have reflected a divergence of interests between the Japanese buyer of technology and MITI's general economic goals. The Japanese firms may have been willing to trade off export markets for lower royalty rates, but given the government's interest in exports, MITI sometimes would not accept such a trade-off. Yet despite MITI's dislike of such restrictions, they still happen in many cases (Peck 1976).

In Korea, which was severely constrained by a shortage of foreign exchange when it was promoting the petrochemical industry, the government had no choice but to rely mainly on foreign investment. The choice of who was to undertake manufacture and what technology they were to employ was therefore inseparable from who was to provide at least some of the capital. The Korean government in 1968 initiated negotiations with all foreign firms capable of supplying the technology in developed countries. Many suppliers were approached: 13 for polyethylene, 9 for vinyl chloride monomer, and similar numbers for other petrochemicals. In almost all negotiations with foreigners (except for caprolactam), the government imposed increasingly stringent conditions until all but one of the foreign contenders dropped out. With the remaining foreign firm, the government signed a contract for provision of the technology; arranging of finance; training of Koreans as technicians, engineers, and managers; supervision of design, construction, and initial production in the petrochemical plant; and organization and responsibilities of the joint venture. In the case of the

Ulsan petrochemical complex, foreign firms were required to submit processing schemes and financing proposals, on the basis of sharing the equity ownership of the joint venture 50–50 with the Korean government. The Korean government put stress on the foreign firms' ability to raise capital, not only their share of the equity but also the amount of debt, because the latter would constitute the major portion of the total capital requirement (Enos and Park 1987). For caprolactam, the government was not able to negotiate what it considered satisfactory terms for a joint venture, so it decided to license a foreign design and itself undertake all the other activities—financing, training, production, and management (Enos 1984).

An example of how the government used the one-buyer policy to press the foreign technology supplier to accept deals favorable to the domestic party is the agreement signed between Dow Chemical Co. and Chungju Fertilizer Company on November 8, 1968. The major clauses were as follows:

1. Dow was to grant an exclusive license for the use of its technology in the joint venture, subject to royalty payment and certain fees for technical assistance.
2. In exchange, the joint venture was to receive all of Dow's "know-how," defined as "all inventions, trade secrets, technical information, data, shop practices, plans, drawings, blueprints, specifications, and methods possessed by Dow on or prior to November 8, 1968."
3. The joint venture would also receive in exchange all information on improvements made by Dow and by its licensees.
4. Dow was to employ and train Korean engineers in numbers and to such an extent that they could completely and independently employ the technology, that is, that they could design the basic plant; design and procure its individual pieces of equipment; supervise the construction; test, start up, operate, and maintain the equipment; and carry out those activities that would lead to process and product improvements.
5. Until the Korean engineers absorbed the technology, Dow would continue to provide engineers from among its own employees. Dow's minimum contribution was listed in terms of the number of men and their responsibilities.
6. It was anticipated that the plant would be operated as intensively as possible to supply the Korean market. If domestic market demand was not sufficient to justify full-capacity operation alone, however, rather than cut back on output the joint venture would sell the excess first to Dow or, if Dow did not want it, in world markets at a price not below, or at terms not more favorable than, Dow itself conceded.
7. Again to the greatest extent possible, domestically produced inputs would be substituted for imported inputs (Enos and Park 1987).

In Taiwan, the main source of technology was transfers from the United States, Japan, and the former West Germany. The main technologies of the first few naphtha-cracking plants were imported from Du Pont and UPM of the United States. All technology cooperation agreements between local firms and foreign firms were subject to government approval. The government spelled out its policy in the "Statute for the Encouragement of Technical Cooperation." According to the 1964 version of this law, an agreement for purchasing a product or process technology could be made only if one of these conditions was met: (1) the agreement involved the production of a new product; (2) the new technology would increase the volume of production, improve quality, or reduce production costs; or (3) the new technology would lead to improvements in management or operation efficiency (Simon 1988).

In the upstream sector, CPC has been naturally the only buyer of foreign technologies for basic petrochemical materials since the early 1960s, which helped its bargaining power in deals with foreign technology suppliers. In the downstream sector, however, there exists internal competition and the government has not actively intervened specifically for the purpose of strengthening domestic firms' bargaining position. Even though the government approves all technology cooperation agreements, it does not oversee their eventual implementation. Nor are local firms required to report the upgrading of a product from first to second generation. This has two important effects. First, the government is not fully aware of the activities of many local producers and thus may duplicate agreements. Second, the government can never be certain if and when a second-generation technology becomes available. Both of these difficulties impede comprehensive government planning involving local technology needs (Simon 1988).

Initiatives to Technology Absorption

In the late 1960s, Korea embarked upon a number of large investment projects in manufacturing, particularly in process industries such as the manufacture of chemical fertilizers, petrochemicals, and oil refining.[10] In order to unbundle technology transfer packages from foreign sources either under licensing agreements or as integral parts of turn-key projects, the need to develop a local capability in project engineering and design services became acute. The particular reasons for this need included:

1. The failure of conventional turn-key projects to allow participation by Korean engineers in the engineering design and thereby develop local capability through "learning by doing."
2. The foreign engineering design firms' lack of knowledge of local production capability, resulting in project specifications for equipment and supplies that could be met only by foreign suppliers, and thereby depriving

local suppliers and manufacturers of a chance to respond even to local demand.
3. The heavy drain of foreign exchange used to pay for project engineering and design services, amounting to, in some instances, almost 10 per cent of total project cost.

A major decision to build up local capability in project engineering and design services was taken in 1969 by President Park, who observed that:

> The majority of major industrial plants, into which a vast amount of foreign and domestic capital investments has been channeled, have been built with foreign capital, foreign technology, and foreign services in all phases of their construction; from basic design to test operation. Therefore, the participation of the Korean engineers in, and the use of domestically available materials for, the construction of these plants has been impossible, while the lack of our technical know-how and the shortage of adequately trained Korean engineers have made it difficult for firms to ask foreign countries for our greater participation in these projects . . . To deal with the situation, the government will henceforth do away with the turn-key job principle to make newly emerging Korean engineering service companies and homemade products take a greater share in these projects. For this purpose, the establishment of joint-venture service companies will be encouraged between foreign engineering service firms of high standing and able engineers at home who have been pooled by industries, and thus form a combination of foreign capital and domestic skills. . . . In addition, the government will encourage the integration of Korean manufacturing industries with an eye to raising the standards of domestic products, and all efforts will be made to search for able brains and excellent engineers hitherto untapped. (Park 1969)

There are a number of significant aspects to this presidential instruction. First, it came out when Korea was about to embark on its first petrochemical complex in Ulsan. Second, it was appropriate to issue such an instruction to resolve conflicting interests even within the government, where some supported the idea of greater local participation, while others felt the efficiency of the tasks at hand to be a matter of immediate importance.

The initial response to the president's instruction took the form of establishing the Korea Engineering Company, Ltd. (KECL) in 1970. This was a joint venture of the government (through the Korea Development Bank) and the Lummus Co. of the United States, with equity participation by several leading Korean enterprises, including the Korea Institute of Science and Technology. Retired General Lee Chong Chan, widely known as a person highly respected by the president, was installed as the first president of the company. The fact that this was done at the urging of President Park indicates the president's commitment to the effort.

During the years 1971–77, KECL carried out more than 60 engineering projects, most of which were detailed design and engineering projects. It also supervised local procurement and plant construction management for its clients. As KECL expanded its scope by acquiring more experience and expertise, it developed a growing number of both private and public clients, and the number of its employees grew from 66 in 1971 to 460 in 1978 (Lee 1981).

To put the nascent engineering services industry on a sound footing, the government of Korea passed the Law for Promotion of Engineering Services in 1973, which stipulated that all government-financed projects should engage local engineering firms as the prime contractor for their engineering services. The only exception to hiring a local contractor was to obtain a waiver from the Ministry of Science and Technology for those projects whose financing required international competitive bidding. This promise, of course, provided little economic rent as most investment projects during this period were financed by loans from bilateral or multilateral sources which were not subject to this regulation. The 1976 revision of the law classified engineering firms into several categories and subcategories in accordance with their areas of competence. For example, plant engineering included subcategories such as chemical plant engineering, machinery plant engineering, power plant engineering, and nuclear power plant engineering. It was an attempt to preserve quality service from engineering firms. The law also contained new provisions for extending favorable tax incentives to local engineering firms. Promoted by such policy measures and by the rising demand for engineering services, private engineering firms began to appear in the early 1970s.

When Korea's first low-density polyethylene plant was constructed, with an output capacity of 50,000 tons per year (which increased to 100,000 tons per year at the second petrochemical complex), along with 60,000 tons per year at a vinyl chloride monomer plant (which increased to 150,000 tons per year at the second petrochemical complex), plus an ethylene dichloride plant with a capacity of 286,000 tons per year as an integral part of the first petrochemical complex in Ulsan, the responsibility for design, construction, and start-up was entirely in the hands of the foreign joint-venture partner, the Dow Chemical Company. Dow, in turn, engaged an American engineering design firm, PROCON, as the prime contractor while a Korean firm, Daelim Engineering Corp., acted as subcontractor. When the second petrochemical complex was built in Yeocheon, with more capacity and incorporating many technological modifications, a foreign engineering company (Fluor Corporation) was again the prime contractor, but with significant participation by a local engineering firm (Daelim Engineering Corp.) which assumed all responsibility for detailed engineering and construction (see Table 4.2). At the same time, local procurement increased significantly, resulting in 16 per cent of equipment and parts for the project being produced locally, as compared to none in the earlier case. "Were a third plant to follow on the first two, it could be designed, constructed and operated entirely by Koreans," local engineers were reported as saying (Enos and Park 1987).

TABLE 4.2 Korean Engineers Engaged in Adopting the Two Petrochemical Techniques, 1970 and 1979

Stage of Adoption	Percentage of Korean Engineers		
	Total Number Engaged	Ulsan Plant (1970–77)	Yeocheon Plant (1975–79)
Design	6	0	50
Securing of finance	3	0	33
Procurement	5	0	40
Construction	25	72	76
Start-up	27	67	67
Operation	46	91	91

Source: Enos (1984:30).

Bolstered by the increasing sophistication of local engineering design capability, the Yeocheon complex built a plant to recover mixed C4, with technology developed by the Lummus but never used at a commercial-scale plant, on extremely favorable terms. Not only were the royalties for that technology at a low level, but the Korean firm that took the risk of applying the commercially untested technology would get 50 per cent of any future royalties the licensor received from licensing that technology subsequent to the operation of the C4 plant in Yeocheon. Moreover, the participation of Korean engineers in various key aspects of plant operations began to expand rapidly. For instance, the computer control system at the Dow Chemical's LDPE plant at the Yeocheon Complex was jointly developed by the Dow and Korean engineers. Korea's rigorous attempts to acquire technological capability in the design, construction, and operation of petrochemical plants, assisted greatly by the sudden surge in petrochemical industrial investment in Korea along with aggressive entry into the international competitive markets for engineering services, provided an invaluable opportunity for selected Korean engineering and design firms to acquire world-class capabilities. The successful completion of an ethylene plant (with an annual capacity of 385,000 tons) on a turn-key basis for the Thai Olefine Corporation in June 1995 by the Daelim Engineering Corporation is such an example.

4.3 MECHANISMS ENSURING POLICY SUCCESS

The rapid development of East Asia's petrochemical industries, particularly in Japan and Korea, stemmed primarily from their extraordinary ability to acquire, absorb, and improve foreign technologies. In contrast, many other countries, such as India and Brazil, started to develop their petrochemical industries in the 1960s and 1970s, but have not yet achieved technological mastery in most of the important technologies after about 30 years of development. While the contrast in performances of East Asia and many other countries is clear, whether this performance difference has to do with a difference in government policies is an extremely controversial question. Section 4.2 shows that the East Asian governments' involvement in the development of domestic technological capabilities was deep and extensive, but what we still need to ask is whether this government intervention did indeed, and through what mechanisms, contribute to the development of this industry.

There are many theoretical arguments against government interventions in the forms described in the previous section (including control over market entry, technology licensing, import restriction, etc.). Two of them are widely heard. The "rent-seeking" argument maintains that such government controls create enormous rents for incumbents in the industry and thus induce wasteful rent-seeking activities as incumbents attempt to maintain their monopoly status and potential entrants attempt to obtain access to a controlled industry. Another argument, based on the "informational problem," contends that while theoretically coordination failure (e.g., due to interenterprise or interindustry spillover effects) by the private sector seems to justify government intervention, it does not in reality do so because the government may not have sufficient information to make the best judgment. In game theoretical terms, because there are too many equilibrium outcomes of a coordination game, no government has the knowledge to choose the best coordination strategy that maximizes efficiency.

In this section, we use the case of the East Asian petrochemical industry to argue that government failures due to rent-seeking and informational problems are not absolute, and can be reduced or even avoided by a government's deliberate efforts, including the creation of certain institutions. By minimizing the side effects of interventions, it is possible for a government to achieve its policy objectives to a maximum extent. The rest of this section examines, in five aspects, how this was made possible in East Asia.

Creating Incentives for Innovation Using Contingent Entry

Government control over market entry using means such as a technology-licensing policy created an environment in which firms competed for valued economic rents, such as access to foreign technology, protected domestic market, cheap credit, and scarce foreign exchange. In short, it created contests. Such contests, if well designed and enforced, can provide additional incentives for both the incumbents and potential entrants to enhance their technical and R&D capabilities, rather than encourage rent-seeking activities.

For economic rents to create incentives for innovation, an important prerequisite is that government control over market entry should have clear and well-enforced rules. In many countries where governments intervene heavily in technology imports and market entry, the distribution of licenses is often arbitrary and strongly influenced by the lobbying of existing firms. The lack of clearly articulated selection criteria and procedures and the tendency to favor incumbents create strong incentives to lobby and discourage innovation. In Japan and Korea, in their early stages of development, however, the governments set forth the criteria in advance of the actual selection and allowed all firms to compete for the privileges (see "Selecting Domestic Players" in Section 4.2). In most cases, the approval of a technology import was contingent on the firms' obtaining (1) the ability to construct a plant with an efficient scale; (2) the required R&D personnel and some experience in basic design, detailed design, construction, and operation; (3) the necessary financial resources, either domestic or foreign investment; and (4) terms of technology import that were acceptable to the government (the government tends to reject technology import contracts with excessively restrictive clauses on information disclosure, participation of local personnel, exports, and so forth). These criteria encouraged both incumbents and potential entrants to develop their technical, R&D, and financial capabilities as well as to seek better deals with foreign technology suppliers. In a sense, all firms were placed on an equal footing.

The dynamic aspect of such contingent entry is worth noting. The staggered approach announced by MITI in the early 1950s clearly conveyed the message that a few years after the first entry, more firms would be allowed to enter the market. With the government's commitment to such a strategy, firms that were denied access to the market in the first round could make long-term plans for development to gain access to the government-protected market in the future. The potential threat from future entrants, which the government promised, in turn forced the first incumbent to innovate in order to secure its leading position in the market.

Of course, capacity-licensing policy could lead to many negative effects, including wasteful rent-seeking activities, if the government was unable to clearly articulate and strictly enforce the rules for entrant selection. The Indian case presented in Vergara and Babelon (1990) illustrates this point. According to them, the capacity-licensing policy adopted by the Indian government to regulate the petrochemical industry has several features: (1) licensing has tended to enhance existing protection of established producers who have also lobbied against granting licenses to new entrants; (2) consequently, existing producers have tended to operate in a seller's market with little incentive to innovate, improve efficiency, or stop uneconomic operations; and (3) there has been little incentive to develop export markets or meet the needs of export segments among users because the domestic market has been able to comfortably absorb the available production under government protection. Even in the late 1980s, the average rate of protection for the major petrochemicals was as high as 400 to 500 per cent.

Ensuring Economies of Scale and International Competitiveness

One of the objectives of the East Asian governments' control over duplicate technology imports was to construct plants of efficient scale that would be competitive internationally, since the technology of the petrochemical industry is characterized by strong increasing returns to scale. To achieve this goal, Japan and Korea set criteria for minimum scales of production in the selection of entrants to the market (see Section 4.2). Although both the Japanese and Korean governments expressed the need to control the monopoly in the market, they were obviously more concerned about excess competition than about lack of competition, at least in the first one or two decades of the petrochemical industries' development. Taiwan also incorporated a minimum-scale requirement in its investment planning for publicly owned enterprises.

To see the reasoning behind the minimum size requirement, one should first understand import restrictions on petrochemical products in the early stages of East Asia's petrochemical industry. According to the well-known infant-industry theory, for a newly developed industry characterized by economies of scale, a large volume of output is necessary to spread fixed costs and to accumulate learning. Before the infant industry reaches a certain level of production, the unit production cost is so high that the industry cannot survive competition with rivals from industrial countries. This provides a case for temporary government protection of the industry, that is, for the government to reserve the domestic market for a small number of domestic producers through trade restriction.

In the presence of trade protection and/or significant transportation costs, the domestic price is higher than the international price, and, as a result, incentive exists to develop plants of small scale with high production costs. Unrestricted market entry therefore leads to too many firms and too small an average plant size that will in the long run be unable to compete internationally. If the government's objective is, as it was for MITI, to increase the long-run competitiveness of the industry, such an outcome is a coordination failure by the private sector. It therefore necessitates government intervention in the form of a requirement for minimum plant size. Setting such a requirement can be viewed as the government's effort to coordinate private investment activities in order to achieve the objective of long-run competitiveness.

In the petrochemical industry, government coordination failures due to informational problems are not a concern as critical as some theorists suggest, because only a very small number of potential investors have the capacity to invest in even small petrochemical plants, and petrochemical products are very homogeneous relative to products in most other sectors. In all three East Asian economies considered in this chapter, the governments were able to estimate reasonably accurately the demand for major petrochemical products such as ethylene and the production capacity needed to meet such needs. Information on potential investors in the upstream sector and demands from the downstream sector were obtained through forums linking the government and the private sector, such as Japan's Petrochemical Cooperative Discussion Group, Korea's Petrochemical Industry Promotion Committee, and Taiwan's investment coordination meetings sponsored by the Industrial Development Bureau. Given reasonable forecasts of demand and supply, there might be as few as two equilibrium outcomes (rather than countless) that the governments would be concerned about when judging whether a minimum size requirement was desirable: the one of free market entry, and the one under the minimum-plant-size requirement. The implications for long-run competitiveness of these two outcomes could then be compared and contrasted and form the basis of decision making.

In contrast to the Japanese and Korean governments, which clearly placed great emphasis on economies of scale and less on monopoly control, the Brazilian government stimulated the creation of many petrochemical enterprises almost simultaneously. The objective of this policy was to avoid monopolies in the petrochemical sector. In the words of Roos (1991), however, the result was not only a fragmented petrochemical sector, but also a large number of small, inefficient producers. A constraint on the development of R&D activities resulting from this policy is the size of the firm: the annual turnover per firm is too small to direct a large amount of capital to R&D. The 1989 survey reported by Roos (1991) shows that 30 per cent of all managers considered their firms too small to invest in R&D, and a further 13 per cent claimed that financial resources were insufficient for R&D activities.

Securing Favorable Terms and Conditions for Domestic Firms in Technology Transfers

As discussed in detail above, all three East Asian economies have used administrative means to assist domestic firms in obtaining better technology transfer deals, in the forms of lower prices, fewer restrictions on the participation of local engineers, export of products, sublicensing of the imported technology, etc. In Japan, MITI applied the staggered entry formula to limit the number of buyers of each technology within a given time interval and clearly expressed its objection to restrictive clauses imposed by foreign technology suppliers. Even more explicit than MITI, the Korean government imposed the one-item, one-plant principle and directly participated in negotiations on technology imports, with a strong emphasis on conditions that guaranteed the participation of local engineers. In Taiwan, state ownership and monopoly of a single large corporation (CPC) in the upstream sector has guaranteed that the government can effectively bargain with foreign technology suppliers, although this advantage in its mid- and downstream sectors has not been apparent due to limited government involvement.

A major effect of the governments' control over market entry was to provide the selected firms with technology on more favorable terms than they would have obtained without such protection. This control can be justified by the rationale of granting monopsonistic positions to domestic buyers when foreign firms monopolize the seller's market. Trade theory (Brander and Spence 1985) shows that in international competition, a domestic monopoly or monopsony can react strategically to the rival country's demand and supply conditions. In contrast, a large number of domestic producers or buyers in the same sector will compete among themselves and reduce their bargaining power with foreigners. This is a typical form of coordination failure by the private sector (a "prisoner's dilemma"): each firm chooses a strategy that maximizes its own interest, but the equilibrium outcome of these actions is in fact detrimental to every player's interest. This provides a case for the government deliberately to limit the number of buyers (e.g., entrants in the petrochemical industry) of foreign technologies, that is, to use its cohesive power to "coordinate" the private sector's technology imports. Again, in the petrochemical industry, the two alternative equilibria—under free technology imports and controlled technology imports—can be assessed with reasonably good information, as the potential buyers are not many and the number of sellers is even smaller. There was no strong evidence showing major government failures in East Asia's petrochemical industry due to informational problems in this regard.

In contrast to those of Japan and Korea, India's technology import agreements involved a great many restrictive clauses that were harmful to the indigenous absorption and dissemination of technology. These restrictive clauses included those on capacity expansion, export, and transfer and improvement of imported technologies. For firms in the private sector, negotiations with foreign partners were not adequately supported by the government. Even in the case of the public sector, the government seemed not to have fully used its ability to obtain favorable terms for domestic firms. In Brazil, influenced by the import-substitution strategy of the government, negotiating less restrictive contracts was not the main priority of Brazilian entrepreneurs in many cases. Using up-to-date technology in their companies was more important. For example, the technology contracts signed to establish the first petrochemical firms in Comarari were, above all, favorable to transnational corporations (TNCs) and did not include many terms concerning the transfer of the whole package of technology. The last phase of technology transfer, involving company expansion with the acquired technology, was almost never arranged in the contracts. Restrictions established in the contracts included limits on the maximum production capacity to be realized with the acquired technology, restrictions on export of production or the production process, and limits on further R&D (Roos 1991).

Promoting "Unpackaging" of Imported Technologies

While 100 per cent TNC subsidiaries and importation of turn-key projects were probably the quickest ways to build up production capacity, the East Asian governments, particularly those of Japan and Korea, consciously realized that this mode of technology transfer would not help the development of local technological capability, because the imported technology was treated as a "black box." Only by "unpackaging" an imported technology could local engineers grasp its contents and eventually reproduce or improve it. The governments of Japan and Korea have deliberately promoted the "unpackaging" of imported technology through three sets of policies (see Section 4.2). First, Japan and Korea restricted foreign direct investment in the early stages of their development, with the objective of maintaining the independence of the industrial sector. Second, instead of importing entire plants, Japan's technology imports concentrated on individual items in the form of patent rights, detailed drawings, operating instructions, manuals, and interchange of personnel between the Japanese buyers and foreign sellers. Third, the Korean government made deliberate efforts to gain access for local engineers to basic and detailed design of the plants, and successfully reduced the need for repeatedly importing the same technology or service.

The benefit of importing packaged technologies—ensuring smooth operation of the plants—is obvious, but its cost is rather subtle. This cost involves the lack of opportunities and incentives for local engineers to engage in technical matters once foreign technicians are present to take care of everything. On one hand, the foreign technology suppliers may tend not to release much technical know-how to local engineers. In joint ventures where foreign equity participation can translate into management control, technical services are often contracted to foreign engineers rather than local engineers. On the other hand, the government does not have sufficient incentive to press the foreign partners hard in negotiations for favorable conditions regarding information release and training of local personnel; the local engineers do not have sufficient incentive to learn technical know-how because they are not responsible for the operation as well as innovation. Roos (1991) pointed out that "the presence of a foreign participant in a joint venture may seriously discourage national R&D, as illustrated by the fact that 46 percent of the managers from Comarari-based firms said they did not need their own R&D center because all research was carried out in the R&D center of the foreign partner."

Theoretically it can be argued that the private sector may underestimate the social cost of packaged technology imports (i.e., the social benefit of unpackaged technology imports) because it does not incorporate the positive spillover effects of unpackaged technology imports in its calculus, thus necessitating government intervention. For example, the experiences that local engineers gain from participating in the design and construction of the first project based on imported technology may not be particularly useful to the operation of this project, but is most useful to the design and construction of the second project that uses a similar technology. If the owners of the two projects differ and the engineers are mobile from the first to the second project, the participation of the local engineers in the first project has a positive spillover effect on the second one. This leads to a less-than-optimal degree of local engineering participation, in the form of too many imports of packaged technology. To ensure an optimal degree of local participation, the government should provide incentives for unpackaged technology imports or impose restrictions on packaged technology imports. This can also be viewed as an example of government coordination, in an area where the private sector cannot coordinate itself to achieve the socially optimal degree of local participation. Again, in the upstream sector of the petrochemical industry, the superiority of the equilibrium under government coordination to the equilibrium without government intervention can be clearly identified, because the number of projects involved is often very small.

In many other developing economies, large foreign equity participation has contributed to the slow process toward technology independence. In India, 100 per cent multinational subsidiaries and joint ventures accounted for three out of four major petrochemical complexes. Foreign equity participation was also extensive in Brazil; more than 60 per cent of the petrochemical firms are joint ventures. From the Brazilian point of view, granting TNCs access to equity participation was necessary for obtaining up-to-date technology. Evans (quoted in Roos 1991) puts it as follows:

> Technology is, of course, one of the multinationals' prime contributions. It would have been possible to purchase most of the technology, but buying technology has its disadvantages. An engineering firm does not have the same interest in future profits that a partner does. Once a plant is constructed, the engineers are not there to deal with the problems. Getting technology from a partner, whose local profits depend on its efficient operation, is the best way to ensure that it will work.

This rationale also reflects many other developing economies' concerns. On the forms of technology imports, many developing countries, including China, India, and Brazil, imported a large number of "packaged" technologies, which were treated as black boxes by the local technicians. In India and Brazil, importing packaged technology is often a result of majority foreign equity participation. In the case of China, there was political pressure to start projects quickly, and decisions were made without adequate technical knowledge or experience. In such situations, the packaged project has many attractions, because searching out alternative approaches, involving perhaps alternative technologies and other collaborators, requires time, resources, and knowledge which the local decision maker may well not possess (Francks 1988). In two major ethylene plants completed in China in the late 1980s, the purchase of foreign equipment and materials accounted for 86.3 per cent of the total foreign exchange spent on the projects, leaving merely 13.7 for foreign technical assistance and technology licensing.[11] Officials of the China Petrochemical Corporation (SINOPEC) admitted that the policy has tended to overemphasize imports of packaged technology and neglected its absorption. The same or similar technology has been imported repeatedly in different projects, and as a result, "domestic R&D became meaningless" (Industrial Policy Study Group 1987). In addition to reasons related to foreign equity participation and domestic political pressure, limited knowledge of the technology to be imported is also responsible for the choice of packaged technology imports. In Brazil, when the Comarari complex was built, the technological knowledge of most Brazilian entrepreneurs and technicians regarding petrochemical products was almost negligible. As a clear illustration of the limits of their technological knowledge, special meetings were organized to teach the entrepreneurs how to read technology contracts (Roos 1991).

Promoting R&D Activities

The terms and conditions of technology transfers are affected by both the supply and the demand sides of the technology. On the supply side, technology suppliers are often monopolistic or oligopolistic and tend to have strong bargaining power. On the demand side, the buyer's bargaining power depends on its indigenous technological capability. R&D expenditure is an important indicator of the efforts made in developing such capabilities. In addition to obtaining favorable terms and conditions, a strong indigenous R&D infrastructure is also a prerequisite to having the ability to assimilate, adapt, and improve the imported technologies. In the words of Nagaoka (1989), "Domestic R&D efforts not only help enterprises 'unbundle' [unpackage] foreign technology and identify the technology components most efficient for importation, but also enhance the utility of imported technology." A weak indigenous R&D infrastructure may be responsible for continuously being dependent on foreign technology.

Theoretically, government promotion of R&D activities is justified by arguments related to spillover effects. R&D activities often produce knowledge that benefit not only the inventor but also others. Therefore, an individual firm, facing the possibility of not reaping all the gains from the investment, will prefer to undertake less than the socially optimal degree of R&D investment. Formal education, on-the-job training, and centralized technology information services face similar problems. The private sector may also underinvest in R&D activities when such activities require a large amount of investment and involve extraordinary risks that the private sector cannot or is not willing to bear. There appears to be a fairly strong case for government programs to encourage private R&D activities, to improve education and vocational training, and to initiate or subsidize centralized consultancy services.

Recognizing the importance of R&D activities, Japan in the early 1950s adopted strategies to strengthen R&D activities by giving the private sector subsidies and providing information services. Under the government promotion, Japan's R&D/sales ratio in the petrochemical industry reached 2.1 per cent in 1970 (Peck 1976). Korea directed its science and technology strategies of the 1970s at strengthening technical and engineering education in adapting imported technology and promoting research for industrial needs. Although Korea's R&D/GNP ratio was modest in the 1970s (0.7 per cent in 1978), the rate of increase in R&D expenditure has been phenomenal, now reaching over 2.5 per cent of GNP with over 80 per cent (in 1993) coming from the private sector.

In contrast to Japan and Korea, the ratios of R&D expenditure to GNP in India and Brazil are much lower. In 1988 India's R&D expenditure to GNP ratio was 0.9 per cent, and in 1985 Brazil's R&D expenditure to GNP ratio was 0.4 per cent (State Statistical Bureau 1993). In TNC subsidiaries and joint ventures in India, until the early 1980s, there were no R&D units even for "application research," and all technical services were left in the hands of foreign collaborators. The R&D/sales ratio of the public companies, although higher than that of most private petrochemical firms, is only 0.4 per cent. In terms of technical personnel, Japan has 15 per cent of its manpower in R&D, while India has only 2 per cent. This low R&D level has acted as a constraint in the development of indigenous technology capabilities. This, in turn, has affected the strength of India's bargaining power while importing technology.

4.4 CONCLUDING REMARKS: DEALING WITH GOVERNMENT FAILURES

It is widely agreed among economists that government intervention creates rents for favored producers and therefore induces wasteful rent-seeking activities. Casual observation suggests, however, that government-created rents did not produce as many wasteful rent-seeking activities in the East Asian economies as in many other countries, such as India. Why? When rents are created by government intervention, the government can limit the diversion of resources into unproductive rent-seeking activities. The East Asian economies achieved this through the creation of contests based on contingent entry and limited terms of protection. Contingent entry bases the distribution of rents on some pre-announced and well-enforced rules that encourage all participants to enhance their technology and financial capability rather than lobbying. As for limited terms of protection, the rationale is that if the monopoly position (and the accompanying rents) is too quickly eroded, the private sector will have little incentive to innovate; however, if the monopoly position lasts too long, the cumulative deadweight loss due to its existence will ultimately cancel out the initial productivity gains.

What institutional, political, and historical factors have contributed to the East Asian governments' ability to control rent seeking is an extremely intriguing question. Although the answer is beyond the scope of this chapter, the strong authority of the East Asian governments relative to the influence of social interest groups has been one of the factors responsible for the government taking initiatives rather than simply accommodating the demands of interest groups. Compared with many other developing countries, Japan and Korea have fewer cases where nongovernmental forces—wealthy families, ethnic or tribal or regional groups, multinational firms, etc.—control government. In addition, what Japan and Korea were able to achieve had to do with the way both governments interacted and teamed up with the private sectors in formulating plans and in delineating the terms of entry and so forth.

Another important argument against government intervention is that effective intervention requires highly detailed information on, among other things, market conditions and the relationship among various private actors' activities, which may not be available to the government (Nagaoka 1989, Matsuyama (Chapter 5 in this volume)). We have shown in this chapter that while a government is not necessarily smarter than the private sector, this argument against government intervention based on informational problems seems to have a damaging effect only on government coordination under significant uncertainty. In the petrochemical case discussed in this chapter, however, uncertainty involved in decision making is not as pervasive as imagined by some scholars. Government coordination in the petrochemical industry—and likely in steel and automobile industries also—suffers only to a limited extent from the informational problem, as the number of players (potential investors or technology buyers) involved is small and the products are very homogeneous relative to those in other sectors. The costs and benefits of alternative equilibria—under government coordination and without government coordination—can be identified with a reasonable level of confidence. In many policy issues discussed in this chapter (e.g., whether to impose a minimum-plant-size requirement, whether to control the number of domestic technology buyers, whether to encourage or limit unpackaged or packaged technology imports, and whether to support R&D activities), the number of possible equilibria can be quite small. The possibility of government coordination failure due to lack of information should therefore not be overemphasized, at least in the petrochemical industry.

Of course, we do not claim that informational problems do not exist in the petrochemical industry. What the East Asian experience shows us is that the government can mitigate this problem by deliberately creating certain institutions. Examples of such institutions include Japan's Petrochemical Cooperative Discussion Group, Korea's Petrochemical Industry Promotion Committee, and Taiwan's investment coordination meetings sponsored by the Industrial Development Bureau. These groups or committees brought together policymakers, industrialists, and experts from academia and petrochemical industrial associations (in Japan, Korea, and Taiwan) in the process of policy formation. Informational exchange between the government and the private sector through such a forum could not only reveal the need for government coordination in certain areas, but also provide the government with enough details on how best to coordinate the private sector's activities.

NOTES

The authors wish to thank K. C. Fung, Ha-Joon Chang, Masahiro Okuno-Fujiwara, Larry Lau, Masahiko Aoki, Vinayak Bhatt, Soon-Yong Yoon, H. K. Tsu, and Martin Chen for helpful discussions and for providing us with useful materials. The views expressed in this chapter are those of the authors and should not be attributed to the World Bank.

[1] See Westphal, Kim, and Dahlman (1985).

[2] Itami (1991) attributes the lackluster performance of the Japanese chemical industry, including the petrochemical industry, to the lack of integration as compared to Western chemical giants.

[3] Calculated from data in Economic Commission for Europe (various issues).

[4] Ibid.

[5] The reader should not interpret the Japanese "staggered entry" approach as MITI's *ex ante* planning of the exact date of entry for each new entrant. Rather, the staggered entry pattern is a result of the application of the rules for selecting entrants. In other words, the date of entry of any particular firm was not planned by MITI in advance; the firm was allowed to enter because MITI considered that it had met the ministry's criteria at that time.

[6] The group guidelines adopted in January 1965 made the following stipulations: (1) in the case of expansion, (a) the accumulative net increase in capacity should not

exceed 350,000 tons per year, and (b) the existing plants shall be given priority in increasing the ethylene output capacity; (2) in the case of newly installed capacity, (a) the center (meaning the naphtha-cracking center that produces ethylene, among others) should have appropriate plans for derivatives from residuals as well as possessing a capacity that carries international competitiveness through economies of scale. The minimum scale envisaged was 100,000 tons per year of ethylene, with appropriate plans for derivatives as well as the full utilization of olefine. If the bulk of the naphtha was to be supplied by pipes from an oil refinery, the acceptable plan had to have the necessary locational condition that would allow the installation of a plant with a capacity in excess of 200,000 tons per year in ethylene. It was again these sets of criteria that led to MITI's approval of the Chiba Plant proposal of the Mitsui Petrochemical Company in May 1965, the Chiba Plant proposal of Sumitomo Chemical in June 1965, and the ethylene plant proposals of Osaka Petrochemical and Showa Tenko Corporation in July 1966.

[7] The development of acrylic fibers in the late 1950s followed a different approach. There was simultaneous entry by four firms, soon followed by two others. Because of this uncontrolled entry, the industry was immediately crowded and characterized by intense competition, which took the form of uncoordinated plant expansion and price wars. One reason for this intense competition might have been that MITI's ability to control market entry by means of the technology-import screening mechanism was somewhat limited because the acrylic fiber industry was less dependent on foreign technology than the other two fibers (Ozawa 1980).

[8] Conversation with CPC's Representative Office in the United States, October 1994.

[9] Since the mid-1960s, class A technology agreements have risen faster than class B technology agreements as MITI relaxed the control over technology imports. See Peck (1976).

[10] This subsection draws heavily on Kim (1984).

[11] Information provided by China Petrochemical Corporation.

REFERENCES

BRANDER, J. and SPENCE, B. (1985), "Export Subsidies and Market-Share Rivalry," *Journal of International Economics*, 18:83–100.

CHU, W. (1994), "Import Substitution and Export-Led Growth: A Study of Taiwan's Petrochemical Industry," *World Development*, 22(5):781–94.

DRAZEN, A. (1990), "Threshold Externalities in Economic Development," *Quarterly Journal of Economics*, 105:501–26.

Economic Commission for Europe (United Nations) (1978, 1981, 1986, 1992), *Annual Bulletin of Trade in Chemical Products*, United Nations, New York.

ENOS, J. (1984), "Government Intervention in the Transfer of Technology: The Case of South Korea," *IDS Bulletin*, (12):26–31 (Institute of Development Studies, Sussex).

——and PARK, W. H. (1987), *The Adoption and Diffusion of Imported Technology: The Case of Korea,* Croom Helm, New York.

Francks, P. (1988), "Learning From Japan: Plant Imports and Technology Transfer in the Iron and Steel Industry," *Journal of Japanese and International Economics*, 2:42–62.

Gerschenkron, A. (1962), *Economic Backwardness: Historical Perspective*, Harvard University Press, Cambridge, Mass.

Industrial Policy Study Group, SINOPEC (1987), "A Preliminary Study of the Industrial Policy of the Petrochemical Industry of China," SINOPEC, Beijing.

Itami, H. (1991), *Nihon no kagakukōgyō* (Japan's chemical industries), NPT Publishing Co., Tokyo, 59.

Kim, C. (1994), *Policy-making on the Front Lines: Memoirs of a Korean Practitioner, 1945–79*, EDI Retrospective in Policy Making, World Bank, Washington.

Kim, H.- K. (1984), "Technology Development Strategies and Experience in Korea," Economic Development Institute Working Paper, World Bank, Washington.

Krueger, A. O. and Tuncer, B. (1982), "An Empirical Test of Factor Productivity in Turkish Manufacturing Industries," *Journal of Development Economies*, 11:307–26.

Lee, G. D. (1980), "The Past and Future of the Petrochemical Industry," *Industry in Free China*, 53(3):2–11.

Lee, J. (1981), "Development of Engineering Consultancy and Design Capability in Korea," in A. Araoz, ed., *Consulting and Engineering Design in Developing Countries*, International Development Research Center, Ottawa.

MITI (1962), *Kagaku kōgyō tōkei nenpō* (Chemical industry annual statistical report), MITI, Tokyo.

——(1990), *Tsūshōsangyō seisakushi*, (Trade and industrial policy history), No. 6, MITI, Tokyo.

Nagaoka, S. (1989), "Overview of Japanese Industrial Technology Development," Industry and Energy Department Working Paper, Industrial Series Paper No. 6, World Bank, Washington.

O'Driscoll, G. P. (1977), *Economics as a Coordination Problem*, Sheld Andrews and Medeed, Inc., Kansas City.

Ozawa, T. (1980), "Government Control over Technology Acquisition and Firms' Entry into New Sectors: The Experience of Japan's Synthetic-Fibre Industry," *Cambridge Journal of Economics*, 4:133–46.

Park, C. H. (1969), "Translation of President Park's Instruction on the Creation of Engineering Service Companies in Korea," May 15, 1969, quoted in A. Araoz, ed. (1981), *Consulting and Engineering Design in Developing Countries*, International Development Research Center, Ottawa.

Peck, M. (1976), "Technology," in H. Patrick and H. Rosovsky, eds., *Asia's New Giant: How the Japanese Economy Works*, Brookings Institution, Washington.

Petrochemical Industrial Association of Japan (1990), *Sekiyukagaku kōgyō sanjūnen no ayumi*, (30-year footprint of the petrochemical industry), Petrochemical Industrial Association of Japan.

Petrochemical Industrial Association of Korea (1994), *Petrochemical Industry in Korea 1994*, Petrochemical Industrial Association of Korea, Seoul.

Petrochemical Industrial Association of Taiwan (1994), *Petrochemical Industries in Taiwan, Republic of China*, Petrochemical Industrial Association of Taiwan, Taipei.

Rodrik, D. (1993), "Trade and Industrial Policy Reform in Developing Countries:

A Review of Recent Theory and Evidence," National Bureau of Economic Research, Working Paper Series No. 4417.

Roos, W. (1991), *Shaping Brazil's Petrochemical Industry: The Importance of Foreign Firm Origin in Tripartite Joint Venture*, Center for Latin American Research and Documentation, Amsterdam.

Rosenberg, N. and Frishtak, C. (1985), *International Technology Transfer: Concepts, Measures, and Comparisons*, Praeger Publishers, New York.

Simon, D. F. (1988), "Technology Transfer and National Autonomy," in E. A. Winckler and S. Greenhalgh, eds., *Contending Approaches to the Political Economy of Taiwan*, M. E. Sharpe, Armonk, N.Y.

State Statistical Bureau (1993), *China Statistical Yearbook 1993*, State Statistical Press, Beijing.

Tattum, L. (1993), "Asia-Pacific Chemical Industry: New Frontiers are Opening," *Chemical Week*, 152(4):19.

Vergara, W. and Babelon, D. (1990), *The Petrochemical Industry in Developing Asia*, World Bank Technical Paper No. 113, Industry and Energy Series.

Wada, M. (1976), "Foreign Technology and Industrial Policy in the Post Second World War Period In Japan," report prepared for UNCTAD/SIDA training course in Sri Lanka.

Wade, R. (1990), *Governing the Market: Economic Theory and the Role of Government in East Asian Industrialization*, Princeton University Press, Princeton.

Westphal, L. E. (1981), "Empirical Justification for Infant Industry Protection," Staff Working Paper No. 445, World Bank, Washington.

——, Kim, L., and Dahlman, C. (1985), "Reflections on the Republic of Korea's Acquisition of Technological Capabilities," in N. Rosenberg and C. Frishtak, eds., *International Technology Transfer*, Praeger Publishers, New York.

5

Economic Development as Coordination Problems

KIMINORI MATSUYAMA

5.1 INTRODUCTION

The major challenge for the theory of economic development is to explain divergent economic performances across economies. In recent years, this problem has motivated a large number of studies in the so-called "new growth theory."[1] One strand of this literature approaches economic development as a coordination problem and portrays underdevelopment as a state of equilibrium, in which the economy fails to achieve necessary coordination among complementary activities.[2] The task assigned to me in writing this chapter is to reexamine the logic of coordination failures in the context of economic development and to draw some implications concerning the role of government in facilitating coordination.

Some economists believe that this literature provides a theoretical justification for active roles of the government, and try to support it empirically by collecting anecdotal evidence, in which the government seems to have improved efficiency through coordination activities. The critics, skeptical of the government's ability to coordinate actions when the private sector fails to do so, *also* believe that this literature tries to justify more interventionist policies. In their effort to refute such a conclusion, the critics question the prevalence of coordination failures in practice and offer anecdotal evidence, in which the private sector seems to have succeeded in coordination without any government guidance.

I do not attempt here to review these arguments and to find the "right" side of this debate. Instead, I intend to explain that this debate is fundamentally misguided as it is based on a wrong presumption; contrary to the common perception, the logic of coordination failures does *not* justify policy activism.

The task of any allocation mechanism requires coordination of a large number of activities, performed by a large number of people, each equipped with what Hayek (1945) called "the knowledge of the particular circumstances of time and place." The major part of this problem is to find out which combination of activities should be coordinated. This problem—not unlike the problem of hundreds of people, scattered in a dense, foggy forest, trying to locate one another—is of such fundamental difficulty that no algorithm can solve it. What the economics of coordination failures tries to show is that *even* the market mechanism cannot solve the problem. More precisely, it projects the view of the world that economic development is a continuous process of system change, in which society tries to discover a better way of coordinating economic activities, and yet, due to the fundamental complexity of coordination problems, there are equilibrating tendencies in which society is evolved into one of a large number of inefficient states. From this perspective, even the most advanced economies fail in coordination. What differentiates the rich from the poor is simply a matter of degree; the former have been *relatively* more successful in coordination than the latter. In this sense, all countries are still developing. And a series of historical accidents, including coordinating efforts of entrepreneurs and of the government, determine the performance of the economy, by pushing it from one state into another in an unpredictable manner, which in turn explain diverse performances across economies, as well as the diversity of the manners in which different economies cope with coordination.

If there are significant coordination failures, then the economy necessarily operates at a position far away from the Pareto frontier. So, it is possible that, after some shocks, society may accidentally discover a better way of coordinating activities. This helps us explain, among other things, why we can find much anecdotal evidence in which government intervention seems to have played an important role in improving coordination. But, it is one thing to say that something is improvable and another to say that we know how to improve it. If the coordination problem were simple enough for even the outsider, such as the economist or the bureaucrat, to know how to solve it, it would have been taken care of a long time ago by those directly involved with the problem.

If there are significant coordination failures, then it is not surprising, and indeed very likely, that we can find some isolated instances in which some entrepreneurs, those lucky enough to stumble upon unexploited opportunities, succeed in solving coordination problems; business sections of newspapers are full of such stories. But this does not refute the prevalence of coordination failures in practice. Quite the contrary. The very facts that these innovators become fabulously rich by doing so and that such innovations are introduced year after year suggest that a large number of coordination problems are yet to be solved, or even identified.

This is not to deny the value of studying how government policies have permanent impact on the way we coordinate our economic activities, or the value of studying how entrepreneurs succeeded in enhancing efficiency through their coordination efforts without any government guidance. It is through accumulation of such evidence that we can acquire better understanding of how our society is organized. However, the sheer abundance of such evidence neither supports nor refutes the benefits of policy activism. It merely suggests the prevalence of coordination failures in our society.

Pointing out that the market mechanism fails in coordination problems does not mean that the government should intervene. In fact, we do great injustice to the achievement of the market if we judge it by an ideal standard there is no way of achieving. But this is different from saying, as mainstream economists are often inclined to do, that the market allocation is "constrained efficient." Such a statement, by arguing that we were seemingly in the best of all possible worlds, does not sit comfortably with the apparent lack of progress in the Third World and the conspicuous roles played by the government in some rapidly growing economies in East Asia. The economics of coordination failures, by arguing that we are far from being efficient, questions the validity of efficiency as the criterion by which we judge economic performances, and hence suggests that the mere evidence of improvement by government intervention does not justify a policy activism.[3]

What, then, are the policy lessons from the literature on the economics of coordination failures? This literature does not intend to argue that there is a single, easily identifiable source of failure that is waiting to be solved. Rather, it argues that coordination problems are inherently difficult; coordination failures are everywhere; whatever coordination mechanism is put in place, they are so pervasive that there is plenty of room for improvement. The only way to sustain continuous improvement is thus to keep searching for a better system. That is why it is essential to maintain the freedom to pursue and experiment with new ways of coordinating economic activities, such as the freedom to form new business enterprises. This is not to deny that the government can sometimes improve coordination. Indeed, the coercive power of the state is the effective means for establishing a particular coordination mechanism. However, precisely because of its coercive power, state-led coordination inevitably leads to tighter enforcement, which limits experiments for further improvement in coordination, thereby making it hard to sustain continuous progress.[4] Freer systems have their own problems, but they are at least open to the discovery of new ways of solving those problems.

It is worth pointing out that recent studies of coordination failures in economic development attempt to formalize the old idea that dates back to Allyn Young (1928), Paul Rosenstein-Rodan (1943), Ragnar Nurkse (1953), Tibor Scitovsky (1954), Albert Hirschman (1957), and Gunnar Myrdal (1958). This early literature, after it enjoyed wide popularity in the 1950s and 1960s, lost much of its intellectual force in subsequent decades. The reason was not because the sources of coordination failures pointed out by these authors proved to be empirically insignificant, but rather because many economists, including some of the authors themselves, had drawn wrong policy lessons from this literature; they had misinterpreted it as a call for a "big push" industrialization, i.e., a synchronized expansion of industries, deliberately coordinated by the central planning board. The eventual collapse of such state-led industrialization programs in many countries diverted the profession's attention away from what nevertheless remains one of the important sources of development failures discovered by the early writers.

It is my ultimate goal in this chapter to discuss the fundamental difficulty of coordination problems in the context of economic development (in Section 5.3) and some implications that follow (in Sections 5.4 and 5.5). Before embarking on this task, it is worth pondering why the economics of coordination failures is widely misinterpreted as a call for more active government intervention (with my sincere apologies if my own writing in this area has been responsible for such misunderstanding). In Section 5.2, I point out some possible reasons by using an abstract coordination game, devoid of any economic content. I hope that clarifying common fallacies and discussing closely connected methodological issues at the outset will help us avoid unnecessary confusion in the discussions to follow.

5.2 *the economics of coordination failures: misconceptions*

The paradoxical nature of the economics of coordination failures is that any attempt to model it necessarily runs the risk of trivializing the difficulty of coordination problems. The theorist naturally tries to come up with a SIMPLE model of coordination problems, so that the reader can EASILY see how the agents living in the model environment may be stuck in a Pareto-dominated equilibrium. The significant part of expositional effort hence has to be spent on demonstrating the existence of other, and better, equilibria. But, such a demonstration itself makes coordination problems look easy and trivial to the reader. Having seen how a better equilibrium can be achieved, some may think that there are obvious things the government can do. Others may find it hard to believe that the private agents miss such obvious gains from coordination. But such readers are making two kinds of error. One is the failure to distinguish between the main results of the model and the mere artifacts of its simplifying assumptions. The other is the failure to make a clear distinction between what is known to the agents living in the model environment and what is known to us (that is, the theorist, the creator of this artificial world, and the reader, who is given the opportunity to look at the structure of the model).

For example, let us look at Figure 5.1, which shows a simple coordination game. It is widely used as the simplest set-up in which one can talk about coordination failures. The game is played by a representative agent against the rest of the agents in society. There are two strategies, I and II, and two equilibria. In one equilibrium, every agent selects I, and in the other, every

	I	II
I	1,1	0,0
II	0,0	2,2

FIG. 5.1 A Simple Coordination Game

agent selects II. Although the former is Pareto-dominated by the latter, I is an optimal strategy for each agent given that the other agents also select I; a unilateral deviation does not improve his/her pay-off. In order to escape from the dominated equilibrium, the agents somehow need to coordinate the complementary changes in their strategies. They are stuck in the dominated equilibrium because of their failure to coordinate. In the context of economic development, an additional interpretation is given in order to explain divergent performances across economies. That is, some societies, "the underdeveloped," play the dominated equilibrium, while other societies, "the developed," play a better equilibrium (in this case, every agent playing II). This simple game captures the economics of coordination failures in its essentials. And it is a useful one, as long as we do not forget that the game is meant only for illustration. Here are some cautionary remarks in interpreting Figure 5.1.

By showing that some societies, "the underdeveloped," play a dominated equilibrium, this game is not trying to argue that these societies fail in coordination completely. In Figure 5.1, every agent playing I happens to be the worst equilibrium outcome, but this is a mere artifact of the two-ness of the game. In general, one can easily imagine that society plays a dominated equilibrium, which in turn dominates other equilibria. This may at first appear obvious but has at least three consequences that are not appreciated sufficiently.

First, pointing out some real-world examples of successful coordination does not refute the prevalence of coordination failures in practice, because even the most primitive society has achieved a certain degree of coordination. (Otherwise, it would hardly deserve to be called a "society.") Second, improving coordination not only means setting up a new system of coordination, but may also mean tearing down the old system of coordination. Steady progress in coordination can be achieved only through the process of "creative destruction." Third, society may be worse off by an attempt to move to another equilibrium by coordinating changes in strategies. For example, coordination failures are sometimes interpreted as a problem of expectations; that is, the agents play a bad equilibrium when plagued by pessimism, while a good equilibrium is associated with optimistic expectations. This interpretation helps us understand why governments occasionally try to generate optimism by preaching the "economics of euphoria."[5] It may work, and there is nothing to lose from attempting to do so if society is in the worst possible equilibrium, as in Figure 5.1. But, generally, such an attempt may cause a backlash and society may find itself in an even worse equilibrium. When the president makes a statement such as "the only thing we have to fear is fear itself," it may indeed help to generate euphoria, but it could also be taken as a sign of despair (particularly when it is not supported by any tangible act of government commitment) and end up making the mood of the nation even more pessimistic. One can never predict how the "market" will interpret and react to statements made by public officials.[6]

Similarly, by showing that some societies, "the developed," play a better equilibrium than others, this game is not trying to argue that these societies have already succeeded in solving the coordination problem. In Figure 5.1, every agent playing II happens to be Pareto optimal, but, in a more general game, the equilibrium played by the most successful societies can be dominated by other equilibria. Again, the Pareto optimality of II is a mere artifact of the two-ness of the game in Figure 5.1. Unfortunately, this tends to trivialize the difficulty of coordination—if somebody else has solved the problem, it cannot be particularly hard—and also to generate the false impression that one simply has to imitate practices in more advanced societies.

By pointing out that the agents are stuck in the dominated equilibrium due to their failure to coordinate complementary changes in their strategies, this game does not intend to argue that, in order to escape from a low-level equilibrium, it is necessary to force a large number of agents to start moving in the same direction simultaneously. In Figure 5.1, all agents are identical and have only one alternative, so that such a "Big Push" or "Great Leap Forward" solution to the coordination problem could work. But again, this is an artifact of the two-ness of the game and the symmetry of the game (another simplifying assumption). In a more general game, with different agents having different sets of strategies and different pay-offs, such a bold move may lead to an even bigger failure. Furthermore, society may be able to escape from a low-level equilibrium even when a small number of agents succeeds in coordinating changes in their strategies. This is because, in the presence of complementarity, the small change initiated by a small group of agents could start a long chain reaction, in which the change in one strategy is continuously supported by changes in complementary strategies.

More importantly, the logic of coordination failures does not require that the agents playing this game, or any agent living in the model environment (e.g., the economist or the bureaucrat), have full knowledge of the structure of the game (that is, the pay-offs, the strategy spaces, or even the set of opponents). In short, they may not know which game they are playing. For example, when all agents play I in Figure 5.1, they may be unaware of the existence of another equilibrium. In order to make I an equilibrium strategy, all the agents need to know is that a deviation from I does not improve their pay-offs. Even if they are sure of the existence of a better equilibrium (e.g., by observing that other societies seem to be doing better), they may not know which combination of strategies constitutes an equilibrium. Of course, in a two-by-two symmetric game, like the one given in Figure 5.1, this would be easy to figure out; one could deduce from the two-ness of the game that all agents must be playing II in a second equilibrium. But, again, there is nothing special about "two," except that it happens to be the smallest integer larger than one. More generally, with N different agents, each of whom has access to M different strategies, there are M^N boxes in a pay-off matrix, each of which contains an N-dimensional pay-off vector. Then, just figuring out which box corresponds to an equilibrium alone becomes a formidable task even when the agents have full knowledge, let alone when they have only partial knowledge of the game. And even if society accidentally discovers a better equilibrium and succeeds in reaching it, this newly attained equilibrium is almost surely dominated by other equilibria that are unknown (at least to the agents living in the model environment).

That the agents have only partial knowledge of the game makes problematic any attempt to learn from the experiences of other societies and to imitate those more successful, as others may not be playing exactly the same game. It is indeed more natural to expect that each society is different in its own way. And it takes only a small change in pay-offs to render a particular strategy profile unqualified for equilibrium. Such sensitive dependence on small (and perhaps imperceptible) differences raises the question of replicability of the experiences of others.

When interpreting a model of coordination failures, such as the one given in Figure 5.1, it is important to keep in mind the enormous complexity of coordination problems each society has to deal with in the real world. Each of us, including the economist and the bureaucrat, possesses only very partial knowledge of the situation. Any model of coordination failures should thus be interpreted as an abstraction of the complex reality, and thinking about policy lessons of this literature requires the intuitive combination of several such models. The trouble begins when we start taking a particular model literally, treating it as a complete description of the real world and assuming that everybody agrees it is a complete description of the real world. It is the approach that Coase (1988:19) termed "blackboard economics." It is the approach in which "the policy under consideration is one which is implemented on the blackboard. All the information needed is assumed to be available and the teacher plays all the parts . . . In the back of the teacher's mind (and sometimes in the front of it) there is, no doubt, the thought that in the real world the government would fill the role he plays." But, of course, "there is no counterpart to the teacher within the real economic system." There is no one who has access to all the information the teacher has on his blackboard.

Of course, some economists, particularly those familiar with Hayek's work, fully understand that the main difficulty of formulating economic policies lies in that we have to cope with uncertainty, about which everybody disagrees. But, blackboard economics has been the dominant approach in the profession since the 1970s, with the rational expectations revolution in macroeconomics and the increasing popularity of game theory throughout almost all areas of economics. It has become almost mandatory to treat a formal model as if it were a complete description of the real world, which includes not only the physical environment, but also the information structure, and to assume that the agents agree on the true structure of the model.[7] Such a modeling exercise undoubtedly requires great intellectual ability and may play a role in developing the skills of an economist. But, it has the danger of misdirecting our attention when thinking about economic policy.

In the next two sections, I intentionally adopt an approach different from "blackboard economics" in my discussion of economic development as coordination problems. In particular, I try to describe the complexity of development processes as it is; I consider the implications from the fact that the agents have to cope with considerable uncertainty, by thinking about the possibility that there are substantial discrepancies between the true structure of the model and the subjective knowledge possessed by the agents living in the model environment, including the government. I hope that this rather nonstandard approach will be more effective in conveying the fundamental difficulty of coordination problems.

5.3 FUNDAMENTAL DIFFICULTY OF COORDINATION PROBLEMS

Economies grow and our standards of living rise not so much because we are becoming better at doing the same activities, but because we continuously develop and add new activities to the list of those we are engaged in. Economic development is also a process of structural change; productivity growth is achieved through the evolution of a highly complex system of activities, generally associated with an ever greater indirectness in the production process and an ever increasing degree of the division of labor. Why have certain countries been more successful than others in developing such a complex economic system? And why does the process of system change proceed at different rates in different countries?

By an activity, I mean all sorts of jobs, tasks, works, services, goods, and products that have potential economic value and are costly to perform and to produce.[8] By an economic system, I mean a combination of highly complementary economic activities (i.e., tasks, services, goods, etc.), which, when taken together, make a coherent whole. The development of a sophisticated economic system requires a high degree of coordination among these diverse activities, performed by a diverse set of agents, each of whom may possess the unique knowledge and technical expertise concerning these activities.

It should be noted that the problem is not merely coordinating day-to-day operations of a fixed set of activities. Because there are innumerable activities, any economic system inevitably has to choose the range of activities that are actually introduced. The major part of this problem is to figure out which set of activities should be activated. It is the problem of discovering a combination that brings about a better outcome for the economy as a whole. Economic progress may thus be regarded as an outcome of a continuous process of adding a new set of activities, while dropping others. This problem would be relatively simple if the value of introducing each activity could be assessed independently of other activities. If this were true in reality, we could achieve steady progress by routinely experimenting with, and determining to adopt or to reject, one activity after another. The problem arises, however, because of the inherent complementarity across activities.

The following metaphor may be apt here. Think of the physical world we live in as a network. It consists of a large number of nodes and a larger number of branches connecting pairs of nodes. Traveling through a node takes a certain amount of time, but this information is available only to the agents living in the node. Our goal is to discover the quickest route from node S (start) to node F (finish). According to this metaphor, each node corresponds to a particular activity; each route corresponds to a particular economic system; a set of nodes that belong to the same route corresponds to a set of complementary activities.[9]

Finding the efficient route would be relatively easy if we knew that every route contained a single node. Then, even when there were thousands of possible routes, one could steadily discover a better one by trying one after another. And once a better route was discovered, one could eliminate old ones without any loss. The problem would be much harder if routes contained multiple branches and they were all interconnected. In this case, whether one should visit a particular node could not be determined solely on the traveling time across the node; one would have to evaluate the total traveling time across an entire itinerary along all possible routes that contained this node. And yet, the number of all possible routes would grow exponentially with the number of nodes. This is a difficult problem to solve, as anyone who has tackled the traveling salesman problem in a puzzle book can testify. The catch is the interconnectedness. Due to the large number of possibilities, it is practically impossible to check all possible routes, but there is no way of reducing the entire problem into a number of separate problems of a manageable size.

Our problem of finding the best route, or the problem of discovering the efficient economic system, is much harder than the traveling salesman problem, which is already very difficult. There are two additional obstacles. One is that the information concerning the traveling time across each node is widely dispersed in a society, so that we somehow need to collect the information. It is as if the traveling salesman first had to make a phone call to obtain information concerning each node, although he knows for sure that he would never visit most nodes. And he may not even know who to call. This difficulty has been pointed out before by many economists, most eloquently and persistently by Hayek (1945, 1974), and yet it is probably worthwhile to repeat it here as it tends to be forgotten whenever theory is applied to real-world problems.

There is another, and in my opinion more serious, obstacle. Unlike the traveling salesman, we do not have a map of the network. It is as if the traveling salesman had to go through a maze. If you have ever tried to escape from a real maze (as opposed to solving a maze in a puzzle book, in which case you are given the diagram of a maze), or if you have ever been lost in a dense, foggy forest and tried to escape from it, then you know that this means that there is no way of knowing all feasible routes; the only way to discover a feasible route is to try one, of which there are so many. This means that there is no way of verifying that the route (or the economic system) discovered is indeed the efficient one. The best one can hope for is to assure that taking a detour here and there along the route will not cut down the traveling time (that is, to verify that it is locally optimal). Even if we are sure as a matter of conviction that there must somewhere be a route better than the current route, it is not even clear where to start a search process.

No algorithm or rule of thumb can guide us "intelligently" through untrod regions of the maze. Likewise, no mechanism can help us discover the efficient economic system. The price mechanism, or the Invisible Hand, is no exception. This is not to deny that the price mechanism may be the best means of utilizing information diversely held in a society, relative to any other mechanisms that ever existed in the human history. However, this is different from saying that the price mechanism can solve the kind of coordination problems we have to deal with in designing an economic system.

In rebuttal, one might argue that the Invisible Hand Theorem, or the first fundamental theorem of welfare economics, demonstrates the efficiency of the price mechanism as a coordination mechanism, and that this theorem does not rule out the possibility of complementarity across goods. But let us read carefully what this theorem has to say. It states that, if there are complete competitive markets, market allocation is efficient; hence, all we have to do is to price all potential activities (competitively). In other words, this theorem claims that there would be no coordination failure, *if* we can make a list of *all* activities we may conceivably be interested in coordinating. But how can we make such a list, when the knowledge concerning the feasibility of each activity, as well as the knowledge concerning possible complementarities across activities, is diversely held in a society?

In the Invisible Hand Theorem, the coordination problem is artificially resolved by the Walrasian auctioneer, who quotes the prices for all potential activities, to which agents can communicate demand and supply simultaneously. But, there is no way of knowing whether the list held by the Walrasian auctioneer indeed includes everything. This is like saying that we know how to discover the most efficient route if all the feasible routes are drawn in your map of the network, when there is no way of knowing if a feasible route, possibly the most efficient one, is missing from your map. And this is not the end of the problem. Even if one succeeded in making the list of everything, it would be impossible to open markets for all: even with very small costs of setting up markets, all the resources in the economy would be absorbed so that nothing would be left over to be used in performing these activities. Hence, one must somehow decide for which combination of activities markets should be set up.

We have thus come back to our original problem of finding the efficient economic system. The paradox is that we need to open all markets in order to collect necessary information to know which markets to open. Of course, in reality, nobody ever designed a system of markets. It has somehow evolved over time. If there are potential gains from trading a particular good, independently of those that are already available in the marketplace, then one may hope that the market for that good will eventually come to exist. However, there is no reason to expect that the markets for a complementary set of goods would ever be developed. (See the Appendix for simple models illustrating this point.)

Of course, the Visible Hand, by entrepreneurs, managers, or bureaucrats, could fill some of the gaps left by the Invisible Hand of the price mechanism. Entrepreneurs in particular have advantages in solving isolated coordination problems with their localized knowledge, through the formation of new organizations, thereby creating the islands of conscious power in the ocean of unconscious cooperation.[10] However, it is optimistic to suppose that such coordination efforts of entrepreneurs, managers, and bureaucrats can solve coordination problems altogether. Furthermore, precisely because of the localized nature of their knowledge, they are powerless in tackling global coordination. Even worse, their successes in local coordination may indeed block the possibility of achieving a better way of coordinating at a global level.

5.4 THE ECONOMICS OF COORDINATION FAILURES: IMPLICATIONS

As a consequence of the fundamental difficulty of the coordination problem, it is inevitable that any mechanism, including the Invisible Hand of the price mechanism, supplemented by the Visible Hand of entrepreneurs and of bureaucrats, cannot find the efficient economic system. Each society, whatever mechanism is used, has evolved into a particular economic system and adopted a particular combination of activities, which are at best locally optimal.

Figure 5.2 schematically illustrates this view of the world. The horizontal axis represents the space of all possible combination of activities, or all possible economic systems. The dimensionality of this space indeed is a very big one (it is an M-dimensional lattice, where M is the number of all potential activities), although it has to be shrunk down to one dimension here. The graph represents the performance of economic systems. The rugged nature of the graph captures the inherent complementarity of activities in each system; the performance of an economy can change drastically by a small change in the selection of activities. (Building only one barrier along a route can turn it into a driver's nightmare.) There are a large number of locally optimal systems, and each society has evolved into one of them. There is no way for a society to search in a systematic way for the global optimum or for other local optima that are more efficient. And a

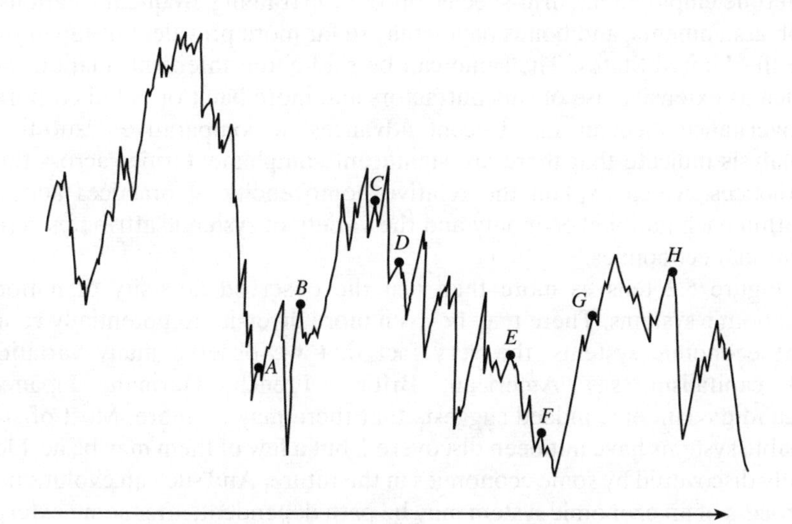

FIG. 5.2 The Complex Nature of Coordination Problems
Note: The horizontal axis represents the space of all possible economic systems, and the graph represents their performance levels.

series of accidents, such as coordination efforts of entrepreneurs and of the government, pushes society out of one local optimum to another. As an illustration of the economics of coordination failures in the context of economic development, Figure 5.2 has several advantages relative to the simple coordination game given in Figure 5.1.

For example, it does not give the impression that developed countries have already succeeded in solving coordination problems and that developing countries fail in coordination completely. Instead, it shows that even the most advanced economies fail in coordination, and even the least developed economies have achieved a certain degree of coordination. What differentiates the rich from the poor is simply a matter of degree; the former have been relatively more successful in coordination than the latter. In this sense, all countries are still developing.[11] This helps us understand why it is so difficult to find empirically any systematic relation between the growth performance of the economies and their initial levels of development.

Figure 5.2 also implies that, even after one controls for the stages of economic development, there may be a great variety in the manner in which different economies cope with the coordination problem. This is a direct consequence of the prevalence of coordination failures; there is only one way of being perfect, but there are millions of ways of being imperfect. This helps us to understand large systemic differences across national economies, in financial markets, in labor markets, as well as in the organization of industry. For example, it has been pointed out that some human resource management practices, such as the seniority system, the corporate union, lifetime employment, firm-specific on-the-job training, frequent rotations in job assignments, and bonus payments are far more prevalent in Japan than in the United States. The same can be said about interfirm relationships, such as extensive use of subcontractors and more bank-oriented corporate governance mechanisms. Recent advances in comparative institutional analysis indicate that there are significant complementarities across these practices, which explain the relative homogeneity of practices adopted within each national economy and the variety of systemic attributes across national economies.[12]

Figure 5.2 tells us more than just the observed diversity of national economic systems. There may be even more diversity to potentially coherent economic systems; the very fact that we observe many variations of capitalism, say American, British, French, German, Japanese, Scandinavian, etc., indeed suggests that there may be more. Most of such viable systems have not been discovered, but a few of them may be accidentally discovered by some economies in the future. And such an evolutionary process of an economic system may be path dependent; after some external shocks, an economy may experience fundamental structural changes, develop a new system, and never return to the original one. For example, an increasingly large number of historical studies show that the Japanese economy before World War II was fundamentally similar in character to the West European and American economies; many of the practices mentioned above, often viewed as uniquely and culturally Japanese, became widespread only after World War II, and their origins can be traced back to a variety of attempts by the government as well as by the private sector to secure access to critical supplies during the turbulent periods of wartime planning and postwar recovery (see Nakamura 1989 and Okazaki 1994).

One can also read many implications from the rugged nature of the graph in Figure 5.2. For example, combining two economic systems does not make a new, coherent system. Because of the fundamental complementarity of a system, one cannot simply pick and choose different parts from different systems without sacrificing their effectiveness. The ruggedness is also highly suggestive of the sensitivity of an economic system, as a small shift of the graph can be shown to have a big effect on performance. Not only may the effectiveness of an economic system be greatly undermined by small errors in selection of activities; it is also highly sensitive to the environment in which the system is applied. These properties of the complementarity all indicate the difficulty of adopting any system that has proved to be successful in other economies, and help us understand why an attempt to transplant foreign technologies or practices to underdeveloped economies often meets with disaster.

The economics of coordination failures is widely interpreted as a call for policy activism. But the view of the world expressed above, and portrayed in Figure 5.2, suggests a more prudent approach. Because of the prevalence of coordination failures, it is not surprising to find some cases where government policies played an important role in improving the way we coordinate our economic activities. Of course, this does not mean the government knew how to improve coordination and to design a new system. Rather, it could have been that the disturbances created by the government had forced the private agents to come up with and experiment with a new way of conducting their businesses and, as a result, they happened to discover a better system. For example, one may be able to point out with the benefit of hindsight that many policies adopted by the Japanese government during World War II turned out to be critical in the evolution of the postwar Japanese economic system. Yet it is clear that these policies were adopted as a part of the war effort, not as part of any grand design to rebuild the postwar Japanese economy. It was what Aoki (in his chapter (8) in this volume) calls "Unintended Fit." Going back to one of the earlier metaphors, imagine that for traveling between two locations in a maze, people have been using a particular route, a meandering one but the quickest among the routes known to them. If somebody builds a wall across this route, they are forced to try alternatives and may very well end up discovering a shortcut. Does this mean we should build another wall? Of course not.

Even if one can establish, as convincingly as Okazaki's study (Chapter 4 in this volume) on postwar Japan and Rodrik's study (1994) on Korea and Taiwan, that government policies sometimes appear to have succeeded in coordination in an intended way, it does not follow that the government was essential in achieving coordination in such instances. Private initiatives could have achieved the same, or even better, results.[13] Furthermore, the sensitive dependence of a solution to the specific nature of the coordination problem raises the question of replicability. Each industry, each region, each country is unique in its own way. Without detailed knowledge of the environment, the effects of policy interventions are extremely difficult to predict, and even small differences in the environment, or small errors in designing policy packages, can render the policy ineffective. In the worst case, such a policy mistake could lead to a major disaster by undermining the entire system.

The very diversity of the manners in which different developed economies cope with coordination also imposes a problem for underdeveloped economies if they try to learn from the experiences of more successful economies. They cannot pick and choose different parts from different systems, because of the complementarity inherent in any system. They somehow need to decide from whom to learn. In the context of transition from the communist regime in Central and Eastern Europe, there is an ongoing debate concerning the choice of a corporate governance mechanism, whether it should be based on the Anglo-American system, which relies heavily on the stock market, or on the French-German-Japanese system, where banks play more significant roles. We can no doubt gain many insights from the debate, but it is unlikely that any consensus could ever be reached in time on what to do about, say, the financial system of Lithuania.

Even if we could decide which system to adopt among all the systems currently known, and then replicate the system completely, it is not at all clear whether this is a desirable thing to do. If the view of the world portrayed in Figure 5.2 is correct, even the most developed economies fail in coordination. All the systems the human society has developed constitute a very small subset of all the potentially coherent systems, many of which would perform much better. The very attempt to replicate the best-known system, if successful, would lead to more uniformity, thereby reducing the possibility that some economies may accidentally discover a new and better system. This point is illustrated in Figure 5.2, where an economy sitting at A performs more poorly than others, and yet this economy has a better chance than other economies of discovering a new system, which could be far better than any existing system.

This is the most fundamental paradox of the coordination problem. Any conscious effort to coordinate a certain set of activities would pose the greatest danger of interfering with our attempt to discover an even better way of coordination, particularly when the effort has succeeded. More generally, this is the critical trade-off that the human being, not being omniscient, has to face in the quest for better knowledge; the dissemination of knowledge leads to a uniformity in our thinking, which hinders the creation of new knowledge. When the World Bank sponsors an interdisciplinary forum like the one for which this chapter was written, inviting scholars from many different fields, it gives us a great opportunity to exchange our ideas and may enrich our understanding of the real world. But if an attempt to reach a consensus has any effect of making us all think alike, such exchanges of ideas would impede the creation of new and possibly better ideas. Similarly, we may miss the great chance of discovering a new economic system, when a group of economists visits developing economies or former communist countries and tries to "educate"—or "indoctrinate" if you prefer—them on how to conduct their businesses.

This seems to be the most important case against a collective approach to coordination problems, the virtue of keeping diversity in coping with uncertainty.[14] Admittedly, the coercive power of the state is useful if it is easy to figure out what should be done, so that coordination failures are caused solely by the inability of the private agents to move in harmony. Very few people deny that the government can play a critical role in establishing and enforcing standards of measurement, traffic rules, property rights, etc.[15] But the sources of coordination failures in economic development are more likely to come from the difficulties of finding out, or reaching any agreement on, what ought to be done and which activities should be coordinated. Precisely because of its coercive power, government-led coordination limits diversity and experimentation, which reduces the chance that society continues to discover a better coordination.

Economic development is an eternal process of innovation, in which economies make progress as they discover a better combination of activities, or a better system of coordination. The discovery of any new system, by its nature, cannot be designed nor even anticipated; all we can do is to design a better search mechanism or discovery procedure. But an attempt to write down such a procedure itself has the danger of conditioning us into certain prescribed patterns of thinking, with stifling effects on innovation. And nothing can be more dangerous than an attempt to design such a mechanism in a collective way, and to put an economy into the straitjacket of a bureaucratic framework, as any attempts to organize, categorize, and even classify search efforts would restrict the directions of search, and slow down the pace of innovations. Indeed, any major innovation, by its nature, inevitably cuts across any existing categories; as we know, any industry or job classification designed by government bureaucrats can quickly become outdated in a fast-growing economy.

Going back to the problem of finding a quicker route in a maze, imagine that we can build a robot and program a particular search algorithm. There is good chance we can continuously come up with shortcuts if we endlessly build new robots, each given a new algorithm, and let them search. But any single robot, sooner or later, will get trapped in a blind alley and stop discovering shortcuts, no matter how sophisticated its algorithm is.

5.5 CONCLUDING REMARKS

The economics of coordination failures argues that coordination failures are everywhere—they are so pervasive that we can always find room for improvement—and that it is therefore important to encourage coordination experiments. The economics of coordination failures does not argue that such an experiment has to be conducted from above (i.e., the government); a better coordination can, and is more likely to, come from below (i.e., the private sector) by means of innovations. After all, Toyota Motors has improved productivity by introducing a new way of coordinating its subcontractors, and many developers have succeeded in capitalizing on complementarities across firms and shops by means of industrial parks and shopping malls. An attempt to coordinate from above, while effective in enforcing a particular coordination mechanism, would inevitably restrict such coordination experiments from below and make it difficult to achieve sustainable improvement in coordination.

The logic of coordination failure does not justify policy activism, any greater role of the government in coordination. However, the argument presented above should not be viewed as a case for a smaller government, either. After all, the prevalence of coordination failures suggests the importance of coordination experiments; there should also be experiments in centralized allocation mechanisms, *as long as such centralization experiments are done in a decentralized way*. The free enterprise system can be viewed as one way of encouraging such experiments, where new methods of centralized coordination are tested within independent enterprises. Likewise, it could be argued that the government in each regional, or even national, economy should be allowed to pursue experiments in its roles of coordination.[16] If no economy has succeeded, as I have argued, in coming even close to the discovery of the ideal economic system, then such experiments, by creating and maintaining the diversity of economic systems, are valuable for discovering better systems. It is thus essential to maintain the political autonomy in which each economy has the freedom to experiment with a new economic system. This is indeed a familiar theme in the writings of economic history. Great mercantile expansions in the Mediterranean, as Hicks (1969) points out, were associated with a system of city-states and their political autonomy. Many historians who ask why Western Europe became the first region in the world to industrialize, most notably Jones (1981) and Rosenberg and Birdzell (1986), attribute the "Rise of the West" to its political fragmentation. As Eric Jones (1981:124) argued, "The multi-cell system possessed a built-in ability to replace its local losses . . . and was more than the sum of its parts." From this point of view, advocating "level playing fields" is misplaced and can be counterproductive, if it means that the organization of society, including its business relations as well the public policies regulating them, should be everywhere alike, as American public rhetoric usually means, even when the intention is to reduce restrictive practices by foreign governments.[17]

At the same time, any example of successful government intervention in coordination, even when it is convincingly demonstrated, should not be interpreted that other governments should intervene in the same way. According to the logic of coordination failures, as I have been trying to explain, it is not surprising that many such examples can be found, and yet they are extremely difficult to replicate. Instead, such an example, or rather the abundance of such examples, should be interpreted as evidence that we are far from having discovered the ideal mechanism, that there is still plenty of room for improvement, that another coordination experiment has succeeded, and hence it is important to encourage further experiments.

Recently, an increasingly large number of works have attempted to look at the experiences of the Japanese economy from new perspectives. The older literature, with its neoclassical perspective, tended to portray Japanese business organizations and practices as signs of backwardness, destined to fade away as the Japanese economy developed. The new literature, exemplified by Aoki (1988), Komiya, Okuno, and Suzumura (1988), Teranishi and Kosai (1993), Aoki and Dore (1994), and Aoki and Patrick (1994), tries to understand the logic, or the internal consistency, of the Japanese economic system. In my view, these studies are important, not because they demonstrate that the Japanese version of capitalism may offer a better role model for developing and transforming economies than the American version of capitalism (as argued by some, but not all, of these authors), but because they keep reminding us that the American system is not the sole model for capitalism. After all, the success of capitalism depends not so much on a particular set of institutions as on its ability to maintain an environment that encourages open experimentation, by preserving the freedom to form new institutions and letting existing institutions be constantly replaced by those that are more successful. Likewise, the papers presented at the conference from which this volume originates, many of which offer interesting case studies of rapidly growing economies in East Asia, are useful, not because they suggest the birth of a "New Asian Paradigm," but rather because they demonstrate the enormous diversity in which different societies deal with the organization of their economies. And the diversity, just like the freedom to pursue something new, is essential for generating sustainable economic progress.

APPENDIX

To understand the inherent difficulty of coordination problems in the presence of complementary activities, let us consider the following example.

There is one final consumption good, and one type of primary source, whose total supply is given by L. Let us call it labor. There are three activities: 1, 2, and 3. Activity 1 transforms c_1 units of labor into one unit of the consumption good. Activity 2 transforms c_2 units of labor into one unit of an intermediate good, which itself has no consumption value. Activity 3 transforms one unit of the intermediate good into one unit of the consumption good by using c_3 units of labor. Figure 5A.1 represents the structure of this economy. Note that this economy can choose between two alternative systems, or two alternative routes from S to F. The first system, $X = \{1\}$, uses Activity 1 only, while the other, $Y = \{2,3\}$, uses the complementary activities, 2 and 3. The optimal allocation can be defined as the solution to the following optimization problem: Choose z_1, z_2, $z_3 \geq 0$, to maximize:

$$U = z_1 + \mathrm{Min}\{z_2, z_3\}, \qquad \text{s.t.} \qquad c_1 z_1 + c_2 z_2 + c_3 z_3 \leq L.$$

It is easy to see that, if $c_1 \leq c_2 + c_3$, the solution is $z_1 = L/c_1$, $z_2 = z_3 = 0$, hence $X = \{1\}$ is the efficient economic system. If $c_1 \geq c_2 + c_3$, then $Y = \{2,3\}$ is the efficient economic system. Our question is whether the agents living in this environment, which of course include the government, can discover the efficient economic system.

The standard neoclassical theory argues that they can solve this problem by making use of the price mechanism. All they have to do is to appoint an auctioneer and let him quote the prices and adjust them until the equilib-

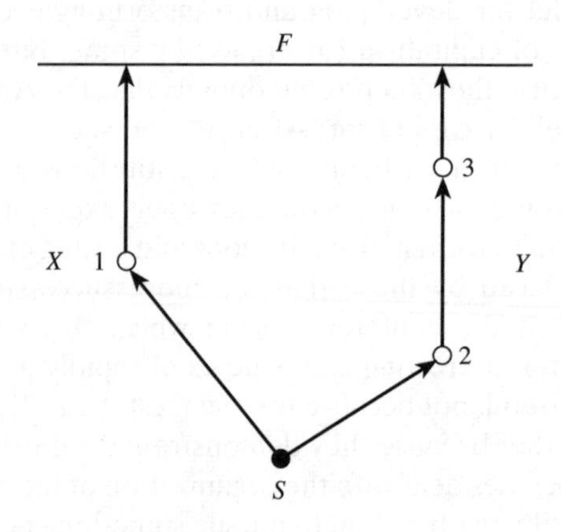

FIG. 5A.1 An Economy with Three Activities

rium prices are found. Taking labor as the numeraire, the auctioneer publicly quotes a price vector (P_1, P_2, P_3). Then, there is positive demand for 2 and 3 if and only if $P_1 \quad P_2 + P_3$, and the agents who have access to Activity J are willing to perform it if and only if $P_J \quad C_J$. Thus, Y is adopted in equilibrium if and only if the equilibrium price vector satisfies $P_1 \quad P_2 + P_3$, P_1 £ C_1, $P_2 \quad C_2$, and $P_3 \quad C_3$. It is easy to check that this occurs if and only if $C_1 \quad C_2 + C_3$; that is, Y is adopted if and only if it is the efficient system. The price mechanism hence can help the economy discover the efficient system.

The trouble with this approach is that it assumes the existence of a market for all three activities. One cannot defend this assumption by saying that the government, or any other agent living in this environment, can design a complete system of markets, as that would assume a significant amount of objective knowledge on the part of the designer. In particular, it assumes that the designer of the system of markets already knows in advance that Figure 5A.1 represents the true structure of the economy, and hence the three activities are only potential activities in this economy. To put it another way, neoclassical theory is not a theory of market formations, but rather a theory of market prices under the assumed existence of markets.

To see whether there is any tendency for the efficient system of markets to develop, suppose that there is a small cost of keeping an open market for any activity, and the government sequentially experiments in a new system of markets, by adding one market to the set of existing markets or by dropping one market from it. Figure 5A.2 illustrates such a search process. With three activities, there are $2^3 = 8$ possible market systems, represented

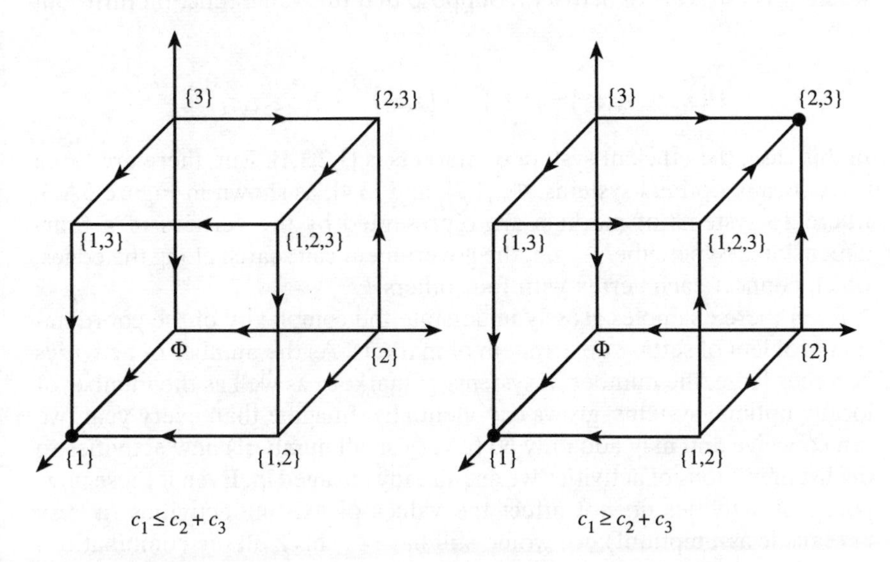

FIG. 5A.2 Search Processes in an Economy with Three Activities

by eight vertices of the unit cube. The government can search only along the edges of the cube. (Note that each vertex is connected to three others, which means that, from any system of markets, the government can experiment with three alternative systems; it can either add a market that does not exist, or drop a market that exists.) Arrows represent the direction of increasing efficiency. For example, suppose that, initially, only the market for Activity 1 exists, {1}, and the government experiments by setting up the market for Activity 2, {1,2}. Then, for any price vector (p_1,p_2), demand for Activity 2 is equal to zero, and the government shuts down the market for 2. Similarly, the government does not see any need for the market for Activity 3.

If $c_1 \leq c_2 + c_3$, the case shown in the left, $X = \{1\}$ is the efficient system and having only the market for 1 open is optimal, and this search process can find it, no matter where the search begins. On the other hand, if $c_1 \geq c_2 + c_3$, the case shown in the right, there are two local optima, $X = \{1\}$ and $Y = \{2,3\}$, of which Y is the efficient system. But the search process may choose system X instead. For example, if the search begins from the origin, Φ, the state in which there is no market, Y cannot be found. In order to discover the efficient system, one needs to coordinate setting up the two markets simultaneously. This example also suggests that the discovery of a sophisticated system may be stalled by the discovery of a less sophisticated one, where the sophistication can be measured by the number of activities involved.

Here is a slightly more complicated example. There are four activities, and $2^4 = 16$ possible market systems. The unit cost of Activity i, measured in labor unit is c_i, and the value of these activities is given by $U(z_1, z_2, z_3, z_4)$, where z_i is the scale of activity i. Suppose that this value function turns out to be:

$$U(z_1, z_2, z_3, z_4) = (z_1 z_2)^{1/2} + (z_3 z_4)^{1/2} + 2(z_1 z_2 z_3 z_4)^{1/4}.$$

In this case, the efficient system of markets is {1,2,3,4}. But, there are three more locally optimal systems, Φ, {1,2}, and {3,4}, as shown in Figure 5A.3, where 16 systems of markets are represented by the vertices of a four-dimensional hypercube. Again, the government can search along the edges, which connect each vertex with four others.[18]

Even these examples grossly understate the complexity of the coordination problem of setting up a system of markets. As the number of activities becomes large, the number of systems of markets, as well as the number of locally optimal systems, grows exponentially. Imagine that, every year, we can conceive and may add only 60 (a very small number!) new activities to the list of millions of activities we are already engaged in. Even if these new, potential activities do not affect the values of existing activities (a very unrealistic assumption!), we would still have to check all the combinations of the 60 activities in order to discover the optimal set of new activities. But

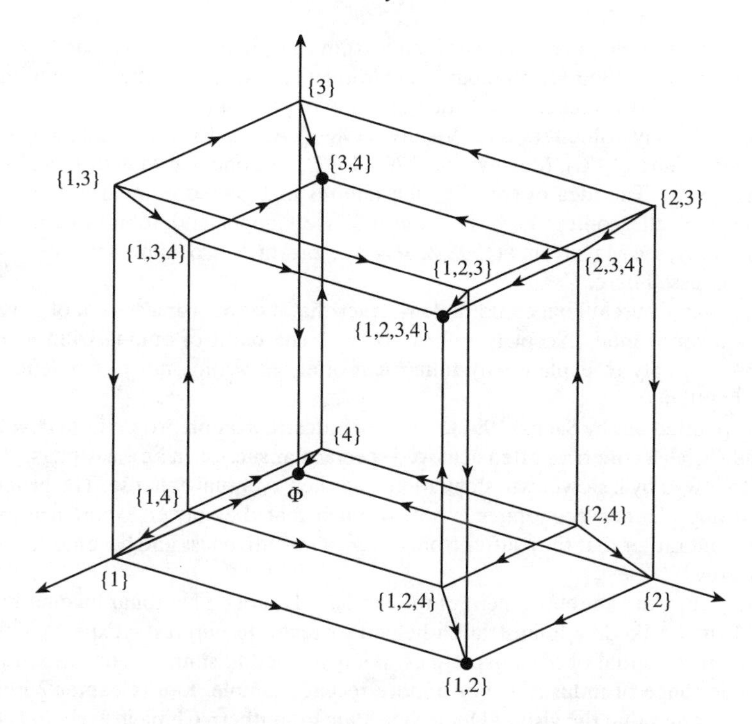

FIG. 5A.3 Search Processes in an Economy with Four Activities

this would mean that, even if we could check the performance of each combination every second, we would need 2^{60} seconds, that is, more than 10 billion years, about the age of our universe. This simple calculation suggests the inadequacy of any coordination mechanism, including the price mechanism, and the prevalence of coordination failures.

NOTES

I have benefited from discussions with the participants of the World Bank/Economic Development Institute Project on Roles of Government in Promoting Economic Development and System Change. I would like to extend my special thanks to the formal discussants, P. Krugman, K. Murdock, and Y. Qian, and to the organizer, M. Aoki, for inviting me to write this chapter. R. Lucas, J. Mokyr, and C. Udry have also given me useful comments on earlier versions.

[1] See Lucas (1988, 1993), Romer (1986, 1990), Grossman and Helpman (1992), and many others. Of course, not everyone would agree. Barro and Sala-i-Martin

(1995), for example, stress the continuity from the previous growth literature by focusing on, using their terminology, "conditional" convergence; they seem to think that "absolute" divergence is outside the scope of growth theory.

[2] See Murphy, Shleifer, and Vishny (1989), Azariadis and Drazen (1990), Rodriguez-Clare (1993), Matsuyama (1991, 1992), Ciccone and Matsuyama (1992), Rodrik (1993). The idea of coordination failures first gained popularity in macroeconomics in the context of business cycles; see Cooper and John (1988). For a broad survey, see Matsuyama (1995a), Section 5 of which also addresses some of the issues discussed here.

[3] Winston Churchill once said of democracy that it is the worst system of government known to man, except for all the others. The point of emphasizing market failures is simply to explain why things can often go wrong, not to condemn the market system.

[4] As pointed out by Sachs (1994), state-led industrialization programs in developing and socialist countries often achieved spectacular success in an early phase, only to be followed by a slowdown, stagnation, and then eventual collapse. The problem of centrally planned economies is not so much that they never experience rapid growth, but rather that they suffer from a lack of inventiveness and become "prematurely grey."

[5] Arguably, the announcement of the famous "Doubling National Income Plan" in 1961 by the Ikeda administration helped to generate optimistic expectations of the growth potential of the Japanese economy and led to simultaneous expansions of a wide range of industries. For a more recent example, Lau (Chapter 2 in this volume) argues that the visit of Deng Xiao-Ping to southern China in early 1992 had the effect of coordinating optimistic expectations. "The announcement of his visit to the public almost three months afterward stimulated an economic boom that continues even today."

[6] The history of financial markets is rich with examples, where the official use of "cheap talk" to build market confidence ended up precipitating crises. Indeed, there was a joke, during the Bretton Woods era, that the public assurance by a finance minister that there will be no devaluation is the best signal of an imminent devaluation.

[7] I should mention that there are several important strands of literature that attempt to move away from this dominant approach. In game theory, there is already a large literature on "evolutive" or learning models of games. See also the recent paper by Kalai and Lehrer (1995) on subjective games, which allow discrepancies between the true structure of the model and the players' perception of it. In macroeconomics, there is the bounded rationality literature, surveyed by Sargent (1993). However, it seems fair to say that these studies have not yet made much impact on policy analysis.

[8] Some readers may object to the fuzziness of my definition of "activity," but this is intentional, because my main concern is to describe a process of system change. An activity, which is performed only as a "task" in a production line under one economic system, can be a "service" readily available in the marketplace under another. I have chosen to use "activity" instead of other terms, as it is most generic in meaning. Indeed, coordination of a certain range of activities itself could be another "activity." I deliberately use this term in a fuzzy way, so that it will not be interpreted in any concrete fashion that assumes a particular form of economic,

political, and social organization. For the same reason, I also make frequent use of "agents." Unlike "consumers," "producers," or "workers," this generic term does not assume a particular pattern of the division of labor prevailing in an economy. "An agent" could also mean all sorts of actors, not only an individual, but also a group of individuals, such as teams, firms, committees, unions, etc.

[9] One minor disadvantage of this metaphor is that all activities in a particular system have to be perfectly complementary to one another. This, of course, helps to simplify the discussion below, but the conclusion does not require perfect complementarity across activities.

[10] This statement is true almost by definition, as I would define "an entrepreneur" as an agent who designs and experiments with a new organization in order to facilitate coordination, and "a manager" and "a bureaucrat" as those who conduct day-to-day coordination within a given organizational framework.

[11] Future archaeologists will surely find the way we organize our society, even in the most advanced one, very primitive relative to theirs, just as we find the organization of the Roman Empire very primitive relative to ours.

[12] See Aoki and Dore (1994) for a most assertive statement of this view.

[13] Okazaki's study stresses the role of government councils in facilitating coordination between shipbuilding and steel industries. But one can also point to the story of Eiichi Shibusawa, a private entrepreneur, who achieved coordination between the cotton-textile and ocean-shipping industries in Japan during the Meiji period (1868–1912).

[14] One may wonder why the diversity in national economic systems can be of any use if you cannot, or should not, replicate the successful experiences of others. At least two reasons may be given. First, the example of others can give you a starting point for a new search: you can learn a lot from your own failure at replicating the successes of others. So, you may want to try replicating others experimentally, even if you don't want to replicate them completely. Second, observing the successes of others makes you aware that you may not be doing as well as you could, which helps to inspire a search for better alternatives. Major innovations in organizations tend to occur only after the current system has become demonstrably inferior to others, as military history amply illustrates (McNeill 1983).

[15] It is worth pointing out another important feature of coordination problems that makes the government better suited than private agents in solving them. For certain cases, even a small degree of noncompliance can greatly undermine the effectiveness of a coordination mechanism. We feel safe to cross intersections with green lights, because we are confident that nearly everyone agrees that "green" means "go" and "red" means "stop." We would not feel safe if we suspected that even 1 per cent of the population might not know the traffic rule. In such a case, the government's enforcement is effective in achieving coordination by making compliance almost universal. The same argument could be made to justify government-led coordination in defense against external attacks and in rescue operations after disasters. The argument may even be extended to support other coordination roles of the government, such as establishing and maintaining standards of measurement, judicial systems, or even monetary systems (mainly through its certification activities such as coinage). However, many of the coordination problems discussed in the economic development literature do not have this feature.

[16] Montinola, Qian, and Weingast (1994) and Qian and Weingast (Chapter 9 in

this volume), argue that the key to understanding recent economic success in China, where, unlike former communist countries in Eastern Europe, political freedom of individuals is still suppressed, is the greater autonomy of local governments, "Federalism, Chinese Style," which leads to more experimentation by local authorities.

[17] Mokyr (1992:21), in his 1990 Davidson Lecture, argues that "pluralism, diversity, and openness to foreign influences are almost always important elements in technological creativity. If different societies follow divergent technological paths, it will always be possible to follow the one that turns out to be the most successful [and] from this point of view the breaking up of the Soviet Union may be good news, whereas the proposed European unification of 1992 may have unexpected long-term negative consequences."

[18] Matsuyama (1995b) discusses in more detail the fundamental complexity of market formation problems. The examples presented there are indeed more subtle in that, unlike in the examples presented here, every activity is of some economic value even when used in isolation, and yet complementarities across activities arise through general equilibrium interactions.

REFERENCES

AOKI, M. (1988), *Information, Incentives and Bargaining in the Japanese Economy*, Cambridge University Press, Cambridge.

——and DORE, R., eds. (1994), *The Japanese Firm: Sources of Competitive Strength*, Oxford University Press, Oxford.

——and PATRICK, H., eds. (1994), *The Japanese Main Bank System: Its Relevance for Developing and Transforming Economies*, Oxford University Press, Oxford.

AZARIADIS, C., and DRAZEN, A. (1990), "Threshold Externalities in Economic Development," *Quarterly Journal of Economics*, 105:501–26.

BARRO, R. J. and SALA-I-MARTIN, X. (1995), *Economic Growth*, Prentice-Hall, New York.

CICCONE, A. and MATSUYAMA, K. (1992), "Start-up Costs and Pecuniary Externalities as Barriers to Economic Development," Working Papers in Economics, E-92-14, Hoover Institution, Stanford University.

COASE, R. H. (1988), *The Firm, the Market, and the Law*, University of Chicago Press, Chicago.

COOPER, R. and JOHN, A. (1988), "Coordinating Coordination Failures in Keynesian Models," *Quarterly Journal of Economics*, 103:441–63.

GROSSMAN, G. and HELPMAN, E. (1992), *Innovation and Growth in the Global Economy*, MIT Press, Cambridge, Mass.

HAYEK, F. (1945), "The Use of Knowledge in Society," *American Economic Review*, 35:519–30.

——(1974), "The Pretence of Knowledge," Nobel Memorial Lecture.

HICKS, J. (1969), *A Theory of Economic History*, Oxford University Press, Oxford.

HIRSCHMAN, A. O. (1957), *The Strategy of Economic Development*, Yale University Press, New Haven.

JONES, E. L. (1981), *The European Miracle: Environments, Economies, and Geopolitics in the History of Europe and Asia*, Cambridge University Press, Cambridge.

KALAI, E. and LEHRER, E. (1995), "Subjective Games and Equilibria," *Games and Economic Behavior*, 8:123–63.

KOMIYA, R., OKUNO, M., and SUZUMURA, K. (1988), *Industrial Policy of Japan*, Academic Press, New York.

LUCAS, R. E., JR. (1988), "On the Mechanics of Economic Development," *Journal of Monetary Economics*, 22:3–42.

——(1993), "Making a Miracle," *Econometrica*, 61:251–72.

MCNEILL, W. (1983), *The Pursuit of Power: Technologies, Armed Forces and Society since 1000 AD*, University of Chicago Press, Chicago.

MATSUYAMA, K. (1991), "Increasing Returns, Industrialization, and Indeterminacy of Equilibria," *Quarterly Journal of Economics*, 106:617–50.

——(1992), "The Market Size, Entrepreneurship, and the Big Push," *Journal of the Japanese and International Economies*, 6:347–64.

——(1995a), "Complementarities and Cumulative Processes in the Models of Monopolistic Competition," *Journal of Economic Literature*, 33.

——(1995b), "New Goods, Market Formations, and Pitfalls of System Design," Paper presented at TCER-NBER-CEPR Trilateral Conference on Transition from Socialist Economies, Tokyo, Japan, January 6 and 7.

MOKYR, J. (1992), "Is Economic Change Optimal?" *Australian Economic History Review*, 32:3–23.

MONTINOLA, G., QIAN, Y., and WEINGAST, B. R. (1994), "Federalism, Chinese Style: The Political Basis for Economic Success in China," unpublished manuscript, Hoover Institution, Stanford University.

MURPHY, K., SHLEIFER, A., and VISHNY, R. (1989), "Industrialization and the Big Push," *Journal of Political Economy*, 97:1003–26.

MYRDAL, G. (1957), *Economic Theory and Under-developed Regions*, Duckworth, London.

NAKAMURA, T. (1989), "Gaisetsu: 1937–1954" (Overview: 1937–1954), in T. Nakamura, ed., *"Keikakuka" to "minshuka"* ("Planification" and "democratization"), vol. 2 of *Nihon Keizaishi* (Japanese economic history), Iwanami Shoten, Tokyo.

NURKSE, R. (1953), *Problems of Capital Formation in Underdeveloped Countries*, Oxford University Press, New York.

OKAZAKI, T. (1994), "The Japanese Firm during the Wartime Planned Economy," in M. Aoki and R. Dore, eds., *The Japanese Firm: Sources of Competitive Strength*, Oxford University Press, Oxford.

RODRIGUEZ-CLARE, A. (1993), "Underdevelopment: A Trap with an Exit," unpublished manuscript, Stanford University.

RODRIK, D. (1993), "Coordination Failures and Government Policy in Intermediate Economies: A Model with Applications to East Asia and Eastern Europe," unpublished manuscript.

——(1994), "Getting Interventions Right: How South Korea and Taiwan Grew Rich," NBER Working Paper No. 4964.

ROMER, P. M. (1986), "Increasing Returns and Long Run Growth," *Journal of Political Economy*, 94:1002–37.

Romer, P. M. (1990), "Endogenous Technological Change," *Journal of Political Economy*, 98: S71–S102.

Rosenberg, N. and Birdzell, L. E., Jr. (1986), *How the West Grew Rich*, Basic Books, New York.

Rosenstein-Rodan, P. N. (1943), "Problems of Industralization of Eastern and South-Eastern Europe," *Economic Journal*, 53:202–11.

Sachs, J. (1994), "Notes on Life-cycles and State-Led Industrialization," mimeo.

Sargent, T. J. (1993), *Bounded Rationality in Macroeconomics*, Oxford University Press, Oxford.

Scitovsky, T. (1954), "Two Concepts of External Economies," *Journal of Political Economy*, 62:143–51.

Teranishi, J. and Kosai, Y., eds. (1993), *The Japanese Experience of Economic Reforms*, St. Martin's Press, New York.

Young, A. A. (1928), "Increasing Returns and Economic Progress," *Economic Journal*, 38:527–42.

PART II

THE MARKET-ENHANCING VIEW

6

Financial Restraint: Toward a New Paradigm

THOMAS HELLMANN, KEVIN MURDOCK, AND JOSEPH STIGLITZ

6.1 INTRODUCTION

This chapter responds to the question of what governments can do to assist the development of the financial sector. While the neoclassical "*laissez-faire*" prescriptions have been challenged—in theory by the development of information economics, and in practice by the mostly disappointing results from financial liberalization—there is no consensus yet of what constitutes a good set of financial policies. The only point on which a consensus seems to exist is that financial policies matter. King and Levine (1993) identify financial depth as the most important explanatory variable in a large set of cross-country regressions.

In this chapter we propose some elements of financial policy that we believe form the core of a government strategy to promote financial deepening. These ideas are influenced by a stylized analysis of the policies pursued by a number of high-performing East Asian economies, and in particular by the Japanese postwar experience (cf. Aoki, Patrick, and Sheard 1994). The concepts are not, however, "culture specific." Rather, we believe they represent a normative analysis of more general validity.

The set of financial policies that we call "financial restraint" are aimed at the creation of rents in the financial and production sectors. For the purpose of this chapter, by rents we do not mean the income that accrues to an inelastically supplied factor of production; rather, we mean the returns in excess of those generated by a competitive market. The essence of financial restraint is that the government creates rent opportunities in the private sector through a set of financial policies. The government sets the deposit rate below the competitive equilibrium level. In order to preserve rents in the financial sector, it must regulate entry and sometimes direct competition. The control of deposit rates may be complemented by a set of controls on lending rates to different sectors. Such controls serve to affect the distribution of rents between the financial and production sectors. We argue in this chapter that rents in the financial and production sectors can play a positive role in reducing information-related problems that hamper perfectly competitive markets. In particular, these rents induce private-sector agents to increase the supply of goods and services that might be underprovided in a purely competitive market, such as the monitoring of investments or the provision of deposit collection. A number of preconditions must be met in order for financial restraint to operate effectively. The economy needs to have a stable macroeconomic environment, where inflation rates are low and predictable. Heavy taxation (whether direct or indirect) of the financial sector is incompatible with financial restraint, and, importantly, real interest rates must be positive.

We think of two broad categories of rent effects. First, giving rents to financial intermediaries and production firms will increase their own equity stakes and make these institutions behave in a more proprietary way. Second, we often think of rents not so much as the transfer of wealth, but as *opportunities* to create wealth. *Rent opportunities* thus link actions of agents to the receipt of the resources. We will focus on instances where the government creates rent opportunities that induce economically efficient actions that private markets would not undertake because of a divergence between private and social returns.

Financial restraint should be clearly differentiated from financial repression. Under a regime of financial repression, the government extracts rents from the private sector, whereas under financial restraint, the government acts to create rents *within* the private sector. See Figure 6.1. We can highlight the flow of rents under financial repression using a two-sector model of the economy—the private sector and the government, as shown in Figure 6.2a. The government extracts rents by holding nominal interest rates well below the rate of inflation. A model of financial restraint requires a four-sector model of the economy—households, financial intermediaries, pro-

Direct rent flow

Inflation	Extraction	Zero	Creation
High	Financial repression	"Southern cone" experiment*	
Low		Free markets	Financial restraint

FIG. 6.1 Rent Effects

* The government extracted rents from the financial sector indirectly through the inflation tax.

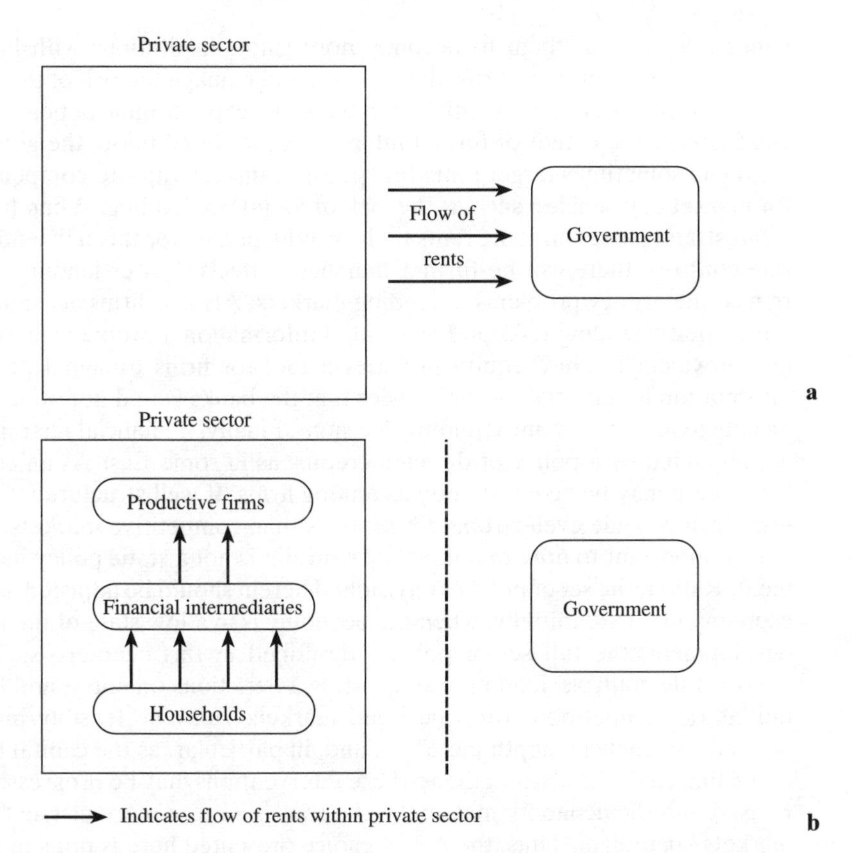

FIG. 6.2 The Flow of Rents under (a) Financial Repression and (b) Financial Restraint

duction firms, and the government, as shown in Figure 6.2b. Under financial restraint, no rents are extracted by the government. Rather, deposit-rate controls create rents that are captured by financial intermediaries and by firms (if additional lending-rate controls are applied as well).

Our chapter clearly relates to the large literature on financial development. While our analysis addresses the same fundamental issues raised by McKinnon (1973) and Shaw (1973), we reach somewhat different conclusions. We agree with McKinnon in warning against the government depriving the private sector of a positive real return on financial assets. We also share Shaw's view that improving the quality of financial intermediation is critical to increasing the efficiency of investment. Our analysis differs, however, from theirs in arguing that selective intervention—financial restraint—may help rather than hinder financial deepening.

Our analysis identifies a number of ways in which financial restraint can foster financial deepening. We argue that rents create "franchise value" for banks that induces them to become more stable institutions with better incentives to monitor the firms they finance and manage the risk of the loan portfolio. Rents create incentives for banks to expand their deposit base and increase the extent of formal intermediation. In addition, the government can sometimes target rents for specific bank activities to compensate for market deficiencies, such as the lack of long-term lending. When financial restraint passes on some rents to the production sector through lending-rate controls, there can be further beneficial effects. Lower lending rates reduce the agency problems in lending markets. Also, as firms accumulate more equity, lending risks and associated informational problems become less prevalent because equity provides a tool for firms to signal private information to financial intermediaries that the banks would not otherwise be able to incorporate into funding decisions. Finally, if financial restraint is accompanied by a policy of directed credits, as in some East Asian countries, there may be "contest" effects among firms. If well structured, "contests" can provide even stronger incentives than competitive markets.

It is important to note that financial restraint is not a static policy instrument. Rather, the set of policies envisioned herein should be adjusted as the economy matures. Initially, when the economy is in a low state of financial development, the full set of policies described in this chapter—such as deposit-rate controls, lending-rate controls, restrictions on entry, and limitations on competition from the bond markets—may be feasibly implemented. As financial depth increases, and, in particular, as the capital base of the financial sector strengthens, these interventions may be progressively relaxed and the economy may make the transition to a more classic "free markets" paradigm. Thus, the policy choice presented here is not simply a static contrast between *laissez-faire* and financial restraint, but a dynamic decision governing the order of financial market development.

The structure of this chapter is as follows. Section 6.2 introduces a simple demand-supply framework of the funds market and explains the basic mechanics of financial restraint. Section 6.3 explains the role of rent creation in the financial sector, discussing the franchise value and the deposit mobilization effects. Section 6.4 discusses the role of rents in the production sector, focusing on equity accumulation mechanisms. Section 6.5 discusses a model of credit rationing that allows us to consider some complications that arise from the implementation of lending-rate controls. Section 6.6 elaborates on directed credits as a tool of industrial policy. Section 6.7 finally touches on some of the governance issues that pertain to the policies proposed in this chapter. It is followed by a brief conclusion.

6.2 THE BASIC FRAMEWORK

We begin our discussion by introducing a simple demand-supply model of the market for loans. This will allow us to examine the effect of interest-rate controls as a mechanism for the creation of rents within the financial sector. In our view of the financial system, there are three sectors:[1] the household sector supplies funds, the corporate sector is a user of funds, and banks act as financial intermediaries.[2] Figure 6.3a shows market equilibrium at an interest rate *r* as the intersection of a household funds supply curve and a corporate funds demand curve.[3]

Note that if funds are lent to risky firms, then *r* represents the expected returns to the bank. The actual rate faced by firms would include an appropriate risk-premium. In Section 6.5 we focus further on the composition of loan demand. In this section and Section 6.3 we concentrate mainly on the supply.[4]

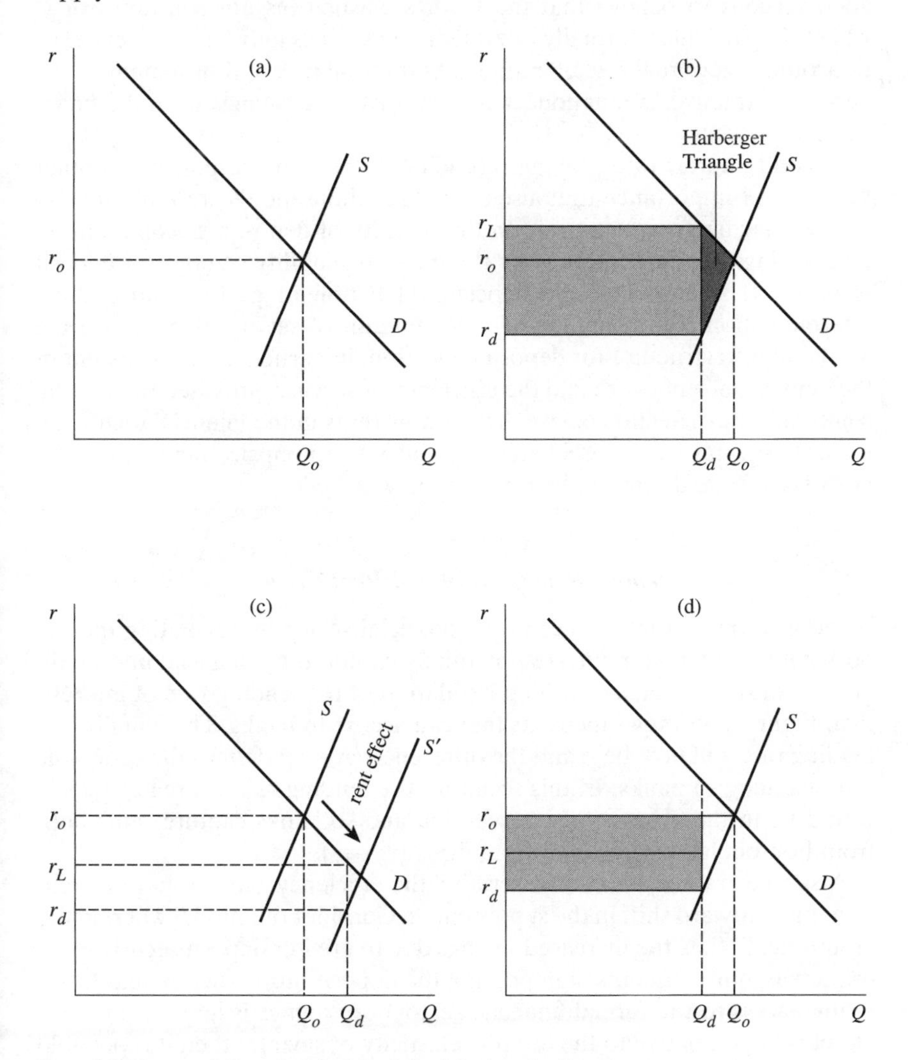

FIG. 6.3 Demand-Supply Model of the Market for Loans

Supply of Loans (Savings)

There has been a considerable debate about the interest-elasticity of savings. Theory cannot predict whether savings should increase or decrease with the interest rate, due to offsetting wealth and substitution effects. The empirical consensus is that national savings respond favorably to higher interest rates, but that this elasticity is very low (cf. Giovannini 1985).[5] As a consequence we draw steep supply curves in the figures (of Figure 6.3). It should be noted that financial savings will be more elastic than national savings (cf. Fry 1995). The government should be aware of the risks of asset substitution, an issue that we discuss in Section 6.3. Further, there are good reasons to believe that the savings elasticity is not constant everywhere. In particular, formally intermediated savings may become very elastic around a zero real rate of interest. At this real rate of return many assets become attractive as inflationary hedges, diverting savings from the financial sector.

Beyond interest rates, savings are likely to be more responsive to other variables of importance to households. First, households are typically risk averse, placing great emphasis on the security of deposits. Second, household savings depend crucially on the mere availability of efficient deposit facilities. It is here that the neoclassical fiction of perfect and costless intermediation is most unhelpful. The amount of savings depends on the available infrastructure for deposit collection, in particular on the extent of the bank branch network and the efficiency of services provided to the local communities. In Section 6.3 we discuss how rents in the financial sector can increase savings by precisely affecting these two nonprice factors, i.e., deposit security and intermediation efficiency.

Deposit Rate Control and Rent Creation

If the government intervenes in the financial sector by regulating the deposit rate of interest, rents are potentially captured by financial intermediaries.[6] Consider a regime with no regulation of the lending rate of interest; then Figure 6.3b shows the rents that can accrue to banks. The equilibrium lending rate will now be r_L and the difference $(r_L - r_d)$ defines the economic rent accruing to banks. In this scenario, the lending rate is greater than it would be in the absence of intervention and so banks capture rents both from households $(r_o - r_d)$ and from firms $(r_L - r_o)$.

A simple graphical way of describing the efficiency gains from rent creation is an outward shift in the supply curve. Consider our model wherein the "rent effect" (i.e., the increased savings due to greater deposit security and/or increased investments in improving the deposit infrastructure and facilitating access to the formal financial sector) on savings is large. If the rent effect is large relative to the interest-elasticity of savings, then it is possible that the total volume of funds intermediated through the formal financial sector is larger than would be available under "free markets." See Figure 6.3c. Now the "excess" demand for loans gives an equilibrium lending rate of r_L and banks capture rents of $r_L - r_d$. Interestingly, despite the rent capture by banks, firms are better off under financial restraint with the rent effect. They obtain a greater volume of loans at a lower rate of interest than they would under the Walrasian equilibrium ($Q_d > Q_0$ and $r_L < r_0$). We can find plausible parameters so that households are also in a more favorable situation under financial restraint because the rent effect, i.e., the greater security and the improved deposit infrastructure, dominates the interest-rate effect (cf. Hellmann, Murdock, and Stiglitz 1994a).

Lending Rate Control and Rent Allocation

Returning to the framework of Figure 6.3b, where the rent effect is assumed away, we can study the effect of a concurrent restriction on the lending rate. Assume that the government intervenes to determine both the deposit rate, r_d, and the lending rate, r_L. Rents clearly still accrue to banks ($r_L - r_d$), and they also accrue to firms if the fiat lending rate is less than the Walrasian interest rate ($r_L < r_o$). See Figure 6.3d. Moreover, if we allow for a sufficiently large rent effect such that the volume of savings is greater under financial restraint, there is no ambiguity—banks capture rents ($r_L - r_d$) and so do firms ($r_o - r_L$). See Figure 6.3c.

In this simplified demand-supply framework, the allocation of rents is simply a function of the fiat deposit and lending rates. In Section 6.5 we further refine the analysis of the distribution of rents by considering how lending rate controls affect the market equilibrium under credit rationing with multiple classes of borrowers.

The Role of Rents

It is important to distinguish the nature of the rents that we are considering in this analysis. The institutional arrangements that are responsible for how rents are created and captured have an important influence on their ultimate efficacy in promoting financial deepening. In particular, we need to distinguish between rent transfers and rent opportunities.

Rent transfers alter the distribution of income without directly altering the incentives of the parties competing for these transfers. Worse, agents may prefer to engage in influence activities aimed at garnering a disproportionate share of the rents rather than making productive investments. Rent opportunities, conversely, are contingent on the agent's action. If the rent opportunities provide an increased return to activities that are underprovided in a competitive equilibrium, then these rent opportunities are welfare enhancing. The policy objective of creating rent opportunities is then to provide appropriate incentives that can induce a market-based outcome to provide socially beneficial activities.

In the case of financial intermediaries, rent opportunities would include incentives to promote deposit mobilization—both in the breadth and the intensity of financial services—and to encourage efficient portfolio allocation and loan monitoring on the part of banks. In the absence of rent opportunities, however, private incentives may be too weak to provide the socially efficient level of financial services. Banks do not capture the full benefit of their services—depositors achieve higher, less volatile returns than are available through self-intermediation, and firms benefit from additional access to financing.[7] We demonstrate in this chapter how financial restraint creates the rent opportunities for banks that facilitate these goals.

The Optimal Level of Financial Restraint

Traditional welfare analysis emphasizes the Harberger Triangle, as depicted in Figure 6.3b. It should be noted that if financial savings are not very elastic, the welfare triangle is small. We argue that the welfare loss has to be traded off against the benefits of financial restraint. If there are agency costs or market failures, creating rents has direct benefits (by reducing the cost of intermediation) that can well outweigh the welfare loss. These welfare gains from rent creation can be depicted as an outward shift in the supply curve. What is important to note about this trade-off is that it suggests that a little financial restraint is good, but that as financial restraint becomes more severe, costs may outweigh the benefits. The welfare loss triangle increases monotonically for lower fiat deposit rates, while the benefits of rent creation may exhibit diminishing returns. Moreover, because of substitution into real assets, the elasticity of savings is likely to increase near-zero real rates of returns (cf. Section 6.3). This will significantly increase the welfare-loss triangle. As a consequence, we argue that while real rates of interest should be below the market-clearing rate, they should also remain positive.[8]

6.3 RENTS TO FINANCIAL INTERMEDIARIES

We emphasize two important roles of the creation of economic rents for financial intermediaries under a regime of financial restraint. First, by creating an ongoing flow of profits from the continuing operation of the bank, these rents create incentives for banks to operate as long-run agents (by creating a "franchise value" for the banks) so that they will work to monitor firms effectively and manage the risk of their portfolio of loans. Consequently, banks have incentives to insure that loans are allocated to their most efficient uses (cf. Bhattacharya 1982) and to monitor firms' use of those funds. Second, by increasing the returns to intermediation, banks have strong incentives to increase their own deposit bases. Banks will thus make investments to attract incremental deposits, for example, by opening new branches in previously unserved rural areas or by making other investments to bring new depositors to the formal financial system. Interestingly, the nature of rents necessary to provide these incentives is very different for these two effects. It is the *average rent* on the bank's entire portfolio that creates franchise value for the bank. Conversely, it is the *marginal rent* on incremental loans that induces banks to seek out additional deposits.

In this section we explain how financial restraint affects financial intermediation. We discuss the principal effects of deposit rate controls: "franchise value creation" and incentives for deposit collection. We also discuss a related policy of maturity transformation. We then discuss how two further policies, restrictions on competition and limiting asset substitution, are complementary policies to financial restraint.

Average Rents Create "Franchise Value" for Banks

One of the major problems of competitive financial systems is their lack of stability. Risk-averse households will only deposit their wealth with financial intermediaries if they have high levels of confidence that their funds will remain safe and that they can withdraw their funds at will. Also, firms require a constant presence of banks to finance their ongoing working-capital expenses. As firms and banks continue to transact with each other, they develop relation-specific capital that reduces agency costs of intermediation. Consequently, both improving the stability of the financial sector and creating incentives to develop higher-quality financial institutions are important goals for the government of a developing country.

Yet financial stability is not easily acquired. Recent discussions of financial instability, such as the S&L crisis in the United States, have highlighted moral hazard as a key contributing factor. If banks are poorly capitalized, they may have an incentive to "gamble on their resurrection" by taking on high and correlated risks (cf. Bhattacharya 1982, Rochet 1992).[9] Moreover, Akerlof and Romer (1993:2) show that when banks' own capital levels are low, managers may seek ways "to go broke for profit at society's expense." Managers find covert ways to siphon off the banks' resources (also called "looting"), and then deliberately allow the banks to go bankrupt. These actions may be initiated by the managers themselves, or by shareholders in a closely held firm.

A remedy to financial instability is to increase the capital base of financial intermediaries.[10] Caprio and Summers (1993) argue that banks should have a franchise value to protect. Only if the right to provide financial intermediation is of significant value will banks refrain from risking their charters by "gambling on resurrection" or "looting."[11] Financial restraint creates rent opportunities in the financial sector. These rents create franchise value that will induce banks to abstain from moral hazard, because banks have an ongoing interest to stay in business. An important aspect of franchise value is that it creates "long-run" equity that can not be appropriated in the short term or wiped out by an adverse macroeconomic shock. One result of Akerlof and Romer's (1993) analysis is that banks with positive net worth may choose to loot themselves if more funds can be extracted in the short term than the banks are worth as ongoing entities. When financial restraint creates a franchise value for a bank, most of its equity value is derived from its continued operation in the future. This equity thus cannot be extracted by the management. Consequently, franchise value creates commitment for the bank to act as a long-run agent.[12]

A neoclassical response to the above argument may be that if franchise value is beneficial, why doesn't the market create it by itself? In Hellmann, Murdock, and Stiglitz (1994b), we develop a formal model that analyzes a bank's incentives to gamble with its deposits. We show that under very plausible conditions, markets cannot create franchise value by themselves.[13] In these cases, deposit rate controls can be used to increase franchise value and prevent gambling.

Another response to the above is that capital requirements are the appropriate instrument to fight moral hazard in banking. In Hellmann, Murdock, and Stiglitz (1994b) we also compare deposit rate controls with capital requirements. We argue that deposit rate controls can be expected to be more effective than capital requirements, especially in the context of a developing economy. Both policies indeed can reduce the incentive to gamble. The difference is, however, that deposit rate controls create an environment where banks are given the opportunity to operate more profitably, and develop franchise value, whereas capital requirements coerce banks' portfolio choices to the point of making gambling unattractive. The economic costs of deposit rate controls are the lost savings due to lower deposit rates (which we argue would be typically small in the positive interest rate range), while the costs of capital requirements are that banks are forced to hold portfolios of government securities that typically yield lower returns than a private-market lending portfolio.[14] This lower rate of return on government bonds implies that the growth of the banking sector will be relatively slower than under deposit rate controls, where banks can accumulate equity faster. Also, fewer funds will be available to private loan markets, which can be particularly costly in developing countries, where private lending activity needs to be developed, rather than restricted.[15] Finally, we argue that deposit rate controls are much easier to monitor. Capital requirements are based on accounting measures of a bank's net worth, which are intrinsically hard to measure and thus susceptible to manipulation. Banks on the other hand don't want to circumvent deposit rate controls, unless they can attract substantial new deposits. But in order to attract new deposits, a bank's intention of paying higher deposit rates must become public knowledge, in which case regulators are likely to obtain this knowledge too.[16]

Moreover, governments may be tempted to augment the incentives of banks to refrain from moral hazard. The government can enforce hefty punishments for failing banks.[17] It is often argued that one of the problems is that the government is unable to commit to *not* rescuing failing banks. While the government may not be able to commit not to rescue the bank, it may well be able to punish management.

An interesting point to note is that financial restraint does not rely on the existence or absence of deposit insurance. Many analyses of financial market failures, such as the problems of looting and gambling on resurrection, suggest that they occur because depositors do not act as an effective monitor because their funds are insured. Looting and gambling on resurrection, however, can occur even in an environment without deposit insurance, where depositors are aware of the risk but do not take action either because the probability of it occurring is sufficiently small or the cost of effective monitoring is sufficiently large. Thus financial restraint may be beneficial even in the absence of deposit insurance. In the more realistic case of explicit (or implicit) deposit insurance, the moral hazard problems of banks become stronger and the role of depositors as monitors becomes weaker, so financial restraint becomes all the more necessary.

There is an important distinction to be made between the rents that are created through financial restraint and direct forms of subsidization. Under financial restraint, a bank may only capture rents as a consequence of its own effort—by attracting new deposits to loan in rent-generating sectors and by rigorous monitoring of its portfolio of loans to ensure maximum return on its investment. When direct subsidies are provided to financial intermediaries, perverse incentives may arise. For example, if the government rediscounts too many loans to priority sectors at a subsidized interest rate, the bank's incentives to seek out incremental sources of deposits may be weakened. The bank may view government rediscount loans as substitutes for deposits and it may be far easier to seek out a greater volume of loans from the government than to develop new branches for deposit collection.[18] Additionally, the government may provide implicit or explicit loan guarantees to these sectors. This will effectively reduce the bank's incentives to monitor the loans it provides to priority sectors. By contrast, the franchise value created by financial restraint does not undermine the commercial profit-maximization orientation of banks.

Finally, it should be noted that franchise value should be supported by an appropriate ownership and governance structure of the financial institutions. The bank's owners must have a long-term perspective. The flotation of a bank's equity on a stock market may be inappropriate, if investors have short horizons (cf. Stein 1989). Also, the bank's shareholders' demands for dividend payments must be subordinated to the preservation of franchise value.

Financial Deepening through Deposit Collection

Creating a network of depository institutions to collect savings and making further investments to integrate depositors into the formal financial sector is an important part of financial deepening for a developing country. Financial restraint, by creating rents that banks may capture when attracting incremental deposits, motivates banks to seek out new sources of deposits. In particular, it may not be profitable for a bank to develop rural[19] branches in a competitive banking environment because rural markets are higher cost relative to urban ones and because developing a network of rural deposits may require large fixed costs before banks may earn returns on their investments.

Lack of capital may present a barrier to the kind of infrastructure investment needed to develop a rural branch network. We assume that new rural branches require significant capital to open and these branches make economic losses during their first years of operation as a new market is being developed. Consequently, investments in rural branches will negatively affect the equity of the bank.[20]

Search (discovery) costs provide another possible explanation for why banks in a competitive market do not make investments to develop a rural branch network. For example, assume that banks do not have perfect information about the potential profitability of a rural catchment area for a new branch. A good catchment could profitably sustain a branch, but a poor one would not, and the bank would have to withdraw from the market, losing its sunk cost of building the branch. The problem with a perfectly competitive market for deposits is that it cannot provide any "patent protection." If a bank discovers a bad catchment, it will bear the search cost, but if it discovers a good catchment, it will face entry of a competitor, so that all rents of discovery are competed away. Under financial restraint, however, rents can be protected, as the deposit rate will not rise to the competitive equilibrium. There is, however, a possibility that rent will be competed away (or at least reduced) through nonprice competition. It is clear that in this case some further policies are necessary to direct competition, and we discuss these below. For the discovery of the good catchment, there is, however, a simple policy that may enhance deposit collection. The government can institute a policy that provides temporary monopoly power for the discovery of good catchments by restricting entry into the area by any second-mover for a fixed period of time.

These ideas are demonstrated in a model developed in Hellmann, Murdock, and Stiglitz (1994a). When competitive entry is allowed, new branch development is suboptimally provided in the resulting equilibrium. Further, the government cannot induce efficient entry by offering a subsidy covering part of the fixed costs of entry due to the nonmonotonicity of returns under competition. If instead the government were to offer "patent" protection to the first entrant, then a well-designed policy will induce efficient entry—either through a one-period patent combined with an optimal subsidy or by offering an optimal duration patent to the first entrant. When the government induces efficient entry exclusively through "patent" protection, the policy has an additional attractive feature that it places no incremental fiscal demands on the government.[21]

The social benefits of such a policy should be clear. First, as will be discussed in Section 6.4, banks are in general unable to capture the full social benefit of the loans they are making: the banks' benefits of collection deposits therefore always underestimate the social value of these deposits. Moreover, there is an external benefit of financial deepening. New branches are now bringing previously self-intermediated funds into the formal financial sector, which can intermediate funds more efficiently. If a rural household previously had only very limited capabilities to transfer resources to the future (perhaps by holding inventory that was subject to waste and infestation), providing a new asset for intertemporal trade-offs should improve the household's welfare.[22]

In addition to incentives to seek out new locations for branches, banks will make investments to bring new depositors to their existing networks to attract incremental savings. The incentive to make these investments comes from the fact that banks enjoy a generous margin on marginal deposits. Increasing the volume of deposits has a strong effect on the banks' profitability. If depositors experience a fixed cost of setting up a bank account, many will not open savings accounts, even though the marginal benefit of holding financial savings is positive. The bank, under financial restraint, will have incentives to pay this fixed cost to bring depositors into its network.

When rents are available, banks essentially are making investments to increase the convenience of access to the formal financial system. We can think of the supply of funds being a function not just of the deposit interest rate, but also of the convenience of the formal financial sector. Banks thus have incentive to make investments that shift out the supply curve of savings in order to capture marginal rents. In a competitive equilibrium, banks will not make these investments because the marginal return to a deposit is zero.

The incentive to increase convenience should not be underestimated, especially in the context of financial deepening. Indeed, one of the institutional challenges in the financial sector is that households have little experience and sometimes unfounded skepticism with depositing their money with formal intermediaries. There is therefore value to educating households about the potential benefits of saving. Moreover, facilitating the first contact with a bank through promotions and sign-up bonuses can be socially beneficial. Banks, however, will only engage in such educational efforts if there are positive rents on the marginal deposit.

A second model developed in Hellmann, Murdock, and Stiglitz (1994a) highlights this effect. When not all potential depositors have joined the formal financial system (i.e., the economy is in a low or medium state of financial deepening), banks have the opportunity to invest in educational advertising campaigns to convince households to open deposit accounts, thereby expanding the scope of the financial system. In a competitive equilibrium, however, no bank will make the investments because the marginal return on deposits is zero while the cost of the campaign is positive. Under deposit rate control, the marginal return to deposits will induce banks to make these investments, increasing total social income.

Note that the deposit collection effect depends on the banks' *marginal* rents. The bank is considering the value that an additional deposit contributes to its profitability. For this reason it is important that the marginal lending rate remain sufficiently high. While the bank may have a significant part of its lending portfolio invested in directed credits (see Section 6.6), it should have the opportunity to invest its residual funds in higher-margin markets that are not affected by directed credits.

The rents from mobilizing additional deposits can also be turned into a policy instrument. In postwar Japan, for example, the government used branch licenses as a "stick and carrot" to enforce a number of policy objectives (cf. Cho and Hellmann 1993). Finally, there remains a question of why the government should mobilize the deposits directly through the post office (as was done in Japan). In so far as the government can provide an appropriate incentive structure, the post office can become a significant substitute to bank branches. It will, however, not be a perfect substitute, as banks can offer a wider range of services. It is also hard to imagine that a post office could be as aggressive in deposit mobilization as private banks.

Maturity Transformation

We emphasize the benefits of enhanced franchise value and deposit collection services as the most important parts of a policy of financial restraint. A policy that can also promote financial deepening in the particular sense of developing long-term credit markets is a policy of maturity transformation. The essence of the policies described in the first two subsections is that the government creates rent opportunities in the private sector that induce banks to engage in more efficient actions. In some circumstances the government can encourage more specific lending practices. Here we focus on the government's role in maturity transformation.

Commercial banks in most developing economies are typically reluctant to engage in long-term lending. On top of the usual agency problems, banks are reluctant to take the inflation risk and the lack of liquidity that accompanies long-term lending. Moreover, bond and stock markets are typically underdeveloped, providing no viable source of long-term funds.[23] For this reason, governments have often chosen to operate development banks that provide long-term capital (for Japan, see for example Packer 1994), i.e., they have addressed the market failure directly. However, when government engages in direct lending, it suffers from agency problems of its own. The danger that "government failure" might outweigh the market failure is apparent.

A promising alternative is that the government assists private banks in engaging in long-term financing. With long-term lending, in addition to the credit risk associated with the loan, private banks also bear inflation risk—about which they have relatively little information and no control. This inhibits the development of a private long-term credit market. This may be addressed by dividing the risk according to who may most efficiently bear it: private banks should bear credit because of their comparative advantage at selecting and monitoring loans, whereas the government should bear inflation risk. By leaving the default risk with commercial banks, they will have strong incentives to monitor those firms, and if necessary take remedial actions (cf. Aoki 1994). This can be achieved through the following mechanism: when a bank provides a long-term loan to a client, it can obtain an equivalent duration loan from the central bank at a lower interest rate that should reflect credit risk.[24] If inflation is different from what is expected, it is the government that bears the loss, whereas if the client performs poorly, the private bank bears the loss.[25]

A policy of supporting long-term lending through automatic rediscounts is in general inflationary.[26] The funds created through discounts should therefore be fully financed by savings generated elsewhere in the economy, such as postal savings. Indeed, many developing countries use postal savings as a source of funds for long-term credit banks. This mechanism, where the private sector is involved in selecting and monitoring long-term borrowers, is preferable to government long-term lending because it utilizes the comparative advantage of the private sector to select and monitor loans.

Having discussed the principal mechanisms of how financial restraint can foster financial deepening, we now turn to a number of policies that support the implementation of financial restraint.

Restrictions on Competition

The argument so far is based on the assumption that the rents generated by the financial sector can persist even in the long run. There is, however, a problem that competition in the banking sector could eliminate those rents. We must distinguish between two potential sources of competition. First, there may be excessive entry into the banking sector, and second, there can be excessive competition among incumbents. While financial restraint prevents price competition, there can be nonprice competition, such as in locality and quality of services. We have already discussed one way competition can be harmful, if banks are discouraged from searching for good locations to open new branches in previously unserved areas because competition prevents them from recouping search costs. There are further socially wasteful forms of competition. For instance, a bank may open a branch next to a competitor's branch. This does not mobilize any new funds; the new branch only competes for existing depositors. This is an instance of socially wasteful duplication as a result of socially unproductive competition.[27]

Apart from these arguments, there is another simple reason why governments would want to restrict competition in financial markets. Competition entails frequent bank failures that threaten the stability of the financial system.[28] By allowing positive profits in the banking sector, the probability of bank failure is reduced. Restrictions on competition in banking can then increase the security of the financial system, which has important external effects on the economy.[29] One possible cost of this policy is that some less efficient banks will be shielded. We argue that this cost may be substantially smaller than the benefits of a safer financial system.

In order to regulate competitive behavior in the banking industry, the government needs to control entry into the industry. This does not mean that the government prevents all entry, but it means that new entry does not erode the rents that are necessary to induce banks to value their franchise. Also, too much entry would prevent most competitors from achieving an efficient scale, thus lowering their ability and desire to invest in better information and monitoring capabilities and worsening the overall quality of intermediation.

Beyond entry control, the government may want to attempt to curb "disruptive" competition by directing competition. There are some broad and objective criteria of competitive behavior that may be used to check such activities. However, implementing government policy in this area may be particularly delicate. The government will often lack the detailed knowledge to distinguish beneficial from disruptive competition. Even when the government has the knowledge, it may be difficult to write rules that effectively curb unproductive competition. An alternative is to rely not on rules, but on discretion. The allocation of certain subsidies (such as central bank credits) or new branch licenses is a case in point. While these can be used as sticks and carrots to induce banks not to engage in unproductive activities, it is also clear that the discretionary nature of these instruments implies a risk that bureaucrats will use them for other purposes.[30]

When financial restraint creates rents to intermediaries, they will make investments to capture additional depositors. This subsection has focused on the need to place restrictions on this competition in order to prevent socially wastefully duplication of activity. However, the investments that banks make can have one of two effects in how they gather increased deposits—bringing new depositors into the formal financial sector versus competing for share against other banks. The first is socially beneficial while the second is not. In countries with low financial depth, and thus a greater potential for deposit creation, a greater mix of the former should result from the increased competitive pressures generated by rents. Consequently, concerns of "excessive competition" remain secondary in the early stages of financial deepening.

Policies to Curb Asset Substitutability

The final set of policies on the deposit side of financial restraint is concerned with restricting households' ability to substitute out of formal sector deposits. We noted in Section 6.2 that saving elasticities are typically very low. There is, however, a concern as to how much of the savings is captured by formal intermediaries, and how much is channeled into alternative savings vehicles. There are four important asset alternatives to consider: securities, foreign deposits, informal market deposits, and inflationary hedges. We discuss each of these below.

In developed countries, bond and stock markets have become an attractive alternative in which households may invest their savings. Their usefulness in developing countries remains limited. In many developing countries, the development of security markets is hardly an issue: these markets would require a critical mass of demand to allow liquidity and a set of highly sophisticated institutions—ranging from broker houses and analysts to well-functioning supervisory boards—that enable the operation of these markets. There is also a well-known free-rider problem in security markets. Investors not only hold smaller, diversified portfolios that give them no incentives to monitor individual firms, but once they discover problems, they also have incentives to sell shares, rather than take remedial actions. In the absence of a set of highly sophisticated institutions, security markets will lack an appropriate governance structure and be prone to extensive fraud.[31]

We would argue that, even if it were feasible, the development of security markets may not be desirable. The main reason is that security markets would compete with the banking sectors for household funds. Security markets can only be used by the largest and most highly reputed firms in the economy. If they were to go to the security markets, banks would lose some of their most profitable business, and there would be a loss of franchise value.[32] It follows that security markets provide an alternative savings vehicle that undermines the rents in the banking sector and may threaten the stability of the financial system.[33]

A second alternative to depositing savings with domestic financial intermediaries is for households to take their funds abroad. This is particularly detrimental to the domestic economy as the funds are not reinvested. The government therefore needs to restrict capital flight through capital controls. While it is clear that no system can perfectly curtail capital flight, there are none the less significant costs for savers to take their funds abroad. The combination of mild financial restraint and a serious attempt to control capital movements can then make capital flight unattractive to the bulk of savers.[34]

A third threat to the formal banking sectors is the informal sector. These markets tend to be much less efficient than the formal sector for a number of reasons: illiquid deposits, poor institutional structure, low contract enforcement, inability to create inside money, limited lending opportunities, and the inconvenience of working in the shadow of legality.[35] Empirical studies suggest that, at least partly because of the above inefficiencies, substitution between the informal and formal markets is limited (cf. Bell 1990, Teranishi 1994b). Moreover, we would argue that the decision to deposit funds in the informal sector is not so much a function of the rate differential (the informal sector invariably pays much higher rates to attract deposits), but mainly a function of the efficiency and safety of the formal sector. In this sense, financial restraint may actually facilitate the flow of funds from the informal sector to the formal sector, and not vice versa.

The fourth asset-substitution opportunity is real assets, such as gold and real estate, as inflationary hedges. These assets typically do not yield real returns, but are not affected by inflation. Real asset substitution becomes an issue whenever real interest rates are negative. Consequently, we emphasize that positive real interest rates are an essential aspect of financial restraint.

6.4 RENTS TO THE PRODUCTION SECTOR

The creation of rents in the production sector may also enhance the efficiency of fund allocation. In particular, we focus on the social losses that arise from agency costs in investment and the role that the creation of equity within the private sector may have on reducing these costs. Furthermore, agency costs increase with the lending interest rate, so lending rate controls may also increase the social return to investment. As a final point, corporations are more prone to save and invest out of retained earnings than households are willing to save out of income. Consequently, the transfer of rents from households to firms should increase investment in the economy. Rents in the production sector are created by financial restraint through controls on the lending rate.

Agency Costs in Investment

Recent information economics has emphasized that banks generally have less information than firms about the projects they finance. Following

Stiglitz and Weiss (1981), we assume that banks can only identify classes of projects. Within a given class, all borrowers are informationally indistinguishable from the bank's perspective, but each potential borrower has private information about the potential return from the project. Banks calculate expected returns for a given class of projects. This depends on the average quality of the pool and the interest rate charged.

Figure 6.4 shows the expected return R to the bank for loans to a particular class of borrowers, as a function of the real interest rate I charged.[36] Note that the maximum return the bank may earn from these borrowers may be achieved by charging an interest rate I_o. The fact that the banks' returns may actually decline for higher interest rates is the result of agency costs. Three main channels may be identified.[37] First, adverse selection arises because increases in the interest rate may reduce the average quality of the applicant pool, as only higher-risk projects continue to apply. Second, moral hazard arises because higher interest rates encourage firms to divert funds to higher-risk activities. Finally, there is an even more direct and simpler effect; even without altering actions, at a higher interest rate there is a higher likelihood of creditors defaulting on their loans. If bankruptcy costs are positive,[38] the social surplus from investment is thus reduced.

Equity Reduces Agency Costs

These agency costs arise because of the debt nature of the contract between the firm and the bank. The firm promises to repay the bank the principal plus interest, and the firm keeps the remainder of the surplus from investment. If the firm fails and cannot repay its loan, it is the bank that suffers the

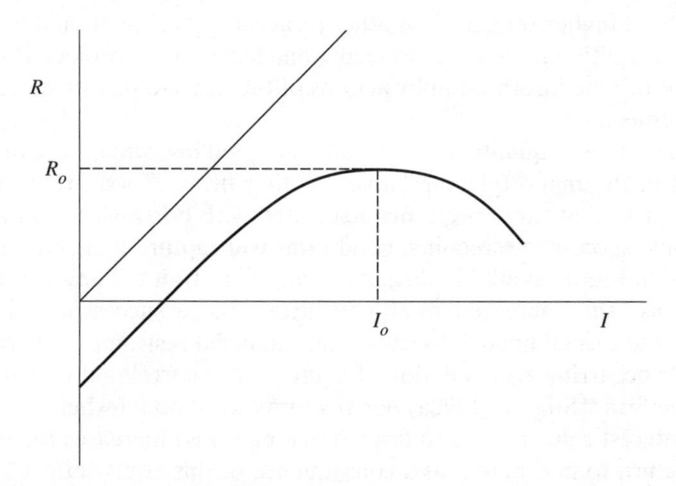

FIG. 6.4 Expected Return to Bank (R) and Real Interest Charged to Firm (I) under Credit Rationing with Agency Costs

loss.[39] This convexity of returns will give firms incentives to take excessive risks.

When firms increase their equity stake in a project, however, these agency costs are reduced. Essentially, the profit function of the firm becomes less convex. We can see this effect by considering each of the three agency-cost models in turn. With adverse selection, the pool of borrowers who are willing to pay a given interest rate is biased toward those with riskier projects.[40] As borrowers increase their equity stakes, this bias is reduced and thus the average riskiness of the projects funded by the banks falls as well. In the moral hazard example, as a firm increases its equity component of the investment, the riskiness of the project it will choose will also decrease. Finally, as a firm increases its equity stake, the probability (and hence the expected cost) of bankruptcy falls unambiguously.

The Dynamic Selection Mechanism

In a market equilibrium where there are agency costs and information asymmetries, many inefficiencies result. In particular, there is red-lining[41] of many socially profitable categories of projects that cannot be financed because banks cannot appropriate a sufficiently large portion of those returns, or because very high-return projects are informationally indistinguishable from low-return projects.[42] As noted above, one way to make rationed projects acceptable to banks is to increase the capital base of those firms wanting to undertake those projects.[43] Not only does the increased equity investment reduce agency costs, but the equity investments act as a signaling device that allows good creditors to distinguish themselves from bad creditors. Firms that have private information that indicate one project should have higher returns than other projects in its class should be willing to devote additional resources to secure financing for the project. Banks can infer this private information by actions of the firms to devote more equity to the project.

Firms with high-quality management and good investment opportunities succeed in the marketplace relative to other firms. If loan rates are also restrained so that there are rents associated with borrowing, and if banks have some success in screening, good firms will capture a disproportionate share of the rents available through financial restraint. They will then be able to use this increased wealth to attract more successfully financing through the formal financial sector. Thus financial restraint accelerates the naturally occurring accumulation of equity that is correlated with the quality of the firm.[44] Stiglitz (1992a) derives formally a model where a decrease in the interest rate charged to firms (creating rents) increases the ultimate social return to investment as a consequence of this equity effect.

If equity is preferable to other forms of finance for investment, then why do not firms just attract more equity finance directly through the stock market? There are a number of reasons. First, it is well known that when firms issue new equity, it creates a negative signal of the firm's prospects (Myers and Majluf 1984; Greenwald, Stiglitz, and Weiss 1984), so new equity is a relatively expensive form of finance. Second, formal equity markets, particularly in developing countries, are only available to the largest firms with well-established reputations. Financial restraint creates a source of equity for less well-established companies. Third, equity captured through new share issues does not have the same positive signal associated with it as equity earned through successful competition. A firm that has large retained earnings is also likely to have good management and positive investment prospects.

Lending Rates and Agency Costs

In the first two subsections, we noted that increased equity investments reduce agency costs. Similarly, when the lending rate charged to firms falls, agency costs are reduced as well. A lower lending rate increases the quality of the pool of applicants, decreases the convexity of the return function for the firm, and reduces the probability of bankruptcy. The benefit of reduced agency costs must be weighed against other costs that restrictions on the interest rate may introduce.

In particular, in order that the profitability of the banks not be squeezed, the deposit rate (the bank's cost of funds) must fall as well. It is worth noting, however, that the deposit rate does not need to fall by as much as the lending rate to preserve the bank's profits. This is because part of the reduced income to the bank from a lower lending rate is offset by lower agency costs. This implies that high-quality firms gain more in income than depositors lose.[45]

A second potential trade-off is that the bank may alter the portfolio of projects to which it provides funds for investment at the lower lending rate. For example, a group of projects with a modest expected return and very little risk will become more attractive than a project with a high expected return and higher risk when the lending rate falls to a sufficiently low level. These adjustments may harm the social productivity of the portfolio of investment. This issue is discussed more fully in Section 6.5.

Retained Earnings and Investment

There is another additional benefit from the creation of rents within the production sector—total investment should increase due to an increase in the supply of funds for investment. Whether within or among corporations, funds within the corporate sector tend to get reused (or "self-intermediated") within the sector. Put differently, the marginal propensity to save is typically very high in the corporate sector. Transferring rents from the household sector to the production sector thus reduces consumption (by households) and increases saving (by corporations).[46]

Firms, then, increase their total investment in tandem with savings, when their income rises.[47] This investment effect actually arises from the decreased cost of intermediation when firms are investing their own capital (retained earnings) as compared with when they must raise funds from outside the firm in the form of either new equity issues or debt borrowing. More capital is consequently available for investment and the marginal cost of investment is lower. Both effects increase total investment in the economy.

Rent Capture or Dissipation

An implicit assumption in our discussion that lending rate controls create rents that are captured in the production sector is that these markets are imperfectly competitive. If markets are perfectly competitive, then the reduced cost of capital implied by the lower lending rate will just be passed on to consumers. This distinction, however, is not critical to our analysis. Even if *all* markets in the economy were perfectly competitive, benefits would accrue to the economy because long-term investments would become more feasible due to the lower cost of capital. For example, investments in innovation are generally underprovided because firms (while bearing all of the cost of investment) do not capture all of the return if the innovation can be imitated. More realistically, markets in developing economies will be characterized by imperfect competition. Firms will thus be able to capture rents in equilibrium.

Note the role that rents may have in facilitating investments in industries experiencing learning. Assuming that financial restraint results in lending rates below those that would have occurred under a Walrasian equilibrium, firms will be more farsighted in their investments due to the lower discount rate on future cash flows. Also, firms that forward price (sell products at below current-period marginal cost) to reflect the future benefit from increased current-period production experience (potentially large) losses. In the absence of perfect information about the firm's long-run profitability, the firm may experience difficulty in attracting financing for these investments in learning (cf. Hellmann 1994). Rents from financial restraint may partially fund these investments.

We have thus seen that rents captured by production firms increase the amount of equity capital available for investment in the economy. Firms may use this equity as a signaling device when undertaking high-return projects to secure financing from the formal financial sector. Rents are created by financial restraint through controls on the lending rate. The analysis in this section does not focus on the complications associated with implementing lending-rate controls; in Section 6.5 we address this issue.

With many classes of borrowers with varying risk-return profiles, this distinction is important. In the next section we discuss the somewhat more involved mechanics of how lending rate controls affect the allocation of funds. The argument that an increased equity base reduces agency costs (even in the presence of these complications) will remain valid.

6.5 LENDING RATE CONTROLS, COMPENSATING BALANCES, AND THE NEGOTIATION FOR RENTS BETWEEN INTERMEDIARIES AND FIRMS

In this section, we discuss how the imposition of lending interest-rate controls affects the market equilibrium with credit rationing. We present a more robust description of the market equilibrium where there is credit rationing and many classes of borrowers, and then we use this framework to analyze the effect of imposing lending rate controls with and without compensating balances. We suggest that the combination of bargaining and administrative guidance may produce outcomes that are superior to both the free-market outcome and that of strict lending controls.

The Market Equilibrium with Many Classes of Borrowers

The allocation problem for the bank is much more complicated than simply determining a single interest rate that maximizes the expected return from a given class of borrowers—the bank must allocate funds across many different classes of borrowers. Some classes of borrowers will provide sufficient expected return to the bank so that all borrowers in this class will be able to attract funds at the equilibrium interest rate. Other classes offer so little return that they will be completely rationed out, i.e., red-lined. Essentially, the bank will consider all classes of borrowers and determine the maximum expected return that it could capture from each class.

Figure 6.5 identifies four classes of borrowers, ranked according to their maximum expected return. To fix our ideas, consider first a monopolistic bank. It would charge each class interest rates of I_1, I_2, I_3, and I_4, respectively, earning expected returns of R_1, R_2, R_3, and R_4. The monopolist would allocate all its funds initially to class (1). If the bank still had funds after satisfying all borrowers in the first class, it would proceed to the second, and so on. For the sake of exposition, let us assume that there are sufficient savings to wholly fund classes (1) and (2) and to partially fund class (3).

Consider now a competitive market with many banks. Competition will drive the interest rate down until the expected return on loans to class (1) equals the marginal expected return, R_3. Hence, only class (3) will be charged the monopolist's preferred interest rate, I_3 (which maximizes the expected return for loans to the class of borrowers). Classes (1) and (2) will

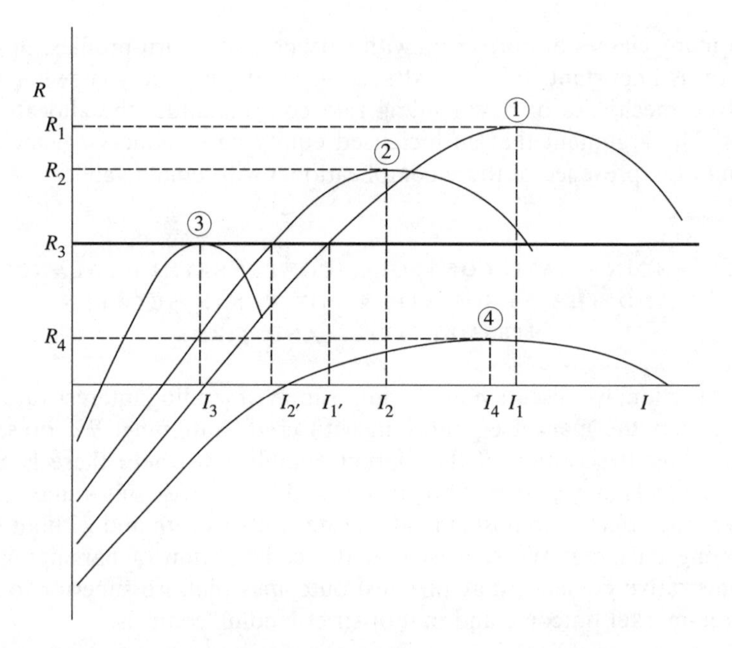

FIG. 6.5 Equilibrium Interest Rates (I) and Expected Return (R) under Credit Rationing with Multiple Classes of Borrowers

be charged interest rates of I_1' and I_2', respectively.[48] Borrowers in class (4) are red-lined (i.e., completely rationed).

Lending Rate Controls

Now suppose the government strictly enforces controls on lending interest rates, so that no borrower may be charged an interest rate greater than I_L (and no compensating balances are held). See Figure 6.6. The preference ordering in terms of expected return to banks changes markedly. Banks can earn the highest return on loans to class (3) (the expected return R_3 is unchanged because $I_3 < I_L$). But the expected return to loans to classes (1) and (2) falls to R_1' and R_2', respectively (with $R_2' > R_1'$). Now the firm will lend first to class (3), then to class (2), with class (1) receiving funds only to the extent that there are residual funds left over from the other two. Worse, if there exists a safe asset (such as short-term government bonds) that gives the bank an expected return of R_{safe}, then class (1) is completely rationed out under interest rate controls. Strict lending rate controls, particularly when there exists large heterogeneity in the portfolio of potential investment projects, greatly distorts the allocation of funds for investment.

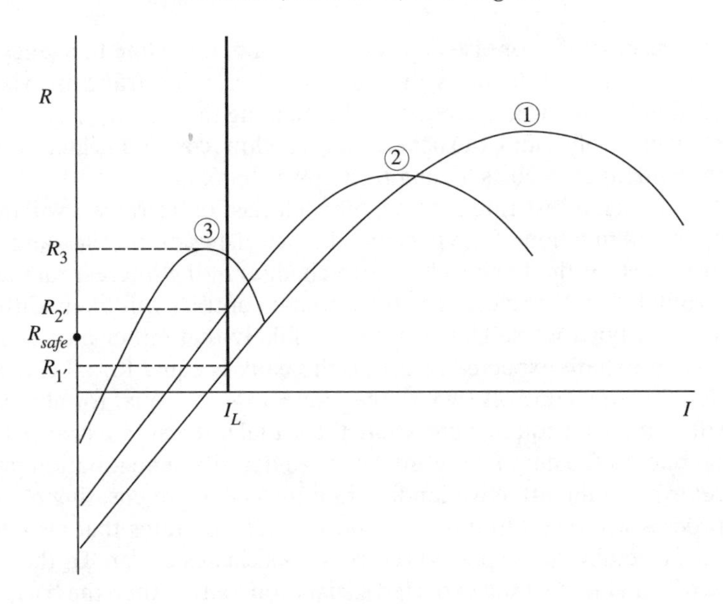

FIG. 6.6 The Effect of Strict Lending Rate Controls

The Socially Efficient Interest Rate Contract

What is the socially efficient interest rate contract for a given class of borrowers? It is clear that when banks are charging the interest rate that maximizes their expected return (I^*), social welfare would increase if the lending rate were to decline. Consider the moral hazard example. At any given lending rate, the firm chooses the investment that maximizes its expected return. Increases in the interest rate unambiguously decrease its expected profits. At I^*, the bank's profits are maximized, so a slight decrease in the interest rate has only a second-order effect on profits, yet it has a first-order increase in the profits of the firm. Essentially, at I^* the bank is trading off the increased *private* return due to the higher interest rate against the decreased *social* return from the changes the interest rate induces in the investment choice of the firm. Similarly, if we consider the agency costs that arise from bankruptcy costs, a decrease in the interest rate unambiguously increases the social return by lowering the probability of bankruptcy.[49]

The socially optimal lending rate contract is determined by the trade-off of reduced firm agency costs from lower interest rates against increased bank agency costs. Other things being constant, the bank's intensity of monitoring is an increasing function of the interest rate. Decreases in the lending rate thus reduce the quality of the investment portfolio of the bank due to this monitoring effect.[50] Further, the bank must earn positive profits on its entire portfolio, or else depositors are vulnerable due to agency costs *of the bank*. This, after all, is the purpose of creating franchise value as described in Section 6.3. Decreases in the lending rate, however, negatively impact bank profits and thus there is a shadow cost associated with increased bank agency costs arising from lower bank profits.

The optimal interest-rate contract for each class of borrowers will thus be a complicated function of the peculiar characteristics of the class and of the responsiveness of the bank's choices to changes in the interest rate and its total profitability. It is clear that the optimal contract will likely differ for each class of borrowers. Thus it is very unlikely that either a competitive equilibrium (where expected return to the bank is equal for all classes) or strict lending rate controls (where the interest rate is equal for all borrowers) will result in an equilibrium where the actual interest rate charged is the optimal one. In the next few subsections, we describe a negotiation process that determines the effective lending rate through compensating balances. This process will result in differing effective lending rates that also do not necessarily equilibrate expected return across classes either. To the extent that factors that impact the expected social return strengthen the bargaining incentives for each party, these differences in the outcomes of the negotiation will, at least in part, reflect differences in the social return.

Negotiation over Compensating Balances

One way to circumvent lending rate controls is for the bank to require compensating balances. The bank lends more funds than are necessary to finance the project with the remainder deposited at the bank and earning the lower deposit interest rate, in order to increase the effective lending rate.[51] If compensating balances were allowed to completely offset the effects of the lending rate restriction, then the equilibrium would exactly mirror the competitive equilibrium and the banks would capture all of the rents from *financial restraint* (cf. Horiuchi 1984). This is, however, an unlikely outcome, as compensating balances are typically illegal, and there is no "market" that would allow for the discovery of the competitive price (i.e., the competitive rate of return).

With financial restraint, the natural outcome is that firms negotiate with the bank over the amount of compensating balances, and thus over the distribution of rents.[52] Little can be said about the precise structure of this bargaining process, but we can identify some reasonable determinants of the outcome.

Consider first the best outcome for the firm. This is when no compensating balances are levied (only the fiat lending rate is charged) and the firm attracts funds for investment. The best outcome for the bank is that the highest possible lending rate is levied. The bargaining game is complicated by threats that either party will withdraw from the negotiation because it perceives better outside opportunities. The determination of these threat points would in general depend on the search costs of either party, on the level of aggregate credit rationing, and the degree of competition between banks. In addition, the slope of the bank's expected return function (as a function of the lending rate) affects the marginal incentive to bargain "harder." The steeper this curve, the greater the benefit to the bank of increasing compensating balances. As this curve approaches a maximum, banks have a very weak incentive to bargain because the agency costs offset the increased return from an increase in the effective lending rate. Firms, in contrast, still retain powerful incentives to reduce their lending rates because they fully capture the benefit of a lower rate. See Figure 6.7.

When governments have "priority lending" systems, one of the most important determinants of bargaining strength is the rank the firm enjoys in terms of government priority. It is reasonable to believe that firms favored by the government find it easier to resist the bank's demands to keep compensating balances.[53] The level of the fiat lending rate is also likely to matter. The government can set different fiat rates for different sectors that indicate the government's priorities. A lower fiat rate also makes it more difficult for the bank to impose compensating balances to achieve a target effective lending rate. It is important to remember that compensating balances are typically illegal. The higher the amount of compensating balances,

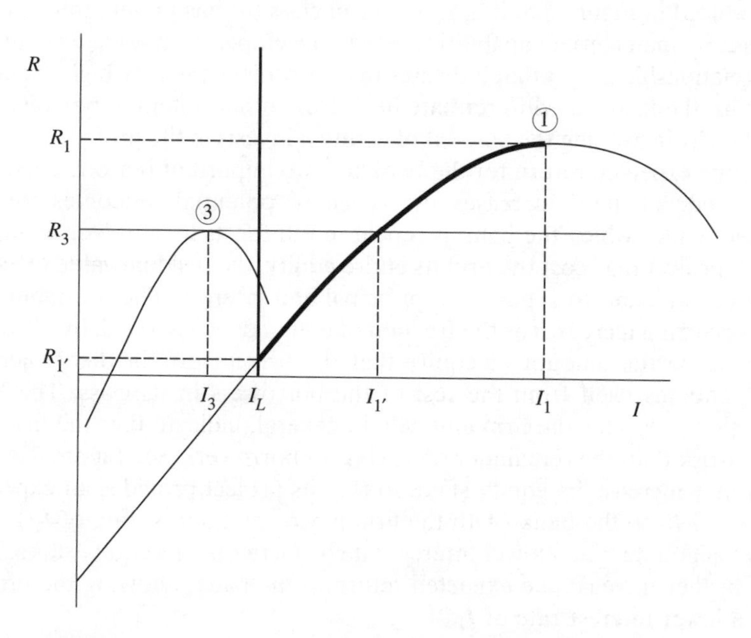

FIG. 6.7 Negotiation between Banks and Firms with Interest Rate Controls and Compensating Balances

the more likely they will attract the attention of the legal enforcement system, resulting in penalties. If the probability of a bank being caught and punished for requiring compensating balances is correlated with the size of compensating balances, then we can expect banks not to charge compensating balances that replicate the competitive equilibrium.

The enforcement of a compensating balances prohibition is a difficult topic. On the empirical side, very little is known—at least to the authors—about the exact extent that compensating balances have been practiced (say in postwar Japan) and about how the government monitored transgressions. On the normative side, however, we would conclude that a strictly enforced lending control can cause serious allocation distortions, by introducing a strong antirisk bias.[54] To the extent that compensating balances counter this bias, they are efficient. If the overall level (and variability) of compensating balances is high, they may, however, undermine the transfer of rents to the production sector.

Negotiations with Equity Signaling

In Section 6.4 we discussed how firms may use their contribution of equity to signal the quality of their investment opportunities. To illustrate this effect of increasing the equity base in a credit-rationing equilibrium with many classes of borrowers, consider again the four classes of borrowers introduced in Figure 6.5. If a borrower in class (4) has private information (about its managerial capabilities, newly developed technologies, marketing relationships, etc.) that indicates that its project has very high expected returns, the firm may differentiate itself from other potential borrowers in its class by increasing the amount of equity it invests in the project. This will raise the expected return for the bank for two important reasons. First, the increased collateral increases the range of potential outcomes for the project under which the bank is repaid in full for its loan. (Even though a failed project may cost the firm its entire equity, the residual value of assets may be sufficient to repay both principal and interest. The probability of this occurring increases as the fraction of equity does.) Second, by *choosing* to increase the amount of equity that the firm invests in the project, it differentiates itself from the rest of the borrowers in its class. This self-selection separates the firm and will, in general, indicate that the firm is a better risk than the remainder of its class of borrowers. See Figure 6.8. The firm may increase its equity stake so that its project provides an expected return of R_3 to the bank (with the firm paying an interest rate of $I_{4'}$), or it may "negotiate" for a lower interest rate by increasing its equity stake. This will further increase the expected return to the bank, allowing the firm to pay a lower interest rate of I_4.[55]

Given that firms can signal their quality through their equity, we would argue that there are essentially three types of firms: those that can bargain

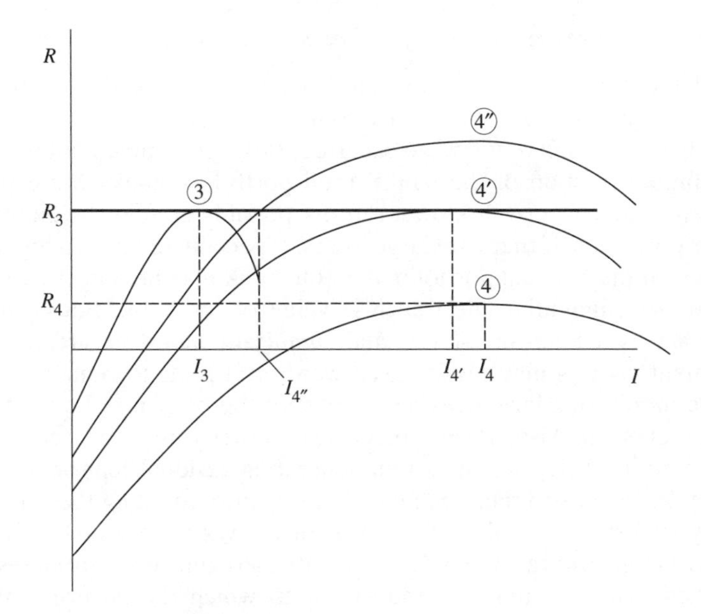

FIG. 6.8 The Equity Selection Mechanism

an effective lending rate (including compensating balances) that is lower than the Walrasian benchmark, those that get a rate above the benchmark, and those that do not get funds even though their expected returns exceed the banks' cost of capital. Some firms will be better off, acquiring rents to further boost their equity base. There are, in general, also some firms that are worse off. If, however, there is a significant rent effect on the supply of funds, as discussed in Section 6.3, then it may even be that all firms are better off.

6.6 DIRECTED CREDITS AND INDUSTRIAL POLICY

Financial restraint, by increasing the set of projects that may receive funds through formal intermediation, may have significant influence on the allocation of invested funds. The potential scope for more direct government intervention into the allocation of funds also increases, and so discussion of directed credits and industrial policy is necessary. Directed credits are not a necessary component of financial restraint. They are, however, a prevalent feature of the financial policies of developing countries. This section attempts to explain under what circumstances such interventions may be justified and, importantly, we note critical *limitations* on the extent to which these inventions may be pursued without interfering with the positive benefits from our proposed policy regime.

Preserving Rents for Financial Intermediaries

Should the government directly intervene in the allocation of invested funds, the expected return to banks from these projects will, in general, be lower than if no intervention had occurred. If the government intervenes in a substantial fraction of the banks' total portfolios, banks can expect to experience (at least private) lower returns, possibly even losses, on this part of their portfolios. If there are large losses, especially relative to the rents it captures on the residual portfolio, then the bank may no longer earn rents on average, eliminating the franchise value of the bank. Banks may no longer act as a long-run player, and significant moral hazard in banks' investment choices may result. Even were total rents to remain positive, positive monitoring incentives on the part of the bank may be reduced as average rents fall. Also, if banks perceive that they will not be free to invest newly mobilized deposits in a rent-generating residual loan market, but rather that the government will coerce them into investing these funds in priority sectors, then banks will not have incentives to develop their branch networks (e.g., in rural areas). Consequently, a regime of financial restraint embodies real limitations on the extent to which the government may pursue directed credit policies.

We can characterize these limitations by considering our earlier demand-supply framework. See Figure 6.9. The bank earns no (or negative) rents on its loans to priority sectors. Loans to nonpriority sectors are invested at higher returns, generating rents so that the bank earns positive profits on its entire portfolio. It is these profits that create the franchise value of the bank. In addition, the bank must be able to invest incremental deposits in the residual market so that it has positive marginal incentives to collect new deposits.

The Information Structure of the Government, Banks, and Firms

In Section 6.4 we noted that banks typically have less information than firms about the quality of individual projects. In general, we would expect the government to have even less information than banks. Yet in order efficiently to affect the allocation of resources, the government requires considerable information. An immediate consequence is that a high threshold (in terms of incremental social return) should be perceived with a high degree of certainty before the government intervenes through directed credits.

There are, however, ways of choosing an appropriate form of intervention to affect at least partially the government's informational disadvantage. In general the government should not intervene by selecting individual projects. Rather, directed credits should be targeted at *sectors*

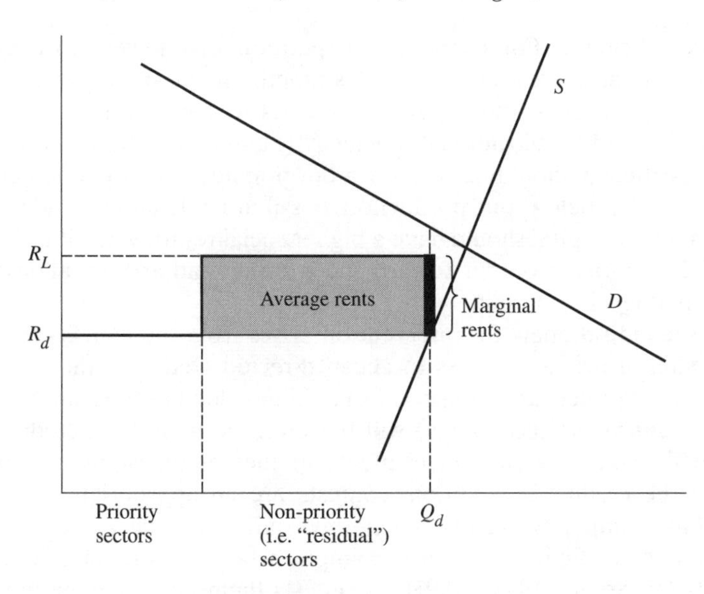

FIG. 6.9 Average Rents, Marginal Rents, and Directed Credits

that have a high social, but low private, return. Private information held by both banks and firms may then be exploited in the intrasectoral allocation of funds.

Rationales for Intervention

We identify two distinct rationales for the government to intervene in the allocation of credit:

1. divergence of private and social return, due to externalities, market failures, and coordination failures;
2. incentive effects derived from the "contest" for rents by firms.

The first point embodies the classic rationale for government intervention. Directing credit to sectors with high social return is justified, as long as the intervention does not create inefficiencies that exceed the gains from the intervention. Note that our framework of credit rationing already identifies some divergence between private and social returns. In the adverse selection model (cf. Stiglitz and Weiss 1981), for example, banks cannot appropriate the full returns, yet these returns do accrue to firms.[56]

Apart from the more traditional analysis of allocative inefficiency due to the divergence of private and social returns, we emphasize that there is often a trade-off between short-term allocative efficiency and long-run dynamic efficiency. For example, competition that lowers cost induces growth and value creation, whereas competition for share just improves allocational efficiency. When transaction costs are high, too many resources may be devoted to allocational efficiency (Summers and Summers 1989). This in particular should be true for a developing economy, when current output lies far below the production possibilities frontier. Under these circumstances, capital should have a higher social return when it is devoted to activities moving output toward the frontier, rather than allocating a suboptimal level of output.

The second rationale for intervention arises from the benefits that may occur when firms view access to cheap directed credits as the prize in a contest. If the rules are understood that value-added performance (lowering cost, improving technology) will be rewarded with these credits, then firms will make increased investments in these dimensions in order to capture the credits. In addition, contests are an appropriate means for rewarding competing agents when environmental uncertainty is large (Nalebuff and Stiglitz 1983), for example, when firms enter new export markets (cf. Stiglitz 1993a, 1993b). Contests themselves may be linked to areas where social and private returns are believed to diverge especially greatly.

Types of Intervention

There are also different types of intervention. The simplest is a direct allocation to specific firms. Except for cases of natural monopoly, this intervention can be problematic. When the government commits to a particular firm, it fails to utilize private information by the bank and the firm. Moreover, if the government distributes such direct favors, it exposes itself to considerable lobbying opportunities that give rise to inefficient rent-seeking behavior or influence costs (cf. Milgrom and Roberts 1990). In many cases a more reasonable policy is to target a specific sector. This allows banks to use their information in selecting the better firms within the sector. Banks also create a buffer between firms and the government, reducing influence costs. And productivity-enhancing contests rather than nonproductive rent seeking are encouraged.

Rather than targeting certain preferred sectors, a government may want to have a restrictive policy that prevents certain sectors from absorbing too large a share of the funds. It may be easier for the government, based on its information structure, to identify sectors that impose a negative externality on other sectors (or at least those that have no positive externality). The government may then want to intervene by expressing a preference for avoiding these sectors, rather than directly intervening to allocate funds to a specific (positive externality) sector. For example, consumption goods generally do not create positive externalities for other sectors in the same way that investment goods do. If the government directs banks to limit their portfolios of consumption-goods (and consumer-durables) projects, then more funds will be available to the investment sectors. The selection mechanism that allocates funds within these sectors will still exploit the maximum amount of private information held by both banks and firms. The only difference is that incremental marginal investment-goods projects will be funded at the expense of marginal consumption-goods projects.

Apart from the level of intervention, there is a question about the type of subsidization.[57] In general we would argue that a fiat lending rate (possibly with a compensating balance that reflects firm risk) is superior to a credit guarantee. This is because the latter gives rise to moral hazard on behalf of both the firm and the bank, as neither party takes responsibility for potential losses. Firms will engage in riskier projects and banks have no incentives to monitor. As discussed in Section 6.3, matters become even worse when banks can obtain preferential loans from the central bank to cover their losses from priority-sector lending, as this may undermine the incentive to collect deposits.

The Effect of Information Coordination and Interdependent Returns

The government may use another type of intervention that is of an entirely different nature from directed credits—information coordination.[58] Just as banks in general have better information than the government in the selection of projects, the information held by financial intermediaries as a group is superior to that held by any individual bank. If banks were to pool their information about potential borrowers and then use the joint information set for the selection of projects (rather than to facilitate collusion, an important distinction), then the efficiency of allocation will be improved.

In our model in Section 6.5, we implicitly assumed that the returns to the many sectors seeking investment funds through the formal financial sector were independent. Hence no one investment affected the expected returns to other sectors. In reality, this is not an accurate assumption. Investments both upstream and downstream from a given sector affect the cost of production and the ultimate demand for a sector's output.

We can identify two different classes of correlated returns—lead-sector dependence and mutual interdependence. In the first case, one sector imposes a substantial positive externality on a number of other sectors (e.g., the electric power industry). Under these circumstances, directing credit to this specific sector may be a justifiable intervention. More commonly, we would expect to see the second class—mutual interdependence. Here, the performance of many sectors depends on the performance of a number of others, but no one sector can be identified as the driving sector. Directing credits to these sectors then is not appropriate, yet the role of coordinating information is more sensible. Banks communicate with each other, improving their joint information set. If we return to the model of Figure 6.5, this should have the effect of raising the expected return curve for the mutually interdependent sectors. Those that should efficiently receive funds do, and projects that do not meet a private hurdle rate are not funded. It is important to note, however, that information coordination may also facilitate collusion. In pursuing a policy of coordination, the government must balance the benefits against the potential risks of collusion.

6.7 THE GOVERNANCE OF FINANCIAL RESTRAINT

While we believe that financial restraint can be a reasonable financial policy, we are aware that it could be badly implemented or corrupted for other purposes. The most significant danger is that financial restraint turns into financial repression. As pointed out in Figure 6.2 in the introduction, financial restraint is based on the idea of rent creation in the private sector, rather than rent extraction from the private sector. While the primary emphasis of this chapter has been on the differences between financial repression and restraint, these two regimes do have one important similarity—in each the government imposes interest rate controls. Figure 6.10 highlights the risk that can occur should the government decide to extract rents from the financial sector.

Governments often attempt to extract rents from the private sector through the inflation tax. The nefarious effects are well known. Not only is

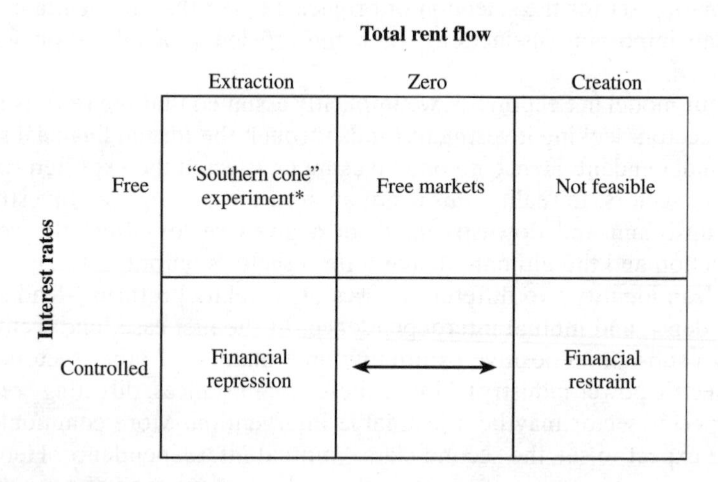

FIG. 6.10 A Cautionary Note
* The government indirectly extracted rents from the financial sector through the inflation rate.

the private sector deprived of the rents necessary to ensure financial deepening, as described in Sections 6.2–6.6, but there is the added curse that high rates of inflation are invariably hard to predict, creating uncertainty in the economy and arbitrarily redistributing rents between lenders and borrowers.

Inflation apart, the financial sector often provides a convenient target for a government in need of additional revenues. Compared to the production sector, accounting in the financial system tends to be superior, thus providing an easy target for taxation. Also, the government can ask for high reserve requirements, or it can require banks to buy government bonds at artificially low interest rates. We emphasize that none of these policies is part of financial restraint, as they extract rents from rather than create rents within the financial sector.

The Optimal Level of Financial Restraint

Assuming now that a government is serious about implementing financial restraint to foster financial deepening and economic growth, there are a number of challenges to be met. The first concern is the extent of deposit rate control. In this chapter we have shown that the benefits to financial restraint can work at modest levels of deposit rate control, but that for very large rate controls, allocational distortions can outweigh the benefits. This leads us to the conclusion that financial restraint should be mild in nature. In particular, we emphasize that the real deposit rate should be positive. Empirical work testing the relationship between interest rate policy and growth has identified a strong correlation between severely negative real interest rates and poor economic growth (cf. Fry 1988), but more recent work has identified that the correlation does not hold once real rates exceed zero.[59] Financial restraint may be positively correlated with growth, as long as the intervention is small (cf. Murdock and Stiglitz 1993).

Controlling the lending rate turns out to be considerably more complicated. In particular, care must be taken not to discriminate against high-risk projects. The government needs to include estimates of risk premia when determining fiat lending rates. As we noted in Section 6.5, when the fiat lending rate is set too low, high-return projects may not receive financing because banks are unable to appropriate sufficient returns. If compensating balances are permitted, then much of the effect of lending restrictions may be obviated.

Lending rate controls are more closely tied to directed credits and industrial policy than are deposit rate controls. If lending rate controls are part of an industrial policy, the government needs to recognize its informational weaknesses (private information about individual risk-return characteristics of project) and strengths (information coordination and recognition of interdependent returns). Experiences in East Asian economies, such as

Korea and Japan, have shown that effective government–business relationships can help to bridge informational gaps and render industrial policies more effective (cf. Cho and Hellmann 1993). Lending rate restrictions are much harder to implement successfully and require greater information on the part of the government. Consequently, the government should phase out lending rate controls at an earlier stage of development.

Bureaucratic Rent Seeking and Financial Restraint

It is obvious that financial restraint, like any other powerful economic intervention, creates opportunities for politicians and bureaucrats to misuse the policy for their special interests.[60] Here we will only mention the commonplace argument that a policy of *financial restraint* may benefit from an insulation of political rent seeking, from reasonably transparent implementation, and from clear rules of accountability for the responsible bureaucrats. This, however, brings up the interesting question of how financial restraint can be phased out as the economy acquires financial depth. The sad truth may be that there exist no strong commitment devices that could tie a government to a promise to relax financial controls at some far date in the future. In fact, it will most likely become the vested interest of the bureaucrats running the system to uphold it long beyond its economic justification.[61] A process of gradually increasing competition in the financial sector, as noted in the next subsection, can create both internal and external pressure for the government to devolve financial restraint, and eventually counterbalance entrenched interests.[62]

The Order of Capital Market Development

The arguments set forth in this chapter are *not* designed to claim that there exists a single optimal level of financial restraint that should be implemented by all governments identically, regardless of the state of financial development. Rather, financial restraint should be a dynamic policy regime, adjusting as the economy develops and moving in the general direction of freer and more competitive financial markets. The policy trade-off is not a static one between *laissez-faire* and government intervention; the relevant question is over the proper order of financial market development.

The free-markets paradigm embodied in the Anglo-Saxon financial system required the substantial development of complementary independent financial institutions—such as Moody's and Standard and Poor's and the investment banks—that either simply do not exist or only exist in rudimentary form in most developing or transitional economies. It is not credible that an economy in a very low state of financial development can move directly to a regime of liberal financial markets. Instead, we would argue that the establishment of a sound banking system should be the first priority of financial policy. Once a sound banking system is in place, there is still ample opportunity to move toward a more market-dominated Anglo-Saxon model, or to continue to develop toward a universal, bank-dominated "Japanese-German" model.[63]

The optimal level of financial restraint—both in terms of the magnitude of the intervention and in terms of the breadth of the intervention—falls as the economy increases its level of financial depth. Some policy options follow a natural sequence. For an economy in a low state of deepening, financial restraint may embody both deposit and lending rate controls, entry restrictions, and limitations on competition from capital markets. As the economy develops, lending rate controls should be relaxed before those on deposits, and the government should develop a private bond market for government securities before introducing competition for the banking sector from corporate bond and stock markets.

6.8 CONCLUSION

Financial restraint is a fundamentally different policy from financial repression. Preconditions for financial restraint are a stable macro environment, low inflation, and positive real interest rates. Most critically, the government, in marked contrast to financial repression, does not extract rents from the financial sector.

The rents created within the private sector serve to strengthen incentives on the part of banks and firms to increase their output of goods and services that are underprovided in a competitive equilibrium. In the financial sector, average rents create a franchise value for banks and induce them to provide better monitoring, while marginal rents encourage banks to develop new sources of deposits, and rents captured by firms allow them to signal private information about investment opportunities. Consequently, a greater volume of funds is intermediated through the formal financial sector with a high degree of allocational efficiency due to strong monitoring and quality information. In the production sector, lower interest rates and greater retained earnings reduce agency costs and allow for a more efficient fund allocation.

One of the most delicate points is the applicability of financial restraint. Does it concern only East Asian economies? Are these policies most applicable for developing economies? Or may they be applied even to developed economies? We would argue that while there are good reasons to believe that aspects of financial restraint also apply to developed countries, it is to developing and transitional economies that they apply best. The premise of this view is that the biggest weakness of many financial systems in these countries is their poor institutional structure. It is here that the benefits of domestic deposit mobilization and increased financial stability and longevity are most needed. In transitional economies, well-capitalized banks can perform an important role in monitoring firms and providing financial discipline.

In many developing economies the experiences with financial repression have been disheartening, leaving the economies in low states of financial development, with weak institutions, poor deposit mobilization, and negative returns to financial assets. The results of financial liberalization, however, have often not lived up to expectations either, at least partly because of a naïve acceptance of neoclassical *laissez-faire* ideas. Financial restraint, by creating the right incentives for the private sector to develop strong financial institutions, may provide a paradigm that is more attractive than either alternative.

NOTES

We would like to thank Masahiko Aoki, Gerard Caprio, Shahe Emran, Maxwell Fry, Masahiro Okuno-Fujiwara, Mushtaq Khan, Hyung-Ki Kim, Ronald McKinnon, Juro Teranishi, participants at the World Bank conferences in Kyoto and Stanford, and participants at seminars in the Stanford Department of Economics and the Stanford Graduate School of Business for their many helpful comments. This chapter represents the views of the authors and does not necessarily represent that of any organization with which they are or have been affiliated.

[1] The government can be thought of as a fourth player. Because we are assuming that it does not extract rents from the financial sector, it only has the role of a regulator.

[2] A more accurate description would be that households are *net* suppliers and corporations are *net* users of funds. This does not affect the analysis.

[3] This simple demand-supply model assumes no transaction costs (including agency and information costs) in intermediation. A simple way of including transaction costs would be to shift the supply curve backward by the amount of funds that get absorbed in transaction. It is clear that an increase in intermediation efficiency will increase the availability of funds.

[4] In focusing on the equilibrium as the intersection of a demand and supply schedule, we ignore the possibility of endogenous credit rationing (cf. Stiglitz and Weiss (1981)). In Section 6.5 we will explicitly consider this.

[5] Note that the determination of the relevant real rate is often far from obvious. If consumers perceive that the current consumer prices are high relative to expected future prices (for example, if future trade liberalization through tariff reductions is expected), then households may choose to defer present consumption. Moreover, certain consumer goods may be temporarily rationed, so that the benefit of saving is not fully reflected in standard calculations of real interest rates.

[6] As with the rest of our discussion, we only consider the distribution of rents within the private sector. Our fundamental assumption is that the government

captures *no rents* from the financial sector. If this assumption is relaxed, then the regime may no longer be appropriately characterized as financial restraint, but rather takes on characteristics of financial repression.

[7] In a perfectly competitive environment, with perfect information, the benefits of these improvements would be fully reflected in the prices banks could charge. In the actual market environment, especially characteristic of less developed countries, neither assumption is plausible. More generally, the need for financial intermediation arises out of imperfect information and transaction costs, in the presence of which markets are almost never Pareto efficient (cf. Greenwald and Stiglitz (1986)).

[8] Again, we emphasize the importance of low and stable inflation rates. When inflation is high and erratic, it is almost impossible to maintain positive deposit rates.

[9] At least in the S&L case, it is widely believed that an important contributing factor to the moral hazard problem was the existence of deposit insurance (Kane 1989, Stiglitz 1992b). We address this issue later in Section 6.3.

[10] There may of course be other remedies. We would argue for instance that good accounting standards and prudential regulation are essential complements to the policies described here.

[11] The argument is of course just a specific application of the general theory of reputation (cf. Klein and Leffler 1981, Shapiro 1983, or Stiglitz 1989).

[12] Aoki (1994) discusses the necessary role rents play in creating incentives for Japanese main banks to perform delegated monitoring tasks without shirking.

[13] Note that we are not saying that *laissez-faire* will never create franchise value, or not create any franchise value. Dinc (1995), for example, identifies cases where franchise value is created endogenously. We emphasize, however, that endogenous franchise value may fail in important sets of circumstances.

[14] Interestingly, there are strong parallels between capital requirements and directed credits. In both cases the government directs the bank's portfolio composition.

[15] Another result derived in Hellmann, Murdock, and Stiglitz (1994a) is that the incentives to collect deposits, as discussed in the next subsection, will be higher under deposit rate controls than under capital requirements. The intuition is that the bank's margins are always higher under deposit rate control.

[16] A bank may also want to circumvent the deposit rate control to individual large clients, in order to retain their business. In these cases, circumvention of the controls may be harder to detect, but would also be on a smaller scale.

[17] An extreme example is Taiwan, where bank managers could be held personally liable for the loans they made.

[18] Note that this argument does not imply that the central bank should never provide cheap rediscounting facilities. Later in Section 6.3, we discuss how rediscounts may assist banks in providing long-term credit, if they are structured appropriately. The key point discussed in the current subsection is that banks must have incentives, on the margin, to seek out additional deposits.

[19] A finer breakdown of deposit markets might consist of primary urban, secondary urban, and rural markets. Banks initially based in the primary urban areas will have incentives to expand the breadth of their branch networks into a wider network by expanding into both secondary urban and more densely populated rural areas. For simplicity, in the remainder of this subsection, we describe bank incentives to expand into new areas as movements to open branches in "rural" areas.

[20] Capital requirements impose a further constraint on such investment. We argue in this chapter that financial restraint may allow for lower capital requirement, so that these types of investment would be easier to undertake.

[21] It should be noted that this policy achieves dynamic efficiency at the expense of near-term allocative efficiency. For the duration of the "patent," the incumbent bank will act like a monopoly, resulting in allocative inefficiency arising from the difference between the monopoly deposit rate and the competitive one. After the patent expires, however, entry will result in allocative efficiency. Thus, in the medium run, all socially efficient entry will have occurred and there will be no further allocative distortions.

[22] In general, banks do not act as discriminating monopolists so those who do avail themselves of the bank's intermediation services enjoy some consumer surplus.

[23] Later in Section 6.3, we argue that repressing the bond and stock market, at least in an initial period, may be an efficient policy.

[24] For an analysis of the Japanese experience with such a system, see Teranishi (1994a). In Japan, however, the government did not provide long-term loans as such, but provided short-term loans on a continuing basis. In this system the government had much more discretion over the decisions made by banks. Inflation risk was absorbed by the government only in so far as the government could honor an implicit contract not to raise short-term Bank of Japan credit rates by the full amount of the inflation.

[25] Note that this policy does not necessarily require that the government subsidize long-term credit, as was the case in Japan.

[26] Note also that rediscounting could attenuate the bank's incentives to pursue deposits. If, however, rediscounting is defined only on a narrow, well-specified set of loan activities, banks will still have incentives to pursue the additional deposit in order to lend it in all other loan markets.

[27] In the United States under regulation Q, banks competed with each other to collect deposits by offering toasters and other gifts to depositors who opened up new accounts. This was probably inefficient because most—although probably not all—new deposits came at the expense of other banks, i.e., banks were competing for share rather than increasing the total supply of funds.

[28] This is an instance where the neoclassical notion of perfect competition as an equilibrium phenomenon is particularly misleading. An evolutionary perspective on competition makes it clear that survival of the fittest banks also implies the frequent exit of less fit banks.

[29] This is witnessed by the numerous accounts of how financial instability can have a disruptive effect on economic activity (cf. Bernanke 1983). Furthermore, if the supply of deposits depends on the security of the financial sector, then the volume of intermediation may increase as well. This reasoning relates to a broader set of results that markets with imperfect competition, such as monopolistic competition or competition for location, are in general not efficient (Stiglitz 1986).

[30] Rather than just contrasting rules with discretion, it may be more helpful to think of rules that can be revised. Regulators may need to learn of the effectiveness of a given set of rules, in order to adapt them to the particular conditions.

[31] It should be noted that even with a set of sophisticated institutions, developed countries have been unable to eradicate these problems.

[32] To a large extent, those benefits are then lost in the transaction cost of the bond issue. The remaining benefits are absorbed by firms and households that enjoy a bond rate that lies between the deposit and lending rates.

[33] Our argument suggests that security markets should not be emphasized in a stage of development where an effective banking system is being developed. As the financial system deepens, security markets can clearly become more useful. Also, there is a debate whether security transactions should be handled by universal banks (cf. Rajan 1992). The analysis of financial restraint suggests that universal banks may be an efficient solution, at least in earlier stages of development, as security transactions would then contribute, rather than undermine, the franchise value of banks.

[34] Capital flight is typically an option only to a few wealthy individuals. Alternative investment options can be provided to these investors. For example the government may allow the establishment of "venture funds" that would operate along the lines of venture capital partnership funds. They invest exclusively in high-risk and -return projects. Investors can buy nontransferable partnership interests. Because of their explicit high-risk orientation, these funds would not be attractive to the bulk of household savings. Moreover, the equity structure of the venture fund, combined with a performance-based management compensation, would reduce the intermediary's agency problems.

[35] Note that for these reasons many informal lenders do not even accept all deposits.

[36] The government must maintain, as a precondition for successful implementation of a regime of financial restraint, a low and stable inflation rate. When there is high (unstable) inflation, the government is implicitly extracting large rents from the private sector. With low and stable inflation, both banks and firms may extract the real interest rate from the nominal interest rate with a reasonable degree of certainty.

[37] The first two effects are discussed in Stiglitz and Weiss (1981), the third in Williamson (1987).

[38] These may arise if there are collection costs or if there is reduced disposal value (arising from a not perfectly efficient market for the disposition of assets from distressed firms).

[39] Of course, if the managers suffer a cost from bankruptcy, they will attempt to avoid failure. If this cost is essentially fixed, however, the managers will still have socially inefficient incentives to take risk because managers do not suffer the full cost of bankruptcy.

[40] This assumes a model of adverse selection where projects have identical expected returns but some are more risky than others.

[41] That is, none of the properties in the red-lined category is given serious consideration for a loan. There is simply a review to determine whether the project falls into the red-lined category.

[42] Moreover, there is a dynamic inefficiency: if a group of borrowers is red-lined, there is no chance for the projects within this group to prove their quality. Private returns to learning are less than social returns if the information discovered by the investment in learning is not appropriable to the lender. Thus, there will be less than the social optimum investment in learning (with potentially no learning) in the competitive equilibrium.

[43] In Section 6.6 we discuss another way to finance such firms, namely, through directed credits.

[44] As firms accumulate large amounts of free cash flows, there is a possibility that they fail to invest it in profitable investment projects (cf. Jensen 1986). This problem, however, is unlikely to be prevalent at least in the earlier stages of development.

[45] The incremental equity resulting from financial restraint conveys additional information because it also reflects the business judgment of lenders. This would not be true if there were automatic rules for access to credit based on publicly available information.

[46] This analysis assumes that households do not fully "pierce the corporate veil," so that they do not completely offset incremental savings held via stock for other savings in their portfolio. Note first that in the presence of costly intermediation (including agency costs), households cannot costlessly offset the saving decisions of corporations. Second, they often do not have the requisite information to do so. In addition, there can be a positive savings effect, due to effects on distribution, if stock is owned by (on average) wealthier individuals who have a relatively high marginal propensity to save.

[47] Fazzari, Hubbard, and Peterson (1988) present evidence that investment is a function of cash flow.

[48] For the purposes of the discussion in this section, we can assume competitive lending markets. Later in this section, we explore the effect of lending rate controls on this equilibrium and the bargaining process of determining compensation balances. The results of this subsection still hold under more robust assumptions.

[49] The effect on social return in the adverse selection case is not as clear. If all firms in the class of borrowers have projects with the same expected returns and only differ in the variance of their returns, then changes in the interest rate have no effect on the social return. If, however, the expected return decreases with increases in variance, then the social return will respond positively to a decrease in the lending rate.

[50] Though this has a second-order effect on the bank's profitability (by the enveloped theorem), it can have a first-order effect on social profitability.

[51] Another method by which banks may circumvent lending rate controls is through packaging loans together, i.e., tying the approval of a low-interest loan to making another loan at a higher lending rate. The "above-market" premium on the second loan may compensate the bank for the below-market rate on the directed credit. In any case, the process by which these compensating loans are determined is very similar to the negotiations over compensating balances discussed below.

[52] The view of bargaining over rents certainly applies well to the Japanese economy (cf. Aoki 1988).

[53] Because (direct) rents on priority-sector loans may be lower for banks than for other sectors, banks may be more vigilant in their monitoring of the use of funds by these firms, limiting their attempts to "overborrow," because the banks would prefer to lend funds to rent-generating sectors.

[54] When setting the fiat lending rates, the government should follow some rough guidelines to minimize this distortion. Fiat lending rates should also account for default risk and agency problems.

[55] As is often the case in signaling models, distortions may occur through excess investment in the signal. These distortions, then, may counteract some of the other social benefits from equity signaling.

[56] An argument can also be made that there is some room for the government to foster "experimentation," or what may be called an entrepreneurial environment: since there is no learning on the group of projects that are red-lined, society never learns about the potential of those sectors.

[57] A full discussion of the tools of industrial policy is beyond the scope of this section. We just concentrate on two tools that pertain to the functioning of financial restraint.

[58] For another view on the issue of information coordination and government policy, see also Chapter 5 in this volume, by Matsuyama.

[59] Most of the effect may be attributable to the negative correlation between high inflation and growth, rather than the direct effect of real interest rates (cf. Murdock and Stiglitz 1993).

[60] Another related problem is that banks must monitor their loan officers carefully. Given that there is credit rationing, there may be large opportunities for bribes.

[61] This would also depend on the organization of the civil service. The Japanese example of *amakudari* (see Aoki 1988) is an example of how to devise innovative structures to reduce the dangers of administrative sclerosis.

[62] In Japan as firms gained increased international stature, they were able to consider issuing bonds in other countries. This created pressure on the government to deregulate bond markets.

[63] The desirability of such a transition depends on the perceived advantages of either system, a topic that has received some attention in the recent literature (cf. Dinc 1995).

REFERENCES

AKERLOF, G. and ROMER, P. (1993), "Looting: The Economic Underworld of Bankruptcy for Profit," *Brookings Papers on Economic Activity*, 2:1–73.

AOKI, M. (1988), *Information, Incentives, and Bargaining in the Japanese Economy*, Cambridge University Press, Cambridge.

——(1994), "Monitoring Characteristics of the Main Bank System: An Analytical and Developmental View," chapter 4 in M. Aoki and H. Patrick, eds., *The Japanese Main Bank System: Its Relevance for Developing and Transforming Economies*, Oxford University Press, Oxford, 109–41.

——PATRICK, H., and SHEARD, P. (1994), "The Japanese Main Bank System: An Introductory Overview" in M. Aoki and H. Patrick, eds., *The Japanese Main Bank System: Its Relevance for Developing and Transforming Economies*, Oxford University Press, New York, 1–50.

BELL, C. (1990), "Interactions between Institutional and Informal Credit Agencies in Rural India," *The World Bank Economic Review*, 4(3):297–328.

Bernanke, B. (1983), "Nonmonetary Effects of the Financial Crisis in the Propagation of the Great Depression," *American Economic Review*, 73(3):257–76.

Bhattacharya, S. (1982), "Aspects of Monetary and Banking Theory and Moral Hazard," *Journal of Finance*, 37(2):371–84.

Caprio, G. and Summers, L. (1993), "Finance and Its Reform: Beyond Laissez-Faire," Policy Research Working Papers, Financial Sector Development WPS 1171, The World Bank, Washington.

Cho, Y. and Hellmann, T. (1993), "The Government's Role in Japanese and Korean Credit Markets: A New Institutional Economics Perspective," Policy Research Working Papers, Financial Sector Development WPS 1190, World Bank, Washington.

Dinc, S. (1995), "Relationship Banking, Integration of Financial Systems, and Path Dependence," mimeo, Stanford University, Stanford.

Fazzari, S., Hubbard, G., and Peterson, B. (1988), "Financing Constraints and Corporate Investment," *Brookings Papers on Economic Activity*, 1:141–206.

Fry, M. (1988), "Financial Development: Theories and Recent Experience," *Oxford Review of Economic Policy*, 6(4):13–28.

——(1995), *Money, Interest, and Banking in Economic Development*, The Johns Hopkins University Press, 2nd edn., Baltimore.

Giovannini, A. (1985), "Saving and the Real Interest Rate," *Journal of Development Economics*, 18:197–217.

Greenwald, B. and Stiglitz, J. (1986), "Externalities in Economies with Imperfect Information and Incomplete Markets," *Quarterly Journal of Economics*, 101:229–64.

————and Weiss, A. (1984), "Informational Imperfections and Macroeconomic Fluctuations," *American Economic Review, Papers and Proceedings*, 74:194–99.

Hellmann, T. (1994), "A Comparison of Incentives and Screening Properties of Short- and Long-term Finance," mimeo, Stanford University, Stanford.

——, Murdock, K., and Stiglitz, J. (1994a), "Deposit Mobilization through Financial Restraint," mimeo, Stanford University, Stanford.

——(1994b), "Addressing Moral Hazard in Banking: Deposit Rate Control vs. Capital Requirements," mimeo, Stanford University, Stanford.

Horiuchi, A. (1984), "Economic Growth and Financial Allocation in Postwar Japan," *Brookings Discussion Papers in International Economics*, No. 18.

Jensen, M. (1986), "Agency Costs of Free Cash Flow, Corporate Finance, and Takeovers," *American Economic Review, Papers and Proceedings*, 76:323–29.

Kane, E. (1989), *The S&L Insurance Crisis: How Did it Happen?* Urban Institute Press, Washington.

King, R. G. and Levine, R. (1993), "Finance and Growth: Schumpeter Might Be Right," *Quarterly Journal of Economics*, 108(3):717–37.

Klein, B. and Leffler, K. B. (1981), "The Role of Market Forces in Assuring Contractual Performance," *Journal of Political Economy*, 89:615–41.

McKinnon, R. (1973), *Money and Capital in Economic Development*, The Brookings Institution, Washington.

Milgrom, P. and Roberts, J. (1990), "Bargaining Costs, Influence Costs and the Organization of Economic Activity," in J. Alt and K. Shepsle, eds., *Perspectives on Positive Political Economy*, Cambridge University Press, Cambridge.

Murdock, K. and Stiglitz, J. (1993), "The Effect of Financial Repression in an

Economy with Positive Real Interest Rates: Theory and Evidence," mimeo, Stanford University, Stanford.

MYERS, S. and MAJLUF, N. (1984), "Corporate Financing and Investment Decisions When Firms Have Information That Investors Do Not Have," *Journal of Financial Economics*, 13:187–221.

NALEBUFF, B. and STIGLITZ, J. (1983), "Prizes and Incentives: Towards a General Theory of Compensation and Competition," *Bell Journal*, 14(1):21–43.

PACKER, F. (1994), "The Role of Long-term Credit Banks within the Main Bank System," EDI Working Papers, 94-6, World Bank, Washington.

RAJAN, R. (1992), "A Theory of the Costs and Benefits of Universal Banking," Center for Research on Security Prices Working Paper 346, University of Chicago, Chicago.

ROCHET, J. (1992), "Capital Requirement and the Behavior of Commercial Banks," *European Economic Review*, 36:1137–78.

SHAPIRO, C. (1983), "Premiums for High Quality Products as Returns to Reputation," *Quarterly Journal of Economics*, 98:615–41.

SHAW, E. (1973), *Financial Deepening in Economic Development*, Oxford University Press, New York.

STEIN, J. (1989), "Efficient Capital Markets, Inefficient Firms: A Model of Myopic Corporate Behavior," *Quarterly Journal of Economics*, 103:655–69.

STIGLITZ, J. (1986), "Towards a More General Theory of Monopolistic Competition," in M. H. Peston and R. E. Quandt, eds., *Prices, Competition and Equilibrium*, Philip Allan, Barnes & Noble Books, Oxford, 22–69.

——(1989), "Imperfect Information in the Product Market," in R. Schmalensee and R. D. Willig, eds., *Handbook of Industrial Organization*, vol. 1, Elsevier Science Publication, Amsterdam, 769–847.

——(1992a), "Explaining Growth: Competition and Finance," mimeo, Stanford University, Stanford.

——(1992b), "Introduction—S&L Bail-Out," in J. R. Barth and R. D. Brumbaugh, Jr., eds., *The Reform of the Federal Deposit Insurance: Disciplining the Government and Protecting the Taxpayers*, Harper Collins, New York.

——(1993a), "The Role of the State in Financial Markets," Proceedings of the Annual Conference on Development Economics, 19–52.

——(1993b), "Some Lessons from the Asian Miracle," mimeo, Stanford University, Stanford.

——and WEISS, A. (1981), "Credit Rationing in Markets with Imperfect Information," *American Economic Review*, 71(3):393–410.

SUMMERS, L. and SUMMERS, V. (1989), "When Financial Markets Work Too Well: A Cautious Case for a Securities Transaction Tax," *Journal of Financial Services Research*, 3(2):163–88.

TERANISHI, J. (1994a), "Savings Mobilization and Investment Financing During Japan's Postwar Economic Recovery," unpublished manuscript.

——(1994b), "Modernization of Financial Markets: An Analysis of Informal Credit Markets in Prewar Japan," *World Development*, 22(3):315–22.

WILLIAMSON, S. (1987), "Costly Monitoring, Loan Contracts, and Equilibrium Credit Rationing," *Quarterly Journal of Economics*, 101:135–45.

7

Government Intervention, Rent Distribution, and Economic Development in Korea

YOON JE CHO

As part of their economic development strategies, most governments in developing countries intervene in the market to affect resource allocation. In the process, economic rent is created. The creation of economic rent and its distribution provide government with perhaps its greatest leverage for affecting the economic behavior of the private sector. In every economy, developing or industrialized, economic rent is created and rent seeking is ubiquitous. The difference among economies may be the relative size of rent created and the way it is distributed—and this seems to have important consequences for the performance of the economy.

Korea is a country where government intervention in the market, especially in the financial market, was extensive, and where substantial economic rent was created and allocated in the course of economic development. However, the areas where major rent was created and the rules by which it was distributed changed over time, with the changes in political regimes and economic policy goals. In retrospect, this brought remarkably different outcomes in the course of Korea's postwar economic development. In the 1950s, rent was created mainly in relation to import restriction and overvalued foreign exchange rates. The sale of government assets, which had been owned by the Japanese during the Japanese occupation period (1910–45), to the private sector also entailed substantial rent. During this period, the government did not have a clear vision for economic development and the development goal was overshadowed by the political agenda related to nation-building. Thus, the creation and distribution of rent was done largely with political considerations in mind rather than clear economic goals.

Change occurred in the 1960s and 1970s in the main area where rent was created. As the Korean government shifted to an export-oriented development strategy, the rent involved with overvalued exchange rates almost disappeared and that involved with the restriction of import quotas diminished. Instead, rent was created mainly in relation to financial allocations—allocation of domestic bank loans as well as foreign loans to priority sectors (e.g., the export sector in the 1960s and the heavy and chemical industries in the 1970s). The government, during this period, created rent with a clear vision of providing incentives to the priority sectors (mainly exports), thereby striving to accelerate economic development. It had a comprehensive development strategy in which credit policies were well coordinated with other economic policies. Although the amounts of rent created and distributed were equally substantial in both periods, the economic performance in the 1960s and 1970s differed widely from that of the 1950s.

This chapter discusses how economic rent was created and distributed in the course of the economic development of Korea, and how the government used this rent to achieve its economic goals. In discussing rent, the chapter focuses mainly on government intervention in the financial market. This study thus attempts to shed some light on the role of government in the early stages of economic development.

The first section briefly discusses the main features of Korean economic policies during the aforementioned periods and the main policy instruments used to achieve economic goals. In this context, it focuses on the areas where economic rent was created and how it was distributed during the 1950s, 1960s, and 1970s. The experience of the 1950s is contrasted with that of the 1960s and 1970s in order to highlight how the areas of rent creation and methods of distribution can have significantly different consequences on economic performance. Section 7.1 also attempts to estimate the relative size of this rent over time. Section 7.2 attempts to assess whether or not government intervention in the market (i.e., the creation and distribution of rent intended to affect industrial behavior) can have a positive impact on economic development in its initial stages by examining the Korean experience. The chapter concludes with brief summary remarks.

7.1 RENT CREATION AND DISTRIBUTION OVER TIME

The 1950s: Import Restriction and Foreign Exchange Allocation

With the end of World War II, Korea gained independence from the Japanese occupation (1910–45). Soon thereafter, it was divided into the two countries of North Korea and South Korea (hereafter, "Korea" refers to the latter). The first Korean government was led by President Rhee Syng-Man. Rhee devoted much of his agenda to building the nation, securing a United States military commitment to ensure Korean security, guiding the country's involvement in the Korean war (1950–53), stabilizing war inflation, and securing US grants for the war-devastated economy.

In the 1950s, the government did not have a comprehensive economic development strategy and economic policy during this time was characterized by an assortment of government regulations that lacked a clear vision or set of policy goals. Since the government's economic policy came under strong US influence, the government did not systematically intervene in the market, and a relatively independent central bank was established following the model of the US Federal Reserve Board, resulting in the private control of banks. Although interest rate regulations and preferential credit programs existed, bank operations were not subject to much government regulation.

However, the government did enact strong regulations with respect to external transactions. It maintained import restrictions and highly overvalued exchange rates. The import restriction policy was adopted not necessarily in accordance with an industrial development strategy, but rather in consideration of the shortage of foreign exchange and the political agenda. Korea did not have any significant exports and the major source of foreign exchange at that time was foreign aid and the local expenditures of the US ground forces. Korea also maintained restrictions on imports, as did most developing countries at that time, for nationalistic reasons. In particular, the government rejected the purchase of Japanese manufactured products. Thus, the government had to ration the scarce foreign exchange mainly to alleviate the shortage of daily necessities and to build factories to produce them. In order to maximize foreign exchange revenues derived from the local expenditures of the US ground forces, the Korean currency remained highly overvalued.

The allocation of import quotas under the strong import restriction that accompanied foreign exchange allocation entailed substantial rent. Importers received windfall gains and prospered; some of the Korean *chaebol* operating in the 1990s were established during this period as major recipients of this rent. The amount of rent that accompanied foreign exchange allocation is estimated to have been roughly 10–14 per cent of annual GNP during this period (see Table 7.1).[1]

In the 1950s, the government had no comprehensive economic development strategy and did not create rent to drive private business in the direction of its economic policy goals. There were no established rules for the allocation of rent or for the explicit and formal institutions in charge of making decisions regarding allocation. The ruling political party and strong political figures intervened in the allocation process. Consequently, there was no clear link between rent distribution and economic considerations for development (Yoon 1991). The allocation of rent was mainly discretionary, and those who received these allocations benefited from windfall gains, portions of which were shared with politicians and bureaucrats.

The 1960s: Rent Creation and Distribution through Credit Market Intervention

Korea's rapid economic growth began in the 1960s. In May 1961, Park Chung Hee, a military general, grasped control of the government in a *coup*

TABLE 7.1 Exchange Rate of the US Dollar and Economic Rent in Relation to Overvalued Exchange Rates (million won, %)

Year	Official Rate[a]	Parallel Market Rate[a]	Total Rent (A)[b]	A/GNP
1953	18.00	37.90	6,873.5	14.3
1954	18.00	43.60	6,228.5	9.3
1955	50.00	96.40	15,841.0	13.6
1956	50.00	96.60	17,992.3	11.8
1957	50.00	103.30	23,569.3	11.9
1958	50.00	118.10	25,755.4	12.4
1959	50.00	125.50	22,936.9	10.4
1960	65.00	145.30	27,583.1	11.2
1961	130.00	150.10	6,535.6	2.1
1962	130.00	134.00	1,687.2	0.5
1963	130.00	174.50	24,933.4	5.1
1964	255.77	290.07	13,870.9	2.0
1965	271.78	323.68	24,050.5	3.0
1966	271.18	302.58	22,495.0	2.2
1967	274.60	305.70	30,981.8	2.5
1968	281.50	309.00	40,229.8	2.6
1969	304.45	339.85	64,555.4	2.6
1970	316.65	348.75	63,686.4	2.5

Notes: [a] Exchange rates are averaged on an annual basis.
[b] Total rent = total imports × exchange rate gap. Imports are valued at CIF and the exchange rate gap is the gap between the official rate and the parallel market rate.

Source: Bank of Korea.

d'état; in 1963, he became president in a popular election. His regime continued until his assassination in 1979. When Park took power, he—and many other Koreans—harbored little confidence in the free market system. He and his economic staff believed the government should guide important prices, such as interest rates, and oversee the allocation of resources. But they gradually began to see the merits of price reforms that allowed important prices such as interest rates and the exchange rate to become closer to market prices. So they implemented price reforms that strengthened guidance in resource allocation.

In the early 1960s, Park's military government established new priorities for Korea's economy by shifting its policy stance from stabilization to growth and from import substitution to export promotion. The overvalued exchange rate was devalued by approximately 100 per cent. Consequently, rent associated with foreign exchange allocation in the 1950s almost disappeared, as indicated in Table 7.1.

The government believed it could accelerate economic growth by taking the lead in mobilizing and allocating resources. In pursuit of this goal, the government launched its first five-year economic development plan and implemented two measures to strengthen state control of the financial market: nationalizing commercial banks, and amending the Bank of Korea (BOK) Act to subordinate the central bank under the government. In addition, it introduced three significant policy reforms: the overhaul of the export credit program, the reform of interest rates, and the facilitation of foreign capital inflow. The government strengthened its control over the financial system and used credit allocation as the major industrial policy instrument. However, it also streamlined relative prices to correspond more closely to market levels during this period; interest rates were substantially increased and the exchange rate overvaluation was corrected.

The rent generated in relation to credit allocation was substantial during the 1960s, not necessarily because the government heavily repressed interest rates, but because the total volume of credit (both bank loans and foreign loans) to be allocated expanded as a result of interest rate reform and government effort to mobilize foreign borrowing.

Expansion of Export Credit Programs

An export credit program to support the export industry was in place as early as the 1950s, but the size of loans then was negligible. When the military government initiated the export-led strategy for economic growth, it naturally strengthened export credit programs to support exporters. Until the mid-1980s, when Korea ran a current account surplus,[2] the system of export financing played a critical role in promoting the export industry.

The short-term export credit system was streamlined in 1961. The essence of the new system was the "automatic approval" of loans by commercial banks to prospective borrowers holding export letters of credit (L/C). Initially, the program covered certain portions of the production costs of goods slated for export. Its coverage expanded rapidly, extending to sales to United Nations forces in Korea in 1961; to exports on a documents-against-payment (D/P), documents-against-acceptance (D/A), or consignment basis in 1965; to construction services rendered to foreign governments or their agencies in 1967; to imports of raw materials and intermediate goods for export-related use or to purchases from local suppliers in 1967; and so on. In each case, the expanded coverage was intended to promote the exploration of new export opportunities and the diversification of export items. These new programs were established after close consultation between the government and exporters.

General trading companies were introduced in the new export-financing system and were provided with financing on the basis of their export performance. To be eligible for financing, these companies had to exceed a specified level of exports which increased year to year, thus linking their export performance to their access to credit. The general trading companies had favorable access to export credit but were required to renew their licenses each year. Those whose exports did not exceed the specified level had their licenses revoked.

The interest rate on export loans was subsidized heavily. When the 1965 interest rate reform was implemented with the doubling of nominal rates (see below), the interest rate on export credit remained untouched. Consequently, the gap between export loans and general loans widened sharply. Interest rates on loans to exporters remained at 6.5 per cent while the general loan rate rose to 26 per cent (see Table 7.2). The rent associated with export credit alone is estimated to have been about 0.5–1.0 per cent of GNP during the 1960s, and about 2–3 per cent of GNP during the 1970s (see Table 7.3).

Interest Rate Reform

The government drastically changed its interest rate policies in 1965. Overnight, it raised the nominal interest rate on (one-year) time deposits from 15 per cent per year to 30 per cent, and the general loan rate from 16 to 26 per cent. However, the reform only partially helped draw the interest rates offered by the banks closer to market rates. Loan-rate increases were selective, excluding export-related, agricultural, and many other categories of investment loans. This action was intended to spur domestic saving to finance ambitious investment programs for economic development. To protect industrial firms from increasing costs incurred from overborrowing, a "negative interest margin" was introduced. At the same time, to protect the profitability of banks, the central bank provided cheap credit to commercial banks, which depended heavily on this credit in the extension of loans to firms.[3] On the other hand, the central bank placed high reserve requirements on commercial banks to contain inflationary pressure due to the expansion of its credit, but it paid interest on this reserve to protect commercial banks' profitability.

The reform successfully attracted private saving. In the first three months, the level of time and savings deposits increased by 50 per cent; over the next four years the level grew at an annual compounded rate of nearly 100 per cent. The stock of M2 relative to GNP increased from 8.9 per cent in 1964 to 31.8 per cent in 1971. Total bank loans increased by an equivalent amount. The annual growth rate of bank loans rose from 10.9 per cent during 1963–64 to 61.5 per cent during 1965–69.

More importantly, the reform helped shift funds from the unregulated informal sector to the banking sector, over which the government tightened its control. This allowed the government to increase controls on financial flow. It increased the total volume of capital to be distributed under government influence. Despite the interest rate reform, bank interest rates were still substantially lower than market rates (Table 7.2). Thus, the allocation of bank credit was accompanied by substantial rent. The rent associated

TABLE 7.2 Comparison of Various Interest Rates and Rent Created in the Financial Sector (%)

Year	Bank Loan Rate		Curb Market Rate (C)	Corporate Bond Rate	Inflation[a]	A – B	C – A	Rent/GNP[b]	Rent/GNP[c]
	General Loan (A)	Export Loan (B)							
1968	25.8	6.0	55.9	—	16.1	19.8	30.1	5.6	—
1969	24.5	6.0	51.2	—	14.8	18.5	26.7	5.5	—
1970	24.0	6.0	50.8	—	15.6	18.0	26.8	7.0	—
1971	23.0	6.0	46.3	—	12.5	17.0	23.3	6.3	—
1972	17.7	6.0	38.9	22.9	16.7	11.7	21.2	6.1	1.5
1973	15.5	7.0	39.2	21.8	13.6	8.5	23.7	7.2	1.9
1974	15.5	9.0	37.6	21.0	30.5	6.5	22.1	8.7	2.2
1975	15.5	7.0	41.3	20.1	25.2	5.8	25.8	9.5	1.7
1976	17.5	8.0	40.5	20.4	21.2	8.5	23.0	8.0	1.0
1977	19.0	9.0	38.1	20.1	16.6	10.0	19.1	6.3	0.4
1978	19.0	9.0	41.7	21.1	22.8	10.0	22.7	8.2	0.8
1979	19.0	9.0	42.4	26.7	19.6	10.0	23.4	9.2	3.0
1980	20.0	15.0	45.0	30.1	23.9	5.0	25.0	10.8	4.4
1981	16.4	15.0	35.4	24.4	17.0	1.4	19.0	8.8	3.7
1982	10.0	10.0	33.1	17.3	6.9	0.0	23.1	11.8	3.7
1983	10.0	10.0	25.8	14.2	5.0	0.0	15.8	8.4	2.2

Notes: [a] GNP deflator.
[b] Rent = total loans × (curb market rate – bank loan rate).
[c] Rent = total loans × (corporate bond rate – bank loan rate).
Source: Bank of Korea.

TABLE 7.3 Rent Created in Export Loans (billion won, %)

Year	Export Loans[a] (A)	(A) × Interest Gap[b] (B)	Rent (B)/GNP
1963	3.9	1.4	0.3
1964	10.0	4.6	0.7
1965	12.1	4.0	0.5
1966	16.6	5.4	0.5
1967	32.4	9.8	0.8
1968	43.4	13.1	0.8
1969	80.7	21.5	0.9
1970	161.6	43.3	1.7
1971	248.5	57.9	1.8
1972	231.8	49.1	1.3
1973	416.2	98.6	2.0
1974	652.6	144.2	2.1
1975	1,042.7	269.0	3.0
1976	1,511.5	347.6	2.9
1977	2,616.0	499.7	2.9
1978	3,764.8	854.6	3.7
1979	5,642.8	1,320.4	4.5
1980	6,957.4	1,739.4	4.7
1981	6,957.4	1,321.9	2.9
1982	8,192.0	1,892.4	3.7
1983	9,232.6	1,458.8	2.5

Notes: [a] Outstanding loans at the end of the year.
[b] Interest gap = curb market rate – export loan interest.
Source: Bank of Korea, *Economic Statistics Yearbook*, various issues.

with domestic credit allocation is estimated to have been around 4–6 per cent of GNP in the 1960s when bank interest rates were significantly high.[4] Real interest rates were very positive in the 1960s. However, interest rates were reduced to support the heavy and chemical industries in the 1970s, and accordingly the rent generated also increased to 6–12 per cent of GNP (Table 7.2).

The interest rate reform of the 1960s has been described by many economists as financial liberalization.[5] This is correct in the sense that the degree of government repression on the interest rate level was substantially reduced. In price terms, therefore, it was substantial liberalization that brought rapid growth of the financial sector. However, as mentioned earlier, liberalization in fact helped to enhance government influence over the total financial flow of the economy by expanding the formal banking sector, which was already under tight government control. Funds shifted from the informal credit market, which lay beyond government control. Therefore, the interest rate policy in the 1960s can be assessed as one of financial restraint.[6] On the other hand, government policy in the financial sector shifted toward more financial repression in the 1970s, as the government reduced interest rates, tightening its control over credit allocation.

However, financial repression in Korea was somewhat different from that usually found elsewhere or that defined in Chapter 6 by Hellmann, Murdock, and Stiglitz in this volume. In Korea, financial repression was not the mechanism for the nonproductive transfer of wealth from the household sector to the government. Rather, that mechanism was the implicit taxation of depositors to subsidize priority industrial sectors. Cheap credit for industrial firms was supported by interest rate control on deposits and the central bank's cheap credit to commercial banks, which sometimes reached 20–30 per cent of the latter's total lending. The interest rates on these loans were very low in order to sustain the profitability of banks.[7]

Most of the central bank credit to commercial banks was to support the policy-based lending of commercial banks such as export bills. In Korea, a substantial part of policy loans was supported by the expansion of high-powered money rather than fiscal funds, as was the case in postwar Japan. This was a fundamental reason why Korea had a relatively unstable inflation rate compared to Japan or Taiwan, despite its conservative fiscal stance. The financial resources to support industrialists in the priority sector were mobilized through implicit taxation on depositors. In Korea, through this implicit taxation, the transfer of wealth took place within the private sector rather than from the private to the public sector as was the case in many other developing countries.

Facilitating the Flow of Foreign Capital

The Korean saving rate remained very low in the 1960s. In order to compensate for the shortage of domestic capital and declining foreign aid, the government normalized its relations with Japan in 1965 and amended the Foreign Capital Inducement Act in 1966, allowing state-owned banks to guarantee foreign borrowing by the private sector. This measure prompted a large inflow of foreign capital, especially from Japan. Since few Korean firms had direct access to foreign borrowing in the 1960s, the government's repayment guarantees to private borrowers through state-owned banks facilitated and reduced the cost of private foreign borrowing. Because domestic interest rates were high, private firms perceived foreign borrowing as a very attractive alternative. Yet each foreign loan had to be approved and allocated by the government, and foreign loans were used selectively to support industrial policy goals. The *ex post* rent associated with foreign loans fluctuated with changes in exchange rates but was quite substantial (Table 7.4). Estimations are presented in Table 7.5.

Rent Distribution in the 1960s

Following the creation of substantial rent in relation to credit allocation, rent distribution was used more effectively as an industrial policy instru-

TABLE 7.4 Cost of Foreign Loans and Domestic Market Rates (%, % point)

Year	Cost of Foreign Loans		Bank Loan Rate	Curb Market Rate (C)	Corporate Bond Yield (D)	C – A	D – A	C – B	D – B
	Nominal (A)[a]	Effective (B)[b]							
1968	7.13	15.28	25.8	55.9	—	48.77	—	40.62	—
1969	10.06	14.07	24.5	51.2	—	41.14	—	37.13	—
1970	6.57	24.61	24.0	50.8	—	44.05	—	26.19	—
1971	5.81	12.70	23.0	46.3	—	40.49	—	33.60	—
1972	6.19	5.84	17.7	38.9	22.9	32.71	16.71	33.06	17.06
1973	10.03	31.79	15.5	39.2	21.8	29.17	11.77	7.41	–9.99
1974	10.19	10.19	15.5	37.6	21.0	27.41	10.81	27.41	10.81
1975	6.63	6.63	15.5	41.3	20.1	34.67	13.47	34.67	13.47
1976	5.38	5.38	17.5	40.5	20.4	35.12	15.02	35.12	15.02
1977	7.50	7.50	19.0	38.1	20.1	30.60	12.60	30.60	12.60
1978	12.31	12.31	19.0	41.7	21.1	29.39	8.79	29.39	8.79
1979	14.44	50.78	19.0	42.4	26.7	27.96	12.26	–8.38	–24.08
1980	16.75	22.90	20.0	45.0	30.1	28.25	13.35	22.10	7.20
1981	14.81	21.59	16.4	35.4	24.4	20.59	9.59	13.81	2.81
1982	9.50	15.85	10.0	33.1	17.3	23.60	7.80	17.25	1.45
1983	10.06	13.86	10.0	25.8	14.2	15.74	4.14	11.94	0.34

Notes: [a] Libor-based cost of borrowing.
[b] Nominal cost adjusted for the annual fluctuation rate of the exchange rate.
Source: Bank of Korea.

TABLE 7.5 Rent Created in Foreign Loan Allocation (million $US, %)

Year	Total Foreign Loans (A)	B × A[a]	C × A[b]	D × A[c]	E × A[d]
1968	1,199	584.8	—	487.0	—
		(11.2)	—	(9.3)	—
1969	1,800	740.5	—	668.4	—
		(11.2)	—	(10.1)	—
1970	2,277	1,003.0	—	596.4	—
		(12.6)	—	(7.5)	—
1971	2,984	1,208.2	—	1,002.7	—
		(12.9)	—	(10.7)	—
1972	3,580	1,171.0	598.2	1,183.6	610.8
		(11.1)	(5.7)	(11.2)	(5.8)
1973	4,257	1,241.8	501.0	315.4	–425.3
		(9.2)	(3.7)	(2.3)	(–3.1)
1974	5,955	1,632.3	643.7	1,632.3	643.7
		(8.8)	(3.5)	(8.8)	(3.5)
1975	8,457	2,932.0	1,139.2	2,932.0	1,139.2
		(14.1)	(5.5)	(14.1)	(5.5)
1976	10,635	3,735.0	1,597.4	3,735.0	1,597.4
		(13.0)	(5.6)	(13.0)	(5.6)
1977	12,649	3,870.6	1,593.8	3,870.6	1,593.8
		(12.3)	(5.1)	(12.3)	(5.1)
1978	14,823	4,356.5	1,302.9	4,356.5	1,302.9
		(8.4)	(2.5)	(8.4)	(2.5)
1979	20,287	5,672.2	2,487.2	–1,700.7	–4,885.7
		(9.1)	(4.0)	(–2.7)	(–7.8)
1980	27,170	7,675.5	3,627.2	6,003.9	1,955.6
		(12.7)	(6.0)	(10.0)	(3.2)
1981	32,433	6,678.0	3,110.3	4,478.7	911.1
		(10.1)	(4.7)	(6.8)	(1.4)
1982	37,083	8,751.6	2,892.5	6,396.7	537.6
		(12.6)	(4.2)	(9.2)	(0.8)
1983	40,378	6,355.5	1,671.6	4,822.6	138.8
		(8.4)	(2.2)	(6.3)	(0.2)

Numbers in parentheses are ratio to GNP.
Notes: [a] B = curb market rate – nominal Libor (London interbank offer rates) rate.
[b] C = corporate bond yield – nominal Libor rate.
[c] D = curb market rate – effective Libor rate.
[d] E = corporate bond yield – effective Libor rate.

ment in the 1960s than in the 1950s. Credit allocation (both domestic and foreign), especially export credit allocation, was linked with the performance of rent seekers: those who were more successful in the export market were rewarded with more allocated credit. In the 1950s, harboring close ties with government officials or politically powerful figures often proved to be enough to receive rent allocations. However, such practices and conditions changed in the 1960s. In addition, industrialists were required to prove they could perform in the international market and meet the criteria set by the government. If they did not perform up to the standards, they faced the revocation of favorable treatment. In the 1950s, the volume of items to be allocated with rent (i.e., foreign exchange) was quite small, but the price subsidy (degree of overvaluation) was significant and the rules for distribution were not clear. In the 1960s, however, the degree of the price subsidy was reduced, the volume of items to be allocated credit (both domestic and foreign) was large, and rent distribution was more closely linked to the performances of rent seekers.

The 1970s: Intensified Rent Creation Associated with Development of the Heavy and Chemical Industries

In the 1970s, the government reverted to lower interest rates while intensifying its controls on credit allocation. Credit policies were made more "selective." This reversion was marked by a Presidential Emergency Decree in 1972, which bailed out many financially insolvent firms by placing an immediate moratorium on all loans in the informal credit markets, and reduced the bank loan rate from 23 per cent to 15.5 per cent.[8] Furthermore, approximately 30 per cent of short-term high-interest commercial bank loans to businesses were converted into long-term loans with concessional terms for repayment on an installment basis, over a five-year period, at an 8 per cent annual interest rate, with a three-year grace period. The lapse back to more repressive financial policies was motivated by the policy shift toward the promotion of the heavy and chemical industries (HCI), which required enormous amounts of cheap financing and constituted a significant departure from the export-oriented, non-sectoral-biased strategy adopted throughout the 1960s.

The government adopted two other important measures to support the HCI drive: it established the National Investment Fund (NIF), and it expanded BOK discounts. HCI development required a large amount of term financing. In December 1973, the government established the NIF to finance long-term investments in HCI plants and equipment.[9] The NIF was mobilized from a combination of funds from private financial intermediaries and the government, but predominantly from the former. Although the NIF did not comprise a large share of total bank loans, it provided more than 60 per cent of term financing for HCI equipment investment in the years 1975–80 (Cho and Kim 1995). BOK also expanded its rediscount facility to support the HCI. Considering the long maturation period of investments in the HCI, BOK also increased the maximum loan period for equipment investment. Furthermore, BOK brought out the "Guide to

Bank Loans," adding HCI to the list of high-priority industries for financial support to induce more lending by banks to the HCI. The Guide curbed, or in some cases prohibited, some service industries from receiving bank financing (Cho and Kim 1995).

As the government pursued HCI development, rent was generated through the restriction on entry and selection of manufacturers in specific industries (since there were economies of scale in production for most HCI) in addition to the allocation of credit. Choosing market entrants and providing financial support were packaged. Since great uncertainty accompanied HCI investment, in the opening stages of the HCI drive, industrialists were reluctant to enter these industries, even with the large rent generation. Later, when the government's determination to stand behind selected market entrants at whatever cost was confirmed, these industrialists competed fiercely to receive selection as HCI manufacturers.

In accordance with the nature of this kind of industrial policy, rent distribution became more discretionary in the 1970s than it had been in the 1960s. Although most selected entrants were already established industrialists (and thus their management capability was proven), there was no explicit criterion for the selection of a specific industrialist or *chaebol* as an entrant to a specific industry. There was substantial room for the discretionary allocation of rent and favoritism. Since the HCI required an immense scale of investment, most of the firms that entered these industries with strong government support, in terms of credit allocation, were the already well-established *chaebol*. Consequently, rent distribution in the 1970s increased the degree of economic concentration in the Korean economy, later becoming a serious burden on economic policy.

7.2 DID GOVERNMENT INTERVENTION AND ECONOMIC RENT PROMOTE RAPID DEVELOPMENT?

In Korea, as discussed earlier, government intervention in the financial market was extensive: the government controlled interest rates and supervised the allocation of bank credit. Economic rent associated with credit allocation (and foreign exchange allocation) was substantial, and its distribution constituted the major government tool for corporate governance and industrial policy. The export drive in the 1960s and the HCI drive in the 1970s were supported by various preferential credit programs and the government's discretionary allocation of credit.

To what extent, then, did credit spur growth in the priority sectors and/or support industrial development? A direct answer to this question is not possible. Since credit supports were provided in conjunction with other incentives, it is not easy to isolate the impact of the credit supports from the other incentives. Thus, we can address this issue only in an indirect manner.

We can first examine the impact of credit supports on the take-off of exports in the 1960s; second, we can discuss the impact of credit supports on the HCI in their rapid growth during the 1970s, to determine their merit and whether rent allocation had occurred.[10]

The Impact on Export Growth

In order for exporters to respond to foreign demand, they should have access to the trade financing necessary to fill export orders (Rhee 1989). In many developing countries, financing mechanisms that are taken for granted in industrial countries, such as short-term money markets and bill discount markets, are rudimentary or nonexistent; such was the case in Korea in the 1960s. Thus, one way to provide a market for bill discounts to exporters was to establish the central bank's rediscount facility (Rhee 1989). Although exporters in Korea in the 1950s received some selective credit supports through lending by the central bank, export credit programs were formalized only in the 1960s. The total amount of credit supported by export credit programs increased from 4.5 per cent of total bank credit in the years 1961–65 to 7.6 per cent (1966–72), and further to 13.2 per cent (1973–81). In addition, as shown in the previous section, interest rate subsidies for export credits were substantial. In the years 1966–72, the interest rate for export credit was 17.1 per cent lower, on average, than the general loan rate. Exporters also received support from various other credit programs (such as equipment funds for export industries) and favorable credit allocations in conformity with government directives or administrative guidance. During Korea's export expansion period, credit subsidies comprised the major component of total export subsidies (Figure 7.1), which peaked in 1967 when the total interest rate subsidy was 2.3 per cent of the total value of exports,[11] far exceeding the fiscal subsidy of 1.0 per cent in the same year.

The extent to which credit subsidies contributed to the take-off of Korean exports in the 1960s is unclear (Figure 7.2 shows the export growth rate throughout the economic development period). A competitive exchange rate (with a major devaluation of the won in 1964) and various institutional supports also contributed to export growth. The expanded accessibility of credit (subsidized by low interest rates) was crucial in enabling Korean exporters to fill foreign orders and to explore foreign markets. In general, access to credit seems to have been more essential for supporting the continuous growth of exports than were interest rate subsidies. But, because export marketing requires substantial fixed costs in the initial stages and involves tremendous externalities,[12] government subsidies may also have made a large contribution because private efforts and investment in the exploration of external markets might not have been sufficient to fuel rapid growth. Alternatively, export marketing could have been subsidized

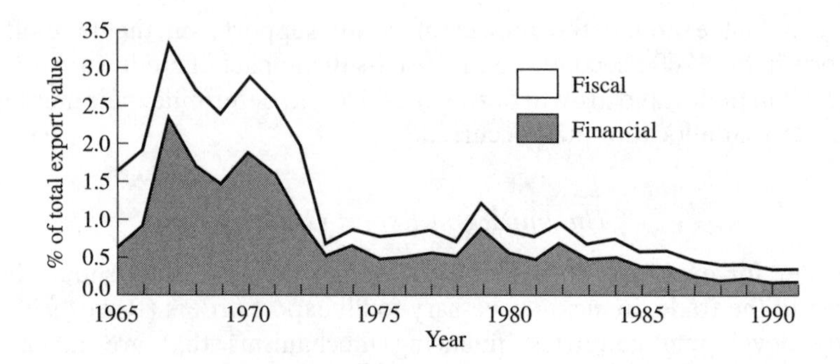

FIG. 7.1 Subsidies to Export, 1965–1991

Note: The amount of financial subsidies is the size of export-related loans multiplied by the interest rate differential between the average loan rate for the manufacturing industry and interest rates for export-related loans. The tax subsidy ratio is the total amount of tax subsidies from export reserves and special depreciation systems divided by the total value of exports. If the amount of the financial subsidy were based on the gap between the market interest rate and the export loan rate, the credit subsidy would be much larger. The tax subsidy from the export reserve system is the amount of tax savings that comes from corporate tax exemptions on the export reserve in a given year. That is, it is calculated by subtracting the net present value of the deferred tax on the export reserve that would be paid over a three-year period after a two-year grace period from the tax on the export reserve that should have been paid in a given year. The tax subsidy from a special depreciation system is the net present value of the tax savings from the added depreciation that is allowed within 30 per cent of the normal depreciation on fixed assets purchased by an exporter.

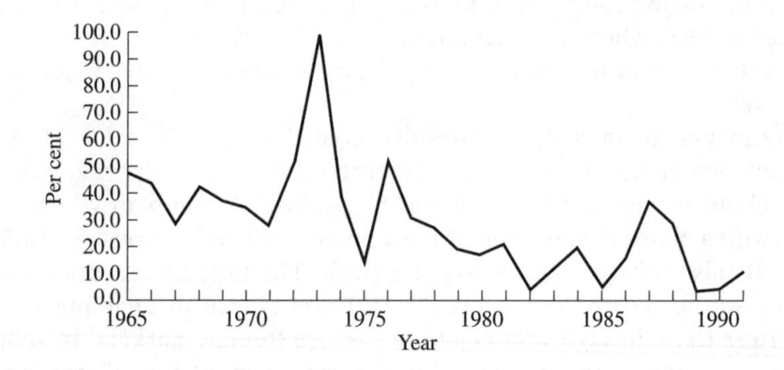

FIG. 7.2 Growth of Exports, 1965–1991

by the budget. But given the poor budgetary situation in the 1960s when total tax revenue fell within the range of 6.8–12.4 per cent of GNP (as discussed earlier), the use of fiscal subsidies was clearly limited. It was also true that using subsidized credit through implicit taxation on the banking system (and consequently on depositors) was politically easier.

Impact on HCI Development

As discussed in the previous section, bank loans were allocated favorably to the HCI in the 1970s. The manufacturing sector received 46.1 per cent of total domestic bank loans in 1970 but contributed only 21.3 per cent to GDP.[13] Within the manufacturing sector, the HCI received 22.6 per cent of total bank loans but contributed only 8.6 per cent to GDP. In 1980, after a decade of the HCI drive, the share of bank credit to the HCI increased further to 32.1 per cent, while its contribution to GDP also rose to 16.5 per cent.

The NIF was the major credit support program for the HCI, providing preferential maturities and interest rates. Credit support was provided not only by explicitly designated credit programs such as the NIF, but also by government directives to banks to provide more credit. The allocation of foreign loans was also a large part of total credit support. In the years 1972–76, for example, industries in the manufacturing sector claimed 66.1 per cent of the total amount of foreign commercial loans. Of this amount, 64.1 per cent went to the HCI (Table 7.6 provides a breakdown of the composition of foreign commercial loans).

The massive credit support made it possible to invest heavily in the HCI during the 1970s. During the late 1970s, almost 80 per cent of all fixed investment in the manufacturing sector went to the HCI. Consequently, the industrial structure and export composition of Korea changed drastically (Table 7.7). The expansion of the HCI in the 1970s is striking. Within a decade, the HCI share of total industrial output grew more than two and half times, and their share of exports tripled. Moreover, HCI shares of bank

TABLE 7.6 Composition of Public and Commercial Loans by Industry (%)

Year	Type of Loan	Agriculture, Forestry, & Fisheries	Manufacturing		Service[a]	Total
			HCI	Light		
1959–66	Public	7.5	11.7	8.3	72.5	100.0
	Commercial	22.3	43.4	31.4	2.9	100.0
1967–71	Public	42.2	6.8	1.6	49.4	100.0
	Commercial	3.6	31.6	23.9	40.8	100.0
1972–76	Public	18.2	6.1	0.0	75.8	100.0
	Commercial	2.2	42.4	23.7	31.7	100.0
1977–82	Public	17.0	1.5	0.3	81.2	100.0
	Commercial	0.6	46.0	10.6	42.8	100.0
1959–82	Public	19.0	3.0	0.4	77.6	100.0
	Commercial	1.6	43.6	15.4	39.5	100.0
	Total	9.6	24.9	8.5	57.0	100.0

Note: [a] Service includes construction, electricity, transportation, etc.
Source: Cha (1986).

TABLE 7.7 Industrial Structure and Export Composition: HCI Trends, 1970–1988 (%)

	1970	1975	1980	1985	1988
Industrial Structure					
Agriculture/fisheries	17.0	12.8	8.3	7.7	6.3
Mining	1.1	0.9	0.8	0.7	0.6
Manufacturing	40.3	50.4	51.0	50.0	52.7
Light	28.4	29.5	24.7	21.7	21.4
HCI	11.9	20.9	26.3	28.3	31.3
Petrochemical	5.9	10.8	12.6	11.4	10.0
Basic metal	2.0	3.4	5.1	4.9	5.3
Metal/machinery	4.0	6.7	8.6	12.0	16.1
Power/gas/construction	9.8	7.7	10.2	10.4	9.3
Service	31.8	28.2	29.7	31.2	29.4
Total	100.0	100.0	100.0	100.0	100.0
Composition of Exports					
Light	49.4	45.6	35.2	30.0	29.1
HCI	12.8	29.0	38.3	47.5	51.4
Petrochemical	5.4	9.2	9.9	12.4	11.0
Basic metal	1.5	4.0	8.1	5.8	5.1
Metal/machinery	5.9	15.8	20.3	29.3	35.4

Source: Bank of Korea, "Input-Output Tables," various issues.

credits, output, and exports within the manufacturing sector also expanded rapidly over time (see Figure 7.3). It is obvious that without government intervention in the allocation of credit, the quick transformation of the industrial composition and discrete jump in the level of industrial development would not have been possible.

Impact on Overall Economic Growth

Did the growth of these credit-supported sectors contribute to the rapid economic growth of Korea? In response to this question, we can only make tentative conclusions. In a sense, it is too early to answer, since Korea is still undergoing economic development and may not yet have fully realized the costs or benefits of financial policies. One solid conclusion pertains to the growth of exports, which was the main engine of rapid growth in Korea during the 1960s and 1970s. To the extent that credit support was indispensable to export growth, credit support, in turn, must have acted as the catalyst for rapid economic growth; but whether the extent of the subsidization implemented was necessary to propel the growth of exports remains questionable. However, the impact of credit support on the HCI drive and its subsequent effect on growth remains controversial (e.g.,

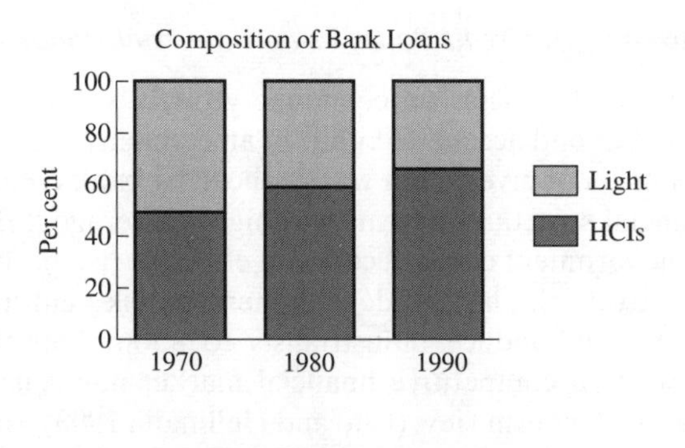

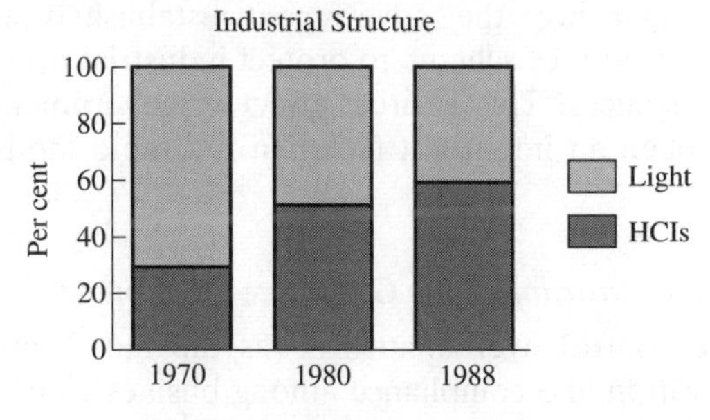

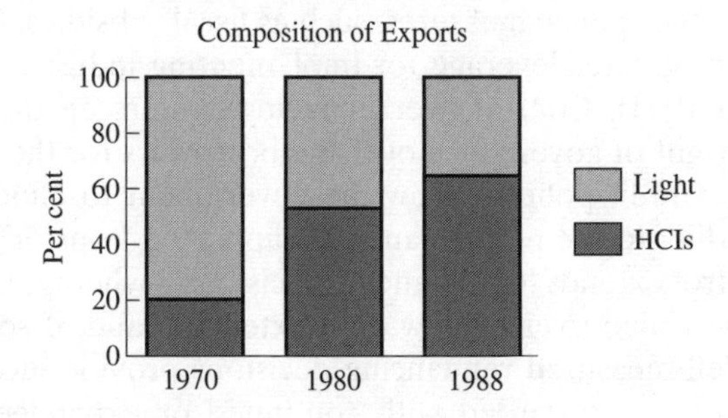

FIG. 7.3 Significance of the HCI and Light Industries in the Manufacturing Sector: Trends

Amsden 1989; Stern et al. 1992; Leipziger and Petri 1992; and World Bank 1987a). Although credit supports were influential in spurring the rapid development of the HCI, credit allocation might have been more efficient had it been allocated more equitably between the HCI and light industry—particularly given the labor endowment in the 1970s.[14] However, by the mid-1980s, the HCI did become the leading export industries in Korea; currently, HCI exports such as steel, metal, general machinery and equipment, electrical and chemical products, etc. constitute 66.1 per cent of Korea's total exports.

The Effectiveness of Credit Policy as an Industrial Policy Instrument

The impact of credit policies on economic growth is not limited to their effect on the cost of and access to credit. In an economy such as Korea's, in which the expansion of investment was financed by bank credit and foreign loans, the financial structure of firms was highly leveraged. By controlling financing, the government could become an effective risk partner for industrialists and motivate the latter's development of risk ventures and entrepreneurship. It could induce industrialists to adopt long-term business perspectives, while a competitive financial market might have prompted firms to take a shorter-term view (Cho and Hellmann 1993). In other words, by controlling financing, the government established a government-industry-bank coinsurance scheme to protect industrial firms from any unexpected circumstances. This indirect effect of government credit policy may also have been an important factor in the rapid industrialization of Korea.

Credit Policy as an Instrument for Corporate Governance

In Korea, state control over financing was the most powerful tool for inducing cooperation and compliance among businesses in the promotion of exports and industrialization. One of the distinct advantages of credit supports over other policy measures, such as fiscal subsidies, is that it gives the government greater leverage for implementing industrial policy (Cho and Hellmann 1993). Control over financing confers on the government some explicit right of governance over the borrowers for the entire period of their loans. Credit policies allow the government to allocate subsidies flexibly, according to the performance of supported firms or industries. In turn, such control extends to refinancing decisions—whether or not existing debt should be rolled over or new debt extended, and, if so, under what conditions. Well-measured refinancing decisions provide incentives: good performance can be rewarded with continued or expanded support; or inappropriate use of funds can be punished with a reduction in or even termination of support, an action that could make a firm's survival untenable. This carrot-and-stick policy underlying credit programs makes them effective tools of government industrial policy, being more effective than fiscal incentives, which stem from legislative initiation and are subject to the rigidity of the implementation process.[15]

But credit policies carry their own risk—the "risk of government failure." In Korea, the government's continuous communication with business leaders and close monitoring of firms through various channels (such as monthly export promotion meetings) helped reduce its risk of failure. Moreover, by controlling the banks, the government created incentives for firms to maximize their assets and growth, rather than to strive for immediate profitability. As long as they satisfied the government by expanding exports and successfully completing the construction of plants, firms ensured their continued credit support and survival. The government thus mitigated the risk of failure by adopting a sounder, more stable investment environment.

Credit Control as an Instrument for Risk Management

Industrial investment in Korea was financed largely by debt, especially during the period of rapid economic growth. Fiscal incentives and low interest rates allowed some firms to accumulate retained earnings, but, in the absence of a well-functioning domestic equity market, huge investment requirements for rapid industrial expansion had to be financed largely with

TABLE 7.8 Growth of the Financial Sector (%)

Year	M2/GNP	M3/GNP	Financial Intermediation Ratio[a]	Domestic Saving Ratio to GNP[b]
1968	26.4	—	—	15.1
1969	32.7	—	—	18.8
1970	32.2	10.0	2.22	15.8
1971	31.7	37.4	2.23	14.7
1972	34.6	40.2	2.36	16.3
1973	36.8	44.5	2.43	22.2
1974	32.4	40.1	2.29	20.2
1975	31.1	38.5	2.26	18.7
1976	30.3	38.1	2.18	24.0
1977	33.0	42.2	2.28	27.4
1978	33.0	42.4	2.28	29.3
1979	32.0	43.3	2.29	28.8
1980	34.0	48.7	2.56	24.8
1981	34.3	51.4	2.71	25.1
1982	39.7	59.6	3.04	26.3
1983	36.9	61.3	3.07	29.6
1984	34.8	64.4	3.72	32.1
1985	36.0	69.9	3.94	32.4
1986	36.4	77.1	3.83	35.9
1987	36.7	85.3	3.79	38.5
1988	37.3	91.6	3.79	40.0
1989	39.6	104.0	4.25	36.8
1990	38.5	111.0	4.33	36.4
1991	39.1	113.9	4.40	36.7
1992	40.3	123.5	4.67	35.4
1993	42.5	132.4	—	35.3

Notes: [a] Domestic stock of financial assets/GNP (at current prices).
[b] Domestic saving ratio = GDP – final consumption expenditure.
Source: Bank of Korea.

bank loans and foreign debt. In the years 1963–71, the debt ratio of the Korean manufacturing sector increased more than fourfold, from 92 per cent to 394 per cent. Even in the 1990s, Korean firms remain highly leveraged, although their debt ratio in the second half of the 1980s declined somewhat with the expansion of the stock market. Consequently, Korean firms became more vulnerable to internal and external shocks.[16] In fact, Korea could have undergone several financial crises had the government not become actively involved in risk management through credit intervention.

The government implemented major corporate bail-outs in 1969–70, 1972, 1979–81, and 1984–88 to ride out recessions and avoid major financial crises. In the credit-based economy, the government made these bail-outs by intervening in credit markets. The government's involvement in restructuring firms and industries and in redistributing losses made risk sharing possible among the members of the economy. Depositors usually incurred the lion's share of this cost, but were also beneficiaries, reaping subsequent rewards from the steady economic growth, increased job opportunities, and higher wages (Woo 1991). The overall size of the financial sector and the total saving rate grew rapidly in Korea although the banking system, subject to heavy government intervention, remained stagnant (Table 7.8).

7.3 AN OVERALL ASSESSMENT

In Korea, government intervention in the financial market was extensive during the process of economic development. The government owned the banking institution, controlled its interest rates, and directed a substantial portion of its loans. This allocation of credit was accompanied by substantial rent, and it constituted a major industrial policy instrument and tool for government control of industrial firms. This strategy— often called financial repression—is viewed by most economists as an ineffective way to achieve high economic growth. It is true that this policy stance in Korea also caused many problems. From time to time it led to the allocation of large amounts of credit to unsuccessful ventures, forcing the government to bail out firms and banks through monetary expansion. It inhibited the development of an efficient banking system and fostered economic concentration. However, the Korean government targeted industrialization and achieved it by allocating cheap credit to large industrialists, forcing them to build industries and increase their exports, while threatening to withdraw the credit if they did not perform up to par. As an additional result, depositors were paid lower rates of return on their deposits but they were rewarded as wage-earners with the expansion of job opportunities and the increase in real wages. Rapid income increases contributed to the accumulation of domestic savings and the subsequent expansion of the financial market. What made this approach work in Korea, while similar policy initiatives led to unsuccessful developmental experiences elsewhere?

This question cannot be answered completely. Only a tentative conclusion can be asserted based on observations on the thrust of policy measures and the overall economic environment prevailing during the process of Korea's economic development. From the observations in this chapter, it is quite obvious that government intervention and the creation of economic rent as such does not contribute to rapid economic development. It could simply nurture widespread corruption in relation to rent-seeking behavior and help sustain economic backwardness, as was manifested in Korea in the 1950s. However, government intervention through the creation and distribution of rent could also be an effective industrial policy measure to help spur economic development, when it is managed carefully as part of a comprehensive economic development strategy with a clear vision.

The major difference between the experiences of Korea in the 1950s and those in the 1960s lay in the areas where rent was created (i.e., import versus export) and the ways it was distributed (i.e., discretionary versus rule based). Providing subsidy (rent) to the export sector, the development of which presented substantial externalities to the economy through the rapid upgrading of technology, etc., can contribute positively to growth in the early stages of development. Rent distribution linked to the performance of exporters in the international market helped expose domestic firms to international competition and encouraged mobilization of high-powered human as well as physical capital in the export sector. Despite the fact that interest rate control entailed substantial subsidies, the level of interest rates remained positive in real terms, and this allowed the rapid growth of financial savings in the 1960s. Although the government's intervention in the financial market and its control over financial institutions afforded it discretion in decision making on rent distribution, the criterion of distribution was monitored reasonably according to the economic development goals. However, when the focus of industrial policy was shifted to HCI development in the 1970s, more room was created for the discretionary allocation of rent, and the extent of rent (or financial repression) was also increased with the widened gap between controlled interest rates and the market rate. This also increased the cost of government intervention. The government was able to partially compensate for the consequently negative impact on financial sector growth by allowing the expansion of nonbank financial institutions and the securities market, which were less regulated during the 1970s.

Overall, what contributed most to the effectiveness of government intervention from the economic development standpoint seem to be effective economic management and the competitive business environment. In Korea, close consultation between government and business and the government's risk partnership with business made what could have been a very distorted investment approach into quite an effective developmental strategy. When the risk capital market was poorly developed, the Korean government controlled banks and effected a close relationship between government, banks, and industry, and thereby made itself an effective risk partner with industry. This implicit coinsurance scheme among the government, industries, and banks allowed the credit-based economy and its highly leveraged corporate firms to explore risky investment opportunities and to operate without the danger of major financial crisis.

However, the Korean experience also suggests that the cost of this approach can be substantial and can be exacerbated as economic development advances. The Korean policy strategy fueled rapid industrialization, but it also dampened efforts to develop an efficient banking system. The government's risk partnership with industrial firms placed a heavy burden on the banking system, loading it with large nonperforming loans, and raised social equity issues. Extensive government intervention in financing, especially in relation to low interest-rate ceilings, slowed the growth of financial savings. Korea was able to overcome this negative impact of government intervention by relying heavily on foreign borrowing. Korea's special relationship with the United States and Japan gave the country access to foreign loans. Furthermore, the perpetuation of strong government intervention in credit allocation when the industrial sector was well established and when economic organizations had become sophisticated placed Korea at greater risk of distorting the allocation of financial resources. The coinsurance scheme among government, industries, and banks fostered a moral hazard for banks and firms, despite contributing to the development of entrepreneurship and the expansion of industrial investment. Consequently, the government became captive to a vicious cycle of intervention. It also became captive to its own bureaucratic interests.

The overall lesson from the Korean experience is that it is possible for governments to intervene productively and effectively in the early stages of economic development. The balance between the role of government and market forces should reflect the financial market, industrial organization, market structure, and political and international environment that face the country. But as economic development advances, the role and scope of government intervention must be reappraised with a view toward fostering greater reliance on market forces.

NOTES

I am grateful for helpful comments from Masahiko Aoki, Hyung-Ki Kim, Masahiro Okuno-Fujiwara, and participants of seminars held for this project in Tokyo and Stanford.

[1] This estimate, however, should be qualified. In a sense, it is purely indicative because there is some doubt whether parallel market rates were at the equilibrium rate. Furthermore, import restrictions allowed importers to monopolize the supply of certain goods, entailing additional rent.

[2] The export credit program has been substantially reduced since the mid-1980s.

[3] Central bank credit to commercial banks constituted 20–30 per cent of total loans extended by the latter during the 1970s.

[4] Again, the rent estimate here may have been exaggerated because it is doubtful that the curb market rate was the equilibrium rate when the financial market was liberalized.

[5] For example, McKinnon (1973) and Shaw (1973).

[6] See Hellmann, Murdock, and Stiglitz, Chapter 6 in this volume.

[7] For instance, the central bank's rediscount rate for export bills was 3.5 per cent in the years 1964–75.

[8] See Cho and Kim (1995) and Kim (1990, 1994) for detailed discussion on the two impacts of the decree.

[9] According to Nam, then Minister of Finance, he was compelled to establish the NIF, given the importance of the heavy industry program, for project financing, thereby attempting to minimize the burden on banking operations.

[10] This part relies on the analysis by Cho and Kim (1995).

[11] Here, the export subsidy is estimated based on the gap between average bank loan rates and the export loan rate. If it was estimated based on the gap between the curb market rate and the export loan rate, as done in this volume by Hellmann, Murdock, and Stiglitz (see Chapter 6), the amount of the subsidy would be much higher.

[12] It is asserted that since Korean export growth was based on the expansion of manufactured exports, the technological effect of export marketing and the informational externality was substantial (see Kim and Roemer 1979, World Bank 1987b).

[13] This reflects the fact that the Korean government's credit allocation favored the manufacturing sector over other sectors.

[14] But in terms of dynamic efficiency, heavy HCI investment might have had some merits.

[15] However, the benefits of the flexibility of credit policies cannot be taken for granted. In particular, poor information on behalf of creditors may turn their potential effectiveness into a large hazard, because renegotiations and refinancing decisions involve delicate trade-offs. In order to use credit effectively as a selection and incentive device, creditors should have the ability to understand two crucial aspects of a firm's performance. First, in order to provide an effective incentive scheme, the creditor should be able to distinguish external factors from managerial performance. Second, in order to make effective selection decisions among external factors, creditors should be able to distinguish cyclical influences from structural ones; in particular, they should have good information on whether financial distress is due to temporary or permanent problems.

[16] This is, to some extent, the result of the government-led industrial financing strategy.

REFERENCES

AMSDEN, A. (1989), *Asia's Next Giant: South Korea and Late Industrialization*, Oxford University Press, Oxford.

CHA, D.-S. (1986), *Waekuk Jabon Doyip Hoykya eui Bunseok* (An analysis of the effect of foreign capital inflow), Korean Institute for Economics and Technology, Seoul.

CHO, Y. J. and KIM, J.-K. (1995), "Credit Policies and Industrialization of Korea," World Bank Discussion Papers, No. 286.

——and HELLMANN, T. (1993), "Government Intervention in Credit Markets in Japan and Korea: An Alternative Interpretation from the New Institutional Economics Perspective," PRE Working Paper Series No. 1190, World Bank, *Seoul Journal of Economics*, 7(4).

KIM, C.-Y. (1990), *Hankuk Kyungje Jeongchaek Samship yeon sa* (A 30-year history of Korean economic development policy: a memoir), Seoul Joong-ang and Ilbo-sa, Seoul.

——(1994), "Policy Making on the Front Lines: Memoirs of a Korean Practitioner, 1945–1979," EDI Retrospectives in Policy Making, World Bank, Washington.

KIM, K. S. and ROEMER, M. (1979), *Growth and Structural Transformation*, Harvard Institute for International Development, Cambridge, Mass.

LEIPZIGER, D. M. and PETRI, P. A. (1992), "Korean Industrial Policy: Legacies of the Past and Directions for the Future," unpublished manuscript.

MCKINNON, R. (1973), *Money and Capital in Economic Development*, Brookings Institution, Washington.

NAM, D.-W. (1979), "Korea's Economic Take-off in Retrospect," paper presented at the Second Washington Conference of the Korea-America Association.

RHEE, Y.-W. (1989), "Trade Finance in Developing Countries," Policy and Research Series, No. 5, World Bank.

SHAW, E. (1973), *Financial Deepening in Economic Development*, Oxford University Press, New York.

STERN, J. *et al.* (1992), *Industrialization and the State: The Korean Heavy and Chemical Industry Drive*, Harvard Institute for International Development, Cambridge, Mass.

WOO, J.-E. (1991), *Race to the Swift: State and Finance in Korean Industrialization*, Columbia University Press, New York.

World Bank (1987a), *Korea: Managing the Industrial Transition*, World Bank, Washington.

——(1987b), *World Development Report 1987*, Oxford University Press, Oxford.

YOON, Y.-J. (1991), "Hankuk eui Kyungje Sungjang Kwajung aesu ei Jungbu Gaeyip Jidae Chuku Hwaldong ae kwanhan Yeonku" (A study on government intervention and rent-seeking behavior in Korean economic development), master's thesis, School of Public Administration, Seoul National University, Seoul.

8

Unintended Fit: Organizational Evolution and Government Design of Institutions in Japan

MASAHIKO AOKI

8.1 INSTITUTIONAL INNOVATION AS A SOURCE OF GROWTH

Imagine that an economy is growing fast because its government is capable of inducing households to save more and accumulate human capital faster. Further, imagine that the government effectively directs, or coordinates, the allocation of the increased resources into the most productive sector. The data generated by such a developmental process would show that the observed growth is realized by the increased mobilization of resource inputs. Putting aside the question of how the government is able to perform the said functions effectively and competently, there is no mystery about the quantity relationship between inputs and outputs.

Indeed, a recent comparative econometrics study by Jong-Il Kim and Lawrence Lau (1994) on sources of economic growth in newly industrializing countries (NICs; Taiwan, Hong Kong, Singapore, South Korea) replicates the above story. Their study does not reject the hypothesis that the phenomenal postwar growth in those economies has been realized simply by continual increase in capital inputs (and human capital inputs to a lesser degree). An implication that the contribution of technological progress to growth has been negligible in those economies has puzzled, even offended, some people. But we should note that their finding does not deny the contribution of the government in mobilizing financial and human resources. Neither does it need to be inconsistent with casual observation that those economies utilize very advanced production technologies generated elsewhere. Simply, the effect of the adoption of sophisticated equipment and know-how may have been fully reflected in the market value of capital inputs (including patents).

As Paul Krugman (1994) argued recently, however, a developmental path based merely on an increase in input cannot be sustained forever, as demonstrated by the example of the former USSR, which eventually failed to maintain the high growth rate it had realized in the 1950s and 1960s. There is a biological limit to human learning as well as a socioeconomic limit on abstention from consumption. To sustain growth per unit of capital, sooner or later a steady rate of technological progress, that is, a productivity increase due to "a new combination of inputs" or some exogenous effects of augmenting the productivity of capital, must set in.

In this vein, the same study by Kim and Lau indicates that the postwar growth pattern of Japan is a little different from that of NICs, and similar to that of other advanced market economies (the United States, United Kingdom, Germany, and France). Technological progress has been an important source of growth in Japan. Their results need to be taken with some caution, particularly because there are other equally important studies denying the primacy of productivity increase as a source of growth in advanced economies.[1] However, let us adopt the following working hypothesis, subject to possible refutation by further empirical studies: something more than a simple mobilization of savings by the government and the importation of foreign technology has been involved in the postwar economic growth process of Japan.

True, the productivity level of Japanese industry has lagged behind that of the United States throughout the postwar period, although the gap has steadily narrowed. In that sense, Japan has indeed been trying to catch up with the Western economies. However, the point is that the gradual closure of the gap cannot be completely attributed to the imitation of Western technology. It is particularly noteworthy that the cross-sectoral pattern of productivity growth in Japan is different from that observed, say, in the United States (Jorgenson 1995). There must have been some homegrown technological progress or a different way of combining inputs in Japan. What was it?

The technological progress captured by econometric studies as an increase in total factor productivity or the capital-augmenting effect is not necessarily restricted to technological innovation in the conventional sense, something that can be discovered in the scientific or corporate laboratory. Commenting on the slower rate of technological progress found in East Asian NICs, Kim and Lau (1994:265) maintained that "it is . . . possible that the growth of the 'software' component of investments, broadly defined to include managerial methods, institutional environment, as well as supporting infrastructure, lags behind the 'hardware' component in the East Asian NICs and hence the capital goods have not been able to realize the full potential productivity." The purpose of this chapter is to focus on the nature of such a "software" component in the productivity increase in the postwar economic growth of Japan and to see if the government played any role in that process.[2]

Did the Japanese government play an active role in designing and developing an institutional environment conducive to a productivity increase that cannot be attributed to a mere increase in resource inputs, including full-priced imported technology? Recently, Japanese academics and columnists have begun to pay unprecedented attention to the origins of the institutional framework of postwar Japanese growth, which can be traced as far back as the wartime period (see, for example, Noguchi 1995 and Okazaki and Okuno 1994). Some argue that those institutions were purposely designed to catch up with the advanced Western economies and that, having fulfilled that purpose, however, their life has now been ended. Implicit or explicit in this argument is that a shift to a *laissez-faire* institutional framework of the Anglo-American type is now on the agenda. This is an echo of the "developmental state theory" of Chalmers Johnson (1982).

However, the developmental state theory or its emergent cousin does not easily resolve the puzzle of why institutions created for central command of the economy can function as infrastructure for technological progress. If the government is indeed able to nurture a new combination of resources in the private sector, why have East Asian NICs not realized rates of technological progress (or quality indices of capital and labor inputs) comparable to Japan's in spite of the introduction of similar government institutions?

My argument will be of an evolutionary nature. I recognize that the matrix of institutions created by the government in the pre- and midwar periods indeed survived into the subsequent period of high growth after the postwar democratic metamorphoses. Those institutions were originally created for the purpose of mobilization and central allocation of financial and labor resources by the government. But, not only did the realization of that purpose fail miserably toward the end of the war, but those institutions also did not (at least primarily) work even in the high-growth period, as the government initially intended. I claim that the direct intervention of the government in the resource-allocation process was not the most important factor in accounting for Japan's sustainable growth, especially the "technological progress" that cannot be attributable to an increase in inputs.

Below I argue that the institutional framework inherited from the war period started to work in the high growth period of the 1950s and 1960s, only when it was found to fit with an evolutionary tendency that had been taking place in the private sector. But this fit was unintended. In finding the fit, institutions modified their functions considerably from the original intention of the government. By this I do not mean the mere conversion of the government toward a "market-friendly" orientation nor the enhanced role of competitive market coordination of resource allocation. Throughout the different phases of the expansion of the Japanese economy from wartime to postwar chaos to the high-growth period, a unique organizational coordination mechanism evolved within and across enterprises, one that would eventually have significant impact on productivity. In other words, one of the important "software" components of investment may be found in the way resource inputs are coordinated within the enterprise.

It was the famous thesis of the late Harvey Leibenstein (1966) that a large proportion of the differential in productivity across developing economies may be attributable to the "X-inefficiency" factor internal to the firm rather than to allocative inefficiency due to various market coordination failures. My thesis is in the same spirit, emphasizing the role of organizational coordination relative to market coordination. I will also emphasize, however, the unintended complementarity between the evolving organizational mode and the institutional framework, in the emergence of which the government had been instrumental. This complementarity is, I will argue, distinct to Japan and has not emerged in other East Asian NICs in clear form.

Under the emerged organizational mode, which will be conceptualized below as a *horizontal hierarchy*, Japanese industry has narrowed the technological gap with the West and even surpassed it in total factor productivity in some markets, while lagging behind in other markets. Parallel to this unbalanced industrial development has been the coevolution of a redistribution mechanism in the Japanese polity, which I call bureau-pluralism. Through this mechanism, economic gains obtained by the industry whose technological and market conditions find a fit with the evolving organizational convention are redistributed to the low-productivity, disadvantaged segments of the economy.

However, emerging international environments are making the maintenance of such a mechanism less tenable. This explains why the Japanese government has lately become increasingly incompetent in problem solving. However, the increasing malfunction of the institutional set-up of Japan has not arisen merely from its out-of-date developmental nature. Rather, it is a symptom of a dilemma existing between the advanced and backward elements of the system. I will argue toward the end of this chapter that this dilemma is not likely to be resolved simply by a "big bang" transition to the Anglo-American competitive market norm. This is not because the Japanese organizational convention is intrinsically superior, but because the Anglo-American-type framework will not easily fit with the existing organizational convention and the government will be unable to change organizational convention by a stroke of the legislative pen. The possible reform of institutions in Japan seems to lie only in an extension of its own evolutionary path and that should be the way for Japan to contribute to the gains from system diversity on a global scale.

8.2 INDUSTRIAL POLICY WAS NOT AN INNOVATION

After the demise of the communist regime, many Japanese bureaucrats and economists started to argue proudly that transitional economies could possibly learn from the Japanese experience of industrial policy, particularly that of the priority production system (*keisha seisan hōshiki*) of the postwar period, to stop the spiral downward movement of industrial output. Jeffrey

Sachs (1995) counterargued that "there are certainly many relevant lessons from the Japanese postwar recovery, but they have little to do with industrial planning, and much more to do with the establishment of a competitive, privately owned economy." I agree with him on the irrelevancy of Japanese industrial policy to transitional economies. I do so, however, on a somewhat different ground related to the issue I am currently dealing with. It was partly from studying the planning mechanism of the former USSR that the Japanese were inspired to design the prototype industrial policy for the execution of the planned wartime economy. Recycling the Japanese experience of industrial policy would hardly have been helpful in resolving problems resulting from the failure of the planned economy.

In 1939 the Japanese army provoked a military confrontation with the Red Army at the border of Manchukuo and Mongolia on the eve of Russian aggression in Poland. The provocation, known as the Nomonhan incident in Japan, developed into a substantial military clash involving mutual air raids on air bases deep inside the border, in which the elite 23rd division of the Japanese Imperial Army was badly defeated. The superiority of the Russian tank brigade was decisive. The industrial capability of the USSR to exhibit such technological superiority came as a great shock to the Imperial Army as well as to the so-called reformist bureaucrats (*kakushin kanryō*) allied with aggressive military officers in Manchukuo. Even before the Nomonhan incident, they had been fascinated by the ability of the Soviet planning apparatus to generate rapid industrial growth and had even implemented some institutional mechanisms to emulate its workings (Okazaki 1993:184–86). In terms of the ability to mobilize resource inputs and direct them to the development of military capability, however, the USSR had been more decisive and thorough.

The Planning Board (Kikakuin), which had been set up in 1937 as an equivalent of *Gosplan*, drafted an "Outline of the Establishment of a New Economic System" in 1940. This plan included such measures as "transforming enterprises to public interest entities" (*kigyō no kōkyō-ka*), "separation of ownership and management," and "restraint of profits." Such an anticapitalist stance provoked vehement protests from the business community, including the Minister of Commerce and Industry, Ichizo Kobayashi, and bureaucrats at the Planning Board were accused of being "Reds." The accusation eventually led to the arrests of several bureaucrats at the Board in 1941 on the charge of violation of the notorious Maintenance of Public Order Act. The Army and Navy ministers had to arbitrate the passage of a moderated plan by cabinet meeting.

After the end of World War II, the General Headquarters (GHQ) of the occupation armies and the Japanese government agreed on the need for establishing an Economic Stabilization Headquarters (ESH; Keizai Antei Honbu) responsible for "top planning and control" of the economy. Professor Hiromi Arisawa of the University of Tokyo, a moderate noncommunist Marxian, advocated the need for giving priority in resource and funds allocation to the production of basic materials and energy sources for reconstruction, coal, and steel. His idea was adopted as the famous priority production system. The director of the ESH which implemented the scheme was one of the bureaucrats arrested in 1941 in the Kikakuin incident.

The purpose of beginning this chapter with such an episode is to illustrate the following point: The industrial policy of Japan may appear unique from the neoclassical perspective of *laissez-faire*. But, if we place it relative to the formidable intellectual and practical impact of the Marxist doctrine of planning and its "successful" implementation in the USSR in the first two-thirds of this century, it hardly stands out as unique or original. The industrial policy or planning may have generated rapid growth through intensified resource inputs into strategic sectors at the sacrifice of others. It may be interesting as well as useful to analyze how such policy could be carried out. However, as Paul Krugman argued, the higher growth rate generated by an increase in the quantity of factor inputs (and possibly by directing such inputs into certain sectors) cannot be sustainable beyond a certain time limit, unless technological progress eventually sets in. In economics, "technological progress" can be anything that can realize residual output gains not attributable to mere increases in factor input. It may include innovation in coordinating the combination of inputs, i.e., organizational and institutional innovations.

8.3 INSTITUTIONAL DESIGN FOR CENTRALIZED CONTROL

The Japanese military government successively introduced various institutional changes in the late 1930s and during the war to facilitate its centralized control over resource allocation for the purpose of increasing wartime production. The following were the most important and relevant for subsequent discussion in this chapter:

1. Shareholders' rights—such as selecting management and deciding on dividend payments—were restrained by the substitution of government control over the selection of top management ("responsible production managers") and dividend ceilings (Okazaki 1993). Heavy triple taxation on profit incomes were imposed on large stockholders, such as *zaibatsu* families, at the levels of subsidiary enterprises, holding companies, and individuals. The stock exchange was closed toward the end of the war.
2. The number of commercial banks was drastically reduced from well over 2,000 at the beginning of the 1930s to 65 at the end of the war by government intervention, and a single bank was designated by the gov-

ernment for each munitions enterprise as the sole intermediary for payment settlement (Teranishi 1990; Aoki and Kim 1995:297–98).

3. Various industrial controlling associations (*sangyō tōsei kai*), supervised by government bureaucrats and staffed by personnel dispatched from enterprises, were formed as intermediaries for information collection, plan-making, and plan implementation between the Planning Board and enterprises (Okazaki 1993).
4. Technologically backward small and medium-sized suppliers were assigned to particular major manufacturers for technical assistance.
5. The enterprise branches of the Industrial Patriotic Society (Sangyō Hōkoku Kai), which comprised both white-collar and blue-collar workers, were formed for the morale enhancement and mutual aid of the families of drafted employees.

It is not necessary to explain how these measures were intended to be used as instruments to exercise centralized control over resource allocation by overriding the decentralized control of stockholders, typified then by *zaibatsu* holding companies. In spite of such institutional change, the government could not stop the dramatic decline in production, not only because of the critical shortage of raw materials, particularly crude oil, but also because of the lack of price incentives for management (Okazaki 1987).

An interesting point is that those measures were not repealed completely after the war, or, when they were, they reemerged in similar forms and evolved as essential elements of the institutional foundation for postwar economic growth. However, I argue below that the functions of these institutions changed considerably from instruments of centralized control of the economy. For that transition to evolve, however, the democratization of the institutions in the postwar reform was essential. The reform included:

1. The *zaibatsu* holding companies were made illegal and their stocks, together with the private holdings of *zaibatsu* families, were transferred to a government committee, which in turn adopted a "stockholder democratization" policy in privatizing transferred stocks. The employees of a company were given priority in purchasing its stock (Miyajima 1995).
2. Each ex-munitions company (most major enterprises) maintained a close relationship with a single bank (often the designated bank described in item (2) of the list of institutional changes above) to resolve the problem of bad debts resulting from the repudiation of wartime obligations by the government (Hoshi 1995).
3. Industrial associations were formed as successors to the controlling associations and placed in close contact with relevant industrial sections of the Ministry of International Trade and Industry (MITI).
4. A large enterprise that rendered technical assistance to particular small and medium-sized enterprises during the war retained the latter as exclusive or semiexclusive suppliers.

5. The enterprise branches of the Patriotic Society were dissolved as prowar organizations, but the Society's organizational basis was transformed into the enterprise union and often its active members assumed the leadership in the widespread "factory control" movement immediately after the end of the war when management confidence and authority was badly shaken.

With (1) and (2) as background, the so-called main bank system gradually emerged in the 1950s. It was initially characterized as a close bank-enterprise relationship formed on the basis of mutual stockholding and key lending in loan consortia. The primary purpose of the formation of cross-stockholding was to insulate managers from outside takeovers and assure them of newly acquired *de facto* control rights in the absence of dominant stockholders as well as direct government interference. However, if government intervention was a nuisance, why then did management also not try to block the formation of industrial associations? If strengthening managerial control and building a managerial empire were the sole objectives, why did they not acquire and integrate subcontracting enterprises? Why did they prefer to deal with enterprise unionists rather than industrial union advocates, when management had rights to bargain with anybody? Was the management of nonfinancial enterprises not fearful that the main bank would try to intervene in management of the enterprise in the hope of reviving the *zaibatsu* under its power? To answer these questions, we now need to take a look at what was taking place within the enterprise at the same time. We will find a subtle fit between the institutional development as described above and internal evolution.

8.4 THE EVOLUTION OF AN ORGANIZATIONAL EXPERIMENT

Relying upon secondary sources accumulated by Japanese labor and economic historians, Andrew Gordon (1985) derived two important points about the nature and role of the prewar labor movement and the evolution of so-called Japanese human resource management. First, in the 1920s and 1930s workers at some major factories organized themselves and were sometimes engaged in militant confrontation with management, but their movement was not driven by the assertion of class interests as much as the aspiration of being recognized as "equal members of their enterprises." Second, innovation in personnel administration, such as seniority wages and "lifetime employment," was not just the result of a unilateral, rationalistic design by management to prevent the frequent mobility of skilled workers. It should be regarded as the result of trilateral interactions involving the government aiming to pacify labor disputes and eliciting workers' cooperation toward war production, management, and workers who aspired to be members of the enterprise.

World War II marked an interesting turning point in how shop floor matters were handled. Because of acute labor and material shortages, various emergencies had to be coped with on an *ad hoc* basis by the collective efforts of workers. Machine breakdowns had to be fixed without the expert help of scarce mechanics. Ways of dealing with shortages of parts and tools had to be improvised on the spot. Frequent absenteeism caused by workers' trips to the countryside to collect food was coped with by sharing jobs among the remaining workers.

Such *ad hoc* adaptation resulted in ambiguous job demarcation. Even the status differentiation between the blue-collar workers and the foreman on the shop floor, as well as between them and white-collar workers, tended to become blurred. The formation of the factory branch of the Industrial Society comprising all workers on an equal membership basis reinforced the sense of employees as members of the enterprise as a community.

The point I would like to make here is the enduring impact of an *ad hoc* team-oriented approach to work organization. Namely, work organization became characterized more by teamwork in which random events were handled collectively. This evolution was indeed in contrast to the contemporaneous evolution in the United States (Baron *et al.* 1986). Facing the same challenge for increasing munitions production during the war, American industry began to adopt the scientific management method on an unprecedented scale. In this method, individual workers were trained to use their work time as efficiently as possible through the calculated division of tasks. It was also designed to train workers to respond individually to minor random events relevant to their own tasks, such as routine adjustment of machines, regular material defects, etc., according to a prescribed manual. Major problems were assumed to be handled by problem-solving specialists, such as machinists, industrial engineers, and inspectors. The machinery and factory layout were designed—and the precautionary inventory of materials, parts, and half-products was planned—to minimize the need for interaction among workers and to control the occurrence of random events that might simultaneously affect their tasks. The American method was apparently much superior at that time in realizing higher productivity, even leaving aside the clear difference in the availability of resources.

After the war, the Japanese factory was in complete confusion. There were not sufficient materials nor power supply. Management lost confidence and workers often took over control of the factory. Even after management regained confidence and authority in the early 1950s after the crushing of the militant labor movement with the help of police and the political backing of GHQ, managers found themselves in no position to reassert managerial authority by breaking up the solidarity of workers and splitting them up to carry out different tasks. As demand for products suddenly expanded during the Korean war, various emergencies on the shop floor had to be quickly dealt with and management again had to rely on workers' *ad hoc* ingenuity and collective efforts at problem solving.

However, the subsequent growth in demand necessitated a more systematic approach to productivity increase. Japanese management, ushered into the international business arena from wartime isolation, marveled at the impressive productivity edge that American industry had realized by the scientific management movement. The Japanese were also impressed with the potential of the quality-control technique developed by W. Edwards Deming. Japanese management ultimately adopted an eclectic approach. The methods of quality-control techniques and time-and-motion studies were introduced to the shop floor with the participation of the workers as a group rather than by relying exclusively upon the research of industrial engineers and imposing their findings on individual workers. Workable *ad hoc* practices on the shop floor were encouraged to be identified and routinized through the collective effort of workers, foremen, and engineers (Cole 1994). There was initial resistance from workers to the extra burden of cooperative problem solving, but they gradually came to terms with management. An unprecedented organizational practice was evolving on a large scale which relied upon the broad information-processing capability of workers on the shop floor. Efficient production and an inventory control method that would come to be widely known later as the "*kanban* system," "zero inventory production system," or "lean production system" actually evolved from such workers' participation (Fujimoto 1995).

8.5 HORIZONTAL AND DECENTRALIZED HIERARCHIES

From the information theoretical viewpoint, the essence of the emergent organizational practice may be conceptualized as a horizontal hierarchy (Aoki 1995). Suppose that the organization is composed of one management and multiple tasks, jointly producing output. To realize higher organizational returns, the activities of those tasks must be coordinated in response to evolving stochastic events that would affect the productivity of individual operational tasks. Suppose that those events can be observed at the operational level with some error, but cannot be transmitted to management either in time for operational decisions or without large noise. In other words, information concerning stochastic events affecting operational tasks is Hayekian, in the sense that it is "knowledge of particular circumstances of time and place" available only to the people on site. Returns to organizational operations will be dependent on who processes such information for operational decisions (i.e., organizational coordination).

The horizontal hierarchy is the method of organizational coordination in which all relevant task units collectively observe the systematic component of stochastic events (i.e., the events that simultaneously affect the productivity of all tasks) and then each task unit attends to the idiosyncratic components of those events (i.e., events that affect the individual productivity of the task). Each task then utilizes the shared and individualized information together for making a choice of its own operational level and orientation according to an organizational rule. The role of management is to mediate the development of the organizational rule such as to maximize the expected organizational returns. Such a mechanism may be called a horizontal hierarchy, as information processing is structured in a hierarchical manner, i.e., collective information processing regarding systematic environments supplemented by individual information processing regarding idiosyncratic environments, without involving the authority relationship in decision making.

In contrast, the essence of the scientific management movement may be conceptualized as a decentralized hierarchy. In this scheme, management decentralizes only the information processing of the idiosyncratic component of stochastic events. Under this mechanism, the factory layout and job classification should be designed so as to control and minimize the systematic effect of stochastic events. To the degree that such control is technically possible, this mechanism can utilize economies of specialization. On the other hand, horizontal hierarchies must depend on the broader scope of information processing at the operational level, with the sacrifice of economies of specialized division of tasks. I will shortly clarify precise conditions under which one of these two hierarchies can be informationally more efficient than the other in the sense of the higher expected returns that it can bring about. In any case, I claim at this stage that the evolving Japanese practice on the shop floor, as well as that across shops, was distinct in its horizontal interaction in information processing, whereas the Western practice was to suppress such interactions through job specialization, the use of precautionary inventory, pooling of information only through the common superior, etc.

8.6 THE COEVOLUTION OF COMPLEMENTARY INSTITUTIONS

At this point, I can argue that there emerged in Japan an unintended fit between the evolving organizational practice described above and the institutional framework the government had initially developed for a different purpose, i.e., the centralized control of resource allocation. This unintended fit included the following aspects.

1. Out of dispersed stockholding by individuals, cross-stockholding among a group of companies was gradually crafted by their managements as a defense against takeover (Miyajima 1995). In the absence of stockholder control, especially that through the active market for corporate control,

the practice of selecting top management through the ranking hierarchy of permanent employees became institutionalized at the enterprise level. This practice functioned as an incentive device for permanent employees to accumulate managerial skills geared toward the administration of horizontal hierarchy (Aoki 1988:ch. 3). Also, the absence of the threat of takeover by outsiders made the commitment of management to long-term employment of blue-collar workers credible, which enhanced the incentives for blue-collar workers to accumulate wide-ranging skills useful in the context of horizontal hierarchy.

2. However, there would be a potential moral hazard problem of free-riding among employees if they were completely insulated from external discipline. Particularly when team-oriented work is involved as in a horizontal hierarchy, this problem may become acute, as metering individual contributions may be difficult. The evolution of the *contingent governance structure* evolved as a response to this potential problem. In this governance structure, the control rights shift from inside management to the main bank, when the financial state of the enterprise is worsened below a threshold point. Below that point, the main bank either rescues the distressed enterprise or harshly penalizes the insiders by the closure of the enterprise, contingent on the degree of financial failure of the enterprise. This governance structure provides the second-best framework for controlling moral hazard in teams (Aoki 1994).

   In order for both the main bank and the enterprise to commit to such a governance structure, main bank rents must be created. If the rent is too high, the enterprise will not find it profitable to maintain the main bank relationship with a particular bank, while if it is too low the main bank will not commit to rescue temporarily distressed enterprises. The appropriate range of the main bank rent is in turn assured, if the number of qualified banks is neither too large nor too small (Dinc 1995).

3. The interests of employees are incorporated at the level of the enterprise by inside management (managerial corporatism). Enterprises in the same industry fiercely compete in the product market, but their common interests in public policymaking are adjusted and mediated by the industrial association to the relevant section of a ministry. The ministry in turn represents the industrial interests under its jurisdiction in interministerial arbitration processes such as budgeting, national plan-making, etc. The prospect of so-called *amakudari*, the arrangement of postretirement jobs in a jurisdictional private sector by the ministry, provides incentives for its bureaucrats to act as quasi-agents of interest groups under their jurisdiction. Such a political-economy regime may be called *bureau-pluralism*, as pluralistic interests are mediated through the bureaucratic process (Aoki 1988:ch. 7). This regime is essentially conservative in being biased toward the vested interests of incumbents recognized by the bureaucratic process against the interests of potential new entrants.

4. The enterprise-specific supplier network, *keiretsu*, based on long-term contracting, facilitated the evolution of a horizontal hierarchy, rather than a decentralized hierarchy, between the manufacturer and the supplier as typified in the auto industry. Both share information relevant to the conceptualization of new product development through the formation of a joint development team. However, the actual design of parts is relegated to the supplier on an approval basis ("design in"). Product market information is also continually shared between them through the use of *kanban* (supply order forms dispatched by the manufacturer to the supplier at frequent intervals according to emergent final demand), but the timely delivery and quality control of the supply in response to the order is the responsibility of the supplier.
5. Enterprise unionism was instrumental for the operation of the information-sharing horizontal hierarchy by facilitating job rotation and joint work responsibilities. If the union had been organized on the principle of job-control industrial unionism, it would have resisted any move to destroy specific job rights (Aoki 1988:ch. 3).

In short, the institutional framework initially introduced by the government to promote the centralized control of resources was transformed and coevolved with internal horizontal hierarchies within and across enterprises. Indeed, I consider such an unintended fit to have been most responsible for the sustained productivity growth in Japanese industries from the

TABLE 8.1 Institutional Evolution in Japan

Institutional Transformation	Wartime Design for Centralized Control	Postwar Democratic Reform	Evolution of Complementary Relationships with Horizontal Hierarchy
Stockholder structure	Restriction of *zaibatsu* stockholders' rights	*Zaibatsu* dissolution and stockholding democratization	Management-crafted cross-shareholding as insulation from takeover
Banks and governance structure	Designated banking system	Bank involvement in cleaning up bad debt problem	Main bank system, contingent governance
Industrial association	Industrial controlling association	Industrial association	Bureau-pluralism
Small and medium-sized enterprise	Assigned to a large enterprise for technical assistance	Relationship maintained	*Keiretsu* (relational contracting)
Workers' organization	Industrial Patriotic Society	Factory control movement	Enterprise unionism

1960s to the 1980s, which cannot be entirely accounted for by simple increases in labor or capital inputs. However, it is important to note that this unintended fit was possible only after the democratic transformation of wartime institutions during postwar reforms (see Table 8.1). It is erroneous to visualize the development of the institution from the war period to the present as a "linear" process, as Noguchi (1995) seems to indicate.

8.7 THE COMPARATIVE INFORMATIONAL EFFICIENCY OF ORGANIZATIONAL MODES

The horizontal hierarchy may process and utilize information more efficiently than a decentralized hierarchy in certain environments, but not in all environments. Theoretically, three dimensions may be important in determining the comparative efficiency of various modes of organizational coordination: stochastic correlation, technological interdependency among various tasks, and the degree of volatility of organizational environments as a whole. It can be theoretically proven that, if the stochastic correlation among the tasks becomes higher than a threshold point, horizontal hierarchy becomes informationally more efficient than decentralized hierarchy, even if the amount of information generated per information processing time becomes lower because of the sacrifice of economies of specialization. Also, the higher the technological complementarity among the tasks, the lower the threshold point would become (Aoki 1995).

Horizontal hierarchy requires workers to have broad skills rather than being specialized in certain functions. Workers must be able to communicate, share knowledge, and collectively act in reaction to emergent events. However, their skills may be attuned to a certain range of variability of environments. If the organizational environment is fairly stable, it may not be worth relying on horizontal coordination, to the sacrifice of economies of task specialization. On the other hand, if the environment is volatile, it would be costly to invest in the accumulation of enterprise-specific skills *ex ante*, as they may easily become obsolete or ineffective under changing situations. For such cases, it would be less costly to employ appropriate specific skills from the outside market, contingent on emergent events. In between, where the organizational environment is continually changing but not wildly, horizontal hierarchy may exhibit higher adaptability (Itoh 1987).

It seems to be precisely in those industries characterized by higher risk correlation, high technological complementarity, and continually changing market and technological environments that Japanese enterprises started to gain competitive strength. For example, the production processes of the assembly industries (e.g., autos and electric machinery) and the continual process industries producing relatively homogenous products (e.g., steel) are comprised of many steps subject to common risks (e.g., the breakdown of the assembly line, product quality affected by events arising at the border of adjacent steps) and technological complementarity (e.g., the requirement of a precise combination of various parts). On the other hand, in a mature industry where the production process is comprised of stochastically independent steps and/or final products are diverse and competing for upstream, in-process products (e.g., the petrochemical industry), a decentralized hierarchy would be informationally more efficient. At the other end of the spectrum, in spite of its strength in manufacturing electric machinery, Japanese industry exhibits a definite weakness in the multimedia industry where industrial standards are still highly uncertain.

We have assumed that the stochastic and technological environments are given. However, they can be targets of business strategy and engineering efforts, thus becoming an endogenous variable of the system. The American automobile industry initially increased its scale on the basis of producing homogeneous models. Henry Ford is said to have once boasted: "we can produce cars in any color for customers, so long as the color is black." But when Japanese manufacturers started to enter the auto markets, they had to face keen competition and tried to capture larger shares of the markets by offering differentiated products in a fairly large variety. To produce a variety of cars in response to continually changing demands, coordination among tasks became essential. Finding that the refinement of horizontal hierarchy could better respond to such a requirement, Japanese manufacturers started to use the introduction of a wider variety as a marketing strategy. This move made technological complementarity among various tasks stronger and horizontal coordination more effective. However, such a strategy can backfire.

The so-called digital revolution, the new possibility of massive data transmission and more efficient interactive communication, has triggered the evolution of a new organizational paradigm in the United States. It has now become feasible for the lower level of a formal hierarchy to have access to information regarding broader environments even beyond the legal boundary of the enterprise. Such a possibility has strategic importance in newly emerging industries such as multimedia where industry standards have not been firmly established and are being continually redefined through interaction among enterprises across different industries and different traditional lines of business. In this situation, the systematic risk, or uncertain events that may affect the productivity of each internal task unit, will not be completely internalized.

There are two very important differences between this development and horizontal hierarchy, although in both the lower level of formal hierarchy seems to have access to information on idiosyncratic as well as systematic risks. First, in the former development, the possibility of horizontal communication extends beyond the boundary of a formal corporation. Under horizontal hierarchies in Japan, horizontal communication is bounded within a single corporation or a closed group of corporations. Second, the purpose of horizontal communication in horizontal hierarchies was for task units to have assimilated information regarding systematic risk as a basis of joint decision making to cope with the high degree of complementarity and stochastic correlation among internal task units. In the new development in the United States, however, access to "data" concerning wider systematic environments may not necessarily lead to the same interpretation among different task units. Interpretation may very well differ, because the new development has been emerging out of a functionally divided decentralized hierarchy. Let us call the emergent organizational form a *differentiated information structure*.

Rigorous analysis can show that the differentiated information structure is informationally more efficient than the horizontal hierarchy, if internal task units are substitutes rather than complementary. This characteristic has an important practical implication. An organizational development parallel to the evolving digital revolution is the increasing reliance on outsourcing by some American manufacturers, especially in the computer and auto industries. This new orientation has been partly learned from the Japanese experience.

But there is an interesting twist. While Japanese manufacturers pursued the increasing diversification of their products, those American manufacturers were pursuing the possibility of the standardization of parts and the modularization of production as a business strategy. Although end products can be highly complex and may be finely customized, this move facilitated the reduction of complementarity among internal task units, as each unit can procure needed parts and information, even from outside the boundary of the corporation, with the aid of digital communications and transportation by air. This has led to the phenomenon commonly referred to as the emergence of the "virtual corporation," i.e., nonpricing, quasi-organizational coordination within the cyberspace beyond the legal boundary of the corporation. In this way, American manufacturers are expanding the business area for which the emergent differentiated information structure generates superior competitive strength. The Japanese relative strength in certain industries built on the refinement of "closed" horizontal hierarchy is now at stake.

8.8 THE DILEMMA OF BUREAU-PLURALISM

In order to consider the political-economy implications of the emerging organizational competition for the Japanese institutional framework, consider the following parable. Suppose that in a relatively small economy, J, a new organizational convention form HH evolved, at a time when the rest of the world was practicing the time-honored organizational form DH. Suppose that the organizational form HH enjoyed absolute cost advantage in industry M (say, machinery), but in traditional sectors A (say, agriculture, retail, service, etc.) productivity was low. Initially, the availability of skills useful for the organizational form HH in industry M was limited so that the supply of products was small relative to global demand. Therefore, the world price of product M was sustained at a higher level at which the dominant organizational form DH could also supply product M profitably. As the organizational form DH was comparatively disadvantageous in industry M, the relatively smaller industry M in economy J was able to reap "quasi-rent" from organizational "innovation." This industry continually ploughed back a part of those quasi-rents for the expansion of its market shares in the world market.

On the other hand, the organizational convention HH was neither productive nor implementable in industry A, yet the skill formation of the workers was geared toward the technological and organizational requirements of that industry so that the workers were not mobile to other organizations, especially to those in industry M, without losing employment value. They therefore tried to defend their interests without leaving industry A through the mechanism of bureau-pluralism. The relevant bureau in the government erected a trade barrier and a portion of the quasi-rents obtained by industry M were redistributed to participants of industry A in the form of price distortion, tax subsidy, etc. As a result, the shift of population from industry A to industry M occurred only at a slow rate consistent with generational turnover. Also, organizational innovation in industry A was suppressed because of the inertia of bureau-pluralism and entry regulation. However, the relatively egalitarian domestic income redistribution was not entirely detrimental to the interests of industry M, as the expansion of domestic markets for its products provided an opportunity for learning by doing for further refinement of the organizational mode HH. Also, the society of economy J enjoyed social stability through the provision of a safety net to every citizen.

However, such a virtuous cycle could not continue forever. Because of trade restrictions against foreign products A, a trade surplus from the export of product M started to accumulate. The foreign exchange rate start to appreciate and exports of product M had to be priced higher abroad, curtailing its exportability. Enterprises in industry M started to invest abroad, building factories along the organizational form HH. Further, foreign enterprises also developed new organizational experiments through the use of new (information) technology, making their products more attractive to consumers.

The opportunity of obtaining quasi-rents started to decline at this stage. Also, the appreciation of domestic currency made foreign direct investment by industry M to newly developing economies more profitable. The more competitive industry M wanted to drift away from the framework of bureau-pluralism, while the less competitive industry A tried to rely more on the protection of bureau-pluralism. However, such protection was no longer sustainable without hurting the competitiveness of comparatively advantageous industry M or causing a partial hollowing of domestic production.

This is the parable of the "dilemma of bureau-pluralism."

8.9 THE VALUE OF ORGANIZATIONAL DIVERSITY AND INSTITUTIONAL REFORM

The various institutions whose origins date back to the wartime period came to serve the development and maintenance of horizontal hierarchy in Japan. There is complementarity among those institutions in that their effectiveness is mutually reinforcing. Because of such a fit, the piecemeal engineering solution of the dilemma of bureau-pluralism may not be viable. But, does this dilemma really mean that the current institutional framework was only effective for the catch-up effort of the Japanese economy and that its life has now run out? Does the Japanese institutional framework need to be transformed into a more advanced form, presumably the Anglo-American *laissez-faire* framework?

Direct answers to such questions are beyond the scope of this chapter. However, the following point may still be raised. The above argument suggests that neither of the organizational conventions that has developed in the United States or Japan may be absolutely superior in all possible dimensions and for every industry. Each may have different implications for the provision of a safety net for citizens, the capability of generating new industries, and producing at cheaper costs and with higher quality, etc. Both conventions have evolved along their respective historical paths. Each has learned and adopted some aspects of the other convention, especially when the other convention appeared to be clearly superior in assimilating more recent technological achievements (Aoki 1995). Yet, differences have remained, exhibiting different implications for comparative advantage, although the realm for comparative advantage of each convention has fluctuated over time and will change in the future. This suggests that there are gains from organizational diversity.

I have shown, however, that such gains cannot be fully exploited only through free trade (Aoki 1993). Is there an alternative way of exploiting possible gains from organization diversity? Note that while the classical source of comparative advantage, various resource endowments, cannot be mobile across economies, organizational forms are a human contrivance. Therefore it may appear that organizational forms are at least in principle transplantable to foreign soil and that organizational diversity may become internalized in each economy. However, as different sets of institutions complement respective organizational forms, one cannot be sure that any organizational form is readily sustainable and viable anywhere. The Japanese institutional framework in particular is built in such a way as to protect the incumbents committed to existing organizational forms by restricting the entry of outsiders and mitigating competitive pressure on insiders to exit. Under such a framework, the domestic realization of organizational diversity will be far more difficult than under the *laissez-faire* framework, although the latter framework also favors particular types of organizational forms (decentralized hierarchies and emergent differentiated structures).

Yet for the dilemma of bureau-pluralism to be resolved, the institutional framework in Japan must be modified in the direction in which private experiments for diverse organizational forms can be viable, especially in industries of relatively low productivity. For that purpose, deregulation of new entry into those industries must be implemented. Organizational diversity is not likely to be achieved, however, by a "big bang" jump to the Anglo-American type regulatory framework. It can be analytically shown that such a roundabout route toward diversity is more costly, as the sustainability of horizontal hierarchies becomes problematic by such a move, even in industries with which they have competitive advantage. Thus the Japanese economy seems to be facing its most difficult challenge, to overhaul the institutional framework that has supported the process of postwar economic growth over almost half a century. A feasible direction is not obvious, however, because that challenge needs to be resolved in a way that reconciles the further evolution of horizontal hierarchies in comparatively advantageous industries, on the one hand, and the inducement of new organizational experiments in industries of lower productivity, on the other.

NOTES

[1] For example, Jorgenson (1995) and his collaborators summarize their extensive econometric studies by saying that the postwar growth of the United States, Japan, and Germany is largely explained by the mobilization of capital including human capital, while productivity played a clearly subordinate role. Their conclusion is based on elaborate estimates of quality indices of labor and capital inputs so that the "residual" component of output growth tended to be smaller.

[2] If we follow the alternative story of sources of economic growth by Jorgenson and others, investments by individuals in human capital by training (and even education) may reflect such "software" component.

REFERENCES

Aoki, M. (1988), *Information, Incentives and Bargaining in the Japanese Economy*, Cambridge University Press, Cambridge.

AOKI, M. (1993), "Comparative Advantage of Organizational Conventions and the Gains from Diversity: An Evolutionary Game Approach," unpublished manuscript, Stanford University.

——(1994), "The Contingent Governance of Teams: Analysis of Institutional Complementarity," *International Economic Review*, 35:657–76.

——(1995), "An Evolving Diversity of Organizational Mode and its Implications for Transitional Economies," *Journal of the Japanese and International Economies* (forthcoming).

——and KIM, H.-K., eds. (1995), *Corporate Governance in Transitional Economies: Insider Control and the Role of Banks*, World Bank, Washington.

——and PATRICK, H., eds. (1994), *The Japanese Main Bank System: Its Relevance for Developing and Transforming Economies*, Oxford University Press, Oxford.

BARON, J. N., DOBBIN, F. R., and DEVEREAUX JENNINGS, P. (1986), "War and Peace: The Evolution of Modern Personnel Administration in U.S. Industry," *American Journal of Sociology*, 92:350–83.

COLE, R. (1994), "Different Quality Paradigms and Their Implications for Organizational Learning," in M. Aoki and R. Dore, eds., *The Japanese Firm: Sources of Competitive Strength*, Oxford University Press, Oxford, 66–83.

DINC, S. (1995), "Integration of Financial Systems and Institutional Path Dependence," unpublished manuscript, Stanford University.

FUJIMOTO, T. (1995), "On the Origin and Evolution of the So-called Toyota Production and Development System," unpublished manuscript, University of Tokyo.

GORDON, A. (1985), *The Evolution of Labor Relations in Japan: Heavy Industry: 1853–1950*, Harvard University Press, Cambridge, Mass.

HOSHI, T. (1995), "Cleaning-up the Balance Sheets: Japanese Experience in the Post-War Reconstruction Period," in M. Aoki and H.-K. Kim, eds., *Corporate Governance in Transitional Economies: Insider Control and the Role of Banks*, World Bank, Washington. 1994, 303–60.

ITOH, H. (1987), "Information Processing Capacity of the Firm," *Journal of the Japanese and International Economies*, 1:299–326.

JOHNSON, C. (1982), *MITI and the Japanese Miracle: The Growth of Industrial Policy*, Stanford University Press, Stanford.

JORGENSON, D. (1995), *Productivity: International Comparisons of Economic Growth*, MIT Press, Cambridge, Mass.

KIM, J-I. and LAU, L. (1994), "The Sources of Economic Growth of the East Asian Newly Industrialized Countries," *Journal of the Japanese and International Economies*, 8:235–71.

KRUGMAN, P. (1994), "The Myth of Asia's Miracle," *Foreign Affairs*, 73:62–78.

LEIBENSTEIN, H. (1966), "Allocative Efficiency vs. 'X-efficiency,'" *American Economic Review*, 56:392–415.

MIYAJIMA, H. (1995), "The Privatization of ex-Zaibatsu Holding Stocks and the Emergence of Bank-oriented Corporate Groups in Japan," in M. Aoki and H.-K. Kim, eds., *Corporate Governance in Transitional Economies: Insider Control and the Role of Banks,* World Bank, Washington. 1994,361–403.

NOGUCHI, Y. (1995), *1940-nen taisei* (The 1940 system), Tōyō Keizai Shinpōsha.

OKAZAKI, T. (1987), "Senji keikau keizai to kaku tosei" (Wartime planning economy and price control), in *Kindai Nihon kenkyū*, 9:175–98.

——(1993), "The Japanese Firm under the Wartime Planned Economy," *Journal of the Japanese and International Economies*, 7:175–203.

——and OKUNO, M. (1994), *Gendai Nihon keizai shisutemu no genryū* (The origin of the contemporary Japanese economic system), Nihon Keizai Shinbunsha, Tokyo.

SACHS, J. (1995), "Reforms in Western Europe and the Former Soviet Union in Light of the East Asian Experiences," *Journal of the Japanese and International Economies* (forthcoming).

TERANISHI, J. (1990), "Financial System and the Industrialization of Japan: 1900–1970," *Banca Nationale del Lavolo*, 174:309–41.

9

Institutions, State Activism, and Economic Development: A Comparison of State-Owned and Township-Village Enterprises in China

YINGYI QIAN AND BARRY R. WEINGAST

9.1 INTRODUCTION

The striking economic success of the East Asian miracles challenges the standard economic wisdom concerning minimum conditions for economic development. A host of recent accounts by economists and political scientists argue that an activist state underpins the growth of the East Asian miracles: government policies and bureaucracies not only promoted market success, but were essential to it.[1] Amsden's (1989:14) study of Korea exemplifies this view: "economic expansion depends on state intervention to create price distortions that direct economic activity toward greater investment."

If governmental activism underpins the economic growth of the East Asian miracles, we are forced to ask how this comes about. Because most poorly performing economies in Latin America, Africa, and Asia also have activist states, it cannot be state activism *per se* that contributes to growth. What causes state activism to promote economic growth in the East Asian miracles, but not elsewhere? The new literature on the state and economic development does not provide the answer.

To address this issue, we investigate the role of the state in Chinese economic reform. For two reasons, modern China presents a natural laboratory for investigating these issues. First, actions by all levels of government are central to China's recent economic success. Second, there is an important diversity of behavior among government-owned firms. The success of Chinese reform rests in large part on the success of new township-village enterprises (TVEs), firms owned by township and village governments. None the less, large numbers of the old state-owned enterprises (SOEs) created during the Maoist era survive with their social obligations largely intact. These firms are rarely efficient. TVEs, in contrast, are much more efficient, often competing successfully in the international market (Che and Qian 1994). The economists' standard understanding of the government-owned firm (e.g., Kornai 1992) affords considerable insight into SOE behavior but little into TVE behavior.

TVEs have considerable incentives to perform efficiently, so they behave far more like private, profit-maximizing firms than do SOEs. One hypothesis about TVE success is that they are actually private firms in disguise. Although this hypothesis is appealing, it is clearly false. TVEs are not private firms because they are set up and maintained by local governments. This hypothesis does not answer the fundamental paradox raised by TVEs: why are these government-owned enterprises structured to behave like private firms? When the United States government sets up corporations, for example, it rarely provides them with incentives to behave efficiently. The same is true with state-owned enterprises throughout the socialist world. The purpose of this chapter is to account for the differences in behavior of these two types of government-owned firm. Despite the new rhetoric about activist government in development, the difference in performance between SOEs and TVEs cannot be accounted for by government ownership, since both are government-owned.

We provide a twofold explanation for the differential between TVE and SOE performances. First, following Wade (1994) among others (Amsden 1989; Campos, Levi, and Sherman 1994; Campos and Root 1994; Clague 1994), we analyze the incentives facing each type of firm. The state saddles SOEs with considerable social goals and punishes managers for failing to meet these goals. These firms cannot go bankrupt, and subsidies are readily provided. Efficient production is clearly a secondary consideration. TVEs, in contrast, do not receive large subsidies or politically motivated loans. They have few politically mandated social burdens, and they must operate under competitive conditions for both capital and labor. Although these firms are owned by governments, the latter are local governments without the political power to protect their firms via trade barriers, inflationary finance, or other administrative means.

At one level, therefore, the explanation for the differential performance of TVEs and SOEs concerns the incentives they face. At a deeper level, however, this explanation remains fundamentally incomplete, for it fails to explain why the governments that create these organizations maintain a particular set of incentives. What prevents the local governments from using TVEs to pursue other political goals? Missing from the new literature on the role of activist government in development is an explanation for the incentive-compatibility of government policies and economic performance: just why do some governments foster markets? Because enterprise incentives are a central instrument of government policy choice, we must explain why some governments choose incentives for efficient production. Put simply, any explanation of the efficacy of governmental activism must explain not only the incentives of organizations created by governments—whether Indian irrigation bureaus, Korean credit allocation bureaus, or Chinese

TVEs—but why a government creates and maintains those incentives. As North (1981, 1990) details, incentives to foster market development are rare throughout history.

The second part of our analysis asks why governments create and maintain incentives that foster market growth. Our approach emphasizes the institutional environment of government (North 1990), in part creating the incentives faced by various governments. Two features of China's institutional environment are central to our analysis: federalism and international competition.

As is well known, Chinese economic reform rests on a foundation of administrative (i.e., political) decentralization, devolving power over the economy from the central government to local governments. Less well known is that this decentralization has created a form of federalism with special properties that we call "market-preserving federalism, Chinese style" (Montinola, Qian, and Weingast 1995; Qian and Weingast 1995; and Weingast 1995).[2] The induced incentives of local governments under this type of federalism are the key to the second part of our analysis. The devolution of power has allowed considerable experimentation and variation in policies. Initially along the south coast but increasingly elsewhere in China, local governments have sought to enhance their power and resources by creating firms with profit-maximizing profiles.[3] As students of federalism have long noted, this system's competitive pressures prevent political encroachments on markets (e.g., Tiebout 1956, Oates 1972). Localities that impose onerous political burdens on their enterprises necessarily place their firms at a competitive disadvantage. These burdens make it harder to attract capital and labor, which favor regions with more profitable enterprises. Market-preserving federalism provides the answer to the question about what makes the creation of profit-maximizing TVEs the incentive-compatible choice for the governments that create these enterprises.

The fiscal component of Chinese federalism illustrates this theme. The arrangements in China afford local governments residual rights to additional revenues (or a substantial portion of revenues) beyond certain specified limits (Oi 1995). A growing local economy implies growing government resources. These incentives have also induced many local governments to provide public goods complementing market development.[4] As the economies of several provinces have grown rich relative to their pasts, the revenue-sharing arrangements of the new fiscal system imply that local and provincial governments have also grown rich.

International competition also limits the political manipulability of local governments. Imposing onerous political burdens on firms competing in international markets would not achieve political goals but would shrink these enterprises' sales and profits. Local governments in the high-growth provinces instead pursue political goals and redistribution from their share of the revenues generated by vibrant, market-oriented firms. Over the long run, the amount of revenue available for public purposes is far larger than from political extraction from local citizens and firms.

The larger lesson of our approach is that the institutional and competitive context of government activism is critical to its consequences. Governments hold both the power to create and maintain competitive markets and the power to confiscate the wealth of their citizens (Diermeier *et al.* 1995, North 1990, Weingast 1995). Particular institutional constraints on government foster policy choices promoting markets rather than political extraction. It is not governmental activism alone that is critical for economic development, for the extractive governments of Africa are also activist. Rather, it is the institutional structure of government that channels governmental activism toward promoting markets.

We develop our argument as follows. Section 9.2 provides the necessary background about SOEs and TVEs, describing their rights, obligations, and incentives. We analyze these differences in the next two sections. Section 9.3 studies the economic implications of these enterprises' incentives. Section 9.4 turns to the problem of the institutional and government environment creating enterprise incentives, analyzing why they are maintained. Our conclusions follow.

9.2 BACKGROUND TO THE GOVERNMENT ENTERPRISES IN CHINA: SOES VERSUS TVES

China's reform experience offers varieties of experiments in enterprise ownership structures, with the majority taking the forms of SOEs and TVEs.[5] This section describes the institutional differences between the SOEs and TVEs, focusing on three dimensions: ownership rights, welfare obligations and employment practices, and budget constraints.

By the end of 1993, China had about 130,000 SOEs, each subordinated to one of the four levels of government: central, provincial (30 provinces in total), prefecture (340 prefectures in total), and county (about 2,100 counties in total).[6] The SOEs constitute the "state sector" of the economy. The number of TVEs totaled about 1.5 million, each owned by one of the 48,000 townships or 800,000 villages. The TVEs are collective enterprises, and collective enterprises, together with the true private enterprises, constitute the "nonstate" sector. All of the TVEs were created after the 1970s, with their numbers rising dramatically during the mid-1980s. Systematic differences in the economic performance of SOEs and TVEs have been documented elsewhere (see, for example, Xu 1991 and Jefferson and Rawski 1994). As new firms in rural areas, TVEs enjoy several advantages over most older SOEs in the urban areas; for example, TVEs usually are smaller and employ a cheaper and younger labor force. At the same time, other factors may disadvantage TVEs, such as a lower level of human resources and technology.

Ownership Rights

Assets in SOEs are legally owned by the whole people of the nation. This ownership grants the central government the legal authority to reallocate the control rights over and residual claims from state-owned assets, even if those rights have been delegated to local governments such as provinces, prefectures, or counties.[7] Changes in control over SOEs have occurred several times since 1949 (Qian and Weingast 1995). An SOE could be subordinated to the central government during the centralization period, and then subordinated to the city government in the decentralization period, and perhaps subordinated to the provincial government later.

In contrast, from the legal point of view, only township and village governments have the authority to reallocate control rights and income from TVE assets. The government regulation specifies that "assets (of a TVE) are owned collectively by the whole of rural residents of the township or village which runs the enterprise; ownership rights over enterprise assets are exercised by the rural residents' meeting (or congress) or a collective economic organization that represents the whole of rural residents of the township or village" (Ministry of Agriculture 1990:81 (Art. 18, ch. 3)). The ownership rights are comprehensive: "the owner of a TVE, according to the law, determines the direction and format of its business operations, selects managers or determines the method of such selection, determines the specific distribution ratios of after-tax profits between the owner and the enterprise, and has the rights over the enterprise concerning its spin-off, merger, relocation, stop-operation, close-down, application for bankruptcy, etc." (Ministry of Agriculture 1990:84 (Art. 19, ch. 3)).

In China, state assets and collective assets (which include TVE assets) have been treated differently by the state. The state, by regulation, cannot transfer collective assets to the state at an arbitrarily low price (*pingdiao*).[8] Land transactions serve as a good example. By Chinese law, land in urban areas is part of state assets while land in rural areas is regarded as a collective asset. During a procurement for land development by the state (say for construction of a highway), the state usually takes away land in urban areas by administrative means but it has to pay a market price for land in rural areas to the community that owns it.

Welfare Obligations and Employment Practice

Historically, SOEs have been saddled with considerable welfare obligations. Employee benefits provided by SOEs are contingent on employment in SOEs, and these have always been high. Perhaps because of the unified ownership, the state has imposed a unified rule requiring state enterprises to provide social welfare such as health insurance, disability insurance, death benefits, and pensions, according to national standards. Furthermore, as a legacy of the planning system, state enterprises remain responsible for providing employees with housing, meal service, day care, medical clinics and hospitals, and, in some cases, even elementary and high schools. This is the well-known practice called "enterprise running social services." It is arguable that economic reforms, in particular fiscal reform, have actually increased the social obligations of SOEs because, facing tight fiscal budgets, all levels of government have tried to download their social responsibilities on to the SOEs.

But for collective enterprises, largely TVEs but also including a small number of urban collectives, there is no unified state regulation of workers' welfare; each enterprise has its own rules (Walder 1994). The level of employee benefits in TVEs, which are outside the government's plan from their inception, is generally low. More importantly, there is no mandate for the provision of employee benefits, which remain at the discretion of the specific township or village. Rich areas have more after-tax profits, so they provide more benefits than do poor areas. Moreover, TVEs provide few or none of the social services mentioned above.

Another difference between SOEs and TVEs concerns employment practices. Workers in SOEs can be laid off only for political or disciplinary reasons, not for economic reasons. This practice is known as the "iron rice bowl." Workers in TVEs, in contrast, can be fired at any time, known in China as the "mud rice bowl." Further, workers in TVEs are not considered "official workers." The state has a commitment only to workers in SOEs. For example, if they become unemployed, the state has the responsibility of finding them other jobs. Workers in TVEs, once laid off, typically return to work on their family land, which was equally distributed to households after the rural reform in the late 1970s. This is regarded as a natural "insurance policy" for rural workers in TVEs, an option not available for most urban SOE workers.

Budget Constraints

Comparing SOEs and TVEs demonstrates not only their different position within the fiscal and monetary systems, but that SOEs have a soft budget constraint. First, consider fiscal subsidies. In 1992, SOEs accounted for approximately 50 per cent of national industrial output and received about 90 per cent of total budgetary subsidies (*Statistical Yearbook of China, 1993*). At the same time, TVEs generated 30 per cent of national industrial output but received only 10 per cent of total budgetary subsidies.

Second, consider bank credits. Every SOE has an account with a state bank branch, enabling the SOE to receive periodically "policy loans" from the bank. Policy loans are not extended on a commercial basis and account for up to 40 per cent of the total outstanding loans of state banks. Many are credits extended to troubled enterprises so they can avoid bankruptcy. These loans are thus subsidies in disguise. State banks, in turn, are able to extend endless policy loans to SOEs because they themselves have soft budget constraints: the state banks often get credit from the central bank, which can resort to monetary expansion. In Table 9.1, the line item, "Credit from the Central Bank" shows that, between 1985 and 1990, state banks in China continuously received credits from the central bank, accounting for about one-quarter to one-third of these banks' total liabilities. The analysis of bank credits reveals that the financial system rather than the government budget has become the most significant source for the soft budget constraint of SOEs (Qian and Roland 1995).

TVEs have harder budget constraints than SOEs for two reasons. First, banks do not extend TVEs policy loans or cheap credit. In cases where TVEs borrow from county branches of the Agriculture Bank of China, they remain second-class citizens compared to SOEs. Second, most TVEs rely on loans from rural credit cooperatives. Unlike state banks, these cooperatives face a hard budget constraint and therefore cannot afford to extend to TVEs loans that cannot be paid back.

Rural credit cooperatives are not formally in China's state banking system. Historically, these cooperatives were created mainly as deposit-taking offices for the Agriculture Bank of China with very few lending activities. The lending activities of rural credit cooperatives have gradually increased since the reform. In contrast to state banks which are net borrowers from the central bank (Table 9.1), rural credit cooperatives have always been net lenders to the state bank—the Agriculture Bank of China (Table 9.2). Thus, unlike state banks, these cooperatives do not receive funds from the government to bail out ailing TVEs.[9]

TABLE 9.1 China: Balance Sheets of State Specialized Banks (share)

	1985	1988	1989	1990	1991	1992	1993
Assets							
Reserves	14.12	10.89	12.60	14.65	16.39	14.34	16.61
Foreign Assets	4.36	4.46	3.83	5.08	5.19	5.73	4.72
Domestic Claims	81.51	84.65	83.53	80.27	78.42	79.93	78.67
Total Assets	100.00	100.00	100.00	100.00	100.00	100.00	100.00
Liabilities							
Domestic Deposits	41.58	47.33	48.03	50.50	53.09	59.82	58.61
Foreign Liabilities	3.12	3.67	3.54	3.73	4.94	4.35	4.01
Credit from Central Bank	33.06	28.40	29.73	28.23	26.94	26.16	30.32
Capital Account	9.61	7.73	7.03	6.19	5.99	5.12	5.42
Others	12.63	12.87	11.69	11.34	9.04	4.55	1.64
Total Liabilities	100.00	100.00	100.00	100.00	100.00	100.00	100.00

Source: International Monetary Fund (1994:281).

TABLE 9.2 China: Balance Sheets of Rural Credit Cooperatives (share)

	1985	1988	1989	1990	1991	1992	1993
Assets							
Reserves at State Banks	50.09	38.95	37.54	35.41	33.62	30.57	30.44
Domestic Claims	49.91	61.05	62.46	64.59	66.38	69.43	69.56
Total Assets	100.00	100.00	100.00	100.00	100.00	100.00	100.00
Liabilities							
Domestic Deposits	90.45	94.05	95.23	98.08	99.44	98.39	95.07
Credit from State Banks	4.11	2.42	2.15	1.92	1.86	1.71	1.33
Others	5.44	3.53	2.62	–0.00	–1.30	0.00	3.60
Total Liabilities	100.00	100.00	100.00	100.00	100.00	100.00	100.00

Source: International Monetary Fund (1994:281).

9.3 INCENTIVES OF GOVERNMENT ENTERPRISES

This section contrasts the incentives facing the two types of government enterprises.[10] Taking the institutional environment—encompassing politics, rules, regulations, and the legal environment—as given, we show why TVEs have profit-oriented incentives and why SOEs do not.

Two principal sets of incentives distinguish TVEs from SOEs. First, the several factors identified above provide *positive* incentives that advantage TVEs. They have more secured property rights, in part due to the residual claims and control by the local community government. Further, they face smaller welfare constraints and obligations toward workers. Second, equally or more important, is the hard budget constraint faced by TVEs, as TVEs' access to credit and subsidies is constrained. The financial constraint imposed upon TVEs provides a critical mechanism of *negative* incentives for TVEs to perform well, otherwise they will go out of business without government bail-out.

For each type of firm, the positive incentives and the negative incentives complement one another. One reason for the soft budget constraint of SOEs is the excess welfare burden imposed by the government, which has to provide policy loans to let them survive (Qian and Roland 1995). On the other hand, the soft budget constraint of SOEs also gives the higher governments the excuse (and legitimacy) to use their discretion to raise more revenue or to intervene to limit the adverse impact of the soft budget constraint, thus leading to insecure property rights. In contrast, decentralized property rights and few welfare obligations provide fewer incentives for the state to extend policy loans to TVEs, hence the hard budget constraint. Further, the hard budget constraint also reduces the chances of intervention by the higher levels of government, which in turn secures property rights.

It is interesting to observe that the fiscal decentralization of authority from the higher- to lower-level governments during the reform has greatly helped TVEs. The same cannot be said of SOEs. The point is that SOEs have been delegated not only rights to revenues, but also many social obligations as well. Therefore, the overall effect is ambiguous. Indeed, as the central government's revenue declined, it downloaded more and more fiscal burdens on to the local governments, especially those obligations for SOE employees. This aspect of decentralization works against providing incentives to enterprises.

Two types of "social services" provided by the government should be distinguished. Those SOEs dating from the planning era reflected government goals at the time (e.g., employment over profitability). In this case, most of the social services provided by the enterprises and the government are *substitutes* for profitable activities. In contrast, the new goals of reform-minded local governments, such as Guangdong, lead them to foster the market. Many of the social services provided after reform, such as infrastructure and enforcement of contracts, are designed to enhance the total value of market activity, net of the costs of these services. This is especially important for the initial development of markets. In this case, they are *complementary* to the profitable activities. Notice how it contrasts with the types of social services mandated for SOEs. The history of the development of TVEs in rural China is also relevant in understanding TVEs. The commune system in rural China between 1958 and 1984 is the basic historical and institutional reason for the rise of TVEs.[11] Originally created for the purpose of organizing agricultural production, the commune system failed miserably. In the late 1970s and early 1980s, land was distributed to households under the reform of the "household responsibility system," but at the same time, townships (formerly communes) and villages (formerly brigades) had become centers for industrial activities. The township and villages inherited physical, human, and institutional capital in the name of collectives, which provide an opportunity for community-based industrialization. What is critical is that at the time when townships and villages have some limited resources to get rich, unlike SOEs, they have no real sources of political rents, only the market. This, combined with considerable competition from other townships and villages, implies that they are highly constrained and face strong competitive discipline. As new, entry-level firms in competitive industries without much government protection, TVEs must compete vigorously with SOEs and other TVEs (and more recently with foreign firms and joint ventures in China) in order to survive, assuming their products are not for export. Exporting TVEs, for example, have to face international competition. Hence, to earn any revenues, TVEs must be profitable.[12] In comparison, SOEs and their political benefactors typically have many ways to create political rents, through tax breaks, budgetary subsidies, "policy loans" at low interest rates, price controls, and all kinds of licenses.

9.4 INCENTIVES OF GOVERNMENTS

The preceding section analyzed the incentives facing government enterprises, thus taking the first of two necessary steps in understanding state capacity. The second step concerns the source of these incentives and how they are maintained. We now turn to the more fundamental question: if the incentives of TVEs explain their success, then what leads local governments to foster an environment promoting profit maximizing while other governments attempt to impose political goals on firms? The answer, we argue, is federalism.

Market-Preserving Federalism and Induced Incentives for Local Governments

To understand the economic role of federalism, we need to study a special type of federalism, *market-preserving federalism*, that encompasses a set of conditions concerning the allocation of authorities and responsibilities among different levels of government (McKinnon 1994; Montinola, Qian and Weingast 1995; Qian and Weingast, 1995; Weingast 1995). Market-preserving federalism is a form of vertical separation of powers and is characterized by five conditions.

1. There exists a hierarchy of governments with a delineated scope of authority so that each government is autonomous in its own sphere of authority.
2. The subnational governments have primary authority over the economy within their jurisdictions.
3. The national government has the authority to police the common market and to ensure the mobility of goods and factors across subgovernment jurisdictions.
4. Revenue sharing among governments is limited, and borrowing by governments is constrained so that all governments face hard budget constraints.
5. The allocation of authority and responsibility has an institutionalized degree of durability so that it cannot be altered by the national government either unilaterally or under the pressures from subnational governments.

These conditions represent an ideal type of institutional arrangement of a market-preserving federalism. All of these characteristics are necessary for federalism to have the desired economic effects. Condition (1) contains the defining characteristic of federalism. Local government autonomy is necessary, for if the central government holds the power to undo the system or to overwhelm the local governments, it can constrain their choices in ways that will destroy the important independence of these governments.

Federalism in India and many Latin American states (e.g., Argentina or Brazil) suffers from this problem; these systems are thus not characterized by market-preserving federalism.

But Condition (1) alone does not generate federalism's market-preserving qualities. These require the addition of Conditions (2) through (5). Condition (2), control over the local economy, combines with local autonomy to imply that local jurisdictions are in competition with one another. From the perspective of preserving market incentives, the authority of the national government over markets is limited to policing the common market across regions, Condition (3), and providing national public goods (e.g., monetary policy), which should not be left to subnational-level governments. Without Condition (3), each subnational government would become something of a *de facto* "national government" in its jurisdiction.

The constraint of Condition (4) has two parts, one for fiscal revenue transfers between levels of governments, and one for borrowing through the financial system (McKinnon 1994). The hard budget constraint in the fiscal channel limits revenue sharing and equalization among governments, especially through soft grants. The hard budget constraint in the financial channel restricts open-ended access to capital markets, especially borrowing from the central bank. The hard budget constraint provides local governments with negative incentives for proper fiscal management. Firms, citizens, and local elites of particular areas typically understand the relationship between the fiscal commitments and tax obligations. Local authorities are discouraged from incurring obligations that citizens and local elites do not deem worth paying taxes for. This constraint also limits the ability of local governments to endlessly bail out ailing enterprises. None the less, it does not prevent the government from providing services deemed valuable to the local economy, for example, infrastructure, education, or housing services that allow a great expansion in the number of workers who come to the area to work in local factories (see, e.g., Tiebout 1956, Oates 1972).

Condition (5) provides for credible commitment to the federal system and thus for limits on the national government's discretionary authority. Not only must there be decentralization, but that decentralization must not be under the discretionary control of the national government, nor under the pressures from some coalitions of subnational governments. Condition (5) concerns the enforcement problem and is critically important.

It should be clear that whether a nation calls itself federal is irrelevant to our definition of market-preserving federalism. What matters is whether the various conditions hold. Notice that not all *de jure* systems of federalism (those calling themselves federal) fit these criteria. In India, Argentina, and Brazil, for example, local governments do not have the critical independent authority over their economies. Although Russia is nominally a federal system, nearly every condition for market-preserving federalism is violated (Qian and Weingast 1995). The relationship between local and national governments remains ambiguous; there is no common market; and the national government retains considerable authority over the economy. Moreover, many systems not normally considered federal meet these criteria, notably, eighteenth-century England during the industrial revolution (Weingast 1995).

Under Conditions (2), (3), and (4), competition among jurisdictions has a positive incentive effect because it induces jurisdictions to provide hospitable environments for firms and the various factors of production such as capital and labor. This typically occurs through the provision of local public goods, such as establishing a basis for secure rights of factor owners, the provision of infrastructure, utilities, access to markets, and so on. Jurisdictions that fail to provide these goods and services find that their firms fare poorly relative to those in other jurisdictions and that factors move to other jurisdictions. These consequences induce strong pressures for the local governments to provide an optimal mix of local public goods and to protect the rights of factor owners.[13] Conditions (2), (3), and (4) also foster experimentation and learning in the presence of problems common to many lower-level governments. As the results of these experiments become known, they can be imitated by others.

Because a local government cannot impose its policies on the entire economy, but only within its borders, a local government that seeks to use its authority to impose political burdens on firms or factors of production within its borders places them at a considerable competitive disadvantage. Suppose, for example, that a particular jurisdiction places an onerous restriction on its enterprises, requiring that enterprises must hire only workers from the locality and that these workers cannot be fired. Restrictions that force political and social goals on to enterprises place local enterprises at a competitive disadvantage relative to enterprises from other jurisdictions that are not bound by such restrictions. This implies that enterprises outside the particular jurisdiction have lower costs and will outcompete firms bound by the restrictions. This greatly reduces the ability of local governments to attempt to manipulate the goals and performance of their enterprises because doing so implies that they are not likely to succeed in the market.

Following the imposition of a system of federalism we should observe a diversity of policy choices and experiments. People in different jurisdictions are likely to have markedly different interests, expectations, and capabilities. They may also appeal to markedly different theories and ideologies to make their decisions. We should therefore observe that they choose a range of policies to promote their goals.

As the results of these experiments and policies become known, individuals and policymakers will update their expectations about the effects of various policies. Thus, decentralization under market-preserving federalism results in an important degree of feedback that would not be present under a unitary system that imposes a single national experiment over all regions.

Thus far, the discussion has focused largely on the benefits of market-preserving federalism, yet this system also has its costs. We raise two: macroeconomic shocks and problems of regional inequality. The trade-off concerning macroeconomic shocks is that granting the national government sufficient power to handle these shocks also grants it a soft budget constraint, allowing all kinds of political and economic mischief. Developing countries have proven notoriously bad at restricting their use of this power to the appropriate circumstances. Countervailing the losses due to the inability to respond to macroeconomic shocks are the savings arising from an absence of the costs resulting from the typical mismanagement of that power.

The problem of regional inequality raises big economic and political concerns, ones that cannot be dealt with satisfactorily in a wholly decentralized manner. In a post-Deng China, for example, these inequalities could lead to political pressure to unravel decentralization. Addressing regional disparities is a task for the national government. Nevertheless, the powers granted to the national government are not straightforward. The problem here, as with the power to deal with macroeconomic shocks, is that if the central government controls this redistribution, the funds can be used for other purposes, potentially conflicting with the central government's hard budget constraint. Any mechanism designed to deal with inequality must also constrain the national government's discretion over how the funds are used. An additional factor in China is that labor migration from poor areas to rich ones implies that funds are moving from rich to poor areas. Indeed, some interior provinces have devised complex mechanisms to help foster this migration and the attending flow of funds back into the province (see examples in Montinola, Qian and Weingast 1995).

Market-Preserving Federalism, Chinese Style

The decentralization in China obviously differs from Western federalism because the latter is associated with strong individual rights, political freedom, and democracy, and is built upon an explicit constitutional foundation. But these are not critically important for our analysis of the economic role of federalism. What we called market-preserving federalism, Chinese style, is a recognition of the fact that China under reform has achieved some of the criteria listed above but not others. At present, China satisfies Conditions (1) and (2), while Conditions (3), (4), and (5) are only partially satisfied. The problematic aspects concern the imperfect common market (Condition (3)), the soft budget constraints (Condition (4)), and the lack of rule-based decentralization with an institutionalized balance of authority.

The degree of imperfection of these conditions varies across levels of government. It turns out that the conditions are better satisfied at the lower levels of government, that is, the township and village governments, than at the higher levels. Two forms of constraint are imposed upon the township and village governments and their enterprises that are absent in upper-level governments and SOEs. The first limit is that these governments do not have the authority or ability to enact protectionist policies. They cannot use political means to protect their enterprises, for example, by erecting trade barriers to keep out competition, simply because the geographic area in one jurisdiction is too small. The second limit is a hard budget constraint. The township and village governments, in contrast to higher levels of governments, do not have easy access to credit. For example, total credit going to the TVE sector was no more than 8 per cent of total outstanding loans, despite the fact that this sector produced more than 25 per cent of total industrial output at the same time (*Almanac of China's Finance and Banking 1992*).

This analysis suggests that the divergent incentives of township/village governments and the higher-level governments are systematic and can be understood from the perspective of federalism. Competition among local governments is benign only if there are no trade barriers and there are hard budget constraints (McKinnon 1994). Only at the township and village levels are these conditions satisfied in China. Because the incentives of the governments differ, so do the incentives of enterprises they control.

An additional aspect of local government incentives concerns the use of revenue or profits controlled by these governments. For the last 10 years, about 90 per cent of after-tax profits in TVEs was used for reinvestment and various public goods, such as education and infrastructure, and 10 per cent for welfare purposes (*Statistical Survey of China 1992, 1993*). This naturally raises the following question: why did China not follow the examples of Latin America or India in which rent seeking and political pressures have led to more government revenue being used for unproductive social expenditures and politically motivated redistribution?

At one level, the regulation by the central government in China helps to avoid that: it requires that the profits from TVEs be mainly used for reinvestment purposes. But at the deeper level we argue that the incentives of local governments to comply with the regulation ultimately derives from interjurisdiction competition, an important consequence of federalism. In China, regional competition to become rich quickly is intense, and every region tries to attract more capital, better quality labor, and better technology. Regional competition changes the calculation of local governments and hence their incentives: competition raises the opportunity costs of using revenue for nonproductive expenditures. Interregional economic competition leads local governments to concentrate spending on productive investment (i.e., growth seeking), while in India or some countries in Latin America, intraregional political competition from interest groups provides local government with incentives toward more spending on welfare redistribution (i.e., rent seeking).

Our explanation for the political foundations of China's economic growth overlaps and disagrees with that of Shirk (1993, 1994) in important ways. Both approaches emphasize the importance of decentralization and the incentives of local governments. Shirk, however, places greater weight on the political organization of local governments and their control over the economy, arguing that local political officials should be viewed as political bosses, creating systems of patronage and loyalty.

We believe that there is considerable truth in Shirk's assertion. None the less, her thesis requires qualification. Local governments do seem to be building systems of patronage. Because their approval is necessary for enterprises and because their protection is part of the maintenance of firm property rights, they play a more central role in the economy than do local governments in, say, the United States. The share of surplus appropriated by local governments and local officials is probably higher for this reason.

We disagree with Shirk on one critical issue. The patronage systems she describes are also present in broad form common to those in Latin America and Africa. And yet those economies have, respectively, performed poorly and abysmally. Thus, the missing component from Shirk's explanation concerns the limits on these systems of political patronage. We argue that the system of federalism, with its jurisdictional competition, places striking limits on this system of patronage and political spoils. So too does competition in the international market. Were the patronage systems to place onerous restrictions or burdens on these firms, they simply could not succeed in international competition. These limits not only underpin China's striking economic success, but suggest how the patronage systems of local Chinese governments differ from those of Latin America and Africa. This question bears further research.

Fiscal Components of Federalism, Chinese Style

Starting in 1980, China implemented a fiscal revenue-sharing system between any two adjacent levels of government.[14] Although schemes vary across both regions and time, the basic idea is that a lower-level regional government contracts with the upper-level regional government on the total amount (or share) of tax and profit revenue (negative values imply a reverse flow of subsidies) to be remitted for the next several years, and the lower-level government keeps the rest.

Consider the fiscal contracting schemes between the central and provincial governments (lower-level fiscal contracting is similar). In the first step, revenue income in each province is divided between central fixed revenue, all of which is remitted to the center, and local revenue, which is subject to sharing. In the second step, a particular formula of sharing is determined. There are six basic types of sharing schemes for the 30 provinces and 5 cities that had independent budget agreements with the center during the period 1988–93 (Bahl and Wallich 1992; see also Wong 1991).

The details of these schemes vary (see Montinola, Qian, and Weingast 1995 for a description). Some provinces and cities keep a fixed proportion of all revenues collected; others retain a certain portion up to a quota, keeping a higher proportion of all revenues above the quota; a few provinces remit a fixed sum; and finally, some of the poorer provinces and cities receive fixed subsidies. The importance of the new fiscal arrangements is that they induce a positive relationship between local revenue and local economic prosperity, thus providing local officials with an incentive to foster that prosperity.

At the macro level, the central fixed revenue (before sharing) increased from 21 per cent of the total in 1981 to 39 per cent in 1991. At the same time, the expenditure of the central government decreased from 54 per cent of the total in 1981 to 40 per cent in 1991 (*Statistical Yearbook of China, 1992*). These changes yield two implications: first, local governments have assumed more responsibility; and second, the total net transfer has become relatively small.

These changes provide substantial independence of the governments in China, from the provincial to the township. Local governments possess not only significant fiscal autonomy from the central government, but considerable independent authority over their economies. The new fiscal system implies that local governments have strong incentives to foster local economic prosperity, for this is the route by which their revenue grows.

Notice the striking contrast between this system and those in the former communist system (including those of the former Soviet Union and Eastern Europe). In the latter, the central authorities retained the right to all residuals "earned" by producers, typically using this authority to take resources from those firms with positive earnings to bail out those with negative earnings. As is well known, this system did not yield incentives to produce. Under the modern Chinese system, all residuals earned by TVEs are retained by the local government.

9.5 CONCLUSIONS

Students of development have recently begun (again) to debate the appropriate role of government. A series of recent studies of the East Asian miracles emphasize the central importance of an activist government in the growth of these economies. Several conclude that an activist government is necessary to promote economic development. The purpose of this paper has been to contest that conclusion, for the evidence does not support the promotion of state activism *per se*. The reason is that nearly all of the most poorly performing economies also have activist governments. It therefore cannot be activism alone that underlies economic growth.

We argue that understanding the positive role of government in economic development requires an analysis of the institutions and incentives of government. To support this claim, we turn to an investigation of the remarkable success of Chinese economic development following the reforms. China provides a natural laboratory for this study, because it contains SOEs established during the old planning era side by side with the new TVEs created under the reform. The old SOEs remain inefficient, have burdensome social mandates and restrictions, and require huge state subsidies. The newer, community-government-run TVEs, in contrast, are more efficient, compete successfully in the international market, and generate much of China's economic surplus.

Because both SOEs and TVEs are government owned, government ownership cannot explain the divergence in their performances. Our explanation of their differential performances has two components. In the first, we parallel a recent literature, arguing that differential incentives explain the difference in performance (Campos and Root 1994; Campos, Levi, and Sherman 1994; Clague 1994; and Wade 1994). In the second, we go beyond that literature to study these organizations' environment. A complete explanation of the performance of government bureaucracies and government-owned firms requires an analysis not only of their incentives, but of the incentives facing the governments within which these are lodged. Why did the latter establish and maintain the relevant incentives facing bureaus and enterprises? The economic success of China necessarily reflects the incentives faced by TVEs, but also the incentives of the governments that establish and maintain them.

This chapter's analysis focuses on China's special form of decentralization, which we call market-preserving federalism, Chinese style. Local governments' independent authority over their economies combines with the fiscal incentives to lead these governments to foster and maintain hospitable economic environments. Governments at the lowest level in the hierarchy, township and villages, do not possess the means to insulate their firms from competition via trade barriers or to bail out ailing firms via macroeconomic tools. Given the structure of federalism, these governments can grow only if their economies grow.

Townships and villages have taken advantage of their authority by creating TVEs. These enterprises face incentives closely corresponding to profit maximizing, and many successfully compete on the international market. As these firms have grown and profited, so too have local governments.

Our analysis suggests some broader lessons for the debate on the role of an activist government for economic development. Critical to the success of local governments in China—and hence of the firms they own—are the incentives facing these governments. We argue that federalism, Chinese style, accounts for the positive incentives of local governments. The restrictions on the central government not only prevent massive market intrusion, but foster competition among local governments. These governments, in turn, compete not only for factors, but for generating surplus. Local governments fostering hospitable economic environments have developed tremendously successful local economies, and they are now being imitated all over China. We thus conclude by emphasizing that, without this system of decentralization inherent in federalism, China is unlikely to have exhibited impressive economic success.

Our analysis also suggests that reform need not be directed by a centralized, national government. In a large country with diverse regions, market-preserving federalism serves as a natural mechanism for creating appropriate incentives for local governments to foster and maintain economic prosperity. Competition among jurisdictions then has important and direct effects for regional development. Market-preserving federalism has proven important in the fast economic growth of many other large states, including England during the industrial revolution and the United States in the nineteenth and early twentieth centuries (Weingast 1995).

Not just any form of decentralization will have the desired effects, however. Federalism is a subset of all possible decentralizations, and market-preserving federalism is a subset of all federalisms. To induce competition among jurisdictions, decentralization must have certain properties. Market-preserving federalism, for example, requires that local governments have political freedom over their local economies. Further, the system of decentralization must have a degree of permanence, implying that it cannot simply remain at the discretion of the national government. The decentralization must be institutionalized so that the national government is constrained from taking back the power granted to local governments. Otherwise, at some future point, the national government will alter or destroy decentralization.

Of course, not all countries are sufficiently large and diverse that federalism is appropriate. Our main point, however, is not that federalism is the solution for all countries. Rather, it is that attention to both the internal incentives of government organizations and their external incentives is critical to development. The recent literature has stressed these organizations' internal incentives, overlooking the external incentives of the larger political system. Both are critical for understanding the performance of public organizations.

NOTES

We thank Masa Aoki, Pranab Bardhan, Cui Zhiyuan, and Dani Rodrik for helpful comments, and Ilse Dignam for editorial assistance.

[1] These accounts differ considerably, both in how they interpret the role of government and in the policy implications they draw. See, e.g., Amsden (1989), Campos, Levi, and Sherman (1994), Clague (1994), Evans (1992), Johnson (1982),

Klitgaard (1991), Rodrik (1994), Root (1994), Stiglitz and Uy (1993), Wade (1994), and World Bank (1993).

[2] Decentralization is an obvious and common theme in the literature on economic reform (e.g., Oi 1995, Shirk 1993, 1994).

[3] Montinola, Qian, and Weingast (1995) also demonstrate how the incentives of federalism were crucial to the diffusion of reform. None the less, economic reform and growth have not been uniform across China.

[4] This is most evident in the Pearl River Delta of Guangdong Province. Examples include the provision of local infrastructure, such as roads and electricity; a predictable set of rights for firms and foreign investment; and land for development of economic zones.

[5] There are also other varieties, such as joint ventures or joint stock companies between the state (possibly with several legal entities) and foreign firms. But so far, the traditional SOEs and new TVEs have accounted for the majority.

[6] Municipalities are included in the last three levels.

[7] There were some lobbying efforts by local governments in 1993 (e.g., Guangdong) to demand regional ownership rights over some assets of those SOEs currently under the supervision of local governments. This effort was unsuccessful. The unitary state ownership right was reasserted in the Party document on the decision of establishment of a socialist market economic structure in November 1993: "For State-owned property in enterprises, the system will be for unitary ownership by the State, supervision by governments at various levels and independent management by the enterprises" (*China Daily*, November 17, 1993, Supplement, p. 1).

[8] Only during the brief Great Leap Forward did the state abuse its power regarding collective assets. Soon after, it retreated, and the collective assets remained reasonably protected from predation by the higher governments (although there have been more incidents of abusing private property rights than collective property rights).

[9] Part of the reason that rural credit cooperatives are net depositors is due to central government regulation. In China, the central government regulates rural credit cooperatives differently from the state banks, limiting their lending activities. For example, rural credit cooperatives are required to keep reserves with the Agriculture Bank of China in proportion to their total deposits ("Zhongguo . . ." (1992), Art. 11, ch. 4, p. 397). The regulation further requires that "total outstanding loans by the year's end should not be more than 75 per cent of total deposits and their own capital" ("Zhongguo . . ." (1992), Art. 12, ch. 4, p. 397). There is no similar regulation for state banks.

[10] Following Campos, Levi, and Sherman (1994), Campos and Root (1994), Clague (1994), and Wade (1994).

[11] In fact, they were called Commune and Brigade Enterprises until 1984 when the commune system was abolished.

[12] Moreover, Montinola, Qian, and Weingast (1995) emphasize that the strong demonstration effects were also important in explaining the fast expansion of TVEs in other parts of the country. Examples include the early success of TVEs in Jiangsu and Guangdong, and the experiences and knowledge about doing business in the market from early interactions with families and enterprises in Hong Kong and Taiwan.

[13] See economic literature on local public goods, e.g., Oates (1972).
[14] See, e.g., Oi (1992, 1995), Oksenberg and Tong (1991), Wong (1991), and Bahl and Wallich (1992).

REFERENCES

Agriculture, Ministry of, ed. (1990), "Zhonghua Renmin Gongheguo Xiangcun Jiti Suoyouzhi Qiye Tiaoli Tiaowen Shiyi" (Explanations of the regulation on township and village collective enterprises of the People's Republic of China), China Legal Press, Beijing.

Almanac of China's Finance and Banking 1992 (1992), The Editorial Office of Almanac of China's Finance and Banking, Beijing.

Amsden, A. H. (1989), *Asia's Next Giant: South Korea and Late Industrialization*, Oxford University Press, Oxford.

Bahl, R. and Wallich, C. (1992), "Intergovernmental Fiscal Relations in China," working paper, Country Economics Department, World Bank, WPS 863.

Campos, E. and Root, H. (1994), "The High Performance Asian Economies," unpublished manuscript, Hoover Institution, Stanford University.

——, Levi, M., and Sherman, R. (1994), "Rationalized Bureaucracy and Rational Compliance," working paper, IRIS Center, University of Maryland.

Che, J. and Qian, Y. (1994), "Understanding China's Township-Village Enterprises," unpublished manuscript, Stanford University.

Clague, C. (1994), "Bureaucracy and Economic Development," *Structural Change and Economic Dynamics*, 5(2) (Dec.):273–91.

Diermeier, D., Ericson, J., Frye, T., and Lewis, S. (1995), "Credible Commitment and Property Rights," unpublished manuscript, University of Rochester.

Evans, P. (1992), "The State as Problem and Solution: Predation, Embedded Autonomy, and Structural Change," in S. Haggard and R. R. Kaufman, eds., *The Politics of Economic Adjustment*, Princeton University Press, Princeton.

International Monetary Fund (1994), *International Financial Statistics Yearbook*, International Monetary Fund, Washington.

Jefferson, G. H. and Rawski, T. G. (1994), "Enterprise Reform in Chinese Industry," *Journal of Economic Perspectives*, 8(2):47–70.

Johnson, C. (1982), *MITI and the Japanese Miracle*, Stanford University Press, Stanford.

Klitgaard, R. (1991), *Adjusting to Reality: Beyond "State Versus Market" in Economic Development*, ICS Press, San Francisco.

Kornai, J. (1992), *The Socialist System*, Princeton University Press, Princeton.

McKinnon, R. I. (1994), "Market-Preserving Fiscal Federalism," unpublished manuscript, Stanford University.

Ministry of Agriculture (1990), Zhonghua Renmin Gongheguo Xiangcun Jiti Suoyouzhi Qiye Tiaoli Tiaowen Shiyi (Explanations of the regulation on township and village collective enterprises of the PRC), China Legal Press, Beijing.

MONTINOLA, G., QIAN, Y., and WEINGAST, B. R. (1995), "Federalism, Chinese Style: The Political Basis for Economic Success in China," *World Politics*, 48(1):50–81.
NORTH, D. C. (1981), *Structure and Changes in Economic History*, W. W. Norton, New York.
——(1990), *Institutions, Institutional Change, and Economic Performance,* Cambridge University Press, New York.
OATES, W. (1972), *Fiscal Federalism*, Harcourt Brace Jovanovich, New York.
OI, J. (1992), "Fiscal Reform and the Economic Foundations of Local State Corporatism in China," *World Politics*, 45:99–126.
——(1995), *Rural China Takes Off: Incentives for Industrialization*, University of California Press, Berkeley.
OKSENBERG, M. and TONG, J. (1991), "The Evolution of Central-Provincial Fiscal Relations in China, 1971–1984: The Formal System," *The China Quarterly*, 1–32.
QIAN, Y. and ROLAND, G. (1995), "The Soft Budget Constraint in China," *Japan and the World Economy*, forthcoming.
——and WEINGAST, B. R. (1995), "China's Transition to Markets: Market-Preserving Federalism, Chinese Style," *Journal of Policy Reform*, forthcoming.
RODRIK, D. (1994), "Taking Trade Policy Seriously: Export Subsidization as a Case Study in State Capabilities," unpublished manuscript, Columbia University.
ROOT, H. L. (1994), *The Fountain of Privilege: Political Foundations of Markets in Old Regime France and England*, University of California Press, Berkeley.
RUBINFELD, D. (1987), "Economics of the Local Public Sector," in A. J. Auerbach and M. Feldstein, eds., *Handbook of Public Economies*, Vol. II, Elsevier, New York, 571-646.
SHIRK, S. L. (1993), *The Political Logic of Economic Reform in China*, University of California Press, Berkeley.
——(1994), *How China Opened Her Door*, Brookings Institution, Washington.
Statistical Survey of China 1992, 1993, China Statistics Publishing House, Beijing.
Statistical Yearbook of China, 1993, China Statistics Publishing House, Beijing.
STIGLITZ, J. and UY, M. (1993), "Financial Policy: Are there Lessons from East Asia?" World Bank–Stanford University Conference on the Asian Miracles, Stanford University, October 25–26.
TIEBOUT, C. (1956), "A Pure Theory of Local Expenditure," *Journal of Political Economy*, 64:416-24.
WADE, R. (1994), "Institutions and Bureaucracies: A Comparative Study of Korea and India," unpublished manuscript.
WALDER, A. (1994), "The Varieties of Public Enterprises in China: An Institutional Analysis," unpublished manuscript, Harvard University.
WEINGAST, B. R. (1995), "The Economic Role of Political Institutions: Market-Preserving Federalism and Economic Growth," *Journal of Law, Economics, and Organization*, Spring: 1–31.
WONG, C. P. W. (1991), "Central-Local Relations in An Era of Fiscal Decline: The Paradox of Fiscal Decentralization in Post-Mao China," *The China Quarterly*, 128:691–715.
World Bank (1993), *The East Asian Miracle: Economic Growth and Public Policy*, Oxford University Press, Oxford.
XU, C. (1991), "Productivity and Behavior of Chinese Rural Industrial Enterprises," unpublished manuscript, Harvard University.

"Zhongguo Nongye Yinhang Nongcun Xinyong Hezuoshe Guanli Zhanxing Guiding Shishi Xize" (Implementation rules of the provisional regulation on supervision of rural credit cooperatives, Agriculture Bank of China), in *Almanac of China's Finance and Banking, 1992* (1992), The Editorial Office of Almanac of China's Finance and Banking, Beijing.

PART III

THE POLITICAL ECONOMY OF DEVELOPMENT AND GOVERNMENT-PRIVATE INTERACTIONS

10

Sectoral Resource Transfer, Conflict, and Macrostability in Economic Development: A Comparative Analysis

JURO TERANISHI

The possibility of falling into a low-level equilibrium trap has been one of the most serious concerns of policy planners in less developed countries, many of them newly independent, since the end of World War II. Reflecting the strong influence of Keynesian thinking, the trap was associated with a low saving–investment balance, rather than a failure to capture externalities associated with learning or knowledge accumulation. This view is most eloquently represented by Ragnar Nurkse's notion of the vicious circle of poverty (1953): on the supply side, a low level of capital accumulation leads to a low level of saving through low real income, and on the demand side, a low level of purchasing power due to low real income results in a low level of investment reflecting poor incentives for investment. Most attention has been paid to investment, however, leaving the supply side of saving to vague ideas of relying on foreign aid, treating saving as a residual or passive factor, or simply resorting to the transfer of agricultural resources.[1] In other words, adequate investment incentives were considered crucial to ignite the engine of industrialization, putting aside the problem not only of sources of savings, but also of income distribution.[2] Thus, government intervention was considered necessary to coordinate properly the pecuniary externality of investment (Rosenstein-Rodan 1943 and Murphy, Shleifer, and Vishny 1989).

Emphasizing the production of import-competing goods was justified by the mere fact that demand for them existed, by the prevailing pessimism about export growth, and by possible strong backward linkage effects, especially in the case of heavy industrial and chemical products (Hirshman 1958). It is possible that a promotion policy of investment has an effect of crowding out consumption, and a high level of investment *ex ante* results in high level of saving *ex post*, so that necessary saving is realized as a result of high investment. (Saving could be treated as passive factor in this case.) Moreover, it is also possible that the production of new equipment is met with sufficient demand, resulting in the virtuous circle of high income and saving that occurred in East Asia. However, the supply-side effect of new investment is not necessarily met with adequate demand: both market and government coordination failures are possible. Further, the crowding out of consumption is liable to be prolonged and have disproportionate effects on social classes or economic sectors, leading to serious sociopolitical problems. In these cases, the sources and levels of saving are no longer passive elements in a development strategy, and how investment is financed matters significantly in determining the course and results of industrialization.

The purpose of this chapter is to investigate the effects of financing industrialization through the policy-based mobilization of agricultural savings in a comparative study of less-developed economies in Asia (mainly East Asia), Latin America, and Sub-Saharan Africa. The pattern and degree of intersectoral transfers of agricultural savings exercise a profound influence on the process of industrialization through their effects on political and macroeconomic stability. On the one hand, an excessive reliance on policy-based resource shifts from agriculture results in declining rural living standards and excessive urbanization, often leading to an expansion of the urban informal sector.[3] Since this tends to give rise to economic classes with a high time preference for consumption, such as low-income workers in the urban informal sector, government consumption is liable to increase in response to their demands, and adverse external shocks like those of the 1970s will compel government to borrow excessively abroad, with inflationary domestic consequences. On the other hand, whenever agriculture is discriminated against *vis-à-vis* industry yet comprises a significant share of total employment or production, government has an incentive to buy the political support of particular sections of the rural constituency. Subsidy of agricultural inputs and directed credit with subsidized interest are frequently used for such purposes, leading to an expansion of current government expenditures and pressure on aggregate demand and the price level.

This chapter is not intended as a proof of these claims, but the following piecemeal propositions are suggested in an attempt to arrive at a deeper understanding of the relationship between financing industrialization and political and macroeconomic stability across these three regions of the developing world.

1. The degree of resource shift from agriculture does not vary significantly by direct or indirect taxation. However, in East Asia indirect taxation on agriculture is largely offset by infrastructure investment, so that the total resource shift from agriculture in the three regions is lowest in East Asia.
2. The rate of urbanization in East Asia lags far behind that in Latin America and Sub-Saharan Africa. The reason may lie in the increased employment opportunities brought about by the ample supply of infrastructure in rural East Asia.
3. During the 1970s, the share of government consumption in GDP increased significantly in Latin America, South Asia, and Sub-Saharan

Africa, but fell in East Asia. An important part of the increase in government consumption is related to spending to secure political support.

4. In both Sub-Saharan Africa and Latin America, the agricultural sector suffered seriously from severe indirect taxation in the form of exchange rate overvaluation. However, in both regions divisible benefits[4] such as subsidized credits were amply supplied to the subset of agricultural actors who supported the incumbent political regime. In Sub-Saharan Africa, divisible benefits were supplied to particular ethnic groups or factions in the rural area regardless of their contribution to production, whereas benefits in Latin America were given to the powerful and productive landlord class. As a result, agricultural production during the 1970s rose in Latin America and fell in Sub-Saharan Africa.
5. In a cross-section regression of developing economies, a strong relationship exists for the 1970s between an increase in foreign debt and an increase in the share of government consumption.

These findings have important implications for policy reforms in developing countries and former socialist economies aimed at the structural transformation from an agrarian to an industrialized economy. Section 10.1 compares the patterns and degree of resource shift from agriculture in the three regions. Section 10.2 deliberates on the determinants of policy-based resource shifts from agriculture. Section 10.3 investigates the possible links between policy-based resource shifts and macroeconomic stability. Section 10.4 explores some implications for policy reform in developing and former socialist economies. The appendix provides a historical perspective on sectoral resource transfers in Japan.

10.1 RESOURCE TRANSFER FROM AGRICULTURE TO INDUSTRY

Let us first look at the various routes of resource transfer from agriculture. During the process of economic development, resources tend to flow out of agriculture through the market mechanism whenever the rate of return on resources in the latter sector is higher than that on the former—a market-based resource shift. But at the same time, government also intervenes in the resource flow and frequently tries to transfer savings from agriculture by various policies—a policy-based resource shift. First, government often mobilizes resources from agriculture by taxing the sector more than it is subsidized: that is, net direct taxation defined as tax minus subsidies. Two representative taxes are an export tax and the compulsory purchase of crops by state marketing boards at below international (border) prices.[5] Subsidies include input subsidies, directed credits, and protection against agricultural imports (the sum of quotas and tariffs). Second, government policies that are adopted for reasons not primarily related to agriculture sometimes result in significant taxation of the sector. Such net indirect taxation consists of two elements: overvalued exchange rates and net protection of nonagricultural goods (equal to quotas and tariffs minus export subsidies). While net direct taxation and indirect taxation prompt a net resource flow out of agriculture, a third method of policy-based resource shift—infrastructure investment—represents a net flow of resources into agriculture. This includes investment in rural transportation, irrigation, agricultural extension services, etc. Total net resource flow from agriculture can be defined as the sum of these items:

1. market-based resource flow;
2. policy-based resource flow:
   (a) net direct taxation;
   (b) net indirect taxation;
   (c) infrastructure investment in agriculture.

During the early period of postwar economic development, significant policy-based taxation occurred in many developing economies as an essential part of the development strategy. This was because everyone accepted that "modernization was an important goal and taxation of agriculture [was] a necessary means to achieve it" (Krueger 1993a:103), and because there was a very strong view that agriculture is less dynamic than industry and that agricultural production was not very responsive to price incentives. Among 18 countries recently studied by the World Bank, such an industrialization strategy existed in Argentina, Chile, Colombia, the Dominican Republic, Ghana, Malaysia, Morocco, Pakistan, and Zambia. In most of the other countries, such a policy was implicit in government revenue from agriculture and its expenditure elsewhere (Schiff and Valdes 1992:205).

Estimates on the amount of resource flows from agriculture exist for some countries in Asia—India by Mundle (1981), Taiwan by Lee (1971), China by Ishii (1967) and Nakagane (1992), Japan by Ohkawa and others (1978), Mundle and Ohkawa (1979), and Teranishi (1976) and (1989).[6] Although similar data on other regions are lacking, the World Bank study referred to above provides us with information in a comparative framework covering three regions. Table 10.1 shows the main results. Since taxation is measured in the form of proportional changes in the relative price of agriculture to nonagriculture, as is roughly explained in the note to Table 10.1, we cannot evaluate the magnitude of taxation, in comparison with GDP or anything else. However, we can derive two important propositions from the table:

1. There is no significant difference in the degree of either direct or indirect taxation on agriculture among the sample countries of the three regions, although there is some variation by individual country.
2. Indirect taxation often is as large as, if not larger than, indirect taxation.

TABLE 10.1 Taxation on Agriculture (%, annual average)

	1960–1972		1976–1984	
	Indirect Tax	Direct Tax	Indirect Tax	Direct Tax
East Asia				
Korea	–34.6	35.4	–13.3	90.8
Malaysia	–9.3	–8.1	–6.4	–11.2
Philippines	–21.3	5.8	–26.7	–10.9
Thailand	–13.9	–33.4	–17.7	–17.7
South Asia				
Pakistan	–38.4	16.1	–27.7	–30.0
Sri Lanka	–27.8	–9.2	–26.7	–10.9
Latin America				
Argentina	–20.3	–21.5	–26.2	–18.5
Brazil	–17.1	45.5	–18.7	0.0
Chile	–23.9	–5.4	–10.7	6.7
Colombia	–24.6	–2.0	–28.1	–4.2
Dominican Republic	–26.0	–24.1	–19.1	–10.6
Sub-Saharan Africa				
Cote d'Ivoire	–17.5	–32.2	–34.5	–39.6
Ghana	–32.9	–37.7	–32.9	n.a.
Zambia	–5.1	–29.6	–51.0	–20.7

Note: Negative (positive) values mean taxation (protection) on agriculture. Taxation rate is calculated on agricultural products, either export goods or import-competing goods for each country. The indirect taxation rate is defined as $(P_A/P_{NA} - P_{A'}P_{NA})/(P_{A*}/P_{NA*})$ and the indirect taxation rate as $(P_{A'}/P_{NA} - P_{A*}/P_{NA*})/(P_{A*}/P_{NA*})$, where P_A = domestic producer price of agricultural goods, $P_{A'}$ = border price of agricultural goods evaluated at the official exchange rate, P_{A*} = border price of agricultural goods evaluated at the equilibrium exchange rate, P_{NA} = price of nonagricultural goods including nontradables with the price of tradables evaluated at the official exchange rate. P_{NA*} = price of nonagricultural goods including nontradables with prices of tradables evaluated at the equilibrium exchange rate. For more details, see Schiff and Valdes (1992:31–35).
Source: Schiff and Valdes (1992:23).

Since indirect taxation is caused mainly by exchange rate overvaluation, these propositions imply that there is no significant difference in the degree of real exchange rate misalignment among the four regions. However, this seems to contradict the frequent observation of overvalued real exchange rates in Latin America and the maintenance of near-equilibrium valuation in East Asia, especially during the 1970s. Let us check the movement of some indices of real exchange rates.[7]

Figure 10.1 depicts an index based on the GNP deflator, and Figure 10.2 shows two other indices based on the CPI/GNP deflator and import price/GNP deflator. The real exchange rate index based on the GNP deflator rose equally in Latin America and East Asia during the 1970s, but the other two

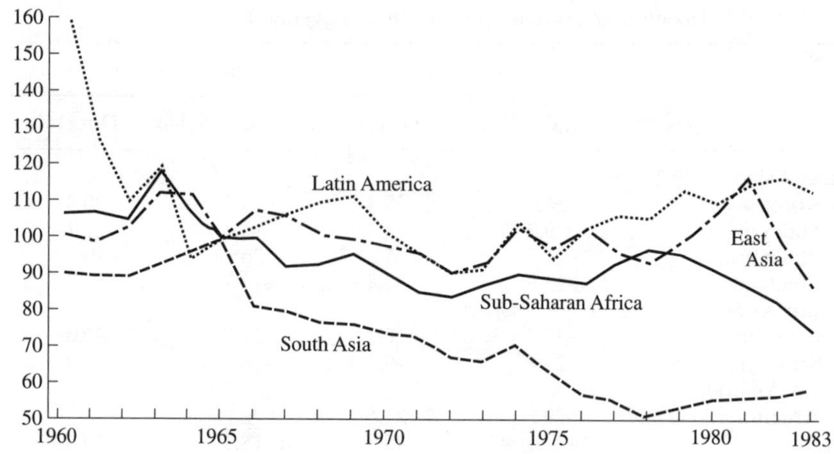

FIG. 10.1 Real Exchange Rate (official rate, 1965 = 100)
East Asia = Philippines, Thailand, Malaysia, Republic of Korea.
South Asia = Bangladesh, Nepal, India, Sri Lanka, Pakistan, Singapore.
Latin America = Bolivia, Honduras, El Salvador, Nicaragua, Dominican Republic, Peru, Ecuador, Jamaica, Guatemala, Costa Rica, Paraguay, Colombia, Chile, Brazil, Panama, Uruguay, Mexico, Argentina.
Sub-Saharan Africa = Zaire, Burkina Faso, Malawi, Niger, Togo, Central African Republic, Kenya, Sudan, Senegal, Mauritania, Liberia, Zambia, Lesotho, Cote d'Ivoire, Zimbabwe, Cameroon.
Note: For each country, the real exchange rate is GNP deflator of the country/(GNP deflator of trading partners × official exchange rate). The real exchange rate of each region is the weighted average (weight calculated by dollar value GNP in 1975) of the sample countries.
The sample for each region is as follows. From all the countries for which data are given, those with incomplete data, with suspect data, noted in Wood (1988:6), and oil-exporting countries in the four regions (Indonesia, Venezuela, Congo) are excluded.
Source: Wood (1988).

indices did not show a rising tendency in either region during the same period. This evidence tends to support the above propositions. It seems that the mistaken view of opposing movements of real exchange rates between regions was derived from the simplistic dichotomy of a shift to export-oriented industrialization in East Asia and maintenance of an import-substitution policy in Latin America during the 1970s. However, it is worth pointing out that while East Asian governments occasionally promoted exports,[8] they generally clung to programs of state-led import substitution through the 1970s and well into the early 1980s. Thailand's fifth national development plan (1981) targeted the development of heavy and chemical industries along its eastern seaboard. Indonesia's third five-year plan (1979) aimed at developing strategic industries such as steel and petrochemicals. In 1981 Malaysia began its fifth five-year plan, and the Philippines embarked

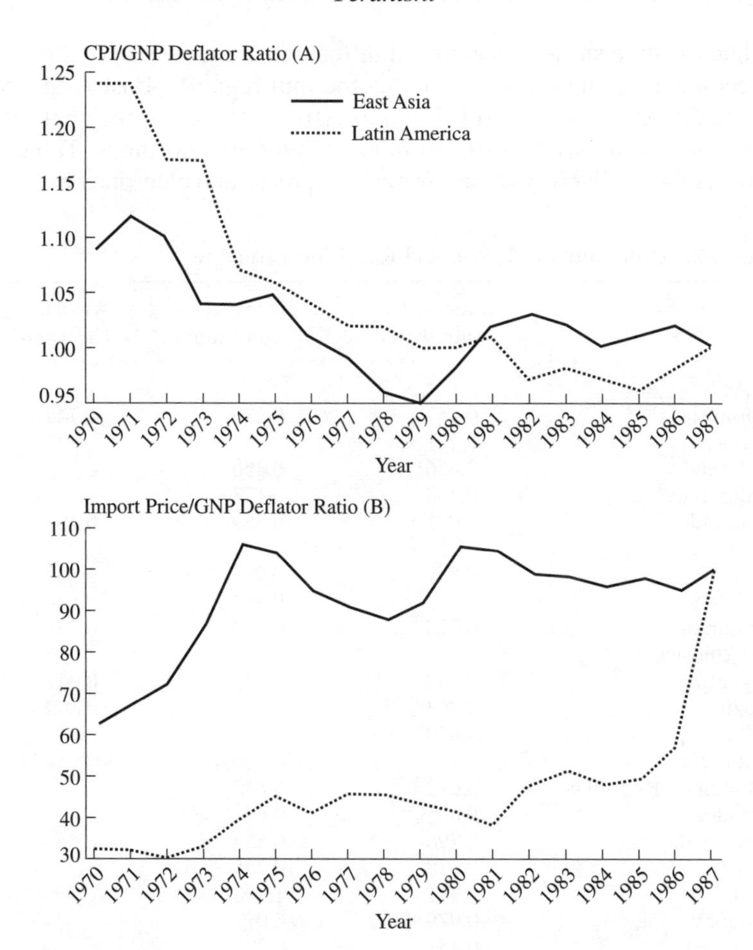

FIG. 10.2 CPI/GNP Deflator Ratio (A) and Import Price/GNP Deflator Ratio (B) (1987 = 100)

Note: Regional data are the weighted average (weighted by the 1980 dollar value GNP) of the sample countries. The sample for each region is the same as Figure 10.1. (Oil-exporting countries, Indonesia and Venezuela, are excluded.)

Source: World Bank (1992), *World Table*.

upon 11 major projects. In the years 1973–79, Korea launched a comprehensive push into heavy and chemical industrialization in an attempt to realize secondary import as well as export substitution. In Taiwan, too, the period 1973–80 is marked by significant government intervention in the promotion of heavy and petrochemical industries. Though these projects were more or less abandoned or faced serious difficulties because of high oil prices and the debt crisis, the lesson remains that many East Asian economies pursued import substitution throughout the 1970s.[9]

While the data show no significant difference in the degree of direct and indirect taxation on agriculture among the four regions—East Asia, South Asia, Latin America, and Sub-Saharan Africa—the cross-regional differences in infrastructure investment in agriculture are enormous. Table 10.2 compares the availability of safe water, sanitation, and electricity among 30

TABLE 10.2 Differential in Urban and Rural Infrastructure

	Access to Safe water	Access to Sanitation	Availability of Electricity
East Asia			
Indonesia	0.457	0.276	0.744
Korea	0.291	—	—
Malaysia	0.456	0.450	0.353
Philippines	0.338	0.173	—
Thailand	0.031	0.359	0.487
South Asia			
India	0.597	0.963	0.400
Pakistan	0.722	0.952	—
Sri Lanka	0.723	0.213	0.771
Latin America			
Argentina	0.738	0.640	0.947
Brazil	0.363	—	0.800
Chile	0.830	—	—
Colombia	—	0.960	—
Dominican Republic	0.612	0.840	—
Ecuador	0.805	0.641	—
Guatemala	0.798	0.556	—
Mexico	0.328	0.765	—
Peru	0.691	1.000	—
Uruguay	0.979	–0.017	—
Venezuela	0.451	0.222	—
Sub-Saharan Africa			
Cameroon	—	—	—
Cote d'Ivoire	—	—	0.785
Ethiopia	—	—	—
Ghana	0.542	0.638	—
Kenya	0.824	0.787	—
Senegal	0.242	0.600	0.855
Sudan	—	1.000	—
Tanzania	—	—	—
Uganda	0.822	0.750	—
Zaire	—	—	—
Zambia	0.508	0.520	—

Note: Latin America and Sub-Saharan countries are those with GNPs in 1991 greater than US $6 billion and $2 billion, respectively. The differential is $(U - R)/U$, where U and R show access or availability in terms of percentage of population.

Source: *World Development Report* (1994:146–47), and World Bank (1993:55).

representative countries over the four regions. The relative difference in the availability of infrastructure between the urban and rural populations is generally large in Latin American and Sub-Saharan African countries but lower in East Asian countries for all three items. It is generally large in South Asia, except for the case of electricity in India, where pumping water by electric motors is the major measure of irrigation.

The data on irrigation ratios in Table 10.3 show a similar pattern of difference in rural infrastructure. The ratios are higher for South and East Asia and lower in Latin America and Sub-Saharan Africa.[10] Note that the ratios kept rising until 1990 in the first two regions, whereas the rise in ratios stopped after 1980 in the latter two regions. It is well known that the rapid development of high-yield crop varieties was possible only with improvements in irrigation. In East Asia, the green revolution resulted in a significant rise in land productivity for rice and maize during the 1970s (Oshima 1987:table 7.2). In Africa, it is said that the green revolution had practically no impact due to the shortage of infrastructure (Clute 1982:14 and Spencer 1994). In Mexico, high-yielding maize was never diffused among small farmers owing to an absence of government support for irrigation and other inputs, while rich wheat farmers were able to adopt new varieties without government support (Griffin 1973). The data on road density also seem to reflect the degree of discrimination against agriculture, since rural road construction is an essential prerequisite for an increase in the production of cash crops, expanded use of agricultural credits, and development of the rural market economy.

Table 10.3 shows that differences in the availability of transportation are also considerable among the regions: the densities in East and South Asia are far higher than in the other two regions. Asia's high road density seems to reflects its high population density. The regression of road density (y) on population density (x) yields:

$$y = 0.03 + 0.62x, \qquad R_2 = 0.702,$$
$$(0.09) \quad (7.81)$$

and the weighted averages of the difference between the actual and predicted value are –0.308 for East Asia, –0.308 for South Asia, 0.536 for Latin America, and 0.036 for Africa.[11] Since India and Sri Lanka have extremely high road and population densities, a revised regression was done excluding the three South Asian countries. The result is:

$$y = 0.08 + 0.40x, \qquad R_2 = 0.819,$$
$$(0.56) \quad (10.3)$$

and the weighted averages of the difference between the actual and predicted values are 0.028 for East Asia, 0.036 for Latin America, and –0.084

TABLE 10.3 Irrigation Ratio and Road Density

	Irrigation Ratio			Road Density		
	1970	1980	1990	1970	1980	1990
East Asia	(0.177)	(0.214)	(0.256)	(0.214)	(0.472)	(0.789)
Indonesia	0.242	0.277	0.345	0.116	0.312	0.643
Korea	0.433	0.595	0.642	0.368	1.579	3.469
Malaysia	0.062	0.067	0.070	0.467	0.623	0.844
Philippines	0.087	0.156	0.196	0.520	0.927	0.746
Thailand	0.143	0.165	0.194	0.189	0.462	0.781
South Asia	(0.234)	(0.282)	(0.313)	(0.940)	(1.785)	(2.279)
India	0.183	0.229	0.255	1.092	2.099	2.555
Pakistan	0.669	0.723	0.795	0.318	0.493	1.126
Sri Lanka	0.220	0.280	0.274	1.423	2.739	3.335
Latin America	(0.068)	(0.096)	(0.101)	(0.099)	(0.156)	(0.217)
Argentina	0.038	0.058	0.062	0.122	0.191	0.209
Brazil	0.015	0.033	0.045	0.060	0.103	0.191
Chile	0.241	0.296	0.279	0.099	0.131	0.147
Colombia	0.049	0.077	0.096	0.058	0.115	0.099
Ecuador	0.183	0.211	0.203	0.105	0.155	0.228
Guatemala	0.037	0.039	0.041	0.215	0.263	0.321
Mexico	0.156	0.203	0.210	0.222	0.351	0.430
Peru	0.393	0.330	0.338	0.038	0.049	0.059
Uruguay	0.027	0.055	0.084	0.346	0.560	0.914
Venezuela	0.080	0.064	0.068	0.204	0.259	0.298
Sub-Saharan Africa	(0.024)	(0.036)	(0.038)	(0.031)	(0.070)	(0.079)
Cameroon	0.001	0.002	0.004	0.020	0.054	0.077
Cote d'Ivoire	0.004	0.012	0.012	0.018	0.103	0.120
Ethiopia	0.006	0.003	0.003	0.201	0.350	0.359
Ghana	0.007	0.014	0.017	0.040	0.096	0.133
Kenya	0.014	0.018	0.022	0.045	0.098	0.121
Senegal	0.024	0.072	0.077	0.109	0.179	0.208
Sudan	0.107	0.143	0.147	0.001	0.013	0.014
Tanzania	0.010	0.036	0.045	0.037	0.038	0.040
Uganda	0.001	0.001	0.001	0.111	0.194	0.121
Zaire	0.001	0.001	0.001	—	—	—
Zambia	0.001	0.004	0.006	0.039	0.075	0.083

Note: The irrigation ratio is irrigation (thousand ha)/arable land and land under permanent crops (thousand ha), and road density is paved road (km)/land area (thousand ha). Figures in parentheses are weighted averages; weights are calculated by the sum of GNP in US dollars for 1970, 1980, and 1990 for each country in the region. The Dominican Republic is not included in the table because of data imperfections.

Source: FAO, *Production Yearbook*, vol. 34 (1980) and vol. 45 (1991). Data on paved roads are from *World Development Report* (1994:140–41). Paved roads in Sri Lanka for 1970 and 1990, paved roads in Uruguay for 1990, and irrigation in Zaire for 1970 are my own estimates.

for Africa. The revised result implies the road density of East Asia is high even if its high population density is taken into consideration.

In sum, it could be argued that there is a considerable difference in regional levels of infrastructural investment in agriculture: highest in East Asia and lowest in Sub-Saharan Africa and Latin America. Since regional differences in direct and indirect taxation are not significant, this amounts to saying that there is a significant difference in the total level of policy-based resource transfer among the regions. In East Asia, the adverse effects of indirect taxation (real exchange rate overvaluation and industrial protection) and direct taxation of agriculture were counterbalanced by government efforts in agricultural development, particularly in the area of infrastructure investment, resulting in a relatively low level of total policy-based resource shift from agriculture. Though agriculture was taxed directly and indirectly in Thailand, marketing roads were built extensively during the 1970s and irrigation of the Chaopraya river area was implemented with the financial aid of the World Bank. In Indonesia, the Suharto government continued the rice production promotion policy initiated in 1964 and finally attained rice self-sufficiency in 1984. At the same time, the government devoted considerable resources to the development of the outer islands by subsidizing the production of cash crops. The Philippines' Masagana 99 program aimed at rice self-sufficiency, and was initiated in the mid-1970s with significant resources devoted to irrigation, extension services, and input subsidization.

10.2 DETERMINANTS OF POLICY-BASED RESOURCE SHIFTS

What determines the level of policy-based resource shift from agriculture? Why was the high growth of the East Asian countries possible without resorting to a significant policy-based resource shift from agriculture? The answer lies in the availability of savings within the industrial sector, in the effect of market-based resource flows, and in the structural characteristics of the agricultural sector. In this section, I first examine the availability of non-agricultural savings, and then move on to the related problem of market-based resource shifts from agriculture, referring to the interaction between policy-based and market-based resource shifts. Finally, the structural characteristics of agriculture are discussed as important determinants of resource flows.

Savings within the Industrial Sector

Needless to say, agricultural savings are not the only source for financing industrialization. Savings emanating from within the industrial sector can become increasingly important as industrialization proceeds.

Under the Kaldorian assumption about the saving rate (the propensity to save from profits is higher than that from wages), the level of saving within the industrial sector depends on the rate of profits, and hence on the real wage rate in particular. In this regard, let us note that labor markets in developing countries are seriously distorted (Krueger 1983 and Squire 1981), and that significant regional differences exist among them (Fields 1984, 1985). Generally speaking, labor markets in Latin America and Africa were more distorted through institutional wage-setting (minimum wage legislation) and by labor market activism, as well as by the influence of public sector employment. In East Asia, the labor market is more flexible owing to weaker enforcement of legislated wage levels (Squire 1981:112), the smaller role played by public sector employment, and, in some countries such as Korea and Singapore, political repression of labor unions.

Regional differences in labor markets can be exemplified by wage rate differentials between the manufacturing and agricultural sectors. According to Fields (1985), the relative wage between manufacturing and agriculture (manufacturing wage/agricultural wage) was 0.92 in Hong Kong (1980), 1.00 in Singapore (1979), and 1.51 in Taiwan (1979). Squire (1981) gives data on the relative wages of low-skilled labor in 23 countries (based on the unpublished work of Peter Gregory). In Latin America he shows figures of 2.08 in Guatemala (1968), 1.84 in Chile (1966), 1.77 in Mexico (1972), 1.58 in Uruguay (1972), 1.50 in Argentina (1972), 1.70 in Panama (1970), 1.14 in Trinidad and Tobago (1968), 1.13 in Venezuela, and 1.11 in Costa Rica (1972). In Sub-Saharan Africa, we see 1.78 in the Ivory Coast (now Cote d'Ivoire) (1965), 1.73 in Cameroon (1972), 1.24 in Malawi (1965), 0.99 in Zambia (1972), and 0.66 in Ghana (1965). For South Asia, we have 1.79 in Pakistan (1972), 1.35 in Sri Lanka (1966), and 1.12 in India (1972). UNDP/World Bank (1992) gives more recent data on relative wages, defined as the ratio of the minimum wage to per-capita value-added in agriculture: 1.2 in Cameroon, 1.8 in Cote d'Ivoire, 1.6 in Ethiopia, 0.2 in Ghana, 1.8 in Kenya, 4.4 in Senegal, 1.2 in Sudan, 2.2 in Tanzania, and 3.1 in Zambia, all referring to the year 1980.

These figures seem to indicate that manufacturing wage rates in East Asia were more or less market determined and close to the level of the supply price of labor from agriculture, while in other regions wage rates were kept at a high, institutionally determined level. It could be argued that there was a tendency for the rate of profit and hence the level of saving within the industrial sector in East Asia to become higher than those in other regions as far as labor market conditions were concerned. In sum, a Lewisian type of accumulation occurred in East Asia but not elsewhere. This might be one of the reasons for the low degree of dependence on agricultural savings in East Asia.

Market-Based Resource Transfers

Given the availability of sources of industrial financing other than agricultural savings, the magnitude of policy-based resource transfer stands in close relationship with the level of market-based resource transfer from agriculture, which depends on the degree of financial development. A readily available index of financial development is the ratio of M2 (money plus quasi-money) to GNP shown in Table 10.4. It is apparent that this index is high for East Asian countries compared with Latin American and African countries. The high M2/GNP in East Asia reflects either the development of modern financial institutions replacing an informal credit system and/or relatively low levels of inflation (the absence of financial repression (McKinnon 1986 and 1988)). Along with financial development, the level of market-based resource transfer hinges crucially on the origins and behavior of business groups in the region.[12] In Latin America, large business groups originated mainly from businesses established by European immigrants, often with special technological knowledge, or from multinational enterprises. Landed elites with a huge wealth base in agriculture were simply not interested in manufacturing in Argentina, and many of the businesses initiated by coffee planters did not succeed in Brazil.[13] On the other hand, it is well known that many of the business groups of East Asia have their origins in opium or sugar: sugar planters, beginning with sugar refining, gradually diversified into transportation and storage, rice milling, lumber, then into banking and other financial business, and finally into modern manufacturing. In this way, much of the resource shift from agriculture to industry was accomplished by large landlord or merchant investment.[14]

Note the two-dimensional relationship between market-based and policy-based resource transfer. On the one hand, whenever business groups invest in industry on their own initiative, the necessity of a policy-based resource shift is reduced. On the other hand, policy-based resource shifts often influence the flow of market-based resources. For example, rural infrastructure investment by government raises the rates of return on private investment and thus promotes the development of rural industry. But higher taxation on agriculture reduces farmer purchasing power and discourages the development of rural industry. In the previous section, we saw that although there is no significant regional difference in direct and indirect taxation on agriculture, infrastructure investment in agriculture was by far the highest in East Asia, so that total policy-based transfer seems to be smaller in East Asia than in other regions. It is plausible that the low level of policy-based resource flows was at least partly offset by the inflow of private capital induced by infrastructure investment. The next section will provide some empirical evidence on this point.

TABLE 10.4 Ratio of M2 to GNP

	1970	1980	1990
East Asia	(0.248)	(0.310)	(0.492)
Indonesia	0.100	0.177	0.488
Korea	0.328	0.341	0.401
Malaysia	0.349	0.534	0.699
Philippines	0.299	0.291	0.341
Thailand	0.283	0.386	0.753
South Asia	(0.256)	(0.372)	(0.449)
India	0.233	0.372	0.463
Pakistan	0.435	0.385	0.374
Sri Lanka	0.245	0.322	0.290
Latin America	(0.222)	(0.262)	(0.293)
Argentina	0.272	0.294	0.265
Brazil	0.211	0.123	0.207
Chile	0.165	0.268	0.465
Colombia	0.198	0.204	0.189
Dominican Rep.	0.199	0.183	0.230
Ecuador	—	—	—
Guatemala	0.185	0.217	0.218
Mexico	—	0.312	0.287
Peru	0.242	0.264	—
Uruguay	0.218	0.399	0.650
Venezuela	0.236	0.361	0.332
Sub-Saharan Africa	(0.226)	(0.230)	(0.264)
Cameroon	0.167	0.246	—
Cote d'Ivoire	0.265	0.339	—
Ethiopia	0.136	0.258	0.576
Ghana	0.193	0.186	0.136
Kenya	0.311	0.317	0.301
Senegal	0.112	0.283	0.269
Sudan	0.171	0.255	0.342
Tanzania	0.243	0.417	0.277
Uganda	0.177	0.137	0.123
Zaire	0.264	0.082	0.146
Zambia	0.300	0.283	0.448

Note: 1990 values are 1989 for Argentina; 1988 for Colombia, Zambia, and Tanzania; 1987 for Brazil, Mexico, and Sudan; and 1986 for Senegal and Uganda. GDP, instead of GNP, is used for Senegal, Sudan, and Uganda.

Source: IMF (1992).

Structural Characteristics of an Agrarian Economy

Given the availability of savings within the industrial sector and given the degree of market-based resource shifts, the levels and patterns of policy-based resource shifts are most affected by the power balance between the urban and rural sectors, and by the internal structure of agriculture.

It is well known that the agricultural sectors of Asia and Africa are mostly composed of small farmers, while agriculture in Latin America is dominated by large farmers. Average arable land per farm is 2.3 hectares in Asia, 0.5 in Africa, and 46.5 in Latin America (Otsuka, Chuma, and Hayami 1992). In Brazil, large farmers (*latifundios* and medium-sized farms) account for 94 and 79 per cent of farmland and production value, respectively. In Argentina, Chile, Colombia, and Guatemala, the corresponding figures were 51 and 41, 92 and 60, 70 and 34, and 73 and 57 per cent, respectively. The remainder is shared by peasants on family farms or *minifundios* (Furtado 1970). In East Asia after World War II, large farmers were eliminated by land reform (Korea and Taiwan), substituted by state ownership (Indonesia), or suppressed by anti-Chinese policy (Malaysia). In Sub-Saharan Africa, large farmers share a rather important position in some countries (those in the White Highlands in Kenya, and rice farmers in Ghana), but these are exceptional.

In Latin America, where large farmers dominate the rural economy, it is reasonable to consider that the magnitude of the total resource flow from agriculture is determined by the power balance between large farmers and the urban sector. Strong antagonism against a landed oligarchy and the weakening of export agriculture after the Great Depression were the basic causes for the significant outflow of resources from agriculture.

What kind of political forces are at work in East Asia and Sub-Saharan Africa, where agriculture is dominated by small farmers? Jeffrey Sachs once argued that the sheer number of farmers in East Asia explains what he considers the pro-agriculture bias in trade policy in the region (Sachs 1985 and 1989:19).[15] But this logic fails to explain the African experience, where small farmers tend to free-ride on the political movements against policies detrimental to their interest. According to Bates (1983:95 and 1981:88), this is because the collective action problem is intensified as the number of farmers rises, since the cost of lobbying rises with communication costs, while the per-farmer benefits of lobbying usually fall. Why then was free-riding prevalent among small farmers in Africa but not in East Asia? The difference between the two regions lies in the nature of land ownership. In Africa, ownership of agricultural land belongs to tribes, so that many small farmers do not own their land. Small farmers are simply given rights to cultivate land while they are in the village. Moreover, the method of cultivation is shifting cultivation, so that there is no incentive for farmers to invest in land improvement (Todaro 1985:301–2). The situation is different for East Asian small farmers, who own land themselves.[16] Any policy that lowers the rate of return on agriculture lowers not only the current income of farmers but also the present value of their assets (land). In the case of Africa, the effect of policy detrimental to agriculture affects only current income of farmers, and it could be avoided simply by migrating to urban areas. Therefore, the incentive for small farmers to resist policies detrimental to agriculture is larger in East Asia than in Africa. This seems to be the fundamental determinant of the difference in the political power of small farmers in Sub-Saharan Africa and East Asia.

Summary of Determinants

In East Asia, the adverse effects of direct and indirect taxation were largely offset by active infrastructure investment. Governments were compelled to increase public investment in agriculture in response to strong concerns over the present value of land held by small farmers. The concomitant low level of policy-based resource shifts from agriculture was offset partly by foreign borrowing and internal accumulation in the industrial sector, and partly by the market-based resource shifts of agro-based business groups and by modern financial institutions. Thus, many East Asian governments during the 1950s and 1960s relied heavily on agricultural support. For example, the Sukarno government in Indonesia (1949–65) was supported by communists, whose main political base was in rural areas. Prior to embarking on an ambitious industrialization plan in the Philippines (1971–74), Ferdinand Marcos adopted the slogan "rice and roads" in an effort to promote the green revolution and road construction, and thereby build a village-level political base.

In both Sub-Saharan Africa and Latin America, strong motivation for industrialization and the political power of the urban sector compelled the government to adopt a policy of shifting resources from agriculture during the early postwar period, relying on direct and indirect taxation of the sector and paying little attention to agricultural infrastructure. This policy was needed also because of a relative shortage of internal accumulation of savings in the industrial sector due to an institutionally high wage rate, and partly because of the absence of market-based resource flows from agriculture. Thus in Latin America during the 1950s and 1960s, development strategy relied heavily on the mobilization of economic surplus in the primary sector. Most of the newly independent Sub-Saharan African countries of the 1950s attempted to industrialize by shifting resources out of agriculture.[17]

Incidentally, it should be noted that I have not taken up the effect of the inflow of foreign savings as a long-term determinant of total resource flow from agriculture. The reason for this lies in the fact that foreign debt should be redeemed by future saving, so that net inflow is zero in the long run. This applies also to foreign direct investment, where the present value of repatriation of profits should be equal to the equilibrium value of investment.[18] Needless to say, this does not deny the role of foreign debt in enabling intertemporal adjustment of expenditures or the role of foreign direct investment as an important tool of technology transfer and managerial skill.

10.3 SECTORAL CONFLICT AND MACROECONOMIC STABILITY IN THE 1970S

During the 1970s, most developing countries fell into macroeconomic difficulties such as fiscal deficits, current account imbalances, and external debt crises. The degree of difficulty varied by region, however: Latin America and Sub-Saharan Africa were hit hardest, and East Asia the least. For example, the number of external debt reschedulings during the years 1981–90 was only 4 in East Asia but 83 in Latin America, and 120 in Sub-Saharan Africa.[19] Needless to say, this point is closely related to the more general topic of the "superiority" of the East Asian model of development or of the East Asian "miracle" (World Bank 1993a), though that will not be discussed here. Instead, this section tries to attribute regional differences to the degree and pattern of policy-based resource transfers before and during the 1970s. First, it is argued that the different degrees of total policy-based resource shifts, especially in infrastructure investment, resulted in different agricultural growth patterns, and consequently variation in rural employment and in the speed of migration to urban areas. Second, this section notes a close relationship between increases in government consumption expenditure and relative growth rates in agriculture and other sectors. It also suggests that government expenditures on the political support or appeasement of disadvantaged sectors, urban in the case of Latin America and rural in the case of Sub-Saharan Africa, were an important cause of expanded government consumption, and hence of the aggravation of fiscal deficits in regions other than East Asia. Finally, it is shown that the increase in government consumption and, during the late 1970s, in total consumption is closely related to rising external debt.

Divisible Benefits

Three measures of policy-based resource shifts were categorized above—net direct taxation, net indirect taxation, and agricultural infrastructure. Let us note the differing political values of the three measures acording to the conception of governments advanced by Bates (1983). Bates emphasized the preference of governments to retain political power. Unlike those that use policy to maximize social welfare or respond to social demands, governments of the type Bates emphasizes use divisible benefits to buy the support of particular interest groups. By doing so, policies against the interest of the rural sector can be adopted even if the total number of farmers is large. While most farmers suffer under these policies, some groups of farmers will enjoy net benefits, since their losses are more than compensated by the provision of divisible benefits. At the same time, increased spending on political activities offers wide opportunities for rent seeking. Among the three measures of intersectoral resource flow, policies related to net direct taxation of agriculture are typical examples of divisible benefits. Directed credit can be allocated to buy political support, and subsidies of agricultural inputs can be used to bribe particular groups of producers. Export taxes, export rationing, and protection against competitive imports are also used to target particular groups. Pricing policy as implemented by government marketing boards can also serve as a divisible benefit for the producers of particular products and discriminate against the producers of others.

In this regard, the argument presented here differs from Bates' approach. Bates emphasizes the indivisibility of pricing policy and contrasts pricing policy with other divisible policy measures. This assumption is generally relevant to monocultural agriculture, but does not apply to agriculture where several kinds of products (sugar, rice, coconuts, cotton, rubber, etc.)[20] are the targets of pricing policy individually, thereby making benefits in principle divisible. By contrast, there is no doubt about the indivisibility of the other two measures of resource flow, indirect taxation and infrastructure investment. These cannot be allocated to particular political groups, although it is true that the costs and benefits of both are more or less proportional to the scale of production (value of exports or land area).

Incidentally, it must be also noted that the greater the sectoral resource shift caused by indivisible measures, the larger the divisible benefits needed to buy political support of particular groups within the sector from which resources are shifted. This is because particular groups will not support the government, whose indivisible policy measures reduce their income, unless the negative income effects are more than offset by positive divisible benefits. It follows that the tendency for governments to try to retain political power through the provision of divisible benefits will be strengthened whenever there are large lopsided shifts in the resource balance due to indivisible policy measures.

From Populism to Authoritarianism

The power balance between sectors changed significantly around 1965–70, especially in Latin America. Before this time the government and urban industrial sectors led development in Latin America and Sub-Saharan Africa. In Latin America, populist governments were established in many countries with the support of heterogeneous coalitions of urban middle-class workers and industrialists. Landed elites were seriously damaged in the Great Depression, and industrialists strengthened their power through the process of spontaneous import substitution during World War II.[21] In Africa as well as South Asia, governments took a strong stance in modernizing and industrializing through import substitution. Many African countries that adopted socialism introduced a Soviet-type dynamic optimizing policy of sacrificing consumption goods during the initial stage of development. Capitalist economies in Sub-Saharan Africa emulated India's pattern of development (the Mahalanobis model) or Nigeria's model, which were themselves products of the Soviet model. In this situation, government elites, motivated by nationalism, exerted strong influence on the economy. Emphasis on the role of the top political leader in the executive branch seems to apply quite well (Haggard 1990). Alternatively, one could argue that the early import substitution policy was made by well-intentioned individuals behaving as benevolent social guardians (Krueger 1993a and 1993b).

However, after around 1965–70, socialist and populist governments were largely replaced by authoritarian or military regimes. This was due to:

1. the failure of import substitution, especially secondary import substitution, for the technical reasons of inefficiency (sub-optimal scale and the absence of internal and external competition);
2. the political failure of populist governments to institutionalize rural poor and urban migrants (Drake 1982); and
3. the failure of populist macroeconomic policy, which invariably produced inflation and both current account and government budget deficits (Sachs 1989).

Military governments took power in Argentina (July 1966–May 1973 and March 1976–December 1983), Bolivia (November 1964–October 1982), Brazil (April 1964–March 1985), Chile (September 1979–March 1990), Ecuador (February 1972–August 1979), Honduras (December 1972–January 1982), Panama (October 1968–August 1975), Peru (October 1968–July 1980), and Uruguay (June 1975–March 1985).[22] Most of these military governments were supported by large farmers, local industrialists, and multinational corporations.[23] A similar shift to authoritarianism occurred in other regions also. In Africa, many socialist countries intensified their political control, and in other countries military rule and authoritarian governments were established during the 1970s. Authoritarian governments were by no means rare in East Asia either. In the Philippines, President Marcos introduced martial law in 1972. The Suharto government in Indonesia after 1965 was based on a coalition of the military and the bureaucracy. Thailand's military regime took a strong authoritarian stance after the coup of October 1976. The authoritarian Park government was established in Korea in 1963.

It is worth emphasizing that regime change in the political realm did not result in a substantial change in economic policy. This is especially true for trade policy. Import substitution continued to be the main direction of trade policy until the early 1980s, and overvalued real exchange rates remained the norm. Yet this entailed an important impact on government expenditure through the political process. Let us consider this point in detail.

In Latin America, the authoritarian regimes established after the mid-1960s adopted economic policies aimed for efficiency under bureaucratic control. In some countries, such as Chile, state enterprises were privatized, and in others, such as Brazil, the number of state enterprises increased significantly. Without exception, these governments encouraged foreign direct investment and pursued market-oriented economic policy by deregulating financial and other markets. With respect to trade policy, however, these governments continued to take an inward-oriented stance. As can be seen in Figures 10.1 and 10.2, the degree of exchange rate overvaluation increased even further during the 1970s,[24] and no significant progress in trade liberalization occurred in Latin American countries. For example, according to the World Bank's evaluation of the trade policy orientation of 14 Latin American countries in the years 1963–73, no country was considered strongly outward oriented, 4 countries were evaluated as moderately outward oriented, 5 countries as moderately inward oriented, and 5 as strongly inward oriented; the corresponding numbers for the period 1973–85 were zero, 3, 7, and 4, respectively.[25]

The continuation of inward-oriented trade policy meant that the net indirect taxation of agriculture stayed more or less the same after the collapse of the populist regimes. Table 10.1, summarizing a World Bank study, shows that the degree of indirect taxation actually increased from the period 1960–72 to the period 1976–84 in three of five Latin American countries. One reason for this is that the authoritarian governments did not abolish import substitution but tried to convert import-substituting industries into export industries instead.[26]

A further reason is that while the authoritarian regimes more or less repressed the urban poor, the political power of the urban sector had grown, partly due to continued urbanization during the 1970s (Table 10.5), to the extent that governments were obliged to overvalue the exchange rate in order to maintain the overall urban standard of living. The overall level of direct taxation did not change during the two periods, either.

Agricultural taxation is costly to large as well as small farmers. Why then did large farmers support the authoritarian regimes? The answer lies in the antipeasant biases in agricultural policy and in the provision of divisible benefits to large farmers. Grindle (1986:56–61) presents a comprehensive list of the unequal effects of agricultural development policy. Credit policy is biased toward large landlords in many Latin American countries. Research and extension efforts are concentrated on irrigation, exemption from import duties on tractors, harvesters, and trucks, and subsidized fuel prices, all benefiting large mechanized landlords with irrigated land.[27] Supporting evidence for Brazil is abundant. Direct credits to agriculture in Brazil were strongly biased toward large farmers. Agricultural credits are supplied by the Banco do Brasil only to farmers at least as large as a minimum profitable agriculturalist, and the smallest loan was 50 times the annual earnings of an industrial worker (Griffin 1973:10).

TABLE 10.5 Urban Populations as Percentage of Total Population

	1960	1970	1980	1991
East Asia	(21.7)	(26.4)	(31.9)	(44.2)
Indonesia	15	17	20	31
Korea	28	41	55	73
Malaysia	25	27	29	44
Philippines	30	33	36	43
Thailand	13	13	14	23
South Asia	(18.5)	(20.6)	(22.8)	(27.6)
India	18	20	22	27
Pakistan	22	25	28	33
Sri Lanka	18	22	27	22
Latin America	(53.2)	(61.2)	(69.5)	(76.5)
Argentina	74	78	82	87
Brazil	46	56	65	76
Chile	68	75	80	86
Colombia	48	57	70	71
Dominican Republic	30	40	51	61
Ecuador	34	40	45	57
Guatemala	33	36	39	40
Mexico	51	59	67	73
Peru	46	57	67	71
Uruguay	80	82	84	86
Venezuela	67	72	83	85
Sub-Saharan Africa	(13.3)	(17.5)	(26.6)	(29.2)
Cameroon	14	20	35	42
Cote d'Ivoire	19	27	38	41
Ethiopia	6	9	15	13
Ghana	23	29	36	33
Kenya	7	10	14	24
Senegal	23	33	25	39
Sudan	10	16	25	22
Tanzania	5	7	12	34
Uganda	5	8	12	11
Zaire	16		34	
Zambia	23	60	38	51

Note: Figures in parentheses are weighted averages; weights are calculated by the sum of GNP for 1970, 1975, and 1980 for each country in the region. Latin American and Sub-Saharan countries are those with GNPs in 1991 greater than US $6 billion and $2 billion, respectively.
Source: World Bank (1981, 1993), *World Development Report*.

Tax policy is also biased toward large farmers. Corporations and the rich benefited from lower tax rates through special provisions in the income tax code and the depreciation provision for fixed investments (*World Development Report* 1990:59). Goodman (1989) presents a succinct summary on the selectiveness and magnitude of institutional credits: only 14–25 per cent of producers benefited from the rural credit system; the estimated subsidies amounted to 3–4 per cent of GDP in 1978; and to Cr. $0.16 for each cruzeiro of credit. Consequently, "feudal" *latifundios* were transformed into large modern enterprises after the mid-1960s, and their main products were changed from the traditional, labor-intensive coffee and sugar cane to wheat and soybeans, which benefit more from mechanization and the use of fertilizer and pesticides.[28]

A similar phenomenon occurred in Sub-Saharan Africa. During the 1970s, when many African countries intensified their authoritarian traits, some military governments, such as Ghana, tried to reverse the antiagriculture bias in their development policies with the support of large mechanized farmers, but they usually failed. Strong demand by urban dwellers and manufacturers for high urban living standards, together with the need to finance the recurring costs of import substitution industries, invariably resulted in a severely overvalued exchange rate. The need to finance recurrent budget deficits in turn kept pricing policy biased against farmers. Similar situations were common in many African countries. As Table 10.1 shows, indirect taxation intensified from the 1960s to the 1970s in all three African countries under study. According to Bates (1983), this did not result in rural opposition, since exchange rate policy is not a divisible cost from the farmers' viewpoint. Rather, agricultural input programs were politicized in a government attempt to buy political loyalty. Thus, divisible benefits in the form of subsidized credits were extended to large farmers in northern Ghana. Leaders of a Senegalese religious sect that earned much of its income from the production of groundnuts, and, not coincidentally, was also a rural base of government support, were major recipients of subsidized credits, land, and other farm inputs. Access to subsidized inputs could best be obtained by most Zambian farmers through membership in agricultural cooperative societies, which were formed and dominated by local units of the government party (Bates 1983:127).

In East Asia, the political process differed substantially from those of the two regions above. Authoritarian governments in the 1970s were established with the support of the military and bureaucracy, but at the same time East Asian governments actively sought rural support. The real exchange rate was overvalued during the 1970s since East Asian governments were also intent on import substitution, at least until toward the late 1970s. However, the government invested significantly in the rural sector, especially in roads and irrigation systems. Agricultural employment, and in particular rural nonfarm working opportunities during the dry season, increased significantly. This kept the expansion of the urban sector to a minimum. After the early 1980s, when expansion of agricultural employment reached its saturation point and outmigration became significant, the government began to emphasize export promotion policy to expand urban employment opportunities.

Rural Economy and Urbanization

The pattern and degree of policy-based resource shifts have significant impact on the development of the rural economy and society. In both Latin America and Sub-Saharan Africa, the overall negative effects of direct taxation and indirect taxation were not offset by infrastructure investment, but only induced an expansion of government expenditures for the purpose of obtaining political support by means of provision of divisible benefits. In Latin America, this had two results. First, large farmers, the chief recipients of divisible benefits, modernized their production system rapidly through mechanization and the use of chemical fertilizers. Since the output of large farms (*latifundios* and medium-sized firms) comprises the majority of agricultural production, this implies an increase in agricultural production in the region during the 1970s, as seen in Table 10.6. Second, significant migration from agriculture occurred during the 1970s. The increase in the share of the urban population is shown on Table 10.5. From 1960 to 1980, the percentage of the urban population increased by 16.3 per cent. Migration was caused first by the sale of family farms and *minifundios* to large farmers under a tax and credit system favoring large farming, and second by a decrease in large farmer demand for labor brought about by mechanization.[29]

In Sub-Saharan Africa, while direct and indirect taxation seriously depressed the agrarian economy, the supply of subsidized agricultural inputs as divisible benefits resulted in a further decline in per capita output after the 1970s (see Table 10.6). This was for two reasons. First, since benefits

TABLE 10.6 The Growth Rate of Per Capita Food and Agricultural Output (per cent)

	Growth Rate in Per Capita Food Production				Growth Rate in Per Capita Agricultural Production			
	1948/52–70	1961–70	1970–80	1980–91	1948/52–70	1961–70	1970–80	1980–91
Developing countries and territories	0.6	0.4	0.5	0.5	0.6	0.2	0.4	0.4
Asia	0.8	0.1	1.0	0.9	0.7	0.1	0.8	0.9
Latin America	0.4	1.2	0.9	0.4	0.2	0.3	0.7	0.2
Africa	0.0	0.0	–1.2	–0.1	0.3	0.2	–1.4	–0.2
Developed market economies and countries	1.1	1.2	1.1	0.6	1.0	1.0	1.1	0.6

Source: United Nations Conference on Trade Development (1991), *Handbook of International Trade and Development Statistics*, United Nations, New York, table 6.5; and Griffin (1973).

were supplied exclusively to supporters of the ruling political party who were not necessarily the dominant producers, the incentives faced by the majority of farmers in the form of overvalued exchange rates and discriminatory pricing policies were overwhelmingly negative, and were rarely compensated for by subsidized inputs. Second, the rationing of divisible benefits led to much unproductive rent seeking. Since rationing was done on the basis of favoritism, most farmers had no alternative to repeated visits and long waits to obtain farm inputs, with a consequent waste of scarce resources (Stryker 1991). Moreover, due to the depression of the agrarian economy, the urban population doubled from 13.3 per cent in 1960 to 26.6 per cent in 1990 (Table 10.6).

A completely different situation, however, emerged in East Asia. Although the direct and indirect taxation of agriculture by the government had negative effects on agriculture, these were more than offset by active government investment in agriculture. As is emphasized by Oshima (1987), infrastructural investment brought significant new rural employment opportunities, first by creating new jobs in weeding, fertilizer supply, and water adjustment; second, by making dry season nonagricultural production possible; and third, by enabling the establishment of factories to process agricultural products. In other words, full employment occurred in rural East Asia before significant rural emigration started. Moreover, landless labor in a literal sense did not exist in East Asia until recently, save for eldest sons who worked temporarily on their parents' farms until they inherited the land from their parents. Table 10.7 compares an index of the development of agrocommerce and industries in rural areas among regions. The figures show the ratios of the rural nonagricultural population, defined as (rural population – agricultural population)/rural population.[30] It is clear that the ratio is highest in East Asia and very low in Latin America and Sub-Saharan Africa. It is also worth emphasizing that the ratio showed a significant increase from 1970 to 1980 in East Asia, while the ratio decreased or stayed the same in other regions.[31]

As a result, urbanization of the population was kept at a minimum in East Asia. Table 10.5 shows that the percentage of the urban population increased quite slowly until 1980 except in Korea. Korea's case, however, is not surprising in view of its high degree of industrialization. Taking the percentage of urban population in 1988 as the dependent variable (y), and per capita GNP in US dollars (x_1) and the ratio of GDP in agriculture to total GDP (x_2) as dependent variables, we have as a regression equation:[32]

$$\underset{(4.10)}{y = -54.9} + \underset{(5.32)}{15.4x_1} - \underset{(1.03)}{18.0x_2}; \qquad R_2 = 0.624,$$

and the difference between the actual and predicted value for East Asian countries is as follows: Fiji (–10.96), Indonesia (–8.87), Korea (–0.16),

TABLE 10.7 Ratio of Nonagricultural Population in Rural Areas

	1970	1980	1990
East Asia	(0.178)	(0.292)	(0.300)
Indonesia	0.202	0.335	0.356
Korea	0.136	0.256	0.201
Malaysia	0.253	0.443	0.469
Philippines	0.210	0.195	0.184
Thailand	0.082	0.216	0.215
South Asia	(0.144)	(0.158)	(0.153)
India	0.133	0.151	0.140
Pakistan	0.215	0.197	0.221
Sri Lanka	0.293	0.269	0.346
Latin America	(–0.007)	(0.031)	(0.026)
Argentina	0.257	0.275	0.260
Brazil	–0.037	0.110	0.028
Chile	0.028	0.158	0.083
Colombia	0.120	–0.141	0.080
Ecuador	0.151	0.295	0.307
Guatemala	0.048	0.068	0.160
Mexico	–0.103	–0.107	–0.110
Peru	–0.098	–0.277	–0.222
Uruguay	0.154	0.016	0.028
Venezuela	0.086	0.097	0.346
Sub-Saharan Africa	(0.029)	(0.017)	(0.039)
Cameroon	0.058	–0.075	–0.035
Cote d'Ivoire	0.075	0.061	0.143
Ethiopia	0.170	0.124	0.251
Ghana	–0.158	–0.055	0.072
Kenya	0.087	0.059	–0.013
Senegal	–0.189	–0.075	–0.266
Sudan	0.024	0.051	0.228
Tanzania	0.076	0.041	–0.184
Uganda	0.066	0.024	0.102
Zaire	–0.057	–0.084	–0.096
Zambia	–0.040	–0.181	–0.379

Note: The ratio of nonagricultural population in rural areas is defined as (rural population – agricultural population)/rural population, where rural population is calculated as (1 – urban population ratio) × population. The agricultural population is defined as all persons depending for their livelihoods on agriculture, comprising all persons engaged in agriculture and their nonworking dependents. The Dominican Republic is not included in the table because of data imperfections.

Source: The urban population is from World Bank (1981, 1992), *World Development Report.* Population and agricultural populations are from FAO, *Production Yearbook*, vol. 34 (1980) and vol. 45 (1991).

Malaysia (–17.07), Philippines (1.26), Singapore (14.21), and Thailand (–27.49). Therefore, except for the Philippines and Singapore, the urbanization rate in East Asia, including Korea, is lower than the average tendency of 66 developing countries.[33]

Government Consumption and Sectoral Growth Rates

Figure 10.3 shows the percentage share of government consumption to GDP for various regions since 1970. In both Latin America and South Asia the share rises during the 1970s. Sub-Saharan Africa's share of government consumption is the highest of all regions, and tends to rise after 1980. By remarkable contrast, the share of government consumption in East Asia declines continuously. Government consumption in GDP statistics indicates current expenditure for the purchase of goods and services by all levels of government. It does not include subsidies supplied directly to the private sector, but it does include the purchase of goods and services by state enterprises and local governments financed by central government subsidies.

I have argued that in Latin America and Sub-Saharan Africa, in particular during the 1970s, government expenditures were utilized to finance various political costs. In Latin America, divisible benefits were supplied to large farmers to compensate for indirect taxation on agriculture produced by trade policy, and in Sub-Saharan Africa, divisible benefits were supplied to buy the political support of particular social groups. Changes in the level of government consumption during the 1970s are closely related to such

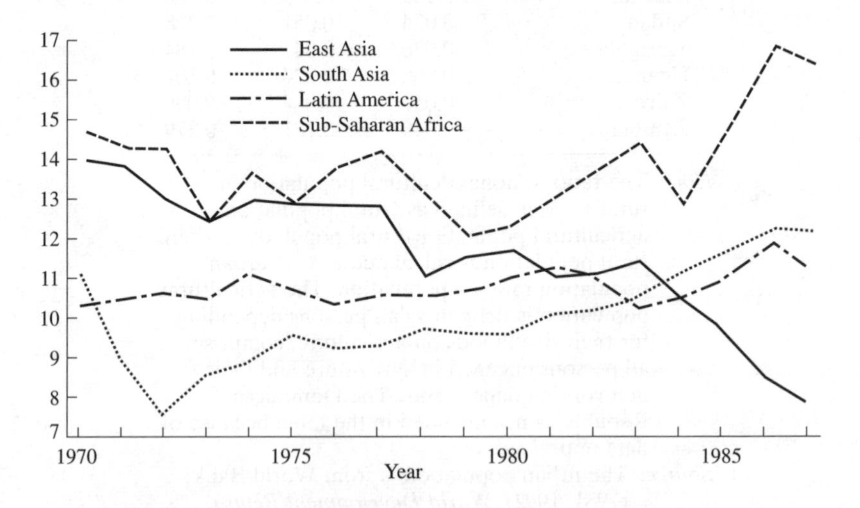

FIG. 10.3 Government Consumption/GDP Ratio
Note: Calculated as government consumption/GDP = 1 – gross domestic savings/GDP – private consumption/GDP.

political expenditures. Part of government consumption was spent directly as divisible benefits and part was spent to appease relatively disadvantaged groups through government policies. Table 10.8 reports the changes in the real expenditures of developing country governments whose real annual expenditures declined more than once during the 1970s. For both total and capital expenditures, the decline was smallest in the categories of social and miscellaneous expenditures, but largest in infrastructure. This suggests that social expenditures and miscellaneous items were the components upon which government expenditure concentrated during the 1970s. The authors of the table conclude that these expenditures are used to finance political costs relating to the prevention of social unrest caused by low living standards. Similarly, Table 10.9 shows the changes in the composition of central government expenditures of non-oil-producing developing countries. While decreases are evident for many of the items from 1972–74 to 1977–79, government spending on housing and amenities, electricity and gas, other economic services, and other expenditures increased. The implications of this table seem to be the same as those of Table 10.8.

Let us assume that changes in government expenditures to finance political costs, either in the form of provision of divisible benefits or as subsidies to disadvantaged sectors, are represented by changes in the composition of government consumption in GDP. Column 1 of Table 10.10 shows the output from a cross-section regression of the changes in the composition of government consumption on the difference between the growth rate of agricultural GDP and the growth rate of total GDP. The growth rate difference has positive effects in Latin America and negative effects in Sub-

TABLE 10.8 Average Rate of Reduction in Real Central Government Expenditures of Developing Countries, 1972–1980

	Total Expenditures	Capital Expenditures
Social	–5.0	–16.7
Defense/Administration	–8.0	—
Production	–11.0	–30.3
Infrastructure	–22.0	–38.1
Miscellaneous	–7.0	–28.8
Total	–13.0	–30.2

Note: Total expenditures are comprised of capital expenditures and recurrent expenditures. Average rate of change in the real central government expenditures (current expenditures divided by GNP deflator or CPI) of the 32 countries (37 cases) where real expenditures were reduced for one or more years.
Source: Hicks and Kubish (1984).

TABLE 10.9 Percentage Composition of Central Government Expenditure (by function, non-oil-producing developing countries)

	1972–74 (A)	1977–80 (B)	(A) – (B)
Defense	14.70	14.42	0.28
Education	11.15	10.88	0.27
Health	5.33	4.31	1.02
Social security and welfare	19.08	15.84	3.24
Housing and community amenities	1.16	1.48	–0.32
Economic services	27.62	25.36	2.26
Agriculture, forest, and fishery	6.63	5.92	0.71
Electricity, gas, steam, and water	2.18	2.57	–0.39
Roads	6.17	4.10	2.07
Other transportation and communication	4.03	3.04	0.99
Other economic services	8.61	9.73	–1.12
Other purposes and general public services	20.96	27.71	–6.75

Source: IMF (1980, 1983), *Government Finance Statistics* (yearbook), Washington, IMF.

Saharan Africa (plus South Asia). The constant dummy variable for Latin America (D_2) has a significant and positive effect on the level of government consumption, but for other regions the constant terms are not significant. These results are by and large in congruence with my arguments above. In Latin America, an autonomous increase in the level of government consumption occurred during the 1970s, and at the same time the share of government consumption rose in countries where the growth of nonagricultural output was relatively low. The latter phenomenon corresponds to the expenditures used to buy the political loyalty of urban dwellers, while the former is a result of the provision of divisible benefits by the authoritarian regime which were more or less built in during the process of political repression. In the case of Sub-Saharan Africa, changes in the share of government consumption are high where the agricultural sector became relatively depressed. This corresponds to the provision of divisible benefits to rural groups and various payments to prevent rural unrest. It also seems reasonable that in East Asia the share of government consumption did not respond to the sectoral growth rate.

External Debt and Consumption

Given that the increases in government consumption during the 1970s in Latin America and Sub-Saharan Africa had the aim of buying political support, the most effective way of financing that expenditure was to borrow from abroad, since this harms no domestic group for the moment. Column 2 of Table 10.10 shows an additional variable representing an increase in external debt. This is highly significant and increases the coefficient of determination.[34] Table 10.11 confirms the close relationship between government consumption and external debt during the 1970s in comparison

TABLE 10.10 Regression Analysis of the Changes in Government Consumption/GNP Ratio

Equation	(1)	(2)
Const.	0.067 (0.020)	–1.098 (0.288)
X_2	—	4.582 (2.338)
D_1	0.472 (0.128)	1.578 (0.445)
D_2	4.021 (2.648)	4.094 (2.825)
D_1X_1	–0.273 (–0.293)	–0.232 (–0.261)
D_2X_1	0.716 (1.738)	0.653 (1.657)
D_3X_1	–1.381 (3.946)	–1.449 (4.325)
R^2	0.297	0.375
Degrees of freedom	45	44

Dependent variable: (average government consumption/GDP ratio during 1980–82) – (average government consumption/GDP ratio during 1970–72).

Independent variables:

X_1 = (average growth rate of GDP in agriculture during 1970–80) – (average growth rate of total GDP during 1970–80).

X_2 = (long-term external debt/GNP ratio in 1981) – (long-term external debt/GNP ratio in 1970).

D_1 = dummy variable with 1 for East Asia.

D_2 = dummy variable with 1 for Latin American countries.

D_3 = dummy variable with 1 for Sub-Saharan Africa and South Asia.

Note: T-values are noted in parentheses. The sample is 51 countries in the four regions (East Asia, South Asia, Latin America, and Sub-Saharan Africa), for which composition of GDP is shown in World Bank (1991), *World Tables*: in East Asia: Indonesia, Korea, Papua New Guinea, the Philippines, and Thailand; in South Asia: India and Pakistan; in Latin America: Argentina, Barbados, Bolivia, Brazil, Chile, Colombia, Costa Rica, the Dominican Republic, Ecuador, El Salvador, Guatemala, Guyana, Haiti, Honduras, Jamaica, Mexico, Nicaragua, Panama, Peru, Trinidad and Tobago, Uruguay, Venezuela; in Sub-Saharan Africa: Benin, Botswana, Burkina Faso, Burundi, Cameroon, the Central African Republic, Congo, Cote d'Ivoire, Ethiopia, Gabon, Gambia, Kenya, Lesotho, Liberia, Madagascar, Malawi, Mali, Mauritania, Rwanda, Senegal, Sierra Leone, Somalia, Sudan, Swaziland, Tanzania, Togo, and Zambia. Data on GDP (in 1987 prices) are from World Bank (1991), *World Tables*.

with other components of GDP. Dependent variables are investment/GDP, saving/GDP, and government consumption/GDP. The independent variable is the change in long-term external debt/GDP during the subperiods.[35] For each subperiod during the years 1971–81, the 56 countries in the sample are divided into two groups depending on the value of the independent variable: countries with an increase in debt higher than the median and those with an increase lower than the median. The following interesting findings emerge.

During the period 1975–78, there is a strong positive relationship between the increase in debt and investment ratios among the group of countries with low rates of increase in external debt; the increase in debt is closely related to government consumption in the group of countries with high rates of increase in external debt, and not only to government con-

TABLE 10.11 Regression Analysis of the Changes in Gross Investment/GDP, Gross Saving/GDP, and Government Consumption/GDP Ratios on the Changes in Debt/GNP Ratio

(A) Dependent Variable: Change in Gross Domestic Investment/GDP Ratio during the Period

	All Countries	Countries with High Increase in Debt[b]	Countries with Low Increase in Debt
1971–75	3.96	7.08	4.17
	(0.59)	(0.47)	(0.40)
	[0.01]	[0.01]	[0.01]
1975–78	3.25	5.24	25.06***
	(0.64)	(0.55)	(3.14)
	[0.01]	[0.01]	[0.27]
1978–81	–7.28	7.81	–17.05*
	(–1.55)	(1.10)	(–1.60)
	[0.04]	[0.04]	[0.09]

(B) Dependent Variable: Change in Gross Domestic Saving/GDP Ratio during the Period[c]

	All Countries	Countries with High Increase in Debt[b]	Countries with Low Increase in Debt
1971–75	1.35	–15.81	22.87
	(0.15)	(–1.01)	(1.13)
	[0.00]	[0.04]	[0.05]
1975–78	–8.75**	–3.97	6.03
	(–1.74)	(–0.43)	(0.67)
	[0.05]	[0.01]	[0.02]
1978–81	–13.58***	6.04	–35.49***
	(–3.42)	(1.32)	(–4.02)
	[0.18]	[0.06]	[0.38]

TABLE 10.11 *Continued*

(C) Dependent Variable: Change in Government Consumption/GNP Ratio during the Period

	All Countries	Countries with High Increase in Debt[b]	Countries with Low Increase in Debt
1971–75	5.10	4.62	6.20
	(1.65)	(0.69)	(1.22)
	[0.05]	[0.02]	[0.05]
1975–78	6.48***	8.38***	0.81
	(4.12)	(3.58)	(0.19)
	[0.24]	[0.38]	[0.00]
1978–81	3.98*	2.92	8.63
	(1.60)	(0.89)	(1.31)
	[0.05]	[0.03]	[0.06]

Independent Variable: Change in Long-term External Debt/GNP Ratio during the Period[a]

Notes: [a] T-values are shown in parentheses and R^2 figures in brackets. Estimates of constants are not shown. The asterisks *, **, and *** show significance at 20, 10, and 1 per cent levels, respectively. The sample comprises the following 56 countries, obtained by excluding 26 countries (15 countries with imperfect data on GDP, 10 countries with imperfect data on debt, and Nigeria which cannot be included in Sub-Saharan Africa) from 82 countries in the four regions (East Asia, South Asia, Latin America, and Sub-Saharan Africa), for which composition of GDP is shown in World Bank (1991), *World Tables*: in East Asia: Indonesia, Korea, Papua New Guinea, the Philippines, and Thailand; in South Asia: India and Pakistan; in Latin America: Argentina, Barbados, Bolivia, Brazil, Chile, Colombia, Costa Rica, the Dominican Republic, Ecuador, El Salvador, Guatemala, Guyana, Haiti, Honduras, Jamaica, Mexico, Nicaragua, Panama, Peru, Trinidad and Tobago, Uruguay, Venezuela; in Sub-Saharan Africa: Benin, Botswana, Burkina Faso, Burundi, Cameroon, the Central African Republic, Congo, Cote d'Ivoire, Ethiopia, Gabon, Gambia, Kenya, Lesotho, Liberia, Madagascar, Malawi, Mali, Mauritania, Rwanda, Senegal, Sierra Leone, Somalia, Sudan, Swaziland, Tanzania, Togo, and Zambia. Data on GDP (in 1987 prices) are from World Bank (1991), *World Tables*.

[b] "Countries with high (low) increase in debt" means countries whose changes in debt/GNP ratio during the period were greater (smaller) than the median. The median changes of debt/GNP were 0.33, 0.066, 0.054, 0.094, and 0.102 for 1971–75, 1975–78, 1978–81, 1971–78, and 1975–81, respectively.

[c] Changes in the composition of GDP are changes in simple annual averages in the compositions as follows: for 1971–75, the change between 1970–72 and 1974–76; for 1975–78, the change between 1974–76 and 1977–79; for 1978–81, the change between 1977–79 and 1980–82; and so on. Changes in the long-term external debt/GNP ratios are changes in the composition from the first year of the period (for 1971, data on 1970 are used) to the end year of the period—for example, for 1975–78, the change between 1975 and 1978. Data on GDP are obtained from World Bank (1991), *World Tables*, and on gross long-term external debt and GNP from World Bank (1985/86), *World Debt Tables*.

sumption but also to total consumption (i.e., a negative relationship between the domestic saving ratio and the increase in debt) in the entire sample. During the years 1978–81, a strong relationship emerges between the total consumption and the increase in debt both for the group of countries with low rates of increase in external debt and for the entire sample.

During the late 1970s, external debt supplied by the international banking system offered a convenient measure to finance not only government but also private consumption. It could be argued that poor people with an extremely high time preference for consumption, probably in the rural sector in Sub-Saharan Africa and in the urban sector in Latin America, exerted a strong influence on the intertemporal choice of national economies (Dornbusch 1984).

10.4 CONCLUDING REMARKS

I have deliberated on the significant effects of policy-based resource shifts from agriculture both on rural socioeconomy and on macroeconomic stability. Those economies on the way to industrialization should pay more attention to balanced growth between agriculture and industry, not only from the viewpoint of the coordination of pecuniary externalities but also from the perspective of sociopolitical and hence macroeconomic stability.[36] It is also important to put due emphasis on the development of markets, especially financial markets, to avoid excessive involvement by government in sectoral resource shifts. However, it is well recognized that it takes time to have a well-developed financial system.

Further, in view of the extremely low taxation capability of developing countries and, in particular, former socialist economies, where the habit of paying taxes simply did not exist, the mobilization of funds for industrialization by measures other than taxation and the financial system is a crucial issue as a second-best policy. Transfer of agricultural surplus is surely one such measure, but the limitations and difficulties related to this measure should be given due consideration. Another representative measure is inflationary finance, but this measure is too risky. It tends to destroy confidence not only in government policy but also in the economic system.[37] A final conceivable measure is implicit taxation on bank depositors by means of regulation of deposit interest rates below the market level. In postwar Japan, a considerable amount of funds is considered to have been shifted from depositors to the industrial sector. It is conceivable that the policy of deposit rate regulation had a favorable side effect of promoting investment in the information-processing capability of banks through an effect on the franchise value of bank charters (see Chapter 6 in this volume by Hellman, Murdock, and Stiglitz). However, it must be noted that the policy entailed not only unfavorable income distribution effects but also serious inefficiencies in the banking industry.[38]

Let me note that emphasis on the balanced growth between agriculture and industry as a principal characteristic of East Asian development is nothing new. In their comparative analysis of newly industrialized countries, Ranis and Orrock pointed out that balanced growth in the rural sector was an essential feature of the East Asian countries' successful economic development (Ranis and Orrock 1985:57). The main message of Oshima (1987) lies in the development of the rural sector as a prerequisite for the industrial development of Asia. More recently, the World Bank (1993a) emphasized the phenomenon of shared growth as an important characteristic of East Asian growth. While the analysis of that study was concerned mainly with intrasectoral equity (sharing income within the corporate sector and equal landholding in agriculture), this analysis, along with Ranis and Orrock (1985) and Oshima (1987), is concerned with the issue of intersectoral equity.

APPENDIX

Sectoral Resource Transfer in Japan

This appendix briefly reviews the main characteristics of the Japanese experience of sectoral resource flows. The whole period may be conveniently divided into three subperiods: before World War I, the interwar period, and after World War II.

Before World War I

The period before World War I was characterized by balanced growth between agriculture and industry, as can be seen by the rather stable share of agriculture in GDP (Table 10A.1). Agriculture retained a high rate of growth mainly because of the diffusion of high-yielding varieties of rice, which were only locally produced before the Meiji Restoration in 1868. During this period, agriculture was taxed quite significantly in order to finance the expenditures of the new government. However, industrialization was mainly financed by the mobilization of accumulated funds of merchants and traditional manufacturers.

The Interwar Period

Agriculture became stagnant during this period partly because of the saturation of the diffusion of high-yielding varieties of rice and partly due to the policy of promoting imports of rice from colonies in order to keep the price of "wage goods" low (see the net import ratio of rice in Table 10A.1). Reflecting the low rate of return to agriculture, landlords tended to shift their funds from agriculture into industry. Table 10A.2 shows that the market-based outflow became quite large after World War I.

Direct taxation on agriculture did not show any significant increase in real terms during the period, partly because the main part of the tax on agriculture was a land tax based on the land price. However, during this period, indirect taxation seems to have become quite large. First, the exchange rate was significantly overvalued until the early 1930s. Second, the policy of importing colonial rice lowered farm income by suppressing the rice price. Income distribution, measured by the Gini coefficient, worsened, and the income disparity between rural and urban households widened (the emergence of the so-called dual structure).

In order to alleviate rising poverty in rural areas, the government expanded infrastructure investment significantly, as is shown in Table 10A.2. Partly as a result of this effect, the urban population ratio did not rise so

TABLE 10A.1 Income Distribution, Urbanization, and Agriculture in Japan

	Urban Population Ratio (%)	Gini Coefficient of Household Income	Net Import Ratio of Rice (%)	Percentage Share of Agriculture in GDP (at Current Price)
1900	11.7[a]	0.417	—	37.7
1905	14.0[b]	—	—	31.5
1910	16.0[c]	0.420	2.2	30.8
1915	16.3[d]	—	4.0	27.8
1920	18.0	0.463	4.6	29.5
1925	21.6	—	17.8	26.9
1930	22.3	0.451	13.5	16.6
1935	30.9	—	23.6	17.3
1940	37.7	0.641	14.8	18.3
1955	56.3	—	—	23.0
1960	63.5	0.376[e]	—	14.9
1965	68.1	0.349[f]	—	11.3
1970	72.1	0.344[g]	—	7.8

Note: [a] 1898; [b] 1903; [c] 1908; [d] 1913; [e] 1962; [f] 1968; [g] 1974.
Source: The urban population ratio is from Japan Statistical Association, *Nihon choki tokei soran* (Tokyo: Sorifu Tokei Kyoku, 1988), vol. 1, p. 155, and the percentage share of agriculture is from vol. 3, pp. 348–49 and 370–71. Gini coefficients are from Mizoguchi and Terasaki (1995) (prewar series in Otsuki, Takamatsu estimates; postwar Mizoguchi, Terasaki estimates). Net import ratio is (import – export)/domestic production. Data obtained from *Long-term Economic Statistics*, vol. 6, p. 150.

much (Table 10A.1) until around 1930, when a rapid expansion of the manufacturing sector owing to exchange rate depreciation and military-related demand induced the start of a significant rural emigration of farmers.

It must be noted that, during this period, investment in the industrial sector was mainly financed within the industrial sector. Although landlords took their assets out of agriculture, the share of agriculture in the economy had become quite small, so that the effect on funding of the industrial sector was not large, as can be seen from the last column of Table 10A.2.

After World War II

Land reform under the occupation forces eliminated the landlord class, and, at the same time, agriculture became a significant protected sector. Rice imports were reduced to zero by a quota system. After 1952, the state marketing system for rice, introduced in 1933, adopted the policy of balancing the income level between farmers and urban households by means of intervention in pricing. Both the producer and consumer prices of rice were

TABLE 10A.2 Sectoral Resource Flow in Japan (¥ million, prewar; ¥ hundred million, postwar)

	Net Direct Taxation on Agriculture (A)	Market-Based Resource Flow from Agriculture (B)	Public Investment in Agriculture	Ratio of (A + B) to Fixed Capital Formation in Nonagricultural Sector (%)
1899–1902	104	1	13	42.0
1903–07	115	13	13	38.4
1908–12	154	4	30	28.0
1913–17	166	43	30	24.2
1918–22	290	208	79	19.4
1923–27	291	24	102	13.8
1928–32	188	–11	114	9.0
1933–37	145	222	132	11.3
1955–59	56	152	8	8.2
1960–64	50	400	23	6.5

Source: Teranishi (1982:258–61).

set considerably higher than the international price. At the same time, the consumer price of rice was made lower than the producer price, and the difference became a source of huge budget deficits.

NOTES

I am grateful for the very helpful comments by Masahiko Aoki, Albert Fishlow, Yujiro Hayami, Kiminori Matsuyama, Ronald McKinnon and other participants at the World Bank workshop on Roles of Government in Economic Development: Analysis of East Asian Experiences in Kyoto during September 16 and 17, 1994 and in Stanford during February 10 and 11, 1995. I am also thankful to David Lane for comments and suggestions of related literature. Recently, I obtained valuable comments from Gustav Ranis and Howard Stein, but I could not follow their suggestions in this version because of time constraints.

[1] This view on saving is symbolized by the Solowian model of economic growth developed during the 1950s, according to which an increase in saving rate does not lead to a change in steady-state growth rate (Sala-i-Martin 1990).

[2] The possibility of aggravation of income distribution was considered only temporal, as is symbolized by Kuznets' hypothesis of a U-shaped curve or Leibenstein's idea of a trickle-down mechanism. On this point, refer to Oman and Wignaraja (1991:16–21) and Woo (1990). The emphasis on the investment side is pointed out in Oman and Wignaraja as well as Maddison (1989:ch. 6).

[3] The urban informal sector comprises a large number of small-scale production

and service activities using simple labor-intensive technology, and is often characterized by tax evasion and various kinds of crimes, including drug trafficking and prostitution.

[4] Divisible benefits are supplied by the government to a sector, but applicable to subsets only of the constituents of the sector. These benefits are discussed in greater detail below.

[5] Domestic purchase prices were depressed below world prices, and the margins, after deducting the administrative costs of the marketing board, became government revenue and were sometimes substantial. In Ghana, for example, the shares of producers' income, marketing board cost, and government revenue were 55, 11, and 35 per cent, respectively, during the regime of President Kwame Nkrumah (1957–66). Under the later military regime (1973–83), however, the corresponding figures were 45, 38, and 17, respectively (Stryker 1991). Note also that another and sometimes more important justification for state intervention in agricultural pricing lies in the price stabilization of agricultural products. Refer to Lele (1988) on this point.

[6] Most of these studies were surveyed and evaluated by Ishikawa (1988). When this chapter was nearly complete, I came to know the recent work of Karshenas (1995), which offers a comprehensive comparative analysis of industrialization and agricultural surplus including the experience of Iran.

[7] The definition of real exchange rate follows the recent theoretical work. On this point, refer to Edwards (1988:5–8). Let us denote the price of tradables by P_T, prices of nontradables by P_N, and GNP deflator by P. Then:

$$P = \alpha P_N + (1-\alpha) P_T$$
$$P^* = \beta P_N^* + (1-\beta) P_T^*$$

where α and β show the share of nontradable in the country and foreign countries, respectively, * indicates foreign countries. Assuming *PPP* on tradables, that is $P_T = eP_T^*$, we have:

$$\frac{P}{eP^*} = \frac{\alpha(P_N/P_T) + (1-\alpha)}{\beta(P_N^*/P_T^*) + (1-\beta)},$$

so that, as P_N/P_T increases (real exchange rate appreciates), P/eP^* increases. Next, let us introduce another assumption that consumption goods are composed of imported goods with price (in foreign currency) P_M and domestic goods with price P, so that:

$$CPI = \gamma P + (1-\gamma) P_M,$$

where γ shows share of domestic goods in the consumption basket. Further let us assume that *PPP* hold with respect to imports, $eP_M = P_T$.
We have:

$$\frac{CPI}{P} = \gamma + (1+\gamma)\frac{P_T/P_M}{(1-\alpha)P_T/P_N + \alpha}$$

and:

$$\frac{eP_M}{P} = \frac{P_T/P_M}{(1-\alpha)P_T/P_N + \alpha}.$$

Therefore, both *CPI*/*P* and eP_M/P move inversely with P_N / P_T.

[8] For example, an export promotion policy was introduced in Korea under the Park regime during the years 1961–73, including tariff exemption of intermediate good imports used for export goods production. A free trade zone was established in Malaysia in 1971. The Export Encouragement Act was introduced in the Philippines in 1970, and subsidized export credits and tariff exemptions for imported raw materials used in exports were introduced in Thailand in 1972.

[9] It must be also noted that in Latin America, too, an import substitution policy was supplemented by encouragement of manufacturing exports during the 1970s and 1980s (Haggard 1990:26).

[10] I am grateful to Toshihiko Kawagoe for the suggestion of the data source for Tables 10.3 and 10.6.

[11] Zaire is excluded from the regression because of the lack of data. Population density is calculated as population (thousands) divided by land area (thousand ha). Data on population are from FAO, *Production Yearbook*, vol. 34 (1980) and vol. 45 (1991).

[12] The importance of the behavior of business groups in latecomer economies in the process of technology import is emphasized in Hikino and Amsden (1994).

[13] Typical roots of conglomerates in Brazil were shopkeepers or engineers, who benefited from government development programs in peripheral regions (Makler 1993).

[14] An important exception is the *chaebol* in Korea. The military regime of General Park Chung Hee provided most of their funding, with pressure for strong economic performance.

[15] It is shown above that the trade policy in East Asia is not necessarily biased toward agriculture.

[16] I am grateful to Yujiro Hayami for suggesting this point.

[17] Zambia was an exception in that it was endowed with rich extractable mineral resources such as copper, although agricultural pricing policy was used politically to enhance national integrity (Pletcher 1986). Another exception was Tanzania, which emphasized agricultural development under the socialist regime of President Julius Nyerere.

[18] World Bank (1993a:33) shows that the inflow of foreign direct investment more or less balanced profits during the 1960s and 1970s.

[19] Kuhn (1990) and OECD (1987:77–80). There was no rescheduling in South Asian countries during the period because of the adoption of a cautious borrowing policy after their experience of several cases of debt rescheduling during the 1970s.

[20] Farmers evade the unfavorable effects of government pricing policy by shifting crops. Even cocoa farmers in Ghana evaded the effects by shifting to rice or cassava production.

[21] Corbo (1988). Refer to Fishlow (1972) for a longer-term perspective on import substitution in Brazil.

[22] Note that no military-backed regimes were established in such large countries as Colombia and Mexico. Sheahan (1980) argues that the relative absence of urban poor in these countries explained this fact.

[23] Not all military governments adopted authoritarian policies (e.g., the policy of the military regime in 1979–80 Brazil was populistic), and not all authoritarian regimes were supported by large farmers and industrialists (e.g., the Peruvian government of 1968–75 adopted policies against the interests of the landed and financial elites).

[24] Another reason for the overvaluation of exchange rates in Latin America lies in the monetarist stabilization policy of the Southern Cone countries. For the mechanism of exchange rate overvaluation see Sachs (1987) and Dornbusch and Pablo (1990).

[25] World Bank (1987), *World Development Report*, 82–83. The degree of outward orientation is judged by the effective rate of protection, direct controls, export incentives, and exchange rate policy.

[26] Chile, where many of the import substitution industries were sacrificed in pursuit of a market-oriented economic system, is an exception.

[27] It must be noted that Grindle utilizes a logic different from mine in explaining the biased targeting of agricultural development policy. In his model, the state elite that aimed at industrialization tried to make the most of the growth potential of agriculture as a source of cheap food for the urban workforce, cheap labor, foreign exchange earnings, and so on. Large farmers were considered to be most suited as the recipients of development subsidies because subsidies for mechanization, etc. could be utilized most efficiently by those endowed with large land areas with sufficient water resources. Thus, according to Grindle, small farmers were discriminated against simply from efficiency considerations because they were settled on land of poor quality, often without access to water. It follows that the recent downfall of small farmers in Latin American countries was an unanticipated consequence of the agricultural development policy for state elites who had believed in a sort of trickle-down mechanism. However, in this chapter I consider that the unfavorable conditions faced by small farmers to have been themselves results of a political process related to the efforts of the government to retain political power.

[28] In this regard, Albert Fishlow made an important point in his comment on this chapter that the importance of large farmers as an economic power declined significantly during the 1970s. This point seems to be underlined, for example, by the low share of agriculture in total exports. However, this does not necessarily seem to imply the decline in their power in the political arena. For example, refer to the following observation: “while large landowners generally lost power to emerging urban industrial interests, the impact of development ideologies allowed them to increase their influence over policy making for the rural sector” (Grindle 1986:56).

[29] The low employment opportunities in commercial agriculture and the worsening of rural poverty during the 1960s and 1970s is succinctly disussed in de Janvry and Sadoulet (1989) and Grindle (1986:ch. 5). The factors behind the upsurge in migration in Brazil, Mexico, and Colombia are extensively analyzed in various chapters in Ishii (1989).

[30] Negative value means the spread of agricultural activity in urban areas. Such a phenomenon is frequently observed in recent Africa. There might be some problem

in data consistency, however, since rural and agricultural populations are taken from different sources.

[31] The importance of agrarian industry and entrepreneurship is also emphasized in Hayami and Kawagoe (1993:ch. 5). Ranis and Stewart (1993) present insightful arguments on the role of rural nonagricultural activities.

[32] The sample is 66 developing countries in East Asia (8), South Asia (5), Latin America (23), and Sub-Saharan Africa (30). All data were obtained from World Bank (1991), *World Table*. OLS was used and figures in parentheses are t-values.

[33] The urban population ratio in Singapore is an exception, for Singapore is basically a city-state. In a comparison with Taiwan, Korea's relative neglect of the agricultural sector is often pointed out (Ranis and Orrock 1985 and Oshima 1987). The analysis here, however, seems to suggest that, even in Korea, the neglect of agriculture was not so pronounced as in regions outside Asia.

[34] Berg and Sachs (1988) also argue that the debts incurred during the 1970s were not the product of calculations of intertemporal efficiency, but resulted from the political needs of the incumbent government.

[35] My analysis follows the examination of the relationship between debt and investment in *World Development Report* 1985, where with a sample of 39 countries, a strong positive relationship was found for the period 1973–78, a weaker but positive relationship was found for 1965–72, and no significant relationship was found for 1979–83.

[36] When I had almost completed this chapter, I read a manuscript by Binswanger and Deininger (1995), which is a comprehensive survey of the political economy of agriculture and agrarian society as well as an ambitious attempt to build a framework of a predictable theory of policy change.

[37] Moreover, this method usually is not effective enough to mobilize sufficient resources. For example, whenever there is a lag between incidence and the collection of tax, the real value of tax tends to be reduced (Tanzi 1978).

[38] On these points, refer to Teranishi (1982 and 1990).

REFERENCES

Bates, R. H. (1981), *Markets and States in Tropical Africa: The Political Basis of Agricultural Policies*, University of California Press, Berkeley.

——(1983), *Essays on the Political Economy of Rural Africa*, Cambridge University Press, Cambridge.

Berg, A. and Sachs, J. (1988), "The Debt Crisis: Structural Explanation of Country Experience," NBER Working Paper, No. 2607.

Binswanger, H. P. and Deininger, K. (1995), "Towards a Political Economy of Agriculture and Agrarian Relations," unpublished manuscript.

Clute, R. E. (1982), "The Role of Agriculture in African Development," *African Studies Review*, 25(4):1–20.

Corbo, V. (1988), "Problems, Development Theory, and Strategies of Latin America," in G. Ranis and T. P. Schultz, eds., *The State of Development Economics: Progress and Perspectives*, Basil Blackwell, Oxford.

Dletcher, J. R. (1986), "The Political Use of Agricultural Markets in Zambia," *Journal of Modern African Studies*, 607–17.

Dornbusch, R. (1984), "External Debt, Deficit Finance and Disequilibrium Exchange Rates," NBER Working Paper, No. 1336.

——and de Pablo, J. C. (1990), "Debt and Macroeconomic Instability in Argentina," in J. Sachs, ed., *Developing Country Debt and Economic Performance*, vol. 2, University of Chicago Press, Chicago.

Drake, W. P. (1982), "Conclusion: Requiem for Populism?" in M. L. Conniff, ed., *Latin American Populism in Comparative Perspective*, University of New Mexico Press, Albuquerque.

Edwards, S. (1988), *Real Exchange Rates, Devaluation, and Adjustment: Exchange Rate Policy in Developing Countries*, MIT Press, Cambridge, Mass.

Fields, G. S. (1984), "Employment, Income Distribution and Economic Growth in Seven Small Open Economies," *Economic Journal*, 94:74–84.

——(1985), "Industrialization and Employment in Hong Kong, Korea, Singapore and Taiwan," in W. Galenson, ed., *Foreign Trade and Investment; Economic Development in the Newly Industrializing Asian Countries*, University of Wisconsin Press, Madison.

Fishlow, A. (1972), "Origins and Consequences of Import Substitution in Brazil," in L. E. di Marco, ed., *International Economics and Development: Essays in Honor of Raul Prebisch*, Academic Press, New York.

Furtado, C. (1970), *Economic Development of Latin America*, Cambridge University Press, Cambridge.

Goodman, D. (1989), "Rural Economy and Society," in E. Bacha and H. Klein, eds., *Social Change in Brazil: 1945–1985: The Incomplete Transition*, University of New Mexico Press, Albuquerque.

Griffin, K. (1973), "Agrarian Policy: the Political and Economic Context," *World Development*, 1(11):1–11.

Grindle, M. (1986), *State and Countryside: Development Policy and Agrarian Policies in Latin America*, Johns Hopkins University Press, Baltimore.

Haggard, S. (1990), *Pathways from the Periphery: The Politics of Growth in the Newly Industrializing Countries*, Cornell University Press, Ithaca.

Hayami, Y. and Kawagoe, T. (1993), *The Agrarian Origins of Commerce and Industry: A Study of Peasant Marketing in Indonesia*, Macmillan, London, and St. Martin's Press, New York.

Hicks, N. and Kubish, A. (1984), "Cutting Government Expenditures in LDCs," *Finance and Development*, 21(3):37–39.

Hikino, T. and Amsden, A. H. (1994), "Staying Behind, Stumbling Back, Sneaking Up, Soaring Ahead: Late Industrialization in Historical Perspective," in W. J. Baumoi, R. R. Nelson, and E. N. Wolf, eds., *Convergence of Productivity: Cross-National Studies and Historical Evidence*, Oxford University Press, Oxford.

Hirshman, A. O. (1958), *The Strategy of Economic Development*, Yale University Press, New Haven.

International Monetary Fund (1992), *International Financial Statistics (1992 Yearbook)*, International Monetary Fund, Washington.

Ishii, A. (1967), "Resource Flow Between Agriculture and Industry: The Chinese Experience," *The Developing Economies*, 5(1):3–49.

ISHII, A. (ed.) (1989), *Raten Amerika no Toshi to Nogyo* (Urban and rural sectors in Latin America), Institute of Developing Economies, Tokyo.

ISHIKAWA, S. (1988), "Patterns and Processes of Intersectoral Resource Flows: Comparison of Cases in Asia," in G. Ranis and T. P. Schultz, eds., *The State of Development Economics: Progress and Perspectives*, Basil Blackwell, Oxford.

DE JANVRY, A. and SADOULET, E. (1989), "Investment Strategies to Combat Rural Poverty: A Proposal for Latin America," *World Development*, 17(8):1203–21.

KARSHENAS, M. (1995), *Industrialization and Agricultural Surplus: Agricultural Surplus: A Comparative Study of Economic Development in Asia*, Oxford University Press, Oxford.

KRUEGER, A. O. (1983), *Trade and Employment in Developing Countries (3, Synthesis and Conclusions)*, University of Chicago Press, Chicago.

——(1993a), *Political Economy of Policy Reform in Developing Countries*, MIT Press, Cambridge, Mass.

——(1993b), "Virtuous and Vicious Circles of Economic Development," *American Economic Review*, 83:351–55.

KUHN, M. G. (1990), *Multilateral Official Debt Rescheduling: Recent Experience*, International Monetary Fund, Washington.

LEE, T.-H. (1971), *Intersectoral Capital Flow in the Economic Development of Taiwan*, Cornell University Press, Ithaca.

LELE, U. (1988), "Comparative Advantage and Structural Transformation: A Review of Africa's Economic Development Experience," in G. Ranis and T. P. Schultz, eds., *The State of Development Economics: Progress and Perspectives*, Basil Blackwell, Oxford.

MCKINNON, R. I. (1986), "Issues and Perspectives: An Overview of Banking Regulation and Monetary Control," in A. H. H. Tan and B. Kupur, eds., *Pacific Growth and Financial Interdependence*, Allen and Unwin, Sydney.

——(1988), "Financial Liberalization in Retrospect: Interest Rate Policies in LDCs," in G. Ranis and T. Paul Schultz, eds., *The State of Development Economics: Progress and Perspectives*, Basil Blackwell, Oxford.

MADDISON, A. (1989), *The World Economy in the Twentieth Century*, OECD, Paris.

MAKLER, H. M. (1993), "Brazilian Financial Conglomerates: Family Capitalism, Diversification and Implications for Hemispheric Integration," a paper presented at the international conference on Financial Justifications in Transition, Universidad Nacional Autonoma de Mexico and Universidad Autonoma Metropolitana, May 27–28, 1993.

MIZOGUCHI, T. and TERASAKI, Y. (1995), "Kakei no shotokubunpu hendo no keizai-shakai oyobi sangyo-kozo-teki yoin" (Long-term analysis of income distribution of households), *Keizai kenkyu*, 46(1):1–19.

MUNDLE, S. (1981), *Surplus Flow and Growth Inbalance: The Intersectoral Flow of Real Resources in India: 1951–1971*, Allied Publisher Private Ltd., New Delhi.

——and OHKAWA, K. (1979), "Agricultural Surplus Flow in Japan 1888–1937," *The Developing Economies*, 17(3):247–65.

MURPHY, K. M., SHLEIFER, A., and VISHNY, R. W. (1989), "Industrialization and the Big Push," *Journal of Political Economy*, 97(5):1003–26.

NAKAGANE, W. (1992), *Chugoku keizai-ron* (The political economy of agro-industrial relationships in contemporary China), Tokyo Daigaku Shuppankai, Tokyo.

NURKSE, R. (1953), *Problems of Capital Formation in Underdeveloped Countries*, Basil Blackwell and Mott Ltd., Oxford.

OHKAWA, K., YUTAKA, S., and TAKAMATSU, N. (1978), "Agricultural Surplus in an Overall Performance of Savings-Investment," in *Papers and Proceedings of the Conference on Japan's Historical Development Experience and the Contemporary Developing Countries: Issues for Comparative Analysis*, International Development Center of Japan, Tokyo.

OMAN, C. P. and WIGNARAJA, G. (1991), *The Postwar Evolution of Development Thinking* (OECD Development Center), Macmillan, London.

Organization for Economic Cooperation and Development (1987), *Financing and External Debt of Developing Countries: 1986 Survey*, OECD, Paris.

OSHIMA, H. (1987), *Economic Growth in Monsoon Asia: A Comparative Survey*, University of Tokyo Press, Tokyo.

OTSUKA, Y., CHUMA, Y., and HAYAMI, Y. (1992), "Land and Labor Contract in Agrarian Economies: Theories and Fact," *Journal of Economic Literature*, 30:1965–2018.

PLETCHER, J. R. (1986), "The Political Use of Agricultural Markets in Zambia," *Journal of Modern African Studies*, 24:607–17.

RANIS, G. and ORROCK, L. (1985), "Latin American and East Asian NICs: Development Strategies Compared," in E. Duran, ed., *Latin America and the World Recession*, Cambridge University Press, Cambridge.

——and STEWART, F. (1993), "Rural Non Agricultural Activities in Development; Theory and Evidence," *Journal of Development Economics*, 40:75–101.

ROSENSTEIN-RODAN, P. N. (1943), "Industrialization of Eastern and South Eastern Europe," *Economic Journal*, 53:202–11.

SACHS, J. (1985), "External Debt and Macroeconomic Performance in Latin America and East Asia," *Brookings Papers on Economic Activity*, 1985(II):523–73.

——(1987), "Trade and Exchange Rate Policies in Growth-Oriented Adjustment Programs," in V. Corbo, M. Goldstein, and M. Khan, eds., *Growth-Oriented Adjustment Programs*, IMF and World Bank, Washington.

——(1989), "Social Conflicts and Populist Policy in Latin America," NBER Working Paper, No. 2897.

SALA-I-MARTIN, X. (1990), "Lecture Notes on Economic Growth (I): Introduction to the Literature and Neoclassical Models," NBER Working Paper, No. 3563.

SCHIFF, M. and VALDES, A. (1992), *The Political Economy of Agricultural Pricing Policy*, vol. 4: *A Synthesis of the Economics in Developing Countries*, Johns Hopkins University Press, Baltimore.

SHEAHAN, J. (1980), "Market-Oriented Economic Policies and Political Repression in Latin America," *Economic Development and Cultural Change*, 28(2):267–91.

SPENCER, D. S. C. (1994), "Infrastructure and Technology Constraints to Agricultural Development in the Humid and Subhumid Tropics of Africa," EPTD, Discussion Paper, No. 3, International Food Policy Research Institute.

SQUIRE, L. (1981), *Employment Policy in Developing Countries: A Survey of Issues and Evidence*, Oxford University Press, Oxford.

STRYKER, J. D. (1991), "Ghana," in A. O. Krueger, M. Schiff, and A. Valdes, eds., *The Political Economy of Agricultural Pricing Policy*, vol. 3: *Africa and the Mediterranean*, Johns Hopkins University Press, Baltimore.

TANZI, V. (1978), "Inflation, Real Tax Revenue, and the Case for Inflationary Finance: Theory with an Application to Argentina," *IMF Staff Papers*, 25(3):417–51.

TERANISHI, J. (1976), "The Pattern and Role of Flow of Funds between Agriculture and Non-Agriculture in Japanese Economic Development," in *Papers and Proceedings of the Conference on Japan's Historical Development Experience and the Contemporary Developing Countries: Issues for Comparative Analysis*, International Development Center of Japan, Tokyo.

——(1982), *Nihon no keizai hatten to kinyu* (Money, banking, and economic development in Japan), Iwanami Shoten, Tokyo.

——(1989), "The Sectoral Flow of Funds in Pre-War Japan: A Reconsideration," in S. Chakravarty, ed., *The Balance between Industry and Agriculture in Economic Development*, vol. 3: *Manpower and Transfers* (Proceedings of the Eighth World Congress of the International Economic Association), Macmillan, London.

——(1990), "Financial System and Industrialization of Japan: 1900–1970," *Banca Nazionale del Lavore*, 174:309–42.

TODARO, M. P. (1985), *Economic Development in the Third World*, Longman, New York.

United Nations Development Programme and World Bank (1992), *African Development Indicators*, World Bank, Washington.

WOO, W. T. (1990), "The Art of Economic Development: Markets, Politics and Externalities," *International Organization*, 44(3):403–29.

WOOD, A. (1988), "Global Trends in Real Exchange Rates, 1960 to 1984," World Bank Discussion Papers, No. 35.

World Bank (various years), *World Tables*, Johns Hopkins University Press, Baltimore.

——(various years), *World Development Report*, Oxford University Press, Oxford.

——(1986), *World Debt Table 1985/86*, World Bank, Washington.

——(1993a), *The East Asian Miracle in Economic Growth and Public Policy*, Oxford University Press, Oxford.

——(1993b), *Global Economic Prospects and the Developing Countries*, World Bank, Washington.

11

The Political Economy of Growth in East Asia: A Perspective on the State, Market, and Ideology

MEREDITH WOO-CUMINGS

11.1 INTRODUCTION: BACK TO HISTORY AND INDUCTION—OR, THE POLITICAL ECONOMY OF ECONOMIC GROWTH

The debate over the reasons for East Asian economic ascendancy has become one of the most important intellectual *causes célèbres* in the closing decades of this century. The public controversy and partisanship over the interpretation of this phenomenon, with its far-reaching implications for development strategy elsewhere, is testimony once again to Lord Keynes's insight (1936:383) that ideas have consequences—even if they emanate from the forgotten texts of "some defunct economist."

Causal arrows explaining the enrichment of East Asia are difficult to draw, however, if only because of the absence of counterfactual evidence. Thus, the proponents of free trade argue that the causal link between selective policy intervention and economic growth and intervention is impossible to establish, and they speculate that East Asian economies might have performed even better without the interventions. Critics counter that if the link between growth and intervention is impossible to test, so also is that between growth and nonintervention: what is sauce for the goose is sauce for the gander.[1]

This is a debate with a pedigree, going back two centuries to Adam Smith and Friedrich List, to Thomas Jefferson and Alexander Hamilton, and the latest incantations are variations on substantially the same theme, with much of the empirical support for the contending arguments often being eclectic and selective. For instance, one can dredge up the lamentable experience of, say, Indonesia's protection of the airplane (or the automobile) industry as an example that industry protection simply does not work—or, on the contrary, that it works just fine because South Korea so successfully protected and developed the shipbuilding sector and a host of other heavy industries.

This bias in case selection grows out of an excessively economistic focus on individual policy output, extruded from the general context of the developmental ensemble involving the state and market, the domestic society and the world, and the ideology facilitating societal mobilization for growth. Without grasping the essential quality of this developmental ensemble—call it political economy—it is impossible to understand the oscillations of economic policy and, more importantly, the parameters of this oscillation.

In truth, most national economies defy categorization as pristine embodiments of axiomatic economic beliefs; rather, suppleness and not authenticity, heterodoxy and not orthodoxy is the hallmark of fine economic management. Thus the economies in Japan, Taiwan, and South Korea are alternately, or sometimes all at once, liberal and illiberal, open and closed, disciplining and protecting, of their markets and industries. One might say the same of the Latin American economies today (if not 20 years ago), as they juggle their residual import-substitution strategies with timely adaptations to stimulate exports, enhance revenues, and sustain increases in agricultural productivity.

This is not to say that the time-honored debate between neoclassical orthodoxy and motley rebuttals based on (equally selective) empirical evidence is the only intellectual fisticuff of practical consequence, crowding out alternative ways of conceptualizing development. Quite to the contrary, in the past two decades a seemingly disparate set of ideas has come forth, taking stock of past failures in explaining economic development and occasioning a rethinking of the ideas that had long dwelt in the shadow of equilibrium economics.

The main thread linking these ideas is the recognition that the market is not the only way information is transmitted and economic life organized, and that nonmarket institutions are integral—and not necessarily inconvenient—parts of economic life. For instance, one variant of this argument takes as its starting point a reformulation of the firm as a "governance structure" (in contrast to the Walrasian perspective which contains no analysis of the internal social organization of the firm), and extends it to larger institutions and processes, such as the state.

Taking institutions and institutional processes seriously also means taking history seriously, something neglected *a priori* in the concept of equilibrium. As Richard Nelson and Sidney Winter (1982:403) put it, "the process of institutional development is an evolutionary process, both linked and akin to the evolution of firms and industries. It is a groping, incremental process, in which the conditions of each day arise from the actual circumstances of the preceding day and in which uncertainty abounds." The evolutionary character of all things—from technology, firms, and industries to institutions—has been charted through useful ideas such as increasing returns, the "lock-in," and path dependency, but the upshot is to render profoundly problematic the very notion of the predictability of economic futures—a disturbing idea offering little consolation even to those skeptical of the *laissez-faire* approach.

If future indeterminacy is a problem, so is overdeterminacy, as embodied in the arguments of "the new institutionalism," with its variant in transaction cost theory. Departing from the conventional view in economics that market transactions are costless, the adherents of this position argue that market exchanges are costly, and so are state interventions. If both state intervention and market transactions are costly, then the question would become *not* whether state interventions are costly *per se*, *but* whether the state can achieve the same allocative efficiency at a lower cost than the market (Chang 1994:54). The merit of this point, despite its functionalist bent, is that the state and its policies become proper objects of study, not to be dismissed as a hindrance to the *ipso facto* smooth functioning of the market: some economists have thus found a way to bring the state back in.

But the argument—interesting as it is in making explicable in economic terms the purpose and agency behind state interventionism in East Asia—is essentially rationalistic, reifying the state as a profit-maximizing agent bent on achieving the highest possible efficiency (a Lone Ranger in a realm bereft of stubborn interests and real people). What is needed is an account of the East Asian method toward nonneoclassical madness, not in terms of cost calculations but in terms of pragmatic and improvised solutions, devised in the face of harsh historical circumstances not of their own choosing.

Much has been made in recent years about the differences between the East Asian and Latin American patterns of economic development, an enterprise made increasingly urgent in the 1980s by the divergence in economic performance of the two areas, with the former galloping ahead with double-digit growth while the latter suffered the blight of the "Lost Decade," or, more tellingly, the "Great Depression of the 1980s." At the root of this divergence, it is often said, is a fundamentally different set of policy choices. The corollary to that argument is that convergence between the two regions requires similar policy choices, in this case the much vaunted export orientation and market liberalization that is said to characterize the pattern of growth in East Asia.

It is true that Latin America and East Asia—Taiwan and South Korea in this instance—followed different paths after completing or "exhausting" the primary stage of import substitution industrialization (ISI) in the late 1950s. Mexico and Brazil, for instance, pursued the second phase of ISI through much of the 1960s and have continued this strategy to date, while experimenting with diversified export promotion schemes. In East Asia, the 1960s saw the beginnings of export oriented industrialization (EOI), which has continued without interruption. But this was judiciously combined with the secondary phase of ISI—meaning a concerted push for heavy and chemical industrialization for much of the 1970s, in South Korea above all but also in Taiwan to a lesser extent.

It cannot be that the persistence of ISI in Latin America is to be explained by "mistaken" policies; by the early 1960s the argument in favor of the manifold virtues of export-led growth had already worked itself into the global economic *zeitgeist*. The point instead is that economic policies are not made in a vacuum devoid of societal interests and historical constraints. Juro Teranishi in this volume (Chapter 10) gets around to this point, in part by arguing that development strategy in East Asia and Latin America is explicable as an attempt by the state to redress the existing sectoral imbalance by utilizing "divisible benefits": put differently, it is a political process whereby the state compensates those sectors adversely affected by its preferred development policies.

This brings us to the core conundrum of this chapter: the nature of the state and its relationship to domestic social forces, in a situation where its ability to make and remake the domestic society is profoundly constrained by history and by the structure of the world at large. The main argument that I advance here is that the East Asian and Latin American newly industrializing countries (NICs) have entered modernity at different points, encumbered by vastly different historical baggage that either hamstrung or facilitated economic development. In both areas, the historical task facing economic policymakers was the same: to overcome the situation of unrelenting peripherality in a world dominated by core economies. But this purpose called for different agents, and I will discuss this issue by emphasizing in turn the structure of the state, its relationship to the outside world and the domestic society, the methods devised to bring about development, and, finally, the question of culture and ideology in overcoming economic backwardness.

11.2 THE EAST ASIAN STATE IN COMPARATIVE PERSPECTIVE: THE BEGINNINGS

Because I use the term "state," and not the more familiar term "government," it would be useful to define what I mean by it. I mean by this term the continuous administrative, legal, bureaucratic, and coercive system that is capable of restructuring its relations to social groups, as well as relations among those groups. The strength of the state depends on how effectively the state alters these structures, and in this context Korea and Taiwan are "strong states." The state is both an agent of class power (thus to fulfill the function of capital accumulation) and of its citizens (thus to fulfill the function of legitimacy), and this balancing act requires a certain "autonomy" and discretion on the part of the state. In this way, state agencies and institutions, and their back-and-forth interaction with social forces, become for many political scientists and sociologists the proper foci of analysis.

But I would also posit something else: the state is also poised between the world system and the domestic system. Depending on the autonomy or the strength of the state, it can either be a *lumpen*, dependent state, or engineer a movement upward in the international system, wresting power away from the external world. Unless we understand the full complexity of the state's relationship to the outside world and domestic sectors—the "give and take," for developing states are not merely "takers," as Stephen Krasner (1985) says—we cannot understand how the international system is constituted, how it is both made and remade.[2]

Let me briefly outline what I consider to be the salient aspects of the Latin American state in relation to the domestic and external society, so as to cameo contrapuntally the "strong" character of the East Asian state. In the context of Latin America, international consideration was foremost in the minds of those development economists who were concerned with national efficacy in harnessing developmental energy and resources. Albert Hirschman (1945), basing his argument on the analysis of the trading structure in Eastern Europe in the interwar period, warned of the compromise to sovereignty when national economies are articulated to the global one through extensive exports of primary commodities. In this regard, ISI in Latin America, which had as its linchpin overvalued exchange rates, was a subtle device to discourage dependence on primary exports by shifting resources to the industrial sector without frontally attacking the powerful agrarian interests (Hirschman 1968). More famously, Raul Prebisch argued that static market signals overestimated the returns to primary exports because of potential deterioration of the terms of trade, and advocated ISI as a way to correct this shift of resources in favor of the core countries.

The Latin American state exercised little autonomy, either *vis-à-vis* the world economy to which it had been articulated since the sixteenth century, as dependency theorists have long argued, or *vis-à-vis* the domestic society whose powerful agrarian interests it was loath to confront. ISI was in that sense a halfway-house solution for the Latin American state to distance itself from both international and domestic forces, while gaining a breathing space, a prophylactic realm, for industrialization at home.

This weakness of the Latin American state—in contrast to the widely touted "strong states" in East Asia—has something to do with the fact that Latin America entered modernity much earlier than Korea or Taiwan, not to mention attaining political independence a century earlier; it also began the protracted process of industrialization much earlier, in the context of restricted enclaves. And by and large it was a process that was guided not by state action, but by individual entrepreneurial initiatives, much as it was elsewhere in the pioneer industrial countries (Dore 1990). In other words, Latin America was never the "late developer" in the classic Gerschenkronian sense, and thus its state never took the commanding role in crash industrialization programs.

The early insertion of the Latin American economies into the world system, combined with the pattern of industrialization that resembles (on its face) the experience of the United States, has resulted in the developmental *gestalt* characterized by the economist Fernando Fajnzylber (1990) as "showcase modernity," aimed not at self-sustaining development but at satisfying a set of elite consumption patterns appropriate for developed countries. More specifically, this showcase consists of the following mutually reinforcing aspects: a consistent pattern of exuberant consumption, heavily skewed in favor of urban elite groups at the expense of the rural and lower-income majorities; industrial sectors oriented primarily toward the domestic market; the insertion of national economies into the international system via trade in natural resources (we might call this the Leontiff Paradox without the paradox); and the dubious leadership role played by either the state or national industry.

The timing and manner of Latin America's insertion into the modern world economy, or Latin America's encounter with modernity through an idiosyncratic internalization of the experience of the United States (in modernization-speak), all seem to point to the weakness of the state as overdetermined in Latin America. It was always a state imbedded in "the interests," even if the interests changed over the decades. The reverse seems true in East Asia: the strength of its states seems overdetermined.

Korea and Taiwan came into modernity suddenly, brutally, in the fearsome grip of the world's late developer *par excellence*, Meiji Japan. This is not to gainsay that both China and Korea had two of the oldest and most sophisticated bureaucratic traditions in the world, or that they could have developed successfully on their own. Taiwan on the eve of Japanese colonization (1895) was more prosperous and more commercialized than the rest of China, with a stable landlord-gentry class providing local social and political leadership (Gold 1986); by 1910 Korea also saw the sprouts of capitalism in its commerce, and more importantly it had a highly sophisticated bureaucracy with an intricate network of checks and balances that was responsible for the half-millennial political stability.

Well suited as these *anciens régimes* were for governing an essentially steady-state economy, in the face of imperialism and competition with modern states, they could not solve the problem of creating adequate authority for the achievement of new, modernizing national goals. The modern state institutions were, then, imposed on Taiwan and Korea by Japan. But a long tradition of bureaucratic statecraft, drawing its legitimacy from the claim that its civil servants were "the best and brightest," helps explain the alacrity with which Koreans and Taiwanese took to Japanese bureaucratic doctrines (which Japan in turn had imported from Prussia.) It survived through the colonial period to facilitate the economic transformation of Korea and Taiwan thereafter. Of course, in many cases the survival was the mundane and predictable result of the continuity of native bureaucrats from Japanese colonialism through to the postwar regimes.[3]

The legacy of Japanese colonialism that produced modern states in Korea and Taiwan is a politically sensitive issue, so sensitive that two of the much-cited English texts on the economic development of Korea and Taiwan, by Alice Amsden (1989) and Robert Wade (1990), hardly discuss it, preferring to treat the colonial period as an aberration. But the origin of the modern state *is* an important issue because the peculiarities of the present are often inexplicable without scrutinizing the origins, or the initial conditions at the founding of institutions. Another way of saying the same thing is that evolution, whether biological or institutional, is really path dependent.

Japanese colonialism left three imprints that are relevant for our consideration here. The first is the nature of the political machinery that was imposed on top of the agrarian economy in Taiwan, and later in Korea. From as early as the 1880s, Japanese interest in Taiwan and Korea sprang from regional security concerns, broadly conceived. In the words of Marius Jansen (1968:182), the compass of Japan's strategic concern was in concentric circles radiating from the homelands: the "cordon of sovereignty" encompassing territory vital to the nation's survival and under formal occupation, and the "cordon of advantages," an outer limit of informal Japanese domination, seen as necessary to protect and guarantee the inner line. The territorial contiguity of Japanese imperialism and this security concern, when combined with the fact that Japan was still a developing country, meant that Japanese policy in its colonies would be significantly different from that of, say, Britain. Japanese control and use of the colonies were much more extensive, thorough, and systematic; the economic structure of the colonies had to undergo radical and brutal transformation tied to the needs of the rapidly growing Japan.[4]

The colonial state was not only unaccountable to social groups in Taiwan and Korea (merely a matter of defining a colonial state). But it was also exempt from the supervisional scrutiny of both the Japanese cabinet and the parliament (it reported to the Ministry of Colonies in Tokyo, which tended to ratify what the colonial governments proposed). This resulting separation both from colonized societies and from superordinate Japanese influence was reinforced by the highly articulate, well-organized, and bureaucratized nature of this state machinery.

The second point worth considering is the relationship between this colonial state and business, especially the prewar *zaibatsu* that came to invest in its colonies. The colonial state offered big business the two fundamental preconditions for business engagement and practice: guarantees of political stability and of state investment in infrastructure necessary for industrialization—political and social overhead, so to speak. But most critical in the Japanese private sector's decision to invest in the colonies was the financial incentive created by the Japanese government: the willingness to share the risk should the investment turn unprofitable. This socialization of financial risks, one might argue, adumbrates the postwar Korean government policy of "financial repression," a tried-and-true, four-decade-long policy of shifting resources from savers to the gigantic and heavily leveraged enterprises, to create in the end a whole constellation of world-class native industrialists.

The prewar Japanese *zaibatsu*, especially the new ones like Nichitsu, really formed the mold from which the latter-day Korean *chaebol* were cast. Despite the gradual transformation since the Meiji period of the *zaibatsu* from family owned firms to joint stock companies, the prewar *zaibatsu* tended to retain dominant ownership and often management control by a family or kinship group and diversification into many industries and oligopolization through mergers and cartels.

The most edifying memory of this colonial political economy for the latter-day industrializers was that the colonial industrialization pattern *worked*, and that its success was based on close collaboration between the state and the *zaibatsu* and the building of the economies of scale. The colonial state's role in the comprehensive and semicoercive channeling of capital to target industries probably was a precedent for the similar mobilization in the 1970s in both Taiwan and South Korea, especially the mid-to-late 1930s "big push" that brought new industries to Korea (steel, chemicals) and Taiwan (aluminum), along with very high growth rates. If a "growth perspective" can only be garnered with an experience of growth, then one might say that the colonial political economy was important in providing such a perspective in postwar years.

True, the Japanese pattern also had a devastating effect on the development of that class that has carried all before it in the modern world, the entrepreneurial element. Certainly there were Koreans and Taiwanese who did quite well under the Japanese, then parlayed their capital and entrepreneurial skill into a fortune in the postcolonial era. But the Japanese presence in the colonies was too overbearing for one to argue the case of entrepreneurial continuity. It was the bureaucrats who "continued" into the postwar period, armed now with a new concept of state-guided development.

The smothering of local entrepreneurial talent, combined with the revolutionary upheaval that bedeviled both countries, further wiping out what little entrepreneurial continuity there might have been, in the end cut both ways in terms of the development of postcolonial Korea and Taiwan; bereft of powerful and entrenched local business interests, the new states were also less hamstrung, especially by interests that were closely tied to the metropole.

The defeat of the Kuomintang in China did not have the effect of transplanting a retreating cluster of businessmen to Taiwan. Few leading mainland capitalists followed Chiang Kai-shek to his island redoubt, preferring instead to go to the United States or Hong Kong; and the few that went to Taiwan thought it was a sojourn, and eschewed significant commitments of capital until a bilateral treat between Washington and Taipei guaranteed the island's security. This also tended to reinforce the state's role in postwar Taiwan—or what Robert Wade (1990) has called "governing the market."

The third point is the relationship between the state and the rural sector. Unlike the European colonialists in Latin America—or for that matter, elsewhere in Southeast Asia—the Japanese colonial government did not drive the peasants off their land to establish plantations, although it did not care to enact reforms to redistribute land, either. Instead, it preferred to use police and administrative methods to root the landlords firmly in the countryside, for a reliable extraction of agricultural outputs and taxes, and to keep the lid on peasant unrest. Korea and Taiwan have some differences here, of course; Korea's landed class was of centuries' duration whereas Taiwan, as a nether-region of China, never had deeply developed landlordism. Instead, it had a significant group of "rich peasants," giving another reason why Japan could achieve extraction of resources in Taiwan through incentives, while often having to use coercion in Korea. By 1945 both countries did have wealthy landlords by virtue of strong growth in the agrarian sector. But the landlords in postcolonial Taiwan and Korea did not have long to enjoy their privileges, unlike the *latifundia* owners in Latin America.

As the historian Bruce Cumings (1981) argues, the defeat of imperial Japan burst asunder the "pressure cooker" that was colonial Korea, leading eventually to war and instability; in the midst of this chaos, even the conservative South Korean state had quickly to enact a thorough and extensive land reform, at the prodding of the United States, lest the revolution in the north spill over. Likewise in Taiwan, land reform in 1950 was swift and decisive, enacted by the Kuomintang with a lot of help from American advisors while nervously looking over its shoulder to the revolutionary mainland—thus to nip peasant upheaval in the bud.

How then do we sum up the colonial legacy for the latter-day industrializers in Korea and Taiwan? One is by noting the relative absence of entrenched interests, both industrial and agricultural—either because local entrepreneurial talents were not nurtured in the smothering intensity of Japanese imperialism, or because they were shattered to smithereens when the colonial pressure cooker blew up in their faces, as in the case of the agrarian interests. This discontinuity had a powerful leveling effect, equalizing incomes more than in most developing countries and providing a fertile ground for instituting effective interventionist states, which were given a relatively free hand to forge a developmental coalition as they saw fit. And it worked because the resources for this coalition did not depend on internal sources but on the external succor of a big power: the United States. But this gets us ahead of our story.

If there were useful absences, so too were there salutary presences and continuities. The bureaucratic structure that was imposed on colonial Korea and Taiwan was a modern, meritocratic, and authoritative one, with much of it (all the offices and substantial personnel) carried forward to independence. The classic colonizer was a careful administrator such as Goto Shumpei, who got his feet wet in Taiwan, later worked in Korea, and helped with the architectonic rebuilding of modern Tokyo after the 1923 earthquake. In many ways he was an early exemplar of the Japanese practice of "administrative guidance," colonial-style. Unlike the politically appointive bureaucracies in Latin America, where tens of thousands of bureaucrats move through revolving doors with each election, and where policy decisions are made with an eye on the next job (Schneider 1991), the civil services in South Korea and Taiwan have continued to be merit oriented in recruitment and promotion, lifelong in tenure, and relatively uncorrupt by comparison to other developing countries (Woo-Cumings 1995). Of course, they both had a much longer civil service tradition to draw upon than just the experience of Japan's bureaucratic colonialism.

So, the state structure was there, and the lessons in form of demonstration effect, the know-how of engineering industrial policy, were there. The disruption caused by colonialism and war in terms of wiping out the entrepreneurial and landowning class meant that state-led industrialization was overdetermined and that the historical task of the Korean and Taiwanese states was to construct, from the vacuum left by colonialism and war, a social class that could carry the burden of industrialization. The ways Korea and Taiwan went about doing this were different, however, and here there is a sharp divergence in how both countries dealt with colonial legacies.

Korea essentially replicated the Japanese pattern of nurturing large conglomerates, at least under Park Chung Hee and Chun Doo Hwan (1961–87), whereas Taiwan nurtured only a couple of big firms, while emphasizing small business. What accounts for the difference? The reasons are primarily historical. Because of Korea's mainland connection to Manchuria and north China, Japanese colonizers and *zaibatsu* corporations developed heavy industries and spent huge amounts on social overhead, especially in northern Korea but also in the south, thus to stitch together a large marketing, communications, and transportation infrastructure in Northeast Asia, tied into the mother country. Taiwan did have heavy industries such as aluminum and electricity generation by the end of the colonial period, but it was much more of a light industrial and agricultural sphere of the Japanese empire, with much of what it produced exported (exporting sugar in great amounts to Japan, for example). This history bequeathed bigness to Korea, small-scale practices to Taiwan.

As Tom Gold (1986) and others have shown, Nationalist rule on Taiwan also brought with it Nationalist methods in the economy—a state-centered rather than firm-centered pattern, often called "bureaucratic capitalism" in the literature. Personal connections in the ruling Kuomintang party were often the avenue to upward economic mobility. An additional Chinese pattern, drawn from the interstitial economic practice of the Chinese diaspora in what Ralph Clough (1978) has aptly called "island China," yielded the family as the prime economic unit, specializing in small business (the stereotypical Chinese laundry or Chinese restaurant throughout the United States is an example of a far wider pattern of family business in Southeast Asia). This tended to promote greater emphasis on small business in Taiwan. Taiwan also sought niches in the world economy, quite like Singapore but quite unlike Korea—the leaders of which always wanted a fully developed industrial structure. For Taiwan, this was something to be accomplished when the mainland was retaken, but not on an island. All of these factors tend toward a divergence in Korean and Taiwan economic practices by the 1980s. But there was still essential similarity up to that point, and great similarity in both cases in regard to something economists do not pay much attention to: security. Here there is also vast difference from the Latin American cases; the relation of these two NICs to the world was also the relation of two highly developed security states to the world, especially in regard to their relations to the United States in the context of the Cold War.

11.3 STATE, INDUSTRY, AND THE POLITICS OF SECURITY IN EAST ASIA

The external context, I emphasized earlier, is of paramount importance in understanding the role of the state in economic development in East Asia, not simply because these states are trading nations but in the sociological sense that the state is situated between, and mediates the relationship between, the domestic and external societies, and that the manner of this articulation tells us much about the efficacy of the state in restructuring the domestic society. This insight, I have argued, is a familiar one for those social scientists writing on Latin America, which is after all the intellectual origination point for dependency theory, proposing a deleterious impact of dependency on the strength of the state and domestic industries.

Strangely enough, external considerations have rarely been part of the discourse on state formation in East Asia, so much so that even the modal paradigm for the East Asian political economy, the so-called "developmental state," is conspicuously silent on the issue. The East Asian developmental state is a world of bureaucrats who, along with business leaders and politicians, pursue a "national interest" that is assumed away in a realm devoid of world politics, the strategic goals of superpowers, the actions of multinational corporations, foreign aid, and so on.[5]

If the American design for East Asia during the Cold War is invoked, one visceral reaction often heard is that South Korea and Taiwan would have developed anyway, with or without the Cold War; it is hard to imagine that the world-beating economic performances of the most educated and hard-working populaces are predicated on, say, foreign aid that seems, elsewhere in the world, of dubious value in ameliorating material conditions. But these are also two states that the United States rescued from certain oblivion in 1950, by fighting the Korean War and interposing the 7th Fleet between Taiwan and the mainland.

Still, in the absence of counterfactual evidence, it is difficult to establish whether geopolitical prerogatives that had the effect of bestowing massive and munificent economic aid to both Taiwan and South Korea were preconditions to growth. But one can make reasonable guesses. Taiwan and South Korea were destitute and enervated in 1950, but perched on the seismic faultline of global politics; their geopolitical situation was both leverage and mortgage to extract maximum "rent" from the global hegemony, with which these states could sustain themselves and incubate the fledgling local capital. In other ways, too, the intensity of security politics was a goad to economic development, as it was for the development of nineteenth-century Germany. Without threats to survival and international competition, a society-wide economic mobilization as occurred in these two countries is hard to imagine and goes some way toward explaining idiosyncratic policy choices.

I will discuss the impact of the Cold War in the following three senses: (1) the role of massive US foreign aid and the Vietnam War, both of which were critical for sustaining postwar security states and jump-starting domestic business; (2) as an important determinant in shifting economic policy orientations; and (3) the institution of the national-security state which was based on a symbiotic relationship between the state and big business, at the expense of labor. Let me discuss them in turn.

The importance of US foreign aid to Taiwan and South Korea cannot be exaggerated. After the Korean War, both Taiwan and South Korea catapulted forward in the American global calculation as bulwarks of anticommunism, whose survival necessitated a massive infusion of capital. In Taiwan over the 1950s economic aid equaled about 6 per cent of GNP and nearly 40 per cent of gross investment, and military aid was even bigger than economic aid (Wade 1990:82). From 1946 to 1976, the United States provided $12.6 billion in economic and military aid to South Korea, and $5.6 billion to Taiwan; combined with additional contributions from Japan and international finance institutions, the total gave South Korea in the midpoint year of 1960 a per capita assistance figure of $600 for three decades, and $425 for Taiwan (Woo 1991:44).

This munificent aid went far toward rehabilitating the recipient countries, helping to stabilize the economy, the society, and the regime; it boosted investor confidence and financed extensive land reforms and other social reforms. It also gave a big push to domestic capitalists who got their start through noncompetitive allocation of import quotas and licenses, access to bank loans, aid funds and material, and the noncompetitive award of government and US military contracts for reconstruction activities (Woo 1991:67).

When the Cold War turned into a regional conflagration in Southeast Asia, US aid to South Korea and Taiwan reversed its historical decline and pumped more resources into these countries. Much as Japan started its postwar take-off with the Korean War, so did Taiwan and South Korea with the Vietnam War. Taiwan benefited from American purchases of agricultural and industrial commodities, use of military facilities and depots for repair of equipment, designation of Taiwan as a site for R&R, and contract work for and in Vietnam.

South Korea's involvement in Vietnam was more direct, having sent more than 300,000 troops by the time the war was over; this was more men per capita than any nation in the world, including the United States. The total cost to the United States of equipping and paying for these was "peanuts compared to what it would be for a comparable number of Americans," but those "peanuts" went a long way to finance Korea's take-off. The total economic and military aid that Korea received as a direct payment for partaking in the Vietnam War came to more than one billion dollars (Woo 1991:93–94).

Less well studied than the direct impact of monetary infusion in East Asia was the role of foreign aid in programmatic shifts in economic policy. To the extent that this is studied, focus has been on the salutary impact of American economic advisors prodding Taiwan and South Korea in the direction of liberalization and export orientation, celebrated by Anne Krueger (1979:82) as "the most dramatic and vivid change in any developing countries since World War II." There is of course truth to that: the Economic Cooperation Administration (ECA) had its biggest operation in South Korea, and the US Agency for International Development shipped off the best and brightest of economic experts to Seoul and Taipei to forge new economic orders. But the Cold War also pushed these countries in other directions, what we might call "the political economy of import substitution industrialization in East Asia," to paraphrase Albert O. Hirschman.

The argument I wish to advance here is that the early phase of ISI in South Korea and Taiwan for much of the 1950s was not an ill-thought-out outcome of home-grown economists (or even a well-thought-out policy in a decade where ISI was a developmental norm and not an aberration) but a catch-as-catch-can political solution to sink foreign aid dollars in infrastructural and industrial development and keep the foreign aid tap open. Open trade or export orientation as a way to earn foreign currency was fiercely resisted, especially as it involved the American effort to create a viable regional market to revive the Japanese economy. Both Chiang and Rhee were aware of the American plan to solve two intractable problems at once—the revival of the Japanese economy, and the maintenance of viability in the two Cold War wards—by linking them in a regional market, which meant recycling US aid dollars in Taiwan and South Korea to purchase goods from Japan: a specter of another Co-Prosperity Sphere. This resistance worked, as did the resulting program of ISI (at least for some years). In the end, however, this policy of making Korea and Taiwan another Japan, while keeping the real Japan at bay (all of it succored by an indulgent America), could not stand. The Decade of Mutual Security was coming to an end, and with it a precipitous reduction in aid toward South Korea and Taiwan; Taiwan was forced to turn outward by the end of the 1950s, and South Korea by the beginning of the 1960s (the South Korean delay had to do with the uncertainty caused by the *coup d'état* in 1961).

If the first phase of ISI in the 1950s was politically motivated, the second phase in the 1970s was no less so and coincided with another shift in hegemonic policy and its adverse effects on the security of South Korea and Taiwan. The new world according to Richard Nixon was an unfriendly and minatory one for the allies, where God only helped those who helped themselves: the Nixon doctrine wrote off Indochina, and shoved off (through protectionism) economic parvenues such as Taiwan and Korea, and further brought mainland China to international limelight and respectability. In what were perceived to be the waning days of the Pax Americana, the first goal in South Korea was to purge all uncertainties from the body politic by tightening the grip of authoritarian politics, and with the steering mechanism thus made predictable, to veer toward the Big Push: massive investments in steel, shipbuilding, machine building, chemicals, and metals. The development of heavy industries also held the promise of a vibrant defense industry, thus to end the reliance on American largess in weaponry and various attendant political kibitzing that came with it.

This conception of national security in the South Korean context meant a clear departure from the export-oriented, non-sectoral biased strategy adopted throughout the 1960s. As Yoon Je Cho argues in this volume (Chapter 7), it also meant that the liberal financial reforms of the mid-1960s came to a grinding halt, replaced by an intensified policy of "financial repression." The nature of these repressive financial policies is well described by Cho and need not detain us. The important point for the purpose of this chapter is to underscore the profound impact of this "financial repression" on reconfiguring the class structure in South Korea, giving a huge boost to a constellation of domestic enterprises, marking their birth as world-class conglomerates. It also altered the nature of the state's relationship to big business, eliminating any arm's-length relationship that might have existed between the state and business.

In a nutshell, what the financial policy of credit allocation and low interest rates—lower than the rate of inflation throughout the 1970s—meant was that bank loans (in the context of the virtually absent equity market) became subsidies for the chosen: the entrepreneurs who had already proven their mettle through good export records, the risktakers who entered into heavy and chemical industries, and the faithful who plunged into the untried sea of international competition with new products, relying on the state's good offices to rescue them, should they fail. It was really these entrepreneurs who made possible the Big Push, the drive for industrial maturation.

To join the hallowed, chosen few, enterprises had to be big, but to remain chosen they had to be gigantic: size was an effective deterrent against default, forcing the government into the role of the lender of last resort. The importance of size in this sense cannot be overemphasized, since highly leveraged firms, exposed to the vagaries of the international market, live with a constant specter of default. It was for this reason that the expression "octopus-like spread of the *chaebol*" came into wide circulation in South Korea. But the *chaebol* tentacles gripped not only the economy but the state as well: big state and big business would have to sink or swim together. A credit-based financial system, mediated by an interventionist authoritarian state, became the basis of Korea Inc.

The flipside of the state-big business symbiosis was an effective suppression of popular protests and a thorough evisceration of labor as a political force. This is in stunning contrast to the situation in Western Europe where the development of governmental institutions of representation was powerfully shaped by an effort to cope with such popular sectors. It is also fundamentally dissimilar to the experience of Latin America, where the evolution of corporatist structures was an intellectual solution to the demands of labor, and where economic policies, such as ISI, obtained political legitimacy through populist attempts to redress the gaping economic inequality. True, oppressive political conditions for labor in Taiwan and South Korea are somewhat mitigated by firm-level paternalism; but labor remains weak and systematically excluded in both countries, still shackled by continuing considerations of national security and international economic competitiveness.

Taiwan's political trajectory is a bit different from Korea's; whereas Park Chung Hee had to create strong authoritarian politics through his Korean Central Intelligence Agency (founded in 1961), the 1972 Yushin Constitution, and periodic declarations of martial law, as well as to create a major ruling party governed with authoritarian internal structure (the Democratic Republican Party), Taiwan had had a Leninist-style central party since Russian advisors helped Sun Yat Sen set up the Kuomintang, and after the disorders in 1947 it ruled Taiwan through martial law for the next 40 years. Still, its financial pattern in relation to industrial development was not the same as the one we have seen in the Korean case—but then it never had been, because Taiwan was not a centerpiece of colonial industrial development, as Korea was.

What the foregoing discussion points to is that the contours of state and society in South Korea and Taiwan are powerfully shaped by international conflicts, from the agony caused by late-blooming Japanese imperial ambition, to civil wars, revolutions, and the Cold War. With the easing of Cold War tensions, combined with greater prosperity in Taiwan and South Korea, both the political terror and developmental frenzy are subsiding. The greatest task for the 1990s will be to redress some of the excesses of the past, in the case of Korea to reassess the relationship between the state and business, and in both cases to find ways to institutionalize popular sectors that had shouldered much of the burden of such rapid development.

11.4 THE CULTURE AND IDEOLOGY OF LATE DEVELOPMENT

In light of our discussion of power and plenty in the context of a security state, it would seem superfluous to comment on the issue of ideology and culture. But a brief discussion may be salutary to underscore a few points.

A consideration of culture and ideology as they contribute to a collective national goal is important. Douglass North (1990:24) writes that without a theory of culture and ideology it is impossible to construct a theory of economic change. Yet when culture is invoked in the East Asian context, it is always in terms of a residual "Confucianism" that is unchanging and overdetermined. East Asian culture often strikes people as something fundamentally different, to the degree that America's premier strategic thinker, Samuel Huntington (1993), argued that Confucian culture was irreconcilably alien to that in the "West." The retinue of these allegedly profound differences often blinds us to the point developed in this chapter: that economic growth in East Asia is not culturally determined, but developed out of a particular late-developing regional context, a particular place called Northeast Asia at a particular time called the Cold War. Furthermore the pursuit of power and prestige, either in the context of the security state or in the context of catching up with the rest of the world, or indeed both, is vastly more effective in harnessing developmental energy than a general appeal to increased welfare, *à la* Latin American "populism"—and this is also a matter of the "culture" of development.

11.5 CONCLUSION

In this conclusion I wish to make two points. One is the often-heard argument that the developmental experience cannot be replicated because of the difference in historical circumstances. Sometimes this argument is nothing but a tautology (they are different because they are different), but in another way the argument rings true: the circumstances that produced the

South Korean and Taiwanese states did not burden them with the structural social inequality that has so dogged the Latin American states; and their placement as frontline Cold War states, making resources so readily available to them, is not likely to be repeated elsewhere. Another way of saying this is that the East Asian "developmental states" are really historical and nonreplicable artifacts.

This does not mean, however, that the East Asian experience is bereft of useful lessons for other economies. The genius of the states in South Korea and Taiwan was in harnessing very real fears of war and instability into a developmental energy, which then could become a binding agent for growth. The lesson for other developing countries is that the state must be able to create collective goals—preferably ones that have a competitive context.

Another lesson may be that the states in Taiwan and South Korea did not veer away from their historical nature; they were born strong, and stayed strong, and the goals of their economic policies were plausible to the collective "we." Hence they were successful in generating compliance and sacrifice.

I think this is a salutary point for Latin America, where the economic devastation of the Lost Decade has generated, in combination with the outside influence, a push toward *laissez-faire* economic policies and the reduced state, in radical disregard for a three-decade process of increasing sophistication of Latin American public administration. But as Albert Fishlow (1990) so successfully argues, the 1980s were a clear break from past growth trends and, to the extent that the 1980s underlined the fragility of the state and its inability to respond to the less favorable external constraints, the task for the future ought to be in fine-tuning and reshaping the state as a better regulator and subsidizer—and not throwing the baby out with the bath water.

NOTES

[1] See for instance, World Bank (1993), and the controversy generated by the report, collected in the special issue of *World Development* (1994).

[2] For an elaboration of this definition of the state, see Woo (1991:ch. 4).

[3] For Korea, see Cumings (1981:chs. 4–5); for Taiwan, see Gold (1988).

[4] For a more extensive discussion of the colonial industrialization in Korea, see Woo (1991:ch. 2). Taiwan experienced less coercion and repression than did Korea, mainly because of the much weaker nationalist impulse in Taiwan.

[5] For a criticism of the "developmental state" paradigm for its inward-looking bias, see T. J. Pempel (forthcoming).

REFERENCES

AMSDEN, A. (1989), *Asia's Next Giant*, Oxford University Press, Oxford.

CHANG, H. (1994), *The Political Economy of Industrial Policy*, St. Martin's Press, New York.

CLOUGH, R. (1978), *Island China*, Harvard University Press, Cambridge, Mass.

CUMINGS, B. (1981), *The Origins of the Korean War, I: Liberation and the Emergence of Separate Regimes*, Princeton University Press, Princeton.

DORE, R. (1990), "Reflections on Culture and Change," in G. Gereffi and D. Wyman, eds., *Manufacturing Miracles*, Princeton University Press, Princeton.

FAJNZYLBER, F. (1990), "The United States and Japan as Models of Industrialization," in G. Gereffi and D. Wyman, eds., *Manufacturing Miracles*, Princeton University Press, Princeton.

FISHLOW, A. (1990), "The Latin American State," *Journal of Economic Perspective*, 3:61–74.

GOLD, T. (1986), *State and Society in the Taiwan Miracle*, M. E. Sharpe, Armonk, N.Y.

——(1988), "Colonial Origins of Taiwanese Capitalism," in E. Winkler and S. Greenhalgh, eds., *Contending Approaches to the Political Economy of Taiwan*, M. E. Sharpe, Armonk, N.Y.

HIRSCHMAN, A. (1945), *National Power and the Structure of Foreign Trade*, University of California Press, Berkeley.

——(1968), "The Political Economy of Import-Substitution Industrialization in Latin America," *Quarterly Journal of Economics*, 1:1–32.

HUNTINGTON, S. (1993), "The Clash of Civilizations?" *Foreign Affairs*, 3:22–49.

JANSEN, M. (1968), "Modernization and Foreign Policy in Meiji Japan," in R. Wald, ed., *Political Development in Modern Japan*, Princeton University Press, Princeton.

KEYNES, J. M. (1936), *The General Theory of Employment, Interest, and Money*, Macmillan, London.

KRASNER, S. (1985), *Structural Conflict: The Third World Against Global Liberalism*, University of California Press, Berkeley.

KRUEGER, A. (1979), *The Developmental Role of the Foreign Sector and Aid*, Harvard University Press, Cambridge, Mass.

NELSON, R. and WINTER, S. (1982), *An Evolutionary Theory of Economic Change*, Belknap Press, Cambridge, Mass.

NORTH, D. (1990), *Institutions, Institutional Change and Economic Perspective*, Cambridge University Press, Cambridge.

PEMPEL, T. J. (forthcoming), "The Developmental Regime in a Changing World Economy," in M. Woo-Cumings, ed., *The Developmental State in Comparative Perspective*.

SCHNEIDER, B. (1991), *Politics within the State: Elite Bureaucrats and Industrial Policy in Authoritarian Brazil*, University of Pittsburgh Press, Pittsburgh.

WADE, R. (1990), *Governing the Market*, Princeton University Press, Princeton.

WOO, J. (Woo-Cumings, M.) (1991), *Race to the Swift: State and Finance in Korean Industrialization*, Columbia University Press, New York.

WOO-CUMINGS, M. (1995), "Developmental Bureaucracy in Comparative Perspec-

tive," in H.-K. Kim, M. Muramatsu, T. J. Pempel, and K. Yamamura, eds., *Japanese Civil Service and Economic Development: Catalysts of Change*, Oxford University Press, Oxford.
World Bank (1993), *The East Asian Miracle*, Oxford University Press, Oxford.
—— *World Development* (1994), 4:615–54.

12

Rents and Development in Multiethnic Malaysia

JOMO K. S. AND EDMUND TERENCE GOMEZ

The neoclassical "counter-revolution" against the rise of development economics (Toye 1987) in the last two decades has focused attention on the alleged wastefulness of distortionary state interventions. The general contention is that development economics exaggerated market failures and provided the rationale for ostensibly developmentalist state interventions by ignoring and underestimating the resultant state failures and their consequences. Most importantly, government interventions have allegedly distorted market processes, causing disequilibrium, undermining competition, and creating rents, which, in turn, encourage wasteful rent-seeking behavior. The state's active participation in the economy is generally seen as significantly affecting the process and pattern of wealth accumulation, involving serious "distortions" to what might be considered the (usually imaginary) "normal" outcome of market operations.

However, while implementation of state policies—necessarily involving wealth or rent-appropriating opportunities—can result in unproductive, corrupt, and wasteful activities in politically modified markets, state intervention can also reshape growth and accumulation processes to facilitate the emergence and development of new economic activities (for example, economic diversification or industrialization), or to favor particular demographic groups (for example, politically favored ethnic, religious, linguistic, regional, or gender groups). Thus, limitations on competition could be necessary and desirable to achieve desired growth as well as distributive goals. Such distortions are recognized, for example, to have been important in facilitating late industrialization in continental Europe, the United States, and Japan in the nineteenth century, as well as similar ambitions in this century, mainly in Japan and former colonial countries.

The "infant industry" argument, for instance, views such protection for new industries as necessary, but temporary, in order to protect those industries until such time that they "grow up" by becoming internationally competitive. Unfortunately, this argument has often been abused in many situations, with many industries protected almost indefinitely; in many instances, protected industries never really had the potential for becoming internationally competitive and were therefore doomed to remain "dwarfs" requiring permanent assistance.

In Northeast Asia, however, it appears that effective protection has generally been conditional upon export performance, hence forcing international exposure upon infant industries almost from the outset, thus helping to ensure their eventual international competitiveness. This argument is most often invoked to support and protect the emergence and consolidation of desirable strategic new industries, which could then stimulate the emergence and development of other desired new industries, that could, in turn, transform a national economy's profile of comparative advantage.

Contrary to the myth that import-substituting industrial policy has been distortionary while export-oriented industrialization has not, it has been shown that both types of industries have benefited from and developed on the basis of various investment incentives provided by governments (for a Malaysian case study, see Rasiah 1996). While these incentives have been different in nature, and hence have had different consequences (e.g., in terms of international trade distortions), all such incentives involve rents and distortions. Bhagwati has recognized this to be true for South Korea, though he finesses it by suggesting that export promotion measures negate the distortionary consequences of import substitution efforts, with near neutral consequences, approximating a "simulated free market" situation (see Wade 1990).

Rents have also been allocated to achieve explicit redistributive objectives, though the very exercise of rent allocation is, of course, redistributive in nature. Thus, while deliberate distortionary interventions favoring investments to achieve growth or developmentalist goals, such as economic diversification or industrialization, can be promoted, such distortionary interventions could just as well only be redistributive in intent, for example, among regions, ethnic or religious groups, and age cohorts, or between genders. Such measures could redistribute economic resources or just entitlements and income flows, with varying implications and consequences. For instance, enhancement of the human resources of a particular demographic group would have different implications for growth, equity, and sustainability than would enhancing the property rights of a select few from that community.

Khan (1989) has made the useful analytical distinction between what he terms corruption and clientelism, where the former merely involves rent transfers, albeit of a morally repugnant nature for some. He argues that corruption in South Korea may be seen as a bargaining outcome between state decision makers and coalitions of beneficiaries, with losses due to the substantial rent-seeking possibilities generally more than offset by gains from the restrictions imposed by the state. In contrast, patron-client relations in Bangladesh are seen as clientelist, where the client bargains for resources on the basis of an organizational ability to disrupt income flows to the patron, due to weak asset rights owing to limited state enforcement capacity, resulting in a loss of resources besides constraining the state to a low level of efficiency.

12.1 MALAYSIAN EXPERIENCE

Because the generation and distribution of rents within a political milieu does not operate in the abstract, but rather is part of a larger framework within which an economy functions and develops, the distribution of rents in the Malaysian context and its impact on the economy are considered in two ways here: first, the ways in which the government has created and allocated rents for postcolonial diversification of the economy, especially to promote industrialization, and second, and "more politically" (mainly because it is explicitly redistributive), the manner in which redistributive goals, especially among ethnic groups, have been pursued. This chapter will thus explore the trade-offs involved between the two—primarily developmentalist and primarily redistributive—types of interventions and the rents created, captured, and deployed therefrom.

To put our discussion of rents in context, some historical and economic background is necessary. The economy of Malaya (as it then was) under British colonialism, which began in 1786, grew impressively to become the empire's single most profitable colony. The economic infrastructure (e.g., railways, roads, ports, utilities, etc.)—so crucial for profitable investment—was generally more developed in Malaya than in most British colonies. Such infrastructure construction was paid for by taxes levied on the population by the colonial government. Colonial monopolies thwarted the development of a local capitalist class producing for the domestic market; instead, local businesses found it more profitable to engage in production for export, commerce, and usury. Malays remained largely marginal to the growing capitalist sector, with the elite integrated into the colonial state apparatus, and the masses remaining in the countryside as peasants. Instead, emerging business opportunities were mainly taken by some of the more urbanized and commercially better connected Chinese.

Although the Malaysian economy has changed significantly since independence in 1957, the many existing differences reflecting uneven development can be traced to the crucial formative decades under colonial rule which shaped the economic structure. For instance, the differences between the east coast and the west coast can be traced to uneven regional growth dating back to the location of the early tin mines, colonial annexation, and infrastructure development on the west coast, as well as subsequent growth building upon existing advantages. Similarly, differences between the rice-growing north and the rest of the peninsula are related to demographic history as well as the British policy of preserving Malay peasants as rice farmers, despite the rational peasant preference for rubber cultivation, which threatened British plantation interests; the urban–rural gap is, of course, related to the typical roles of town and country in capital accumulation. The relative backwardness of the peasantry compared to plantations is only the most obvious of various differences in the rural economy. Ethnic differences often coincide with class and occupational differences originating in the colonial economy.

Helped by favorable commodity prices and some early success in import-substituting industrialization, the Malayan and then the Malaysian economy sustained a high growth rate with low inflation until the early 1970s. Official statistics for 1957 and 1970 point to a worsening distribution of income over the 1960s, a growing gap between town and country and growing inequality among all the major ethnic groups, with inequality within the Malay community increasing most—from a situation of least intra-ethnic inequality in 1957 to one of greatest inequality in 1970. However, this growing inequality not only resulted in growing interclass tensions, but was primarily perceived in racial terms, not least because of political mobilization along ethnic lines. Hence, Malay resentment of domination by capital was expressed primarily against ethnic Chinese, who comprise the bulk of businessmen, while non-Malay frustrations were directed against the Malay-dominated postcolonial state machinery widely identified with the United Malays' National Organization (UMNO), the dominant partner in the ruling Barisan Nasional (National Front) coalition.

Such popular ethnic perceptions resulted in widespread racially inspired opposition to the ruling government of the 1960s. The decade was marked by an import-substituting industrialization program that generated relatively little employment and petered out by the mid-1960s, and rural development efforts that emphasized productivity increases while avoiding redistribution in favor of the poorly capitalized, land-hungry peasantry. The general election results and "race riots" of May 1969 reflected the ethnic dimensions of the new postcolonial socioeconomic class structure. Meanwhile, the emerging Malay middle class, who had nominal political control, perceived the gradual decline of British economic hegemony giving way to Chinese ascendance. This "political-bureaucratic" fraction became more assertive from the mid-1960s, establishing clearer dominance after May 1969.

Malaysia's export-led growth record in the last century has been quite impressive. During colonial times, Malaya was, by far, Britain's most profitable colony, credited with providing much of the export earnings that financed British postwar reconstruction. The colonial authorities, who generally considered the colonies as suppliers of raw materials and importers of manufactured goods, allowed only a few types of industries to develop. Most industries then were set up to reduce transport costs of exported or imported goods, such as factories for refining tin ore and bottling imported drinks. Local industries developed most when economic relations with the colonial powers were weak, e.g., during the Great Depression and the Japanese Occupation.

To understand the nature of state interventions, it is useful to consider them in their larger context. For this purpose, it is convenient to distinguish the following five periods to appreciate the origins and significance of various interventions since the late colonial period. Such an overview also offers more understanding of the circumstances in which policies have been made and implemented.

Late Colonial Period, c1950–1957

In the face of a communist-led insurgency, the British colonial government initiated social reforms, including rural development efforts to consolidate a Malay yeoman peasantry, protect labor, and allow limited popular political participation through elections. Many redistributive efforts undertaken by postcolonial governments have actually built upon and elaborated reforms dating from this period.

Postcolonial Conservatism (Tunku Abdul Rahman, 1957–1969)

After independence, generally *laissez-faire* policies were pursued—with some "mild" import-substituting industrialization, some agricultural diversification, greater rural development efforts, and modest but increasing ethnic affirmative action policies. Government intervention was limited and constrained by a conservative fiscal policy as well as by the commitment to preserving existing property rights inherited from the colonial period.

Growing State Intervention (Razak, 1969–1976; Hussein, 1976–1981)

The New Economic Policy (NEP)—ostensibly to improve interethnic relations through poverty reduction and interethnic economic redistribution—provided the legitimization for increasing state intervention and public-sector expansion, especially to create a Malay business community and middle class; export-oriented industrialization succeeded in reducing unemployment, while increased petroleum revenues financed rapidly growing public expenditure.

Heavy Industrialization (Mahathir, 1981–1985)

In the face of declining private, including foreign, investments, countercyclical public expenditure expansion from 1980 was followed by increased fiscal discipline from mid-1982, but through government-sponsored joint ventures with Japanese partners, technology and finance were obtained to develop heavy industries—constituting a second round of import-substitution.

Partial Economic Liberalization (Mahathir, 1986–present)

In the mid-1980s, the Malaysian economy was in a severe recession, which was exacerbated by fiscal and debt crises, problems with heavy industries, as well as massive ringgit depreciation. The situation was compounded by a political crisis involving a power struggle between Mahathir and some of his senior party leaders which the prime minister barely managed to stave off. Various measures of economic liberalization were subsequently promoted, including privatization, improved official support for the private sector, increased investment incentives, and reduced regressive "supply-side-oriented" tax reforms. Export-oriented industrialization, with increased investments from East Asia, has sustained rapid growth since 1987. After 1990, the initially tentative efforts at economic liberalization were consolidated and reiterated as part of a modernizing, industrializing national vision to achieve developed country status by the year 2020. Privatization has been effectively deployed to create a more competent, politically influential, new rentier elite in the private sector.

Various tables provide details illustrating the main economic trends identified in this chapter; these include some macroeconomic features of the Malaysian economy in the postcolonial period showing rapid growth in relation to a changing public-private mix (Table 12.1), rapid structural change (Table 12.2), the rapidly changing composition of exports (Table 12.3), the growth of public expenditure in the 1970s and early 1980s (Table 12.4), and the primarily "economic" and "social" (rather than "security") orientation of public expenditure (Table 12.5). The changing ethnic distributions of corporate wealth (Table 12.6), the significant reduction in poverty over the 1970s and 1980s (Table 12.7), and changing ethnic distributions in the professions (Table 12.8) together suggest significant progress in reducing interethnic economic differentials. Thus, the tables illustrate the arguments in the text, suggesting the successful deployment of rents to achieve specific policy objectives, particularly growth of the manufacturing sector and interethnic redistribution.

12.2 POST-COLONIAL ECONOMIC DIVERSIFICATION

After independence in 1957, and especially during the 1960s, the Malaysian economy diversified from the twin pillars of the colonial economy, rubber and tin. The Malaysian economy continued to experience rapid economic growth in the first quarter-century after independence (see Table 12.1). The average annual growth rate of the gross domestic product (GDP) in Penin-

TABLE 12.1 Gross National Product by Expenditure Category, 1956–1994 (percentages)

	1956–60[a]	1961–65	1966–70	1971–75	1976–80	1981–85	1986–90	1991–94
Consumption	79.2	82.4	79.9	77.3	69.9	72.8	69.6	67.3
Private[b]	64.5	66.8	63.0	59.9	53.3	55.1	54.0	53.5
Public	14.7	15.6	16.9	17.4	16.6	17.7	15.6	13.8
Investment	12.6	16.8	17.0	25.7	27.2	35.7	29.3	36.5
Private	9.9	9.5	11.0	17.8	17.3	18.1	18.0	24.3
Public	2.7	7.3	6.0	7.9	9.9	17.6	11.3	12.2
Net Foreign Trade	8.2	0.8	3.1	–3.0	2.9	–8.5	6.9	0.9
Gross National Savings[c]	16.6	15.3	18.0	22.0	29.8	27.1	30.9	32.3

Notes: [a] Peninsular Malaysia only.
[b] Includes inventories.
[c] Gross capital formation plus balance on current account of the balance of payments.

Sources: Bank Negara Malaysia, *Money and Banking in Malaysia*, table 1.9.
Malaysia (1986).
Ministry of Finance, Malaysia, *Economic Report*, various issues.
Bank Negara Malaysia, *Annual Report*, various issues.

sular Malaysia was 5.8 per cent during the years 1957–70 (Rao 1980), while the GDP for the whole of Malaysia rose by an average of 7.8 per cent per year between 1971 and 1980 (Malaysia 1981). Malaysia's considerable export earnings ensured that it did not suffer from shortages of either savings or foreign exchange, contributing to investments, growth, and structural change.

Primary commodity production continued to dominate the economy in the early years after independence. However, in view of colonial Malaya's heavy dependence on rubber and tin export earnings, following sharp rubber price fluctuations during the 1950s and in anticipation of the inevitable exhaustion of tin deposits, diversification of the economy upon decolonization seemed imperative.

However, economic diversification remained limited before the 1970s (see Table 12.2). Thus, despite the promotion of import-substituting industrialization and the uncertainties that overdependence on tin and rubber production posed for the economy, these commodities remained the mainstays of the country's economy at the end of the 1960s. From 1951 to 1969, in spite of declining rubber exports due to falling prices, among other reasons, rubber and tin still accounted for almost 80 per cent of Malaysia's gross export earnings (see Table 12.3). The continued dominance of foreign capital meant that the surplus generated was often channeled overseas.

In 1957 the primary sector (agriculture and mining) accounted for 45 per cent of the GDP, the tertiary sector (services) for 44 per cent, and the secondary sector (manufacturing and construction) for only 11 per cent (see Table 12.2); by the late 1960s, there had been little structural change in the economy in terms of either relative production shares or employment. Efforts were stepped up to diversify agricultural exports in the early 1970s. Cocoa and palm oil production, for example, were encouraged with crop-specific incentives, with Malaysia going on to become the world's largest exporter of both agricultural products.

Thus, Malaysia extended its colonial global preeminence in rubber, tin, and pepper to palm oil, tropical hardwoods, and cocoa through diversifica-

TABLE 12.2 Gross Domestic Product by Sector, 1955–1994 (percentages)

	1955[a]	1960[a]	1965	1970	1975	1980	1985	1990	1994
Agriculture	40.2	40.5	31.5	30.8	27.7	22.8	20.7	18.7	14.8
Mining	6.3	6.1	9.0	6.3	4.6	10.0	10.4	9.8	7.5
Manufacturing	8.2	8.6	10.4	13.4	16.4	20.0	19.6	26.9	31.5
Nontradables	45.3	44.8	49.1	51.3	49.5	47.2	49.3	46.1	48.8

Note: [a] Peninsular Malaysia only.
Sources: Bank Negara Malaysia, *Money and Banking in Malaysia*, table 1.2.
Ministry of Finance, Malaysia, *Economic Report*, various issues.
Bank Negara Malaysia, *Annual Report*, various issues.

TABLE 12.3 Exports by Major Groups, 1960–1993

	1960	1965	1970	1975	1980	1985	1990	1993
Agriculture	66.1	54.5	59.2	52.8	43.6	32.7	22.3	15.3
Rubber	55.1	38.6	33.4	21.9	16.4	7.6	3.8	1.7
Timber	5.3	9.5	16.5	12.0	14.1	10.3	8.9	6.1
Palm oil	2.0	3.1	5.3	15.4	10.3	11.8	6.2	5.2
Others	3.7	3.3	4.0	3.5	2.8	3.0	3.4	2.3
Minerals	22.2	30.0	25.9	22.6	33.8	34.0	17.8	9.4
Tin	14.0	23.1	19.6	13.1	8.9	4.3	1.1	0.4
Petroleum	4.0	2.3	3.9	9.3	23.8	22.9	13.4	6.6
Liquefied Natural Gas	—	—	—	—	—	6.0	2.8	2.1
Others	4.2	4.6	2.4	0.2	1.1	0.8	0.5	0.3
Manufactures	8.5	12.2	11.9	21.4	21.6	32.1	59.3	74.3
Other exports	3.2	3.3	3.0	3.2	1.0	1.2	10.6	1.0
Total	100.0	100.0	100.0	100.0	100.0	100.0	100.0	100.0

Sources: Tan Tat Wai (1985).
Bank Negara Malaysia, *Annual Report*, various issues.

tion of primary sector production. Petroleum exports have been growing since the mid-1970s (see Table 12.3), and petroleum gas as well as cocoa production have become increasingly significant since the early 1980s. Since the late 1960s, the export orientation of the Malaysian economy has been sustained by Malaysia's new industries, which have been largely export oriented.

Meanwhile, biased and conservative postcolonial rural development efforts contrasted with British colonial neglect, especially in the pre-World War II period. Initially, such government efforts were aimed at consolidating a politically loyal Malay yeoman peasantry for counterinsurgency purposes in the late colonial period and to capture the rural vote after independence. Since the early 1980s, however, more official attention has been given to the development of commercial agriculture—involving larger farms using more profitable, productivity-raising, and cost-saving modern management methods—for export markets.

In the mid-1970s, petroleum production—off the east coast of Peninsular Malaysia—began providentially, as oil prices soared after 1973. Since the early 1980s, petroleum gas production—almost exclusively for the Japanese economy—has come onstream, offering yet another primary commodity engine for the future growth of the Malaysian economy.

12.3 IMPORT-SUBSTITUTING INDUSTRIALIZATION

Besides retaining the open, export-oriented economy following independence in 1957, the government also promoted some import-substituting industrialization (ISI) to encourage industries to manufacture goods previously imported. The most important incentive for such industries was probably the tariff protection the government offered. From 1958, the Pioneer Industries Ordinance offered tax relief on profits for new, mainly import-substituting manufacturing firms, the length of such relief dependent on the size of a company's investments. While this legislation involving tax incentives tended to reflect infant-industry protection arguments and was legislated to be temporary (though, in practice, it could be extended through various means), tariff protection tended to be more longstanding in nature. The investment incentives were also not structured to encourage eventual exports of initially import-substituting manufacturing.

The government also promoted ISI by offering infrastructure and credit facilities. Total public development expenditure for infrastructure, particularly for transport, power, and communications, was increased (see Table 12.4). Under the First and Second Malaya Plans (1955–65) and the First

TABLE 12.4 Public Sector Expenditure as a Percentage of Gross Domestic Product, 1971–1994

Year	General Government Expenditure[a]			Non-financial Public Enterprises (NFPE) Expenditure			Total Public Sector Expenditure
	Current	Development	Total	Current	Development	Total	
1971	21.2	9.7	30.9	3.1	1.2	4.3	35.2
1972	24.8	10.4	35.2	4.6	1.1	5.7	40.9
1973	20.6	7.2	27.8	3.3	1.3	4.6	32.4
1974	21.0	8.7	29.7	3.7	1.5	5.2	34.9
1975	24.9	11.0	35.9	4.1	2.1	6.2	42.1
1976	23.3	9.5	32.8	3.8	2.3	6.1	38.9
1977	25.8	10.7	36.5	3.0	2.1	5.1	41.6
1978	23.7	10.9	34.6	2.4	1.6	4.0	38.6
1979	24.9	10.2	35.1	3.2	2.0	5.2	40.3
1980	28.1	15.2	43.3	9.2	3.9	12.1	55.4
1981	29.9	22.5	52.4	14.0	4.0	18.0	70.1
1982	29.0	19.4	48.4	15.1	6.5	21.6	70.0
1983	28.5	15.6	44.1	14.6	9.4	24.0	68.1
1984	27.1	12.0	39.1	15.0	8.4	23.4	62.5
1985	29.5	10.2	39.7	15.3	9.7	25.0	64.7
1986	31.7	12.1	31.5	26.4	7.6	28.0	65.5
1987	37.9	10.9	48.8	30.2	4.8	35.0	83.8
1988	37.2	13.4	50.6	31.1	5.6	36.7	87.3
1989	26.9	10.3	37.2	28.1	4.6	32.7	69.8
1990	26.2	12.2	38.4	27.9	3.9	31.8	70.2
1991	23.8	10.2	34.0	26.2	4.0	30.2	64.2
1992	26.1	9.3	35.4	22.5	4.6	27.2	62.6
1993	23.7	8.6	32.3	22.1	5.1	27.2	59.5
1994	22.7	9.5	32.2	19.8	6.7	26.5	58.5

Note: [a] "General government" refers to the federal government, state governments, and four local governments.
Source: Ministry of Finance, Malaysia, *Economic Report*, various years.

Malaysia Plan (1966–70), almost half of the total public development expenditure was invested in developing such infrastructure (Schatzl 1988:35). (see Table 12.5).

With the government providing lucrative opportunities, foreign manufacturing investment in the country grew, though ISI in Malaysia was initially led by British investors anxious to preserve, if not expand, their market shares from the colonial period. British capital in Malaysia increased from RM946.9 million to RM1,439.8 million between 1960 and 1971, i.e., by 77 per cent during a period of relatively low inflation (Junid 1980:25). Since the incentives provided by the government tended to favor large, capital-intensive, foreign companies, the development of domestic industries remained limited; their development was also restrained by the government's continued commitment to economic openness and by Malay concern that ethnic Chinese would be the primary beneficiaries of protected domestic industrialization. The extent of domestic capital participation in Malaysian ISI in the 1960s was thus rather minimal, primarily involving ethnic Chinese in relatively simple food, plastic, and wood-based industries. With limited incentives and support from the government, the manufacturing and technological base developed by Malaysians then continued to remain small and often dependent on foreign technology (Khor 1983:25).

Most of the import-substituting industries established by foreign companies were, however, set up as their subsidiaries merely to finish goods produced with imported materials or to replace imports of finished goods with imports of semifinished goods for very profitable sale within the protected domestic market. The automobile assembly industry, for example, simply replaced imports of finished cars with imports of kits to be assembled in Malaysia. Furthermore, the technologies used were imported from the parent companies abroad and were capital-intensive; hence, while wages increased, not many workers were required. These capital-intensive industries thus tended to generate relatively little employment, allowing overall unemployment to rise.

The size of the local market was also limited by the level and distribution of income, which reflected the pace and nature of economic growth in the country (Jomo 1990:12). Facing rapid population growth and a decline in international demand for agricultural products, increases in incomes in the 1960s were heavily skewed, perpetuating widespread poverty and growing inequality. Despite fairly steady and relatively high economic growth and low inflation in the first dozen years after independence, income inequalities increased, while ISI failed to sustain its momentum and to significantly reduce unemployment (Jomo and Ishak, 1986). The size of the local market was clearly limited by the level and distribution of income.

With the profitability of manufacturing activities largely due to protection as well as other incentives provided by the government, companies were quite prepared to offer influential, usually ethnic Malay politicians or

TABLE 12.5 Sectoral Allocations in Malaysian Development Plans, 1950–1995 (%)

	DDP (1950–55)		FFYP (1956–60)		SFYP (1961–65)		1MP (1966–70)		2MP (1971–75)		3MP (1976–80)		4MP (1981–85)		5MP (1986–90)		6MP (1991–95)
	Plan	Actual	Plan	Actual	Plan	Actual	Plan	Actual	Plan	Actual	Plan	Actual	Plan	Actual	Plan	Actual	Plan
Economic sector	90.6	91.9	69.2	78.9	68.8	66.5	59.0	63.3	71.6	72.3	59.3	64.0	60.6	75.3	76.0	64.8	56.8
Agriculture	22.4	26.0	23.1	23.6	25.5	17.7	23.2	26.3	23.1	21.7	20.8	22.1	16.4	11.8	17.2	20.8	16.4
Infrastructure	68.2	85.9	44.7	54.0	42.1	46.6	33.9	33.7	32.8	34.1	24.8	26.6	29.8	36.2	44.7	32.8	30.0
Industry	n.a.	n.a.	1.4	1.3	1.2	2.2	1.9	3.3	15.7	16.5	13.7	15.3	14.4	27.3	14.1	11.3	10.5
Social sector	9.4	8.1	18.5	14.4	22.8	15.6	21.4	17.8	14.0	13.7	17.6	17.2	21.7	13.5	13.1	24.8	24.5
Education	6.0	5.5	8.3	6.3	12.1	8.9	10.3	7.8	7.4	6.9	6.9	7.3	9.3	6.3	8.1	16.1	15.5
Health	2.2	3.1	4.3	1.3	6.7	3.8	4.2	3.5	2.2	1.8	1.7	1.5	1.6	1.0	1.0	2.6	4.1
Housing	1.2	n.a.	5.9	6.8	3.7	2.6	4.6	4.9	2.3	2.4	5.5	6.1	8.3	5.3	2.9	4.1	1.5
Other services	n.a.	n.a.	n.a.	n.a.	0.3	0.3	2.3	1.6	2.1	2.7	3.5	2.3	2.5	0.8	1.1	1.9	3.5
General	n.a.		12.3	6.7	8.4	17.9	19.0	18.9	14.4	14.8	23.1	18.8	17.7	11.2	10.9	10.4	18.7
Administration	n.a.	n.a.		6.7	4.1	6.3	2.8	3.2	3.6	3.6	2.8	2.2	1.8	1.1	4.0	7.2	15.3
Security		n.a.	n.a.		4.3	11.6	16.2	15.7	10.8	10.4	20.3	16.6	15.9	10.1	6.8	3.2	3.4
Total	100.0	100.0	100.0	100.0	100.0	100.0	100.0	100.0	100.0	100.0	100.0	100.0	100.0	100.0	100.0	100.0	100.0

Note: DDP = Draft Development Plan; FFYP = First Five-Year Plan; SFYP = Second Five-Year Plan; 1MP = First Malaysia Plan; 2MP = Second Malaysia Plan; 3MP = Third Malaysia Plan; 4MP = Fourth Malaysia Plan; 5MP = Fifth Malaysia Plan; 6MP = Sixth Malaysia Plan. n.a. = not available.

Source: Calculated from Malaysia Plan documents.

former civil servants minority ownership and directorships on the boards of subsidiary companies in Malaysia. The enhanced political clout thus secured provided political access and protection. In these circumstances, the expenditure of resources to protect their markets and to enjoy other incentives in Malaysia was a small price to pay for the handsome monopoly profits to be enjoyed (Edwards and Jomo 1993:330–34). Thus, in the Malaysian situation, the main beneficiaries of most of the rents deployed to promote industrialization were the foreign (mainly British and later Japanese) and Chinese-Malaysian investors—as well as their mainly ethnic Malay politician and bureaucrat allies—who dominated the first round of import substitution in the 1960s.

12.4 EXPORT-ORIENTED INDUSTRIALIZATION

By the mid-1960s, the problems of ISI had become quite apparent. In 1965, the Federal Industrial Development Authority (FIDA) (now known as MIDA, the Malaysian Industrial Development Authority) was set up to encourage industrial investment. By this time, many transnational corporations, in order to reduce production costs, were planning to relocate their more labor-intensive production processes abroad, often in Latin America or East Asia. Foreign experts and international consultants encouraged the Malaysian government to switch to export-oriented industrialization (EOI), which it did in the late 1960s.

Thus, as in the rest of East Asia, with the exhaustion of ISI, the government began to promote EOI, although no significant attempt was made to reduce or remove the incentives provided during its active promotion of ISI. In 1968 the Pioneer Industries Ordinance was replaced by the more wide-ranging Investment Incentives Act which provided tax holidays to approved firms for up to eight years. Among other incentives offered under the Act were income tax exemption for the employment of at least a certain number of workers (to encourage employment), exemption from import duties on capital equipment and raw materials for export-oriented production, investment tax credits, other export incentives, and accelerated depreciation allowances; a new tariff policy on imported consumer goods was also adopted to continue to protect the domestic market (Khor 1983:48).

The labor laws were also amended in 1969 to help create more attractive labor regulations and industrial relations for such industries (see Jomo and Todd 1994). These new export-oriented industries seeking cheap labor succeeded in reducing unemployment at the expense of wages until the tighter labor market pushed wages back up in the late 1970s and early 1980s, and again from the late 1980s.

Under the Free Trade Zone Act of 1971, new industrial estates or export processing zones known as free trade zones (FTZ) were established to encourage investments, particularly from companies manufacturing for export. The Act provided exemptions from customs regulations for FTZ companies for the purpose of importing and exporting equipment, inputs, and outputs for export oriented industries; later, licensed manufacturing warehouses (LMWs) were introduced to allow greater flexibility in the location of such export-oriented industries. Within a decade, FTZ firms came to dominate Malaysian manufactured exports, overtaking the resource-based industries processing raw materials for export.

With the new policy direction, the government continued to rely even more on foreign capital to promote industrialization; it was still wary that growth would otherwise probably contribute more to wealth accumulation among the Chinese (Bowie 1991). Domestic capitalists had even fewer opportunities to benefit from EOI than from ISI. The foreign firms in the FTZs mainly used imported equipment and materials for production and were not under any pressure from the government to set up joint ventures with domestic firms unless they produced for the local market. Thus, foreign firms continued to dominate these industries, especially with their control over technology and marketing (Jomo 1993:6–7).

The promotion of EOI, with its new, attractive investment opportunities, gave fresh impetus to industrial growth. With the incentives provided to promote manufacturing, especially EOI, the average annual growth rate of manufacturing output exceeded 10 per cent between 1970 and 1980, before declining to an average of 4.9 per cent during the years 1981–85, and then rising again after 1986. By the end of the 1970s, manufacturing had become a major net foreign exchange earner, reducing Malaysia's dependence on primary exports; manufacturing's share of Malaysia's GDP more than doubled from 13 per cent in 1970 to 31.5 per cent in 1994 (see Tables 12.2 and 12.3).

However, much export-oriented manufacturing in Malaysia is still limited to the relatively low-skill, labor-intensive aspects of production, e.g., electronic component assembly. Though more skilled and complex production processes have developed, Malaysia remains far from the top of the new international division of labor, in which Singapore, for example, has emerged as a sort of regional center. The potential and likelihood of further progress will be determined by the interests and preferences of foreign investors, especially transnational corporations, and their perceptions of future prospects in host countries such as Malaysia.

Thus, the promotion of export-oriented manufacturing was conceived as distinct from the promotion of import substitution. The result has been a dualism in the manufacturing sector, with the import-substituting sector integrated into the otherwise mainly naturally protected "national economy" involving "nontradables," developing separately from the internationally competitive export-oriented enclaves of FTZs and LMWs. Only resource-based industries, mainly processing primary products for export, involved significant linkages between the two (Jomo and Edwards 1993).

Hence, EOI has significant, but none the less limited, potential for sustained industrial development, especially in view of the foreign dominance as well as the technological and marketing dependence involved in the Malaysian case. Malaysia has undoubtedly been an attractive investment site for foreign investors for a variety of reasons, including its good infrastructure and political stability. However, the primary emphasis on interethnic redistribution in the last quarter-century has strongly affected government investments in education and human-resource development. Consequently, full employment and related wage pressures since the early 1990s may deter investments in more sophisticated industries requiring more technologically skilled workers.

The conclusion of the Uruguay Round of negotiations of the General Agreement on Tariffs and Trade (GATT) is likely to strengthen the various advantages enjoyed by transnational corporations. The agreement on Trade-Related Investment Measures (TRIMs) will eventually eliminate many of the remaining restrictions on foreign investments in Malaysia, while the one on Trade-Related Intellectual Property Rights (TRIPs) will strengthen transnational corporate claims to monopoly rents associated with intellectual property (copyright, patents, trade marks, etc.). Similarly, the General Agreement on Trade in Services (GATS) will eventually remove most obstacles to a greater foreign presence in the Malaysian services sector, including industry-related services. Thus, economic liberalization is likely to further limit the trade policy instruments that might be deployed for the purpose of late industrialization.

12.5 HEAVY INDUSTRIALIZATION

After Mahathir Mohamad took over as the fourth prime minister of the country in mid-1981, the government placed new stress on heavy industrialization in line with his desire to transform Malaysia into a newly industrializing economy. In an attempt to diversify the country's industrial sector while keeping Malaysia's EOI policies in place, he launched his heavy industrialization program in the face of widespread criticism, even from within his own cabinet. If there was a coherent rationale or plan for this major new initiative, it was never disclosed to the public, or even to the cabinet (Chee 1994).

Claiming reluctance on the part of private capitalists to participate in these heavy industry projects in view of the huge capital investments required and their own limited technological expertise (Anuwar 1992), the Mahathir government bypassed the domestic manufacturing sector, though some observers insist that this was yet another deliberate policy of "ethnic

(Chinese) bypass." Instead, the government channeled responsibility to a newly incorporated public sector agency, the Heavy Industries Corporation of Malaysia (HICOM), which mainly collaborated with Japanese companies, to develop a variety of industries, ranging from steel and cement production to the manufacture of a national car. To finance the heavy industrialization initiative, the government resorted to massive borrowings from abroad, again mainly from Japanese official and private sources.

As a result of these investments in heavy industries, public sector investment in commerce and industry leapt from RM0.3 billion in 1978–80 to RM0.9 billion in 1982 and to RM1.5 billion in 1984. Many of the companies established through HICOM, however, turned out to be financially losing concerns, at least in the early years. In 1989 even the government's *Mid-Term Review of the Fifth Malaysia Plan* had conceded that although "the public sector continued to play the leading role in the development of heavy industries . . . in general, the performance of heavy industry projects sponsored by the public sector was far from satisfactory. A number of these projects suffered from heavy financial losses due to the sluggish domestic market and the inability of the industries concerned to compete in international markets" (Malaysia 1989:196). Eventually, the government even brought in Japanese and ethnic Chinese managers to replace the ethnic Malays running the heavy industries that had been established.

While the government had been able to sustain these losses during the early 1980s, its capacity to do so diminished as the economy slipped into recession as well as fiscal and debt crises, the yen appreciated, and actual production operations ran into serious problems in the mid-1980s. Falling oil prices in the early and mid-1980s, the collapse of the tin market in 1985, and the declining prices of Malaysia's other major exports—rubber, cocoa, and palm oil (after 1984)—all contributed to the economy registering minus 1 per cent growth rate in 1985; in the following year, the growth rate was only 1 per cent. Weakening revenue earnings from commodities strengthened the government's resolve to promote manufacturing exports once again.

12.6 INTERETHNIC REDISTRIBUTION

Historically, the significance of redistributive efforts by the state in Malaysia increased with the growing hegemony of UMNO in the ruling Barisan Nasional coalition. By the late 1960s, despite the government's declared desire to promote Bumiputera—the term means indigenous people, and mainly refers to the Malays—capitalism, Malay ownership of assets in the corporate sector did not increase appreciably; Bumiputera ownership of shares in all major sectors of the economy was still insignificant in 1970. Ownership of the economy was still primarily in the hands of

TABLE 12.6 Malaysia: Ownership of Share Capital (at par value) of Limited Companies,[a] 1969–1992

Ownership Group	1969		1970		1971		1975		1980[b]	
	RM mill.	%	RM mill.	%	RM mill.	%	RM mill.	%	RM mill.	%
Malaysian residents	1,746.3	37.9	1,952.1	36.6	2,512.8	38.3	7,047.2	46.7	18,493.4	57.1
Bumiputera individuals and trust agencies(*)	70.6	1.5	125.6	2.4	279.6	4.3	1,394.0	9.2	4,050.5	12.5
Bumiputera individuals[c]	49.3	1.0	84.4	1.6	168.7	2.6	549.8	3.6	1,880.1	5.8
Trust agencies[d](**)	21.3	0.5	41.2	0.8	110.9	1.7	844.2	5.6	2,170.4	6.7
Other Malaysian residents[e]	1,958.0	59.6	1,826.5	34.3	2,223.2	3.9	5,653.2	37.5	14,442.9	44.6
Chinese	1,064.8	22.8	1,450.5	27.2	—	—	—	—	—	—
Indians	41.0	0.9	55.9	1.1	—	—	—	—	—	—
Others	—	—			—	—	—	—	—	—
Nominee companies	98.9	2.1	320.1	6.0	—	—	—	—	—	—
Locally controlled companies	471.0	10.1			—	—	—	—	—	—
Federal and state governments	21.4	0.5	—	—	—	—	—	—	—	—
Foreign residents	2,909.8	62.1	3,377.1	63.4	4,051.3	61.7	8,037.2	53.3	13,927.0	42.9
Share in Malaysian companies	1,235.9	26.4	—	—	2,159.3	32.9	4,722.8	31.3	7,791.2	24.0
Foreign controlled companies in Malaysia	282.3	6.0	—	—	—	—	—	—	—	—
Net assets of local branches[f]	1,391.6	29.7	—	—	1,892.0	28.8	3,314.4	22.0	6,135.8	18.9
Total[g]	3,286.0	100.0	5,329.2	100.0	6,564.1	100.0	15,084.4	100.0	32,420.4	100.0

Notes: [a] The classification of ownership of share capital (at par value) as adopted by Department of Statistics (1969–85) was based on the residential address of the shareholders and not by citizenship. Residents are persons, companies, or institutions that live in or are located in Peninsular Malaysia, Sabah and Sarawak. The definition, therefore, also includes foreign citizens residing in Malaysia.

[b] Figures for 1980 are based on Department of Statistics (1969–85).

[c] Includes institutions channeling funds of individual Bumiputera such as the Muslim Pilgrim Saving and Management Authority(LUTH), MARA Unit Trust Scheme, cooperatives and the ASN scheme.

[d] Shares held through institutions classified as trust agencies such as the National Equity Corporation (PNB), National Corporation (PERNAS), the Council of Trust for Indigenous People (MARA), state economic development corporation (SEDCs), Development Bank of Malaysia (BPMB), Urban Development Authority (UDA), Bank Bumiputera Malaysia Berhad, Kompleks Kewangan Malaysia Berhad (KKMB), and Food Industries of Malaysia (FIMA). Category also includes the amount of equity owned by government through other agencies and companies which have been identified under the Transfer Scheme of Government Equity to Bumiputera.

[e] Includes shares held by nominees and locally controlled companies (LCC). LCC record the total value of share capital of limited companies whose ownership could not be disaggregated further and assigned beyond the second level of ownership, to specific ethnic groups.

foreigners, who held a 60.7 per cent stake in the modern corporate sector, while the Chinese, controlling a significant 22.5 per cent, lagged a distant second. Even with the inclusion of shares owned by government agencies, Bumiputera control of the economy stood at only a meager 2.4 per cent (see Table 12.6).

In addition, Malays were largely outside the modern, urban, and corporate sectors, with very few businessmen or managers outside the public sector (see Table 12.6); the main occupations of the community continued to be largely in low-productivity peasant agriculture and the public sector. Between 1957 and 1970, there was an overall increase in income inequality among all ethnic groups, with the greatest increase among ethnic Malays (Jomo and Ishak 1986).

The redistributive commitment of the Malaysian government—particularly, but not only along interethnic lines—was enhanced from the early 1970s, and has, arguably, been the primary consideration in state

1982		1983		1985		1988		1990		1992	
RM mill.	%	RM mill.	%	RM mill.	%	RM mill.	%	RM mill.	%	RM mill.	%
31,903.5	65.3	33,010.6	66.4	57,666.6	74.0	73,889.2	75.4	71,631.5	66.0	76,061.8	58.2
7,597.3	15.6	9,274.7	18.7	14,883.4	19.1	19,057.6	19.4	20,877.5	19.2	23,730.5	18.2
3,636.1	7.5	3,762.2	7.6	9,103.4	11.7	12,751.6	13.0	15,322.0	14.1	20,778.2	15.9
3,961.2	8.1	5,512.4	11.1	5,780.0	7.4	6,306.0	6.4	5,555.5	5.1	2,952.3	2.3
24,306.2	49.7	23,735.9	47.7	42,783.2	54.9	54,831.6	56.0	59,974.4	55.3	64,805.1	49.5
16,345.5	33.4	—	—	26,033.3	33.4	31,925.1	32.6	49,296.5	45.5	49,484.0	37.8
423.7	0.9	—	—	927.9	1.2	1,153.0	1.2	1,068.0	1.0	1,391.5	1.1
772.9	1.6	—	—	987.2	1.3	1,022.6	1.0	389.5	0.3	1,455.8	1.1
2,443.2	5.0	—	—	5,585.1	7.2	7,943.6	8.1	9,220.4	8.5	12,473.8	9.5
4,320.9	8.8	—	—	9,249.7	11.8	12,787.3	13.1				
—	—	—	—	—	—	—	—				
16,970.0	34.7	16,697.6	33.6	20,297.8	26.0	24,081.8	24.6	27,525.5	25.4	42.374.1	32.4
10,319.1	21.1	9,054.3	18.2	12,672.8	16.2	15,516.8	15.8				
—	—	—	—	—	—	—	—				
6,651.2	13.6	7,643.3	15.4	7,625.0	9.8	8,565.0	8.8				
48,873.8	100.0	49,708.2	100.0	77,964.4	100.0	97,971.0	100.0	108,377.4	100.0	130,909.8	100.0

[f] This refers to the difference between the total assets in Malaysia and total liabilities in Malaysia of the companies incorporated abroad. This approach had to be used for Malaysian branches of companies incorporated abroad as the criterion on equity share capital could not be applied to these companies.

[g] Excludes government holdings other than through trust agencies, except for 1969.

(*) The amount held by this group in 1992 consists of RM13,496 million owned by Bumiputera as direct investors and RM7,282 million as investments in institutions channeling Bumiputera funds such as the ASN and ASB schemes, LUTH and LTAT.

(**) Refers to shares held through traditional trust agencies such as PNB, PERNAS and SEDCs. It also includes the amount of equity owned by the government through other agencies and companies which have been identified under the Transfer Scheme of Government Equity to Bumiputera. The figures from 1990 exclude BBMB, consistent with the decision of the Committee on Investment Coordination that BBMB is no longer classified as a trust agency.

Sources: *Second Malaysia Plan*, 1971, p. 40; *Third Malaysia Plan*, 1976, p. 184; *Fourth Malaysia Plan*, 1981, p. 62; *Mid-Term Review of the Fourth Malaysia Plan*, 1984, p. 101; *Fifth Malaysia Plan*, 1986, p. 107; *Mid-Term Review of the Fifth Malaysia Plan*, 1989; *Sixth Malaysia Plan*, 1991; *Mid-Term Review of the Sixth Malaysia Plan*, 1994.

interventions and rent redistribution since then. In the aftermath of the events of May 1969, the New Economic Policy (NEP) was introduced in 1970, ostensibly to create the socioeconomic conditions for "national unity" through poverty reduction (supposedly irrespective of race) and restructuring society to achieve interethnic economic parity, especially between the predominantly Malay Bumiputeras (indigenes) and the predominantly Chinese non-Bumiputeras. The NEP was the new regime's response to the demands of the ascendant Malay political elite for greater government intervention in what was then a relatively *laissez-faire* economy. Besides the politically popular policy to reduce poverty (see Table 12.7), it soon became evident that interethnic wealth and occupational restructuring (see Table 12.8) was the main emphasis of the NEP for the ascendant Malay middle class; the government aimed to attain at least 30 per cent Bumiputera ownership of the economy by 1990 and to create a viable Malay business community. To achieve this objective, state involvement in the economy

TABLE 12.7 Peninsular Malaysia: Incidence of Poverty[a] by Rural-Urban Strata, 1970, 1976, 1984, and 1987

Stratum	Households, 1970[b]			Households, 1976[c]			Households, 1984[d]			Households, 1987[e]	
	Total ('000)	Poor ('000)	Incidence of Poverty (%)	Total ('000)	Poor ('000)	Incidence of Poverty (%)	Total ('000)	Poor ('000)	Incidence of Poverty (%)	Poor ('000)	Incidence of Poverty (%)
Rural[f]	1,203.4	705.9	58.7	1,400.8	669.6	47.8	1,629.4	402.0	24.7	485.8	17.3
Rubber smallholders	350.0	226.4	64.7	126.7	73.8	58.2	155.2	67.3	43.4	83.1	40.0
Padi farmers	140.0	123.4	88.1	187.9	150.9	80.3	116.6	67.3	57.7	54.4	50.2
Estate workers[g]	148.4	59.4	40.0	—	—	—	81.3	16.0	19.7	11.7	15.0
Fishermen	38.4	28.1	73.2	28.0	17.6	62.7	34.3	9.5	27.7	10.7	24.5
Coconut smallholders	32.0	16.9	52.8	19.3	12.4	64.0	14.2	6.6	46.9	4.9	39.2
Other agriculture[h]	144.1	128.2	89.0	528.4	275.4	52.1	464.2	158.8	34.2	—	—
Other industries[i]	350.5	123.5	35.2	510.5	139.5	27.3	763.6	76.5	10.0	—	—
Urban	402.6	85.9	21.3	530.6	94.9	17.9	991.7	81.3	8.2	82.6	8.1
Agriculture	—	—	—	24.8	10.0	40.2	37.5	8.9	23.8	—	—
Mining	5.4	1.8	33.3	4.5	0.5	10.1	7.8	0.3	3.4	—	—
Manufacturing	84.0	19.7	23.5	55.3	9.5	17.1	132.3	11.3	8.5	—	—
Construction	19.5	5.9	30.2	34.7	6.1	17.7	86.6	5.3	6.1	—	—
Transport and utilities	42.4	13.1	30.9	53.2	9.1	17.1	73.9	2.7	3.6	—	—
Trade and services	251.3	45.4	18.1	242.0	33.7	13.9	472.7	21.9	4.6	—	—
Activities not adequately defined	—	—	—	116.1	26.0	22.4	180.9	30.9	17.1	—	—
Total	1,606.0	791.8	49.3	1,931.4	764.4	39.6	2,621.1	483.3	18.4	485.8	17.3

Notes: [a] The incidence of poverty for 1970 was based on the per capita poverty line income, while those for 1976, 1984, and 1987 are based on the respective gross poverty line incomes.

[b] *PES* is a sample survey covering 25,000 households in Peninsular Malaysia.

[c] The *Agricultural Census, 1977* (for reference year 1976) covered 188,000 households in Malaysia.

[d] The *Household Income Survey, 1984* is a sample survey covering 60,250 households in Malaysia.

[e] Malaysia (1989): 54–55.

[f] Households have been redefined on the basis of the industry and occupation of the head of household.

[g] Statistics on estate workers for 1970 were derived from indirect sources and, therefore, are not comparable with 1984. The PES did not make any distinction between estate workers and laborers on small holdings. The *Agricultural Census, 1977* did not cover estates, and, therefore, estimates on estate workers are not available for 1976.

[h] Includes other agricultural farmers such as oil palm smallholders, pepper smallholders, pineapple and tobacco farmers, and livestock and poultry farmers.

[i] Includes households engaged in mining, manufacturing, construction, transport, utilities, trade and services.

Sources: Department of Statistics, *Post Enumeration Survey (PES) of the Population Census, 1970*, Government Printers, Kuala Lumpur; *Agricultural Census, 1977*; *Household Income Survey, 1984*; and Malaysia (1989).

TABLE 12.8 Malaysia: Registered Professionals[a] by Ethnic Group, 1970–1992

Year	Bumiputera		Chinese		Indian		Other		Total	
	No.	(%)	No.	(%)	No.	(%)	No.	(%)	No.	(%)
1970[b]	225	(4.9)	2,793	(61.0)	1,066	(23.3)	492	(10.8)	4,576	(100)
1975[c]	537	(6.7)	5,131	(64.1)	1,764	(22.1)	572	(7.1)	8,004	(100)
1979	1,237	(11.0)	7,154	(63.5)	2,375	(21.1)	496	(4.4)	11,262	(100)
1980	2,534	(14.9)	10,812	(63.5)	2,963	(17.4)	708	(4.2)	17,017	(100)
1983	4,496	(18.9)	14,933	(62.9)	3,638	(15.3)	699	(2.9)	23,766	(100)
1984	5,473	(21.0)	16,154	(61.9)	3,779	(14.5)	675	(2.6)	26,081	(100)
1985	6,318	(22.2)	17,407	(61.2)	3,946	(13.9)	773	(2.7)	28,444	(100)
1988	8,571	(25.1)	19,985	(58.4)	4,878	(14.3)	762	(2.2)	34,196	(100)
1990	11,753	(29.0)	22,641	(55.9)	5,363	(13.2)	750	(1.9)	40,507	(100)
1992	15,505	(31.9)	26,154	(53.8)	6,091	(12.5)	820	(1.7)	48,570	(100)
Increases										
1970–88	8,346	(28.2)	17,192	(58.0)	3,812	(12.9)	270	(0.9)	29,620	(100)
1980–88	6,037	(35.1)	9,173	(53.4)	1,915	(11.2)	54	(0.3)	17,179	(100)
1985–88	2,253	(39.2)	2,578	(44.8)	932	(16.2)	–11	(–0.2)	5,752	(100)
1990–92	3,752	(46.5)	3,513	(43.6)	728	(9.0)	70	(0.9)	8,063	(100)

Notes: [a] Architects, accountants, engineers, dentists, doctors, veterinary surgeons, surveyors, lawyers.
[b] Excluding surveyors and lawyers.
[c] Excluding surveyors.
Sources: Malaysian plan documents.

progressed rapidly with the incorporation of public enterprises. The state's extensive direct participation in the economy was facilitated by a gradual shift to deficit financing and the fortuitous availability of oil exports from off the east coast of the peninsula from the mid-1970s almost coinciding with the international oil price increases.

State intervention as well as public sector investments became important means for private wealth accumulation and patronage. Public and Bumiputera enterprises were generally assured of favorable government treatment, particularly through licenses, contracts, and access to finance and information, especially if supported by influential politicians; in many cases, politicians also became actively involved in business. This enabled many such enterprises to advance rapidly in areas of business in which government regulation and political patronage were crucial, such as real property, transport, plantations, mining, and finance. By the late 1970s, politically linked Bumiputera businessmen figured increasingly prominently as corporate leaders and shareholders of major publicly listed companies.

State ownership as well as measures to increase Bumiputera ownership were only two of several problems encountered by non-Bumiputeras and foreigners after the advent of the NEP; various laws and regulations were also promulgated to increase Bumiputera participation. The Petroleum Development Act (PDA) and the Industrial Coordination Act (ICA) were enacted by the government in 1974 and 1975, respectively; both were roundly condemned by foreign and Chinese business groups. Foreign oil companies were upset with the government's intended use of the PDA to bring the country's petroleum industry under the control of the national oil agency, Petroleum Nasional Berhad (Petronas). The ICA mainly alarmed Chinese investors, who perceived the Act as an attempt to control the country's manufacturing sector to secure the advancement of Malay interests in that sector. Meanwhile, the Investment Incentives Act was also used by the government to ensure that foreign companies adhered to the NEP guidelines on Bumiputera equity participation and employment.

The ICA gave the government increased authority over the establishment and growth of manufacturing enterprises and provided the bureaucracy with the means to ensure that the development of the manufacturing sector would be in line with the ethnic redistributive policies of the NEP. Following the promulgation of the Act, there was a marked slump in foreign and domestic private investments except in the oil industry and the FTZs which were exempted from the ICA guidelines. Among the Chinese, the ICA provoked much consternation, prompting the Chinese Chambers of Commerce and even UMNO's leading partner in the ruling Barisan Nasional coalition, the business-conscious Malaysian Chinese Association (MCA), to protest the legislation, particularly the ICA's mandatory ruling that foreign and Chinese companies ensure a minimum of 30 per cent

Bumiputera ownership in all their ventures beyond a certain size. Many Chinese reacted by investing abroad while others joined efforts to pool resources in new corporate institutions in an effort to gain economic strength (see Gomez 1991). The government eventually conceded by amending the ICA, first in 1977, and again on several subsequent occasions, making a few concessions each time. The essential premise of the ICA, however, remained intact; licenses would be required from the Ministry of Trade and Industry, except for small firms, and these could be revoked if requirements for Bumiputera ownership and employment were not met. Both Chinese and foreign companies began to actively solicit business ties with politically influential Malays willing to lend their names for a price without taking on executive roles after becoming owners and directors of the companies (Bowie 1991:103–4).

In addition to such legislation, in 1968 the government set up a regulatory body, the Capital Issues Committee (CIC), to regulate the growth of the capital market. By the 1970s, the CIC had obtained much more clout to ensure the indigenization of corporate stock. The CIC's approval was required, for example, before companies obtained public listing and before quoted companies could change their equity structures or the nature of their operations (Low 1985:88). In 1992 the CIC was replaced with the Securities Commission, which has more wide-ranging powers. The Foreign Investment Committee (FIC) was established to oversee major issues involving foreign investments, particularly to ensure conformity with NEP guidelines. Non-Bumiputeras also felt that Malay control over other discretionary powers of the state—such as licensing, concessions for logging and mining, land alienation, protective tariffs, and import controls—constrained and hindered their business prospects (Low 1985:83).

Foreign investors were also perturbed when state-owned agencies began acquiring foreign-owned companies. When the Bumiputera trust agency, Perbadanan Nasional Berhad (Pernas), successfully took over the British-owned London Tin and Anglo-Oriental tin-mining conglomerates in 1976, and then secured control of the British-owned, Southeast-Asian-based multinational Sime Darby, foreign investors became increasingly concerned about their economic interests in Malaysia in the face of what was described as "back-door nationalization" (see Gale 1981:86–138). In 1981 two other foreign-owned plantation giants, Guthrie Corporation and Dunlop Estates Berhad, were taken over by another government-owned trust agency, Permodalan Nasional Berhad (PNB), and the MCA-controlled Multi-Purpose Holdings Berhad, respectively (see Gomez 1994:203–6).

Following the implementation of the ICA, Bumiputera—including state—participation in government-approved manufacturing projects began to grow rapidly between 1975 and 1985, with equity participation always above 40 per cent, well exceeding 50 per cent in two years (Yasuda 1991:340–41). Declining Bumiputera investment in the sector since 1986 has been consistent with economic liberalization since then, especially after the severe recession in the mid-1980s. The government's liberalization initiatives, including some deregulation, succeeded in attracting much foreign investment from the late 1980s, especially from the East Asian region (see Yasuda 1991:340–41). Chinese equity participation in the manufacturing sector between 1975 and 1990 only exceeded 30 per cent in four years, though it had been prominent in the sector prior to the ICA.

Recognizing that legislation such as the ICA and the PDA, as well as regulatory bodies such as the CIC and FIC, were meant to regulate and pressurize the private sector to comply with the NEP employment and ownership objectives, some Chinese tried to conceal the extent of their investments by setting up diverse and widespread cross-holding networks. Others who were already prominent businessmen or who owned listed vehicles had little choice but to restructure, contributing to a spate of rights issues from the late 1970s. A number of prominent Chinese businessmen such as Robert Kuok, Tan Chin Nam, and Khoo Kay Peng diversified their operations overseas (see Tan 1993). Chinese firms that had dominated small manufacturing enterprises were most affected by the new government regulations. Although often rather efficient, these small-scale manufacturers faced many difficulties in a sector dominated by large, often foreign operations.

As Chinese dissatisfaction with the NEP mounted, there was a corresponding reluctance to invest in the economy, causing capital flight. The ICA resulted in a significant drop in private investment, almost 60 per cent of which has been attributed to Chinese reluctance to invest in the economy. According to a Morgan Guaranty estimate, the total capital flight during the period 1976 to 1985 amounted to about RM30 billion (Khoo 1994:165).

Despite this capital flight and the relative decline of domestic private investment, the share of ethnic Chinese corporate ownership rose to 40.1 per cent in 1980 from 30.4 per cent in 1971 (see Table 12.6). Despite this significant gain by Chinese capital, compared with the 1960s, its access to state power clearly was more limited, necessitating new business strategies. One strategy used by many of the bigger Chinese business interests has been to coopt influential UMNO politicians and former Bumiputera civil servants as directors and shareholders of their companies. The more important ties between Chinese businesses and the political elite, however, appear to have been forged through more indirect means. Chinese businessmen have, for instance, been known actively to fund ambitious politicians as a means to gain access to government patronage. In fact, as UMNO became increasingly factionalized, the support of Chinese businessmen became crucial for political campaigns.

Political factionalism often involved rival patronage, sometimes involving state-owned enterprises. Clientelism, usually structured and legitimated in terms of ethnic interests and interethnic redistributive objectives, often involved inefficient state interventions resulting in public enterprises coming under growing criticism for poor performance, waste, inefficiency, and corruption. These factors contributed to growing losses and wasted investment resources, which in turn increased the government's fiscal and debt burdens, hampering sustained economic growth. By the mid-1980s, however, as the economy slipped into recession, a drastic policy response became imperative as the financial requirements to develop and maintain losing public enterprises rapidly mounted, increasingly involving foreign borrowing (Jomo 1990).

12.7 ECONOMIC LIBERALIZATION

To help revive the economy after the economic crises of the mid-1980s, the Mahathir administration introduced a range of economic liberalization measures (Jomo 1994). To encourage foreign investment, the Promotion of Investments Act was enacted in 1986, providing generous tax holidays and pioneer status for a period of five years, renewable in some cases for up to 10 years, particularly for those investing in manufacturing, agriculture, and tourism. To promote domestic private investment, the ICA was also amended in 1987 to raise the investment and employee exemption levels for licensing purposes (Koh 1990:233–34). The government even suspended or relaxed some NEP requirements to attract new investments. These policy moves, coupled with changed economic conditions in the region, resulted in a resurgence of export-oriented manufacturing, largely under the auspices of foreign capital, mainly from East Asia, which reinvigorated the economy enough for it to register over 8 per cent growth annually since 1988 (Jomo and Edwards 1993:33–38).

Privatization was also introduced in 1983, ostensibly to curb inefficiency, poor management, and weak financial discipline in the public sector. This reversal of the rapid expansion of public enterprises under the NEP, especially in the 1970s, has been encouraged by multilateral financial agencies, such as the World Bank and the Asian Development Bank (ADB), and by conservative governments in Britain and the United States in the 1980s. The introduction of privatization in Malaysia was also apparently due to Mahathir's opinion that public enterprises should only serve as a temporary vehicle for creating a Bumiputera property-owning class. Nevertheless, substantial public enterprise spending—mainly to finance the new heavy industries—continued until the mid-1980s, four years after Mahathir's appointment as prime minister. Mahathir was also believed to have been considering privatization as an important means for sponsoring the emergence and consolidation of a new Malay rentier elite, which he hoped would somehow transform itself into an internationally competitive industrial community. Thus, it seems probable that even without the prompting of multilateral funding agencies, redistribution through privatization had long been seen by Mahathir as an important policy tool for the promotion of Bumiputera capitalism.

Some proponents of privatization claimed that because the private sector—and not the public sector—was now viewed as the main vehicle for economic development, this would check political influence on the economy through public enterprises, especially for purposes of patronage. This view, however, ignores the reality of political capture of the privatization process itself, with "cronies" of the national executive well placed to capture the most lucrative opportunities arising from privatization (see Jomo 1995). With the privatization policy, allegations of political nepotism and patronage have grown. In particular, the policy's commitment to achieving the NEP objectives (mainly referring to wealth redistribution in favor of Bumiputeras, and perhaps the creation of a "Bumiputera commercial and industrial community") and its "first-come, first-served" criterion have provided opportunities for politically well-connected businessmen to gain priority over others. Many privatizations have not even involved the formality of an open tender system, and thus many beneficiaries have been chosen solely on the basis of political and personal connections.

A number of major non-Bumiputera corporate groups have also emerged during the NEP era, especially with economic liberalization, despite the policy bias in favor of the development of Malay capital. Unlike Chinese companies that developed before the NEP with far less political patronage, the characteristic trait of many of these newly emerging Chinese companies, as with most new Bumiputera conglomerates, is that their corporate development has mainly been achieved through share maneuvers, asset shifting, and speculative transactions utilizing the stock market. Even established Chinese business groups have had to forge and maintain close links with influential UMNO politicians to protect and enhance their corporate holdings. Thus, in spite of the more limited role played by the state in the economy following privatization in terms of property rights, the dependence of non-Bumiputera and Bumiputera business groups operating in the domain of the "national economy" on senior politicians for corporate survival and success is another indication of the increasing concentration of political power in the hands of the UMNO leadership.

12.8 EFFECTS OF RENTS ON ECONOMIC DEVELOPMENT

The preceding review of rent creation, distribution, and deployment in the Malaysian economy suggests a combination of different forces at work, of which the focus has been on two in particular. On one hand, rents have been created and allocated in ways that encourage investment in new productive activities, which have accelerated the diversification of the economy from its colonial inheritance. Such rents have emphasized industrialization, initially on the basis of import substitution, then export promotion and heavy industrialization as well. The other important goal of rent creation and deployment in Malaysia has been redistribution, especially along interethnic lines.

The availability of natural resource rents—most notably from petroleum, natural (petroleum) gas, tin, and timber—has been very significant for growth, exports, government revenue, and hence fiscal capacity, allowing the government greater latitude and capacity than most other governments in the world. In the case of timber, only a small fraction of the rents has been captured by the state governments, which control all land and natural resources (other than petroleum and natural gas which fell under the ambit of the federal government following the promulgation of the Petroleum Development Act (PDA) of 1974). The PDA enables the federal government to successfully capture much of the resource rent from petroleum and natural gas resources, providing a modest proportion to the government of the state where the deposits are located. Timber rents have also been captured by the mainly Bumiputera politicians, royalty, and others who secure logging concessions, as well as their mainly ethnic Chinese logging operator partners and, frequently, Japanese *sogo sosha* financiers.

"Timber politics" dominates in timber-rich Sarawak and Sabah (INSAN 1988) as "land politics" and other "resource politics" do in other states—involving a great deal of wasteful resource rent seeking in the form of political expenses. Yet, it should not be forgotten that such rent seeking occurs in essentially oligopolistic environments, ensuring that rents are not all dissipated in the process due to political "entry barriers" and the net gains are handsome enough to be very attractive. Such rents have not been restructured to reward productivity-enhancing investments until recently, when bans on log exports have encouraged investments in wood processing with inefficient outcomes (Vincent and Hadi 1992).

The more effective linkage of rent access and capture to the achievement of specific policy objectives has reduced rent dissipation as well as enhanced efficacy in the use of rents as incentives. For example, the greater use of performance criteria by the public sector has probably reduced wastage and inefficiency besides rewarding businesses for efficiency and achieving policy objectives. For example, allowing a company to collect tolls on a privatized highway as soon as it is built creates an incentive for the company to speed up construction of the highway and thus collect more tolls.

Nevertheless, accumulation in the "internationalized" export-oriented sectors of the economy has not been undermined by the magnitude and nature of these rents, and has instead ensured much of the growth and dynamism of the Malaysian economy. The continued and recently enhanced allocation of rents in favor of industrialization, especially of the export-oriented variety, has ensured rapid growth, particularly in recent years, albeit under foreign control, which raises grave doubts about the sustainability of the process. While rents have effectively served as incentives for foreign investors to relocate export-oriented production in Malaysia, which has been responsible for the rapid growth of such manufacturing in the 1970s and since the late 1980s, some government policy reforms—including more effective implementation and enforcement (e.g., with the introduction of "one-stop agencies")—have minimized clientelist pay-offs to government officials and politicians for such firms, which essentially operate within the realm of the global rather than the national economy.

The economic effects of redistributive state intervention have been quite different from those intended to enhance structural change and economic diversification, but also more varied. Economic rents have been structured and offered by the government in various ways to favor certain demographic groups or regions. Of these, the most important measures have been undertaken for the purpose of interethnic redistribution ("NEP restructuring"), particularly in favor of the predominantly Malay Bumiputeras at the expense of the predominantly Chinese non-Bumiputeras. Here, one might distinguish between those discriminatory measures that enhance economic resources (e.g., education, training) and those that simply transfer economic resources. Also, one can distinguish among determinants of access, say, between schemes equally accessible to all from an ascriptively favored group and those involving further selection or allocation processes, which may encourage rent-seeking behavior.

Since the 1970s, the allocation of rents by the state has ostensibly been primarily intended to redistribute wealth in favor of Bumiputeras and to promote the development of Bumiputera capitalists. However, although yielding handsome pecuniary returns, substantial profits, and capital gains, the business operations of those benefiting from state-allocated rents are mainly "nonentrepreneurial" in character in a Schumpeterian sense, e.g., in the relatively protected import-substituting manufacturing sector, services, and other "nontradables," such as real property, construction, and infrastructure, while others have gained primarily from major, often complex financial and other corporate maneuvers, rather than from significant productivity gains or other improvements in terms of international competitiveness.

It should be stressed that some redistributive interventions have made some contributions to enhancing productivity. For example, ethnically biased investments in human resource development have certainly contributed to productivity gains—e.g., by overcoming various colonial, cultural, and urban biases, and facilitating employment in modern economic activities characterized by high productivity growth—though it is unclear what the overall economic effects of ethnic bias have been. While violating ethnically blind meritocratic principles undoubtedly breeds ethnic frustrations among those discriminated against, there is no clear evidence that greater investments among the less academically successful are economically wasteful, i.e., that the social rates of return to educational investments among the less educationally successful are lower than those for the more successful, especially since the latter tend to cost more. There is also evidence that some redistributive programs have favorable consequences for productive investments, e.g., the provision of credit without collateral to poor people by the Grameen Bank-like Ikhtiar scheme has facilitated very productive investments reflected in high repayment rates as well as other indicators.

On the other hand, interethnic redistributive interventions that have been easily captured and abused have had some unfavorable outcomes for efficiency. Such abuse has been facilitated by limited accountability on the part of the government, enhanced by minimal transparency of the rent allocation processes ("executive prerogatives"), rather than by organizational incapacity on the part of the state, judging by its governance capacity in other regards, which suggests that the lack of transparency is deliberate. Thus, while some state interventions in the economy—and the rents thus created—have enhanced accumulation, economic diversification, and late industrialization, not all interventions—especially those ostensibly oriented to redistribution—have contributed to productivity enhancement.

Furthermore, simple wealth transfers do not seem to have such positive consequences for productivity enhancement, but, on the contrary, seem to have adverse consequences by discouraging productive investments. For example, the ICA requirement that private manufacturing firms beyond a certain size have to ensure that at least 30 per cent of equity is owned by Bumiputera interests has probably adversely affected the development of the manufacturing sector. Such conditions have probably discouraged investments in manufacturing as businesses anticipate losses from discounted transfers to their Bumiputera partners. It is likely that investors would be less reticent in making productive investments if they did not have to incur such additional costs. Hence, it can be argued that such rent transfers have contributed little to enhancing the productive capacity of the Malaysian economy. However, in so far as these constitute straightforward transfers, there is relatively little rent dissipation except for investors incurring additional transaction costs, e.g., in trying to identify and perhaps even help finance suitable Bumiputera partners.

Without such intervention, it is unlikely that Bumiputera business interests would have made such significant inroads into sectors of the economy long dominated by ethnic Chinese. Such bias in favor of cronies, however, is readily perceived as ethnic or national bias, thus not just exacerbating ethnic relations, but also discouraging investments by those who see themselves as less favored or likely to be discriminated against. Perhaps recognizing that this could impair the need for the government to be seen to be creating a "level playing field" or "fair environment," the Mahathir administration reversed the earlier ascendance of the public sector and the bureaucracy with policies such as "Malaysia Incorporated" (which sought to get the public sector to collaborate more effectively with the private sector after relations worsened over the 1970s) and privatization. The apparent success of Malaysia's campaigns to attract private investments since the mid-1980s has also enhanced state sensitivity to foreign and Chinese capital. The executive has consequently been perceived as more restrained in favoring the Malay business elite since the mid-1980s. Also, by providing lucrative business opportunities to some Chinese and Indian businessmen, the state has managed to reduce some ethnic dissent among the non-Malay communities. Hence, the impressive economic recovery since 1987 and government efforts to deregulate and to de-emphasize the NEP—long sought by many non-Bumiputeras—have shifted some non-Bumiputera sentiment to the regime since the late 1980s as the Mahathir administration's economic and cultural liberalization became more pronounced with the declaration of his Vision 2020 to achieve developed country status by the year 2020 (Jomo 1994).

NOTE

We wish to thank Ha-Joon Chang for his useful comments and suggestions on earlier drafts.

REFERENCES

Anuwar, A. (1992), "The Role of the State and Market Mechanisms in Malaysia," paper presented at the Second East-Asia and East-Central Europe Conference, April 22–30, Budapest.

Bowie, A. (1991), *Crossing the Industrial Divide: State, Society, and the Politics of Economic Transformation in Malaysia*, Columbia University Press, New York.

Chee, P. L. (1994), "Heavy Industrialisation: A Second Round of Import Substitution," in Jomo K. S., ed., *Japan and Malaysian Development: In the Shadow of the Rising Sun*, Routledge, London.

Edwards, C. and Jomo K. S. (1993), "Policy Options for Malaysian Industrialisation," in Jomo K. S., ed., *Industrialising Malaysia*, Routledge, London.

Gale, B. (1981), *Politics and Public Enterprise in Malaysia*, Eastern Universities Press, Petaling Jaya.

Gomez, E. T. (1991), *Money Politics in the Barisan Nasional*, Forum, Kuala Lumpur.

——(1994), *Political Business: Corporate Involvement of Malaysian Political Parties*, Centre for Southeast Asian Studies, James Cook University, Townsville.

Institute of Social Analysis (INSAN) (1988), *Logging Against the Natives of Sarawak*, Institute of Social Analysis, Kuala Lumpur.

Jomo K. S. (1990), *Growth and Structural Change in the Malaysian Economy*, Macmillan, London.

——(1994), *U-Turn?: Malaysian Economic Development Policies After 1990*, Centre for Southeast Asian Studies, James Cook University, Townsville.

——ed. (1993), *Industrialising Malaysia: Policy, Performance, Prospects*, Routledge, London.

——ed. (1995), *Privatizing Malaysia: Rents, Rhetoric, Realities*, Westview Press, Boulder.

——and Edwards, C. (1993), "Malaysian Industrialisation in Historical Perspective," in Jomo K. S., ed., *Industrialising Malaysia*, Routledge, London.

——and Ishak Shari (1986), *Development Policies and Income Inequality in Peninsular Malaysia*, Institute for Advanced Studies, University of Malaya, Kuala Lumpur.

——and Todd, P. (1994), *Trade Unions and the State in Peninsular Malaysia*, Oxford University Press, Kuala Lumpur.

Junid, S. (1980), *British Industrial Development in Malaysia, 1963–1971*, Oxford University Press, Kuala Lumpur.

Khan, M. H. (1989), "Clientelism, Corruption and Capitalist Development: An Analysis of State Intervention With Special Reference to Bangladesh," Ph.D. diss., University of Cambridge.

Khoo, B. T. (1994), "Mahathir Mohamad: A Critical Study of Ideology, Biography and Society in Malaysian Politics," Ph.D. diss., Flinders University, Adelaide.

Khor, K. P. (1983), *The Malaysian Economy: Structures and Dependence*, Maricans, Kuala Lumpur.

Koh, W. (1990), "Government Policies, Foreign Capital, State Capacity: A Comparative Study of Korea, Indonesia and Malaysia," Ph.D. diss., Northern Illinois University, De Kalb.

Low, K. Y. (1985), "The Political Economy of Restructuring in Malaysia: A Study of State Policies with Reference to Multinational Corporations," M.Ec. thesis, University of Malaya, Kuala Lumpur.

Malaysia (1981), *Fourth Malaysia Plan, 1981–1985*, Government Printers, Kuala Lumpur.

——(1986), *Fifth Malaysia Plan, 1986–1990*, Government Printers, Kuala Lumpur.

——(1989), *Mid-Term Review of the Fifth Malaysia Plan, 1986–1990*, Government Printers, Kuala Lumpur.

Ministry of Finance, Malaysia (1989), *Economic Report, 1989/1990*, Government Printers, Kuala Lumpur.

Rao, V. V. B. (1980), *Malaysia: Development Pattern and Policy, 1947–1971*, University of Singapore Press, Singapore.

Rasiah, R. (1996), "State Intervention, Rents and Malaysian Industrialization," in J. Borrego, Alejandro Alvarez, and Jomo K. S., eds., *Capital, the State and Late Industrialization: Comparative Perspectives from the Pacific Rim*, Westview, Boulder.

Schatzl, L. H. (1988), "Economic Development and Economic Policy in Malaysia," in L. H. Schatzl, ed., *Growth and Spatial Equity in West Malaysia*, Institute of Southeast Asian Studies, Singapore.

Statistics, Department of, Malaysia (1969–85), *Ownership Survey of Limited Companies*, Kuala Lumpur.

TAN, B. K. (1993), "The Role of the Construction Sector in National Development: Malaysia," Ph.D. diss., University of Malaya, Kuala Lumpur.

TAN TAT WAI (1985), "Lessons from Development Policy of a Resource Rich Country: Malaysia," First Progress Report to the Development Studies Division, United Nations University.

TOYE, J. (1987), *Dilemmas of Development: Reflections on the Counter-Revolution in Development Theory and Policy*, Blackwell, Oxford.

VINCENT, J. and YUSOF, H. (1991), "Deforestation and Agricultural Expansion in Peninsular Malaysia," Harvard Institute for International Development, Development Discussion Paper No. 396 (September).

WADE, R. (1990), *Governing the Market: Economic Theory and the Role of Government in East Asian Industrialization*, Princeton University Press, Princeton.

YASUDA, N. (1991), "Malaysia's New Economic Policy and the Industrial Coordination Act," *The Developing Economies*, 29(4):330–49.

13

Toward a Comparative Institutional Analysis of the Government-Business Relationship

MASAHIRO OKUNO-FUJIWARA

13.1 INTRODUCTION

In this chapter, I attempt to present an abstract model of the government-business relationship and to identify institutional structures that determine the nature as well as the outcome of that relationship in different societies. In the designing and implementing of economic policies, the nature and means of interaction within the government and those between the government (especially the administration) and the private business sector play important, and sometimes critical, roles. However, there seem to be distinctive differences in different countries, such as the United States and Japan, both in how government itself is organized and in how such interactions occur; these differences seem to be institutionalized in each society. I try to capture these institutional differences across societies and attempt to identify their relative merits in coordinating the interests of various political actors in the private sector, inducing their innovation incentives and directing their investments to certain activities. By doing so, I hope this analysis will shed some light on analytical comparisons of the workings of the government-business relationship across different societies.

At the same time, I believe these institutional structures play key roles in promoting economic development and in encouraging industrialization of society. Several proponents of the "developmental state" view[1] have stressed that a *strong* government, which relies heavily upon direct state intervention over the use of a competitive market mechanism, may have an advantage in industrializing a developing economy, possibly at the cost of repressing democracy. However, this view seems conjectural, expressing the authors' beliefs without providing a useful analytical framework that would help readers understand what constitutes a strong government and how strong governments have such an advantage over a democratic government. I hope that the following analysis, though it is also tentative and conjectural, will fill in this lacuna.

The model outlined below strives to provide an analytical framework to scientifically evaluate the validity of the view that differences in government regimes and institutions are sometimes critical in promoting industrialization. To support this framework, I attempt to examine, with the help of economic theories such as incentive theory and contract theory, the relative merits and demerits of the institutional structures behind the government-business relationship in achieving desirable resource allocations. These merits and demerits may depend upon the parameters surrounding the economy, especially the difference in the stage of economic development. In particular, I examine their impact on economic development in both postwar and contemporary Japan.

This chapter is organized as follows. In Section 13.2, a model of a typical government-business relationship is formulated with emphasis on *ex ante* policy rules and *ex post* negotiation to revise them. Several extreme forms of governments are identified. The extent of the government's bargaining power, defined by the government's ability to exert its power over the private sector, reflects the difference between the degree of functional separation of powers within the government as well as the relative size of the government's litigation costs compared to those of the private sector. Whether government is jurisdictionally centralized or decentralized is defined by the relative level within the government (typically within its administrative branch) at which the main activity of coordinating public interests takes place. Section 13.3 discusses *ex post* negotiation to coordinate interests among the government (again, its administrative branch) and various private groups, using the theory of bargaining, and identifies the main factors that dictate the bargaining outcome. Section 13.4 analyzes *ex ante* incentives of the government and private firms in the light of the different institutional structures, using contract and incentive theories. Section 13.5 discusses and evaluates the relative merits and demerits of different regimes of the government in view of various criteria, though these discussions are of a preliminary nature. Section 13.6 presents a brief historical account of the government-business relationship in postwar Japan, arguing that the relationship may have contributed to the success of industrialization in the 1950s and 1960s. Section 13.7 concludes.

13.2 MODEL OF A GOVERNMENT-BUSINESS RELATIONSHIP

What is the government and what does it do in relation to the business sector? In this section, I present an abstract model of government activities which, I hope, will enable us to analyze the roles and consequences of different institutional regimes that determine the outcome of the government-business relationship. By so doing, I hope to be able to identify how typical governments interact with the private sector and what institutional factors determine the outcome of such interactions.

A Model

Let us begin by formulating the various activities of government in an extremely simplified form:

1. Government, especially the legislative and administrative branches by negotiating with private sectors to coordinate their interests, decides its policy and determines a (*ex ante*) rule to implement it, which determines a set of alternative *ex post* actions $Y^{ea} = \{y_1, \ldots, y_n\}$[2] that private firms can employ.
2. Private firms carry out (*ex ante*) investments, x, such as product development and plant construction in view of the desired *ex post* action, y, in the set of alternative actions.
3. Uncertainties that are difficult to foresee *ex ante* (or states of nature, will be denoted as s), such as a change in external economic conditions or a technological breakthrough, are unfolded and become fixed.
4. In view of developments in stages (2) and (3), government and some selected parties in the private sector who have power to influence decisions (*insiders*, for short) negotiate over (*ex post*) rules, or a new set $Y^{ep}(x,s)$ of *ex post* actions, to implement after coordinating their interests.
5. A dispute may occur between government and private firms and/or among private firms concerning the validity of the *ex post* rules or the lawfulness of a private firm's action, which will be settled through certain channels depending upon the institutional structure of the society.
6. Private firms perform their (*ex post*) business activities under the *ex post* implementation rule, or choose a particular y from $Y^{ep}(x,s)$, and a society's outcome, $z(x,y,s)$, is determined.

An example may help readers understand these components.[3] During the late 1980s and early 1990s, with foreign diplomatic pressure and the general public's cry for deregulation behind it, the Ministry of Finance (MOF) laid out a plan to liberalize regulated deposit rates and other bank activities in Japan. MOF's publicly stated position at that time was to let the market mechanism decide the winner of the competition, by not providing public rescue for those financial institutions that could not survive the process of deregulation. The retiring president of the Bank of Japan (BOJ) publicly announced as late as autumn 1994 that bankruptcies of small banks with financial difficulties would be unavoidable and possibly desirable. This was stage (1).

With this government announcement, private banks had alternatives over various actions of x, ranging from keeping their financial position slim in anticipation of severe competition in the future to expanding their business aggressively, accepting the risk of holding excessively bad loans and hoping MOF and BOJ would offer help when things turned bad. This was stage (2). In the early 1990s, the stock market crashed and land prices, which were the crucial element in the health of Japanese financial institutions, which must hold property as collateral, started to decline drastically. Financial difficulties arose for many banks, and the collapse of the credit system was widely feared. This was stage (3), or the unfolding of a particular state of nature, s.

The government started to rescue some selected banks[4] with voluntary cooperation from private financial institutions. The *ex ante* principle of not helping those banks that fell into financial difficulties was abandoned and the banking industry started to look for public rescue. This was stage (4). There may be no explicitly written new *ex post* rule and the proposed new rule may be disputed in the media and/or courts (stage (5)), but those precedents that are accumulated as emergency measures will act as a *de facto* new rule. Private banks decide their new business policies, y, based on the development of stages (1)–(5). This is stage (6), which determines the ultimate social outcome (denoted as $z = z(x,y,s)$) such as whether a particular bank with financial difficulty will be rescued by the concerted efforts of the public and private sectors.

The chronological order of stages (4)–(6) may vary across societies depending upon institutional structures. In fact, the typical chronological order in the United States may be better approximated by the government as:

4. A private firm takes an action that may be beyond the conventional interpretation of the law (with respect to the *ex ante* rule) or improper (violating the society's value system).
5. Courts decide the appropriateness of the firm's action and/or lobbying activities and election results change the government's rulings.
6. A new *ex post* rule is set in lieu of the court's verdict.[5]

None the less, in the text to follow I employ the chronological ordering set out at the beginning of this section. When the negotiation in stage (4) between the government and selected parties of the business sector takes place, they anticipate the subsequent developments of (5) and (6). As long as we analyze stages (4)–(6) using subgame perfect equilibrium as a solution concept, which presumes an equilibrium outcome under rational expectation, the result is likely to remain qualitatively unaffected even if we change the chronological order.

Functional Separation of Powers and Jurisdictional Partition

The way the government–business relationship functions depends upon the structure and the nature of the government itself. We can classify governments from two different viewpoints.

First, government, especially its administrative branch, can be classified in view of how easily it can implement its preferred policies through stages (4)–(6). A government has *large* bargaining power if it can implement its favorite policies relatively easily, while a government with *small* bargaining power cannot. The strength of the government, in my view, stems from its relative bargaining power *vis-à-vis* the private sector. In the following, I discuss two institutional factors that determine the relative strength of the government's bargaining power.

One institutional factor that determines the relative bargaining power of the government is the functional separation of powers. In any democratic government, authority is functionally allocated according to the different functions of the government, described as (1), (4), and (5) above. At one extreme of this viewpoint is a *functionally separated* government with rigid *separation of powers*, that is, legislation, administration, and judicature. In this type of government, the different functions of government are controlled by separate and independent bodies; the legislature is mainly responsible for activity (1), the administrative body for (4), and the courts for (5). As explained in the sections to follow, in such a government policies are likely to be implemented on the basis of explicitly written laws and legislation enacted by the legislature, and the implemented policies are constantly checked through judicial processes, or in a *rule-based* manner. Such a government tends to have relatively small bargaining power as the private sector can resort to other branches if policies that are unacceptable to it are chosen by a branch of the government.

Another factor that determines the relative bargaining power of the government is the size and relative magnitude (between the government and private sector) of litigation costs. Even if powers are functionally separated within the government, whether or not the private sector can resort to the checks-and-balances mechanism, especially to the judicial process, is another matter. If litigation costs are large, especially for the private sector in comparison with those for the government, the private sector cannot effectively utilize the rescue from the judicial process, and the government will have relatively large bargaining power. The bargaining power of a functionally separated government is small only if litigation cost is nonsignificant for private firms.

At the other extreme is a *nonseparated* government where either the government activities of (1), (4), and (5) are all carried out by a single decision-making body or the private sector finds it difficult to appeal to other branches of the government for institutional reasons, such as high litigation costs. Even if different functions of the government are nominally controlled by separate bodies, when institutional factors make the preferences of those bodies essentially identical, the power of such a government is concentrated—for example, in the hands of the president—and those in power can implement their preferred policies in different branches of the government. In this type of government, policies may be implemented even if written laws explicitly prohibit them, because laws and rules are written with large room for discretion. Private firms follow government policies either because the government has omnipotent power, that is, in an *authority-based* manner, or because they fear the government's unfavorable treatment in future, that is, in a *relation-based* manner. These governments have relatively large bargaining power.

Second, government, again especially its administrative body, can be classified by the level of the government where the main action of stage (4) activity takes place. The administrative branch usually consists of many bodies such as ministries and bureaus. These are sometimes classified into the upper government, such as the president's or prime minister's office, whose main responsibility is to coordinate policies over various sections of the administrative branch, and the lower government, such as ministries and bureaus that oversee certain government activities and/or those portions of the private sector under their jurisdiction, whose main responsibility is to make policy decisions and to implement them within its jurisdictions.

In this viewpoint, at one extreme is a government with central jurisdictional power, or a jurisdictionally centralized government, where all decisions concerning various sectors across the society are controlled or coordinated by the executive office, such as the president's or prime minister's office (i.e., the upper government). In particular, negotiations for policy revisions in stage (4) take place in an integrated form at the level of the upper government among the executive office, relevant bodies of the lower government, and concerned parties of the private sector. The other extreme is a government with decentralized jurisdictional powers, or a jurisdictionally decentralized government. In this type of government, the jurisdiction of each ministry and bureau usually is clearly and mutually exclusively defined, that is, jurisdiction is strictly partitioned, and authority in the jurisdiction is delegated to ministries and bureaus. Negotiations in stage (4) are fragmented at the level of the lower government between the private sector and the ministry in charge.

The motivation as well as the preference of bureaucrats of the administrative branch, who are key participants at the bargaining table, play important roles in drafting agreements. Because this branch of the government is organized as a hierarchy, bureaucrats have a natural interest in their own promotion which may be made more likely by their contribution to the ministry to which they belong. It follows that bureaucrats in a jurisdictionally decentralized government often find their sources of power in close relationships with and strong support from corporate executives/professionals in the industry under their jurisdiction, thereby contributing to the increase of their ministry's political power.

On the other hand, in a jurisdictionally centralized government, political power is concentrated at the central executive office.[6] In such a government, bureaucrats look for promotion opportunities and sources of power in the executive office's endorsement of their policies. They spend more time and other resources in persuading senior officers and/or in lobbying for the support of the executive office, rather than in collecting relevant industry data and/or in fostering information networks with the corporate executives of their jurisdiction.

It follows that, in a government with central jurisdictional powers, major decisions for policy revisions are made at the higher level by bureaucrats with wider perspectives but with relatively little access to information about individual industries. In a jurisdictionally decentralized government, however, negotiations for revisions are made at lower levels of individual ministries and/or bureaus in a segregated manner. In addition, such a government tends to have a stricter jurisdictional partition and the interests of relatively few parties in the private sector—for example, incumbent firms in the industry of which the ministry is in charge—will be reflected at the bargaining table. The voices of outsiders, such as consumers, buyers of intermediate products and potential entrants, seldom affect policy revisions.[7] This does not imply, however, that there is no coordination across different sectors of the society by a jurisdictionally decentralized government, because there are other means for such coordination; political parties occasionally play such a role in the legislative branch and/or bureaucrats find the source of their power in this coordination.[8]

Types of Government

Putting these two dimensions together, we can classify four typical types of government. The first is an *authoritarian* government, where functional powers are only minimally separated and jurisdictional power is centrally held. A powerful central office, whose power is checked neither by the legislative body nor by the judicial branch of the government, controls the entire economy. This type of government is not only able to exert strong bargaining power over the private sector but also, as an organization, strictly controlled by the central executive office. This type is sometimes criticized as nondemocratic and/or repressive because of its dictatorial or totalitarian nature. Several East Asian governments during the heyday of their economic development were criticized for these characteristics.

The second type is a *rule-based* government, in which a relatively strong central office controls the lower governments irrespective of their jurisdictional powers but in which the separation of functional power is strict and the government's bargaining power over private sectors is limited. This type of government is probably closest to what many people ordinarily view as a democratic government, because the power of each functional branch is checked by the other branches while administrative decisions are made by the top executive office in a centrally coordinated manner. Among the governments of the advanced economies, the US government is probably the closest to this type.

The third type is a *relation-based* government, where either functional powers are not clearly separated or litigation costs are high, while coordination for policy revisions is carried out in the lower levels of government. This type of government may not resemble the textbook democracy because the separation of legislative, administrative, and judicial functions within the government is not sufficiently clear. However, the checks-and-balances mechanism among different branches of the government, such as ministries and bureaus which compete with each other in their jurisdictional authorities, may help the voices of minorities to be heard within the government. There is good reason to believe that the postwar Japanese government is of this type.[9]

The fourth type is a relatively fragmented and possibly disorganized government, in which the government's bargaining power is probably the smallest due to the rigid functional separation of power, while coordination of policy revisions and/or implementations takes place at lower government levels in a segregated manner. In such a government, it is relatively difficult to coordinate decision making among different branches and, even if coordination occurs, it is relatively difficult for the government to commit to a certain policy philosophy.

Other characteristics of governments are of importance in the discussion to follow. For example, there are wide varieties of side payments potentially available between the government and private business, which enable private business to bend the government's decision by offering its price. This possibility ranges from mere bribery to lobbying for political rents in the congress. The ease of making side payments differs depending upon the institutional structure of the government. Another important factor is the motivation of bureaucrats. Bureaucrats have their own preferences to determine their actions. For historical and cultural reasons, some governments seem to have better disciplined bureaucrats with higher morals. Institutional structures within the government also affect the preference of bureaucrats, as "influencing activities"[10] such as lobbying for their own promotion and securing better political resources are sometimes effective means to improve their positions within the government organization.

I analyze the merits and demerits of these different types of government, especially the first three, in the rest of this chapter.

13.3 *EX POST* NEGOTIATIONS

In this section, I analyze how *ex post* negotiations among insiders take place in stage (4). As stressed in the previous section, this is an analysis of a negotiation game in stage (4) anticipating future developments in stages (5) and (6). Put another way, implicit in the following is an analysis of a subgame perfect equilibrium of the game consisting of stages (4)–(6).

Ex Post *Negotiation and Default Outcome*

Stages (1) and (4) are important for the discussion below because they tend to contradict each other. To explain, let us first consider how the decision in stage (4) is made. Given the *ex ante* choice, x, as well as the unfolded state of nature, s, a negotiation in (4) by *insiders* yields an *ex post* policy rule $Y^{ep}(x,s)$. The situation in (4) is depicted in Figure 13.1. If the *ex ante* rule were to prevail or if $Y^{ea} = Y^{ep}(x,s)$, private firms would choose the action y_0 from Y^{ea} that maximizes their pay-off from Y^{ea}. The resulting outcome, $z(x,y_0,s) = z_0$, will be evaluated by the government as g_0 and by the private firms as f_0. This pay-off vector, $P_0 = (g_0,f_0)$, will sometimes be referred to as the default pay-off. On the other hand, if the negotiation in (4) were to result in a new set, $Y^1 = Y^{ep}(x,s)$, private firms would choose an action y_1 which would result in a pay-off vector $P_1 = (g_1,f_1)$. It should be noted that both the default pay-off, P_0, and a pay-off (or pay-offs) realized by a policy revision, P_1, depend upon the *ex ante* rule and, more importantly, on the realized state of nature, s. Thus the decision in (4) will effectively determine

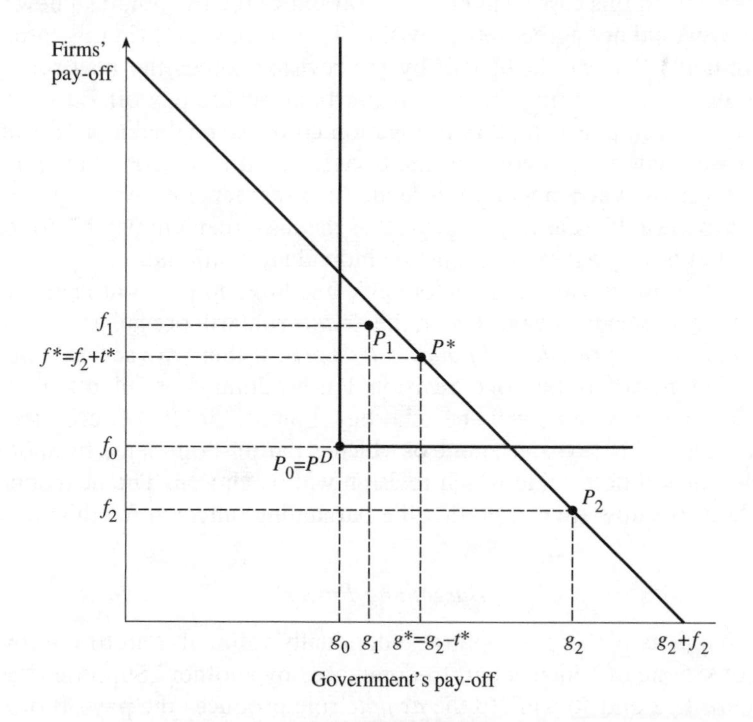

FIG. 13.1 Bargaining Game and Default Outcome

the choice of the *ex post* action, y, in stage (5) and, consequently, the ultimate outcome $z(x,y,s)$ and its associated pay-offs. In order to explain the decision in (4), therefore, it is easier to think of stage (4) as if the government and private firms negotiate over the choice of y itself.

Bargaining with No Side Payments

Then how does the negotiation in (4) determine the bargaining outcome y, or the bargaining pay-off outcome (g,f)? This depends critically upon the availability of side payments between the two parties. It is natural to think there is no possibility of side payments, or of money (pay-off) transfer, between government and private firms, as explicit bribery is prohibited in any democratized country. If side payments are not allowed and if litigation costs are negligible,[11] the *ex ante* rule would prevail even *ex post* if and only if there is no action y_i which assures a pay-off higher than the default pay-off to both government and private firms. It is rather straightforward to see why. If such y_i exists, because y_i Pareto improves y_0, both parties should agree to revise the rule so that y_i would be chosen by firms. On the other hand, if no such y_i exists, by employing a new *ex post* rule (which would produce a pay-off of P_2 in Figure 13.1, for example), at least one negotiating party (firms, in this case) will be worse off under the hypothetical new rule and they would not agree to the revision. Even if the party (in this case, the government) that would benefit by the revision forces the new rule, the opposing party can bring the case to court and secure pay-off P_0.

It is worth emphasizing that if litigation costs are negligible, as assumed in this subsection, P_0 is equal to the disagreement payoff, $P^D = (g^D,f^D)$, the pay-off vector when negotiation leads to disagreement. Any agreement must provide at least as large a pay-off as the disagreement pay-off for each party, that is, any agreement must be individually rational.

In sum, if side payments are impossible and litigation costs are negligible, even if unforeseeable events occur, the *ex ante* rule will prevail *as long as no Pareto-improving revision of policy rules exists*. If there are several Pareto-improving revisions but one revision Pareto-dominates all other alternatives, this revision will be chosen. Finally, if there are several Pareto-improving revisions, none of which is Pareto-dominated by another, bargaining will determine which revision will be chosen. The next subsection discusses how we can predict the bargaining outcome for this case.

Bargaining Power

What happens if there are plural individually rational, Pareto-improving revisions, none of which is Pareto-dominated by another? Suppose P^D is as in Figure 13.2 and sticking to the *ex ante* rule produces the pay-off of $P_0 = P^D$, while revising it to a new rule (1) yields the pay-off of P_1, and revising

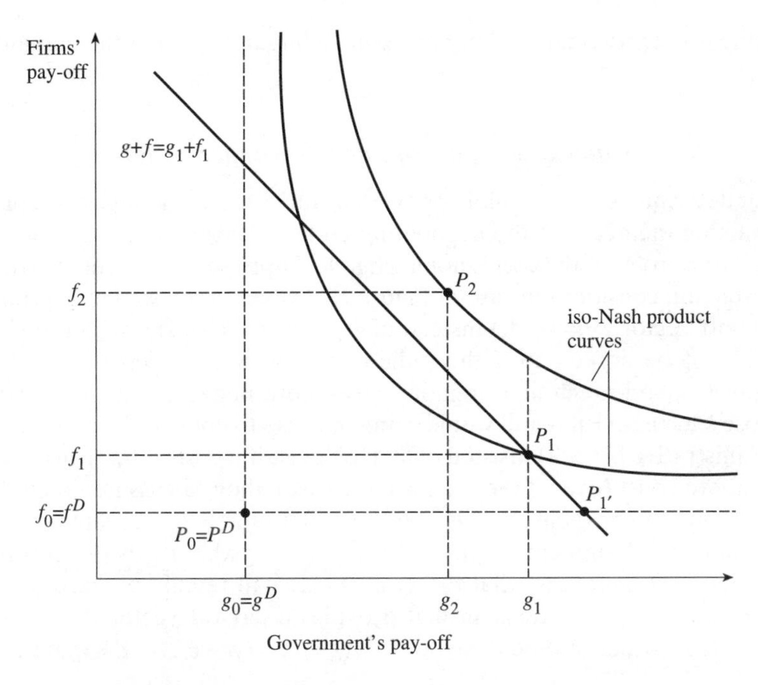

FIG. 13.2 Nash Bargaining Solution without Side Payments

it to yet another new rule (2) yields the pay-off of P_2, which are both feasible and individually rational (and no other choice exists), but neither Pareto-dominates the other. In this case, the relative bargaining power of the two parties will determine which of the two alternatives will be chosen by the negotiation.

In our set-up, two factors affect their bargaining power. First, the disagreement pay-off partly determines the strength of their bargaining power, as it is the pay-off that each negotiating party can assure itself of having when the bargaining breaks down. The lower the disagreement pay-off, the less advantageous the strategic position of the party becomes, and the weaker his bargaining power is. Second, factors such as bargaining skills and/or those implicit in the bargaining rule may influence the bargaining outcome.

In the following, however, I use the theoretical prediction of the Nash Bargaining Solution, which assumes equal bargaining skills and/or the symmetric bargaining rule. Under this bargaining solution, an outcome is chosen from the set of individually rational outcomes so as to maximize the Nash product, $(g_1 - g^D) \times (f_1 - f^D)$.[12] In Figure 13.2, two iso-Nash product curves are depicted and, under the assumed situation, P_2 gives a larger Nash product than P_1 and should be chosen by the negotiation. It follows that the higher the bargaining member's disagreement pay-off, the larger his bargaining power becomes and he can assure a larger pay-off at the bargaining table.

Litigation Costs and Functional Separation of Power

What determines the bargaining power, or the disagreement pay-off, of the bargaining members at the negotiating table in stage (4)? Litigation costs play critical roles, if the cost is nonnegligible. Suppose side payments are not allowed and consider the case of Figure 13.3 where a revision may produce a pay-off vector $P_1 = (g_1, f_1)$ instead of $P_0 = (g_0, f_0)$. Clearly, such a revision would not be agreed to if the judicial branch were independent of the administrative branch and litigation costs were negligible, as firms would oppose such a revision and would bring the case to court if the government (administrative branch) insisted on it. However, if it costs c_f for firms to take the case to court (even if they can win the case), they can assure themselves only a pay-off (or their disagreement pay-off) of $f^D = f_0 - c_f$. Similarly, the government's disagreement pay-off is $g^D = g_0 - c_g$ where c_g is its respective litigation cost. It follows that the *ex ante* rule will remain effective only if there exists no policy revision that provides a pay-off vector that Pareto-dominates the disagreement payoff, $P^D = (g^D, f^D) = (g_0 - c_g, f_0 - c_f)$, that is, only

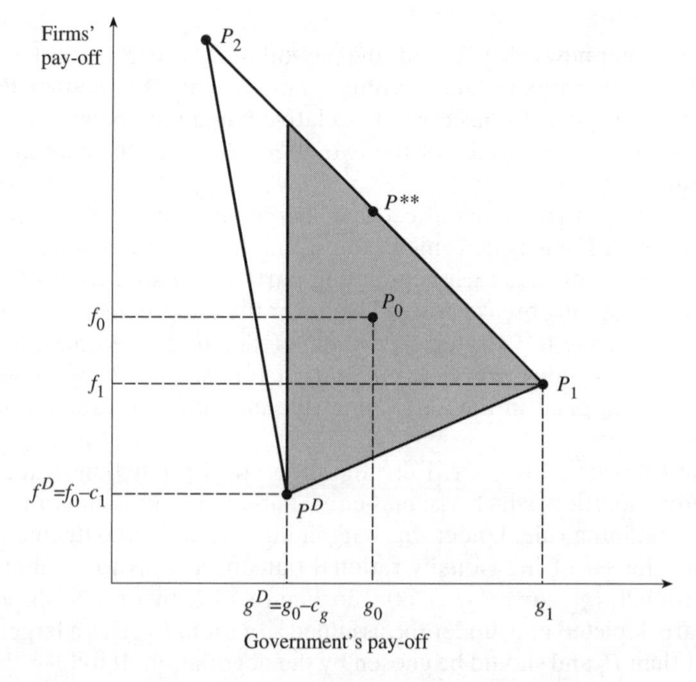

FIG. 13.3 Litigation Costs and Average Pay-Offs in Repeated Game

if there exists no policy revision that is individually rational. If litigation costs are high, as in the case of Figure 13.3, P_1 may Pareto dominate P^D even if it does not Pareto-dominate P_0, and a revision would be agreed to for implementing the pay-off outcome of P_1.

Note that the litigation costs in this framework may consist of two factors: functional separation of powers and actual litigation costs. When functional powers within the government are not strictly separated, the private sector cannot win the default outcome even if it can bring the case to court. Because the court is controlled by the same group that controls the administrative branch, the judicial process is not the last resort for the private sector. Put another way, with a functionally nonseparated government, litigation costs for the private sector are prohibitively high.

An extreme, but important, case for the following discussion is a situation in which the government has absolute bargaining power, a regime of the government-business relationship called "predatory" in the following sections. This can be approximated where $g^D = g_0 > -\infty$ but $f^D = -\infty$, that is, while the government incurs no litigation cost even if the firms bring a case to court to assure the default outcome, they must pay prohibitively high litigation costs to defend it. In this case, private firms will have no bargaining power, and any negotiation will result in the outcome (or adoption of a new rule) that provides the largest pay-off to the government. Needless to say, compared to other types, the authoritarian government has a relatively large bargaining power and is potentially predatory.

When powers are functionally separated but litigation costs do matter, the relative costs between the government and private sector become important. If costs are relatively high for the private sector but low for the government, the situation is similar to that discussed above, with the extreme case of a predatory government. When the costs for the two parties are of similar size but large, the set of individually rational pay-off outcomes expands and the *ex post* renegotiation becomes more likely to yield outcomes that are different from the default outcome. In other words, such a government produces more flexible *ex post* policy revisions.

Let me add two further observations. First, I have assumed so far that the autonomous court will always enforce the default outcome. This is not necessarily the case when some state of nature unanticipated when the *ex ante* rule was chosen has been realized. For example, if a structural change has occurred in the society, the *ex ante* rule may be found inappropriate by an autonomous court and a policy revision may be accepted, especially when the revision is found to improve the society's welfare. As discussed below, there is good reason to believe that the independent court of a functionally separated government tends to honor such revision and, hence, has *ex post* flexibility against structural change in the society. On the other hand, courts that are controlled by the same group as the administrative branch are likely not to admit such revisions and hence are *ex post* inflexible.

Second, with a jurisdictionally decentralized government, *ex post* negotiation is carried out in a segregated manner, between an individual ministry or bureau and the members who have stakes in the destiny of the rule. Members at the bargaining table are fewer with relatively similar interests. It follows that revisions that Pareto-improve insiders are more likely to exist and an agreement for a revision is more likely to be made, allowing more flexible adjustments of policies. On the other hand, a government with centralized jurisdictional powers must take into account the possible implications on other bargaining tables and/or the diverse interests of bargaining participants, making it more difficult to reach an agreement. In short, a jurisdictionally centralized government is less likely to reach an agreement in the *ex post* bargaining.

Bargaining with Side Payments

If side payments are possible in stage (4), however, the result may be critically different, as part of a player's pay-off can be transferred to other parties in the form of (monetary) transfer, which enlarges the set of feasible pay-offs. For example, without side payments, suppose there is only one possible *ex post* rule revision, yielding the pay-off of P_2 in Figure 13.4. The possibility of side payments enlarges the set of feasible pay-offs from a singleton set $\{P_2\}$ to all pay-off vectors southwest of the line AP^*P_2B. This line has a slope of -1 and represents all the payoffs (g,f) whose sum is $g + f = g_2 + f_2$. It follows that a revision of the *ex ante* rule takes place if and only if the total pay-off under a revision, $g_2 + f_2$, exceeds the total default pay-off, $g_0 + f_0$. In Figure 13.4, for example, an agreement with a revision (and hence enforcing P_2) with transfer of t^* from the government to private firms would assure the pay-off vector of P^*, which Pareto-dominates $P_0 = P^D$. The actual size of the transfer, or t^*, depends upon the bargaining power of the respective players.

Under the Nash Bargaining Solution, the transfer will be:

$$t^* = \left[(g_2 - g_0) - (f_2 - f_0)\right]/2.$$

This solution would assure the ultimate outcome of:

$$(g^*, f^*) = \left(g_0 + \left[(g_2 + f_2) - (g_0 + f_0)\right]/2,\quad f_0 + \left[(g_2 + f_2) - (g_0 + f_0)\right]/2\right),$$

which maximizes the Nash product:

$$\left(g_1 - g_0 + t\right) \times \left(f_1 - f_0 - t\right)$$

for t. That is, the surplus generated by the bargaining agreement:

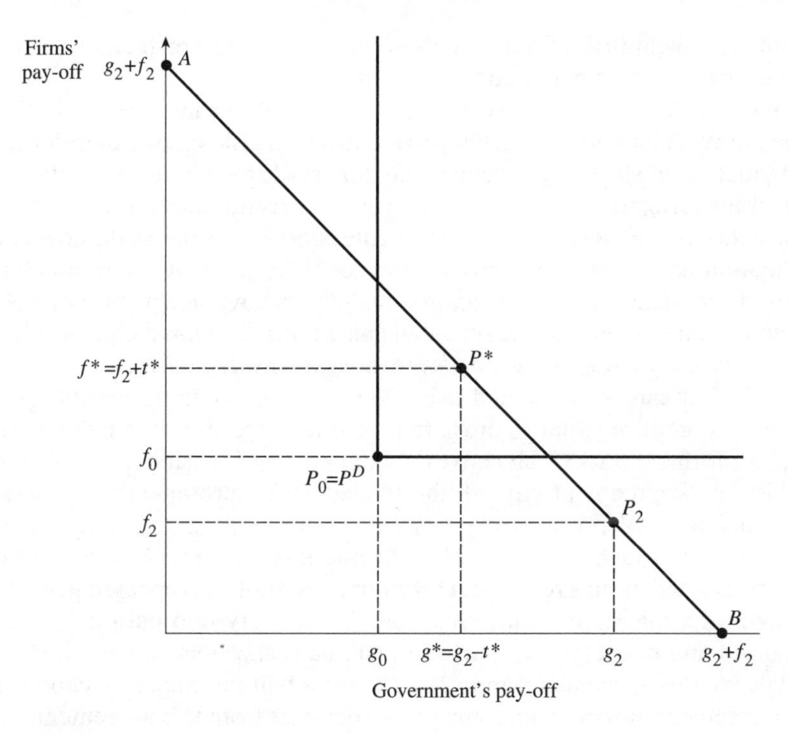

FIG. 13.4 Bargaining with Side Payments

$$\left(g_1 + f_1\right) - \left(g_0 + f_0\right)$$

is equally divided by the two parties.[13]

If we compare two regimes with the same litigation costs but one with side-payments and the other without, side payments, it is easier to come to agreement with side payments because monetary compensation is an extra means to expedite a compromise. Such a regime achieves as large a total pay-off (for insiders) as, and sometimes a strictly larger total pay-off than, the latter regime, possibly at the cost of outsiders. This difference arises because side payments permit more flexible *ex post* adjustments of policy rules. One should note, however, the resulting pay-off outcome for firms with side payments may be less than that without side payments. Figure 13.1 demonstrates that a case such as P_1 will be chosen without side payments while P^* will be chosen with side payments.

Long-Term Relationship between Government and the Business Sector

As argued in Section 13.6, the contemporary Japanese government has implemented its policies through a long-term interdependent relationship with incumbent firms. Four aspects of this regime are worth emphasizing in view of the *ex post* negotiation.

First, such relations are likely to produce repetitive interactions between the government and incumbent private firms. In this regime, therefore, the negotiation in stage (4) becomes only a part of the long-term relationship or, in the terminology of the repeated game literature, only a single *stage* of the entire repeated game that is their true concern. As the well-known Folk Theorem illustrates, any convex combination of individually rational pay-offs of the stage game can be approximated as an average pay-off of a Nash equilibrium outcome of the repeated game *if the discount factors of players are sufficiently close to one or players are sufficiently patient.*

This fact can be explained using Figure 13.3, assuming feasible policy revisions produce either P_1 or P_2. In Figure 13.3, the area within the triangle $P_1P_2P^D$ forms the set of all convex combinations of feasible pay-offs. Since P^D is the disagreement pay-off, the shaded area represents the set of individually rational portions of feasible pay-offs. Any individually rational pay-off vector such as P^{**}, which is the midpoint between P_1 and P_2, can be approximated as an average equilibrium pay-off of the repeated game by a self-enforceable agreement, such that: (1) in every odd period P_1 will be realized and in every even period P_2 will be realized as long as all players abide by this agreement; and (2) all players will permanently choose the disagreement outcome once any player deviates from this agreement. Such an agreement will be a (subgame perfect) Nash equilibrium if discount factors are close to 1. In other words, a long-term closed relationship enables pay-off averaging, an incomplete form of side payments. It follows that long-term relationships, even without side payments, permit a limited *ex post* flexibility. The extent of flexibility is greater than in the case without a long-term relationship and without side payments, but less than in the case with side payments.

A second point, which is critical for the following discussion, is the fact that the size of the disagreement pay-off may be strongly affected by the repeated game nature of the situation. In the repeated game, the penalty for disagreement may be much larger than in a mere one-shot game. In order to see this, note that the relevant penalty of choosing disagreement in a particular stage game consists of not only the cost of the immediate litigation process but also the pay-off difference between two ensuing subgames, one after agreement and the other after disagreement. The additional penalty, the pay-off difference of the two ensuing subgames, can be as large as the difference of keeping the agreement forever and perpetuating the disagreement outcome, as the example of the agreement in the previous paragraph indicates. In other words, the breakdown of negotiation in a particular stage game may imply the breakdown of the relationship between the government and private firms forever, so that the subsequent hostile relationship would mean a continuous battle in court, providing a prohibitively high penalty for disagreement. In summary, the repetitive nature of the game substantially amplifies the penalty associated with the disagreement compared with the case when the game is played as a one-shot game, contributing to the flexibility of the bargaining outcomes.

The third important aspect of this regime is those institutional arrangements that assure the rigidity of bargaining members, such as entry regulations. When entry is free and members of the industry change over time, a long-term agreement that calls for intertemporal trade-offs is likely to be nonself-enforceable. That is, any intertemporal agreement that forces an immediate sacrifice by a member in exchange for promised benefits in the future is unlikely to be enforced either because new entrants oppose providing the promised benefits to the incumbent or because an incumbent, anticipating such developments, finds the agreement noncredible. In this respect, if a threat of new entry exists, the nature of the government-business relationship, which is always potentially repetitive in nature, will become a one-shot game.

It follows that, in order to maintain a closed, long-term relationship between the government and private incumbent firms, and to maintain the self-enforcing property of long-term agreements, it is critical that new entry be effectively limited. Strict entry regulations founded upon a clear legal basis may be one possibility. Even if entry regulation is neither strict nor based upon a clear legal basis, if litigation costs are substantial, entry may be effectively blockaded. For example, a petition to new entry to a regional trucking industry in Japan was held up for more than five years, because the government office simply ignored the petition by refusing to formally receive it.[14] Because litigation costs for administrative suits in Japan are extremely high, the applicant could do nothing other than wait.

The fourth important aspect of this regime, which may be unique to Japan, is the existence of an additional bargaining forum, such as industry associations, that facilitates the bargaining.[15] Although it has not been stressed so far, *ex post* bargaining in reality is likely to take place with more than two participants, each with independent preferences. This is so because private firms have heterogeneous, sometimes diametrically opposite, interests and it is difficult to coordinate their interests even if they belong to the same industry. Industry associations, which themselves are a forum for coordinating interests among member firms, can aggregate such heterogeneous interests with the help of a long-term implicit agreement that trades immediate costs for future benefits.

Needless to say, facilitation of the bargaining process using industry associations is likely to be achieved at the cost of those who are left out of the bargaining process, such as consumers, because it is likely to create semicartel behavior. If bargaining takes place in the lower government levels in a segregated manner, society's overall interests will tend to be undervalued. It also implies that an individual industry's interests will be reflected more strongly than otherwise and insiders' accumulated vested interests are likely to be reflected strongly in the bargaining outcome. It also follows that policy decisions that require coordination of interests across industries tend to be difficult, unless the society has relatively uniform interests.

13.4 *EX POST* INCENTIVES OF GOVERNMENT AND PRIVATE FIRMS

In this section, I extend the analysis to stages (1) and (2), and analyze the incentives of the government in writing *ex ante* rules as well as the investment incentives of the private sector.

Incentives of Government

In writing an *ex ante* rule in stage (1), the relevant branch of the government must be fully conscious of the possible developments in stages (4)–(6). It follows that a functionally nonseparated government with large litigation costs (government with relatively large bargaining power) and a government with strict separation of powers with negligible litigation costs (government with small bargaining power) are likely to write fundamentally different *ex ante* rules. Let us begin with the case of the former government, whose legislative, administrative, and judicial branches are controlled by a single agency and/or litigation costs are significant for private firms but negligible for the government.

For such governments, there is little incentive to write a narrowly defined *ex ante* rule, as writing such rules will restrict their powers to implement better *ex post* rules when unexpected contingencies arise.[16] It is in their interests to write a broadly defined rule that leaves room for *ex post* discretion, with which they can exploit advantage through negotiations where the government has a large bargaining power thanks to asymmetric litigation costs. By so doing, the government can realize those outcomes that best fit its preference.

At the same time, if such a government is jurisdictionally decentralized as well, it has an additional incentive to leave more room in drawing an *ex ante* rule. Being less afraid of opposition to *ex post* policy revisions from parties who have no immediate connection to the ministry's constituency, a jurisdictionally decentralized government is more confident that any *ex post* revisions will reflect the government's (or the ministry's) interest. It means that such a government may find it even more advantageous to write *ex ante* rules in vague language, leaving many things to *ex post* renegotiation and discretion.

On the other hand, if the government is functionally separated and litigation costs are negligible, its incentive is quite different. First of all, the branch that is responsible for stage (1), usually the legislative branch, may have a different preference from that of the branches responsible for (4) and (6), the admininstrative and judicial branches. It follows that the legislative branch has little incentive to write an *ex ante* rule that leaves room for *ex post* reinterpretations. It is more likely to write a stricter rule with fewer opportunities for *ex post* bargaining, which has a better chance of surviving *ex post* renegotiation, securing the outcomes this branch likes.

Moreover, if the judicial branch is autonomous and independent from the rest of the government, it is likely to deliver rulings that reflect the aggregate interests of the society. Hence, even if the legislative and administrative branches of the government are controlled by the same decision unit, it is not in their interests to write an *ex ante* rule with room for discretion. Writing such a rule would result only in outcomes that may be undesirable for these two branches of government, by increasing the possibility of reinterpretation by courts.

To sum up, the extent to which *ex ante* rules leave room for *ex post* discretion is likely to be determined by the type of government. A jurisdictionally decentralized government and/or a government with large bargaining power is likely to write rules with ample room for discretion, while a jurisdictionally centralized and/or functionally separated government is likely to write stricter rules.

Hold-Up Problem

Recent developments in contract theory and transaction cost economics revealed the fact that commitments to contracts provide better *ex ante* incentives but that *ex post* renegotiation facilitates adjustments for unraveled uncertainties and newly revealed information. More specifically, if players expect the outcome of the game to be mainly determined by *ex post* negotiation, *ex ante* incentives will deteriorate and the hold-up problem will emerge. *Ex post* negotiations would allocate a share of returns to those players at the bargaining table according to their bargaining power, whether or not they had contributed to making such returns possible. Thus, a part of the returns for *ex ante* efforts may be captured by those free-riders who are not responsible for these *ex ante* efforts. Anticipating less than full returns to be appropriated, suboptimal levels of *ex ante* efforts are chosen, the well-known "hold-up problem."[17]

On the other hand, in order to provide a proper incentive for *ex ante* efforts, it is not sufficient to write an agreement that promises to appropriate full returns to the investor, because the agreement may be invalidated by *ex post* renegotiations. What is important is a commitment to this agreement or the belief that the agreement will not be changed by renegotiation. This is not a problem in a world full of uncertainties, because a contingent contract is available in such a world, that is, all players agree with and commit *ex ante* to a (possibly complex) contingent plan according to which the returns will be allocated appropriately for each contingency. Writing a full contingent plan that leaves no room for any Pareto-improving revision in any contingencies, players expect the plan to remain unchanged even after renegotiation. Contingent contracts may not be practical in the real world, however. Many contingencies are difficult to describe fully *ex ante*, because identifying each contigency and spelling them out fully requires prohibitively high costs, and because some contingencies are not verifiable by third parties, notably by courts, making agreements unenforceable from legal viewpoints.

It follows that, in many real-world situations, relatively simple contracts which must call for inefficient solutions if unspecified contingencies occur are used more widely. Renegotiation will be called for in such contingencies in order to find and implement more efficient solutions. Writing government laws and legislation is no different and *ex ante* rules written in stage (1) are likely to be relatively simple, leaving many decisions for *ex post* renegotiation in stage (4). It follows that the overall social efficiency of the private firms' *ex ante* investment decisions is likely to be affected by the hold-up problem.

Private Firms' Incentives

Hold-up problems that occur in the government-business relationship appear in different forms depending upon the type of government. This subsection discusses those differences.

We start with an authoritarian government with the extreme case of a predatory government. A predatory government, that has infinite power against the private sector at the bargaining table in stage (4), can choose any revision it likes as long as the private firms' pay-off outcome is at least as large as the individually rational level. If side payments are allowed, any pay-off that exceeds the firms' individually rational pay-off level, a kind of quasi-rent, will be taken away by the government in the form of monetary transfer (with side payments and a predatory government, P_1' in Figure 13.2 will be chosen). For firms in this regime, there is no incentive for making risky investments because neither innovation nor risk taking will result in any extra profit, unless such investments are promoted by the government itself. It follows that, under such a regime, firms will have a strong incentive not to carry out investments of their own, unless they are sure that the government will permit the fruits of the investment to be appropriated by the investors. In this sense, a predatory government has the power to implement its preferred policy, both from *ex ante* and *ex post* viewpoints, but, by this very fact, it may fail to generate proper incentives for innovations and investments by private firms.

Hold-up problems in the sense described above appear in a straightforward form in a relation-based government with relatively large, but not infinite, litigation costs, where an incomplete form of side payments exists. Recall that, with side payments, part of the returns from investment may be taken away by the government in the form of monetary transfer and the investment incentive is reduced (though not as much as under a predatory government). A well-known example in Japan is that financial institutions have little incentive to develop novel financial products because the Ministry of Finance, being a benevolent supervisor of the banking industry as a whole, would not allow the product to be marketed until the inventor's rivals were ready to release similar products.

For both authoritarian and relation-based governments, whose functional powers are not well separated, an additional problem may exist for private firms' incentives to innovation. Note that, under these governments, private firms will find it difficult to secure the default outcome through judicial processes, as the ultimate result tends to be dictated by the preference of the administrative branch of the government. Bureaucrats in this branch, either controlled by those in power in an authoritarian government or having stakes in the power structure of the ministry for which they work in a jurisdictionally decentralized government, tend to ignore structural changes that occur in the society for the sake of past decisions made by those in power or people who held the same positions before. Private firms, anticipating such predilections by the administrative branch, will not invest in innovative activities to meet the novel situation created by structural changes.

On the other hand, a rule-based government with a strict functionally separated government is likely to provide a larger incentive in promoting private firms' *ex ante* investment. Future business environments are relatively clear and investors feel assured of receiving full returns from their investment as long as it satisfies the *ex ante* rule. In addition, a relatively autonomous judicial branch may assure private firms in making innovative and risk-taking investments whose results are not allowed to be utilized under the *ex ante* rule, because they might be rewarded if courts find the resulting innovation improving social welfare, especially when there is a structural change in the business environment.

In sum, strict rules with less room for discretion, together with an autonomous judicial process that assures a relatively inexpensive avenue to guarantee the default outcome, provide a power to commit to an *ex ante* rule, and private investments that are consistent with the rule are more likely to be efficiently carried out. Such a regime is probably most effective in inducing innovative and risk-taking investments by private firms. On the other hand, a predatory government, which can enforce its preferred revision at the renegotiation table, is most suited in directing private firms' investments to the direction the government likes most. A relation-based government seems to be somewhere between these two governments.

13.5 TYPE OF GOVERNMENT AND ITS PERFORMANCE

The primary economic role of government is to promote economic welfare. Traditional economic theory has emphasized the market-sustaining role of government. This role of government is to *sustain* the market mechanism, by correcting market failures, by controlling the economy's aggregate demand, and by maintaining and improving income equality in the society, using coercive measures such as regulation, taxation, and public goods provision, or using macroeconomic policies that manage aggregate demand. The background philosophy is that government is called in when and only when the market cannot solve the problem well, and the government is to constantly uphold the working of the market. Recently, another role of government has attracted research attention, which is *guidance* of the market mechanism. The guiding role of government is to help the economy move in a certain direction by providing incentives and by coordinating private activities. It includes helping the private sector to industrialize in developing economies using, for example, industrial policies, and promoting the innovative activities, such as R&D, of the private sector in developed economies.

The role of guiding the economy may be further divided into two roles. One is the coordination in macro resource allocation, which is to provide various incentives to private firms in directing resources toward a particular industry, such as an exportable industry or a high technology industry, from other sectors of the economy. Another role is the coordination in micro corporate strategies, which is to help private firms improve their products by disseminating information about a new method of quality control, training workers for new jobs, and promoting the standardization of their products and their informational exchange, etc.[18]

Among the roles of government for sustaining the market mechanism, there are several policy measures that would promote economic growth and, hence, would complement the guiding role. They include those measures that provide proper incentive systems, especially to innovation and product/process improvements in the private sector, by establishing an appropriate property rights system such as a patent system, and by providing pecuniary and nonpecuniary incentives for R&D.

It is probably worth emphasizing that these two basic roles of government, sustaining and guiding, often conflict with each other, partly because these two roles represent two different views about the relative ability of government and the private sector. Those who support the guiding role emphasize that government has a better ability to steer the economy, citing the fact that the private sector often fails in coordinating its activities and government can solve this problem by rendering its resources. On the other hand, critics of this view stress the possibility of government failure, saying there is no guarantee that an active government can solve a coordination failure that the private sector cannot.[19] Hence, they call for a more limited role of government in promoting private firms' activities in a certain direction.

In addition, in providing these two roles, the performance of government may differ depending upon different institutional arrangements within the government. In this section, I attempt to analyze the comparative advantage of each type of government in pursuing such roles from a theoretical viewpoint. Some of the evaluations offered are preliminary in nature, and further research, in both theoretical analysis and case studies, is necessary.

Authoritarian Government

An authoritarian government has a natural advantage in its guiding role. Having a large bargaining power, it has the means to guide and even to force the private sector to act in the way it prefers in achieving a certain goal. Being *ex post* flexible, it can easily and freely adjust its policies to achieve the same goal when unforeseen events make its original plan unworkable.

There are several important reservations about this ability of a government with a large bargaining power. If side payments are possible in the form of outright bribery or political contributions, those governments such as predatory governments will take away from firms all the benefits in excess of their individually rational pay-offs. Any profit that would have been accruable to the private sector in other regimes would be taken away, and the proper investment incentives of firms will be severely hampered.

Government's guiding roles include coordination in macro resource allocation as well as coordination in micro corporate strategies. For an authoritarian government to carry out such roles successfully and improve social welfare, there is an important precondition. Government bureaucrats must have at least as much knowledge and as good analytical capabilities as, and preferably better than, the private sector has. Otherwise, the market mechanism, based upon competitive pressures through which firms intensively look for cost reductions, new products, innovations in organizational form, etc., will find a better solution.

Being jurisdictionally centralized, an authoritarian government can coordinate the interests of industries across society and, hence, it is probably more able to coordinate macro resource allocation. However, individual firms and their cooperative initiatives are relatively more effective in coordinating organizational innovations and corporate and/or intercorporate strategies.

It follows that for authoritarian, especially predatory, governments to coordinate private activities successfully, it is essential that there are both a bureaucracy with the ability to analyze, design, and implement an appropriate economic plan and also the social system and the bureaucratic culture that maintains the moral discipline within the government. This type of government may be more effective, especially in view of its lack of ability to coordinate micro corporate strategies, with a private sector that is controlled by a few dominant conglomerates, which can pursue the role of micro coordination by themselves, than a government supported by networks of numerous small and medium-sized independent firms, where coordination failures among firms are numerous and complicated.

Needless to say, an authoritarian government is not very effective in its sustaining role. Its policies are prone to discretionary revisions that are likely to be dictated by the government's presuppositions, the future business environments for private firms are not well articulated in advance, and incentives for innovative activities are severely limited. Another, and probably critical, deficiency of an authoritarian government is in its noneconomic aspect. With a limited functional separation of powers and the concentration of power within the government, this government lacks transparency in decision making and is prone to rent-seeking activities. If a particular group, such as the landlord class, of the society dominates the government, the interest of other groups may be seriously contained. Only when it is controlled by a disciplined group that aims for society's overall well-being can this government attain a desirable goal.

Relation-Based Government

This government has many similarities with an authoritarian government in its ability to fulfill the guiding roles. Because of its large bargaining power, such a government is again more effective for guiding roles. Its strength lies especially in its ability to coordinate micro corporate strategies. The power of each ministry is restricted within its jurisdiction, and thus government has natural interests in promoting such coordination within its jurisdiction, which can be a specific industry (such as the manufacturing industry for the Ministry of International Trade and Industry (MITI)) or a certain aspect of business activities (such as labor relations for the Ministry of Labor). Being less connected to the central executive office of the government, career bureaucrats of the ministries have relatively large influence over decision making, and jurisdiction-specific knowledge is better accumulated within each ministry and is better reflected in policy decisions.

A relation-based government is not normally very effective in coordinating macro resource allocation, because the demarcation of jurisdictional boundaries often impedes such coordination. However, coordination of macro resource allocation is often carried out by negotiation between relevant ministries and bureaus in such a government. If, and only if, these different governmental bodies in the administrative branch have a uniform policy target as well as an agreed plan to achieve it, this role can be effectively realized, as we shall see for the case of Japan in the next section.

For both guiding roles, however, the relative superiority of the government's knowledge and its ability with respect to the private sector is again essential for its effectiveness.

A relation-based government, too, cannot coordinate the innovative activities of private firms well. However, at least compared with an authoritarian government, this type of government can promote its sustaining role to some extent. Because its power is less concentrated and is held by various ministries and bureaus of the lower government, it cannot drastically revise original policies because doing so often requires support from other ministries which have some but minor stakes in the jurisdiction. Furthermore, bargaining for revisions is done at the lower levels of the government, making the voices of private firms relatively well heard; new business, which is not allowable by the *ex ante* rule, may be permitted by the government if it is found suited to the interests of both the ministry and the firm. Coordination in micro corporate strategies, such as helping to improve work environments and/or promoting product standardization, also supports innovative activities of the private sector.

Most critical policy decisions are made at the lower level of the government at each individual ministry, and thus the interests of outsiders are not well reflected in public policy. Consumers, potential new entrants to industry, and users of the products produced by the industry may find such a government frustrating for this reason. Moreover, rents may be created and accrued by the firms and bureaucrats (e.g., in the form of ex-bureaucrats obtaining postretirement jobs).

Rule-Based Government

With only a small bargaining power, a rule-based government is likely to be inferior in guiding roles. Its strength lies in its capability to achieve its sustaining roles. Hold-up problems and other incentive problems for innovation are least serious with this type of government because future business environments are most transparent, partly reflecting its inability in revising *ex ante* policies and partly reflecting its ability in providing multiple routes, such as the legislative and judicial branches, for private firms to have their voices heard in the government.

Among the guiding roles, this type of government implements coordination of macro resource allocation by traditional coercive policy measures, such as taxation and public goods provision, with the legislative branch as the major forum for coordinating the interests of the society. The resulting resource allocation tends to be more of a compromise of various interest groups than a directed public intervention.

We should note that, compared with other types of government, rule-based government does not necessarily solve rent-seeking problems better. In rule-based government, the decisions of *ex ante* rules are more critical and rent-seeking activities tend to concentrate in the political forum instead of the administrative arena. In fact, in the United States where the government is considered closer to the rule-based type, policy decisions seem to be influenced more heavily by lobbying activities in Congress.

In short, various types of government have relative merits (and demerits) in pursuing different goals. There is one more critical element in the relative effectiveness of different types of government: the internal and external conditions of the economy, such as the developmental stage of the economy relative to the rest of the world. This is so because the active guiding roles of the government are effective if it is simply following a successful precedent. With such a precedent, the possible lack of relevant information, and the knowledge and ability of bureaucrats in comparison with private firms presents fewer problems, while the government's coordination (of firms' coordination failures) may work more effectively. Pursuing economic development through industrialization is one such example because there are several successful precedents. In a developed economy, however, the sustaining role of the government is more important as a source of growth because such an economy must seek its source of economic development in innovative ideas, which are better left for the private sector.

I shall provide a brief historical account of the government-business relationship in Japan in order to illustrate this last point, taking industrial policy as an example.

13.6 THE GOVERNMENT-BUSINESS RELATIONSHIP IN JAPAN: A HISTORICAL PERSPECTIVE

Industrial policy in Japan had its heyday in the 1950s and early 1960s. In those days, a typical policy came in three steps. First, those industries with a high probability of technological advance and demand expansion in the future were discovered or identified. In order to make such forecasts, private information exchange networks and/or government committees and councils were utilized to facilitate and encourage the exchange of information.

Second, in order to promote these industries, several measures were employed. The government intervened in resource allocation by issuing licenses and permits; providing incentives to affect corporate decisions in the form of financial assistance such as low-interest loans, subsidy payments, and preferential taxes; and employing indicative measures such as announcing long-term economic plans and provision of information. Funds and materials were allocated (not by power but by providing various incentives) across industries/sectors after careful coordination among MITI,

MOF, the Bank of Japan, the banking industry, and major manufacturing industries. At the same time, MITI promoted tie-ups and mergers of private firms, provided various forms of assistance, and applied administrative guidance[20] in order to achieve intended resource allocations.

Third, information concerning new business opportunities was shared by all firms in an industry, and a strong desire was generated among private firms to take advantage of those advantageous policy measures, before other firms could do the same, in order to gain a strong foothold within the industry as quickly as possible. So-called "excess competition" arose as firms rushed to expand equipment and investments to levels that far surpassed their capacity. Also facing pressures to maintain job opportunities for those employees who insisted on job security, Japanese firms set their targets not on profits but on market share.

Even if firms found their new business to be in trouble and massive dismissals in the workforce became inevitable, responsibility also fell to the ministry or bureau whose jurisdiction covered the firm's activities and that had endorsed the business and conceived the policy measures concerned. In such instances, the government could not help but extend assistance to relieve these enterprises that were caught in dire situations. In fact, the government employed various measures to avoid the occurrence of such systemic risks; the various measures enacted after the oil shocks in 1973 and 1979 were typical examples. However, firms that anticipated such government responses actually strengthened their move toward excess competition.

In short, the postwar Japanese industrial policy utilized government "management" of competition among private firms with the help of relation-based policy implementation on one hand and government provision of various incentive mechanisms to realize the intended macro resource allocation on the other hand.[21] This system had its roots in the tightly regulated and controlled economic system that developed during the war.

Between 1940 and 1945, the Japanese government-business relationship was drastically restructured to promote the planned economy, which was instituted for the execution of the Sino-Japanese and Pacific wars, by moving to a controlled and/or a regulated economy. In this system, in order to execute the Goods Mobilization Plan, which was drawn up by the Planning Board and other related government agencies, every economic activity (production, distribution, pricing, consumption, etc.) of all aspects of the nation (such as trade, fund allocation, labor employment, transportation, equipment formation, etc.) was controlled by the government. To facilitate the working of this system, several institutional reforms were enacted to induce corporate objectives to move from pursuit of profit toward cooperation for the war effort. For example, the influence of shareholders on corporate management was minimized by introducing a ceiling on dividends and regulations on executives' compensation, and by reforming commercial law to contain the power of a general meeting. Moreover, the Japanese economy was reorganized into a unified vertical hierarchy, consisting of central planning bureaus, control associations in each industry, and each individual firm and plant. As a result, firms became puppet institutions that simply implemented government orders, and their daily activities completely bound by the controlling bureaucracy. The postwar Japanese government-business relationship until at least the 1960s was strongly influenced by the legacy of this wartime system.[22]

Despite its historical origins and the many criticisms of it, the relation-based nature of the Japanese government may have contributed to the social welfare of the country. In particular, there are good reasons to believe that part of the "success" of the Japanese economy in the first half of the postwar period may be ascribed to the fact that the relation-based regime dominated the design and implementation of public policies in Japan. Discussion follows of some those reasons.

First of all, in order to reconstruct an economy that had been destroyed during the war and to achieve an industrialization with strong emphasis on heavy and high technology industries, two alternative routes existed for postwar Japan. One was to rely mainly on the market mechanism to determine resource allocations, with the government playing only a sustaining role. The other was to utilize discretionary governmental intervention and/or to coordinate corporate activities to achieve industrialization and other policy goals. Needless to say, the latter was the route chosen.

The latter alternative of government-guided industrialization is inferior in inducing innovation and invention in the private sector, but it does have some ability to induce innovation. Japanese bureaucrats often set out self-imposed rules in applying their policies in order to assure their fairness and to counter political pressures. These rules, adopted as a self-imposed control, tended to provide advantages to larger and older enterprises. The typical example is the MOF/BOJ convoy policy for the banking industry. Under this policy, permits for new branches and lending from the BOJ were granted according to the market share of each bank, a sort of *performance-based criterion*.[23] These rules aggravated excess competition because the larger a firm's share, the better the treatment it obtained from the government. Excess competition also provided an incentive to win and expand. However, the rule of competition was less clear and not committed to by the government, and the distribution of the returns on efforts was determined by negotiation among the concerned parties. Consequently, incentives were directed toward incremental improvements so that firms could get ahead of their rivals, and not toward invention of truly novel products. As is often stated, the postwar "success" of Japanese manufacturing has its roots in its ability to improve the production process, thereby cutting production costs and providing quality improvements for existing products, but not in its ability to introduce truly innovative new products or design completely novel concepts.

More importantly, the period of reconstruction and high growth in postwar Japan was unique in the following sense. The closure of the country for almost two decades during the two wars had made Japan's technology and industrial structure obsolete, far behind those of the industrialized nations. To reconstruct and industrialize, the country did not need drastic innovations. What was important was to coordinate public and private business in order to catch up with the advanced nations' industrial structure as well as their technology. This strategy required knowledge about the kind of industries that had high growth potential and about the necessary policy prescriptions for promoting them. Compared with corporate executives, bureaucrats had better access to this knowledge immediately after the war as the country was still essentially closed and, by negotiation and fine tuning, they could coordinate and encourage the private sector's effort.

Moreover, the Japanese in those hard days were unanimous in their desire to promote economic growth. Bureaucrats were no exception, as exemplified by the cooperative efforts between MOF and MITI in directing funds and other resources into growing industries. In other words, despite the fact that the Japanese government is of a jurisdictionally decentralized nature, coordination in macro resource allocation was effectively carried out through joint efforts among several ministries that coordinated their policies to achieve the goal of industrialization and high economic growth.[24]

A second reason for Japan's success was that the early postwar period was one of social disruption and large-scale structural transformation. These changes included three drastic reforms (land, labor, and economic reforms) ordered and implemented by the occupation force in the late 1940s; the Korean War boom and reconstruction in the 1950s; the high economic growth with real GNP growing at more than 10 per cent annually in the 1960s; and the oil crisis and subsequent recession in the early 1970s. For example, the workforce moved from rural to urban areas at the rate of 800–1,200 thousand a year on average, changing the percentage of the workforce in the agricultural sector from 50.0 per cent in 1950 to a mere 19.7 per cent in 1970. The industrial structure was drastically transformed so that the production share in the manufacturing sector of the heavy and chemical industries rose from 43.6 per cent in 1950 to 63.6 per cent in 1970.

With these large-scale social transformations, many people and firms would have lost their economic base for living and social unrest would have occurred, had the transformation been completely dictated by market forces. In particular, small banks with bases in declining industries and small plants in rural areas might have been eliminated by larger urban competitors. With the emerging contemporary economic system, which emphasized long-term relationships such as stable long-term employment, the failures of these banks and firms would have created a chain reaction of bankruptcies and resulting unemployment in a particular region, which might have led to political and/or social chaos. In order to effect a smooth transition, it was essential to assist those negatively affected by economic change and to provide help to declining industries. The relation-based regime seems to have contributed significantly because of its advantage in taking account of *ex post* considerations flexibly.

Third, bureaucrats of this period had relative autonomy from political influence and their quality and morals were high. This reflected the fact that during the war bureaucrats had controlled and dominated policy decisions, with the parliament transformed into a puppet institution. Moreover, as is well known, the Japanese bureaucrats of that time were of high quality and were highly motivated because of the legacy of high morals they had inherited from the classic bureaucrats of the prewar period. These characteristics of the Japanese bureaucracy of those days seem to have contributed to its success in containing rent-seeking activities.

13.8 CONCLUDING REMARKS

In this chapter, I have presented a theoretical model of the nature of the government-business relationship taking in the institutional structures behind it, analyzed the possible advantage of various types of government, and examined aspects of the government-business relationship in postwar Japan.

Three major types of government have been identified—authoritarian, relation-based, and rule-based—on the basis of their capabilities in directing private business activities and the level of government at which main coordination activities take place. I have argued that a government with a large bargaining power, such as an authoritarian or a relation-based government, is relatively more effective in active guidance, such as coordinating macro resource allocation and coordinating micro corporate strategies. On the other hand, a government with a small bargaining power, such as a rule-based government, has a relative advantage in carrying out its role of sustaining the market mechanism by, for example, providing a clear business environment.

The government regime in Japan can be roughly described as relation-based, with the government-business relationship having a long-term repeated nature and government agencies being endowed with a relatively large amount of discretion. Compared with an alternative rule-based government, this relation-based regime may well have contributed to the "success" of the Japanese economy in the first half of the postwar period. I have also emphasized that this positive appraisal depends heavily upon the external conditions of the Japanese economy as well as the traits of its bureaucratic system at the time.

It should be emphasized that external conditions faced by other East Asian countries when they started their economic development were very similar to those in postwar Japan. Industrialization being the ultimate goal of their economic policy, they tried to follow previous successful examples such as postwar Japan, but faced the potential social disturbances that industrialization causes. Although I am not familiar with the details of the regimes of the government-business relationship in these societies, casual observation suggests that the regimes of many East Asian countries, such as China, Korea, Taiwan, and Singapore in the 1970s and/or 1980s, are likely to be characterized as authoritarian. The governments of these countries at these times were controlled strongly either by military groups and/or by parties that had an asymmetrically strong political power in the society. Some governments were even criticized as being repressive. None the less, the discussion in this chapter suggests that authoritarian government has the ability to achieve industrialization effectively by directing private resources to desirable sectors, given their economic environments.

This suggests that institutional structures behind the government-business relationship can have a significant impact on whether a country can successfully achieve economic development. In fact, several economists as well as political scientists, including the late Yasusuke Murakami, have conjectured that "developmentalism," an industrialization strategy that places higher priority on industrialization than on full democratization of the society, may be more effective than classical economic liberalism, which places strong preference on democratization over industrialization. According to Murakami (1992), for example, successful industrialization would naturally lead to the democratization of a society, while the reverse does not necessarily follow. Further serious research to examine this conjecture may be valuable for the designing of policies to help industrialize developing countries as well as to help facilitate the transition of former socialist regimes to market economies. Undoubtedly, fuller understanding of institutional arrangements behind the government-business relationship is an important requirement of such research.

Finally, let me emphasize that my assessment of the government-business relationship in contemporary Japan is quite different. With Japan now being one of the leading countries in the world in terms of its share of GDP, together with its preeminence in high technology industries and large investments in research and development activities, the advantage to Japan of having relation-based governments guiding the private sector has diminished significantly, if not completely disappeared. The country has now matured in terms of both economic affluence and the diversity of social values and preferences, and the public's unanimous desire for economic growth at the cost of public intervention no longer exists. Other forms of government must be sought to meet the country's new environment and its developmental stage. For this new regime, a rule-based government is one, but certainly not necessarily the only, candidate. Other East Asian countries will soon face a similar problem, if they do not already do so.

NOTES

I would like to thank Masahiko Aoki, Thomas Hellmann, Yoshitsugu Kanemoto, Ikuo Kume, Chiaki Moriguchi, Akira Morita, Michio Muramatsu, James Murdock, Kohsuke Ohyama, Tadashi Sekiguchi, Barry Weingast, and participants of the World Bank conferences for their valuable comments on and helpful discussions of earlier versions.

[1] See, e.g., the writings of Johnson (1982), Wade (1990), and Amsden (1989).

[2] This set may be contingent upon observable and verifiable information signaled by the realization of uncertainties in stage (3).

[3] Readers not familiar with the Japanese economy may imagine instead the savings and loan (S&L) incidents in the United States during the 1980s, which is a story rather similar to the following accounts. For details of the S&L incidents, interested readers are referred to, e.g., Kane (1993).

[4] A typical example is as follows. In December 1994, BOJ announced a rescue plan for two small regional banks in Tokyo that were burdened by large, bad loans. The rescue plan consisted of the establishment of a new special bank financed by: (1) investment of ¥20 billion (about US$200 million) by BOJ, (2) the same amount of investment by other large city banks, and (3) a gift of ¥40 billion from the Deposit Insurance Corporation. In addition, another new institution, which would help collect these banks' bad loans, was created by a low-interest loan (of an estimated ¥100 billion) from the Tokyo municipal government and private financial institutions.

[5] Several recent developments in US telecommunications regulation seem to be better approximated in the latter framework.

[6] A notable example may be the US government where the top layer of each department is filled by political appointees.

[7] In contemporary Japan, for example, the power structure that controls each individual industry is often dominated by the triad of politicians, bureaucrats, and business people, sometimes called a policy community, which holds a tight nexus that effectively controls and practically determines many critical policy decisions. A policy community, consisting of an industry association of the industry in question, a government agency in charge, and a relevant subcommittee of the Policy Research Committee of the Liberal Democratic Party (while the LDP dominated Japanese politics), acts as an exclusive policy-making institution. Three additional institutional features—(1) the *nawa-bari* of government agencies, which is an agreement of demarcation for exclusive administrative jurisdictions among various government ministries; (2) the *zoku* members of the parliament, who act essentially for the interest of firms in each individual industry; and (3) the existence of industry associations, which integrate diverse interests of member firms and act for the industry as a whole—contribute to the fragmentation of policy decisions.

[8] See discussion of the Japanese case in Section 13.7.

[9] The strict jurisdictional partitioning of the Japanese government is well known as *nawa-bari*. See, e.g., Okuno-Fujiwara (1993). Its legislature is heavily controlled by the administrative branch, as most legislation is written and prepared by bureaucrats, while litigation costs are significantly high. For example, it takes an average of 10 years for the Supreme Court to reach final verdicts in administrative suits. See Miyazaki (1986).

[10] See Milgrom and Roberts (1988 and 1992).

[11] This is an important caveat, to be addressed below.

[12] For the details as well as the justification of the Nash Bargaining Solution, see, e.g., Kreps (1990) and Osborne and Rubinstein (1990).

[13] If we assume asymmetric bargaining power between the two parties, the ultimate pay-off is favored for the party with the larger bargaining power. See Roth (1979).

[14] Interested readers are referred to Okuno-Fujiwara (1992).

[15] Industry associations play the role of an intermediary by coordinating member firms' interests and by acting as subordinates of the government agency in charge of implementing its policy. To make this role effective, industry associations accept former bureaucrats from the agency to fill their most senior positions.

[16] This conclusion holds only when more narrowly defined rules will not benefit the government by changing private firms' behavior. In reality, however, one of the most important factors the government must take into account in writing these rules is the effect on the private firms' actions (especially in stage (2)). In this subsection, however, I ignore this effect because this problem will be taken up in the next two subsections.

[17] For the hold-up problem and contract theory in general, see, e.g., Grossman and Hart (1986) and Milgrom and Roberts (1992).

[18] See, e.g., Chapter 3 by Okazaki in this volume.

[19] Okazaki's chapter in this volume may be seen as emphasizing the guiding role, while Matsuyama's (Chapter 5) emphasizes the sustaining role.

[20] Through "administrative guidance," a ministry realizes its policy objectives through the subject's "voluntary" cooperation. Because of the closed and long-term relationship between the agency in charge and the industry association in question, information is exchanged on a daily basis, and administrative and other related activities are implemented behind the scenes.

[21] For fuller accounts of postwar Japanese industrial policy, see Komiya, Okuno, and Suzumura (1988) and Itoh, Kiyono, Okuno-Fujiwara, and Suzumura (1991).

[22] For details of this wartime development, see Okazaki and Okuno-Fujiwara (1993).

[23] See the Introduction to this volume as well as World Bank (1993).

[24] For details, see e.g., Okuno-Fujiwara (1994). This aspect of the Japanese bureaucracy is emphasized by Aoki (1988), who coined the word "bureau-pluralism" for it.

REFERENCES

Amsden, A. H. (1989), *Asia's New Giant: South Korea and Late Industrialization*, Oxford University Press, Oxford.

Aoki, M. (1988), *Information, Incentives, and Bargaining in the Japanese Economy*, Cambridge University Press, Cambridge.

Grossman, S. and Hart, O. (1986), "The Costs and Benefits of Ownership: A Theory of Vertical and Lateral Integration," *Journal of Political Economy*, 98:1119–58.

Itoh, M., Kiyono, K., Okuno-Fujiwara, M., and Suzumura, K. (1991), *Economic Analysis of Industrial Policy*, Academic Press, New York.

Johnson, C. (1982), *MITI and the Japanese Miracle*, Stanford University Press, Stanford.

Kane, E. (1993), "What Lessons Should Japan Learn from the U.S. Deposit-Insurance Mess?" *Journal of the Japanese and International Economies*, 7:329–55.

Komiya, R., Okuno, M., and Suzumura, K., eds. (1988), *Industrial Policy of Japan*, Academic Press, New York.

Kreps, D. (1990), *A Course in Microeconomic Theory*, Princeton University Press, Princeton.

Milgrom, P. and Roberts, J. (1988), "An Economic Approach to Influence Activities in Organizations," *American Journal of Sociology*, 94:S154–79.

——(1992), *Economics, Organization and Management*, Prentice Hall, Englewood Cliffs, New Jersey.

Miyazaki, Y. (1986), "Gyosei fufuku shinsa seido no un-yo to mondai ten" (Workings and problems of the review system for discontent against public administration), *Shakai kagaku kenkyu*, 38(2):85–134.

Murakami, Y. (1992), *Han koten no seiji keizai-gaku* (Anticlassical political economy), Chuo Koron-sha, Tokyo.

Okazaki, T. and Okuno-Fujiwara, M., eds. (1993), *Gendai Nihon keizai shisutemu no genryū* (Origins of the contemporary Japanese economic system), Nihon Keizai Shinbunsha, Tokyo. English translation forthcoming from Oxford University Press.

Okuno-Fujiwara, M. (1992), "The Japanese Government's Relationship with Industry," unpublished manuscript.

——(1993), "Government-Business Relationship in Japan: A Comparative Institutional Analysis," unpublished manuscript.

——(1994), "Fund Allocation System in Japan around 1957: Why It Did Not Create Rent Grabbing," unpublished manuscript.

Osborne, M. J. and Rubinstein, A. (1990), *Bargaining and Markets*, Academic Press, San Diego.

Roth, A. (1979), *Axiomatic Models of Bargaining*, Springer-Verlag, Berlin.

Wade, R. (1990), *Governing the Market: Economic Theory and the Role of the Government in East Asian Industrialization*, Princeton University Press, Princeton.

World Bank (1993), *The East Asian Miracle: Economic Growth and Public Policy*, Oxford University Press, New York.

INDEX

Note: Most references are to East Asian countries, unless otherwise indicated.